Georg Gottlob   Moshe Y. Vardi (Eds.)

Database Theory – ICDT '95

5th International Conference
Prague, Czech Republic, January 11-13, 1995
Proceedings

Springer-Verlag

Berlin Heidelberg New York
London Paris Tokyo
Hong Kong Barcelona
Budapest

Series Editors

Gerhard Goos
Universität Karlsruhe
Vincenz-Priessnitz-Straße 3, D-76128 Karlsruhe, Germany

Juris Hartmanis
Department of Computer Science, Cornell University
4130 Upson Hall, Ithaka, NY 14853, USA

Jan van Leeuwen
Department of Computer Science, Utrecht University
Padualaan 14, 3584 CH Utrecht, The Netherlands

Volume Editors

Georg Gottlob
Institut für Informationssysteme, Technische Universität Wien
Paniglgasse 16, A-1040 Wien, Austria

Moshe Y. Vardi
Department of Computer Science, Rice University
P.O.Box 1892, Houston, TX 77251-1892, USA

CR Subject Classification (1991): H.2, F.1.3, F.4.1, I.2.1

ISBN 3-540-58907-4 Springer-Verlag Berlin Heidelberg New York

CIP data applied for

© Springer-Verlag Berlin Heidelberg 1995
Printed in Germany

Typesetting: Camera-ready by author
SPIN: 10479308   45/3140-543210 - Printed on acid-free paper

Lecture Notes in Computer Science 893

Edited by G. Goos, J. Hartmanis and J. van Leeuwen

Advisory Board: W. Brauer D. Gries J. Stoer

Foreword

Database research is a field of computer science where theory meets applications. Several database concepts and methods that yesterday were regarded as issues of more theoretical interest are fundamental parts of today's implemented systems. Examples abound in the fields of database design, query languages, query optimization, concurrency control, statistical databases, and many others.

The papers presented in this volume were presented at ICDT'95, the International Conference on Database Theory, in Prague, January 10-13, 1995. ICDT is an international forum for research on the principles of database systems. It is organised every two years and has a tradition of being held in beautiful European cities, Rome in 1986, Bruges in 1988, and Paris in 1990. From 1992 on, when the conference was held in Berlin, ICDT has been merged with another series of conferences on theoretical aspects of database systems, known as the Symposium on Mathematical Fundamentals of Database Systems (MFDBS). MFDBS was initiated in Dresden in 1987, and continued in Visegrad (1989) and Rostock (1991). ICDT should enhance the exchange of ideas and cooperation within a unified Europe and between Europe and the other continents.

ICDT'95 was organized jointly by:
> Faculty of Electrical Engineering, Czech Technical University of Prague;
> Christian Doppler Laboratorium für Expertensysteme, Wien;
> Vienna University of Technology

The conference was also sponsored by
> International Thomson Publishing UK;
> IDOMENEUS: Network Esprit Network of Excellence;
> COMPULOG NET: Network of Excellence in Computational Logic;
> The Joint Center of CTU Prague and FAW Linz
> The International Science Foundation
> Creditanstalt Bankverein

In addition to 29 technical papers selected from 116 submissions, the conference featured the following two invited presentations: *Data on Air – What's in it for the Database Theorist* by Tomasz Imielinski and *Spatial Databases, the Final Frontier* by Jan Paredaens. The conference also featured the following state-of-the-art tutorials: *Parallel Database Systems* by Gerhard Weikum and *Languages for Polynomial-time Queries – an Ongoing Quest* by Phokion G. Kolaitis.

The members of the program committee were:

Paolo Atzeni (Italy)	Jan Van den Bussche (Belgium)
Stefano Ceri (Italy)	Jan Chomicki (USA)
Janos Demetrovics (Hungary)	Georg Gottlob (Austria) co-chair
Stephane Grumbach (France)	Ravi Krishnamurthy (USA)
Georg Lausen (Germany)	Heikki Mannila (Finland)
Marina Moscarini (Italy)	Jaroslav Pokorný (Czech Republic)
Doron Rotem (USA)	Joachim Schmidt (Germany)
Odet Shmueli (Israel)	Letitia Tanca (Italy)
Bernhard Thalheim (Germany)	Mars K. Valiev (Russia)
Moshe Y. Vardi (USA) co-chair	Gottfried Vossen (Germany)
Peter Widmayer (Switzerland)	

External reviews were provided by:

Foto Afrati	Meike Albrecht	Andreas Benczur
Marco Cadoli	Luca Cabibbo	S. Castano
Surajit Chauduri	Amy Chen	Qiming Chen
Marco Colombetti	Anuj Dawar	M.I. Dekhtyar
A.Ya. Dikovsky	Marie Duzi	Thomas Eiter
Martin Erwig	Shi Fei	Andrew U. Frank
Piero Fraternali	Mike Freeston	O.Yu. Gorochinskaya
Ralf Hartmut Güting	Alois Heinz	Friedbert Huber-Wäschle
Willem Jonker	Gerti Kappel	Peter Kirschenhofer
Brigitte Kröll	Eva Kuehn	Gabriel Kuper
Nicola Leone	Bertram Ludäscher	R. Manthey
V. Markowitz	Tibor Markus	Bernd Meyer
Thomas Mueck	Peter Muth	Otto Nurmi
Frank Olken	Pekka Orponen	Stefano Paraboschi
G. Pernul	Riccardo Torlone	Lajos Ronyai
Kenneth A. Ross	Yehoshua Sagiv	Vladimir Sazonov
Marco Schaerf	Peter Schäuble	Hans-Jörg Schek
Klaus-Dieter Schewe	Gary Schloss	Markus Schneider
Michael Schrefl	Heribert Schuetz	Konrad Schwarz
Wolfgang Slany	Eljas Soisalon-Soininen	Hua Nam Son
Christian Stary	Ulrike Stege	P. Stepanek
Alexei P. Stolboushkin	Markus Stumptner	Jianwen Su
Christophe Tollu	Riccardo Torlone	Bela Uhrin
Heinz Uphoff	P. Vana	Helmuth Veith
Mark Wallace	Gerhard Weikum	O. Wolfson
Pierre Wolper	Haiyan Ye	

Conference Organization Committee

Marcela Bezoušková (Czech Republic)   Marie Duží (Czech Republic)
Jitka Ešpandrová (Czech Republic)   Marcus Herzog (Austria)
Dušan Húsek (Czech Republic)   Ludmila Kolářová (Czech Republic)
Lenka Lhotská (Czech Republic)   Vladimír Mařík (Czech Republic) co-chair
Jaroslav Pokorný (Czech Republic)   Katrin Seyr (Austria)
Wolfgang Slany (Austria)   Olga Štěpánková (Czech Republic) co-chair

We would like to sincerely thank all program committee members, as well as the external referees, for their care in evaluating the submitted papers.

Prague, January 1995   Georg Gottlob and Moshe Y. Vardi
                                       Program Co-Chairs

Table of Contents

Session 5: Query Languages II

Session 6: Advanced Models

Session 7: Probabilistic Methods

Session 8: Constraints and Dependencies

Session 9: Nonmonotonic Semantics II

Session 10: Datalog Analysis

Session 11: Query Languages III

Data on Air - What's in it for the database theorist
(Invited Paper)

Tomasz Imielinski

Department of Computer Science
Rutgers University
New Brunswick, NJ 08903
e-mail:{imielins}@cs.rutgers.edu

Abstract. Mobile and Wireless Computing is a new emerging computing paradigm posing many challenging data management problems. We provide a brief introduction to wireless technology, identify new research challenges and investigate their technical significance. New research problems emerge due to mobility of users, narrow wireless bandwidth and limitations of battery power.

1 Introduction

Wireless technology is gaining popularity very rapidly. Many predict a new emerging, gigantic market with millions of mobile users carrying small, battery powered terminals equipped with wireless connection.

The objective of this short paper is to sketch some of the research problems which emerge in the vision of mobile and wireless computing and which may be of interest to theoretical database community [1].

However, let me start with a disclaimer. If you are the kind of person who likes to ask *"Is this a database problem?"* this paper is probably not for you. In my opinion there are no new, clean and clear database problems anymore. In the age of integration of telecommunication networks, multimedia, distributed systems etc. researchers who are sticking to just one background in the name of of research purity will be left in the dust[2]. This is the time for database people to *learn* and *expand*. One natural area of expansion is, in my view, a growing synergy between databases and telecommunication networks. The research area which I would like to describe is a prime example of such a synergy.

In the future, users equipped with small handheld terminals will query information resources on the worldwide computer network via "wireless exit ramps". Typical applications will range from yellow pages (find me the nearest pizza restaurant, closest Skoda Dealer etc..) to traffic, weather and travel information (For example: is my plane late?). Wireless networks will include cellular, satellite

---

[1] For a more elaborate exposition of research challenges see [2]

[2] For example: is querying the World Wide Web a database problem? A Network problem? An Information Retrieval problem?

and the future PCS (Personal Communication) networks outdoors and wireless LAN indoors.

This paper addresses some of the issues which I characterize as data management problems in mobile and wireless computing[3] and combine knowledge and expertise of databases, distributed systems and telecommunication networks.

It is useful to group the major challenges to data management brought by the vision of mobile computing into the following categories:

1. Mobility Management and Scalability

   Location dependent applications will require the ability to query data which changes with location. Querying such data requires new, more general, models and solutions for query evaluation and optimization.

2. Bandwidth Management

   Wireless bandwidth will drop by two orders of magnitude when moving from indoor to outdoor environment. Typical wireless LAN such as Wavelan support 2Mb/s while cellular solutions such as CDPD provide only up to 19.2 Kb/s. Hence, the proposed solutions will have to be bandwidth efficient. Better organization of data on the communication channels could significantly improve bandwidth utilization. We will show that there is a strong connection between data organization methods which were developed for the disk storage and the data organization on the communication channels.

3. Energy Management and Portability

   Perhaps the most surprising limitation, at least to computer scientists, is that the lifetime of a battery is expected to increase only 20% over the next 10 years [5]. This is an extremely slow rate especially comparing to the fast progress in the areas of memory capacity and CPU speed. Hence, there seems to be a *long term* need for energy efficient solutions in all aspects of the systems software including, as we will show later in the paper, data management. Such solutions will either increase the lifetime of a given battery set or will reduce the size of the battery set without affecting the time between successive recharges. The latter, will increase the portability of the palmtop by reducing the battery weight.

   Energy management will affect the way data is disseminated in the wireless environments. Index based and Hashing based organization schemes are demonstrated to be very effective addressing methods for data streams on wireless communication channels.

   Portability will require new innovative user interfaces to concisely present query answers considering screen limitations of the small palmtop terminals.

Due to lack of space we will elaborate here only on two research issues: one dealing with querying location dependent information and another which deals with efficient organization of telecommunication data.

---

[3] The term "mobile databases" is a rather unfortunate characterization of the field. It is too narrow. This research is not about just databases, static or mobile...

2   Location Dependent Information Services

In a mobile environment, location of a user is an important and possibly frequently changing attribute. Location can be defined as a *cell* in which a user currently resides[4], in which case no distinction is made between two locations within the same cell. In case the *GPS* (Global Positioning System) is used, the location of the user can be determined much more precisely.

The value of the location attribute can either be stored in some database[5] or found out by performing a network search, for example by broadcasting a special WHERE_IS data packet[6]. Usually, a combination of a database lookup and network search is necessary in order to determine the location of the user since in most of the cases the database can only know the user's location approximately and further search is necessary to find out the exact location.

Let us start first with the problem of establishing a location of a user in the mobile network. Although this problem will be handled by the network layer protocols (such as MobileIP), the general location dependent queries will have to understand the network costs of locating a user.

Suppose that A wants to establish the location of B. Obviously we want to avoid searching the whole network. A standard scheme used in current cellular networks associates each user with his/her *Home Location Server* (HLS) which always knows the location of the user. If A wants to find out where B is he/she contacts B's home location server. B, on the other hand always informs his/her home location server upon moves. This results with many possibly unnecessary messages (location updates) from the user to his/her HLS even if this location information is not really needed (nobody requested the information). Additionally, two users, say from Prague, who are at a conference in Australia will still have to look for each other thru the remote Prague server (this is called triangular routing problem).

A number of alternative location schemes have been proposed which involve caching location information and providing different levels of granularity for location information. For example, the whole area can be partitioned into *zones* and the user will inform about his/her location only upon crossing the borders between *partitions* and not upon each and every move. Consequently, the network knows the location of the user only up to a certain degree of precision and the exact location of the user within a partition can only be determined by search within a partition [3].

It is important to understand the network costs which are involved in the process of finding out about unknown location of a user when dealing with location depedent queries.

---

[4] A cell is understood as area under radio coverage of one base station just as in cellular telephony
[5] Usually, in the cellular networks such a database is stored at the so called Home Location Register (HLR) placed in the switch nearest to the permanent location of the user
[6] Similarilly to Columbia's MobileIP protocol

2.1 Querying Location Dependent Data

Viewing location as an attribute implies that it can be a subject of more complex queries such as "Find the closest doctor to the campus" (where with doctors being possibly mobile or "Find the number of policemen in the stadium area." Such queries combine *spatial* or *geographic* information with possibly frequently changing location information. Other queries may not directly target the location attribute but may require information which is stored on the mobile terminal, with unknown location. For example, the latest sales figures for a group of travelling salesmen may require accessing sales figures on a bunch of mobile terminals.

Ad-hoc queries like this may be formed by users; they also may be formed by the network or the system administrator in order to dynamically balance the system's load. For example, the system may decide on the type of message routing or frequency allocation on the basis of locations of individual users (in the former case) or some aggregate information such as Count in the latter case.

We will assume the presence of location database (such as previously described home location register) which stores information about user's locations. Unfortunately, as we already indicated, this location information is almost never precise, in fact quite often may be simply incorrect[7]. However, there is always an option to *complete* the imprecise data in the location database by performing network search and of course paying for this[8]. This is an interesting option especially in comparison to the traditional databases where incomplete information cannot just be completed at request but is more of a permanent feature. This additional option to make information more complete at additional cost can lead to new models of query processing:

Given a fixed *budget* what is the "best" answer[9] a query which can be obtained possibly by "completing" some of the incomplete data values by performing network search. The cost of query evaluation is a combination of the database and network search, involving database access, and communication components. More precisely, given a query which depends on the location attribute (such as closest doctor or a number of taxi cabs in the area) we have the following options to evaluate it:

- Rely only on the database information (that is information stored at the location servers) while processing a query: Since the data in the database may be imprecise the answer to the query will also be imprecise and possibly carry an error as well. But the *communication* effort will be zero.
- Send additional messages to find out exact locations of objects which are relevant to the query. Here, at the expense of additional communication we can find out a more precise (closer to the actual) answer to the query.

---

[7] The cost of keeping such a database always up to data will simply be prohibitive - each move of a user would cause a database update

[8] No free lunch here!

[9] Best in terms of some predefined metric. Most of the queries which we consider here return numerical values

Obviously, we will be interested in exchanging as few messages as possible since communication cost is always substantial.

Hence, we will face a tradeoff between communication cost and the required precision of an answer to a query. Our aim is to achieve "maximal precision" for a fixed communication cost. Here we present three examples illustrating the basic tradeoffs between communication and computation.

Example
How many taxi cabs are in the campus area?

Example Consider the query to find the number of taxi cabs in the campus area. Suppose that the database knows only the "partitions" (zones) in which the taxi cabs are located, bounds (between 3 and 6 taxis) can be obtained immediately from the database. The partitions are explicitly represented as numbered rectangles on the figure 1. Improving the bounds will require additional messaging. For example, we can find out the exact locations of taxis 5 and 6 and improve the gap between the lower and the upper bound in the answer by 2. An interesting question is by how much can we improve the bound given that we can use only K messages.

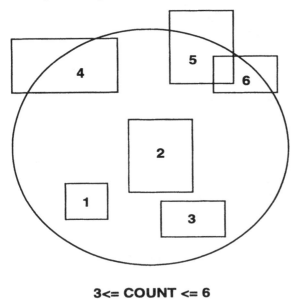

3<= COUNT <= 6

Fig. 1. Users in a given area

Querying changing locations requires careful combination of spatial query processing with the management of incompletely specified data. Incompletely specified location can be "completed" in the run time of a query by additional messaging. Thus, a query optimization problem has the additional new dimension: cost of acquiring data during the query's run time.

Example Another example of an aggregate query is to find the distance to the closest doctor. The doctors are known to be in partitions 1, 2, or 3. The closest distance can either be MIN if a doctor is found in partition 1 or MAX if the doctor is found in partition 2. The closest distance will lie within these bounds.Again, these bounds can be improved upon additional messaging to improve the location information.

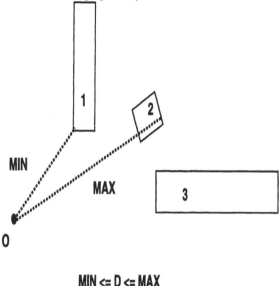

Fig. 2. Nearest Object

Incremental Query Evaluation

Answers to location dependent queries change while the users move. An interesting problem is to how to provide the "refresh" capability for the location dependent query answer without resending the new answer on location changes and consuming in this way costly network resources. For example, the answer to a query about directions to the nearest hospital can change upon move etc. In an implementation effort to extend Mosaic for wireless and mobile environments which we are currently undertaking, this problem manifests itself through "location dependent pages". A location dependent page changes its content on the basis of location - acting like a window to the surarounding world. If a page contains an image (map) there is an obvious need for incremental updates.

General Model

Querying location dependent information is a special case of quering update intensive, sensory data such as the data stored in many scientific databases. Such sensory information could include fast changing temperature, velocity, energy etc. There is a need for a general model for such fast changing sensory environments. The common features between location and sensory data can be summarized as follows:

– Data changes possibly more often than it is queried. Hence, precise tracking of data values by the database usually makes no sense.

- Exact measurement of data is an option which can be excercised at additional cost by a query.
- Query answers are almost never precise. Thus, the numerical error is a feature rather than a bug.

There is a clear need for a query optimization and query evaluation models which will involve "completing the data" in the run time of the query.

Knowledge about Locations

Let us now come back to more elementary questions dealing with location management which involve simple applications such as e-mail.

User profiles dealing with their mobility patterns can be effectively used to improve the efficiency of the network layer's mobility management. Interesting questions involve specification of user mobility profiles which will probably include a mixture of temporal and spatial information (e.g. between 11 and 12 I am usually in my office, after 12 you can find me in the lab) and their use in helping out the network to locate a given user[10].

For example, the sender may know the most likely locations of the receiver of the message and may instruct the network to try these locations first. The sender may know the receiver's informing strategy ("Mary would have notified me if she was going to go to Manhatan tonight"). The receiver may know about the sender's searching strategy ("John is first going to try my office number"). Finally, the receiver may or may not know the sender's search strategy. We can continue along this path and consider higher levels of "mutual" knowledge. Interesting questions involve utilizations of these differerent levels of knowledge in providing more efficient mobility management. One interesing "metastrategy" would ask the user to inform the network about his/her moves only when the moves are "surprising" - i.e. inconsistent with the user's profile.

Caching Location Information

Caching location information could be a very effective way of improving performance of location management methods. However, careful solutions are required to handle cache invalidations. Invalid cache may mislead the sender and increase his/her search cost significantly. On the other hand we cannot make the receiver (callee) responsible for invalidating every possible cache which may exist in the network storing his/her location. Cache invalidation based on expiration dates could offer an attractive alternative. For example, assume that the server in California has cached the location of a particular user in New Jersey to be in New Brunswick. The locationi information itself may be hierarchically structured so the most significant bits represent the state, then county and finally the township. Different expiration dates are assigned to different portions of the address and thus the state part may be stored for a week, the county part for a day and the city part for a few hours from the time it was first cached. Thus a few hours after the cache was created in California the most specific part of

---

[10] In the future networks may offer discounts to cooperative users who offer their profiles with, hopefully proper privacy and security measures. Allocation and replication of such profiles is another interesting problem

the location will explore but the information about the state and the county will still persist - it will be invalidated later on. Consequently, the cache information in California will only be approximate (and still could be incorrect if the user in fact made a wider area a move).

3 Data Organization on Air

We have argued in [6] that dissemination of information in wireless environment will be done using two basic modes: the *on demand* mode which is the standard client server mode of interaction and the publishing mode which amounts to periodic multicasting of the most important (most frequently accessed) information. For example, flight departures schedules may be periodically broadcasted (published) at the airport, where they are likely to be of interest, while they will be provided only "on demand" outside of the airport. In this way, bandwidth can be saved since it is no longer necessary to hadle repeated requests for the same information. Battery power at the client's machine is saved as well, since in the publishing mode the client does not have to transmit a costly uplink request - it simply waits and filters the incoming stream of data.

We view periodic publication mode as a form of storage "on air" in which air becomes a form of public storage medium. How to organize and data and directory information on the publishing channel is an interesting problem similar to disk organization in database systems. There are, however, important differences which make this problem a good candidate for further research. Below, we provide some basic explanations.

3.1 Publishing Mode - Energy Saving Access

Before demonstrating the energy saving advantages of the publishing mode let us explain the distinction between the active and doze modes.

Active and Doze modes

We assume that the client's CPU has the ability to operate in at least two major modes: the *active mode* and the *doze mode*. The doze mode describes a low power operation mode where CPU performs only a very limited set of operations. In the AT&T's Hobbit chip the doze mode requires 5,000 times less power than the active mode. By *low power operations* we mean operations which can be performed by the client *in the doze mode*. We are interested to maximize the use of low power operations in client server interactions. Below, we list some of the operations which can be provided without involving (waking up) the CPU:

- Filtering by matching multicast addresses:
  Assuming that the client is equipped with an Ethernet Card or a pager, such as the one used by Embarc or the new *Inflo* receiver [11] it can match the predefined set of packet addresses without waking up the CPU and utilizing only the low energy consuming circuits of Ethernet card or the pager.

---

[11] Recently announced by Motorola and NewsPager Corporation of America

– Filtering by matching a specific timestamp
Since clock can be operated as a low energy circuit, matching a predefined
timestamp can be performed entirely in a doze mode without waking up
the CPU. In this way the client can wake up at the specific time to receive
relevant information.
– Storing in a buffer
Receivers used in pagers such as Embarc and the recently announced *Inflo*
are capable of storing up to 120 Kbytes of data (Inflo). This buffer is built as
a low energy circuit, which does not require CPU to operate in active mode.

Queries per Watt?, Queries per Hz?

In cellular telephony one of the most important performance criteria is the
cell capacity: the number of telephone calls which may be handled by the cell
per unit of time. In the future - a *query* - a single request for a page (of some
standarized size) will be an analog of a telephone call[12]. Consequently, we believe
that future cell capacity will be measured as a number of *queries* which the
local MSS can handle per unit of time as well as a number of queries which a
mobile client can issue before it runs out of batteries. This leads us to two major
performance indexes: *queries per Hz*[13] and *queries per Watt* which measures a
number of queries which a given client can process from a one Watt battery.

We will structure the client server interactions in a way which maximizes both
queries per Hz as well as queries per Watt by using low energy operations and
minimizing such energy consuming tasks as client's initiated transmissions. This
in turn, will lead to a different structuring policy for a server which, at least for
the most frequently accessed data items will operate in *publishing mode* rather
than in *on-demand mode*. In publishing mode, the server periodically publishes
information without waiting for the explicit request for it. Publishing mode is
currently used by all major media such as TV, radio and newspapers. Publishing
mode requires no transmission from the client, but may require continuous tuning
for the client which wants to locate a data item it is interested in. Thus, in order
to further minimize the energy it is necessary to provide the client with the
ability of *low power filtering* operations. This can be accomplished by making
sure that the client remains in the doze mode and wakes up only when the
"relevant' data is being published.

Summarizing, the low energy information system will be structured using the
following principles:

– The server periodically publishes the most frequently accessed data items.
The rest of the data items are provided "on demand" in the usual client-
server mode of operation This minimizes the number of transmissions from
the client, since accessing published data items requires only "listening."

---

[12] The concept of a query is used here in much more narrow sense than in standard
database literature and it is closer to a file system's page request. Page is Mosaic-like
page though, rather than disk sector equivalent volume of data
[13] Maximizing the number of queries which the wireless link with a given bandwidth
can handle in a unit of time

– The client has the ability of selectively listening to the published information by remaining in a doze mode and waking up only when relevant information is published. This avoids excessive energy consumption on the client's side due to continuous tuning to the published information in the active mode.

The published information can be viewed as a *cache* or cache on the air [6]. The client first tries to locate the item it is looking for on the cache and only upon cache miss, does it submits a request to the server. Hence, transmission from the client takes place only upon cache miss. Additionally, the cache itself is *addressable* in order to enable selective listening on the client's side. The addressing of server's published information should be done in such a way that address matching is a low power operation, i.e., address matching is performed in the *doze mode* without engaging the CPU.

This can be implemented using two basic operations which can be performed while in doze mode:

The publishing channel can be viewed as a virtual memory which is addressable in such a way that address matching is a *low power operation*. Technically, the address of a page on the network is an element of the cartesian product:

$$TIME * CHANNEL$$

The TIME domain is the set of timestamps and the CHANNEL domain is the set of multicast addresses[14]. For example, the IBM stockquote may be published at 11:30 AM on the multicast address 255.6.4.2. For selective tuning it is imperative to provide a directory information to the clients. The directory provides the mapping between the pages and their addresses.

In [6] a number of methods have been proposed to multiplex the directory (index) information together with the data on the same channel, in case the address refers simply to the time of the publication of a data item. One can extend these methods to the situations when the address is a hybrid of temporal and multicast addressing. The mapping between the data items and the addresses can be performed by a hashing function, which when applied to a data item returns the multicast address.

For instance, in a stock market information service, each stock quote can be mapped to a multicast address. There are 28 bits available for *multicast groups*, which provide an address space of 2^{28} addresses. A hashing function which is known to the receiving client is applied to the name (or its three letter abbreviation) of the stock that it is interested in, to obtain the multicast address. This is the finest possible granularity of indexing which leads to non-efficient use of packets since usually a single packet can carry numerous stock quotes, not just one. In case numerous stock quotes are "packed" into one packet only one multicast address is needed for every (such) group of stocks. Hashing into *buckets* rather than single addresses can accomplish this goal.

The client then, joins such a multicast group and is able to filter the relevant packets using Ethernet card only, without waking up the CPU and the whole IP protocol stack. This protocol has actually been implemented and the details are

---

[14] In IP, this constitutes all 32 bit addresses starting with 1111.

reported in an upcoming technical report. It also describes how more complex events (triggers) such as "New High" or stock going up by more than a predefined threshold can be implemented.

To accommodate a free style, ad hoc mode of querying, the directory has to be explicitly published as well. In [6] we discuss in detail how the index information (directory) can be multiplexed together with the data on the downlink channel in case, temporal addressing is used. For multicast addressing, a hashing function which maps the keys of data items (or pages) to the multicast addresses has to be provided to the clients.

Since the hashing function takes much less space than the full directory it can be provided to the clients on a "one to one" basis upon crossing a cell boundary (as part of the registration).

Virtual Network Memory

In this way the communication channel, or the network, can be viewed as a database with a new extended form of address which could be a mixture of multicast and temporal components. The address which reads "tune at 11:30AM to the channel 164.5.6.4" to get this data items, seems to be a fairly unortodox way of database addressing. It looks like the concept of a *stream* similar to the one used in dataflow computing would be a right model for the network based memory. This leads to a concept of virtual memory which includes not only the memory of the client (internal and external) and the server (external and internal) but also the network itself. This addressing of such distributed shared memory should be entirely transparent to the client analogously to the way virtual memory concept hides the real physical address of data from the application.

Querying Streams

Querying continous stream of information such as broadcasted data calls for new methods of query evaluation and is an interesting area of future research [4]. The answer to the query should dynamically change along with the incoming data stream which is a mixture of metadata and data. The stream model captures well general context of querying network residing data both on fixed as well as on the wireless medium.

4 Other research issues

Due to the lack of space we have concentrated on two major research issues dealing with mobility management and with new modes of information dissemination. There is a number of other important research issues in mobile and wireless computing which may be of interest to the database community. We should mention quite a few here:

- Disconnection Management
  The mobile clients will be disconnected most of the time in order to save energy. How are we going to ensure data consistency and support concurrency control for transactions issued by such frequently disconnected

clients? In case several users, say traveling salesmen, share a common inventory database this will be a pressing issue especially assuming a low bandwidth of outdoor radio. Indirect solutions which are easy on wireless link and run mostly on the fixed part of the network will be necessary. New caching methods will be necessary in which invalidation messages are efficiently distributed. Solutions which assume stateless servers will be more practical.

- Replication and Migration of Data
  The network should be able to balance its load in order to adjust to changing distributions of mobile users. There will be an increased need for dynamic replication and data migration methods such as [7]
- Innovative User Interfaces - Answer Presentation
  There is a clear need for new family of user interfaces to support database access from small palmtop terminals. How should a large answer to a query be presented on the small screen of a palmtop terminal? New abstraction and approximation methods are necesary to represent query answers with possibly increasing levels of precision.

5 Summary

The problems described in this paper are only beginning to be addressed. The recent, NSF sponsored, *Mobidata* workshop at Rutgers (Nov,1,1994) [1] has a chance of stimulating more research in this area[15]. Recent Sigmod and IEEE Distributed Computing Conference (1994) both had sessions on mobile computing.

I would like to encourage database researchers to learn about new exciting technologies and to take a broader view of database research. Yes, there is life after Datalog...

References

1. Proceedings of the Mobidata Workshop, Rutgers University, Editors: Tomasz Imielinski and Hank F. Korth, November, 1994.
2. T. Imielinski and B. R. Badrinath, "Wireless mobile computing: Challenges in data management," In *Communications of the ACM*, October 1994, pp. 19–27.
3. T. Imielinski and B. R. Badrinath, "Querying in Highly distributed environments," In the Proceedings of the 18th VLDB, August 1992, pp. 41–52.
4. D. B. Terry, D. Goldberg, D. A. Nichols, and B. M. Oki, "Continous queries over append-only databases," Proc of the ACM SIGMOD, June 1992, pp. 321–330.
5. Samuel Sheng, Ananth Chandrasekaran, and R. W. Broderson, "A portable multimedia terminal for personal communications," IEEE Communications Magazine, December 1992, pp. 64–75.

---

[15] The report about the workshop will be soon available through Rutgers's WWW Mobile Computing site at http://paul.rutgers.edu/ acharya/dataman.html This site contains also other information about the DataMan project on Mobile and Wireless Computing

Spatial Databases,

The Final Frontier

Jan Paredaens
University of Antwerp, Belgium
pareda@wins.uia.ua.ac.be

During the last decade database systems are used to represent spatial information mainly in the two-dimensional plane or the three-dimensional space. Applications that rely on spatial databases can be found in CAD-CAM, VLSI, robotics, historical databases, geographical information systems, architectural sciences, visual perception and autonomous navigation, tracking, environmental protection and medical imaging.

Following [Gut94b] a spatial database is a database system that offers spatial data types in its data model and query language and supports such data types in its implementation, providing at least spatial indexing and efficient algorithms for spatial join.

A spatial database system should
- contain an elegant framework to combine geometric and thematic information;
- be as general as possible and not be designed for one particular area of applications;
- have a formally defined semantics that is closed under set theoretic, geometric and topological operations and that is defined in terms of finite representations;
- be independent of a particular DBMS but cooperative with any DBMS;
- use efficient implementation techniques, especially for the operations on n-dimensional objects;
- have an up-to-date visual user interface and a gateway to multimedia.

The first spatial database systems that were build do not support all these criteria. Their main issue was to extend existing database management systems by introducing rather trivial spatial data types and extending SQL in an ad hoc way. There was, and still is, a lack to understand the more fundamental issues that are involved in geometric data types. In traditional database systems we have a clear understanding of which part of the information retrieval is handled by the DBMS, and which part is handled by the application software. A projection, for instance, is part of the query language, the calculation of the standard deviation, is not. How do we make such a distinction in the case of a spatial database? Which is the range of data models that can be acceptable candidates for a spatial DBMS and which are the typical features and properties of spatial data manipulation languages?

We believe, that after a few years of experiments, it is now time to investigate deeper those characteristics that distinguish the spatial database systems from the traditional ones. As the authors say in [Gue90]: 'The challenge for the developers of DBMSs with spatial capabilities lies not so much in providing yet another special-purpose data structure that is marginally faster when used in a particular application, but in defining abstractions and architectures to implement systems that offer generic spatial data management capabilities and that can be tailored to the requirements of a particular domain'.

Looking to the literature, we see that only a few researchers have paid attention to the basic issues of spatial data. One of the reasons of this lack of interest could be the vast know-how that is needed in three totally different areas of science: databases and information systems [Kem87], geography and cartography [Col68], and abstract and computational geometry [Pre85] and topology [Ale61]. We are convinced that the contribution of each of them is inevitable in a solid theory of spatial information systems. They are the basis of the so-called geomatic data models.

This paper is divided into two parts. In Section 1 we discuss five different geomatic data models. All of them are intentional, i.e. they give a finite representation of the mostly infinite and even non-enumerable

6. T. Imielinski, S. Vishwanathan, and B. R. Badrinath, "Energy efficient indexing on air," *In Proc of ACM SIGMOD*, May 1994, pp. 25–36.
7. Y.Huang, P. Sistla and O.Wolfson, "Data Replication for Mobile Computers" *In Proc of ACM SIGMOD*, May 1994, pp. 13–25.

set of points of the spatial objects that are described by the database. In the Raster Model an object is given by a finite number of its points. These points are equally distributed following an easy geometric pattern, which is normally a square. In the Spaghetti Model an object is intentionally deduced from its contour, which is a polyline. The Peano Model also uses a finite number of object-points, but here these points are distributed non-uniformly, according to the form of the object. This distribution method is based on the well-known Peano curve. In the Polynomial Model we use a calculus, extended with comparisons between polynomials. In the PLA-Model, finally, only some kind of topological information is handled without dealing with the exact position and form of the spatial objects.

In Section 2 we try to focus on the typical geomatic operations and we introduce different kinds of spatial queries. Therefore we generalize the well-known concept of genericity of Chandra and Harel [Cha80]. A taxonomy of genericity-classes is given. We end with investigating two of these classes more deeply: the isometry-generic queries and the topology-generic queries.

On many occasions we will introduce open problems, open areas or topics that have to be studied. We are convinced that a lot of research has to be done in the field of geomatic data types and geomatic operations and we hope that this text can motivate some of the young and intelligent researchers to pay more attention in the future to this unexplored forest that is irrigated by three main rivers: geometry, information sciences and geography.

1 Geomatic Data Models

Four main characteristics distinguish geomatic data models from the classic ones:

- geomatic data models are used to represent information about the n-dimensional real space IR^n. The latter is an infinite, even a non-enumerable, set of points. So, in general, the information we want to represent is infinite in nature. This prevents us to use extensional data models. Different intentional techniques are used in geomatic data models for representing this infinite information. The data model that will be used in a particular geomatic database depends on the operations that have to be defined and on the efficiency needs of the implementation;

- the intentional aspect of geomatic data models has a particular influence on the operations, those that are defined within the model as well as those that are user-defined [Gut89]: the data model has to be closed for all the operations. Since geomatic applications ask typically for a rich set of operations, the above property can be hard to be fulfilled;

- the information that is represented in geomatic applications has usually not the elegant geometric properties of a man-created structure, but is mostly the visualization of a symmetryless phenomenon proceeded from nature. This induces that the intentional information is mostly vast and that we need particular algorithms for implementing the datastructure. These algorithms are based on algebraic, geometrical and topological properties;

- the notion of genericity distinguishes the typical abstract operations that are independent from the contents of the information, from the operations whose result is intrinsically influenced by this contents. This notion of genericity, which has been formally defined for classical data models [Cha80], seems to break up in a hierarchy for geomatic data models.

In this section we give an overview of some well-known geomatic data models: the Raster Model, the Spaghetti Model, the Peano Model, the Polynomial Model and the PLA-Model.

1.1 The Raster Model

In the Raster Model [Gut93a,Gut93b,Sam90] the geomatic information is intentionally represented by a finite number of raster points with the semantics that the infinite number of points in the environment of a raster point p have the same properties as p. The raster points are uniformly distributed over the object that is considered. Although this is a quite natural definition, some problems can arise since the environment of a raster point is not always homogeneous as to the relevant properties. In Figure 1 for instance most of the points in the environment of raster point G are not on the line b, (an infinite number of) others are. This fundamental problem gives rise to a number of anomalies in the natural extension of classical operations to the Raster Model.

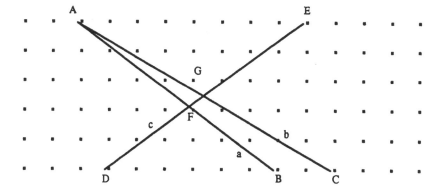

Figure 1

We can illustrate this in Figure 1. In the Raster Model a line is represented by two of its raster points. Theoretically this gives a problem to represent those lines that do not contain any raster point, but in most applications these lines can be approximated sufficiently by representable lines. In Figure 1, the line a is represented by A and B, b by A and C and c by D and E. Clearly the two lines b and c intersect although their real-intersection-point is not a raster point. The model could define the model-intersection-point to be the nearest raster point to the real-intersection-point, here this is F, but then we deduce in the model that F is on line b. Since F is also on line a it is the raster-intersection-point of a and b, but A is also the raster-intersection-point of a and b, since it is a raster point as well as the real-intersection-point of a and b. This kind of problems is handled in [Gut93a,Gut93b].

1.2 The Spaghetti Model

In the Spaghetti Model, or Vectorization Model [Lau92], the information in an n-dimensional space is represented only using m-dimensional hyperspaces, with m < n. This means that in a three-dimensional space we only consider polyhedra, the boundaries of which contain planar facets, segments and points.

In the two-dimensional case we only consider polygons, the boundaries of which contain segments and points. More concretely we use here:
- points;
- graphs, whose datastructure is a finite set of pairs of points;
- polylines, whose datastructure is a finite sequence of points;
- polygons that are represented by non-selfintersecting closed polylines;
- complex polygons, that can contain holes, which are again complex polygons (up to a finite level);
- objects are sets of polygons, points or graphs.

Hence we have

POINT = (x: REAL, y: REAL, a: DOM)
GRAPH = (g: {(p1: POINT, p2: POINT)}, a: DOM)
P_LINE = (p: POINT*, a: DOM)
POLYGON = P_LINE
COMPLEX_POLYGON = POLYGON |
      (p: POLYGON, holes: {COMPLEX_POLYGON}, a: DOM)
OBJECT = {(id: KEY, p: POINT, a: DOM)} | {(id: KEY, g: GRAPH, a: DOM)} |
      {(id: KEY, c: COMPLEX_POLYGON, a: DOM)}.

'a: DOM' denotes one or more thematic attributes.
Figure 2 shows one object that contains two complex polygons and one object that contains a graph.

The reason why this model is so popular is the existence of very efficient algorithms for detecting properties in this model [Sam90]. We are thinking of verification algorithms to detect wether two polygons overlap, whether a point lies in a polygon or on a segment, whether two segments intersect, whether a polyline selfintersects, whether a polygon is contained in another one, etc. Furthermore the model is simple to use and offers in most applications a sufficient approximation to reality. Also the technique of 'recursive holes' has some unexpected applications, such as the representation of a third dimension in a two-dimensional space (like isobars and isotherms).

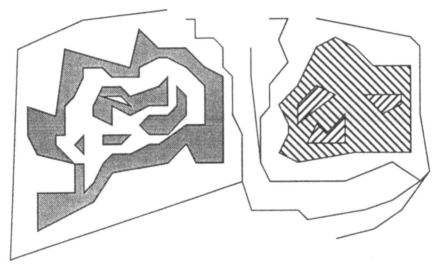

Figure 2

The Spaghetti Model is a widely discussed model [Bur77,Gue88] and numerous query languages [Cha94, Rig94,Gut94a,Ege94b] and algebras [Gut88,Gut89] can be found in the literature that are based on a spaghetti-like model.

1.3 The Peano Model

In contrast to the Spaghetti Model, some models try intentionally to represent every point of an object, in the same sense as the Raster Model. Such models are sometimes called the 'Pizza' Models. The Peano Model is such a model. It is an elegant marriage of two different well-known techniques: space-filling curves and quadtrees.

A space-filling curve is an infinite sequence of curves, whose limit fills a given square. Two of the most well-known examples are the Peano curve [Pea90] and the Hilbert curve. They are illustrated in Figures 3 and 4.

The quadtree [Sam90] is a generalization of the binary tree in which every node is a leave or has four children. Each node represents a quadrant of its parent. The quadtree is an appropriate implementation technique for the two-dimensional information of a square. It is illustrated in Figure 5.

[i,j] indicates the subsquare with edge-length j, whose left bottom unit subsquare is labeled by i. Remark that the unit subsquares are labeled according to the second Peano curve of Figure 3. There is a very handsome technique to calculate the label of a unit square:

$$label(u) = interleave(u_x, u_y)$$

where
- label(u) is the binary representation of the label of the unit subsquare u;
- u_x and u_y are the binary coordinates of u;
- interleave shuffles its two binary arguments.

The Peano Model [Lau92] is particularly interesting to represent surfaces or volumes. As in the Raster Model the information is represented by a finite number of points, but these points are not uniformly distributed as is the case in the Raster Model. Actually it is a special kind of the relational model where each relation contains tuples that represent subsquares. Each Peano relation has the form

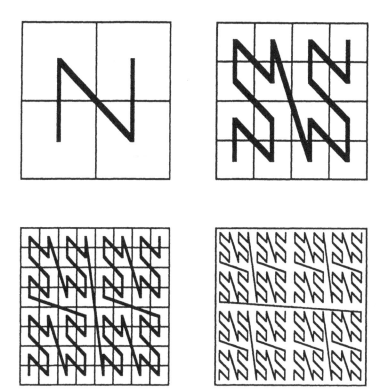

Figure 3

PR(OID, P, S, A$_1$, ... , A$_n$)

where
- PR is the name of the Peano relation;
- OID is the object identifier of which the subsquare is a part;
- P is the Peano key, that is the label of the bottom-left unit subsquare of the square that is represented;
- S is the edge-length of the subsquare;
- A$_1$,..., A$_n$ are attributes.

Figure 6 contains the Peano relation of Figure 5.

Clearly we will always endeavor a maximal quadrant compaction.

On this model, the Peano algebra was defined with 12 operators on relations:
- union, intersection, difference;
- translation of an object, rotation of a object over k*90 degrees;
- scaling of an object with a factor 2^i;
- symmetry according to an axis;
- extracting, which is deleting all objects outside a given window;
- duplication of an object;
- changing the unit, which looses some information;
- classical projection and join.

Consider the following example of a land registry [Lau92]. It contains three relations:

LAND_OWNER(Parcel-ID, Landowner-ID)
PR-PARCEL(Parcel-ID, P, S)

Figure 4

and a relation for a planned road passing through the area of the land registry

PR-ROAD(P, S)

We want the land-owners, together with their parcels that are affected.

Therefore we first calculate the join of PR-PARCEL and PR-ROAD obtaining

A1(Parcel-ID, P, S)

containing all the parcels that are affected. Then we join A1 with LAND_OWNER in order to get

A2(Landowner-ID, Parcel-ID, P, S), which is projected to obtain

A3(Landowner-ID).

The Peano Model is an elegant model for a direct representation of areas and volumes that is not based on contours. Because of its relationship with Peano curves it is efficiently implementable. To our knowledge the fundamental properties of this model and this algebra have not yet been investigated.

Some possible directions are:

- Is the algebra, as it is proposed above, complete, or are there other relevant operators we cannot express? What is the characterization of the operations that we can express by this algebra?

- How do we generalize this model to more dimensions, and with an additional technique to represent objects of a lower dimension (for instance curves in a two-dimensional space)?

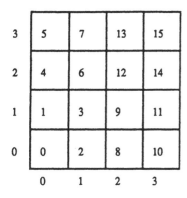 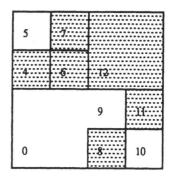

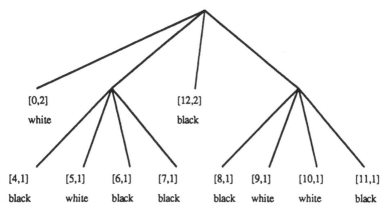

Figure 5

ZOOM_IN	OID	P	S	A
	background	0	2	white
	head	4	1	black
	background	5	1	white
	head	6	1	black
	head	7	1	black
	head	8	1	black
	background	9	1	white
	background	10	1	white
	head	11	1	black
	head	12	2	black

Figure 6

- The basic polygon-structure is here the square. What about using triangles or hexagons? What do we gain or lose?

- We only can handle a finite part of the n-dimensional space. How the Peano Model can it be extended such that we can also handle objects with an infinite length, surface or volume?

- An analogous model can be build, based on other space-filling curves, like the Hilbert curve f.i., although the way to calculated the square labels will be not so elegant.
  Also other trees like octtrees or R- and R$^+$-trees [Sam90, Hoe94] can be considered.

- In [Sch89] the authors develop an algebra on regions. It is one of the rare algebras on a Pizza Model. Such algebras have to be studied furthermore and their relation to the Peano Model for the implementation should be investigated.

1.4 The Polynomial Model

In the Polynomial Model [Kan90,Par94a,Par94b] the information is stored in relations. Each relation contains a finite number of tuples. A relation has at most one spatial attribute for representing a spatial object. Furthermore it can have a number of thematic attributes that represent non-spatial information.
Each tuple has a component for every attribute. In the case of the spatial attribute this component represents the spatial properties of an entire object. In the case of a thematic attribute the component is an atomic value.
The spatial properties of an object are described by a semi-algebraic set of the form

$$\{ (x_1, ..., x_n) \mid x_1, ... , x_n \in IR \wedge \Phi(x_1, ... , x_n) \}$$

where $\Phi(x_1, ... , x_n)$ is a semi-algebraic formula that contains boolean operators, existential and universal quantifiers and whose terms are comparisons, using $<, \leq, >, \geq, =, \neq$, between polynomials whose coefficients are rational numbers. $x_1, ... , x_n$ are the free variables of Φ.

Remark that the coefficients of the polynomials are rational numbers in order to be representable.

$$\{ (x_1,x_2) \mid (81 < (x_1 - 6)^2 + (x_2 - 5)^2) \wedge ((x_1 - 6)^2 + (x_2 - 5)^2 < 121) \}$$

and

$$\{ (x_1,x_2) \mid \exists x_3 \; \exists x_4 \; ((x_3 - 6)^2 + (x_4 - 5)^2) = 100 \wedge ((x_3 - x_1)^2 + (x_4 - x_2)^2 < 1) \}$$

are two semi-algebraic sets that both represent Figure 7.

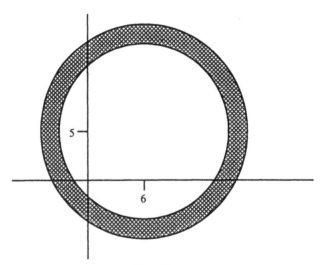

Figure 7

In general, it is decidable whether two semi-algebraic sets are equivalent, in the sense that they represent the same geometrical object [Par94b]. This result is far from trivial and is based on the famous Tarski Theorem [Tar51] that says that every semi-algebraic formula is equivalent to a semi-algebraic formula without quantifiers.

Consider now the spatial relation SR = (SA; TA_1, ... , TA_k) where the SA is the spatial attribute and TA_1, ... , TA_k are the thematic attributes. A tuple of this relation has the form

$(\Phi; a_1, \dots, a_k)$, with the Φ being a semi-algebraic formula and the a_i's being atomic values.

The extension of this tuple is the set $\{ (x_1, \dots, x_n; a_1, \dots, a_k) \mid \Phi(x_1, \dots, x_n) \}$.

In Figure 8 we give a spatial relation together with the representation of its extension on a part of the first quadrant.

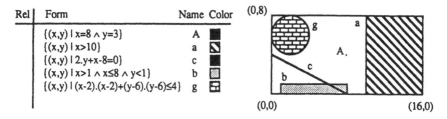

Rel	Form	Name	Color
	$\{(x,y) \mid x=8 \wedge y=3\}$	A	■
	$\{(x,y) \mid x>10\}$	a	◨
	$\{(x,y) \mid 2.y+x-8=0\}$	c	■
	$\{(x,y) \mid x>1 \wedge x\leq8 \wedge y<1\}$	b	▨
	$\{(x,y) \mid (x-2).(x-2)+(y-6).(y-6)\leq4\}$	g	▦

Figure 8

In the Polynomial Model a query Q is a partial recursive function on the set of relations for which there is a function Q_e with:

- Q_e can be expressed by $\{ (x_1, \dots, x_n, y_1, \dots, y_k') \mid \Psi(x_1, \dots, x_n, y_1, \dots, y_k') \}$
  where $\Psi(x_1, \dots, x_n, y_1, \dots, y_k')$ is a formula that contains boolean operators, existential and universal quantifiers and whose terms have the form $(x'_1, \dots, x'_n, y'_1, \dots, y'_k) \in SR$, $y'_i = y'_j$, $y'_i = c$ or are comparisons, using $<, \leq, >, \geq, =, \neq$, between polynomials whose coefficients are rational numbers. $x_1, \dots, x_n, y_1, \dots, y_k'$ are the free variables of Ψ.
  $\{ (x_1, \dots, x_n, y_1, \dots, y_k') \mid \Psi(x_1, \dots, x_n, y_1, \dots, y_k') \}$ is called a formula of the polynomial calculus;
- the diagram of Figure 9 being commutative.

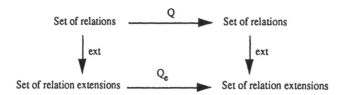

Figure 9

Reconsider Figure 8. Figure 10 gives the queries for respectively:
- Give the name of the shaded objects.
- Show the shaded objects, translated by 4 units to the right.

$$\{ (n) \mid \exists x \exists y (x, y; n, \textbf{◨}) \in Rel \}$$

$$\{ (x, y) \mid \exists n \exists x' ((x', y; n, \textbf{◨}) \in Rel \wedge x = x'+4) \}$$

Figure 10

Figure 11 shows a second example: the relation with its attributes, the question in English, the query and an example of the answer.

SR_Geo(Plane; Ident)

Give the topological boundary for each figure in the given plane.

{ (x, y; n) | (x, y; n) ∈ SR_Geo ∧ ∀ r ∃ x' ∃ y' ((x-x').(x-x')+(y-y').(y-y')<r.r ∧ (x', y'; n) ∉ SR_Geo) }

Given   Answer

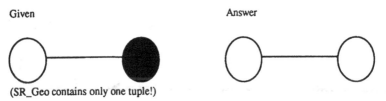

(SR_Geo contains only one tuple!)

Figure 11

Here is a wide range of research problems:

- Is the definition of a tuple relevant and fundamentally different if we consider the coefficients of the polynomials to be integers, algebraic numbers or belonging to some other enumerable field?

- Try to characterize the expressive power of this query language and also of the sublanguages where we restrict Ψ to be quantifierless, or a conjunction, or containing no polynomial part, or where all polynomials have a degree at most one, etc.

- We know that it is undecidable whether two given queries are equivalent. But what about queries of the above sublanguages?

- Give an appropriate implementation model with an optimization method for the Polynomial Model.

- Are the following queries expressible by the polynomial calculus: the transitive closure, whether an object is connected, whether an object contains only a finite number of points, whether an object is the union of a finite number of line segments, of filled squares, of filled triangles, of disks, etc. ?

1.5 The PLA-Model

The so-called PLA-Model was introduced by the Census Bureau of the United States in 1979 [Cor79]. It contains topological information on points, lines and areas, that are called zero-cells, one-cells and two-cells respectively [Lau92].

The two-dimensional plane is described by a number of cells, each having an identifier. Furthermore the following types of information is given:
- every one-cell has two zero-cells, indicating that every line has exactly two endpoints;
- every one-cell has two two-cells, indicating that every line is the border between exactly two areas;
- every two-cell is surrounded by a cycle of one-cells and zero-cells, indicating the border of an area;
- every zero-cell is surrounded by a cycle of one-cells and two-cells, indicating the neighborhood of a point.

Furthermore we suppose that all intersections of lines are points and all intersections of areas are lines. This condition settles the planarity of the model.

Consider the example of a PLA-database in Figure 13, illustrated in Figure 12.

Ri represents the information of type i.

Clearly Figure 14 is also represented by the PLA-database of Figure 13.

Hence the exact position of the cells nor their length or surface is not given by this representation. Only the interrelation of the position of the lines, the areas and the points, i.e. its topological properties are determined. If we are only interested in this kind of information, this model does not contain any redundancy.

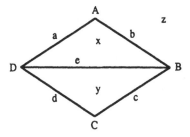

Figure 12

R1	1-cell	from	to
	a	D	A
	b	A	B
	c	B	C
	d	C	D
	e	B	D

R2	1-cell	left	right
	a	z	x
	b	z	x
	c	z	y
	d	z	y
	e	y	x

R3	2-cell	point	line	#
	x	A	b	1
	x	B	e	2
	x	D	a	3
	y	B	c	1
	y	C	d	2
	y	D	e	3
	z	A	b	1
	z	B	c	·2
	z	C	d	3
	z	D	a	4

R4	0-cell	line	area	#
	A	b	x	1
	A	a	z	2
	B	c	y	1
	B	e	x	2
	B	b	z	3
	C	d	y	1
	C	c	z	2
	D	a	x	1
	D	e	y	2
	D	d	z	3

Figure 13

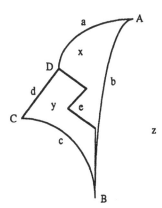

Figure 14

Several topics are here interesting to be discussed:

- Clearly the relations R1, R2, R3 and R4 satisfy some constraints, s.a.: If A is an endpoint of a in R1 then a has to occur in the environment of A in R4. Which are the necessary and sufficient constraints for this model to represent the information in the full two-dimensional plane? What is the complexity for verifying these constraints?

- Suppose we want to use this model to represent the information of a bounded part of the plane, with possible holes. Suppose furthermore we do not stick to planarity, but that we want to model overlays with areas that overlap and lines that cross without having a crossing point. Which are the necessary and sufficient constraints in that case?

- Suppose we want to use this model to represent the information on a sphere. What are the constraints in that case?

- Clearly, it is decidable whether two PLA-databases are equivalent, in the sense that they represent topologically isomorphic information. What is the complexity of such a verification algorithm?

- For which kind of transformations is this model closed? Which kind of queries in this model give a result that can be expressed in this model? Design a suitable query language for the PLA-Model.

1.6 Other Models

Numerous other models could be considered for representing geomatic data. One point for instance could be represented by:
- by its Cartesian coordinates (complete geomatic information);
- by its pole coordinates (complete geomatic information);
- by indicating that its distance to a given point p is smaller then a given number r (partial information);
- by indicating its quadrant (also partial information);
- just by indicating it is in the plane (here we do not have any information at all);
- etc.

A polyline could be represented by:
- the sequence of the endpoints of its lines (complete information);
- the sequence of the direction-coefficients of its lines (partial information);
- for each of its points, whether it is more to the north, to the west, to the south or to the east of its predecessor (more partial information);
- the number of its lines (more partial information);
- its two endpoints (partial information);
- etc.

A region could be represented by:
- the Raster Model, the Peano Model, the Polynomial Model, the Spaghetti Model (could be complete or incomplete information);
- the PLA-Model (partial information);
- its surface (partial information);
- a square, it is contained in (also partial information);
- etc.

Clearly the more partial the information is, the lesser queries can be asked to the database.

It would be very interesting to study a general framework that clarifies the information hierarchy of the different geomatic models and that defines a hierarchy of query languages on these models.

2 Geomatic Genericity

Genericity is a well-known concept in the theory of computable queries in databases. Indeed, a query in the relational model is called computable iff it is a Turing-Computable function on a representation of the database, that is also generic. By a generic function Q we mean here a function whose result is invariant on any permutation ϕ of the universal domain of the database.

Formally this means that if D and D' are two relational databases such that D' = φ(D), for some permutation φ, then Q(D') = φ.Q(D). It is well-known that all the operation in the relational algebra are generic (except for the selections of the form $\sigma_{A=c}$ and $\sigma_{A>B}$). On the other hand, the algebra is not complete for the generic functions, since the transitive closure, for instance, is a generic function that cannot be expressed by the algebra.

A weaker kind of genericity, the C-genericity, where C is a subset of the universal domain, has been introduced: a function Q is called C-generic if its result is invariant on any permutation φ, for which φ(c) = c for all c ∈ C. Obviously $\sigma_{A=c}$ is {c}-generic.

In the sequel we will try to understand what genericity means in the context of geomatic data models. We will see that there is no unique intuition of geomatic genericity. In the next subsection we give a taxonomy. Afterwards we will focus on two types of geomatic genericity: the isometry- and the topology-genericity.

2.1 Taxonomy

A lot of examples are given in this section, most of them concern a database that contains information about persons and the place they live. By place we mean the geomatic information of their home. The database also contains geomatic information about one region Reg. This could be expressed in one of the five models of Section 1 or in some other model. The next queries are illustrated in Figure 15.

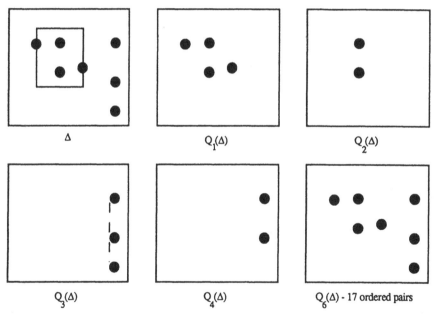

Figure 15

A first simple kind of query is

Q_1: Give the home of the persons that live in Reg.

This query commutes with every permutation of the points of IR^2. Indeed, if φ is an arbitrary permutation on the plane, φ: IR^2 --> IR^2, then we have that

$$Q_1.\phi = \phi.Q_1$$

This question is independent of any geometric, geomatic or topological property of the region. We mean that, if we first select the wanted locations and then apply some permutation φ, we get the same result as first doing the permutation ϕ and then ask the question. We say that Q_1 is **permutation-generic**. This type of genericity is identical to the genericity in the relational model, as explained above. Remark that it can be expressed in any of the five models of Section 1.

Consider now a second question

Q_2: Give the home of the persons that live in the interior of Reg.

By interior we mean here the topological interior. It is clear that this query does not commute with every permutation. Indeed, take only one person living in (0,0), the region being the closed disk with center (0,0) and radius 1 and consider the permutation that interchanges (0,0) and (2,2) and fixes the rest. Obviously (2,2) is not in $Q_2.\phi(\Delta)$, while it is in $\phi.Q_2(\Delta)$, where Δ is the database.

However, Q_2 commutes with every continuous permutation. Therefore we call it **topology-generic**. Such queries can be expressed in the Polynomial, the PLA- and the Spaghetti Model but not in the Raster, nor in the Peano Model.

An affinity is a permutation that preserves collinearity. They give rise to the **affinity-generic** queries, being those queries that commute with the affinities. The query Q_3 is obviously an affinity-generic query:

Q_3: Give the triples of homes of those persons that live on one line.

We can prove that Q_4,

Q_4: Give the homes of those persons that live closest to the region.

is not affinity-generic, but it commutes with all similarities. A similarity is a permutation that preserves the angles. Such queries are called the **similarity-generic** queries.

The next question

Q_5: Give the pairs of homes of those persons that live exactly 10 from each other.

This query is obviously not similarity-generic but it commutes with every isometry. An isometry is a permutation that preserves the distances. Therefore we call this query **isometry-generic**. It can be expressed in all models of Section 1 except for the PLA-Model.

The next class contains the **direct-isometry-generic** queries. These queries commute with the direct-isometries, those permutations that preserve the distance and the clock-orientation.

Finally, we have the **translation-generic** queries. They commute with the translations.

Q_6: Give the ordered pairs of homes of those persons, the first lives west of the second

illustrates the translation-generic queries. They can be expressed in all models of Section 1 except for the PLA-Model.

Just for fun, we can speak about the identity-generic queries, as those queries that commute with the identity. Clearly every query does.

In general we say that **G-generic** queries, for any group G of permutations of $\mathbb{R}^2$, are those queries that commute with all permutations of G.

Other interesting groups that could be considered in this context are:
- those permutations that fix the first quadrant:
- those permutations that fix the x-axis and the y-axis:
- those permutations that fix the points with equal thematic information:
- the reflection on a given axis:
- the horizontal translations:
- the homothecies with (0,0) as center:
- etc.

We can easily deduce that

G is a subgroup of G' iff all G'-generic queries are G-generic.

The genericity classes above form a hierarchy in the sense that permutation-genericity => topology-genericity => affinity-genericity => similarity-genericity => isometry-genericity => direct-isometry-genericity => translation-genericity => identity-genericity.

A negative result is that it seems to be undecidable whether a query, expressed in the polynomial calculus, is G-generic, for most groups G. This result has to be reexamined also for other models. Because of this undecidability result it is (at least theoretically) important to find sublanguages of the polynomial calculus in which the G-genericity is decidable for most groups G.

The great challenge is here to find for each group G, a sound and complete language for the class of G-generic queries. The challenge becomes still harder if we add the geomatic model as an additional parameter to the problem.

More research has still to be done in order to generalize this concept of genericity to queries where the result has not the same dimension as the database, or where the result only contains thematic information, such as boolean queries for instance.

In the final two subsections we focus on two very important genericity classes, namely the isometry- and the topology-genericity.

2.2 Isometry-Genericity

In this section we discuss the isometry-generic queries, namely the queries that commute with every isometry. It is well-known that the isometries of the two-dimensional space are generated by the rotations, the translations and the reflections. Since the two former are also generated by the latter, we know that each isometry is generated by a finite number of reflections.

In this chapter we will use the Polynomial Model and the polynomial calculus. We limit our discussion to the case that the database only contains one relation, which has no thematic attributes and that the only spatial attribute is two-dimensional. In this case a database can be viewed as the content of a plane.

Quantifiers seem to play an important role in this calculus. We have proved [Par94a,Par94b] that, when an isometry-generic query can be expressed without using quantifiers, then this query is trivial in the sense that it always results in the empty relation, in the full plane, in the database or in the complement of the database.

Intuitively an isometry-generic query cannot give any privilege to one fixed point, one fixed line, one fixed line segment, one fixed direction, one fixed angle or one fixed object. This is the intrinsic reason why the following queries are not isometry-generic:
- give the points of the database that have a positive x-coordinate;
- give the points of the database that are closer then 10 to (0,0);
- translate the database 5 in the direction of the x-axis;
- rotate the database 90 degrees around (0,0);
- rotate the database 30 degrees around its gravity center;
- reflect the database along the x-axis.

On the other hand, a particular distance or the gravity center may play a role. Also topological issues can be used. The following queries are isometry-generic:
- give the points p in a database for which there is at least one point q in the database such that the distance between p and q is exactly 10;
- give the points in the database that are most remote from the gravity center;
- give the result of the homothecy with center the gravity center and ratio 2;
- give the topological boundary of the database;
- give the disc with the same gravity center as the database and whose radius is the maximal distance between two points of the database;
- give the points that are the gravity center of three points q, q' and q" of SR, with the distance between q and q' being the square of the distance between q and q", and with the distance between q and q' being the third power of the distance between q' and q".

Now that we have a good intuition of isometry-generic queries, we can try to find a sound and complete language for expressing them. We use the Polynomial Model.
The polynomial calculus is clearly not sound since we can express the first non-isometry-generic query above by

$$\{ (x,y) \mid (x,y) \in SR \wedge x > 0 \}$$

The polynomial calculus without quantifiers is not complete as we have seen above. The calculus without polynomials is not sound nor complete, nor is the calculus without using SR.

This is illustrated with the following examples:
- $\{ (x,y) \mid (y,x) \in SR \}$ is not isometry-generic;
- $\{ (x,y) \mid x = 0 \}$ is not isometry-generic;
- give the topological border of SR is generic but cannot be expressed without using SR or without using polynomials.

We now define the IsoLanguage, which is sound for the isometry-generic queries:
- a query has the form $\{ p \mid \Lambda(p) \}$, where p is a point-variable;
- $\Lambda(p)$ is a combination of terms using universal or existential point-quantifiers, universal or existential real-quantifiers, the disjunction, conjunction and the negation;
- a term is
    - a comparison using $<, \leq, =, \geq, >, \neq$ and real atoms;
    - a comparison using $=, \neq$ and point-atoms;
    - SR(pa), pa being a point-atom;
- a real atom is
    - a polynomial with real coefficients and real variables;
    - d(pa,qa), where pa and qa are point-atoms and d denotes the distance between pa and qa;
- a point-atom is a point-variable or is GrC(Q), where Q is a query and GrC denotes the gravity center of Q.

Let us illustrate the IsoLanguage by giving the representation of the isometry-generic queries above.
p, q, ... represent point-variables, x represents a real variable:
- $\{ p \mid SR(p) \wedge \exists q (SR(q) \wedge d(p,q)=10) \}$
- $\{ p \mid SR(p) \wedge \forall q(SR(q) => d(p,GrC(\{ p' \mid SR(p') \})) \geq d(q,GrC(\{ p' \mid SR(p') \})) \}$
- $\{ p \mid \exists q \exists x(SR(q) \wedge d(p,GrC(\{ p' \mid SR(p') \})) = 2.x \wedge x=d(q,GrC(\{ p' \mid SR(p') \})) \}$
- $\{ p \mid SR(p) \wedge \forall x (x > 0 => \exists q (\neg SR(q) \wedge d(p,q) < x)) \}$
- $\{ p \mid \exists q \exists q' (d(p,GrC(\{ p' \mid SR(p') \})) \leq d(q,q')) \}$
- $\{ p \mid \exists q \exists q' \exists q'' (SR(q) \wedge SR(q') \wedge SR(q'') \wedge p = GrC(\{ p_1 \mid p_1=q \vee p_1=q' \vee p_1=q'' \}) \wedge d(q,q'')=y \wedge d(q',q'')=z \wedge d(q,q')=y^2 \wedge d(q,q')=z^3) \}$

It is still an open problem whether IsoLanguage is complete for the isometry-generic queries.

2.3 Topology-Genericity

In this section we discuss the topology-generic queries, namely the queries that commute with every continuous permutation of $\mathbb{R}^2$. We use the natural classical topology on $\mathbb{R}^2$ [Ale61]. We limit our discussion to the case that the database only contains one relation, which has one thematic attribute that contain the object identifiers and one two-dimensional spatial attribute. In this case a database can be viewed as a collection of two-dimensional objects.

Topology-generic queries are those that only use topological properties. Here are some examples:
- give the connected objects of the relation;
- give the objects that overlap with some other objects;
- give the topological boundary of each object;
- give the objects whose interior includes some other objects;
- give the objects that have some holes;
- give the objects that have more than five holes.

Queries that use the shape of an object, its surface, a distance, the gravity center, etc., are not topology-generic:
- give all the triangles in the relation;
- give the points of the objects in the relation that are closer then 10 to (0,0);
- translate the the objects of the relation 5 in the direction of the x-axis;
- rotate the objects of the relation 90 degrees around (0,0);
- give the gravity center of each object.

Max Egenhofer has studied the topological issues that are related with geomatic data types very extensively [Ege88,Ege89,Ege91,Ege93,Ege94a,Ege94b].

In [Ege91,Ege93] the 9-intersection model is given for topological relations in $\mathbb{R}^2$.
This model is based on the overlapping properties of the interior (A°,B°), the complement (A⁻,B⁻) and the boundary (δA,δB) of two two-dimensional objects A and B.

There are 3 x 3 = 9 combinations for the intersections of A°, A⁻, δA and B°, B⁻, δB. They are represented in Figure 16.

$$R(A,B) = \begin{pmatrix} \delta A \cap \delta B & \delta A \cap B° & \delta A \cap B⁻ \\ A° \cap \delta B & A° \cap B° & A° \cap B⁻ \\ A⁻ \cap \delta B & A⁻ \cap B° & A⁻ \cap B⁻ \end{pmatrix}$$

Figure 16

Each of these intersections can be empty ($\emptyset$) or not empty ($\neg\emptyset$). Hence there are $2^9=512$ different possible values of such matrices, i.e. 512 possible different topological relationships between two objects. Exactly one these topological relationships holds between any two objects in $\mathbb{R}^2$. However only 8 of these relations can be realized for two-dimensional objects. These eight possibilities are illustrated in Figure 17.

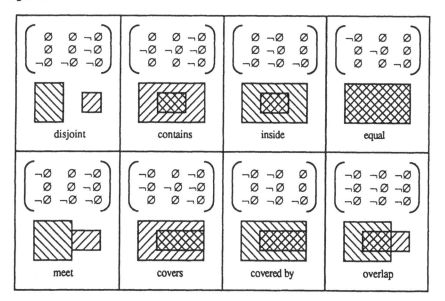

Figure 17

Clearly, when we consider three objects, we need a 3 x 3 x 3 matrix. For n objects, we need an n-dimensional 3 x 3 x ... x 3 matrix.

We call now the contents of two relations SR and SR' Egenhofer equivalent (notation SR $\sim_E$ SR') if they contain the same object identifiers and if their topological relationship is given by the same matrix.

Note that the relation containing (A ; { (x,y) | x=0 ∧ y>0 }) and (B ; { (x,y) | x=0 ∧ y<0}), the relation containing (C ; { (x,y) | x=0 ∧ y>0 }) and (D ; { (x,y) | x=0 ∧ y≤0}) and the relation containing (E ; { (x,y) | x=0 ∧ y≥0 }) and (F ; { (x,y) | x=0 ∧ y≤0}) are not equivalent since
$A^- \cap \delta B = \delta A \cap B^- = C^- \cap \delta D = \{ 0 \}$ and $\delta C \cap D^- = E^- \cap \delta F = \delta E \cap F = \emptyset$.

Let us call a query Q Egenhofer-generic iff SR $\sim_E$ SR' implies Q(SR) $\sim_E$ Q(SR'). 'Give the interior of the objects in the given plane' is an example of an Egenhofer-generic query.

We conjecture that topology-generic queries are also Egenhofer-generic. The inverse does not hold since relations with only one object, with the same identifier, are always Egenhofer equivalent.

The relationship between both kinds of genericity should be studied in detail in order to help us understand the role of topology in genericity and query languages.

There is also a relationship between the PLA-Model and Egenhofer equivalent relations. Indeed, suppose that a relation can be represented by zero-, one- and two-cells is indicated in Section 1.5. We conjecture that two relations have the same representation in the PLA-Model iff they are Egenhofer equivalent.

Acknowledgment

The author is very indebted to Jan Van den Bussche, Dirk Van Gucht and Bart Kuijpers for their fruitful cooperation.

References

[Ale61] Alexandroff P., Elementary Concepts of Topology, Dover Pub., Inc., New York, 1961.

[Bur77] Burton W., Representation of many-sided polygons and polygonal lines for rapid processing, Comm. of the ACM 20, 3, p. 166-171, 1977.

[Cha94] Chan E., Zhu R., QL/G - A Query language for Geometric data Bases, TR CS-94-25, Univ. of Waterloo, 1994.

[Cha80] Chandra A., D. Harel, Computable queries for relational database systems, Journal of Comp. and System Sciences, 21, 2, p. 156-178, 1980.

[Col68] Cole P., King C., Quantitative Geography, John Wiley, London, 1968.

[Cor79] Corbett J.P., Topological Principles in Cartography, Technical paper 48, US Bureau of the Census, Washington DC, 1979.

[Ege88] Egenhofer M., A. Frank, Towards a spatial query language: User interface considerations, Proc. of VLDB, 1988.

[Ege89] Egenhofer M., A Formal definition of Binary Topological Relationships, LNCS 367, p. 457-472, 1989.

[Ege91] Egenhofer M., Reasoning about Binary topological Relations, LNCS 525, p. 143-160, 1991.

[Ege93] Egenhofer M., Topological Relations between Regions in R^2 and Z^2, LNCS 692, p. 316-336, 1993.

[Ege94a] Egenhofer M., R. Franzosa, On the equivalence of topological relations, Int. J. Geographical Information Systems, p. 523-542, 1994.

[Ege94b] Egenhofer M., Spatial SQL: a Query and Presentation Language, IEEE Transactions on Knowledge and Data Engineering, Vol. 6, No.1, 1994.

[Gue88] Guenther O., Efficient structures for geometric data management, LNCS 377, Springer-Verlag, 1988.

[Gue90] Guenther O., A. Buchmann, Research Issues in Spatial Databases, Sigmod Record Vol 19,4, p. 61-68, 1990.

[Gut88] Guting R., Geo-Relational Algebra: A model and query language for geometric database systems, Proc of Extending databse Technology, Venice, p. 506-527, 1988.

[Gut89] Guting R., Gral: An Extensible Relational Database System for Geometric Applications, Proc 15th VLDB, Amsterdam, p. 33-44, 1989.

[Gut93a] Guting R., M. Schneider, Realm-based Spatial Data Types: The ROSE Algebra, TR 141-3-93 of Fern Universität, Hagen, 1993.

[Gut93b] Guting R., M. Schneider, Realms: A Foundation for Spatial Data Tyes in Database Systems, 3rd Int. Symp. on Large Spatial Databases, p. 14-35, Singapore, 1993.

[Gut94a] Guting R., GraphDB: A Data Model and Query Language for Graphs in Databases, Informatik Berichte 155-2/1994, FemUniversitat, Hagen, 1994.

[Gut94b] Guting R., An Introduction to Spatial Database Systems, VLDB Journal, 3, 4, 1994.

[Hoe94] Hoel E., Performance of Data-parallel Spatial Operations, VLDB94, p. 156-167, Chili, 1994.

[Kan90] Kanellakis P., G. Kuper, P. Revesz, Constraint query languages, Proc. 9th Symp. on Princ. of Database Systems, p. 299-313, 1990.

[Kem87] Kemper A., M. Wallrath, An analysis of geometric modeling in database systems, Computing Surveys, 19, 1, p. 47-91, 1987.

[Lau92] Laurini R., D. Thompson, Fundamentals of Spatial Information Systems, Academic Press, APIC Series 37, 1992.

[Par94a] Paredaens J., J. Van den Bussche, D. Van Gucht, Towards a theory of spatial database queries, Extended abstract, Proc. 13th Symp. on Princ. of Database Systems, Minneapolis, p. 279-288, 1994.

[Par94b] Paredaens J., J. Van den Bussche, D. Van Gucht, Full paper of 'Towards a theory of spatial database queries', in preparation.

[Pea90] Peano G., Sur une courbe qui remplit toute une aire plane, Mathematische Annalen, 36(a), p. 157-160, 1890.

[Pre85] Preparata F., M. Shamos, Computational Geometry, Springer-Verlag, 1985.

[Rig94] Rigaux Ph., M. Scholl, Multiple Representation Modelling and Querying, IGIS94, 1994.

[Sam90] Samet H., The Design and Analysis of Spatial Data Structures, Addison-Wesley, 1990.

[Sch89] Scholl M., A. Voisard, Thematic Map Modeling, Proc. SSD, p. 167-192, also in LNCS 409, Springer-Verlag, 1989.

[Tar51] Tarski A., A decision method for elementary algebra and geometry, University of California Press, 1951.

Tutorial on Parallel Database Systems

Gerhard Weikum

Department of Computer Science
University of the Saarland
P.O. Box 151150
D-66041 Saarbrücken, Germany
E-mail: weikum@cs.uni-sb.de

Parallel database technology has evolved to a point where commercial systems appear to be fairly mature. Algorithms and run-time mechanisms for both speeding up query response time and scaling up transaction throughput are well understood. However, using a parallel database system effectively under real application workloads entails a number of complex optimization problems with respect to query processing policies, data placement, and resource management. These policy issues are still largely unexplored, from a theoretical as well as practical perspective. This tutorial gives an overview of the state of the art in parallel database technology, and points out important avenues of further research with emphasis on data placement issues.

Data placement for parallel systems poses a number of hard optimization problems. Since database systems process enormous volumes of data (in the order of Terabytes and more), the data cannot be dynamically redistributed between different processors or disks at acceptable speed on a per query basis. Therefore, the partitioning of the data (i.e., relations or object sets) and the assignment of the resulting partitions onto disks and processors has a paramount impact on the degree of parallelism and the achievable speedup. Most partitioning methods aim to maximize the degree of parallelism for an individual query of a given class, but tend to ignore the adverse effect that high intra-query parallelism may have on query throughput. Practically viable partitioning methods should be able to accomodate constraints on throughput and explicit goals for the response time of specific query classes. The allocation of data partitions must also counteract the skew in the access frequency distribution that is typically exhibited by real application data. Finally, it is desirable that reorganizations of the partitioning and allocation scheme can be performed incrementally and possibly in a parallel manner, to support dynamic adaptation of the data placement in response to evolving data access patterns, without bringing the system off-line. All these requirements should be satisfied not only for a single parallel computer with homogeneous disks and processors but also for a heterogeneous server farm with non-uniform performance capacity in terms of disk speed, processor speed, and memory size.

References

General References

1. DeWitt, D.J., Gray, J.: Parallel Database Systems: The Future of High Performance Database Systems, Communications of the ACM Vol.35 No.6, 1992, pp. 85-98
2. Graefe, G.: Query Evaluation Techniques for Large Databases, ACM Computing Surveys Vol.25 No.2, 1993, pp. 73-170, particularly Sections 9 and 10 on Parallel Query Execution and Parallel Algorithms
3. Mohan, C., Pirahesh, H., Tang, W.G., Wang, Y.: Parallelism in Relational Database Management Systems, IBM Systems Journal Vol.33 No.2, 1994, pp. 349-371
4. Valduriez, P.: Parallel Database Systems: Open Problems and New Issues, Distributed and Parallel Databases Vol.1 No.2, 1993, pp. 137-165

Data Placement Issues

5. Abdel-Ghaffar K.A.S., El Abbadi, A., Optimal Disk Allocation for Partial Match Queries, ACM Transactions on Database Systems Vol.18 No.1, 1993, pp. 132-156
6. Azar, Y., Broder, A.Z., Karlin, A.R., Upfal, E.: Balanced Allocations, ACM SIGACT Symposium on Theory of Computing, Montreal, 1994
7. Azar, Y., Naor, J., Rom, R.: The Competitiveness of Online Assignment, 3rd ACM/SIAM Symposium on Discrete Algorithms, 1992
8. Berson, S., Ghandharizadeh, S., Muntz, R., Ju, X.: Staggered Striping in Multimedia Information Systems, ACM SIGMOD International Conference on Management of Data, Minneapolis, 1994
9. Chen, P.M., Patterson, D.A.: Maximizing Performance in a Striped Disk Array, ACM SIGARCH International Symposium on Computer Architecture, Seattle, 1990
10. Copeland, G., Alexander, W., Boughter, E., Keller, T.: Data Placement in Bubba, ACM SIGMOD International Conference on Management of Data, Chicago, 1988
11. Devine, R.: Design and Implementation of DDH: A Distributed Dynamic Hashing Algorithm, 4th International Conference on Foundations of Data Organization and Algorithms, Chicago, 1993
12. Dowdy, L.W., Foster, D.V.: Comparative Models of the File Assignment Problem, ACM Computing Surveys Vol.14 No.2, 1982, pp. 287-313
13. Du, H.C., Sobolewski, J.S., Disk Allocation for Cartesian Product Files on Multiple Disk Systems, ACM Transactions on Database Systems Vol. 7 No.1, 1982, pp. 82-101
14. Faloutsos, C., Metaxas, D., Disk Allocation Methods Using Error Correcting Codes, IEEE Transactions on Computers Vol.40 No.8, 1991, pp. 907-914

15. Faloutsos, C., Bhagwat, P., Declustering Using Fractals, 2nd International Conference on Parallel and Distributed Information Systems, San Diego, 1993

16. Ghandeharizadeh, S., DeWitt, D.J.: A Multiuser Performance Analysis of Alternative Declustering Strategies, 6th IEEE International Conference on Data Engineering, Los Angeles, 1990

17. Ghandeharizadeh, S., DeWitt, D.J.: Hybrid-range Partitioning Strategy: A New Declustering Strategy for Multiprocessor Database Machines, 16th International Conference on Very Large Data Bases, Brisbane, 1990

18. Ghandeharizadeh, S., Ramos, L., Asad, Z., Qureshi, W.: Object Placement in Parallel Hypermedia Systems, 17th International Conference on Very Large Data Bases, Barcelona, 1991

19. Ghandeharizadeh, S., Meyer, R., Schultz, G., Yackel, J.: Optimal Balanced Partitions and a Parallel Database Application, Operations Research Society of America (ORSA) Journal of Computing Vol.5 No.2, 1993

20. Ghandeharizadeh, S., Wilhite, D., Lin, K., Zhao, X.: Object Placement in Parallel Object-Oriented Database Systems, 10th IEEE International Conference on Data Engineering, Houston, 1994

21. Ghandeharizadeh, S., DeWitt, D.J.: MAGIC: A Multiattribute Declustering Mechanism for Multiprocessor Database Machines, IEEE Transactions on Parallel and Distributed Systems Vol.5 No.5, 1994, pp. 509-524

22. Himatsingka, B., Srivastava, J., Li, J., Rotem, D.: Latin Hypercubes: A Class of Multidimensional Declustering Techniques, Technical Report TR 94-09, Computer Science Department, University of Minnesota, Minneapolis, 1994

23. Himatsingka, B., Srivastava, J.: Performance Evaluation of Grid Based Multi-Attribute Record Declustering Methods, 10th IEEE International Conference on Data Engineering, Houston, 1994

24. Houtsma, M.A.W., Apers, P.M.G., Schipper, G.L.V.: Data Fragmentation for Parallel Transitive Closure Strategies, 9th International Conference on Data Engineering, Vienna, 1993

25. Hua, K., Lee, C.: An Adaptive Data Placement Scheme for Parallel Database Computer Systems, 16th International Conference on Very Large Data Bases, Brisbane, 1990

26. Johnson, T., Krishna, P.: Lazy Updates for Distributed Search Structures, ACM SIGMOD International Conference on Management of Data, Washington, 1993

27. Kamel, I., Faloutsos, C.: Parallel R-Trees, ACM SIGMOD International Conference on Management of Data, San Diego, 1992

28. Kim, M.H., Pramanik, S., Optimal File Distribution for Partial Match Queries, ACM SIGMOD International Conference on Management of Data, Chicago, 1988

29. Kim, M.Y., Tantawi, A.N.: Asynchronous Disk Interleaving: Approximating Access Delays, IEEE Transactions on Computers Vol.40 No.7, 1991, pp. 801-810

30. Kouramajian, V., Elmasri, R., Chaudhry, A.: Declustering Techniques for Parallelizing Temporal Access Structures, 10th IEEE International Conference on Data Engineering, Houston, 1994

31. Kroell, B., Widmayer, P.: Distributing a Search Tree Among a Growing Number of Processors, ACM SIGMOD International Conference on Management of Data, Minneapolis, 1994

32. Lee, E.K., Katz, R.H.: An Analytic Performance Model of Disk Arrays and its Application, ACM SIGMETRICS International Conference on Measurement and Modeling of Computer Systems, Santa Clara, 1993

33. Lee, L.-W.: Optimization of Load-Balanced File Allocation, Ph.D. Dissertation, Department of Electrical Engineering and Computer Science, Northwestern University, Evanston, Illinois, 1994

34. Li, J., Srivastava, J., Rotem, D.: CMD: A Multidimensional Declustering Method for Parallel Database Systems, 18th International Conference on Very Large Data Bases, Vancouver, 1992

35. Litwin, W., Neimat, M.-A., Schneider, D.A.: LH* - Linear Hashing for Distributed Files, ACM SIGMOD International Conference on Management of Data, Washington, 1993

36. Litwin, W., Neimat, M.-A., Schneider, D.A.: RP*: A Family of Order-Preserving Scalable Distributed Data Structures, 20th International Conference on Very Large Data Bases, Santiago de Chile, 1994

37. Matsliach, G., Shmueli, O.: A Combined Method for Maintaining Large Indices in Multiprocessor Multidisk Environments, IEEE Transactions on Knowledge and Data Engineering Vol.6 No.3, 1994, pp. 479-496

38. Nelson, R., Tantawi, A.N.: Approximate Analysis of Fork/Join Synchronization in Parallel Queues, IEEE Transactions on Computers Vol.37 No.6, 1988, pp. 739-743

39. Scheuermann, P., Weikum, G., Zabback, P.: Data Partitioning and Load Balancing in Parallel Disk Systems, Technical Report 209, Department of Computer Science, ETH Zurich, January 1994, submitted for publication

40. Scheuermann, P., Weikum, G., Zabback, P., "Disk Cooling" in Parallel Disk Systems, Bulletin of the IEEE TC on Data Engineering Vol.17 No.3, September 1994

41. Seeger, B., Larson, P.-A.: Multi-Disk B-Trees, ACM SIGMOD International Conference on Management of Data, Denver, 1991

42. Severance, C., Pramanik, S., Wolberg, P.: Distributed Linear Hashing and Parallel Projection in Main Memory Databases, 16th International Conference on Very Large Data Bases, Brisbane, 1990

43. Srivastava, J., Niccum, T.M., Himatsingka, B., Data Declustering in PADMA: A PArallel Database MAnager, Bulletin of the IEEE TC on Data Engineering Vol.17 No.3, September 1994

44. Tomasic, A., Garcia-Molina, H.: Query Processing and Inverted Indices in Shared-Nothing Text Document Information Retrieval Systems, VLDB Journal Vol.2 No.3, 1993, pp. 243-275

45. Vingralek, R., Breitbart, Y., Weikum, G.: Distributed File Organization with Scalable Cost/Performance, ACM SIGMOD International Conference on Management of Data, Minneapolis, 1994

46. Wolf, J.L.: The Placement Optimization Program: A Practical Solution to the Disk File Assignment Problem, ACM SIGMETRICS International Conference on Measurement and Modeling of Computer Systems, Berkeley, California, 1989

47. Zabback, P.: I/O Parallelism in Database Systems (in German), Doctoral Thesis, Department of Computer Science, ETH Zurich, April 1994

48. Zhou, Y., Shekhar, S., Coyle, M.: Disk Allocation Methods for Parallelizing Grid Files, 10th IEEE International Conference on Data Engineering, Houston, 1994

Other Optimization Issues

49. DeWitt, D.J., Naughton, J.F., Schneider, D.A., Seshadri, S.: Practical Skew Handling in Parallel Joins, 18th International Conference on Very Large Data Bases, Vancouver, 1992

50. Frieder, O., Baru, C.K.: Site and Query Scheduling Policies in Multicomputer Database Systems, IEEE Transactions on Knowledge and Data Engineering Vol.6 No.4, 1994, pp. 609-619

51. Ganguly, S., Hasan, W., Krishnamurthy, R.: Query Optimization for Parallel Execution, ACM SIGMOD International Conference on Management of Data, San Diego, 1992

52. Hasan, W., Motwani, R.: Optimization Algorithms for Exploiting the Parallelism-Communication Tradeoff in Pipelined Parallelism, 20th International Conference on Very Large Data Bases, Santiago de Chile, 1994

53. Hong, W., Stonebraker, M.: Optimization of Parallel Query Execution Plans in XPRS, Distributed and Parallel Databases Vol.1 No.1, 1993, pp. 9-32

54. Lo, M.-L., Chen, M.-S., Ravishankar, C.V., Yu, P.S.: On Optimal Processor Allocation to Support Pipelined Hash Joins, ACM SIGMOD International Conference on Management of Data, Washington, 1993

55. Rahm, E., Marek, R.: Analysis of Dynamic Load Balancing Strategies for Parallel Shared Nothing Database Systems, 19th International Conference on Very Large Data Bases, Dublin, 1993

56. Shekita, E.J., Young, H.C., Tan, K.-L.: Multi-Join Optimization for Symmetric Multiprocessors, 19th International Conference on Very Large Data Bases, Dublin, 1993

57. Wolf, J.L., Yu, P.S., Turek, J., Dias, D.M.: A Parallel Hash Join Algorithm for Managing Data Skew, IEEE Transactions on Parallel and Distributed Systems Vol.4 No.12, 1993, pp. 1355-1371

58. Wolf, J.L., Turek, J., Chen, M.-S., Yu, P.S.: Scheduling Multiple Queries on a Parallel Machine, ACM SIGMETRICS International Conference on Measurement and Modeling of Computer Systems, Nashville, Tennessee, 1994

Languages for Polynomial-Time Queries –
An Ongoing Quest

Phokion G. Kolaitis

Computer and Information Sciences
University of California, Santa Cruz
Santa Cruz, CA 95064
U.S.A.
kolaitis@cse.ucsc.edu

During the past twenty years, a major direction of research in database theory has focused on the development of progressively more powerful languages for relational queries. Much of the work in this area has concentrated on the problem of finding languages that capture exactly the queries that are computable in polynomial-time in the size of the database. The quest for such languages has resulted into an extensive interaction between database theory, finite model theory, and computational complexity. Although satisfactory answers have been obtained in certain important special cases, a solution to the general problem remains elusive. The aim of this tutorial is to describe some of the main results obtained so far and to present a status report on this problem.

References

1. S. Abiteboul and V. Vianu. Generic computation and its complexity. In *Proc. 23rd ACM Symp. on Theory of Computing*, pages 209–219, 1991.
2. F. Afrati, S. S. Cosmadakis, and M. Yannakakis. On Datalog vs. polynomial time. In *Proc. 10th ACM Symp. on Principles of Database Systems*, 1991.
3. A. V. Aho and J. D. Ullman. Universality of data retrieval languages. In *Proc. 6th ACM Symp. on Principles of Programming Languages*, pages 110–117, 1979.
4. J. Cai, M. Fürer, and N. Immerman. An optimal lower bound on the number of variables for graph identification. *Combinatorica*, 12(4):389–410, 1992.
5. A. Chandra and D. Harel. Horn clause queries and generalizations. *Journal of Logic Programming*, 1:1–15, 1985.
6. A. Chandra and D. Harel. Structure and complexity of relational queries. *Journal of Computer and System Sciences*, 25:99–128, 1982.
7. A. Dawar. *Feasible computation through model theory*. PhD thesis, University of Pennsylvania, Philadelphia, 1993.
8. R. Fagin. Finite-model theory—a personal perspective. *Theoretical Computer Science*, 116(1):3–31, 1993.
9. Y. Gurevich. Logic and the challenge of computer science. In E. Börger, editor, *Current trends in theoretical computer science*, pages 1–57, Computer Science Press, 1988.

10. Y. Gurevich. Toward logic tailored for computational complexity. In M. M. Ricther et al., editor, *Computation and Proof Theory, Lecture Notes in Mathematics 1104*, pages 175–216, Springer-Verlag, 1984.

11. Y. Gurevich and S. Shelah. Fixed-point extensions of first-order logic. *Annals of Pure and Applied Logic*, 32:265–280, 1986.

12. L. Hella. Logical hierarchies in PTIME. In *Proc. 7th IEEE Symp. on Logic in Computer Science*, pages 360–368, 1992.

13. L. Hella, Ph.G. Kolaitis, and K. Luosto. How to define a linear order on finite models. In *Proc. 9th IEEE Symp. on Logic in Computer Science*, pages 40–49, 1994.

14. N. Immerman. Descriptive and computational complexity. In J. Hartmanis, editor, *Computational Complexity Theory, Proc. Symp. Applied Math., Vol. 38*, pages 75–91, American Mathematical Society, 1989.

15. N. Immerman. Relational queries computable in polynomial time. *Information and Control*, 68:86–104, 1986.

16. N. Immerman and E. S. Lander. Describing graphs: a first-order approach to graph canonization. In A. Selman, editor, *Complexity Theory Retrospective*, pages 59–81, Springer-Verlag, 1990.

17. Ph. G. Kolaitis and J. K. Väänänen. Generalized quantifiers and pebble games on finite structures. In *Proc. 7th IEEE Symp. on Logic in Computer Science*, pages 348–359, 1992.

18. C. H. Papadimitriou. A note on the expressive power of Prolog. *Bulletin of the EATCS*, 26:21–23, 1985.

19. M. Y. Vardi. The complexity of relational query languages. In *Proc. 14th ACM Symp. on Theory of Computing*, pages 137–146, 1982.

Distributed Query Optimization in Loosely Coupled Multidatabase Systems

Silvio Salza[1], Giovanni Barone[1] and Tadeusz Morzy[2]

[1] Dipartimento di Informatica e Sistemistica, Università di Roma "La Sapienza"
Via Salaria 113, I-00198 Roma, Italy
Email: {salza,barone}@dis.uniroma1.it
[2] Institute of Computing Sciences, Technical University of Poznań
ul. Piotrowo 3A, 60-965 Poznań, Poland
Email: morzy@pozn1v.tup.edu.pl

Abstract. A multidatabase system (*MDBS*) is a database system which integrates pre-existing databases, called component local database systems (*LDBSs*), to support global applications accessing data at more than one *LDBS*. An important research issue in *MDBS* is query optimization. The query optimization problem in *MDBS* is quite different from the case of distributed database system (*DDBS*) since, due to schema heterogeneity and local autonomy of component *LDBSs*, is not possible to assume that the query optimizer has a complete information on the execution cost and database statistics. In this paper we present a distributed query optimization algorithm that works under very general assumptions for *MDBSs* with relational global data model. The algorithm is based on the idea of delegating the evaluation of the execution cost of the elementary steps in a query execution plan to the *LDBS* where the computation is performed. The optimization process is organized as a sequence of steps, in which at each step all *LDBSs* work in parallel to evaluate the cost of execution plans for partial queries of increasing size, and send their cost estimates to the other *LDBS* that need them for the next step. The computation is totally distributed, and organized in order to perform no duplicate computation, and to discard as soon as possible the execution plans that may not lead to an optimal solution.

1 Introduction

The need for integrating information from various decentralized organizations motivates the design of *multidatabase systems* (*MDBSs*). A multidatabase system is a database system implemented to connect several, autonomous, and (possibly) heterogeneous pre-existing database systems, called *local database systems* (*LDBSs*), which allows users to execute transactions accessing data residing at more than one *LDBS*. Heterogeneity and local autonomy are two main features of a *MDBS* that distinguish it from a conventional distributed database system (*DDBS*). Heterogeneity refers to the various types of component *LDBSs*, which may have different user interfaces, data models, query languages, and query optimization strategies. Local autonomy means that each *LDBS* maintains total autonomy and responsibility over its own data, and allows only indirect access to it. It reflects the fact that *LDBSs* were designed and implemented independently, and were initially totally unaware of the integration process.

A consistent research work has been performed in the last years on *MDBS*, especially in the area of schema integration [10, 11, 12]. Another important topic that has received recently considerable attention is transaction management [3, 4, 8, 9], but the focus has been mainly on concurrency control, and only few papers have been published on *multidatabase query optimization (MQO)* [2, 6, 7, 15]. This is due to several reasons, mainly the initial idea that this problem is not substantially different from the classical *distributed query optimization (DQO)* problem, and can be easily reduced to it if the proper information on execution cost and database statistics is available at global level. However this is in clear contrast with local autonomy of component *LDBSs*, and the needed local information may not be available to the global query optimizer, thus preventing the use of classical *DQO* algorithms. These refer to an homogeneous database architecture, and assume that the global query optimizer has all the local and global information on execution costs, access methods and database statistics, that it needs to select the optimal execution plan for the global query. Therefore, new methods to extract or estimate the necessary local query optimization information without violating local autonomy have been proposed [2, 15].

In [6, 7] some important issues concerning the *MQO* problem are presented, stressing the difference between *DQO* and *MQO*, and discussing the problems arising from the heterogeneity and local autonomy of component *LDBSs*. In [7] the architecture of a multidatabase query optimizer is presented. In [2] the authors propose a classification of database management systems (*DBMS*) from the viewpoint of their degree of heterogeneity with respect to the construction of a multidatabase query optimizer. Three categories of database systems are distinguished: 1)*proprietary DBMS*, providing both cost functions and database statistics to the multidatabase management system, 2)*conforming DBMS*, providing some important database statistics but not the cost functions, either because of the lack of such abstraction, or because this information is proprietary information of the *DBMS*, and 3)*non-conforming DBMS*, incapable of providing either database statistics or the cost function. The *MQO* problem in the context of proprietary *DBMS* is similar to the classical *DQO* problem. For conforming *LDBSs* a *calibration method* is proposed in [2], to deduce the necessary information. The idea is to use a synthetically created database, and to run a set of queries against this database, to deduce the coefficients in cost formulas for the underlying *LDBS*. This approach has several shortcomings [15]: 1) it may not be possible (or allowed) to create the calibrating database at some local sites, 2) the deduced cost formulas cannot be applied if some details of the local physical organization (e.g. indices) are not known. Finally, this approach is inadequate for *MDBS* including object-oriented or non-conforming *LDBSs*. To overcome some of these shortcomings, in [15] the authors suggest to obtain estimates of cost formula coefficients by using statistical sampling, i.e. grouping all possible queries on each *LDBS* into classes, and running a sample query workload for each class to deduce a cost formula for it. This approach has some shortcomings as well: 1) it is inadequate for *MDBS* including object-oriented *LDBSs* and 2) the estimation process heavily depends on the system contention.

In this paper we present a distributed query optimization algorithm for the general case of *MDBS* including also non-conforming *LDBS*. The algorithm refers to an execution model that we define in the paper, in which a global query is evaluated as a sequence of steps each performed in a different *LDBS* and consisting in evaluating of a local subquery and joining the result to an intermediate relation imported from another *LDBS*. The optimization algorithm is based on the idea of delegating the evaluation of the execution cost of these elementary steps to the *LDBS* where the computation is performed, since in the general case the cost functions and database statistics are only locally available.

The algorithm has a number of steps which is linear with the number of *LDBS* involved in the query. At each step all *LDBSs* work in parallel to evaluate the cost of execution plans for partial queries of increasing size, and send their cost estimates to the other *LDBS* that need them for the next step. The flow of information between the *LDBSs* is organized in order to avoid any duplicate computation, and to discard as soon as possible those execution plans that may not lead to an optimal solution.

The paper is organized as follows. In Section 2 we define the *MDBS* model, and discuss the basic assumptions on the architecture of the *LDBSs*. Then, in Section 3, we define the query execution model for local and global queries. In Section 4 we formulate the multidatabase query optimization problem. In Section 5 we discuss the characteristics of the cost function. Section 6 presents distributed and decentralized query optimization algorithm. Finally Section 7 deals with complexity analysis, and Section 8 gives the final conclusions.

2 The MDBS Model

For our purposes we define a *MDBS* as a collection of sites $\mathcal{S} = \{\mathcal{S}_1, \ldots, \mathcal{S}_n\}$ with component local database systems $LDBS_1, \ldots, LDBS_n$, autonomous and possibly heterogeneous, that are organized according to the following architecture [14]:

- each *LDBS* may adopt its own local data model;
- at the *MDBS* level there is a common global data model;
- each *LDBS* has a *local schema* that is the schema managed by local database management system;
- each *LDBS* has a *component schema* that is the translation of the local schema into the global data model;
- each *LDBS* has an *export schema* which is the portion of the component schema that is available at the *MDBS* level;
- each *LDBS* (which manages the federation) has a *federated schema* which is the union of some of the export schemas of the *LDBSs* in the *MDBS*.

Without any loss of generality we assume in the remainder of the paper that the export schema of each *LDBS* coincides with its component schema, and that all the sites have the same federated schema. Although we do not make any particular assumption on local data models, we assume that the global data model, and hence all the export schemas and the federated schema, are relational.

All the sites are connected by a network about which we do not make any special assumption, other than that all sites are, either directly or indirectly, connected to each other, and that each component *LDBS* may determine at any time the transmission cost of a message to any other site.

3   Global Queries and Query Execution Model

Due to autonomy of *LDBSs*, there is a clear distinction in a *MDBS* between *local queries* and *global queries*. A local query is a query on the local schema that accesses only data controlled by a single *LDBS*. It is locally submitted to and executed by the *LDBS*, without the control of the *MDBS*. A global query is a query on a federated schema that accesses data controlled by more than one *LDBS*. It is submitted to the *MDBS* that coordinates its execution by interacting with the *LDBSs*. For sake of simplicity, we restrict ourselves to considering SPJ global queries, i.e. with select, join and project operations only. This is indeed a quite general class of queries, since more complex queries that include unions are usually decomposed during the optimization process into a set of SPJ queries that are optimized independently.

In evaluating a global query it can be necessary to perform some joins across local databases, i.e. having as operands relations from different export schemas. Therefore, it is necessary to define an execution model to specify how these operations are performed. In this paper, without violating the local autonomy and without making any specific assumption on the local data models, we introduce at the *MDBS* level a new operation that we call *extract-join* and that can be performed by each participating *LDBS*. It consists of computing a local subquery on the export schema of a *LDBS* and joining the result with an *imported relation* (i.e. a partial result transferred from another site). More precisely, we mean that the two operations (i.e. the join and the local subquery) are performed together, since it is reasonable to assume that the local system can take advantage of the join selectivity while computing (extracting) the local relation.

According to this execution model, a global query $\mathcal{Q}$ is decomposed into a set of *local subqueries* $\mathcal{Q}_i$ (one for each site i involved in the query) connected by *global join* operations. The decomposition can be accomplished according to the following heuristics:

- all relations from the same *LDBS* that are in the global query, are included in the corresponding local subquery; cartesian products are eventually generated for those relations with no local join condition on them;
- select conditions are *pushed* into local subqueries whenever possible (i.e. as long as only local attributes are involved); the remaining select conditions are expressed by the corresponding join conditions;
- each local subquery incorporates a projection which eliminates all attributes which are neither in the final result nor involved in some global join; the

latter attributes will be eventually eliminated later, after performing the corresponding joins.

Formally we represent a global query with a *query graph* $\mathcal{G}(V_{\mathcal{G}}, E_{\mathcal{G}})$, with $V_{\mathcal{G}} = \{Q_i\}$ and $E_{\mathcal{G}} = \{c_{ij}\}$, i.e. where each vertex represents a local subquery Q_i on site i, and each edge represents a join condition c_{ij} (with $i, j = 1, \ldots, n$ with $i \neq j$) between two local subqueries Q_i and Q_j. To simplify the notation, and without any loss of generality, we assume that all the sites of the *MDBS* are involved in the global query, and hence, the graph has always n nodes. We shall also use in the remainder of the paper the terms query and query graph indifferently. In Figure 1 the query graph for a global query involving four sites is shown.

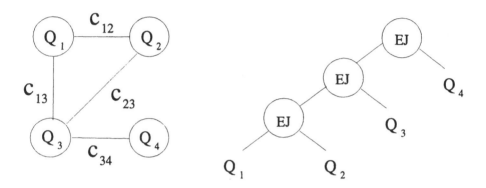

Fig. 1. Query graph and query execution plan

In our model the definition of the extract join operations leads to a strictly sequential execution of global queries. The execution is a sequence of steps, each performed in a given site and consisting in receiving from some other site an intermediate result, computing an extract join, and sending it to the next site. Formally this can be expressed by a *Query Execution Plan (QEP)*, $\mathcal{P} = Q_{i_1} Q_{i_2} \ldots Q_{i_n}$, which represents the sequence of extract-join operations through which the global query is computed, assuming that Q_{i_n} is evaluated first, then the result is sent to site i_{n-1} to be extract-joined with $Q_{i_{n-1}}$, and so on. The *execution space*, i.e. the set of all possible *QEP* for a given query, defined by the execution model defined above, corresponds to the space of *left-deep plans* in centralized database systems, where extract-join operations correspond to classical join operations and local subqueries correspond to stored relations [5, 13].

We denote with $\mathcal{R}(\mathcal{P})$ the set of local subqueries Q_i in the execution plan, and we call it the *query set* of $\mathcal{P}$. A *QEP*, such that its query set does not cover all the local subqueries in the query graph, is called a *Partial Query Execution Plan (PQEP)* of the given global query. On the other hand, each *PQEP* corresponds to a *partial query*, and to a subgraph of the original query graph. We say that two *QEPs* (or *PQEPs*) $\mathcal{P}_1$ and $\mathcal{P}_1$ are *comparable* if $\mathcal{R}(\mathcal{P}_1) = \mathcal{R}(\mathcal{P}_2)$, i.e. if they have the same query set, and therefore compute the same (partial) query.

Finally, to avoid cartesian products, we restrict ourselves to consider only *valid* execution plans $\mathcal{P} = \mathcal{Q}_{i_1} \mathcal{Q}_{i_2} \ldots \mathcal{Q}_{i_n}$, where $\{i_1, \ldots, i_n\}$ is a permutation of $\{1, \ldots, n\}$ and for any $r \in \{1, .., n-1\}$ there is at least an $s \in \{r+1, .., n\}$, such that in the global query there is a join between the two corresponding local queries $\mathcal{Q}_{i_r}$ and $\mathcal{Q}_{i_s}$ (i.e. $c_{i_r, i_s} \in V_{\mathcal{G}}$).

Given two (valid) *PQEPs* $\mathcal{P}_1 = \mathcal{Q}_{i_1} \ldots \mathcal{Q}_{i_k}$ and $\mathcal{P}_2 = \mathcal{Q}_{j_1} \ldots \mathcal{Q}_{j_r}$, we define their *composition* as the *PQEP* $\mathcal{P} = \mathcal{P}_1 \oplus \mathcal{P}_2 = \mathcal{Q}_{i_1} \ldots \mathcal{Q}_{i_k} \mathcal{Q}_{j_1} \ldots \mathcal{Q}_{j_r}$. Note that, in order to produce a valid *PQEP*, $\mathcal{P}_1$ and $\mathcal{P}_2$ must be *composable* i.e. there must be no duplicate local subqueries ($\mathcal{R}(\mathcal{P}_1) \cap \mathcal{R}(\mathcal{P}_2) = \emptyset$) and at least one interdatabase join condition between the local subquery of $\mathcal{Q}_{i_k}$ and a local subquery $\mathcal{Q}_{j_l}$ of $\mathcal{P}_2$.

Example 1. Consider the global query $\mathcal{Q}$ from Figure 1. A possible *QEP* for $\mathcal{Q}$ is: $\mathcal{P}_1 = \mathcal{Q}_1 \mathcal{Q}_2 \mathcal{Q}_3 \mathcal{Q}_4$. First, the subquery $\mathcal{Q}_4$ is executed in site 4 and the result is sent to site 3 to be extract-joined with $\mathcal{Q}_3$. Next, the result of *PQEP* $\mathcal{P}'_1 = \mathcal{Q}_3 \mathcal{Q}_4$ is extract- joined with $\mathcal{Q}_2$, and finally, the result of *PQEP* $\mathcal{P}''_1 = \mathcal{Q}_2 \mathcal{Q}_3 \mathcal{Q}_4$ is extract-joined with $\mathcal{Q}_1$ in site 1. The query set of $\mathcal{Q}$, $\mathcal{R}(\mathcal{P}_1) = \{\mathcal{Q}_1, \mathcal{Q}_2, \mathcal{Q}_3, \mathcal{Q}_4\}$. Another valid *QEP* is $\mathcal{P}_2 = \mathcal{Q}_1 \mathcal{Q}_2 \mathcal{Q}_4 \mathcal{Q}_3$, it differs from $\mathcal{P}_1$ because the *PQEP* $\mathcal{Q}_3 \mathcal{Q}_4$ has been replaced by $\mathcal{Q}_4 \mathcal{Q}_3$; these two *PQEPs* are, of course, comparable. □

4 Global Query Optimization

Given a global query $\mathcal{Q}$, let us consider the execution space E_Q, consisting of all possible valid execution plans $\mathcal{P}$ for $\mathcal{Q}$ in a given execution model, and a cost function $C(\mathcal{P})$ that associates an execution cost to each $\mathcal{P}$. We may now formulate the global query optimization problem as finding in the search space E_Q the execution plan(s) with the least execution cost. Formally:

$$min_{\mathcal{P} \in E_Q} C(\mathcal{P})$$

Any global query optimization algorithm is therefore characterized by: 1) an execution space E, 2) a cost function C, and 3) a search strategy that penetrates the space E for selecting the optimal *QEP*. The execution space is determined by the query execution model which, in general, represents all the degrees of freedom in the query evaluation process: i.e. access methods, join methods, ordering of joins, etc. In our approach, we consider the decomposition of the global query into local subqueries as a preliminary step, and then restrict the optimization problem to selecting the best ordering of the extract-join operations. More precisely there we may distinguish between two optimization levels:

- *global optimization*: selecting the optimal *global* execution plan;

- *local optimization*: selecting the best *local* execution plans, i.e. the best way to perform each extract-join in the global *QEP* in the local site where it must be executed.

The problem arises since the two levels are strictly interconnected, and, because of the autonomy of the sites, the local optimization part can only be performed locally. The same kind of stratification is in the cost function, since no site has a complete information on other component *LDBSs* (database profiles, access methods, local cost functions, etc). Therefore, no single site can evaluate (or estimate) the cost of a *QEP*. On the other hand, each site can solve its own local optimization problem and evaluate the expected cost of performing the extract-join operation and of sending the result relation to the next site, provided that a suitable information on the extensional characteristics of the imported relation is supplied to it. Moreover note that all the local optimization problems are independent, since the way each extract-join is performed does not affect in any way the rest of the computation.

This means that the total execution cost of a *QEP* can be computed *incrementally* through the cooperation of all the sites involved. Each site evaluates the cost of its own extract-join and the characteristics of the result, and sends this information to the next site (or sites). Due to the (presumably) small number of *LDBSs* in a *MDBS*, and therefore of sites involved in the query, it makes sense to consider an exhaustive approach, i.e. taking into account all the valid *QEPs* and computing the exact optimum. The problem is then to parallelize the cooperative optimization process, and to achieve the efficiency by avoiding to perform unnecessary or duplicate computations.

The basic idea of the optimization algorithm we propose is the following. All the sites work in parallel in a sequence of steps. At each step every site evaluates the cost of a set of *PQEPs* and the characteristics of the corresponding result relations. This information is sent to the subset of sites which need it as an input to the next step, i.e. to compute further *PQEPs*. As the algorithm progresses, larger and larger *PQEPs* are considered, until in the last step the optimum *QEP* is found. The delicate part, that we shall discuss in the next sections, is actually how to manage efficiently the flow of information among the sites, and how to discard as soon as possible those *PQEPs* that may not lead to the optimal solution.

5 The Cost Function

The optimization algorithm we propose does not refer to any particular cost function. Given a *PQEP* $\mathcal{P} = \mathcal{Q}_{i_1} \ldots \mathcal{Q}_{i_k}$ and a site $m \notin \{i_1 \ldots i_k\}$ in the *MDBS*, let $C(m, \mathcal{P})$ be a cost function that gives the total execution cost of evaluating, in the order specified by the *QEP* $\mathcal{P}$, the partial query associated to it, and making the result available in node m.

The only restriction we put on the cost function, is that it must be *tail consistent*, i.e. given two comparable *PQEPs* $\mathcal{P}_1 = \mathcal{Q}_i \mathcal{P}'_1$ and $\mathcal{P}_2 = \mathcal{Q}_i \mathcal{P}'_2$ and a site i, then their costs $C(m, \mathcal{Q}_i \mathcal{P}'_1)$ and $C(m, \mathcal{Q}_i \mathcal{P}'_2)$ for any site m must have the same ordering as that of the costs $C(i, \mathcal{P}'_1)$ and $C(i, \mathcal{P}'_2)$.

Such a property of the cost function is indeed very important, since it allows to perform a pruning of the search space during the optimization process, by discarding a *PQEP* any time a comparable one is found to have a better cost. More precisely we say that $\mathcal{P}_1$ *dominates* $\mathcal{P}_2$ in a site m according to the cost function C, if $\mathcal{P}_1$ and $\mathcal{P}_2$ are comparable and $C(m, \mathcal{P}_1) \leq C(m, \mathcal{P}_2)$. Actually, in our execution model, all the cost functions we may reasonably think about, involving local execution cost and transmission cost, are tail consistent. This derives from the incremental way in which computation is performed.

In our multidatabase model, without any substantial loss of generality, we assume that the structure of the cost function makes evident that each step depends on the site in which the corresponding extract-join is performed and on the transmission cost to the next site, that, consistently with the assumptions made in Section 2, can also be considered dependent from the source site. Therefore, we may assume for the cost function the following form:

$$C(m, \mathcal{Q}_i) = F_i(m, \mathcal{Q}_i, \emptyset)$$
$$C(m, \mathcal{Q}_i\mathcal{P}) = C(i, \mathcal{P}) + F_i(m, \mathcal{Q}_i, \mathcal{P})$$

where $F_i(m, \mathcal{Q}_i, \mathcal{P})$ represents the cost of computing in site i the extract-join between the local query $\mathcal{Q}_i$ and the imported intermediate result specified by $\mathcal{P}$, plus the cost of sending the result in site m.

Note that the *incremental* cost computed by F_i only depends on information *local* to site i, and on *extensional parameters* (i.e. cardinality, number of distinct attribute values etc.) of the intermediate result defined by $\mathcal{P}$. This means that the components of the query execution cost can be *only* locally computed, as we have already pointed out.

An exact evaluation of the execution cost of a given *QEP* would require to know the exact values of the extensional parameters of all the intermediate results, plus such detailed information on local databases that is actually unrealistic to suppose to be available. Therefore, as usual in query optimization, we assume that the optimization algorithm relies on *cost estimates* that are computed from partial information maintained by local systems and from estimates of the extensional parameters of the intermediate results.

We shall then consider, instead of the original cost functions , a set of *cost estimators* Φ_i. Estimator $\Phi_i(m, \mathcal{Q}_i, \Pi(\mathcal{P}))$ is available at site i, and computes a cost estimate of performing in i the extract-join between the local query $\mathcal{Q}_i$ and the imported relation defined by $\mathcal{P}$. The computation is based only on local information, which we consider as being part of the function itself, and on estimates of the extensional parameters of the imported relation $\Pi(\mathcal{P})$. We then introduce an additional function at each site, say $\Theta(\mathcal{Q}_i, \Pi(\mathcal{P}))$, to compute the parameter estimates for the result of the extract-join.

Formally we replace in the original formulation of the optimization problem the cost C defined above, with the cost estimate Γ defined by:

$$\Gamma(m, \mathcal{Q}_i) = \Phi_i(m, \mathcal{Q}_i, \emptyset)$$

$$\Gamma(m, \mathcal{Q}_i \mathcal{P}) = \Gamma(i, \mathcal{P}) + \Phi_i(m, \mathcal{Q}_i, \Pi(\mathcal{P}))$$
$$\Pi(\mathcal{Q}_i \mathcal{P}) = \Theta(\mathcal{Q}_i, \Pi(\mathcal{P}))$$

Of course, when the optimization algorithm is based on a cost estimate, it will select an optimal QEP only if Γ is a *correct estimator* of the cost function , i.e. if for any two comparable $PQEP$ $\mathcal{P}_1$ and $\mathcal{P}_2$, and for any site m, the estimates $\Gamma(m, \mathcal{P}_1)$ and $\Gamma(m, \mathcal{P}_2)$ have the same ordering than the corresponding costs $C(m, \mathcal{P}_1)$ and $C(m, \mathcal{P}_2)$.

6 The Distributed Optimization Algorithm

Let us consider a global query with query graph $\mathcal{G}$, and let us assume that all the n sites in the multidatabase are involved in the query, i.e. there is a node in $\mathcal{G}$ for every site in the *MDBS*. We shall therefore use in this and the following sections the terms node and site interchangeably.

To formally express the optimization algorithm sketched at the end of Section 4, we first give some additional definitions:

- given a node i in $\mathcal{G}$ and an integer $k = 1 \ldots n - 1$; we denote as *k-neighbors* of i, all the nodes in $\mathcal{G}$ that are connected to i by an acyclic path of length k. We denote with Ξ_i^k the set of all the k-neighbors of i;
- given a PQEP $\mathcal{P} = \mathcal{Q}_{i_1} \ldots \mathcal{Q}_{i_k}$; we denote by $\Psi(\mathcal{P})$ the set of all the nodes in $\mathcal{G}$ that are the neighbors of the nodes $i_1, \ldots, i_k$, non including themselves, i.e. all the nodes x in $\mathcal{G}$ that have a local query $\mathcal{Q}_x$ *composable* with the partial query defined by $\mathcal{P}$.
- we call *cut point* of the graph $\mathcal{G}$ each node that if removed from the graph makes it become disconnected. Let Ω be the set of all the nodes of $\mathcal{G}$ that are not cut points. Note that the last operation of a valid QEP can only be performed in a node $i \in \Omega$ (otherwise the QEP will include a cartesian product).
- we denote with $\Lambda(m, \mathcal{P})$ a *PQEP estimate*, i.e. the estimate sent to node m about the execution cost and the extensional characteristics of the result of the query defined by $PQEP$ $\mathcal{P}$.

According to these definitions the algorithm can then be formulated as follows:

Algorithm 6.1. Given a global query Q of size n the algorithm requires $n + 1$ steps:

step 0 Each node i evaluates the cost estimates for the $PQEP$ $\mathcal{Q}_i$ composed only its own local subquery, and sends the corresponding $PQEP$ *estimate* $\Lambda(m, \mathcal{Q}_i) = \{\mathcal{Q}_i, \Gamma(m, \mathcal{Q}_i), \Pi(\mathcal{Q}_i)\}$ to each neighbor node $m \in \Psi(\mathcal{Q}_i)$.

step k Each node i waits for $PQEP$ estimates from all its k-neighbors. If the k-neighbors set Ξ_i^k is empty the node is not involved in further steps. Otherwise, when it gets all of them, selects from each set of comparable $PQEPs$ the one with the least estimated cost and discards the others. Then for each of the surviving $PQEPs$, say $\mathcal{P}_x$, and for each node $m \in \Psi(\mathcal{Q}_i\mathcal{P}_x)$ it computes the $PQEP$ estimate $\Lambda(m, \mathcal{Q}_i\mathcal{P}_x)$ and sends it to node m. This way each $PQEP$ estimate computed in the step is sent to all the nodes that have a composable local query.

step n-1 A node i is involved in this step if and only if $i \in \Omega$ (i.e. it is not cut point. Note that all the $PQEP$ estimates it gets from its (n-1)-neighbors relate to $PQEP$ which are comparable among them. It selects the best one, say $\mathcal{P}_x$, and then computes the cost estimate $\Gamma(w, \mathcal{Q}_i\mathcal{P}_x)$ for its *candidate* optimal QEP (where w is the node where the result of the query has to be delivered). The estimated cost of the candidate is sent to all the other nodes in Ω.

step n Each node in Ω waits for cost estimates from all the other nodes in Ω. Each of them may now determine which candidate is optimal. The node corresponding to the optimal candidate informs the remaining nodes (not in Ω) about the optimal plan. □

At the end of the last step each site of the $MDBS$ knows the optimal QEP and therefore is ready to cooperate in the query evaluation. That is, it may determine from the optimal QEP from which site it has to wait for an intermediate result, which extract join it has to perform, and to which site it has to send the result.

Note that all each site needs to know about the query is the local query $\mathcal{Q}_i$ it has to compute, and the topology of the query graph $\mathcal{G}$. In fact, it can derive from the topology of the graph all the information about the sets Ξ_i^k, Ψ and Ω that it needs to perform correctly the steps of the algorithm.

The following example illustrates how the algorithm works:

Example 2. Let us consider the query $\mathcal{Q}$ from Example 3.1, whose query graph is presented in Figure 1. The steps $0 \div (n-1)$ of the algorithm during the optimization of $\mathcal{Q}$ are summarized in Table 1. Each step in the table consists of two parts: the set of $PQEP$ evaluated in the step and the set of $PQEP$ estimates sent to other sites. The $PQEPs$ marked with $*$ represent the ones discarded before the evaluation. Note that $\Omega = \{\mathcal{Q}_1, \mathcal{Q}_2, \mathcal{Q}_4\}$ and $\mathcal{Q}_3$ is the only cut point in the query graph $\mathcal{G}$. In the last step, each node in Ω waits for cost estimates of candidate $QEPs$ from all the other sites in Ω. The node corresponding to the optimal candidate plan informs the site $\mathcal{Q}_3$ (the only site not in Ω) about the optimal plan. □

It is clear from the example that Algorithm 6.1 is organized in such a way that dominated $PQEPs$ are discarded at the beginning of each step by the node to which they have been sent, and that just retains the best one for any set of comparable $PQEPs$. To prove the optimality of the algorithm we need then to show that all non-dominated $PQEPs$ are considered, and therefore that discarding dominated $PQEPs$ does not prevent the generation of the optimal QEP.

To do that we first prove the following lemma:

Lemma 1. *If the cost function C and its estimator Γ are tail-consistent, any valid* PQEP *of size k for the query $\mathcal{Q}$ is either generated by Algorithm 6.1 in step $k-1$, or it is dominated by some other* PQEP *generated in that step.*

site	1	2	3	4
step				
0	$\mathcal{Q}_1$	$\mathcal{Q}_2$	$\mathcal{Q}_3$	$\mathcal{Q}_4$
	$(2, \mathcal{Q}_1)$	$(1, \mathcal{Q}_2)$	$(1, \mathcal{Q}_3)$	$(3, \mathcal{Q}_4)$
	$(3, \mathcal{Q}_1)$	$(3, \mathcal{Q}_2)$	$(2, \mathcal{Q}_3)$	
			$(4, \mathcal{Q}_3)$	
1	$\mathcal{Q}_2$	$\mathcal{Q}_1$	$\mathcal{Q}_1$	$\mathcal{Q}_3$
	$\mathcal{Q}_3$	$\mathcal{Q}_3$	$\mathcal{Q}_2$	
			$\mathcal{Q}_4$	
	$(3, \mathcal{Q}_1\mathcal{Q}_2)$	$(3, \mathcal{Q}_2\mathcal{Q}_1)$	$(2, \mathcal{Q}_3\mathcal{Q}_1)$	$(1, \mathcal{Q}_4\mathcal{Q}_3)$
	$(2, \mathcal{Q}_1\mathcal{Q}_3)$	$(1, \mathcal{Q}_2\mathcal{Q}_3)$	$(4, \mathcal{Q}_3\mathcal{Q}_1)$	$(2, \mathcal{Q}_4\mathcal{Q}_3)$
	$(4, \mathcal{Q}_1\mathcal{Q}_3)$	$(4, \mathcal{Q}_2\mathcal{Q}_3)$	$(1, \mathcal{Q}_3\mathcal{Q}_2)$	
			$(4, \mathcal{Q}_3\mathcal{Q}_2)$	
			$(1, \mathcal{Q}_3\mathcal{Q}_4)$	
			$(2, \mathcal{Q}_3\mathcal{Q}_4)$	
2	$*\mathcal{Q}_2\mathcal{Q}_3$	$\mathcal{Q}_3\mathcal{Q}_1$	$*\mathcal{Q}_1\mathcal{Q}_2$	$\mathcal{Q}_1\mathcal{Q}_3$
	$\mathcal{Q}_3\mathcal{Q}_2$	$*\mathcal{Q}_1\mathcal{Q}_3$	$\mathcal{Q}_2\mathcal{Q}_1$	$*\mathcal{Q}_3\mathcal{Q}_1$
	$*\mathcal{Q}_3\mathcal{Q}_4$	$\mathcal{Q}_3\mathcal{Q}_4$		$*\mathcal{Q}_2\mathcal{Q}_3$
	$\mathcal{Q}_4\mathcal{Q}_3$	$*\mathcal{Q}_4\mathcal{Q}_3$		$\mathcal{Q}_3\mathcal{Q}_2$
	$(4, \mathcal{Q}_1\mathcal{Q}_3\mathcal{Q}_2)$	$(4, \mathcal{Q}_2\mathcal{Q}_3\mathcal{Q}_1)$	$(4, \mathcal{Q}_3\mathcal{Q}_2\mathcal{Q}_1)$	$(2, \mathcal{Q}_4\mathcal{Q}_1\mathcal{Q}_3)$
	$(2, \mathcal{Q}_1\mathcal{Q}_4\mathcal{Q}_3)$	$(1, \mathcal{Q}_2\mathcal{Q}_3\mathcal{Q}_4)$		$(1, \mathcal{Q}_4\mathcal{Q}_3\mathcal{Q}_2)$
3	$\mathcal{Q}_2\mathcal{Q}_3\mathcal{Q}_4$	$\mathcal{Q}_1\mathcal{Q}_4\mathcal{Q}_3$	—	$\mathcal{Q}_1\mathcal{Q}_3\mathcal{Q}_2$
	$*\mathcal{Q}_4\mathcal{Q}_3\mathcal{Q}_2$	$*\mathcal{Q}_4\mathcal{Q}_1\mathcal{Q}_3$		$*\mathcal{Q}_2\mathcal{Q}_3\mathcal{Q}_1$
	$(2, \mathcal{Q}_1\mathcal{Q}_2\mathcal{Q}_3\mathcal{Q}_4)$	$(1, \mathcal{Q}_2\mathcal{Q}_1\mathcal{Q}_4\mathcal{Q}_3)$	—	$(1, \mathcal{Q}_4\mathcal{Q}_1\mathcal{Q}_3\mathcal{Q}_2)$
	$(4, \mathcal{Q}_1\mathcal{Q}_2\mathcal{Q}_3\mathcal{Q}_4)$	$(4, \mathcal{Q}_2\mathcal{Q}_1\mathcal{Q}_4\mathcal{Q}_3)$		$(2, \mathcal{Q}_4\mathcal{Q}_1\mathcal{Q}_3\mathcal{Q}_2)$

Table 1. Steps of the algorithm.

Proof. The lemma is obvious for $k = 1$, since all $PQEP$ of size 1 are generated in step 0. Let us now assume that the lemma is true for $k - 1$, and let $\mathcal{Q}_x\mathcal{P}_{k-1}$ be a valid $PQEP$ of size k, then one of the following two cases holds:

a) $\mathcal{P}_{k-1}$ has been generated by the algorithm in step $k - 2$; then it is sent to site x since it is *composable* with $\mathcal{Q}_x$;

b) otherwise the algorithm must have generated in step $k-2$ a $PQEP$ $\mathcal{P}'_{k-1}$ that dominates $\mathcal{P}_{k-1}$, and must have sent it to site x.

In either case the algorithm, that at the beginning of each step selects the best among any set of comparable $PQEP$, would generate in step k a $PQEPs$ $\mathcal{Q}_x\mathcal{P}"_{k-1}$ where $\mathcal{P}"_{k-1}$ is either $\mathcal{P}_{k-1}$, or $\mathcal{P}'_{k-1}$, or a third one that dominates them. In any of this cases $\mathcal{Q}_x\mathcal{P}_{k-1}$ cannot have better cost than $\mathcal{Q}_x\mathcal{P}"_{k-1}$ since the cost function and its estimator are tail-consistent. Therefore the lemma is proved by induction. □

We may now easily prove the optimality of the Algorithm 6.1 by stating the following theorem:

Theorem 2. *For any global query Q, If the cost function C and its estimator Γ are tail-consistent, the Algorithm 6.1 always finds a QEP with the least estimated cost.*

Proof. The proof follows directly from Lemma 6.1, since in step $n-1$ of the algorithm all non-dominated QEP are generated, and then exhaustively compared in the last step. □

It can also be proved that the algorithm is efficient, in the sense that no duplicate or no useless computations are carried on. In fact from the structure of the algorithm it follows that: 1) the execution cost of each $PQEP$ $\mathcal{P}_k = Q_x\mathcal{P}_{k-1}$ is evaluated only once in node x, 2) the corresponding $PQEP$ estimates are sent only to the sites that have a local query composable with the $PQEP$, and no $PQEP$ $\mathcal{P}_k = Q_x\mathcal{P}_{k-1}$ with a dominated tail $\mathcal{P}_{k-1}$ is ever generated.

7 Complexity Analysis

The computational complexity of the algorithm may be measured with respect to: 1) the number of steps in the algorithm, 2) the number of $PQEPs$ evaluated, and 3) the number of messages.

As we already mentioned in the previous section, the number of steps in the algorithm is always linear with the size n of the query. i.e. with the number of sites involved.

The number of $PQEPs$ evaluated by the algorithm heavily depends on the topology of the query graph. In the worst case, i.e. when the query graph is fully connected, the complexity is $O(n2^n)$. To prove this, consider that the total number of $PQEPs$ of length k is $\binom{n}{k}$. Since all the $PQEP$ of length $k-1$ comparable to a given $PQEP$ are $(k-1)!$, from the above follows that the total number of $PQEPs$ evaluated is:

$$\sum_{k=1}^{n} \binom{n}{k} k = n2^{n-1} = O(n2^n)$$

The number of messages sent during the optimization of a given query Q also depends on the topology of the query graph. In the case of the fully connected query graph the of messages is $O(n^2 2^n)$. This can be proved by considering that for $k = 1 \ldots n - 1$ each $PQEP$ of length k generated by the algorithm is sent to all the remaining $n - k$ sites not included in the $PQEP$, and since in the last step each candidate QEP is sent to $n - 1$ sites, the total number of messages is:

$$\sum_{k=1}^{n} \binom{n}{k} k(n-k) = n(n-1)2^{n-2} + n(n-1) = O(n^2 2^n)$$

The complexity dramatically decreases for simpler graph structures. For instance, for linear queries it can be shown that the total number of $PQEP$ evaluated is $O(n^2)$. Consider the following argument: each PQEP of size k involves k 0 sites, and it is sent at most to two sites. In turn each site at the beginning of step k gets at most two classes of comparable $PQEPs$ of size $k-1$, i.e. at most two non-dominated $PQEPs$ of length k-1 and then evaluates at most two $PQEPs$ of length k. Therefore for n sites over n steps we get that the total number of $PQEPs$ is $O(n^2)$. A similar argument can be used for the number of messages that is $O(n^2)$, since each $PQEP$ is sent at most at two neighbor sites, and this is a constant number with n and does not change the order.

8 Conclusions

In this paper we propose a new decentralized and distributed algorithm for query optimization in a multidatabase environment. The algorithm optimizes a global query through the synergic action of all component local database systems, and works in the general case of multidatabase systems including also non-conforming local systems, i.e. when cost functions and database statistics may not be available at the multidatabase level.

The main idea behind the algorithm is to delegate the evaluation of the execution cost of each elementary step of a query execution plan to the local system where the computation would be performed, since, in the general case, the cost functions and database statistics may be only locally available. All local systems perform this evaluation process in parallel, and cooperate in sending to each other the cost estimates of the partial execution plans. Duplicated and unnecessary computation is avoided by discarding as soon as possible all the partial execution plans that are dominated by some equivalent one.

The optimality of the algorithm is formally proved in the paper for a quite general class of cost functions that we call *tail-consistent*, a property that directly derives from the incremental way in which query evaluation is performed in our global query execution model.

The main advantages of the algorithm are: (1) it does not require any assumption about local execution models and optimization strategies, (2) it is robust to dynamically changing environment (changes of relations sizes, access methods, etc.), (3) it preserves completely the local autonomy of sites, and (4) it is totally decentralized, in the sense that no single site is responsible for supervising the query optimization process.

The approach proposed in this paper can be extended consider more general global query execution models. Here we restricted to an execution space composed only by strictly sequential query execution plans. In a further work we intend to extend the search space to include more complex execution plans (e.g. bushy plans), that would potentially allow more parallelism.. Another direction we plan for further investigation is to consider approximate query optimization algorithms to reduce the complexity of the optimization process.

References

1. W. Du, A. K. Elmagarmid, *Quasi serializability: a correctness criterion for global concurrency control in InterBase*, Proc. of 15th Int. Conf. VLDB, 1989, pp. 347-355.
2. Du, W, et al., *Query optimization in heterogeneous DBMS*, Proc. of the 18th VLDB Conference, Vancouver, 1992, pp. 277-291,
3. A. K. Elmagarmid, W. Du, *A paradigm for concurrency control in heterogeneous distributed database systems*, Proc. of 6th Int. Conf. on Data Engineering, 1990, pp. 37-46.
4. D. Georgakopolous, M. Rusinkiewicz, A. Sheth, *On serializability of multidatabase transactions through forced local conflicts*, Proc. 7th Int. Conf. on Data Engineering, 1991, pp. 314-323.
5. Y. E. Ioannidis and Y.C. Kang, *Left-Deep vs. Bushy Trees: An Analysis of Strategy Spaces and its Implications for Query Optimization*, Proc. of ACM-SIGMOD Conf. on Management of Data, Denver, USA, 1991, pp.168-177
6. W. Lu, et al., *On global query optimization in multidatabase systems*, Proc. of 2nd Int. Workshop on Research Issues on Data Eng., Tempe, 1992, pp. 217-227,
7. W. Lu, et al., *Multidatabase query optimization: issues and solutions*, Proc. of 3rd Int. Workshop on Research Issues on Data Eng., Vienna, 1993, pp. 137-143,
8. S. Mehrotra, R. Rastogi, Y. Breitbart, H. F. Korth, A. Silberschatz, *The concurrency control problem in multidatabases: characteristics and solutions*, Proc. of ACM SIGMOD Conf., 1992, pp. 288-296.
9. P. Muth, W. Klas, E. J. Neuhold, *How to handle global transactions in heterogeneous database systems*, Proc. 8th Int. Conf. on Data Engineering, 1992, pp. 192-198.
10. Proc. of Int. Workshop on Multidatabase and Semantic Interoperability, Tulsa, UK, 1990.
11. Proc. of Int. Workshop on Interoperability in Multidatabase Systems - RIDE, Kyoto, Japan, 1991.
12. Proc. of Int. Workshop on Interoperability in Multidatabase Systems - RIDE, Vienna, Austria, 1993.
13. S. Salza, T. Morzy, M. Matysiak, *Tabu Search optimization of large join queries*, Proc. of 4th Int. Conf. EDBT'94, Cambridge (UK), 1994, pp. 151-161 (Lecture Notes on Computer Science).
14. A. Sheth, J. Larson, *Federated database systems for managing distributed, heterogeneous, and autonomous databases*, ACM Computing Surveys, 22:183-236, 1990.
15. Zhu, Q, Larson, P-A, *A query sampling method for estimating local cost parameters in a multidatabase system*, Proc. of 10th Int. Conf. on Data Eng., Houston, 1994, pp. 144-153.

On the Complexity of Generating Optimal Left-Deep Processing Trees with Cross Products

Sophie Cluet[1] and Guido Moerkotte[2]

[1] INRIA, Domaine de Voluceau, 78153 Le Chesnay Cedex, France
[2] Lehrstuhl für Informatik III, RWTH-Aachen, 52056 Aachen, Germany

Abstract. Producing optimal left-deep trees is known to be NP-complete for general join graphs and a quite complex cost function counting disk accesses for a special block-wise nested-loop join [2]. Independent of any cost function is the dynamic programming approach to join ordering. The number of alternatives this approach generates is known as well [5]. Further, it is known that for some cost functions — those fulfilling the ASI property [4] — the problem can be solved in polynomial time for acyclic query graph, i.e., tree queries [2, 3].
Unfortunately, some cost functions like sort merge could not be treated so far. We do so by a slight detour showing that this cost function (and others too) are optimized if and only if the sum of the intermediate result sizes is minimized. This validates the database folklore that minimizing intermediate result sizes is a good heuristic. Then we show that summarizing the intermediate result sizes has the ASI property. It further motivates us to restrict the subsequent investigations to this cost function called C_{out} for which we show that the problem remains NP-complete in the general case.
Then, we concentrate on the main topic of the paper: the complexity of producing left-deep processing trees possibly containing cross products. Considering cross products is known to possibly result in cheaper plans [5]. More specifically, we show that the problem (LD-X-Star) of generating optimal left-deep processing trees possibly containing cross products is NP-complete for star queries. Further, we give an algorithm for treating star queries which is more efficient than dynamic programming. The NP-completeness of LD-X-Star immediately implies the NP-completeness for the more general tree queries.

1 Introduction

Not only in deductive databases but also in object bases, where each single dot in a path expression corresponds to a join, the optimizer is faced with the problem of ordering large numbers of joins. The standard and, maybe even today, prevailing method to determine an optimal join order is dynamic programming [6]. In 1984, the proof for the NP-completeness of join ordering for cyclic queries was presented together with an algorithm ordering joins for tree queries optimally in $O(n^2 \log n)$ time [2].[3] This algorithm was subsequently improved to $O(n^2)$

---

[3] n denotes the number of relations.

time complexity [3]. A heuristic for join ordering applying this algorithm to the minimal spanning tree of the join graph started the investigation of non-trivial heuristics for join ordering [3]. However, these algorithms rejected cross-products. Lately, Ono and Lohman gave real world examples that abandoning cross products can lead to more expensive plans than those which incorporate a cross product [5]. Furthermore, they gave $n2^{n-1} - n(n + 1/2)$ as the number of processing trees generated by dynamic programming in order to derive the cheapest left-deep processing tree possibly containing a cross product.

The question arises whether there exists a polynomial algorithm for treating the problem of generating optimal left-deep trees considering cross products. For general query graphs, this is unlikely, since already the generation of ordinary left-deep trees without cross products is NP-complete. For tree queries, the complexity of generating optimal left-deep trees possibly containing cross products is — so far — an open question. In this paper, we show that even for star shaped query graphs, which are a special case of a general tree query, the optimization problem is NP-complete.

Of course, every complexity result for an optimization problem highly depends on the chosen cost function. For example, in [2], a complex cost function counting disk accesses for a special block-wise nested-loop algorithm was used. Furthermore, the proof exploits some special features of this cost function, not present in other cost functions. Within this paper, we concentrate on a very easy cost function: the sum of the sizes of the intermediate results. Let us call this cost function C_{out}. This choice is motivated by several facts. First, it is a very simple cost function. Second, as will be shown, NP-completeness for C_{out} implies NP-completeness for other cost functions, too. More specifically, we will show that optimizing other cost functions is equivalent to optimizing C_{out} which formally justifies the database folklore that optimizing intermediate result sizes is a good thing to do.

The paper is organized as follows. In the next section, we first give a short introduction to the problem and present our notation. We then motivate our decision for considering C_{out} as a basic cost function for our complexity investigation on generating optimal left-deep processing trees possibly containing cross products. Section 3 then presents the proof of the NP-completeness of the LD-X-Star problem and ends with the sketch of an algorithm more efficient than dynamic programming. Section 4 presents open problems for future research.

2 Preliminaries and First Results

2.1 The Join-Ordering Problem

Let us first introduce the join-ordering problem. An instance of a join-ordering problem is fully described by the following parameters. First, n relations $R_1, \ldots, R_n$ are given. Associated with each relation is its *size* $|R_i|$, also denoted by n_i. Second, a *query graph* whose nodes are the relations and whose edges connect two relations by an undirected graph constitutes the second parameter.

The edges of the query graph are labeled by their according *selectivity*. Let (R_i, R_j) be an edge in the query graph. Then, the associated selectivity is $f_{i,j}$. We assume that $0 < f_{i,j} < 1$. If there is no edge between R_i and R_j, i.e., we have a cross product, we assume $f_{i,j} = 1$.

Since there exist several implementations for a join, there exist several cost functions. The most common implementations of a join operator are

1. hash loop join
2. sort merge join
3. nested loop join

The according cost functions are usually given as (see, e.g., [3]):

$$C_{hl}(R_i \bowtie R_j) := |R_i| 1.2$$
$$C_{sm}(R_i \bowtie R_j) := |R_i|(1 + \log(|R_i|)) + |R_j|(1 + \log(|R_j|))$$
$$C_{nl}(R_i \bowtie R_j) := |R_i||R_j|$$

These cost functions are mostly applied for main memory databases.

Sometimes, only the costs of producing the intermediate results is counted for. This makes sense if, e.g., the intermediate results must be written to disk, since then the costs for accessing the disk clearly outweigh the CPU costs for checking the join predicate. This cost function is called C_{out}:

$$C_{out}(R_i \bowtie R_j) := |R_i||R_j|f_{i,j}$$

Compared to the cost function used in [2] to proove the NP-completeness of join ordering, this cost function is very simple. Hence, the question arises if join ordering is still NP-complete for this simple cost function. As we will see, the answer is yes. Before we proove this, we need some more definitions.

For all cost functions, we will assume a binary equivalent whose input are just the sizes n_i and n_j of the according relations R_i and R_j. For example, for C_{out}, we have

$$C_{out}(n_i, n_j) := n_i n_j f_{i,j}$$

The problem considered in this paper is the complexity of computing an optimal *join-order*, i.e., a left-deep join-processing tree. More formally, given an instance of the join-ordering problem, we ask for a sequence s of the n relations such that for some cost function C_x the total cost defined as

$$C(s) := \sum_{i=2}^{n} C_x(|s_1 \ldots s_{i-1}|, s_i)$$

is minimized. Some definitions are needed in order to understand the definition of the cost function. Producing left-deep trees is equivalent to fixing a permutation π of the relations, or fixing a sequence $s_1, \ldots, s_n$ of all relations. The latter is what we do. By $|s_1, \ldots, s_i|$, we denote the intermediate result size of joining the relations $s_1, \ldots, s_i$. For a single relation s_i, we also write within cost functions s_i instead of $|s_i|$ or n_{s_i} in order to denote its size.

2.2 The ΣIR Property

The goal of this section is to cut down the number of cost functions which have to be considered for optimization. More specifically, we will argue that it is already quite interesting to just consider C_{out}. For this, we define an equivalence relation on cost functions.

Definition 1. Let C and C' be two cost functions. Then

$$C \equiv C' :\Leftrightarrow (\forall s \; C(s) \text{ minimal} \Leftrightarrow C'(s) \text{ minimal})$$

Obviously, $\equiv$ is an equivalence relation.

Next, we overload the binary C_x cost functions for a single join with those resulting from applying it to each join necessary to join a sequence s of relations. For example, we define

$$C_{out}(s) := \sum_{i=2}^{n} |s_1, \ldots, s_i|$$

Now we can define the ΣIR (Sum of Intermediate Results) property.

Definition 2. A cost function C is $\Sigma IR :\Leftrightarrow C \equiv C_{out}$.

Let us consider a very simple example. The last element of the sum in C_{out} is the size of the final join (all relations are joined). This is not the case for the following cost function:

$$C'_{out}(s) := \sum_{i=2}^{n-1} |s_1, \ldots, s_i|$$

Obviously, we have C'_{out} is ΣIR. The next observation shows that we can construct quite complex ΣIR cost functions:

Observation 3. *Let C_1 and C_2 be two ΣIR cost functions. For non-decreasing functions $f_1 : R \to R$ and $f_2 : R \times R \to R$ and a constant c we have that*

$C_1 + c$
$C_1 * c$
$f_1 \circ C_1$
$f_2 \circ (C_1, C_2)$

are ΣIR. Here, $\circ$ denotes function composition and $(\cdot, \cdot)$ function pairing.

There are of course many more possibilities of constructing ΣIR functions.

For the above cost functions C_{hl}, C_{sm}, and C_{nl}, we derive for a sequence s of relations

$$C_{hl}(s) = \sum_{i=2}^{n} 1.2|s_1, \ldots, s_{i-1}|$$

$$C_{sm}(s) = \sum_{i=2}^{n} |s_1, \ldots, s_{i-1}|(1 + \log(|s_1, \ldots, s_{i-1}|)) + \sum_{i=1}^{n} |s_i|(1 + \log(|s_i|))$$

$$C_{nl}(s) = \sum_{i=2}^{n} |s_1, \ldots, s_{i-1}| * s_i$$

We investigate which of these cost functions are ΣIR.

Let us consider C_{hl} first. From

$$C_{hl}(s) = \sum_{i=2}^{n} 1.2|s_1, \ldots, s_{i-1}|$$

$$= 1.2|s_1| + 1.2 \sum_{i=2}^{n-1} |s_1, \ldots, s_i|$$

$$= 1.2|s_1| + 1.2 C'_{out}(s)$$

and Observation 3, we conclude that C_{hl} is ΣIR for a fixed relation to be joined first. If we can optimize C_{out} in polynomial time, then we can optimize C_{out} for a fixed starting relation. Indeed, by trying each relation as a starting relation, we can find the optimal. Thus, we stay within PTIME.

Now, consider C_{sm}. Since

$$\sum_{i=2}^{n} |s_1, \ldots, s_{i-1}|(1 + log(|s_1, \ldots, s_{i-1}|))$$

is minimal if and only if

$$\sum_{i=2}^{n} |s_1, \ldots, s_{i-1}|$$

is minimal and $\sum_{i=1}^{n} |s_i|(1 + log(|s_i|))$ is independent of the order of the relations within s — that is constant — we conclude that C_{sm} is ΣIR.

Last, we have that C_{nl} is not ΣIR. To see this, consider the following counter example with three relations R_1, R_2, and R_3 of sizes 10, 10, and 100, resp. The selectivities are $f_{1,2} = \frac{9}{10}$, $f_{2,3} = \frac{1}{10}$, and $f_{1,3} = \frac{1}{10}$. Now,

$$|R_1 R_2| = 90$$
$$|R_1 R_3| = 100$$
$$|R_2 R_3| = 100$$

and

$$C_{nl}(R_1 R_2 R_3) = 10 * 10 + 90 * 100 = 9100$$
$$C_{nl}(R_1 R_3 R_2) = 10 * 100 + 100 * 10 = 2000$$
$$C_{nl}(R_2 R_3 R_1) = 10 * 100 + 100 * 10 = 2000$$

We see that $R_1 R_2 R_3$ has the smallest intermediate result size but produces the highest cost. Hence, C_{nl} is not ΣIR.

The rest of the section deals with the complexity of producing optimal left-deep join trees, that is, we do not consider cross products yet. The next subsection deals with the general problem, Sect. 2.4 treats tree queries.

2.3 On the Complexity of Optimizing C_{out}

Since the cost function C_{out} is much simpler than the cost function used to proove the NP-completeness of the general join ordering problem [2], we give a simple sketch of a proof that the join-ordering problem remains NP-complete even if the simple cost function C_{out} is considered. This seems necessary, since the proof in [2] makes use of some special features of the cost functions which are absent in C_{out}.

Theorem 4. *The join-ordering problem with the cost model C_{out} is NP-complete.*
Proof (sketch of). Obviously the join-ordering problem $\in$ NP. We will restrict the join-ordering problem to the Clique problem which is known to be NP-complete [1]. (The question asked in the Clique problem is, whether a graph G contains a clique of at least size K or not.) We will represent all n nodes in a graph G by relations of cardinality 1. If there is an edge between two nodes in G, then the selectivity between the corresponding relations is set to $\frac{1}{2}$. Let G be a graph where each relation has at least one connection to another relation. Now, it is obvious that if there is a clique of size K, then the optimal sequence must start by the K relations involved in this clique.

From this it also follows that the more general problem, where cross products are considered, is NP-complete too.

2.4 Tree Queries, C_{out}, and the ASI Property

In this subsection, we assume that the query graph is acyclic, i.e., a tree. Still, we do not consider cross products. For two special cases of a tree, we know the number of alternatives generated by the dynamic programming approach to join-ordering [5]. For chain queries, i.e., where the query graph is a chain, dynamic programming generates $(n-1)^2$ alternatives. For star queries, i.e., where there exists one relation to which all other relations are connected and there exists no other connection, dynamic programming generates $(n-1)2^{(n-2)}$ nodes. Note that the dynamic programming approach is independent of the chosen cost function. Nevertheless, the question arises, whether one can do better with specialized algorithms, if something is known about the cost functions.

The answer is yes, if the cost function has the ASI (Adjacent Sequence Interchange) property [4]. For these cost functions, there exist polynomial time algorithms (the fastest is $O(n^2)$) producing optimal left-deep trees for tree queries [2, 3]. Let us shortly review this approach.

From a query graph, a *precedence tree* is constructed by arbitrarily choosing one relation as a root and directing the edges away from it. The main idea then is, to produce for every possible precedence graph the optimal solution and take the cheapest of these. The optimal solution for a precedence graph is obtained by an algorithm that is an adaptation of the Monma/Sydney procedure for *job sequencing* with precedence constraints[4]. The ASI property allows to assign a rank to each relation such that if a sequence of relations is ordered by rank, it is optimal. Furthermore, if two relations linked by a precedence edge have unordered ranks, it guaranties that the two relations have to stick together in the optimal sequence. Thus, the idea is to (i) stick together relations that cannot be parted in the optimal sequence and (ii) merge the different chains using rank ordering.

Let us now come back to this ASI property. The selectivity $f_{i,j}$ of an edge within the original query graph corresponds to a selectivity of an edge within the precedence graph. For notational convenience, this selectivity is renamed to f_j, if the relation R_i is the (immediate) predecessor of the relation R_j within the precedence graph. We will rename the root node to R_1 and define f_1 to be 1.

Assume that we can write a cost function in the following form where f_i is used for denoting the selectivity attached to the relation s_i, given s_{i-1}.

$$Cost(s) = \sum_{i=2}^{n} [|s_1 \ldots, s_{i-1}| * g_i(s_i)]$$

$$= \sum_{i=2}^{n} [(\prod_{j=1}^{i-1} f_j * s_j) * g_i(s_i)]$$

for some arbitrary functions g_j. Then, for sequences S_1 and S_2 of relations, we can define this cost function recursively by

$$C(\epsilon) = 0$$
$$C(R_j) = 0 \qquad \text{if } R_j \text{ is the root}$$
$$C(R_j) = g_j(n_j) \quad \text{else}$$
$$C(s_1 s_2) = C(s_1) + T(s_1) * C(s_2)$$

with

$$T(\epsilon) = 1$$
$$T(s) = \prod_{i \in [1,n]} (f_i * s_i)$$

We have that C is well-defined and, for all sequences s, $C(s) = Cost(s)$.

Definition 5. A cost function C has the ASI property, if and only if there exists a rank function $rank(s)$ for sequences s, such that for all sequences a and b and all non-empty sequences v and u the following holds:

$$C(auvb) \leq C(avub) \Leftrightarrow rank(u) \leq rank(v)$$

For a cost function of the above form, we have the following Lemma:

Lemma 6. *Let C be a cost function which can be written in the above form. Then C has the ASI property for the rank function*

$$rank(s) = \frac{T(s) - 1}{C(s)}$$

for nonempty sequences s.

Since C_{hl} and C_{nl} can be written in the above mentioned special form for cost functions, they have the ASI property and tree queries involving these cost functions can be solved in polynomial time [3]. Further, C_{sm} cannot be written in the above form. This is the reason why it was so far abandoned from being treated by the Monma/Sidney-procedure [3]. Nevertheless, since C_{sm} is ΣIR, it suffices to show that C_{out} has the ASI property. If so, we can also treat tree queries involving C_{sm} in polynomial time. But obviously, C_{out} can be written in the above form with $g_j(s_j) = f_j s_j$. Hence,

Observation 7. C_{out} *has the ASI property.*

Summarizing, for tree queries, especially for chain and star queries, optimal left-deep trees can be constructed in polynomial time for all cost functions mentioned in this section; moreover, for all cost functions being ΣIR or having the ASI property.

Let us take a look at the *rank* function for C_{out}, in case of one relation only:

$$rank(s_i) = \frac{T(s_i) - 1}{C(s_i)} = \frac{f_i s_i - 1}{f_i s_i}$$

Since $\frac{x-1}{x}$ is strictly increasing, ordering by *rank* is the same as ordering by $f_i s_i$, for sequences consisting of a single relation.

All this only holds if we do not consider cross products. But as pointed out by Ono and Lohman, introducing cross products can lead to considerably cheaper plans [5]. Consequently, the next section deals with the complexity of constructing optimal left-deep join trees where some joins may in fact be cross products. Further, the dynamic programming approach considers $n2^{n-1} - \frac{n(n+1)}{2}$ — independently of the join graph [5] and the cost function. The question arises, whether we can do better for tree queries and the C_{out} cost function.

3 Star Queries

Consider a star query where the inner relation — or *center* is called R_0 and the relations $R_1, \ldots, R_n$ are the *satellites*. In any plan, there must exist a k such that some relations $s_1, \ldots, s_k$ are connected by a cross product, then, R_0 is joined and subsequently all the missing relations $s_{k+1}, \ldots, s_n$. The only cost function we will consider for the rest of the paper is C_{out}. Hence, we will write C instead of C_{out}.

The following is helpful in reducing the search space to be considered in order to find an optimal solution.

Lemma 8.

Any optimal sequence must obey

$$(1) \quad s_1 \quad \leq \quad s_2 \quad \leq \ldots \leq s_k$$
$$(2) \quad f_{s_{k+1},0} s_{k+1} \leq f_{s_{k+2},0} s_{k+2} \leq \ldots \leq f_{s_n,0} s_n$$

We call a sequence $s_1, \ldots, s_k$ size-ordered, if and only if $s_1 \leq \ldots \leq s_k$, and we call it ρ-ordered, if and only if $f_{s_1,0} s_1 \leq \ldots \leq f_{s_k,0} s_k$. Instead of $f_{s_i,0}$, we will also write simply $f_{i,0}$ or f_i, if a sequence s is implied by the context.

Something can also be said about the placement of R_0:

Lemma 9.

$$C(s_1 \cdots s_k R_0 s_{k+1} \cdots s_n) < C(s_1 \cdots s_{k-1} R_0 s_k s_{k+1} \cdots s_n)$$
$$\Leftrightarrow$$
$$s_k < \prod_{j<k} f_j n_0$$

Also, on the relations to the left and right or R_0, we have:

Lemma 10.

$$C(s_1 \cdots s_k R_0 s_{k+1} \cdots s_n) < C(s_1 \cdots s_{k-1} s_{k+1} R_0 s_k \cdots s_n)$$
$$\Leftrightarrow$$
$$s_k + s_k f_k (\prod_{j<k} f_j) n_0 < s_{k+1} + s_{k+1} f_{k+1} (\prod_{j<k} f_j) n_0$$
$$\Leftrightarrow$$
$$s_k - s_{k+1} < [s_{k+1} f_{k+1} - s_k f_k] n_0 \prod_{j<k} f_j$$

We next consider the cost differences of some more complex swap operations on sequences.

Lemma 11. *Let*

$$s = s_1 \cdots s_{k-1} s_k R_0 s_{k+1} \cdots s_{l-1} s_l s_{l+1} \cdots s_n$$
$$s' = s_1 \cdots s_{k-1} s_l R_0 s_{k+1} \cdots s_{l-1} s_k s_{l+1} \cdots s_n$$

Then

$$C(s) = \sum_{i=2}^{k-1} \prod_{j \leq i} s_j$$
$$+ (\prod_{j<k} s_j) n_k$$
$$+ (\prod_{j<k} s_j) s_k (\prod_{j<k} f_j) f_k n_0$$
$$+ [(\prod_{j<k} s_j) s_k (\prod_{j<k} f_j) f_k n_0] * (\sum_{i=k+1}^{l-1} \prod_{k+1 \leq j \leq i} f_j s_j)$$
$$+ [(\prod_{j<k} s_j) s_k (\prod_{j<k} f_j) f_k n_0] * (\prod_{k+1 \leq j < l} f_j s_j) * f_l s_l$$
$$+ [[(\prod_{j<k} s_j) s_k (\prod_{j<k} f_j) f_k n_0] (\prod_{k+1 \leq j < l} f_j s_j) f_l s_l] * \sum_{i=l+1}^{n} \prod_{l < j \leq i} f_j s_j$$

Analogously for s'. Thus

$$C(s) < C(s')$$

$$\Leftrightarrow$$

$$s_k + s_k f_k n_0 \prod_{j<k} f_j (1 + \sum_{i=k+1}^{l-1} \prod_{k+1 \leq j \leq i} f_j s_j)$$

$$<$$

$$s_l + s_l f_l n_0 \prod_{j<k} f_j (1 + \sum_{i=k+1}^{l-1} \prod_{k+1 \leq j \leq i} f_j s_j)$$

Hence, $s_k < s_l \wedge s_k f_k < s_l f_l \Rightarrow C(s) < C(s')$.

This is an important observation since we can now derive that if there is no contradiction between the order implied by the size and the one implied by the $s_i f_i$, then ordering the satellites by their size already results in an optimal order, except that the placement of R_0 within the sequence is unknown. But placing R_0 can easily be done using Lemma 9. To summarize:

Theorem 12. *If there is no contradiction between the size-rank and the ρ-rank of the satellites of the star query, optimal left-deep processing trees possibly containing cross products can be generated in polynomial time $(O(n \log(n)))$.*

This already looks promising. But the following theorem is slightly discouraging for general star queries. Denote by *LD-X-Star* the problem of generating an optimal join sequence under the consideration of cross products.

Theorem 13. *LD-X-Star is NP-complete.*

Proof. Obviously, LD-Star $\in$ NP. We show that LD-Star is NP-hard by reducing 3DM to LD-Star.

Let

$$X = \{x_1, \ldots, x_q\}$$
$$Y = \{y_1, \ldots, y_q\}$$
$$Z = \{z_1, \ldots, z_q\}$$
$$M = \{m_1, \ldots, m_n\} \subseteq X \times Y \times Z$$

be an instance of 3DM. W.l.o.g. we assume

1. $n > q$ and
   (Other instances can be checked immediately anyway.)

2. z_q occurs at least in two elements of M.
   (If z_q does not occur at all, we are done. If it occurs only once, we can reduce it to a problem of size $q - 1$ and $n - 1$.)

   We will number the x_i, y_i and z_i subsequently and use the symbols to identify the numbers.

Denote by p_i the i-th prime number greater than or equal to 5. Then we define

$$x_i := p_i \qquad\qquad 1 \le i \le q$$
$$y_i := p_{q+i} \qquad\qquad 1 \le i \le q$$
$$z_i := p_{2q+i} \qquad\qquad 1 \le i < q$$
$$A := \prod_{j=1}^{q} x_j \prod_{j=1}^{q} y_j * \prod_{j=1}^{q-1} z_j$$
$$z_q := A^2$$
$$B := A^3$$

Note that we can apply a sieve method to get all the needed polynomial number of primes in polynomial time.

Map each $(a_j, b_j, c_j) \in M$, $1 \le j \le n$, to a relation R_j and define

$$n_j := a_j * b_j * c_j$$
$$f_j := \frac{1}{n_j^2}$$

Last, define for relation R_0 its size $n_0 := B^2$. Again, these numbers can be constructed in polynomial time. We will show that:

there exists a solution to 3DM $\Leftrightarrow$ the optimal solution $s R_0 \bar{s}$ of the transformed LD-Star problem fulfills $||s|| = q$ and $|s| = B$.

Clearly, if there is no solution to the 3DM problem, no such $s R_0 \bar{s}$ exists. Indeed, the conditions we imposed on s ($||s|| = q$ and $|s| = B$) guaranty that it has to contain the 3DM solution. Hence, it remains to proove that if 3DM has a solution, then the optimal join order $s R_0 \bar{s}$ fulfills $||s|| = q$ and $|s| = B$ where $s = s_1 \ldots s_l$ is size-ordered and $\bar{s} = s_{l+1} \ldots s_n$ is ρ-ordered.

Let us first compute the cost $C(s R_0 \bar{s})$ using the recursive definition given in the previous section. Knowing that $||s|| = q$ and $|s| = B$, we have:

$$C(s) = \sum_{i=2}^{q} \prod_{j=1}^{i} s_j$$
$$= s_1 s_2 + s_1 s_2 s_3 + \ldots + s_1 s_2 \ldots s_q$$
$$= s_1 s_2 + s_1 s_2 s_3 + \ldots + |s|$$
$$\frac{C(s)}{|s|} = \frac{1}{s_3 s_4 \ldots s_q} + \frac{1}{s_4 \ldots s_q} + \ldots + \frac{1}{s_q} + 1$$
$$= 1 + \sum_{i=3}^{q} \prod_{j=1}^{q} \frac{1}{s_j}$$
$$=: 1 + C_1(s)$$
$$C(\bar{s}) = \sum_{i=q+1}^{n} \prod_{j=q+1}^{i} \frac{1}{s_j}$$
$$C(s R_0 \bar{s}) = C(s) + T(s) C(R_0) + T(s R_0) C(\bar{s})$$
$$= |s|(1 + C_1(s)) + \frac{|s| n_0}{s_1^2 s_2^2 \ldots s_q^2} + \frac{s_1 s_2 \ldots s_q n_0}{s_1^2 s_2^2 \ldots s_q^2} C(\bar{s})$$

$$= |s|(1 + C_1(s)) + \frac{|s|^3}{|s|^2}(1 + C(\bar{s}))$$

$$= |s|(2 + C_1(s) + C(\bar{s}))$$

Now, note that the conditions imposed on s guaranties that z_q appears once and only once in s and, accordingly, at least once in $\bar{s}$ (since z_q occurs at least in two elements of M). Thus, knowing that s is size ordered and $\bar{s}$ is ρ-ordered, we have:

$$C_1(s) = \frac{1}{z_q y_{s_q} z_{s_q}}(1 + \frac{1}{z_{s_{q-1}} y_{s_{q-1}} z_{s_{q-1}}}(1 + \ldots))$$

$$C(\bar{s}) = \frac{1}{z_q y_{\bar{s}_1} z_{\bar{s}_1}}(1 + \frac{1}{z_{\bar{s}_2} y_{\bar{s}_2} z_{\bar{s}_2}}(1 + \ldots))$$

Now, knowing that all x_i's y_i's are bigger than 4, we can derive the following upper-bound for $C(sR_0\bar{s})$:

$$C(sR_0\bar{s}) < |s|[2 + \frac{1}{4z_q}] \tag{1}$$

Let us now estimate the cost of any $C(uR_0\bar{u})$ for size-ordered u and ρ-ordered $\bar{u}$ where

$$u = u_1 \ldots u_k$$

$$\bar{u} = u_{k+1} \ldots u_n$$

and $1 < k < n$ (the cases $u = \epsilon$ and $\bar{u} = \epsilon$ trivially result in costs higher than $C(sR_0\bar{s})$).

Analogously to $sR_0\bar{s}$, we have:

$$C_1(u) := \sum_{i=3}^{k} \prod_{j=i}^{k} \frac{1}{u_j}$$

$$C(\bar{u}) := \sum_{i=k+1}^{m} \prod_{j=k+1}^{i} \frac{1}{u_j}$$

$$C(uR_0\bar{u}) = |u|(1 + C_1(u)) + \frac{n_0}{|u|}(1 + C(\bar{u}))$$

$$= |u|(1 + C_1(u)) + \frac{|s|^2}{|u|}(1 + C(\bar{u}))$$

With K defined as

$$K := \frac{|s|}{|u|}$$

we have

$$C(uR_0\bar{u}) = \frac{1}{K}|s|(1 + C_1(u)) + K|s|(1 + C(\bar{u}))$$

$$= |s|[K + \frac{1}{K} + \frac{1}{K}C_1(u) + KC(\bar{u})] \tag{2}$$

Note that $K + \frac{1}{K}$
- ≥ 2
- strictly decreasing for $K < 1$
- strictly increasing for $K > 1$

For $K \geq \frac{3}{2}$ and $K \leq \frac{1}{2}$, it follows from (1) and (2) that $C(uR_0\bar{u}) > C(sR_0\bar{s})$.

Hence, we can assume that $\frac{1}{K} > \frac{1}{2}$. Assume that u_k does not contain z_q. Then $\frac{1}{K}C_1(u) \geq \frac{1}{2}\frac{1}{z_{q-1}x_qy_q} \geq \frac{1}{2z_q}$ and, hence, $C(uR_0\bar{u}) > C(sR_0\bar{s})$.

Assume $u_k = z_q x_{u_k} y_{u_k}$. Then we define P such that $K = \frac{|s|}{|u|} = \frac{|s|}{Pz_q}$. Then $K = \frac{A}{P}$. Since both A and P are odd, we can conclude for $A \neq P$ that either $A \geq P + 2$ or $A \leq P - 2$. For the first case, we have

$$K = \frac{A}{P} \geq \frac{P+2}{P} \geq 1 + \frac{2}{P} > 1 + \frac{2}{A} = \frac{A+2}{A}$$

We now proove that for $K = \frac{A+2}{A}$:

$$K + \frac{1}{K} > 2 + \frac{1}{4z_q} \tag{3}$$

Since $K > 1$ and, hence, $K + \frac{1}{K}$ is strictly increasing, $C(uR_0\bar{u}) > C(sR_0\bar{s})$.

Equation (3) now follows from (remember that $z_q = A^2$):

$$\frac{A+2}{A} + \frac{A}{A+2} > 2 + \frac{1}{4A^2}$$

$$\Leftrightarrow$$

$$\frac{2A^2 + 4A + 4}{A^2 + 2A} > \frac{8A^2 + 1}{4A^2}$$

$$\Leftrightarrow$$

$$8A^4 + 16A^3 + 16A^2 > 8A^4 + 16A^3 + A^2 + 2A$$

$$\Leftrightarrow$$

$$15A^2 - 2A > 0$$

$$\Leftrightarrow$$

$$A(15A - 2) > 0$$

The latter is true since $A > 1$.

Now consider the second case. Here, we had $A \leq P - 2$ and hence $\frac{P}{A} \geq \frac{A+2}{A}$. Thus $K = \frac{A}{P} \leq \frac{A}{A+2}$. From (3) we know that $K + \frac{1}{K} > 2 + \frac{1}{4z_q}$ for $K = \frac{A+2}{A}$, and hence also for $K = \frac{A}{A+2}$. Since $K < 1$ and, hence, $K + \frac{1}{K}$ is strictly decreasing, $C(uR_0\bar{u}) > C(sR_0\bar{s})$.

Summarizing, any optimal sequence $uR_0\bar{u}$ must obey $|u| = A^3$ with one occurrence of z_q in u. Since $|u| = A^3$ and $u_k = z_q x_{u_k} y_{u_k}$ implies that $||u|| = q$, we are done.

From the above lemmata, we can infer an algorithm with complexity in the worst case of $\sum_{i=0}^{c} \binom{n}{i}$ where c is the number of cross products to consider. All we have to do is to generate systematically subsets of the relations $R_1, \ldots, R_n$, which will precede R_0 within the join graph. Since we can stop as soon as the rank of R_0 becomes smaller than the size of any of the remaining relations, we can be sure that we do not consider sets containing more relations than necessary. Further, if the rank of R_0 is still bigger than the size of a remaining relation, we can expand the set. Hence, we have a procedure that is within the claimed complexity class. Note, that it is faster than dynamic programming, if the number of cross products is less than the total number of relations.

4 Conclusion and Future Work

We have shown that the problem of constructing optimal left-deep processing trees for star queries is NP-complete. Hence, it is NP-complete for tree queries. The first open question to answer is whether there exists a polynomial algorithm for treating chain queries, i.e. those, whose join graph is a chain, or whether this problem is NP-complete, too.

Also open for future research is the complexity of generating optimal bushy trees, where except for number of plans dynamic programming generates [5], nothing is known.

References

1. Garey, J., Johnson, D.: Computers and Intractability: a Guide to the Theory of NP-Completeness. Freeman, San Francisco (1979)
2. Ibaraki, T., Kameda, T.: Optimal Nesting for computing n-Relational Joins. ACM. Trans. on Database Systems, **9(3)** (1984) 482—502
3. Krishnamurthy, R., Boral, H., Zaniolo, C.: Optimization of Nonrecursive Queries. Proc. Int. Conf. Very Large Databases (VLDB), (1986), 128—137
4. Monma, C., Sidney, J.: Sequencing with Series-Parallel Precedence Constraints. Math. Oper. Res,. 4 (1979), 215—224
5. Ono, K., Lohman, G.: Measuring the Complexity of Join Enumeration in Query Optimization. Proc. Int. Conf. Very Large Databases (VLDB), (1990), 314—325
6. Selinger, P., Astrahan, M., Chamberlin, D., Lorie, R., Price, T.: Access Path Selection in a Relational Database Management System. Proc. Int. Conf. Management of Data (ACM SIGMOD), (1979), 23—34

Querying Disjunctive Databases Through Nonmonotonic Logics

Piero A. Bonatti[1] and Thomas Eiter[2]

[1] Dipartimento di Informatica, Università di Torino, Corso Svizzera 185,
10149 Torino, Italy. email: bonatti@di.unito.it
[2] Christian Doppler Lab for Expert Systems, Institut für Informationssysteme,
TU Wien, Paniglgasse 16, A-1040 Wien, Austria.
email: eiter@vexpert.dbai.tuwien.ac.at

Abstract. In this paper we study the expressive power of major non-monotonic formalisms – among them circumscription, default logic, and autoepistemic logic – used as query languages over disjunctive databases. For this aim, we define the semantics of query expressions formulated in different nonmonotonic logics. The expressive power of the languages that we consider has been explored in the context of relational databases. Here, we extend this study to disjunctive databases; as a result, we obtain a finer-grained characterization of the expressive capabilities of those languages and interesting fragments thereof.
In particular, we show that there exist queries that cannot be expressed by any preference-based semantics (including the minimal model semantics and the various forms of circumscription), but which can be expressed in default and autoepistemic logic. Secondly, we show that default logic, autoepistemic logic and some of their fragments express the same class of Boolean queries, which turns out to be a strict subclass of the Σ_2^P-recognizable Boolean queries. Then we prove that under the assumption that the database consists of clauses whose length is bound by some constant, default logic and autoepistemic logic express *all* of the Σ_2^P-recognizable Boolean queries, while preference-based logics do not.

1 Introduction

Disjunctive databases provide one possibility for representing incomplete information – a topic which has been receiving much attention in the areas of databases, logic programming and AI, cf. [12, 16, 9].

Query languages for retrieving information from disjunctive databases are an open area of research. In the framework of relational databases, many alternative query languages have been proposed; they have been extensively studied in the literature (cf. [25, 14, 6, 7, 2] for fundamentals and overviews) and, in particular, they have been compared to each other by characterizing their *expressiveness*, i.e., the class of queries that they can express. These relationships are quite well understood [7, 2]. The study of query languages for disjunctive databases, constituted by collections of ground clauses rather than facts, is much less established. Work on querying incomplete databases is related; cf. [12, 1] for relations with null values, and [26] for the similar proviso of missing unique names axioms in logical databases. However, such work is basically concerned with expressing disjunctive information of the type "$p(a)$ or $p(b)$" instead of "$p(a)$ or $q(b)$", i.e., disjunctions involving ground facts from the same relation, rather than ground facts from distinct relations.

Advanced query languages for relational databases are typically non-monotonic, i.e. after extending the database some facts may no longer be derivable. Indeed some query languages are built on well-known nonmonotonic formalisms such as logic programming languages, circumscription and default logic [24, 8, 5]. The use of nonmonotonic formalisms as query languages is justified by their expressive power; see [5] for motivating examples.

In this paper we study the expressive power of major non-monotonic formalisms used as query languages over disjunctive databases. We will pay particular attention to *positive* disjunctive databases which, roughly speaking, are sets of positive clauses. Such databases enjoy nice properties that make them suitable for implementations. For instance, deciding whether a clause is entailed by such a database can be done in polynomial time.

The main contributions of this paper are the following:

- We define the semantics of query expressions formulated in different non-monotonic logics.
- We prove that the minimal model semantics (and, more generally, circum-scription; cf. [10]), default logic [23] and autoepistemic logic [20] cannot express all the PTIME-recognizable properties of positive disjunctive data-bases; this result is surprising, because in the framework of relational data-bases these logics are able to express every Σ_2^p-recognizable query. More surprisingly, the same negative result holds for all model-preference based logics, some of which are tremendously powerful (not even recursively enu-merable), and for the perfect and the stable models semantics of logic pro-grams (cf. [10]). This kind of negative results is usually proved by means of persistency properties, cf. [15]; for default logic we use a new technique based on a counting argument.
- If we impose a constant bound on the length of database clauses, then default logic and autoepistemic logic can express every Σ_2^p-recognizable query, while model-preference based logics (including circumscription and the minimal model semantics) cannot express all of the PTIME-recognizable ones. It follows that default logic and autoepistemic logic are strictly more expressive than disjunctive datalog, in the framework of bounded databases. This result is somewhat unexpected: in the framework of relational databases, these formalisms have exactly the same capabilities.
- We identify some interesting subsets of default and autoepistemic logic and give a complete picture of their mutual relationships. For instance, we show that prerequisites do not increase the expressive power of default logic, and that inconsistent stable expansions do not increase the expressive power of autoepistemic logic.

Due to space limitations, we cannot present in detail all concepts and proofs. Details and proofs of all results can be found in the full paper [3].

2 Preliminaries

A *relational scheme* over a domain Dom is a list $\overline{R} = R_1, \ldots, R_z$ of relation (or predicate) symbols R_i of arity $a_i \geq 0$ $(i = 1, \ldots, z)$. We assume that Dom, which will not be explicitly mentioned, is countably infinite. A *disjunctive database over* $\overline{R}$ is a pair $D = (U, \phi)$, where $U \subseteq$ Dom is a finite set of constants (universe) and ϕ is a conjunction of first order formulas

$$A_1 \vee \cdots \vee A_l \leftarrow B_1 \wedge \cdots \wedge B_m, \qquad l > 0, \ m \geq 0, \qquad (1)$$

where $A_1, \ldots, A_l, B_1, \ldots, B_m$ are ground atoms, built from the predicate symbols in $\overline{R}$ and from the constants in U. The empty conjunction (denoted by $\top$) represents the empty database; the universe of D is denoted by $U(D)$. The set of disjunctive databases over $\overline{R}$ is denoted by $\mathcal{D}(\overline{R})$. A disjunctive rule of form (1) is *positive* if $m = 0$; a disjunctive database (U, ϕ) is *positive* if ϕ is a conjunction of positive rules.

For any integer $d \geq 1$, we denote by $\mathcal{D}(\overline{R})_{\leq d}$ the set of databases (U, ϕ) from $\mathcal{D}(\overline{R})$ such that for each clause C occurring in ϕ, the *dimension* of C, which is the number of its disjuncts, is not larger than d. Notice that $\mathcal{D}(\overline{R})_{\leq 1}$ corresponds in an obvious way to the relational databases over $\overline{R}$, i.e., the finite structures $\langle U, r_1^{a_1}, \ldots, r_z^{a_z} \rangle$ where $r_i^{a_i} \subseteq U^{a_i}$.

A clause C *subsumes* a clause C' iff every disjunct of C is also a disjunct of C'. A disjunct of a clause C is *redundant* if it equals a distinct disjunct of C. A conjunct C_i of a CNF sentence $C_1 \wedge \cdots \wedge C_n$ is *redundant* if it is subsumed by some C_j where $j \neq i$.

A sentence ϕ is in *normal form* iff ϕ is in CNF, it contains no redundant conjuncts, and its conjuncts contain no redundant literals; a database $D = (U, \phi)$ is in normal form iff ϕ is.

Clearly, by removing redundant literals and clauses, every CNF-sentence ϕ (resp. disjunctive database D) can be transformed in quadratic time into a logically equivalent normal sentence (resp. disjunctive database), that will be denoted by ϕ^* (resp. D^*); this sentence (resp. database) is unique modulo the ordering of clauses and their disjuncts. Positive databases enjoy the following properties:

Proposition 1. *For all positive databases* $D = (U, \phi)$: (a) *for all non-tautological clauses* C, $\phi \models C \iff C$ *is subsumed by some conjunct of* $\phi \iff C$ *is a prime clause of* ϕ. (b) *for all positive databases* $D_1 = (U, \phi_1)$, ϕ_1 *is logically equivalent to* ϕ *iff* $\phi^* = \phi_1^*$ (*up to clause and literal ordering*).

2.1 Default Logic

A default theory ([23]; cf. [17, 19] for a background) $T = \langle W, \Delta \rangle$ is a pair of a set W of first-order formulas and a set Δ of default rules

$$\frac{\alpha(\mathbf{x}) : \beta_1(\mathbf{x}), \ldots, \beta_n(\mathbf{x})}{\gamma(\mathbf{x})}$$

such that the *prerequisite* $\alpha(\mathbf{x})$, the *justifications* $\beta_1(\mathbf{x}), \ldots, \beta_n(\mathbf{x})$ and the *consequent* $\gamma(\mathbf{x})$ are first-order formulas whose free variables are among those of $\mathbf{x} = x_1, \ldots, x_m$. When $n = 0$, then $\top$ (truth) is implicitly assumed as the justification of the default. We will omit writing $\alpha(\mathbf{x})$ if the prerequisite is $\top$; such defaults will be called *prerequisite-free*. A default is *closed* if it has no free variables, and *open* otherwise; the same notion is defined for default theories in the obvious way.

The semantics of a closed default theory $\langle W, \Delta \rangle$ is based on *extensions*. Formally, an extension E can be characterized through a quasi-inductive construction as follows. Let E be a set of first-order formulas. Define

$$E_0 = W, \quad \text{and for } i \geq 0$$
$$E_{i+1} = \text{Th}(E_i) \cup \{ \gamma \mid (\alpha : \beta_1, \ldots, \beta_n / \gamma) \in \Delta, \, \alpha \in E_i, \, \forall j. \neg \beta_j \notin E \}$$

where $\text{Th}(\cdot)$ denotes classical deductive closure. Then, E is an extension of T iff $E = \bigcup_{i=0}^{\infty} E_i$. Each extension E can be constructed from its *generating defaults*. For a set S of formulas and a set Δ of defaults, let

$$\text{GD}(\Delta, S) = \{ \delta \in \Delta \mid \delta = (\alpha : \beta_1, \ldots, \beta_n / \gamma), \, S \vdash \alpha, \, \forall j. \, S \nvdash \neg \beta_j \}$$

be the generating defaults of S w.r.t. Δ. Furthermore, denote by $\text{CONS}(\Delta)$ the set of the consequents of the defaults in Δ.

Lemma 2. [23, Theorem 2.5] *Let E be an extension of the closed default theory $T = \langle W, \Delta \rangle$. Then, $E = \text{Th}(W \cup \text{CONS}(\text{GD}(\Delta, E)))$.*

3 Query Languages for Disjunctive Databases

Query languages for relational databases are a well-studied topic in the theory of relational databases, cf. [25, 6, 14, 2]. The notion of a query (which maps each relational database onto another relational database) can be naturally extended to disjunctive databases.

Let $\overline{R}$ and $\overline{S}$ be relational schemes. A *database mapping* or *query* is a recursive function $q : \mathcal{D}(\overline{R}) \to \mathcal{D}(\overline{S})$ such that $U(q(D)) = U(D)$; moreover, we require q to be invariant under isomorphism (i.e., *generic* in the sense of [2]) and under logical consequence, i.e., $q(D) = q(D')$ if D and D' are logically equivalent. The latter condition insures that queries are not sensitive to the syntactic representation of disjunctive information. The pair $(\overline{R}, \overline{S})$ is called the *input/output scheme of* q and is denoted by $IO(q)$; it is assumed that $\overline{R}$ and $\overline{S}$ are disjoint.

The queries which compute relations, i.e. such that $q(D) \in \mathcal{D}(\overline{R})_{\leq 1}$ for all D, are of natural interest; they deduce only atomic facts from the database. An important special case of such relational output-queries are those where $\overline{S}$ consists of a single 0-ary relation symbol P, i.e., a propositional letter. Such *Boolean* queries model yes/no queries on disjunctive databases.

Boolean queries naturally correspond to *database properties*. For a given relational scheme $\overline{R}$, a database property is a predicate $\mathbf{P}$ which associates with every database D over $\overline{R}$ a truth value $\mathbf{P}(D)$ from $\{true,\ false\}$ and which is closed under isomorphism and logical equivalence. The database property corresponding to a Boolean query $q : \mathcal{D}(\overline{R}) \rightarrow \mathcal{D}(S)$ is denoted by $\mathbf{P}_q$; for all $D \in \mathcal{D}(\overline{R})$, we have $\mathbf{P}_q(D) = true$ iff $q(D) = (U(D), S)$ and $\mathbf{P}_q(D) = false$ iff $q(D) = (U(D), \top)$.

Let $\mathbf{C}$ be any complexity class (based on the Turing machine model). Following the approach in [25, 13], we say that a database property is $\mathbf{C}$-*recognizable* (or, *in* $\mathbf{C}$) if, given D, deciding whether $\mathbf{P}(D) = true$ is in $\mathbf{C}$; a query q is $\mathbf{C}$-*recognizable* (or, *in* $\mathbf{C}$) if, given D and a ground clause C, deciding whether $C \in q(D)$ is in $\mathbf{C}$.[3]

4 Nonmonotonic Logics as Query Languages

In this section we define the semantics of preference-based logics and default logic as query languages for expressing Boolean properties of disjunctive databases; a generalization to relational-output queries is straightforward.

We follow the deductive view of datalog and other logical query languages. Roughly speaking, the answer to the query expressed by a theory T in a logic L evaluated against a disjunctive database $D = (U, \phi)$ is "yes" iff a designated output letter P is entailed in L by the union of T and ϕ, where T is instantiated over D.

Notation. For all sets of first-order formulas T and any set U, we will denote by $[T]_U$ the set of closed instances of the formulas of T, obtained by binding their free variables to elements of U in all possible ways.

We first define the semantics of first-order query expressions T under preferential semantics. For all disjunctive databases $D = (U, \phi)$ define

$$T + D = [T]_U \cup \{\phi\}$$

Definition 3. Let T be a set of first-order formulas on a relational vocabulary including $\overline{R}$ and a propositional letter S not occurring in $\overline{R}$, and let $\prec$ be a strict partial order (preference relation) on the models of T. Then, T expresses under the brave preferential semantics the Boolean query $q : \mathcal{D}(\overline{R}) \rightarrow \mathcal{D}(S)$ iff for all $D \in \mathcal{D}(\overline{R})$,

$$\mathbf{P}_q(D) = true \text{ iff } S \text{ is true in at least one } \prec\text{-minimal model of } T + D.$$

Similarly, T expresses under the cautious preferential semantics the Boolean query $q : \mathcal{D}(\overline{R}) \rightarrow \mathcal{D}(S)$ iff for all $D \in \mathcal{D}(\overline{R})$,

$$\mathbf{P}_q(D) = true \text{ iff } S \text{ is true in all } \prec\text{-minimal models of } T + D.$$

---

[3] We assume a natural encoding in which U is described by its cardinality written down in unary notation. Equivalently w.r.t. to polynomial time computability, we could represent U by an enumeration of its elements, cf. [13].

Note that the standard minimal model semantics for logic programs is a preference based logic where $\prec = \subseteq$. Similarly, monotonic logics are special cases of preference-based logics, where $\prec$ is empty.

Next we define the semantics of a default logic query. Let $T = \langle W, \Delta \rangle$ be a default theory, whose underlying first-order language is function-free and quantifier-free and includes the predicates from $\overline{R}$. [4] By $[\Delta]_U$ we denote the set of all ground instances of defaults from Δ obtained by binding their free variables to elements of U in all possible ways. Finally, for all disjunctive databases $D = (U, \phi)$ define

$$T + D = \langle \{\phi\} \cup [W]_U, [\Delta]_U \rangle.$$

Definition 4. Let $T = \langle W, \Delta \rangle$ be a default theory. Then, T *expresses* the Boolean query $q : \mathcal{D}(\overline{R}) \to \mathcal{D}(S)$ under the *brave* semantics iff for all databases $D \in \mathcal{D}(R)$,

$$\mathbf{P}_q(D) = true \text{ iff } T + D \text{ has an extension which contains } S.$$

The definition of the cautious semantics is *mutatis mutandis*. Now each database property $\mathbf{P}$ over $\mathcal{D}(\overline{R})$ under brave (as well as cautious) default semantics might be expressed by means of a suitable Boolean query $q : \mathcal{D}(\overline{R}) \to \mathcal{D}(S)$ such that $\mathbf{P}_q = \mathbf{P}$. However, it will be convenient – and probably more appealing – to adopt the following definition, which is simpler to handle and yields the same notion of expressive power:

Definition 5. T expresses $\mathbf{P}$ over $\mathcal{D}(\overline{R})$ under the *brave* semantics iff for all databases $D \in \mathcal{D}(R)$, $\mathbf{P}(D) = true$ iff $T + D$ has an extension.

5 Expressive Power

It has been recently shown that the brave version of parallel circumscription captures the Σ_2^p-recognizable database properties of relational databases (provided that the language contains equality) [8]. We are going to prove that this result cannot be generalized to disjunctive databases. Actually, we will prove a stronger result, namely, that *all preference-based semantics have the same limitation*. For this purpose, consider the following property:

Definition 6. Let R be an a-ary predicate symbol in $\overline{R}$. For all $D = (U, \phi)$ define $\mathbf{P}_R(D) = true$ iff for some tuples $\mathbf{c}_1, \ldots, \mathbf{c}_n$ in $U(D)^a$, $\phi \models R(\mathbf{c}_1) \vee \ldots \vee R(\mathbf{c}_n)$ and $\phi \not\models R(\mathbf{c}_i)$ $(i = 1, \ldots, n)$.

To give an intuitive meaning to the above property, we remind that certain null values, that represent unknown attributes belonging to some fixed range $\{v_1, \ldots, v_n\}$, can be specified by disjunctions of the form $R(c, v_1) \vee \ldots \vee R(c, v_n)$. From this point of view, a database (U, ϕ) has the property $\mathbf{P}_R$ iff D contains a proper null value.

---

[4] The restriction to a function and quantifier-free first-order language is common in database theory.

Theorem 7. *The property* $\mathbf{P}_R$ *cannot be expressed by any first order theory under any brave preferential semantics.*

The proof of this theorem is based on the following lemma:

Lemma 8. *Let* $\prec$ *be any binary relation over the set of interpretations, and for all sets of sentences* S, *let* $MM(S)$ *denote the set of* $\prec$-*minimal models of* S.[5] *For all sets of sentences* S *and* $\{\sigma_1, \ldots, \sigma_n\}$ *we have:* $MM(S \cup \{\sigma_1 \vee \ldots \vee \sigma_n\}) \subseteq MM(S \cup \{\sigma_1\}) \cup \ldots \cup MM(S \cup \{\sigma_n\})$.

Proof. (of Theorem 7) Suppose that some theory T expresses $\mathbf{P}_R$ under some preferential semantics based on a preference relation $\prec$, i.e. for all databases $D = (U, \phi)$, $\mathbf{P}_R(D) = true$ iff the output proposition P is true in some $\prec$-minimal model of $[T]_U \cup \{\phi\}$. Then, for any given universe U and for any distinct tuples of U-constants $\mathbf{c}$ and $\mathbf{d}$, $[T]_U \cup \{R(\mathbf{c}) \vee R(\mathbf{d})\}$ must have a minimal model M where P is true. By Lemma 8, M must be a minimal model of either $[T]_U \cup \{R(\mathbf{c})\}$ or $[T]_U \cup \{R(\mathbf{d})\}$; but neither $(U, R(\mathbf{c}))$ nor $(U, R(\mathbf{d}))$ have the property $\mathbf{P}_R$, therefore T does not express $\mathbf{P}_R$; a contradiction. $\square$

A similar result can be obtained for the property $\mathbf{P}_{MM}$ defined as follows: $\mathbf{P}_{MM}(D) = true$ iff $D = (U, \phi)$ and ϕ has at least two distinct minimal models (i.e. D is truly disjunctive and it is not equivalent to any relational database).

Both $\mathbf{P}_R$ and $\mathbf{P}_{MM}$ can be computed on positive databases in polynomial time. Thus, there exist properties of positive databases that are computable in polynomial time, but cannot be expressed under any brave preferential semantics. The same holds for cautious preferential semantics. (This can be easily derived from the database property complementary to $\mathbf{P}_R$.)

Remark. The above results can be extended also to the *stable model semantics* [21] – one of the major semantics for disjunctive logic programs – although it is not really a preferential semantics, but rather an hybrid between a preferential semantics and the semantics of default logic. By means of Lemma 8 it is easy to prove the following proposition:

Each stable model of $T + D$, where $D = (U, R(\mathbf{c}_1) \vee \cdots \vee R(\mathbf{c}_n))$ is also a stable model of $T + D'$, for some database $D' = (U, R(\mathbf{c}_i))$ $(1 \le i \le n)$.

It follows that no disjunctive logic program expresses $\mathbf{P}_R$ or $\mathbf{P}_{MM}$ under the stable model semantics (the proof is similar to that of Theorem 7; apply the above proposition instead of Lemma 8). Moreover, through similar techniques, one can extend the proof to the *perfect model semantics* [22] (the above property of stable models applies to perfect models, too.) Similar results have already been proved for other important semantics of disjunctive logic programs, cf. [4].

---

[5] By $\prec$-minimal models we mean those models M such that for no model N, $N \prec M$.

5.1 Expressive Power of Default Logic

Default logic can express the property $\mathbf{P}_R$. The default theory $T_R = \langle W_R, \Delta_R \rangle$, whose formulas and defaults are as follows, is suitable for this purpose:

$$(\mathrm{F})\, C(\mathbf{x}) \wedge R(\mathbf{x}) \to S \qquad (\mathrm{D1})\, \frac{:\, C(\mathbf{x})}{C(\mathbf{x})} \qquad (\mathrm{D2})\, \frac{:\, \neg C(\mathbf{x})}{\neg C(\mathbf{x})}$$

$$(\mathrm{D3})\, \frac{C(\mathbf{x}) \wedge R(\mathbf{x}):}{\perp} \qquad (\mathrm{D4})\, \frac{:\, \neg S}{\perp}$$

The predicates C and S are new and do not occur among the database predicates $\overline{R}$. Intuitively, the extension of C describes a clause $R(\mathbf{c}_1) \vee \cdots \vee R(\mathbf{c}_n)$, where $C(\mathbf{x})$ means that $R(\mathbf{x})$ occurs in the clause. The clause is selected by the defaults (D1)-(D2); the default (D3) assures that the clause is truly disjunctive, i.e., does not contain some $R(\mathbf{c}_i)$ such that $\phi \models R(\mathbf{c}_i)$. The formula (F) and the default (D4) check that the clause is implied by ϕ, by assuring that the propositional variable S is derivable.

Proposition 9. *For every database $D = (U, \phi)$ over $\overline{R}$, the default theory $T_R + D$ has an extension iff $\mathbf{P}_R(D) = true$.*

Now the question is: what is the class of properties of disjunctive databases that can be expressed through default logic? From well-known results on the complexity of propositional default logic, we obtain easily the following upper bound for the expressive power of default logic.

Theorem 10. *The database properties expressible in default logic are Σ_2^p-recognizable.*

Proof. As shown in [11], deciding whether a propositional default theory has an extension is a Σ_2^p-complete problem. For every default theory T and database D, the size of $T + D$ is polynomial in the size of T plus the size of D. Hence, the result follows. □

Moreover, there exist database properties defined in default logic which are Σ_2^p-hard to compute (cf. Lemma 19 below). Thus, default logic seems to be powerful; the question is whether it is a well-balanced query language, i.e., can default logic express *all* the Σ_2^p-recognizable properties of disjunctive databases?

The answer is no. We will prove this result in two steps; first we will show that prerequisite-free default logic has the same expressive power as unrestricted default logic; then we will show that prerequisite-free default logic cannot express a simple property of positive databases.

Theorem 11. *For all default theories $T = \langle W, \Delta \rangle$ there exists a prerequisite-free default theory $\mathrm{pf}(T) = \langle W, \mathrm{pf}(\Delta) \rangle$ that expresses the same property as T.*

The proof – which is omitted here – describes pf(Δ), which roughly speaking simulates the defaults of T without deriving their consequents.[6] Now consider the following property:

Definition 12. For all positive databases $D = (U, \phi)$ from $\mathcal{D}(\overline{R})$, $\mathbf{P_{ev}}(D) =$ *true* iff the dimensions of the clauses in ϕ^* are all even.

Theorem 13. $\mathbf{P_{ev}}$ *is not expressed by any prerequisite-free default theory, under brave reasoning.*

It follows easily from this theorem that there exists a Σ_2^p-recognizable database property over general disjunctive databases which cannot be expressed in default logic: Simply extend the definition of $\mathbf{P_{ev}}$ such that $\mathbf{P_{ev}}(D) = \mathbf{P_{ev}}(D')$ if D is logically equivalent to a positive database D', and $\mathbf{P_{ev}}(D) = $ *false* otherwise; call this property $\mathbf{P_{ev,p}}$.

Basically, the proof of Theorem 13 goes as follows: we exploit two interpolation properties of DL (Lemmas 14 and 15) to prove that, in order to distinguish the databases with property $\mathbf{P_{ev}}$ from the ones that do not have this property, we need numerous defaults (Lemma 16); then we show that no fixed default theory can provide so many defaults.

Lemma 14. *Let $T_1 = \langle W_1, \Delta \rangle$ and $T_2 = \langle W_2, \Delta \rangle$ be closed prerequisite-free default theories such that, for some W, $W_1 \models W$ and $W \models W_2$. If T_1 and T_2 have extensions E_1 and E_2 (respectively) such that $\mathrm{GD}(\Delta, E_2) = \mathrm{GD}(\Delta, E_1)$ then also the theory $T = \langle W, \Delta \rangle$ has an extension E such that $\mathrm{GD}(\Delta, E) = \mathrm{GD}(\Delta, E_1)$.*

Lemma 15. *Let $T_1 = \langle \{ \phi_1 \}, \Delta \rangle$ and $T_2 = \langle \{ \phi_2 \}, \Delta \rangle$ be prerequisite-free closed default theories. If T_1 has an extension E_1 and T_2 has an extension E_2 such that $\mathrm{GD}(\Delta, E_2) = \mathrm{GD}(\Delta, E_1)$ then also the theory $T = \langle \{ \phi_1 \vee \phi_2 \}, \Delta \rangle$ has an extension E such that $\mathrm{GD}(\Delta, E) = \mathrm{GD}(\Delta, E_1)$.*

Lemma 16. *Let $D_1 = (U, \phi_1)$ and $D_2 = (U, \phi_2)$ be non-equivalent positive databases with property $\mathbf{P_{ev}}$, and let $T = \langle W, \Delta \rangle$ be a prerequisite-free theory that expresses $\mathbf{P_{ev}}$. For all extensions E_1 and E_2 of $T + D_1$ and $T + D_2$ (respectively) we have $\mathrm{GD}([\Delta]_U, E_1) \neq \mathrm{GD}([\Delta]_U, E_2)$.*

Proof. (of Theorem 13) Suppose that the theorem is not valid, i.e. assume that there exists a prerequisite-free theory $T = \langle W, \Delta \rangle$ that expresses $\mathbf{P_{ev}}$; we will derive a contradiction.

Let U be any universe with cardinality $n = 4i$ with i integer. Let m be the cardinality of the corresponding Herbrand base; note that $m = 4j$ for some integer j.

---

[6] It was already known that every default theory can be translated into an equivalent prerequisite-free theory, but it was not known how to translate Δ into a single theory pf(Δ), preserving the meaning of Δ for *all* possible input databases D.

Let $S = \{D_1, \ldots, D_N\}$ be the set of normal positive databases with universe U that have the property $\mathbf{P_{ev}}$. To prove the theorem it suffices to show that the following inequalities hold for some polynomial $p(n)$ in n:

$$N \leq 2^{p(n)} \tag{2}$$

$$N \geq 2^{2^{n/2}} \tag{3}$$

In fact, (2) and (3) imply $2^{2^{n/2}} \leq 2^{p(n)}$ but for sufficiently large universes we have $2^{2^{n/2}} > 2^{p(n)}$, hence a contradiction.

First we prove (2). By assumption, T expresses $\mathbf{P_{ev}}$, therefore, for all $D_h \in S$, $T + D_h$ has an extension E_h. Note that distinct normal databases are not equivalent; therefore, by applying Lemma 16 to all pairs of databases of S we derive that each extension E_h corresponds to a distinct set of generating defaults $GD([\Delta]_U, E_h)$. The number of possible sets of generating defaults is bounded by 2^l, where l is the cardinality of $[\Delta]_U$, therefore $N \leq 2^l$. Moreover, l can be expressed as a polynomial in n, say $p(n)$, where the exponents are determined by the number of free variables in the defaults of Δ. It follows that $N \leq 2^{p(n)}$, which proves (2).

We are left to prove (3). The number of normal clauses of dimension $2j$ is:

$$\binom{m}{2j} = \binom{m}{m/2} \geq 2^{m/2} \geq 2^{n/2}$$

therefore, the number of databases of S that contain only clauses of dimension $2j$ is at least $2^{2^{n/2}}$. Disequation (3) follows immediately. □

Since $\mathbf{P_{ev}}$ can be computed on databases in polynomial time (because ϕ^* can), we conclude that:

Corollary 17. *There exist PTIME-recognizable properties of positive databases that cannot be expressed through brave reasoning in prerequisite-free default logic.*

However, for the class of bounded databases, i.e., the databases in $\mathcal{D}(\overline{R})_{\leq d}$, for a fixed constant d, we have the following.

Theorem 18. *For every Σ_2^p-recognizable property $\mathbf{P}$ defined over $\mathcal{D}(\overline{R})_{\leq d}$, for d a constant, there exists a default theory T that defines $\mathbf{P}$ under brave reasoning.*

This result can be intuitively grasped through two facts. First, each database from $\mathcal{D}(\overline{R})_{\leq d}$ can be represented in a relational database over some scheme $\overline{R}'$. Second, all Σ_2^p-recognizable queries over relational databases can be expressed in default logic [5]. Recall that we can think of a relational database over $\overline{R}'$ as a database $D \in \mathcal{D}(\overline{R}')_{\leq 1}$, where the clauses in D (which are facts) correspond to the tuples stored in the database relations. The following lemma rephrases the main result in [5].

Lemma 19. *Let* **P** *be a Σ_2^p-recognizable database property over $\mathcal{D}(\overline{R})_{\leq 1}$. Then, there exists a set of defaults Δ such that for every $D = (U, \phi) \in \mathcal{D}(\overline{R})_{\leq 1}$, the default theory $\langle \mathrm{COMP}(D), [\Delta]_U \rangle$ has an extension iff $\mathrm{P}(D) = true$, where $\mathrm{COMP}(D)$ consists of all ground atoms occurring in ϕ and the negations of all ground atoms over U not occurring in ϕ.*[7]

Thus, intuitively, T can be composed of two subtheories $T_1 = \langle \emptyset, \Delta_1 \rangle$ and $T_2 = \langle \emptyset, \Delta_2 \rangle$, such that T_1 transforms the input (disjunctive) database D into a relational database D', and T_2 tests whether D' has the property P' corresponding to **P**.

It is interesting to see that model-preference based logics cannot express all the Σ_2^p-recognizable properties over bounded databases.

Theorem 20. *For all $d > 1$, the properties P_{MM} and P_R restricted to $\mathcal{D}(\overline{R})_{\leq d}$ cannot be expressed by any first order theory under any brave preferential semantics.*

As a consequence, as far as bounded databases are concerned, default logic is strictly more expressive than any model-preference based logic whose brave semantics is in Σ_2^p.

6   Conclusion

The main results of the paper for brave semantics are summarized in Fig. 1 and Fig. 2. An arrow from A to B means that every property which can be expressed in A can also be expressed in B. Dotted arrows correspond to obvious relations; the other arrows illustrate results of the paper. P_R, P_{MM} and $\mathrm{P}_{ev,p}$ are the simple disjunctive database properties introduced in Sect. 5. A picture of the results for the dual cautious semantics can be obtained by replacing Σ_2^p, P_R, P_{MM} and $\mathrm{P}_{ev,p}$ with Π_2^p and the respective complementary properties.

The figures also include results on autoepistemic logic (AEL) [20] as a query language; its semantics is defined in a similar way as the semantics of default logic. The language of AEL is a modal language with one modal operator L, to be read as "know" or "believe"; for an extensive treatment, cf. [18, 17]. An autoepistemic theory is a set of autoepistemic formulas, and called *closed* if all of its members are closed, and *open* otherwise. The semantics of closed autoepistemic theories is based on *stable expansions*, which are the counterparts of default extensions. A set of sentences S is a stable expansion of an autoepistemic theory T iff it satisfies the following fixpoint equation:

$$S = \{\phi \mid T \cup \{L\psi \mid \psi \in S\} \cup \{\neg L\psi \mid \psi \notin S\} \vdash \phi\},$$

where $\vdash$ denotes classical derivability. Prerequisite-free AEL is the fragment where all formulas in T are of the form

$$\neg L\beta_1 \wedge \cdots \wedge \neg L\beta_n \rightarrow \phi, \qquad n \geq 0, \tag{4}$$

---

[7] COMP(ϕ) yields the completion of ϕ under the closed-world assumption.

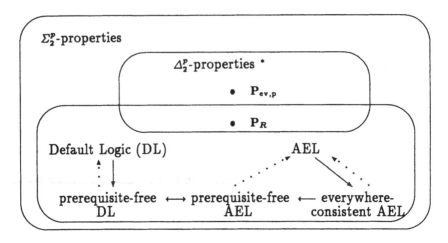

Fig. 1. Expressiveness for unbounded databases

* Over positive disjunctive databases, P_R, P_{MM}, and $P_{ev,p}$ are polynomial-time recognizable.

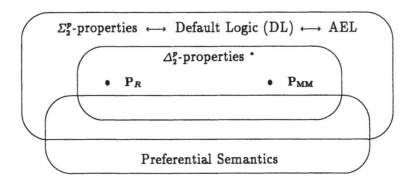

Fig. 2. Expressiveness for bounded databases

* Over positive disjunctive databases, P_R, P_{MM}, and $P_{ev,p}$ are polynomial-time recognizable.

where $\beta_1, \ldots, \beta_n$ and ϕ are objective (L does not occur); everywhere consistent AEL is the subclass of AEL theories T such that for each database D, the instantiation $T + D$ (defined similarly as for default theories) has only consistent expansions.

The proofs for the results in Figs. 1 and 2 are constructive; they allow to effectively transform a query expressed in any of those fragments into an equivalent query expressed in any other of the fragments. Moreover, the transformations are polynomial.

The study of expressiveness w.r.t. generalizations of relational databases leads to deeper understanding of logical formalisms, because it provides a finer-grained characterization of their expressive capabilities. For instance, in the area of relational databases, DL, AEL and DATALOG under the minimal model semantics express exactly the same class of queries (cf. [8]). However, in the area of bounded disjunctive databases, DL and AEL are strictly more expressive than DATALOG using minimal models, which cannot express P_R (or its complement in the cautious version); moreover, no (brave or cautious) preferential-based semantics for DATALOG (or any other first-order query) is capable of this. Similarly, perfect and stable model semantics do not express all the queries in PTIME.

Acknowledgements

The authors would like to thank Georg Gottlob for numerous discussions and for his important suggestions, which had a strong influence on this work, Mirek Truszczyński for his valuable hints and comments, and Victor Vianu for providing references to related work. This paper has been written while the first author was visiting the Institut für Informationssysteme, TU Wien, supported by the Austrian FWF through the Lise-Meitner Fellowship M0066-PHY.

References

1. Abiteboul, S., Kanellakis, P., Grahne, G.: On the Representation and Querying of Sets of Possible Worlds. Theoretical Computer Science **78** (1991) 159–187
2. Abiteboul, S., Vianu, V.: Expressive Power of Query Languages. In Ullman, J. (ed.) Theoretical Studies in Computer Science. Academic Press, 1992
3. Bonatti, P. A., Eiter, T.: Querying Disjunctive Databases Through Nonmonotonic Logics. Technical Report CD-TR 94/70, CD-Laboratory for Expert Systems, TU Vienna, Austria, 1994. Forthcoming. Preliminary version available from the authors.
4. Bonatti, P. A.: Autoepistemic Logics as a Unifying Framework for the Semantics of Logic Programs. Journal of Logic Programming (to appear). Preliminary version in Apt, K. (ed.) *Proc. of the Joint International Conference and Symposium on Logic Programming*, MIT Press, 1992
5. Cadoli, M., Eiter, T., Gottlob, G.: Using Default Logic as a Query Language. In Proc. Fourth International Conference on Principles of Knowledge Representation and Reasoning (KR-94), 99–108, 1994
6. Chandra, A., Harel, D.: Horn Clause Queries and Generalizations. Journal of Logic Programming **2** (1985) 1–15
7. Chandra A. K.: Theory of Database Queries. In Proc. PODS-88, 1988
8. Eiter, T., Gottlob, G., Mannila, H.: Adding Disjunction to Datalog. In Proc. Thirteenth ACM SIGACT SIGMOD-SIGART Symposium on Principles of Database Systems (PODS-94), 267–278, May 1994
9. Etherington, D. W.: Reasoning with Incomplete Information. Morgan Kaufmann Publishers, Inc., Los Altos, 1988
10. Fernández, J., Minker, J.: Semantics of Disjunctive Deductive Databases. In Proc. 4th Intl. Conference on Database Theory (ICDT-92), LNCS 646, 21–50, Springer-Verlag, 1992

11. Gottlob G.: Complexity Results for Nonmonotonic Logics. Journal of Logic and Computation **2** (1992) 397–425
12. Grahne G.: Updates and Counterfactuals. In Proceedings Second International Conference on Principles of Knowledge Representation and Reasoning (KR-91), 269–276, 1991
13. Gurevich Y.: Logic and the Challenge of Computer Science. In E. Börger, editor, Trends in Theoretical Computer Science, Chapter 1. Computer Science Press, 1988
14. Kanellakis, P.: Elements of Relational Database Theory. In J. van Leeuwen (ed.) Handbook of Theoretical Computer Science, Volume B, Chapter 17. Elsevier Science Publishers B.V. (North-Holland), 1990
15. Kolaitis, P., Vardi, M.: On the Expressive Power of Datalog: Tools and a Case Study. In Proceedings PODS-90, 61–71, 1990
16. Lobo, J., Minker, J., Rajasekar, A.: Foundations of Disjunctive Logic Programming. MIT Press, Cambridge, MA, 1992
17. Lukasiewicz, W.: Non-Monotonic Reasoning. Ellis Horwood Limited, Chichester, England, 1990
18. Marek, W., Truszczyński, M.: Autoepistemic Logic. Journal of the ACM **38** (1991) 588–619
19. Marek, W., Truszczyński, M.: Nonmonotonic Logics – Context-Dependent Reasoning. Springer-Verlag, 1993
20. Moore R.: Semantical Considerations on Nonmonotonic Logics. Artificial Intelligence **25** (1985) 75–94
21. Przymusinski, T.: Stable Semantics for Disjunctive Programs. New Generation Computing **9** (1991) 401–424
22. Przymusinski, T.: On the Declarative and Procedural Semantics of Stratified Deductive Databases. in Minker, J. (ed.) Foundations of Deductive Databases and Logic Programming, 193–216. Morgan Kaufman, 1988
23. Reiter, R.: A Logic for Default Reasoning. Artificial Intelligence **13** (1980) 81–132
24. Schlipf, J.: The Expressive Powers of Logic Programming Semantics. Technical Report CIS-TR-90-3, Computer Science Department, University of Cincinnati, 1990. Preliminary version in Proc. PODS-90, 196–204. To appear in the Journal of Computer and System Sciences
25. Vardi, M.: Complexity of relational query languages. In Proceedings 14th STOC, 137–146, 1982
26. Vardi, M.: Querying Logical Databases. Journal of Computer and System Sciences **32** (1986) 142–160

DATALOG Queries [*]
with Stratified Negation and Choice:
from $\mathcal{P}$ to $\mathcal{D}^P$

Sergio Greco,[1] Domenico Saccà[1] and Carlo Zaniolo[2]

[1] DEIS, Univ. della Calabria, 87030 Rende, Italy
{ greco, sacca }@si.deis.unical.it
[2] Computer Science Dept., Univ. of California, Los Angeles, CA 90024
zaniolo@cs.ucla.edu

Abstract. This paper introduces a unified solution to the problem of extending stratified DATALOG to express DB-complexity classes ranging from $\mathcal{P}$ to $\mathcal{D}^P$. The solution is based on (i) stratified negation as the core of a simple, declarative semantics for negation, (ii) the use of a "choice" construct to capture non-determinism of stable models (iii) the ability to bind a query execution to the complexity class that includes the problem at hand, and (iv) a general algorithm that ensures efficient execution for the different complexity classes. We thus obtain a class of DATALOG programs that preserves computational tractability, while achieving completeness for a wide range of complexity classes.

1 Introduction

The issue of designing declarative, logic-oriented database languages with sufficient expressive power is the key motivation of much of current research on databases and knowledge bases. The introduction of DATALOG represents a major breakthrough in this line of work, due to DATALOG's ability of expressing recursive queries. DATALOG is a rule-based language that has simple and elegant semantics based on the notion of minimal model—or equivalently, on the notion of least fixpoint. This second semantics leads to an operational semantics that is amenable to very efficient implementation as demonstrated by recent work on deductive database systems.

Unfortunately, the basic DATALOG language (no negation or function symbols) is still severely limited in its expressive power and cannot express many of the queries of practical interest. The exact expressive power of DATALOG is not yet understood but it has been shown that DATALOG only captures a proper subset of the monotonic polynomial-time queries [3].

In order to support non-monotonic queries, negation is allowed in the bodies of the rules. Of a particular interest is *stratified negation*, which avoids the semantic and implementation problems connected with the use of non-monotonic

---

[*] The work of the first two authors has been supported by the CNR project "Sistemi Informatici e Calcolo Parallelo" and by the MURST project "Metodi Formali per Basi di Dati".

constructs in recursive definitions [4, 6, 27]. We will write DATALOG$^{\neg s}$ to denote DATALOG with stratified negation. Simple, intuitive semantics, leading to efficient implementation exists for DATALOG$^{\neg s}$. Unfortunately, DATALOG$^{\neg s}$ cannot express all polynomial-time queries, and can only express a proper a proper subset of fixpoint queries [14].

The simplest step toward greater expressive power is to remove the condition that negation must be stratified. Unfortunately, the relaxation of the stratification assumption for non monotonic programs opens a pandora box of semantic and computational problems. Take for instance the concepts of *stable models* [8] and *well-founded models* [28]. The well-founded model semantics defines a unique "intended" model for each program, which can be computed in polynomial time. Several programs, however, do not have a well-founded total model: the meaning of portions of these programs, therefore, remain undefined. In terms of expressibility, well-founded semantics can express all fixpoint queries, but neither can express all polynomial time queries, nor it can express queries in $\mathcal{DB}\text{-}\mathcal{NP}$.

A dramatic leap in expressive power is provided by the concept of stable models, which has emerged as the compendium of many concepts and theories developed over the years by AI researches working on non-monotonic reasoning, default theories and autoepistemic logic. This gain in expressive power, however, is not without complications. One is the non-deterministic nature of such semantics that follows from the fact that a program can have several stable models. Nevertheless, deterministic query semantics can be ensured by requesting answers that hold true for *some* stable model (*possibility semantics*), or for *all* stable models, (*certainty semantics*); these are known in AI as membership and entailment semantics, respectively. The two semantics capture the classes $\mathcal{NP}$ and co$\mathcal{NP}$, respectively. However, there remain the following two problems:

1. The usage of unrestricted negation in programs is often not simple nor intuitive, and, e.g., might lead to the writing of programs for which no total stable model occurs (a similar problem also exists for well-founded models)
2. exponential-time algorithms are needed to compute stable models (as expected in situations where programs express NP-hard problems). Unfortunately, we do not know how to ensure that these exponential algorithms compute efficiently on programs that solve polynomial-time problems.

With current research focusing on overcoming these limitations, several proposals have been put forward that give up declarative semantics and fall-back on procedural semantics, e.g., based on the inflationary fixpoint computation procedure [2, 1, 15]. This paper is largely inspired by the conviction that model-theoretic semantics offers important benefits, and, therefore, we should strive to preserve it. Thus, we propose a novel approach whereby stratified DATALOG programs are extended to include (1) an explicit non-deterministic construct called *choice* whose semantics is defined in terms of stable models but can be implemented very efficiently, and (2) the use of quantifiers in the query goals to achieve the desired levels of expressive power and computational efficiency in a more controlled fashion, that allows a user to match the expressive power of the semantic used with the intrinsic complexity of the problem at hand.

This paper proposes an approach that allows users to express easily and compute efficiently problems ranging from the (whole) class $\mathcal{P}$ to the classes $\mathcal{NP}$ and co$\mathcal{NP}$. In this way, the ability of expressing $\mathcal{NP}$-hard problems is not at the cost of gross inefficiencies in solving polynomial problems. Since many practical problems fall in the class $\mathcal{D}^p$ [12, 20], we also introduce the capability of capturing this class. Furthermore, the paper presents of a unifying algorithm that automatically adapts to the complexity of the problem at hand. The algorithm shows how to make stable model semantics amenable to effective implementations. In summary, the paper presents a simple framework for exploiting recent advances in in model-theoretic semantics for non-monotonic DATALOG, without surrendering naturalness and efficiency of stratified negation.

2   Preliminary Definitions

We assume the reader is familiar with the concepts of relational databases and of the DATALOG language [13, 26] as well as of logic programming [16].

The semantics of logic programs is given in terms of total stable model semantics [8] which we briefly recall next.

Given a logic program P and an interpretation M (i.e., a subset of the Herbrand base), M is a (total) stable model of P if it is the minimal model of the program $gl(P, M)$ defined as follows: $gl(P, M)$ is obtained from the ground instance of P by (i) deleting all rules which have some negative literal $\neg b$ in their body with $b \in M$, and (ii) removing all negative literals in the bodies of the remaining rules.

A logic program may have 0 or one or several stable models and deciding whether it admits at least one stable model is $\mathcal{NP}$-complete [17].

Positive (i.e., negation free) programs have a unique stable model, corresponding to the minimum model.

Given a program P and two predicate symbols p and q, we write $p \rightarrow q$ if there exists a rule where q occurs in the head and p in the body or there exists a predicate s such that $p \rightarrow s$ and $s \rightarrow q$. If $p \rightarrow q$ then we say that q depends on p; also we say that q depends on any rule where p occurs in the head.

A program is stratified if there exists no rule r where a predicate p occurs in a negative literal in the body, q occurs in the head and $q \rightarrow p$, i.e., there is no recursion through negation. Also stratified programs have a unique stable model, corresponding to the stratified fixpoint.

A DATALOG⁻ program P is a function-free logic program whose predicates are partitioned into extensional and intensional predicates (EDB and IDB predicates, respectively). A DATALOG⁻ program P has associated a relational database scheme $DB_P = \{r \mid r$ is an EDB predicate symbol of $P\}$. EDB predicates are seen as database relation schemes, whose attribute domain is a countable set U, and they never occur in the rule heads as they are assumed to be defined by some database. A database D on a scheme DB_P is a set of finite relations, one for each EDB predicates in P. The relation associated with an EDB predicate r is denoted $D(r)$. Thus, any (finite) database D over DB_P is considered as a set of facts $\{r(t)|t$ is a tuple in some relation r of $D\}$. The set of all databases on DB_P is denoted $\mathbf{D}_P$.

We assume that the semantics of a program P applied to database D is given by the stable models of $P \cup D$.

If a DATALOG⁻ program P is positive then it is simply called a DATALOG program and, then, the unique stable model of P applied to a database D can be computed in time polynomial in the size of D. We point out the we are referring to the so-called *data complexity* [29] for which the size of P is assumed to be a constant.

If a DATALOG⁻ program is stratified then it is called a DATALOG⁻ˢ *program*. The unique stable model of a DATALOG⁻ˢ program P applied to a database D can be computed in time polynomial in the size of D.

A (*ground*) DATALOG⁻ *query* Q is a pair (G, P) where G is a conjunction of ground literals, called *query goal*, and P is a DATALOG⁻ program. $\mathbf{Q}^{\neg}$ denotes the set of all possible DATALOG⁻ queries, i.e., all possible query goals on all possible DATALOG⁻ programs.

3 Semantics and Complexity of DATALOG⁻

We assume that the reader is familiar with the basic notions of complexity classes [12, 20] and of query language complexity evaluation (see, for instance, [1, 2, 5, 11, 13, 14, 15, 25, 29]).

The *answer* to a query $Q = (G, P)$ on a database D over DB_P is defined as follows:

1. under the *non-deterministic semantics* — $Q_!(D)$:,
    (a) *true* if there is a stable model M of $P \cup D$ for which G is true in M
    (b) *false* if either there exists no stable model or there is a stable model M of $P \cup D$ for which G is false in M
    i.e., for some queries both a *true* and *false* answer is correct.
2. under the *possibility semantics* — $Q_\exists(D)$:
    (a) *true* if there is a stable model M of $P \cup D$ for which G is true in M, and
    (b) *false* otherwise;
3. under the *certainty semantics* — $Q_\forall(D)$:
    (a) *true* if for each stable model M of $P \cup D$, G is true in M, and
    (b) *false* otherwise;

We shall also denote the query Q on a database D under semantics T by $(T(G), P)(D)$, where the subscripts !, $\forall$, $\exists$, respectively, stand for non-deterministic semantics, possibility semantics and certainty semantics. Moreover, the reference to the database is omitted whenever it is clear from the context.

Any query $Q = (G, P)$ in $\mathbf{Q}^{\neg}$ can be considered as a function from the collection $\mathbf{D}$ of all databases over DB_P to $\{true, false\}$. It turns out that we can describe the complexity of a query under a given semantics as the complexity of the recognizing whether a given database input has a *true* answer or not under that semantics.

The expressive power of the above semantics is given by the set of all the functions that can be formulated by all possible queries and will be denoted by $DB_T(\mathbf{Q}^\neg)$. To measure expressive powers, for each Turing Machine complexity class C, there is a corresponding class $DB\text{-}C$ denoting the class of all the above functions for which the recognition problem is in C. In particular, we have the class $DB\text{-}\mathcal{P}$, $DB\text{-}\mathcal{NP}$, $DB\text{-co}\mathcal{NP}$ and $DB\text{-}\mathcal{D}^p$.

Under the non-deterministic semantics, the answer to a query can be both *true* and *false*, therefore, queries cannot be considered as functions. However, the only bound queries of practical interest have only one answer; i.e., these queries are actually deterministic, and non-determinism is only used to increase the expressive power and/or to simplify the formulation. (For instance, to test whether a relation has an even number of tuples, we can write a DATALOG$^\neg$ program which non-deterministically partitions the tuples into a number of pairs; there will then be as many stable models as the number of 2-combinations of all tuples but the result will be the same no matter which stable model is selected.) Therefore, from now on, we shall only consider deterministic queries. Thus, under the non-deterministic semantics $\mathbf{Q}^\neg$ will actually denote only the set of all possible DATALOG$^\neg$ queries which are deterministic.

Observe that the problem of whether a query on a given database is deterministic under the non-deterministic semantics is in $\mathcal{D}^p$; worse, the problem of whether a query is deterministic for all databases is not decidable at all. In our view, this is not a real problem as we assume that the programmer has the responsibility to write deterministic queries in the same way as it is his/her responsibility to write a correct (and terminating) program. If the query turns out not to be deterministic, he/she will eventually get an answer that is not be appropriate as for the case of wrong programs.

Because of the above restriction, queries can be considered as functions also under the non-deterministic semantics and also their expressive power can be then expressed in terms of the above DB complexity classes.

The following results are known in the literature.

Fact 1 *(see [17, 24])*

1. $DB_\exists(\mathbf{Q}^\neg) = DB - \mathcal{NP}$;
2. $DB_\forall(\mathbf{Q}^\neg) = DB - co\mathcal{NP}$. □

Let us now denote the set of all DATALOG queries by $\mathbf{Q}^+$ and the set of all DATALOG$^{\neg s}$ queries by $\mathbf{Q}^{\neg s}$. Any query in $\mathbf{Q}^+$ and in $\mathbf{Q}^{\neg s}$ is deterministic.

Fact 2 *(see [3, 19, 14])*

$$DB_F(\mathbf{Q}^+) \subset DB_F(\mathbf{Q}^{\neg s}) \subset DB - \mathcal{P}$$

where F is any of the three types of semantics. □

Next we show the expressive power of non-deterministic semantics for deterministic queries.

Proposition 1. $\mathcal{DB}_!(\mathbf{Q}^\neg) = \mathcal{DB} - \mathcal{NP}$.

Proof. (Membership to $\mathcal{DB}\text{-}\mathcal{NP}$.) Take any query $Q = (G, P)$ in $\mathbf{Q}^\neg$ and a database D over DB_P; we want to recognize whether $Q_!(D)$ is *true*. To this end we just guess an interpretation M of $P \cup D$ and test in (deterministic) polynomial time whether (i) M is a total stable model and (ii) G is in M. To verify that M is a stable model can be done in polynomial time as we only need to compute the least fixpoint of $gl(P, M)$ and test whether it coincides with M.

(Completeness.) We use Fagin's result [7] that every $\mathcal{NP}$ recognizable database collection is defined by an existential second order formula $\exists R\Phi$, where R is a list of new predicate symbols and Φ is a first-order formula involving predicate symbols in a database scheme Z and in R. As shown in [15], this formula is equivalent to one of the form (*second order Skolem normal form*)

$$(\exists S)(\forall X)(\exists Y)(\theta_1(X,Y) \vee \ldots \vee \theta_k(X,Y))$$

where S is a superlist of R, $\theta_1, \ldots, \theta_k$ are conjunctions of literals involving variables in X and Y, and predicate symbols in S and DB_P. Consider the following program P:

$$
\begin{array}{ll}
s_j(W_j) \leftarrow \neg \hat{s}_j(W_j). & (\forall s_j \in S) \\
\hat{s}_j(W_j) \leftarrow \neg s_j(W_j). & (\forall s_j \in S) \\
q(X) \quad \leftarrow \theta_i(X,Y). & (1 \leq i \leq k) \\
g \qquad \leftarrow \neg q(X). & \\
p \qquad \leftarrow g, \neg p &
\end{array}
$$

The first two groups of rules define an instance of the predicates in S. Therefore, the first three groups of rules implement the above second order formula. The fourth rule checks whether there is some X for which the formula is not satisfied. The fifth rule force the global program to have a total stable model only if g is false. Note that, if g is true the program does not have total stable model. Thus, the program P has a stable model and then the query goal $\neg g$ is true under the non-deterministic semantics iff a database belongs to the collection. $\square$

Observe that the restriction that $\mathbf{Q}^\neg$ only contains deterministic queries under the non deterministic semantics is not necessary for Proposition 1 to hold. Notice also that the expressive power of the non-deterministic semantics coincides with that of possibility semantics.

In order to provide more flexibility in expressing queries (and without any additional cost as we shall discuss later), we allow to combine possibility and certainty semantics. Thus, we write *compound* query goals having the following form $\exists(G_1) \wedge \forall(G_2)$, where G_1 and G_2, are related in useful ways to be discussed later. In particular, if $G_1 = G_2$, then the program must have at least one stable model and G_1 must hold true in each such a model (see *definite semantics* [22]).

Proposition 2. $\mathcal{DB}_{\exists\forall}(\mathbf{Q}^\neg) = \mathcal{DB} - \mathcal{D}^p$.

Proof. A compound query corresponds to the conjunction of a query under the possibility semantics and a query under the certainty semantics. The result follows from the fact that possibility semantics captures $\mathcal{NP}$ and certainty semantics captures $co\mathcal{NP}$, $\square$

4 Choice and Stratification in DATALOG Queries

The *choice* construct (supported in $\mathcal{LDL}$++ [18] and, in some form, in Coral [21]), is used to enforce functional constraints on rules of a logic program. Thus, a goal of the form, `choice((X),(Y))`, in a rule r denotes that the set of all consequences derived from r must respect the FD $X \rightarrow Y$. In general, X can be a vector of variables—possibly an empty one denoted by "( )" —and Y is a vector of one or more variables.

As shown in [23] the formal semantics of the construct can be given in terms of stable model semantics as follows. A rule of the form

$$p(X, Y, W) \leftarrow q(X, Y, Z, W), \ choice((X), (Y)), \ choice((Y), (Z))$$

is rewritten as:

$$
\begin{aligned}
p(X, Y, W) &\leftarrow q(X, Y, Z, W), \ chosen(X, Y, Z). \\
chosen(X, Y, Z) &\leftarrow q(X, Y, Z), \ \neg diffchoice(X, Y, Z). \\
diffchoice(X, Y, Z) &\leftarrow chosen(X, Y', Z'), \ Y \neq Y'. \\
diffchoice(X, Y, Z) &\leftarrow chosen(X', Y, Z'), \ Z \neq Z'.
\end{aligned}
$$

where the *choice* predicates have been substituted by the *chosen* predicate and for each *choice* predicate there is a *diffchoice* rule. Let P be a DATALOG⁻ program with choice constructs. If P is stratified modulo choice (i.e., by removing the choice predicates) the stable model is not in general unique but existence of at least one is guaranteed. (This result remains valid also when choice predicates occur in recursive rules [9].) Moreover, if P is stratified modulo choice then one of the stable models can be computed in polynomial time [23, 9, 10].

Let us now study the expressive power of queries on DATALOG$^{\neg s,c}$ programs, i.e., DATALOG$^{\neg s}$ programs with choice constructs. Let $\mathbf{Q}^{\neg s,c}$ denote the set of all queries on DATALOG$^{\neg s,c}$ programs. Again we restrict our attention to deterministic queries; therefore, under the non-deterministic semantics, $\mathbf{Q}^{\neg s,c}$ is actually only a subset of all possible queries.

Theorem 3.

1. $\mathcal{DB}_!(\mathbf{Q}^{\neg s,c}) = \mathcal{DB} - \mathcal{P}$.
2. $\mathcal{DB}_\exists(\mathbf{Q}^{\neg s,c}) = \mathcal{DB} - \mathcal{NP}$.
3. $\mathcal{DB}_\forall(\mathbf{Q}^{\neg s,c}) = \mathcal{DB} - co\mathcal{NP}$.
4. $\mathcal{DB}_{\exists\forall}(\mathbf{Q}^{\neg s,c}) = \mathcal{DB} - \mathcal{D}^p$.

Proof. (1) Papadimitriou has shown that stratified negation (actually a reduced version of it) plus an ordering on the domain captures $\mathcal{P}$. Computing a stable model of any query in $\mathbf{Q}^{\neg s,c}$ over any database D can be done in polynomial time since it is sufficient to extend the stratified fixpoint with a simple polynomial-time implementation of the choice construct. Since $\mathbf{Q}^{\neg s,c}$ only contains deterministic queries, the answer does not depend on which stable model is returned. Hence the expressive power cannot go beyond $\mathcal{P}$. Thus, it is sufficient to introduce an ordering on the domain and to be able to find the minimal and the maximal element in the domain. This can be done using choice and stratified negation, as reported in the following program:

$$min(X) \quad \leftarrow domain(X), \ choice((), (X)).$$
$$succ(X, Y) \leftarrow succ(\_, X), \ min(Z), \ domain(Y), \ Y \neq Z,$$
$$choice((X), (Y)), \ choice((Y), (X)).$$
$$max(X) \quad \leftarrow domain(X), \ \neg succ(X, \_)$$

(2) We follow the lines of the proof of Proposition 1 but this time we use a DATALOG$^{\neg s, c}$ program P defined in the following way:

$$label(1).$$
$$label(2).$$
$$\hat{s}_j(W_j, K) \leftarrow label(K), \ choice(W_j, K). \qquad (\forall s_j \in S)$$
$$s_j(W_j) \quad \leftarrow \hat{s}_j(W_j, 1). \qquad\qquad\qquad (\forall s_j \in S)$$
$$q(X) \quad\quad \leftarrow \theta_i(X, Y). \qquad\qquad\qquad (1 \leq i \leq k)$$
$$g \quad\quad\quad \leftarrow \neg q(X).$$

It is easy to see that, given the query goal $\neg g$, the query on a database is true under the possibility semantics iff the database belongs to the collection.

(3) Consider the program P in the above proof of Part (2). This time it is required to check whether a database does not to belong to the collection. This happens iff given the query goal g, the query on a database is true under the certainty semantics.

(4) By combining the proofs of Part (2) and (3). $\qquad\qquad\qquad\qquad\square$

Observe that, this time the proof of Part (1) of Theorem 3 strongly depends on the restriction that $\mathbf{Q}^{\neg s, c}$ only contains deterministic queries.

Proposition 4. *Let Q be a query in $\mathbf{Q}^{\neg s, c}$ and D be a database. Then*

1. *$Q_!(D)$ can be solved in time $p(||D||)$;*
2. *$Q_{\exists}(D), \ Q_{\forall}(D)$ or $Q_{\exists\forall}(D)$ can be solved in time $\mathcal{O}(K \times p(||D||))$*

where p is a polynomial in the size of D and K is the number of stable models of the program $P \cup D$.

Proof. Each of the stable models of a DATALOG program with choice can be computed in polynomial time [23, 9, 10]. Finding any stable model is sufficient to solve the query under non-deterministic semantics. For the other semantics, in the worst case we have to find all stable models. This can be done with a simple exhaustive search scheme for generating all possible selections in the choice constructs. Every selection will produce a different stable model in polynomial time. $\qquad\qquad\qquad\qquad\square$

Proposition 4 clarifies the results of using choice models instead of unrestricted stable models as the basis of computation. The number of choice models of a program can be exponential, and so is the number of stable models of a program. However, computing each choice model is polynomial-time, while computing each stable model is exponential-time. Thus, by using choice models, answering queries under the possibility or certainty semantics remains exponential, but polynomial problems can now be computed in polynomial time, by requesting a non-deterministic semantics.

5 Examples

We next present some classical graph problems which can be easily expressed in DATALOG$^{\neg s,c}$. The first two examples will present two classical problems which are polynomial and $\mathcal{NP}$-complete, respectively.

Example 1. Spanning tree in a graph. We are given an undirect graph whose arcs are stored as pairs of edges $g(X,Y)$. A spanning tree for this graph, starting from the source node a, can be defined by the following program ST:

> spanning-tree(X, Y) ← connected(X), g(X, Y), Y ≠ a, X ≠ Y, choice(Y, X).
>
> connected(a)
> connected(Y) ← connected(X), spanning-tree(X, Y).
>
> non-spanning-tree ← g(X, Y), ¬spanning-tree(_, Y).

The choice goal here ensures that no node in the connected subgraph constructed by the transitive closure has two incoming arcs, thus delivering a tree. The graph has a spanning tree connecting all nodes to the source node a if the query

$$(!(\neg non\text{-}spanning\text{-}tree), ST)$$

has answer *true*. The query is obviously deterministic. To understand the relevance of non-deterministic semantics, observe that the same query also returns the correct answer under the possibility semantics. Computation under possibility semantics is as efficient as that under non-deterministic semantics if the graph has a spanning tree. But when this is not the case, then the possibility semantics insists in trying all other selections for choice (and there can be an exponential number of these), while the non-deterministic semantics stops after the first faliure.   □

Example 2. Hamiltonian path in a graph. We are given a undirected graph whose nodes and arcs are stored as facts of the form $n(x)$ and $g(x,y)$, respectively. Consider the following DATALOG$^{\neg s,c}$ program HP which selects a simple paths in the graph:

> simple-path(X, Y) ← connected(X), g(X, Y), first(Z), Y ≠ Z, Y ≠ X,
>   choice((X), (Y)), choice((Y), (X))
>
> first(X) ←   n(X), choice((), (X)).
> connected(Y) ← first(Y).
> connected(Y) ← connected(X), simple-path(X, Y).
>
> non-HP-path ← n(X), ¬simple-path(_, X).

The graph has an Hamiltonian path if there is a simple path which visits all nodes exactly once, that is if the query $(\exists(\neg not\text{-}HP\text{-}path), HP)$ has answer *true*.   □

The next example shows how the program of Example 2 can be replicated to express problems in the classes co$\mathcal{NP}$ and $\mathcal{D}^p$.

Example 3. Unique Hamiltonian path. Consider the following DATALOG$^{\neg s,c}$ program UHP which selects three simple paths in the graph that are labeled 1, 2 and 3 respectively. The predicate *diff-2-3* verifies that the path with label 3 is different from the path with label 2.

```
label(1).
label(2).
label(3).
simple-path(L, X, Y) ← connected(L, X), g(X, Y), first(L, Z), Y ≠ X, Y ≠ Z,
                       choice((X), (Y)), choice((Y), (X))

first(L, Y) ←      label(L), n(Y), choice((L), (Y))
connected(L, Y) ← first(L, Y).
connected(L, Y) ← connected(L, X), simple-path(L, X, Y).
non-HP-sp(L) ←    n(X), ¬simple-path(L, Y).

diff-2-3 ← simple − path(2, X, Y₁), simple − path(3, X, Y₂), Y₁ ≠ Y₂.
two-HP ←   ¬non-HP-sp(2), ¬non-HP-sp(3), diff-2-3.
```

The query $(\exists(\neg non\text{-}HP\text{-}sp(1)), UHP)$ solves the $\mathcal{NP}$-complete problem of whether the graph has a Hamiltonian path. The query $(\forall(\neg non\text{-}HP\text{-}sp(1)), UHP)$ solves the co$\mathcal{NP}$-complete problem of whether all maximal simple paths are Hamiltonian. Finally the query $(\exists(\neg non\text{-}HP\text{-}sp(1)) \wedge \forall(\neg two\text{-}HP)), UHP)$ solve the $\mathcal{D}^p$ problem of whether the graph has a unique Hamiltonian path — note that this problem has not been proven to be $\mathcal{D}^p$-complete as it belongs to the class $\mathcal{US}$, i.e., problems with a unique solution [12, 20]. □

For the program of Example 3, deterministic queries expressible under a non-deterministic semantics are of little practical interest. However, we observe that for this example and others discussed in [22], it is useful to combine fully unbound queries under non-deterministic semantics with bound queries under possibility semantics—under the reasonable assumption is that the stable model chosen for the non-deterministic part is the same used for the existential part of the query. For instance, the query $sp(1, X, Y) \wedge \exists(\neg non\text{-}HP\text{-}sp(1))$ outputs a Hamiltonian path if one exists or returns false otherwise.

6 Implementation

In this section we shall provide an implementation scheme for the computation of choice stratified queries under the various types of semantics.

We first consider the case of non-deterministic semantics. Let a query $Q = (!G, P)$ and a database D be given. In order to solve the query, we have to find a stable model of $P \cup D$. To this end we extend the choice fixpoint proposed for positive choice programs [23, 9, 10] to cope with stratified negation. Therefore we find a stratification for the program P and divide it into a number of subprograms $P_1, \ldots, P_n$, each corresponding to a stratum. Then for each subprogram P_i we fire the function *choice_fixpoint*, passing the stable model of P_{i-1} as input set of facts; for the subprogram P_1 the input set of facts is the database D. Thus we use the following algorithm:

Algorithm 1 *[Non-Deterministic Query Evaluator]*
Input: $Q = (!G, P) : Query; \ D : Facts;$
Output: *true/false*
var: LP : *List of Programs;* n : *int;* M_P, M : *Facts;*
begin
    $compute\_strata(\ P, n, LP);$
    let $LP = [P_1, \ldots, P_n];$
    $M := D;$
    for $i := 1$ to n do begin
        $M_P := M;$
        $choice\_fixpoint(P_i, M_P, M)$
    end;
    return $G \in M$
end.

Observe that the database as well as interpretations are represented as sets of facts (type *Facts*). The function *compute_strata* implements one of well-known methods for finding a stratification; a detailed description of the function *choice_fixpoint* can be found in [10]. Obviously the overall algorithm runs in time polynomial in the size of D.

We next give a unique implementation scheme for the other semantics. For the the sake of presentation, under the compound semantics we shall only consider a subclass of queries that is amenable for a simple implementation. As shown next, the restriction to this subclass does not reduce the generality of our approach.

Let $Q = (\exists(G_1) \wedge \forall(G_2), P)$ be a **DATALOG**$^{\neg s, c}$ query. Then Q is *choice disconnected* if $H_1 \cap H_2 = \emptyset$, where H_1 (resp. H_2) is the set of choice rules defining a predicate on which some goal in G_1 (resp., G_2) depends.

Let **Q**$^{\neg s, c_d}$ denote the set of all choice disconnected queries. The next result shows that the class **Q**$^{\neg s, c_d}$ has the same expressive power as the class **Q**$^{\neg s, c}$.

Proposition 5. $\mathcal{DB}_{\exists \forall}(\mathbf{Q}^{\neg s, c_d}) = \mathcal{DB} - \mathcal{D}^p$.

Proof. For the combination of the proofs of Part (2) and (3) of Theorem 3, it is enough to consider two separated problems. □

Every query in **Q**$^{\neg s, c}$ can be made choice disconnected by simply replicating some of the rules. For instance, the query in the Example 3, finding the unique Hamiltonian path, is not choice disconnected but can be put in this format by simply replicating the labeled rules for each value of the label and moving the label from the argument of each predicate into the name of the predicate symbol—e.g., $sp(L)$ becomes sp_1, sp_2 and sp_3 in the corresponding replicated rules.

We are now ready to describe an implementation algorithm for a choice disconnected query. By simply considering the existential goal or the universal goal as true we get a query under the possibility semantics and the certainty semantics respectively. Therefore the algorithm works for these two semantics as well.

Let $Q = (\exists(G_1) \land \forall(G_2), P)$ be a query in $\mathbf{Q}^{\neg s, c_d}$ and let g_1, g_2 be the predicate symbols of G_1 and G_2, respectively. We divide the program P into three subprograms:

- P_1 (resp., P_2) consists of all rules r having p as head predicate symbol such that g_1 (resp., g_2) depends on p and p depends on some choice rule;
- $P_0 = \{r | r \in P - (P_1 \cup P_2)$ and g_1 or g_2 depends on $r\}$.

By definition of choice disconnected query, $P_1 \cap P_2 = \emptyset$; also, by construction, $P_1 \cap P_0 = P_2 \cap P_0 = \emptyset$. Moreover, P_0 is a stratified program without choice, P_1 and P_2 are $\mathbf{DATALOG}^{\neg s, c}$ programs. Consider a stratification for each of the three subprograms. For the sake of presentation, we assume that possible choice rules are all in the same stratum. Then, by construction, the choice rules are in the first stratum both in P_1 and in P_2.

We can now write the algorithm for solving the query Q:

Algorithm 2 *[Choice-Disconnected Query Evaluator]*
Input: $((\exists(G_1) \land \forall(G_2)), P) : query; D : Facts;$
Output: *true/false;*
var: $P_0, P_1, P_2 : Program; M_0, M_2, M : Facts;$
begin
    let $P = P_0 \cup P_1 \cup P_2$;
    $stratified\_fixpoint(P_0, D, M_0)$;
    if $solve(G_2, false, P_2, M_0, M_2)$ **then**
        return $solve(G_1, true, P_1, M_2, M)$
    else
        return $false$
end.

Let D be the initial database, the algorithm proceeds as follows:

1. first, using the classical stratified fixpoint, it computes a set of facts that are relevant for resolving the two goals and are common to every stable model as they do not depend on choice rules; let M_0 be this set of facts;
2. next, using the function *solve* (below defined), it computes the query (G_2, P_2) over the database M_0 under certainty semantics; say M_2 the set of facts computed;
3. finally, using the function *solve*, it computes the query (G_1, P_1) over the database M_2 under possibility semantics; say M the set of facts computed.

The function *solve* has five arguments. The first argument denotes the query goal, the second one denotes the semantics of the query, i.e., it is true if we are looking for any model and false otherwise, the third one denotes the input program, the last two arguments denote the input and output set of facts, respectively. The procedure *solve* is defined as follows:

function *solve(G : Goal; isAny : Bool; P : Program; M_0, M : Facts):Bool;*
var *Previous_choices : list of Choices; Last_choices : Choices; choice:Bool;*
     LP: List of Programs; n: int;
begin
    if $P = \emptyset$ **then begin**
       $M := M_0$;
       return $(G = true)$
    end
    compute_strata(P, n, LP);
    let $LP = [P_1, \ldots, P_n]$;
    Previous_choices := [];
    repeat
       $choice := choice\_fixpoint(P_1, M_0, M, Previous\_choices, Last\_choices)$
       if *choice* **then begin**
          append(Previous_choices,Last_choices);
          for $i := 2$ **to** n **do**
             $M := T^{\infty}_{P_i \cup M}(\emptyset)$;
       end
    until *(not choice)* **or** *(isAny and $G \in (M \cup \{true\})$)* **or** *(not isAny and $G \notin M$)*;
    return $(G \in (M \cup \{true\}))$
end;

Note that the type *Facts* is considered as a sub-type of *Program* so that $P_i \cup M$ represents a program; indeed M can be thought of as defining the EDB predicates of P_i. The type *Choices* describes a complete set of choices and also includes suitable information in order to allow the function *choice_fixpoint* any time is fired to select a set of choices different from the previous ones stored in *Previous_choice*.

The function *choice_fixpoint* used here is a simple extension of the original function used for the non-deterministic semantics. The new function returns the set of choices that have been performed and, when called again, it receives all previously performed sets of choices in order to select a new set of choices at any time. The function returns the value *false* when all possible choices have been explored. Therefore, the procedure must be only extended to handle the list of previous sets of choices in order to select the next set of choices or to eventually report that no more choices are available. Of course this part can be easily implemented in time polynomial in the size of M; hence, since also the fixpoint is computed in time polynomial in the size of M and the size of M is polynomially bounded by the size of the input database D, the function *choice_fixpoint* runs in polynomial time.

Not surprisingly, the overall algorithm runs in exponential time because of the iterations of "repeat" in the function *solve*. This cycle is executed a number of times equal to the number of different sets of choices carried out by the procedure *choice_fixpoint* which is, clearly, exponential and is equal to the number of stable models. It is interesting to observe the behavior of this function in the two cases it is used. When it works on P_1, the iteration is kept on until a set of choices is found which satisfies the goal — this corresponds to solve a query under the possibility semantics. On the other hand, when it works on P_2, the iteration is stopped as soon as a set of choices is found which does not satisfy the goal — this corresponds to solving a query under the certainty semantics.

7 Conclusion

The table in Figure 1 summarizes the results that we have obtained about the expressive power of various classes of **DATALOG** queries. The fact that the expressive power of stable model semantics can be achieved using simple declarative constructs such as stratified negation and choice is of obvious conceptual interest. The practical significance of these results follows from the fact that programs with these constructs always have a well-defined semantics (i.e., never lack a total stable model), have simplicity and intuitive appeal and have an efficient implementation algorithm. In fact, the class of queries for which we have presented an effective implementation scheme has an expressive power (namely, $\mathcal{D}^p$) higher than the class of classical queries under the possibility or certainty semantics.

Query	Complexity	Reference
$!(\mathbf{Q}^\neg)$	$\mathcal{DB}\text{-}\mathcal{NP}$	this paper
$\exists(\mathbf{Q}^\neg)$	$\mathcal{DB}\text{-}\mathcal{NP}$	Marek-Truszcynski [17]
$\forall(\mathbf{Q}^\neg)$	$\mathcal{DB}\text{-}\mathrm{co}\mathcal{NP}$	Marek-Truszcynski [17]
$\exists\forall(\mathbf{Q}^\neg)$	$\mathcal{DB}\text{-}\mathcal{D}^p$	this paper
$!(\mathbf{Q}^{\neg s,c})$	$\mathcal{DB}\text{-}\mathcal{P}$	this paper
$\exists(\mathbf{Q}^{\neg s,c})$	$\mathcal{DB}\text{-}\mathcal{NP}$	this paper
$\forall(\mathbf{Q}^{\neg s,c})$	$\mathcal{DB}\text{-}\mathrm{co}\mathcal{NP}$	this paper
$\exists\forall(\mathbf{Q}^{\neg s,c})$	$\mathcal{DB}\text{-}\mathcal{D}^p$	this paper

Fig. 1. *Expressive Power* **DATALOG**$^\neg$ *and* **DATALOG**$^{\neg s,c}$

References

1. S. Abiteboul, E. Simon, V. Vianu. Non-Deterministic Language to Express Deterministic Transformation. In *Proc. of the Ninth ACM PODS Conference*, 1990.
2. S. Abiteboul and V. Vianu. Datalog Extensions for Databases Queries and Updates. In *Journal of Computer and System Science*, 43, pages 62–124, 1991.
3. F. Afrati, S. S. Cosmadakis, M. Yannakakis. On Datalog vs. Polynomial Time. In *Proc. of the Tenth ACM PODS Conference*, pages 13–25, 1991.
4. C. Apt, H. Blair, A Walker. Towards a Theory of Declarative Knowledge. In *Proc. Work. on Found. of Deductive Database and Logic Prog.*, (IMinker Ed.), 1988.
5. A. Chandra and D. Harel. Structures and Complexity of Relational Queries. In *Journal of Computer and System Science*, 25, pages 99–128, 1982.

6. A. Chandra and D. Harel. Horn clause and generalizations. In *Journal of Logic Programming*, vol. 2, No. 1, pages 1–15, 1985.
7. R. Fagin. Generalized First-Order Spectra and Polynomial-Time Recognizable Sets, in *Complexity of Computation (R. Karp, Ed.)*, SIAM-AMS Proc., 1974.
8. M. Gelfond and V. Lifschitz. The stable model semantics of logic programming. In *Proc. of the Fifth Intern. Conf. on Logic Programming*, pages 1070–1080, 1988.
9. F. Giannotti, D. Pedreschi, D. Saccà, and C. Zaniolo. Nondeterminism in deductive databases. In *Proc. 2nd DOOD Conference*, pages 129–146, 1991.
10. S. Greco, C. Zaniolo, and S. Ganguly. *Greedy by Choice*. In *Proc. of the Eleventh ACM PODS Conference*, pages 105–163, 1992.
11. N. Immerman. Languages that Capture Complexity Classes. In *SIAM Journal of Computing*, 16(4), pages 760–778, 1987.
12. D. S. Johnson. A Catalog of Complexity Classes, In *Handbook of Theoretical Computer Science*, Vol. 1, (Ed. J. Leewen) North-Holland, pages 67–161, 1990.
13. P. C. Kanellakis Elements of Relational Databases Theory. In *Handbook of Theoretical Computer Science*, (Ed. J. Leewen) North-Holland, pages 1075–1155, 1990.
14. P. Kolaitis. The Expressive Power of Stratified Logic Programs. *Information an Computation*, 90, pages 50–66, 1990.
15. P. Kolaitis and C. Papadimitriou. Why not negation by fixpoint. In *Journal of Computer and System Science*, 43, pages 125–144, 1991.
16. J. W. Lloyd. *Foundations of Logic Programming*, Springer Verlag, Berlin, 1987.
17. W. Marek, M. Truszczynski. Autoepistemic Logic. *Journal of ACM*, 38(3):588–619, 1991.
18. S. Naqvi and S. Tsur. *A logic language for data and knowledge bases.* Computer Science Press, 1989.
19. C. Papadimitriou. A Note on the Expressive Power of Prolog. In *Bull of the EATCS*, 26, pages 21–23, 1985.
20. C. Papadimitriou. *Computational Complexity*. Addison-Wesley, 1994.
21. R. Ramakrisnhan, D. Srivastava, and S. Sudanshan. CORAL — Control, Relations and Logic. In *Proc. of 18th VLDB Conference*, 1992.
22. D. Saccà. The Expressive Powers of Stable Models for Bound and Unbound Queries. this volume, 1994.
23. D. Saccà and C. Zaniolo. Stable models and non-determinism in logic programs with negation. In *Proc. of the Ninth ACM PODS Conference*, pages 205–217, 1990.
24. J. S. Schlipf. The expressive power of the logic programming semantics. In *Proc. of the Ninth ACM PODS Conference*, pages 196–204, 1990.
25. J. S. Schlipf. A Survey of Complexity and Undecidability Results in Logic Programming. *Work. Structural Compl. and Recursion-Theoretic Met. in L. P.*, 1993.
26. J. D. Ullman. *Principles of Databases and Knowledge Base Systems*, Vol. I and II. Computer Science Press, 1988.
27. A. Van Gelder. Negation as failure using tight derivations for general logic programs. *Journal of Logic Programming*, vol. 6, No. 1, pages 109–133, 1989.
28. A. Van Gelder, K.A. Ross, and J.S. Schlipf. The well-founded semantics for general logic programs. *Journal of ACM*, 38(3):620–650, 1991.
29. M. Vardi. The Complexity of Relational Query Languages. In *Proceedings of the 14th ACM Symposium on Theory of Computing*, pages 137–146, 1982.

On the Kolmogorov Expressive Power of Boolean Query Languages

extended abstract

Jerzy Tyszkiewicz*

Mathematische Grundlagen der Informatik,
RWTH Aachen, Ahornstraße 55,
D-52074 Aachen, Germany.
jurek@mephisto.informatik.rwth-aachen.de

Abstract. We develop a Kolmogorov complexity based tool to measure expressive power of query languages over finite structures. It works for sentences (i.e., boolean queries), and gives a meaningful definition of the expressive power of a query language in a single finite model.

The notion of *Kolmogorov expressive power* of a boolean query language L in a finite model $\mathfrak{A}$ is defined by considering two values: the Kolmogorov complexity of the isomorphism type of $\mathfrak{A}$, equal to the length of the shortest binary description of this type, and the number of bits of this description that can be reconstructed from truth values of all queries from L in $\mathfrak{A}$. The closer is the second value to the first, the more expressive is the query language. After giving the definitions and proving that they are correct, we concentrate our efforts on first order logic and its powerful extensions: inflationary fixpoint logic and partial fixpoint logic. We explore some connections between the proposed Kolmogorov expressive power of boolean queries in these languages and their standard expressive power. We show that, except of being of interest for its own, our notion may have important diagnostic value for database query optimisation.

1 Introduction

1.1 The Aim of the Paper

We develop a Kolmogorov complexity based notion of the expressive power of a logic in a finite structure. Recently, the main theoretical efforts in the finite model theory are shifting from considering the expressive power of logics over classes of ordered finite structures, to the unordered ones, and from the class of all finite models to particular, restricted classes, arising from combinatorics and database theory. In this direction we reach the limit: the notion we propose measures the expressive power of a logics in a single, finite structure. The price we pay for reaching this limit is that our method gives meaningful results only when we restrict our attention to sentences. The main idea is quite simple: we

---

* Supported by the Polish KBN grant 2 P301 009 06 and by the German DFG.

measure, in the terms of Kolmogorov complexity, how much of the isomorphism type of the finite structure can be reconstructed from results of evaluation of all sentences in the logic.

From the database theoretic point of view, the notion we propose indicates how large portion of the collected data can be retrieved by boolean queries. The rest, due to the limitations of expressive power of the query language, remains "invisible" to the user.

In the paper, apart from giving all the necessary definitions and proving that they are correct, we begin the study of the Kolmogorov expressive power of the fixpoint extensions of first-order logic. Since even the first-order logic with unrestricted number of variables appears to be too strong for our purposes, we deal with finite-variable fragments of these logics. We prove interesting connections of the introduced notion and the standard descriptive complexity of logics.

We describe also an example, showing that by theoretical investigations one can prove nontrivial results involving the proposed notion. It concerns mainly the interactions of the Kolmogorov expressive power of first-order logic and the *split* technique for optimising fixpoint and partial fixpoint queries, demonstrated in [ACV, AG]. From our results it follows, that any speedup of query evaluation obtained by *split* always indicates that the Kolmogorov expressive power of the query language is limited. In the model considered in [ACV], where the authors proved surprisingly low average complexity results for these query languages, the Kolmogorov expressive power is extremely low. We then extend that model in a simple way, getting a broad spectrum of behaviours of both computational complexity, and Kolmogorov complexity of the considered query languages.

1.2   The Intuitive Basis

Suppose that we have a query language L, consisting of boolean queries only, and a finite structure $\mathfrak{A}$. Then if IT IS NOT POSSIBLE to reconstruct the isomorphism type of $\mathfrak{A}$ from results of evaluation of all queries in L, then certainly some of the information about the structure cannot be retrieved. For we could change $\mathfrak{A}$ into a nonisomorphic structure $\mathfrak{A}'$, preserving the results of evaluation of all queries. So at least the information corresponding to the difference between isomorphism types of $\mathfrak{A}$ and $\mathfrak{A}'$ is lost. On the other hand, if IT IS POSSIBLE to reconstruct the finite structure from the queries evaluation results, then all of the information is accessible. Of course, nobody wants to perform such a reconstruction, but the theoretical possibility of doing so is a guarantee that the user has unlimited access to all the collected data. But so far this is only a qualitative notion.

Now we want to turn the above notion into a quantitative one[2], giving rise to the stratification of expressive powers of query languages with respect to a fixed finite $\mathfrak{A}$: *the more of the isomorphism type of $\mathfrak{A}$ can be reconstructed, the more expressive is the query language.* What remains to be decided, is the unit

---

[2] However, the quantitative notion we propose does not allow to express precisely the qualitative one. So they should be considered as two independent (but closely related) types of inexpressibility statements. See remark at the end of Section 3.

of measure for this kind of expressive power. We choose it to be a *bit* in the sense of *Kolmogorov complexity*.

2 Preliminary Notions and Notation

A *signature* (typically σ) is a finite collection of relation symbols, each one with a fixed arity. We work exclusively with finite structures (typically $\mathfrak{A}$, $\mathfrak{B}$, ...) over σ. The universe set $|\mathfrak{A}|$ of $\mathfrak{A}$ is always some initial segment of the natural numbers. The cardinality of $|\mathfrak{A}|$ is denoted $\|\mathfrak{A}\|$. A *query* (typically p) is a mapping from structures over σ into the structures over τ, preserving the universe of the structures, computable, and *generic*: for any isomorphism $\alpha : \mathfrak{A} \to \mathfrak{B}$, it must be the case that $p(\alpha(\mathfrak{A})) = \alpha(p(\mathfrak{A}))$. A query p is called *boolean* if τ consists of exactly one predicate, which is 0-ary. In this paper, we usually do not distinguish between queries and logical formulas, by which they are expressed. Thus a boolean query is just a sentence. The complexity classes of queries are defined in the natural fashion, based on the time and space complexity of the associated functions on encodings, which are defined below.

The following definitions apply to any such language, **consisting of total queries, only.** All the definitions can be given in a pretty the same way for any query language, which has decidable halting problem over finite structures. At the expense of more complicated definitions, this can be also done for the class of all total queries in any given query language L, even if this class is not recursive.

Definition 1. 1. The set $\mathbf{N}$ of natural numbers is identified with the set $\{0, 1\}^*$ of finite binary strings, in the way defined by ordering $\{0, 1\}^*$ by increasing length first, and then lexicographically in each length class. In particular, 0 is the empty word. We will use $lh(x)$ to denote the length of the word x.

2. σ is a finite, purely relational signature.

3. Σ is the class of all finite structures over σ.

4. L is a recursive query language, and L_0 is the set of boolean queries in L. Both are recursive.

5. We fix some recursive bijective enumeration $\ell : \mathbf{N} \to L_0$ of all boolean queries in L.

6. We fix a recursive surjective encoding enc $: \Sigma \to \mathbf{N}$ of structures in Σ as binary words, such that $\mathfrak{A} \cong \mathfrak{B}$ iff enc($\mathfrak{A}$) = enc($\mathfrak{B}$). This can be done for graphs by choosing enc($\mathfrak{A}$) to be the lexicographically least concatenation of the rows of the adjacency matrix among all graphs $\mathfrak{B} \cong \mathfrak{A}$, and similarly for general structures.

7. If $p \in L_0$ and $\mathfrak{A} \in \Sigma$, then $p^{\mathfrak{A}} \in \{0, 1\}$ is the truth value of p in $\mathfrak{A}$.

8. If $\mathfrak{A} \in \Sigma$, then $L_0^{\mathfrak{A}} \in \{0, 1\}^{\mathbf{N}}$ is the function (or, equivalently, an infinite binary string) $\lambda n.\ell(n)^{\mathfrak{A}}$.

9. We fix a *recursive query evaluation function* eval $: \mathbf{N}^2 \to \{0, 1\}$ such that $p^{\mathfrak{A}} = \text{eval}(\ell^{-1}(p), \text{enc}(\mathfrak{A}))$. □

Definition 2. The tuple made of all the following components: algorithm for identifying binary words and natural numbers, algorithm for enumeration ℓ, algorithm of the encoding function enc of structures as binary words and algorithm computing the eval function we denote Rep. □

2.1 Kolmogorov Complexity

The discussion of the Kolmogorov complexity is to be found in the book [LV2] or in the article [LV1]. We sketch briefly the basic notions, following these sources. However, the exposition is slightly changed, to meet our specific needs. In the sequel, $\log n$ means always the least natural m such that $2^m \geq n$.

Let $\{0,1\}^{\leq\infty}$ stand for the union $\{0,1\}^{\mathbb{N}} \cup \{0,1\}^*$.

Let $\psi(\cdot, \cdot)$ be any partial-recursive function $\{0,1\}^* \times \{0,1\}^{\leq\infty} \to \{0,1\}^*$. The second argument for ψ can be infinite. This may be understood that ψ is computed by a Turing machine, whose first input tape contains the first argument, and the second input tape the second argument; therefore it does not cause any problem, if any of them is infinite.

Definition 3. We define the *Kolmogorov complexity of a string* $x \in \{0,1\}^*$ *relative to a string* $y \in \{0,1\}^{\leq\infty}$ *via decoding function* ψ *to be*

$$C_\psi(x|y) = \min\{lh(z) : \psi(z,y) = x\}.$$

$C_\psi(x|y)$ says how many bits we must add to y in order to describe x uniquely, where the method of understanding descriptions is given by ψ. □

Let $\mathbf{M} = M_0, M_1, M_2, \ldots$ be the enumeration of all two-tape Turing machines with separated input and output tapes, working with two element tape and input/output alphabet $\{0,1\}$, and indexed by all strings in $\{0,1\}^*$. Let $\phi(\cdot, \cdot)$ be the universal partial-recursive function $\{0,1\}^* \times \{0,1\}^{\leq\infty} \to \{0,1\}^*$ associated with $\mathbf{M}$, i.e., let

$$\phi(z,y) = \begin{cases} x & \text{if } M_z \text{ started with } y \text{ on the input tape} \\ & \text{halts with } x \text{ on the output tape,} \\ \text{undefined} & \text{otherwise.} \end{cases}$$

Theorem 4. *For every partial-recursive function* $\psi : \{0,1\}^* \times \{0,1\}^{\leq\infty} \to \{0,1\}^*$ *there exists a constant* c_ψ *such that for all* $x \in \{0,1\}^*$, $y \in \{0,1\}^{\leq\infty}$

$$C_\phi(x|y) \leq C_\psi(x,y) + c_\psi.$$

□

The above theorem, called The Invariance Theorem, justifies the following definition:

Definition 5. The *Kolmogorov complexity of a string* $x \in \{0,1\}^*$ *relative to a string* $y \in \{0,1\}^{\leq \infty}$ is defined as $C(x|y) = C_\phi(x|y)$.

The *Kolmogorov complexity of a string* $x \in \{0,1\}^*$ is defined as $C(x) = C(x|0)$. (Recall that our convention of identifying natural numbers and binary words means that 0 is the empty word.) □

The point here is that the Kolmogorov complexity of a string depends on that string, and *the choice of the function* ϕ. Theorem 4 says that for every other possible choice the value of the complexity does not increase more than by an additive constant. This means, that the complexity is determined "up to an additive constant term". In a strict sense, $C(x|y)$ states how many bits of additional information must be added to the string y to determine string x uniquely.

Definition 6. We extend the definition of C_ϕ for infinite recursive strings $x = x_0 x_1 x_2 \ldots \in \{0,1\}^{\mathbf{N}}$ in the following way:

$$\widehat{C}_\phi(x|y) = \min\{lh(z) : \forall n \in \mathbf{N}, \phi(\langle z, n \rangle, y) = x_n\}.$$

We set for x as above

$$\widehat{C}(x|y) = \widehat{C}_\phi(x|y).$$

. This means that $\widehat{C}(x|y)$ is equal to the length of the shortest program (for ϕ) that, given y, computes x as a function. Similarly as for finite strings we set also

$$\widehat{C}(x) = \widehat{C}(x|0).$$

□

The invariance theorem can be easily extended also for the above $\widehat{C}$, and therefore the definition is also correct.

Formally C for finite strings and $\widehat{C}$ for infinite strings are different functions. But we will write in the sequel C for both — happily their domains are disjoint, and therefore it will be always clear from the context, which function we mean.

3 The Kolmogorov Expressive Power

We set $C^{\mathrm{Rep}}(\mathfrak{A}) = C(\mathrm{enc}(\mathfrak{A}))$ and $I^{\mathrm{Rep}}(\mathfrak{A}) = C^{\mathrm{Rep}}(\mathfrak{A}) - C(\mathrm{enc}(\mathfrak{A}) \mid L_0^{\mathfrak{A}})$. The pair $\langle C^{\mathrm{Rep}}(\mathfrak{A}), I^{\mathrm{Rep}}(\mathfrak{A}) \rangle$ gives the information about expressive power of L_0 in $\mathfrak{A}$, yielding both the real information content of $\mathfrak{A}$ and the quantity of information that can be retrieved from $\mathfrak{A}$ by boolean queries in L_0. Of course, these quantities depend *a priori* on all the parameters fixed in Rep.

So before we start investigating properties of the Kolmogorov expressive power of query languages, we should first demonstrate that these quantities do not depend on the choices we have made: of the encoding function enc to represent finite structures as words, of the enumeration ℓ of queries in L_0, etc.

Theorem 7. *For any other than* Rep *system* Rep$'$ *representing all structures over σ and the query language L in the sense of Definitions 2, there is a universal constant c such that for every two isomorphic structures $\mathfrak{A}, \mathfrak{B} \in \Sigma$*

$$|I^{\mathrm{Rep}}(\mathfrak{A}) - I^{\mathrm{Rep}'}(\mathfrak{B})| \leq c \quad and \quad |C^{\mathrm{Rep}}(\mathfrak{A}) - C^{\mathrm{Rep}'}(\mathfrak{B})| \leq c.$$

Proof. The proof is easy. One can simply recursively translate all the encodings, enumerations, etc., forming the system Rep into ones forming the system Rep$'$, and the constant c is in principle the length of the algorithm (encoded for the reference function ϕ) that computes the translation and its converse. $\qquad\square$

Since all of Kolmogorov complexity is defined up to an additive constant term, we deduce that the choices we have made in Definition 1 are unessential.

This in turn justifies the following definition.

Definition 8 (The Kolmogorov expressive power). The *Kolmogorov complexity of a finite structure* $\mathfrak{A} \in \Sigma$ is defined as

$$C(\mathfrak{A}) = C^{\mathrm{Rep}}(\mathfrak{A}),$$

and the *information expressible in L_0 about* $\mathfrak{A}$ as

$$I_{L_0}(\mathfrak{A}) = I^{\mathrm{Rep}}(\mathfrak{A}).$$

The *Kolmogorov expressive power of L_0* is the function $\mathrm{KE} : \Sigma \to \mathbf{N} \times \mathbf{N}$ defined as

$$\mathrm{KE}(\mathfrak{A}) = \langle C(\mathfrak{A}), I_{L_0}(\mathfrak{A}) \rangle.$$

$\qquad\square$

Remark. Let us note, that, since all the introduced quantities are defined "up to an additive constant", some of subtle inexpressibility results cannot be formulated in our framework. E.g., a result stating that for every n there are two nonisomorphic graphs $\mathfrak{A}, \mathfrak{B}$ on the same vertex set of cardinality n, which are indistinguishable by all sentences of a logic L, says that one bit of information (the difference between $\mathfrak{A}$ and $\mathfrak{B}$) cannot be retrieved by sentences of the logic. But this bit gets lost in the constant indeterminacy of Kolmogorov complexity. Most of what we can express is either that $I_L(\mathfrak{A}) = C(\mathfrak{A}) - O(1)$ (the highest possible expressive power), or that $I_L(\mathfrak{A}) = O(1)$ (the lowest possible expressive power), where $O(1)$ stands for a number bounded by a constant independent of $\mathfrak{A}$.

4 The Query Languages

The definitions form the previous section apply to almost any reasonable query language. The limitation is that all its queries should be total. In this paper we intend to deal with some specific query languages: inflationary fixpoint logic IFP and partial fixpoint logic PFP.

We assume that the reader is already familiar with first-order logic FO. IFP and PFP were introduced to remedy an important weakness of FO, namely the lack of any recursion mechanism. E.g., FO fails to express the transitive closure of a graph, or that a graph is connected.

The two query languages we shall define below were introduced in [Ch, CH], in a different notation. As a matter of fact, each one of them allows a number of different definitions, though of the same expressive power over *finite*[3] models. Both of them allow iterating a FO formula up to a fixpoint. The difference is in the form of iteration.

Definition 9 (IFP and PFP queries). We choose for PFP the definition given in [AV1], and for IFP the definition from [GS].

Let $p(R, \mathbf{x})$ be a k-ary first order formula over $\sigma' = \sigma \cup \{R\}$, where R is k-ary and does not occur in σ.

Then the formula $[\text{PFP } p(R), R](\mathbf{t})$ is in PFP (respectively, $[\text{IFP } p(R), R](\mathbf{x})$ is in IFP), where $\mathbf{x}$ is a k-tuple of variables; the semantics of the formulas is as follows:

Let $\mathfrak{A}$ be a finite structure over σ, and let $\mathfrak{A}[R = S]$ be the structure over σ' resulting from $\mathfrak{A}$ by assigning to R the relation $S \subseteq |\mathfrak{A}|^k$. Then let $P^0 = \emptyset$, and

PFP case: $P^{i+1} = \{\mathbf{a} \in |\mathfrak{A}|^k \mid \mathfrak{A}[R = P^i] \models p(\mathbf{a})\}$.

The sequence P^i need not be convergent. **If it is**, then the limit is denoted by P^∞ (and is equal to $P^{2^{\|\mathfrak{A}\|^k}}$); otherwise the default value for P^∞ is $\emptyset$. Finally,

$$\mathfrak{A} \models [\text{PFP } p(R), R](\mathbf{a}) \quad \text{iff} \quad \mathbf{a} \in P^\infty.$$

IFP case: $P^{i+1} = P^i \cup \{\mathbf{a} \in |\mathfrak{A}|^k \mid \mathfrak{A}[R = P^i] \models p(\mathbf{a})\}$.

The sequence P^i is ascending, so it must converge to a limit P^∞ (and $P^\infty = P^{\|\mathfrak{A}\|^k}$). Finally,

$$\mathfrak{A} \models [\text{IFP } p(R), R](\mathbf{a}) \quad \text{iff} \quad \mathbf{a} \in P^\infty.$$

$\square$

The sets of queries we have just defined are denoted by PFP and IFP, respectively. FO^k, IFP^k and PFP^k stand for the sets of those queries in FO, IFP and PFP, respectively, in which only k variables are used.

4.1 The Descriptive Expressive Power of PFP and IFP

We say that a query language L *captures* a complexity class C iff every query $p \in L$ is computable in C and vice versa: every query p which is computable in C is definable in L.

The following theorem summarises some of the information about the descriptive power of IFP and PFP.

---

[3] This is an important restriction. Over infinite models these definitions give rise to query languages of different expressive powers.

Theorem 10. *1. Over ordered finite structures* IFP *captures* PTIME, *[I, V]*.

2. Over ordered finite structures PFP *captures* PSPACE, *[AV1, V]*.

3. Over arbitrary finite structures neither IFP *nor* PFP *can express the boolean query* EVEN.

4. The standard (descriptive) expressive powers of IFP *and* PFP *are equal if and only if* PTIME=PSPACE, *[AV2]*. □

4.2 The Normal Form Theorem

We are going to present a very powerful normal form theorem for PFP queries, proved first by Abiteboul and Vianu in [AV2]. This is the basis for an interesting optimisation method, called *split*, and will be shown in this paper to lead to a result concerning limitations of the Kolmogorov expressive power of query languages.

Namely, for every signature σ and every natural k there exists a query ϖ_k in IFP^{2k+2}, with output signature τ_k, which in arbitrary $\mathfrak{A} \in \Sigma$ computes an equivalence relation $\equiv_k$ on k-tuples of elements of $|\mathfrak{A}|$, a pre-ordering $\preceq_k$ of $|\mathfrak{A}|^k$, and a tuple of additional binary and unary relations $\mathbf{R}$ over $|\mathfrak{A}|^k$. Moreover, the following additional requirements are satisfied:

1. $\equiv_k$ is a congruence on $|\mathfrak{A}|^k$ with respect to the remaining relations in $\varpi_k(\mathfrak{A})$.
2. The structure $\pi_k(\mathfrak{A}) = \langle |\mathfrak{A}|^k, \preceq_k, \mathbf{R}\rangle / \equiv_k$ is *linearly ordered* by $\preceq_k$.
3. For every k-ary query p in PFP^k over σ there exists an unary query $p^\bullet$ in IFP over σ_k satisfying that $p(\mathfrak{A})$ is equal to $\bigcup p^\bullet(\pi_k(\mathfrak{A}))$. (Recall that $p^\bullet(\pi_k(\mathfrak{A}))$ is a set of $\equiv_k$-equivalence classes of k-tuples over $|\mathfrak{A}|$.) $p^\bullet$ can be constructed effectively from p.
4. Moreover, if p is in IFP, then $p^\bullet$ is also a query from IFP.

In particular, it follows from the above that no formula in PFP^k can distinguish between $\equiv_k$ equivalent tuples of elements of its input.

There is also an important query ϱ_k of the form $[\mathrm{IFP}\ r(R), R](\mathbf{x})$ in IFP^k, such that for every $\mathfrak{A} \in \Sigma$, every stage S^i of ϱ_k consists of the union of the first i equivalence classes of $\equiv_k$ in the ordering $\preceq_k$ defined by $\pi_k(\mathfrak{A})$.

The query[4] π_k, reducing computations of queries over any unordered structure $\mathfrak{A}$ to the computations over the ordered structure $\pi_k(\mathfrak{A})$ is a very powerful technique. It serves as a basis for very important theoretical results, e.g., the proof of the point 4 of the last theorem is based on this approach. It is also useful for results much closer to the practice, concerning query optimisation. E.g., the *split* optimisation technique is based on the fact, that often the value $\|\pi_k(\mathfrak{A})\|$ is much smaller than $\|\mathfrak{A}\|$. Then the computation of p represented as "superposition" of π_k and $p^\bullet$ can be much more efficient than the straightforward computation of p, suggested by semantics. We refer the reader to papers [AG, ACV], where this method is presented in more detail. It should be noted that *split* presented in [AG] is generally more complicated that the method of [ACV], since it is

---

[4] Formally only ϖ_k is a query, since π_k does not preserve the universe of its argument.

more practice-oriented, and allows avoiding the overhead of computing $\|\pi_k(\mathfrak{A})\|$ when it is of cardinality comparable to $\|\mathfrak{A}\|$. Nevertheless, we use the name *split* for both, having in mind all the methods based on the low cardinality of $\|\pi_k(\mathfrak{A})\|$.

5 Basic Properties

5.1 KE of First-Order Logic and its Extensions

The main difference between Kolmogorov expressive power and descriptive expressive power is that in the descriptive case queries are tested one by one against all finite models, while in the Kolmogorov case models are tested one by one against all the boolean queries. So the results are in a sense orthogonal. In this section we will show some of the differences and similarities between the descriptive complexity and Kolmogorov expressive power of fixpoint extensions of first-order logic. They will serve us as tools in proving more advanced results in the next section. We begin with a discussion of the right choice of the query languages to deal with. From now on we drop the "0" subscript of L_0 when speaking about boolean queries from L.

Proposition 11. *For arbitrary finite structure $\mathfrak{A}$ the Kolmogorov expressive power of the fragment Σ_2 of FO is already maximal, i.e.,*

$$I_{\Sigma_2}(\mathfrak{A}) = C(\mathfrak{A}) - O(1).$$

Proof. It is well known, that for every finite $\mathfrak{A}$ the query 'the structure is isomorphic to $\mathfrak{A}$' is definable in Σ_2. Now we need only constant number of extra bits to write a program that will reconstruct the isomorphism type of $\mathfrak{B}$ from $(\Sigma_2)^{\mathfrak{B}}$. Indeed, it is enough to search in this string for the first true query 'the structure is isomorphic to $\mathfrak{A}$' to recognise and output $enc(\mathfrak{A})$ — the (encoding of the) isomorphism type of $\mathfrak{B}$. $\square$

We have seen, that even the full first-order logic appears to be to strong in our context. Therefore we should restrict our attention somehow. It is quite natural in the finite model theory to restrict the number of variables in a formula. And this is our choice in this paper.

The first result indicates the difference between Kolmogorov complexity and descriptive complexity, showing that the Kolmogorov expressive powers of PFP^k and IFP^k are the same as that of FO^k. This is untrue in the descriptive sense, since PFP and IFP are known to be stronger than FO.

Theorem 12. *For arbitrary structure $\mathfrak{A} \in \Sigma$ the quantities: $I_{FO^k}(\mathfrak{A})$, $I_{IFP^k}(\mathfrak{A})$ and $I_{PFP^k}(\mathfrak{A})$ are equal up to an additive constant, independent of $\mathfrak{A}$.*

Proof. Since $FO^k \subseteq IFP^k \subseteq PFP^k$, it is enough to show, that $C(\mathfrak{A} \mid (PFP^k)^{\mathfrak{A}}) \leq C(\mathfrak{A} \mid (FO^k)^{\mathfrak{A}}) + O(1)$.

Suppose that $\phi(x, (PFP^k)^{\mathfrak{A}}) = enc(\mathfrak{A})$ for some string $x \in \{0,1\}^*$. In the process of this computation several times the values $p^{\mathfrak{A}}$ are accessed for $p \in PFP^k$. It is enough to show, that each such access can be substituted by a call of a finite-length subroutine T, which computes the correct value $p^{\mathfrak{A}}$, accessing only $(FO^k)^{\mathfrak{A}}$. This will show, that $\mathfrak{A}$ can be also computed by ϕ from $(FO^k)^{\mathfrak{A}}$, x and finitely many additional bits.

Observe, that for every PFP^k formula $[PFP \ p(R), R](\mathbf{x})$ its stages P^i are FO^k definable. This is so also for the stages S^i of ϱ_k.

When called with argument $p \in PFP^k$, the subroutine T looks through $(FO^k)^{\mathfrak{A}}$ for the first (in the listing) true sentence of the form $\forall \mathbf{x} (S^i(\mathbf{x}) \leftrightarrow S^{i+1}(\mathbf{x}))$. There is such a sentence, since ϱ_k is in IFP^k, and therefore its sequence of stages converges. Now T rewrites p into first-order p', substituting every subformula of the form $[PFP \ q(R), R](\mathbf{y})$ by $(\forall \mathbf{x}(Q^{2^i}(\mathbf{x}) \leftrightarrow Q^{2^i+1}(\mathbf{x})) \wedge Q^{2^i}(\mathbf{y})$. Finally it returns the value $(p')^{\mathfrak{A}}$, found in $(FO^k)^{\mathfrak{A}}$.

Indeed, this value is correct, since if $\|\pi_k(\mathfrak{A})\| \leq i$, then by the Normal Form Theorem the sequence of stages for arbitrary formula in PFP^k must either reach a fixpoint in at most 2^i stages, and then this fixpoint is the meaning of this formula, or else the default value $\emptyset$ is used. $\quad\square$

There are, however, similarities between Kolmogorov and the descriptive notions. In the descriptive case over classes of ordered structures a query language usually achieves the maximum of expressive power (e.g., IFP the power of PTIME, and PFP of PSPACE). The same is true about Kolmogorov expressive power. This will be shown in the following theorem:

Proposition 13. *Suppose that a query $p(x, y)$ defines a linear ordering of a finite structure $\mathfrak{A}$. Then there is a constant k, independent of $\mathfrak{A}$, such that FO with k variables and with p added as a language primitive has the maximal Kolmogorov expressive power:*

$$I_{FO^k[p]}(\mathfrak{A}) \geq C(\mathfrak{A}) - O(1).$$

Proof. The proof is quite straightforward — having ordering we need only few extra variables plus first-order connectives and quantifiers to be able to write the query 'the structure is isomorphic to $\mathfrak{A}$' for each particular $\mathfrak{A}$. $\quad\square$

It seems that it would be nice to have a kind of converse of the above. We will indeed prove some kind of such a converse for query languages that extend the fixpoint query language. Accidentally, the same result indicates also connections of Kolmogorov expressive power with the *split* technique.

We will use the following equality, following easily from the "symmetry of information" equality known for Kolmogorov complexity, to estimate $I_L(\mathfrak{A})$ in terms of $C(L^{\mathfrak{A}})$, which is easier to compute:

Lemma 14. *Let L be any boolean query language consisting of total queries. Then*

$$I_L(\mathfrak{A}) = C(L^{\mathfrak{A}}) + O(\log C(L^{\mathfrak{A}})),$$

for all finite structures $\mathfrak{A} \in \Sigma$. $\quad\square$

The next lemma can be proven by analysis of the query π_k, provided in [D]:

Lemma 15. *For every finite structure $\mathfrak{A}$ over σ and every fixed k, if $\|\pi_k(\mathfrak{A})\| = n$, then $C(\pi_k(\mathfrak{A})) \leq n^2 \log k + O(n \log n)$.* $\square$

Now the promised weak converse of the Proposition 13.

Theorem 16. *Suppose that $\mathfrak{A}$ is finite and $\|\pi_k(\mathfrak{A})\| = n$. Then*

$$I_{\text{PFP}^k}(\mathfrak{A}) \leq n^2 \log k + O(n \log n),$$

where the constant implied by the O-notation does not depend on $\mathfrak{A}$.

Proof. By the Normal Form Theorem, every boolean query p in PFP^k can be evaluated in two phases: first the quotient finite structure $\pi_k(\mathfrak{A})$ is constructed. Then the remaining part of the evaluation is performed by $p^\bullet$ in $\pi_k(\mathfrak{A})$. In particular, if $\pi_k(\mathfrak{A}) \cong \pi_k(\mathfrak{B})$, then $(\text{PFP}^k)^{\mathfrak{A}} = (\text{PFP}^k)^{\mathfrak{B}}$.

Let now $\mathfrak{A} \in \Sigma$, and $\|\pi_k(\mathfrak{A})\| = n$. Let us see, that the result of evaluation of each PFP^k query p in $\mathfrak{A}$ can be recovered from a description of $n^2 \log k + O(n \log n)$ bits. Indeed, the structure $\pi_k(\mathfrak{A})$ can be described uniquely by at most that many bits, by Lemma 15. Now, having $\pi_k(\mathfrak{A})$, we consider consecutively all finite $\mathfrak{B} \in \Sigma$ and compute $\pi_k(\mathfrak{B})$, searching for the first $\mathfrak{B}$ such that $\pi_k(\mathfrak{B}) \cong \pi_k(\mathfrak{A})$. There is at least one such $\mathfrak{B}$ (namely, $\mathfrak{A}$ itself), and therefore this search will terminate. Then, having such $\mathfrak{B}$, we evaluate the boolean query p in $\mathfrak{B}$. The result is guaranteed by the Normal Form Theorem to be identical as in $\mathfrak{A}$.

The whole process of reconstruction of the truth value of p requires $n^2 \log k + O(n \log n)$ bits describing $\pi_k(\mathfrak{A})$, plus a finite number of bits, necessary to formalise the above discussion. As the discussion is independent of p, it yields an algorithm for computing consecutive bits of $(\text{PFP}^k)^{\mathfrak{A}}$ as a function. Therefore $C((\text{PFP}^k)^{\mathfrak{A}}) \leq n^2 \log k + O(n \log n)$. By Lemma 14 we get the thesis. $\square$

Remark. Let us shortly discuss what the last theorem really states, and what it doesn't.

1. The first, simple corollary is that for fixed k always $\|\pi_k(\mathfrak{A})\|$ is at least of order of magnitude $\sqrt{I_{\text{FO}^k}(\mathfrak{A})}$, and that $\pi_k(\mathfrak{A})$ is ordered. So the theorem really states some kind of converse of the Theorem 13. Of course, it allows one to prove lower bounds on complexity of IFP and PFP in terms of $I_{\text{FO}^k}(\mathfrak{A})$.

2. The statement shows also, that whenever the optimisation by *split* gives any real benefit, due to small size of $\|\pi_k(\mathfrak{A})\|$, it indicates the limitation of the expressive power of boolean queries. Moreover, the better is the result of optimisation, the more restrictive is the bound on the expressive power of boolean queries.

3. The Theorem 16 above gives only a *theoretical* upper bound on the expressive power. The real value of $I_{\text{PFP}^k}(\mathfrak{A})$ can be much (even exponentially) smaller. The main reason is that seldom the real information content of $\pi_k(\mathfrak{A})$ is maximal possible, and also seldom all the information present in $\pi_k(\mathfrak{A})$ can be really retrieved from $\mathfrak{A}$ by queries with only k variables.

6 KE and the *Split* Optimisation

Proofs in this section are omitted, since they require a substantial amount of combinatorial and logical results to be proven first, and our space is limited. In this section we assume the we consider finite models over a fixed signature σ with at least one at least binary symbol. Our intention is to demonstrate, that we can prove some nontrivial results concerning the Kolmogorov complexity in a slightly more practical setting. Since the Kolmogorov complexity itself is noncomputable, we prove results concerning the *average value* of this complexity, and its connections with average time and space complexity of query evaluation.

Definition 17. For a finite signature σ the *capacity of σ* is the polynomial

$$\mathrm{cp}_\sigma(x) = \sum_{R \in \sigma} x^{\mathrm{arity}(R)}.$$

$\square$

The sense of capacity is that the value $\mathrm{cp}_\sigma(n)$ gives the theoretical upper bound on the Kolmogorov complexity of n-element *ordered* structure over σ.

Definition 18. Let X be a finite set, and $f : X \to \mathbf{N}$ any function. Then *the average value of f on X* is defined as

$$\mathrm{average}_{x \in X}(f(x)) = \frac{\sum_{x \in X} f(x)}{|X|}.$$

Thi average is equal to the expected value of f with respect to the probability distribution on X that makes all the instances $x \in X$ equiprobable. $\square$

Let $\Sigma(n)$ stand for the set of all finite databases over σ with the universe set $\{0, \ldots, n-1\}$. Let us see first, what happens about the complexity of finite structures in the average case.

Theorem 19. $\mathrm{average}_{\mathfrak{A} \in \Sigma(n)} C(\mathfrak{A}) = \mathrm{cp}_\sigma(n) - n \log n - O(\log n).$ $\square$

Let us analyse an example situation, exactly the same as considered by the authors in [ACV]. They assumed equal probabilities on all n element input structures over σ, and showed a surprising result that the average case sequential complexity of PFP queries is DSPACE($\log n$), and that the average parallel complexity of IFP is in uniform AC_0, i.e., the queries are computable on a PRAM with polynomially many processors in constant average time. What we show now, is that the price to pay for this is very high for a user that uses only boolean queries, in the sense that on average he can get only a constant number of bits of information about the database, out of the quantity established in the proposition above.

Theorem 20. *For every* $k \in \mathbf{N}$ $\mathrm{average}_{\mathfrak{A} \in \Sigma(n)}(I_{\mathrm{PFP}^k}(\mathfrak{A})) = O(1).$ $\square$

We have seen that the Kolmogorov expressive power of PFP^k is very low when we consider all databases with n-element universe set. A simple method to improve the expressive power of the query language under consideration is to mark some elements in the finite structure as "important". Formally, we introduce a new unary relation symbol $U \notin \sigma$, and let $\sigma' = \sigma \cup \{U\}$. The intended meaning is that elements a of the finite structure $\mathfrak{A} \in \Sigma'$ satisfying $U(a)$ are important. If we consider all possible choices of U, it doesn't help: we are back in the situation covered by Theorem 20. We must limit the choice of U. So let us fix some recursive function $i : \mathbf{N} \to \mathbf{N}$, and assume that in a finite structure of n elements we mark $i(n)$ elements as important. So let $D_n^i \subseteq \Sigma'(n)$ consist of all structures $\mathfrak{A}$ satisfying $|\{a \in |\mathfrak{A}| : U(a)\}| = i(\|\mathfrak{A}\|)$. By symmetry we may assume $i(n) \leq n/2$. Now we consider the average Kolmogorov expressive power and the average query complexity in all such databases. First of all we look at the average value of the complexity of structures themselves:

Theorem 21. *Let* $i(n) \leq n/2$ *be as above. Then* $\text{average}_{\mathfrak{A} \in D_n^i}(C(\mathfrak{A})) = \text{cp}_\sigma(n) + i(n) - n\log n - O(\log n)$.

It appears that the Kolmogorov expressive power of the query languages depends in a strong and rather unexpected way on the growth rate of $i(n)$:

Theorem 22. *For arbitrary function* $i(n) \leq n/2$:

1. *If* $i(n)/\log n \to 0$, *then for every* k *large enough* $\text{average}_{\mathfrak{A} \in D_n^i}(I_{\text{FO}^k}(\mathfrak{A})) = \text{cp}_\sigma(i(n)) - i(n)\log i(n) - O(\log i(n))$.
2. *If* $i(n)/\log n \to \infty$, *then for every* $k \in \mathbf{N}$ $\text{average}_{\mathfrak{A} \in D_n^i}(I_{\text{PFP}^k}(\mathfrak{A})) = O(1)$.

$\square$

Let us observe, that in the item 1 above the quantity looks exactly like the average complexity of an $i(n)$-element structure, by Theorem 19. And this is not an accident, the equality comes from the fact, that with large probability for $\mathfrak{A} \in D_n^i$ we can from $L^{\mathfrak{A}}$ reconstruct the isomorphism type of the substructure of $\mathfrak{A}$ consisting of all elements in U, and nothing else. So this supports the idea of marking elements as important. What we mark as important, becomes really visible to the query language — provided we do not want too many elements to be important. $\bullet$

We have seen, that successful optimisation by *split* technique implies a bound on the Kolmogorov expressive power of the query language. Here we see that this expressive power is limited on average. The question is: can we prove in these cases that the queries have lower average complexity than the pessimistic PTIME for IFP and PSPACE for PFP?

Theorem 23. *For arbitrary function* $i(n) \leq n/2$:

1. *If* $i(n)/\log n \to 0$, *then on average PFP queries in* D_n^i *are computable in* DSPACE$(\max(\log n, 2^{O(i(n))}))$, *and in parallel every IFP query can be computed on a PRAM with polynomially many processors in average time* $2^{O(i(n))}$.

2. If $i(n)/\log n \to \infty$, then on average PFP queries in D_n^i are computable in DSPACE($\log n$), and on average IFP queries can be computed in uniform AC_0. □

Remark. The other interesting observation is that if $i(n)/\log\log n \to 0$, we get the same average sequential space complexity of DSPACE($\log n$) for PFP, as established in [ACV], and also for IFP the NC_1 average parallel complexity (i.e., the queries are computable on a PRAM with polynomially many processors in average time $\log n$), but without the collapse of IFP and PFP down to FO, as it is the case in [ACV].

Acknowledgements. I wish to thank Andrzej Tarlecki, who asked me the question if the restricted Kolmogorov expressive power had anything to do with optimisation of queries. The critical comments of the anonymous referees helped me in improving the paper. I owe also many thanks to my son Michal, who let me finish this paper before he was born.

References

[ACV] S. Abiteboul, K. Compton and V. Vianu, 'Queries are easier than you thought (probably)', in: *Proc. ACM Symp. on Principles of Database Systems, 1992.*

[AG] S. Abiteboul and A. Van Gelder, 'Optimizing active databases using the split technique', in: *Proc. ICDT'92*, Springer Lecture Notes in Computer Science 646.

[AV1] S. Abiteboul and V. Vianu, 'Datalog extensions for database queries and updates', *Journal of Computer and System Sciences*, 43(1991), pp. 62–124.

[AV2] S. Abiteboul and V. Vianu, 'Generic computation and its complexity', in: *Proc. ACM SIGACT Symp. on the Theory of Computing*, 1991, pp. 209–219.

[Ch] A. Chandra, 'Programming primitives for database languages', in: *Proc. ACM Symp. on Principles of Programming Languages 1982*, pp. 50–62.

[CH] A. Chandra and D. Harel, 'Computable queries for relational data bases', *Journal of Computer and System Sciences* 21(1980), pp. 156–178.

[D] A. Dawar, 'Feasible computation through model theory', *PhD Thesis*, University of Pennsylvania, 1993.

[GS] Y. Gurevich and S. Shelah, 'Fixed-point extensions of first-order logic', *Annals of Pure and Applied Logic*, 32(1986), pp. 265–280.

[I] N. Immerman, 'Languages that capture complexity classes', *SIAM Journal of Computing* 16(1987).

[LV1] M. Li and P. Vitányi, 'Kolmogorov complexity and its applications', in: J. van Leeuven (ed.) *Handbook of Theoretical Computer Science*, North Holland, Amsterdam, 1990.

[LV2] M. Li and P. Vitányi, *An introduction to Kolmogorov complexity and its applications*, Springer Verlag, New York, 1993.

[V] M. Vardi, 'Complexity of relational query languages', *Proc. 14th Symposium on Theory of Computation* 1982, pp. 137–146.

On Two Forms of Structural Recursion

Dan Suciu[1] and Limsoon Wong[2]

[1] University of Pennsylvania, Philadelphia. Email: suciu@saul.cis.upenn.edu
[2] Institute of Systems Science, Singapore. Email: limsoon@iss.nus.sg

Abstract. We investigate and compare two forms of recursion on sets for querying nested collections. The first one is called *sri* and it corresponds to sequential processing of data. The second one is called *sru* and it corresponds to data-parallel processing. A uniform first-order translation from *sru* into *sri* was known from previous work. The converse translation is by necessity more difficult and we have obtained three main results concerning it. First, we exhibit a uniform translation of *sri* queries into *sru* queries over the nested relational algebra. We observe that this translation maps PTIME algorithms into exponential-space queries. The second result proves that *any* uniform translation of *sri* queries into *sru* queries over the nested relational algebra must map some PTIME queries into exponential-space ones. In fact, in the presence of certain external functions, we provide a PTIME *sri* query for which any equivalent *sru* query requires exponential space. Thus, as a mechanism for implementing *algorithms* over complex objects, *sru* is strictly less powerful than *sri*. This inefficiency is in contrast to a previous result that uniformly translates efficient *sri* programs into efficient *sru* programs, but over a language with higher-order functions. Our third result proves that, in the absence of external functions, higher-order functions do not add more expressive power to the nested relational algebra with *sri* or *sru*. However, elimination of higher-order functions cannot be done uniformly, because in the presence of certain external functions, more expressive power can be gained from the higher-order functions. These three results suggest that higher-order functions could be useful in query languages.

1   Introduction

Structural recursion is an attractive paradigm for programming with sets. It can be conceived in two distinct ways, corresponding to the two distinct universal properties that the finite set construction enjoys [7]. The first gives rise to a form of structural recursion that Tannen, Buneman, and Wong call *sri* [8]. It is closely related to the *set_reduce* of Stemple and Sheard [19] and the *fold* operator in functional programming languages [5]. Essentially, *sri* defines a function g on a set O by iteration in an order-independent manner over the elements of O. Namely, it allows us to define g by:

$$g(\{\}) = e$$
$$g(\{x\} \cup O) = i(x, g(O))$$

Here i is a previously defined function and e is some value. We write $sri(i, e)$ to denote the function g thus defined. In order for g to be well defined, i has to satisfy the following two conditions: $i(x, i(y, a)) = i(y, i(x, a))$ (commutativity), and $i(x, i(x, a)) = i(x, a)$ (idempotence). This form of recursion is related to the primitive recursion schema in the theory of recursive functions [16].

The second form of structural recursion is called sru by Tannen, Buneman, and Wong [8], from *structural recursion on the union presentation*. It is related to the *hom* operator of Machiavelli [17] and the *pump* operator of FAD [4]. Essentially, sru allows us to define a function h on a set O in a divide-and-conquer manner. To compute h, one has to divide O recursively in an order-independent way into ever smaller subsets until one reaches sets with 0 or 1 elements. More precisely, sru allows us to define some function h by:

$$h(\{\}) = e$$
$$h(\{x\}) = f(x)$$
$$h(O_1 \cup O_2) = u(h(O_1), h(O_2))$$

We use $sru(u, f, e)$ to denote the h thus defined. Note that it is not well defined unless the following conditions are satisfied: $u(e, a) = u(a, e) = a$ (identity), $u(a, b) = u(b, a)$ (commutativity), and $u(a, a) = a$ (idempotence).

When sri and sru are considered as candidates to be incorporated in a database query language, it is necessary to compare the relative expressive power of the two resultant languages. A straightforward and efficient translation of sru into sri is described in Tannen and Subrahmanyam [7]. This translation is first-order expressible. This implies that any reasonable language augmented with sri is at least as powerful as the same language augmented with sru. Furthermore, any efficient *algorithm* expressed in the language with sru is tranlated into an efficient one in the language with sri. Tannen and Subrahmanyam also give a simple translation of sri into sru. However, this translation uses higher-order functions. This paper investigates translations of sri into sru over query languages for complex objects without higher-order functions.

We use the nested relational calculus $\mathcal{NRC}$ of Wong [23] as the ambient query language in this investigation. $\mathcal{NRC}$ has the same power as the query languages for nested relations of Thomas and Fischer [22], Schek and Scholl [18], Colby [9], etc. We add the two forms of structural recursion above to $\mathcal{NRC}$. Our first result is a *uniform* translation of queries in $\mathcal{NRC}(sri)$ into queries in $\mathcal{NRC}(sru)$. This translation works in the presence of arbitrary external functions. However, the translation is expensive.

Our second result proves that *any* uniform translation of queries from $\mathcal{NRC}(sri)$ into $\mathcal{NRC}(sru)$ has to be expensive. In particular, any such uniform translation must map some PTIME algorithms into exponential space ones. It should be stressed that this result does not compare the relative expressive power of the two languages, which is the same. Rather, this result compares their ability to express efficient *algorithms*. It is in the same spirit as that of Abiteboul and Vianu [3], proving that *parity* cannot be expressed in PTIME by a Generic Machine, and as that of Suciu and Paredaens [21], proving that Abiteboul and

Beeri's algebra for complex objects needs exponential space to express transitive closure. Our result depends on the particular evaluation strategy considered, which is the unoptimized "call-by-value" evaluation strategy, and may not hold for more advanced evaluation techniques. A weakness of our result is that we do not have a particular PTIME query in $\mathcal{NRC}(sri)$ for which no equivalent PTIME query in $\mathcal{NRC}(sru)$ exists. However, given certain external functions, we can construct such a query; see Proposition 3.

In the context of database query languages and ordered databases, it is known [20] that first-order logic extended with *divide and conquer recursion*, which is a form of recursion closely related to sru, captures the complexity class NC, while first-order logic extended with sri captures PTIME. Here NC is the class of functions computable by polynomially many processors in polylogarithmic parallel time. NC is known to be included in PTIME, but it is unknown whether they are equal. Thus our result here (Theorem 2) can be interpreted as saying that there is no uniform translation of a certain query language for PTIME into another query language for NC.

Our third result is motivated by the efficient translation of sri into sru using higher-order functions given by Tannen and Subrahmanyam [7]. While practical programming languages with higher-order functions such as ML and Scheme exists, they have received little attention in the context of database query languages. This efficient translation of sri into sru using higher-order functions together with the proven inefficency of any uniform translation of $\mathcal{NRC}(sri)$ into $\mathcal{NRC}(sru)$ suggests that higher-order functions could be useful in query languages. Our third result proves that the expressive power of $\mathcal{NRC}(sru)$ and $\mathcal{NRC}(sri)$ is not changed by adding higher-order functions to them. However, we also show that higher-order functions can increase expressive power given certain additional primitives.

Organization Section 2 introduces $\mathcal{NRC}$, $\mathcal{NRC}(sru)$, and $\mathcal{NRC}(sri)$. Section 3 presents the uniform translation of sri into sru. This translation proves that $\mathcal{NRC}(sru)$ and $\mathcal{NRC}(sri)$ have the same expressive power, even in the presence of external functions. Section 4 proves that any such translation is very costly, in the sense that the translated query has to create large objects. Section 5 considers the influence of intermediate higher-order functions on the expressive power of our languages. We prove that over complex objects the same expressive power is preserved when higher-order functions are added to our languages; but when certain external functions are also added to our languages, the presence of higher-order functions increases expressive power.

2 Languages to be Studied

As our ambient language in comparing the two forms of structural recursion we use the nested relational calculus $\mathcal{NRC}$ of Wong [23]. It is a language having the same expressive power as other tractable formalisms for complex objects, such as Thomas and Fischer's algebra [22], Schek and Scholl's NF^2 [18], Colby's recursive algebra [9], Abiteboul and Beeri's algebra without powerset [2], etc.

$\mathcal{NRC}$ is a strongly typed language. The complex object types are given by the grammar:

$$s, t ::= b \mid unit \mid s \times t \mid \{s\}$$

Here b ranges over base types such as booleans $\mathbf{B}$. An object of type $s \times t$ is a pair whose first component is an object of type s and whose second component an object of type t. An object of type $\{s\}$ is a finite set whose elements are objects of type s. The only object of type $unit$ is the empty tuple $()$.

$\mathcal{NRC}$ defines two kinds of expressions: *complex objects expressions* and *function expressions*. A complex object expression denotes a complex object. We write $e : t$ to mean that e is a complex object expression and the complex object it denotes has type t. A function expression denotes a function from complex objects to complex objects. We write $e : s \to t$ to mean that e is a function expression with domain s and codomain t. The language is parameterized by a collection Σ of constants c and external functions p. Each $c \in \Sigma$ has some fixed type t_c and each $p \in \Sigma$ has some type $d_p \to c_p$. For each type s, $\mathcal{X}_s$ is an infinite set of *variables* of type s. $\mathcal{NRC}$ is defined by the following rules:

$$\frac{x \in \mathcal{X}_s}{x : s} \qquad \frac{p \in \Sigma}{p : d_p \to c_p} \qquad \frac{x \in \mathcal{X}_s \quad e : t}{\lambda x.e : s \to t} \qquad \frac{e_1 : s \to t \quad e_2 : s}{e_1 \, e_2 : t}$$

$$\frac{c \in \Sigma}{c : t_c} \qquad \frac{}{() : unit} \qquad \frac{e_1 : s \quad e_2 : t}{(e_1, e_2) : s \times t} \qquad \frac{e : s \times t}{\pi_1 \, e : s} \qquad \frac{e : s \times t}{\pi_2 \, e : t}$$

$$\frac{}{\{\} : \{s\}} \qquad \frac{e_1 : \{s\} \quad e_2 : \{s\}}{e_1 \cup e_2 : \{s\}} \qquad \frac{e : s}{\{e\} : \{s\}} \qquad \frac{e_1 : \{t\} \quad e_2 : \{s\}}{\bigcup \{e_1 \mid x \in e_2\} : \{t\}}$$

$$\frac{}{true : \mathbf{B}} \qquad \frac{}{false : \mathbf{B}} \qquad \frac{e_1 : \mathbf{B} \quad e_2 : s \quad e_3 : s}{if\ e_1\ then\ e_2\ else\ e_3 : s} \qquad \frac{e_1 : s \quad e_2 : s}{e_1 = e_2 : \mathbf{B}}$$

The meanings of these expressions are as follows. $\lambda x.e$ is the function f such that $f(x) = e$. $e_1 e_2$ is *function application*, and applies the function e_1 to the complex object e_2. (e_1, e_2) forms a pair whose first component is e_1 and second component e_2. $\pi_1 e$ retrieves the first component of the pair e. $\pi_2 e$ returns the second component of the pair e. $\{\}$ is the empty set. $\{e\}$ forms the singleton set containing e. $e_1 \cup e_2$ is the union of sets e_1 and e_2. $\bigcup \{e_1 \mid x \in e_2\}$ is the set denoted by $sru(\cup, \lambda x.e_1, \{\})(e_2)$, i.e. $e_1[o_1/x] \cup \ldots \cup e_1[o_n/x]$, where $e_2 = \{o_1, \ldots, o_n\}$. A **query** of type $s \to t$ is a closed function expression $e : s \to t$.

We extend $\mathcal{NRC}(\Sigma)$ with the two constructions $sru(u, f, e)$ and $sri(i, e)$ defined in Section 1. For this, we add the following typing rules:

$$\frac{u : t \times t \to t \quad f : s \to t \quad e : t}{sru(u, f, e) : \{s\} \to t} \qquad \frac{i : s \times t \to t \quad e : t}{sru(i, e) : \{s\} \to t}$$

We write $\mathcal{NRC}(sri)$, $\mathcal{NRC}(sru)$, $\mathcal{NRC}(sri, \Sigma)$, and $\mathcal{NRC}(sru, \Sigma)$ for the extensions of $\mathcal{NRC}$ and $\mathcal{NRC}(\Sigma)$ with sri and sru respectively. In the remainder of this paper, we consider several aspects of the question of $\mathcal{NRC}(sru, \Sigma) = \mathcal{NRC}(sri, \Sigma)$ for various signatures Σ.

3 Equivalence in the Absence of Higher-Order Functions

In the absence of external functions, $\mathcal{NRC}(sri)$ and $\mathcal{NRC}(sru)$ have the same expressive power as that of Abiteboul and Beeri's algebra (with *powerset*) [8], which in turn has the same expressive power as $\mathcal{NRC}(powerset)$. In this section we extend the equivalence of $\mathcal{NRC}(sri)$ and $\mathcal{NRC}(sru)$ to the equivalence of $\mathcal{NRC}(sri, \Sigma)$ and $\mathcal{NRC}(sru, \Sigma)$, where external functions are present in Σ. We do that by constructing a *uniform* translation between the two languages.

Informally, a **uniform translation** from $\mathcal{NRC}(sri, \Sigma)$ to $\mathcal{NRC}(sru, \Sigma)$ is a translation having the following property. Let $i : s \times t \to t$ and $e : t$ be two additional variables. Then the translation should map the expression $sri(i, e)$ to some expression E in $\mathcal{NRC}(sru)$ having i and e as free variables such that $sri(i, e)$ and E are equivalent, for every instantiation of i and e.

From a practical point of view, the uniformity of a translation is connected to the possibility of separate compilation and polymorphism. We want to be able separate the translation or compilation of $sri(i, e)$ from the translation or compilation of i and e. Tannen and Subrahmanyam [7] give the following uniform and efficient translations between sru and sri:

$$sru(u, f, e)(O) \stackrel{\text{def}}{=} sri(\lambda(x, y).u(f(x), y),\ e)(O).$$

$sri(i, e)(O) \stackrel{\text{def}}{=} sru(U, I, id)(O)(e)$, where id is the identity function, I is a function such that $I(x) = \lambda y.i(x, y)$, and U is function composition, that is $U(x, y) = \lambda z.x(y(z))$.

The first definition gives us a uniform translation from $\mathcal{NRC}(sru)$ to $\mathcal{NRC}(sri)$. The second translation, from sri to sru, assumes a language with higher-order functions. In particular $sru(U, I, id)$, I, and U are all higher-order functions. Unlike general purpose functional languages, database query languages usually do not have higher-order functions and thus cannot express the above uniform translation of sri into sru.

We show that a different uniform translation of sri to sru that does not use higher-order functions is possible.

Theorem 1. *There exists a uniform translation of $\mathcal{NRC}(sri)$ into $\mathcal{NRC}(sru)$. Therefore, for any set Σ of external functions we have:*

$$\mathcal{NRC}(sri, \Sigma) = \mathcal{NRC}(sru, \Sigma) \ .$$

The idea is to observe that the computation of $sru(u, f, e)(O')$ is given by a balanced binary tree, whose leaves are labeled with the elements of O'. In order to compute $sri(i, e)(O)$ where $O = \{o_1, \ldots, o_n\}$, one has to apply i consecutively n times. One can do that with a balanced binary tree, provided the tree has height n and therefore 2^n leaves. Thus, in the translation, we define O' to be a set with 2^n elements.

Due to the way our translation works, a PTIME query in $\mathcal{NRC}(sri)$ may get translated into a query in $\mathcal{NRC}(sru)$ that has exponential complexity. For example, the implementation of transitive closure in $\mathcal{NRC}(sri)$ by Tannen, Buneman, and Naqvi [6] has polynomial complexity. But its translation to $\mathcal{NRC}(sru)$

via Theorem 1 results in an implementation having exponential complexity. Of course, this does not rule out the existence of efficient expressions for transitive closure in $\mathcal{NRC}(sru)$. Nonetheless, we conjecture that there is no PTIME expression for transitive closure in $\mathcal{NRC}(sru)$.

4 The Cost of the Translation

We prove in this section that any uniform first-order translation from $\mathcal{NRC}(sri)$ to $\mathcal{NRC}(sru)$ is inherently expensive. More precisely, we show that for a certain external function i and constant $\mathbf{e}$, the expression $sri(\mathbf{i}, \mathbf{e})$ denotes a query for which any "algorithm" in $\mathcal{NRC}(sru)$ requires exponential space, whereas the "algorithm" denoted by $sri(\mathbf{i}, \mathbf{e})$ is in PTIME. This shows a mismatch in the ability of $\mathcal{NRC}(sri, \Sigma)$ and $\mathcal{NRC}(sru, \Sigma)$ in expressing *algorithms*. It also implies that any expression in $\mathcal{NRC}(sri)$ in which sri is used in an essential way, is mapped by any uniform translation into an expression in $\mathcal{NRC}(sru)$ denoting an exponential-space algorithm.

This result is of a different nature than inexpressibility results showing that a database query language cannot express certain queries. It states that of the two equivalent languages, $\mathcal{NRC}(sri, \Sigma)$ and $\mathcal{NRC}(sru, \Sigma)$, the former can express certain queries in a more efficient way than the latter. It is in the same spirit as the result [3] stating that *parity* cannot be expressed in PSPACE on a Generic Machine and the result [21] stating that $\mathcal{NRA}(powerset)$ cannot implement transitive closure efficiently (even though it *can* express it.) Our result here is somewhat weaker than these: in the absence of external functions we do not know any particular query that can be expressed more efficiently in $\mathcal{NRC}(sri)$ than $\mathcal{NRC}(sru)$. However, we conjecture that $\mathcal{NRC}(sru)$ cannot express transitive closure in PTIME, while $\mathcal{NRC}(sri)$ obviously can [6].

We start by defining an evaluation strategy for $\mathcal{NRC}(\Sigma)$. As in Suciu and Paredaens [21], this strategy is essentially the *eager* or *call-by-value* evaluation strategy in programming languages, presented in a natural deduction style. Our result holds *only* in conjunction with this evaluation strategy.

First, let us define a grammar for *complex objects O*:

$$O ::= c \mid true \mid false \mid () \mid (O, O) \mid \{O, \ldots, O\}$$

where c stands for some constant such as a number, a string, etc.; (O_1, O_2) is a pair; and $\{O_1, \ldots, O_n\}$ is a set. The notation for a complex objects is subject to the restriction that the sets have no duplicates and we consider two sets to be equal if they differ only in the order of their elements. For example, $\{c_1, c_2\}$ and $\{c_2, c_1\}$ denote the same complex object, while $\{c_1, c_2, c_1\}$ is illegal. Complex objects are *typed*; for example, $\{O_1, O_2, O_3\}$ is of type $\{t\}$, provided that O_1, O_2, O_3 are all of type t.

Recall that $\mathcal{NRC}$ has two kinds of expressions: complex object expressions and function expressions. We want to define a binary relation $e \Downarrow O$ between an expression e and a complex object O, by induction on the structure of e. Its intended meaning is "e fully evaluates to O." However, since $\mathcal{NRC}$ is a language with variables, we are forced to evaluate expressions e with free variables, which have been bound to complex objects. Following Curien [11] we define an **environment** to be a set of the form $\rho = \{x_1 := O_1, \ldots, x_n := O_n\}$, where x_1, ..., x_n are variables and $O_1, \ldots, O_n$ are complex objects. Finally we define below the relations $\rho \bullet e \Downarrow O$ and $\rho \bullet e(O) \Downarrow O'$, with the intended meaning: "under the environment ρ, the complex object expression e fully evaluates to O" and "under the environment ρ, the function expression e applied to O fully evaluates to O'." We write $\rho, x := O$ instead of $\rho \cup \{x := O\}$.

$$\frac{c \in \Sigma}{\rho \bullet c \Downarrow c} \qquad \frac{p \in \Sigma \quad p(O) = O'}{\rho \bullet p(O) \Downarrow O'} \qquad \frac{}{\{\ldots, x := O, \ldots\} \bullet x \Downarrow O}$$

$$\frac{\rho, x := O \bullet e \Downarrow O'}{\rho \bullet (\lambda x.e)(O) \Downarrow O'} \qquad \frac{\rho \bullet e_2 \Downarrow O \quad \rho \bullet e_1(O) \Downarrow O'}{\rho \bullet e_1 \, e_2 \Downarrow O'}$$

$$\frac{}{\rho \bullet () \Downarrow ()} \qquad \frac{\rho \bullet e_1 \Downarrow O_1 \quad \rho \bullet e_2 \Downarrow O_2}{\rho \bullet (e_1, e_2) \Downarrow (O_1, O_2)} \qquad \frac{\rho \bullet e \Downarrow (O_1, O_2)}{\rho \bullet \pi_1 e \Downarrow O_1} \qquad \frac{\rho \bullet e \Downarrow (O_1, O_2)}{\rho \bullet \pi_2 e \Downarrow O_2}$$

$$\frac{}{\rho \bullet \{\} \Downarrow \{\}} \qquad \frac{\rho \bullet e \Downarrow O}{\rho \bullet \{e\} \Downarrow \{O\}} \qquad \frac{\rho \bullet e_1 \Downarrow O_1 \quad \rho \bullet e_2 \Downarrow O_2}{\rho \bullet e_1 \cup e_2 \Downarrow O}$$
$$\text{where } O = O_1 \cup O_2$$

$$\frac{\rho \bullet e_2 \Downarrow \{O_1, \ldots, O_n\} \quad \rho, x := O_1 \bullet e_1 \Downarrow O'_1 \quad \ldots \quad \rho, x := O_n \bullet e_1 \Downarrow O'_n}{\rho \bullet \bigcup\{e_1 \mid x \in e_2\} \Downarrow O'}$$
$$\text{where } O' = O'_1 \cup \ldots \cup O'_n$$

$$\frac{}{\rho \bullet true \Downarrow true} \qquad \frac{}{\rho \bullet false \Downarrow false}$$

$$\frac{\rho \bullet e_1 \Downarrow true \quad \rho \bullet e_2 \Downarrow O}{\rho \bullet (if \ e_1 \ then \ e_2 \ else \ e_3) \Downarrow O} \qquad \frac{\rho \bullet e_1 \Downarrow false \quad \rho \bullet e_3 \Downarrow O}{\rho \bullet (if \ e_1 \ then \ e_2 \ else \ e_3) \Downarrow O}$$

Recall that a query is a function expression e with no free variables. The evaluation $\{\} \bullet e(O) \Downarrow O'$ of a query e applied to a complex object O under this operational semantics should be viewed as a *derivation tree* whose root is labeled by $\{\} \bullet e(O) \Downarrow O'$ and whose nodes are labeled by the rules above. Note that for a certain query e, the height of the tree is independent of O but its width may vary with O (see the rule for $\bigcup\{e_1 \mid x \in e_2\}$).

This operational semantics is extended to $\mathcal{NRC}(sru, \Sigma)$ by adding the following three evaluation rules for sru.

$$\frac{\rho \bullet e \Downarrow O}{\rho \bullet sru(u, f, e)(\{\}) \Downarrow O} \qquad \frac{\rho \bullet f(O) \Downarrow O'}{sru(u, f, e)(\{O\}) \Downarrow O'}$$

$$\frac{\rho \bullet sru(u, f, e)(\{O_1, \cdots, O_{\lfloor n/2 \rfloor}\}) \Downarrow O' \quad \rho \bullet sru(u, f, e)(\{O_{\lfloor n/2 \rfloor + 1}, \cdots, O_n\}) \Downarrow O'' \quad \rho \bullet u(O', O'') \Downarrow O \quad n \geq 2}{\rho \bullet sru(u, f, e)(\{O_1, \cdots, O_n\}) \Downarrow O}$$

Note that the evaluation of expressions in $\mathcal{NRC}(sru)$ is not deterministic due to the last rule for sru, which says that we may choose any way of splitting the set $\{O_1, \ldots, O_n\}$ into two roughly equal disjoint halves. However, the well-definedness preconditions on sru guarantee the uniqueness of the output. Also, in contrast to $\mathcal{NRC}(\Sigma)$, for queries e in $\mathcal{NRC}(sru)$, the height of the evaluation tree for $\{\} \bullet e(O) \Downarrow$ varies with O. But the height is bounded by a polylogarithm of the size of O.

Similarly, we extend the operational semantics for $\mathcal{NRC}(\Sigma)$ to $\mathcal{NRC}(sri, \Sigma)$ by adding the two rules below. Note that the height of an evaluation tree $\{\} \bullet e(O) \Downarrow$ is bounded by a polynomial of the size of O.

$$\frac{\rho \bullet e \Downarrow O}{\rho \bullet sri(i, e)(\{\}) \Downarrow O}$$

$$\frac{\rho \bullet sri(i, e)(\{O_2, \cdots, O_n\}) \Downarrow O \qquad \rho \bullet i(O_1, O) \Downarrow O'}{sri(i, e)(\{O_1, \ldots, O_n\}) \Downarrow O'}$$

Next, we define the size of complex objects. Up to a constant factor, $size(O)$ gives us the number of symbols needed in the notation for O, assuming one symbol suffices for any value at base types. Formally, $size(c) = 1$, for constants c of base types, $size(true) = size(false) = size(()) = 1$, $size(O_1, O_2) = size(O_1) + size(O_2) + 1$, and $size\{O_1, \cdots, O_n\} = size(O_1) + \cdots + size(O_n) + 1$.

We define $complex(T) = \max(\{size(O'') \mid O'' \text{ occurs in } T\})$, for some derivation tree T. For a query e and complex object O, the **complexity** of the evaluation $\{\} \bullet e(O) \Downarrow$ is defined to be: $complex(e, O) = \min(\{complex(T) \mid T \text{ is a}$ derivation tree of $\{\} \bullet e(O) \Downarrow O'\})$.

Since the height of a tree T is polynomially related to $complex(T)$, the latter gives a rough approximation of the space needed to compute $e(O)$, according to the choices embodied by T. Then $complex(e, O)$ gives us the smallest amount of space needed to evaluate $e(O)$, among all possible nondeterministic choices.

Now suppose there is a measure $\# : b \rightarrow \mathbf{N}$ on complex objects of base type b. Extend this measure to all types as follows:

$\#(c) = 0$, if $t_c \neq b$.
$\#(O_1, O_2) = \max(\#(O_1), \#(O_2))$.
$\#\{O_1, \cdots, O_n\} = \max(\#(O_1), \cdots, \#(O_n))$.

This measure is domain dependent and unrelated to the size of the complex objects. It only becomes interesting through its interaction with the external functions in Σ. Throughout this section, we assume that any external function p in Σ only increases the measure of its argument by a constant amount; that is, there is c_p such that for every O, we have $\#(p(O)) \leq c_p + \#(O)$. This means that, for any evaluation tree T of $e(O)$, we have $\#(e(O)) \leq \#(O) + c \cdot height(T)$ for some constant c, depending only on Σ, leading us to the following theorem:

Theorem 2. *Suppose that every primitive p in the language increases the measure of its input object only by a constant amount. Then the following hold:*

1. *For every query e in $\mathcal{NRC}(\Sigma)$ or $\mathcal{NRC}(powerset, \Sigma)$, there is a constant c_e such that for every complex object O, we have $\#(e(O)) \leq c_e + \#(O)$.*

2. *For every query e in $\mathcal{NRC}(sru, \Sigma)$, there are constants c_e and p_e such that for every complex object O, we have $\#(e(O)) \leq c_e \cdot \log^{p_e}(\text{complex}(e, O)) + \#(O)$.*

3. *For every query e in $\mathcal{NRC}(sri, \Sigma)$, there are constants c_e and p_e such that for every complex object O, we have $\#(e(O)) \leq c_e \cdot (\text{complex}(e, O))^{p_e} + \#(O)$.*

The intuition behind it is that the measure of complex objects may increase only by applying external functions, and that the number of successive applications of external functions is bounded by the depth of the derivation tree. Hence it suffices to observe that the depth of the derivation tree T for an expression e is: constant, when e is in $\mathcal{NRC}(\Sigma)$ or $\mathcal{NRC}(powerset, \Sigma)$; polylogarithmic in the complexity of T, when e is in $\mathcal{NRC}(sru, \Sigma)$; and polynomial in the complexity of T, when e is in $\mathcal{NRC}(sri, \Sigma)$. The function *powerset* is handled as an external function, and it preserves the measure of its input.

The bounds given above are also tight. In fact, we prove that in the presence of certain external functions, *sri* is strictly more efficient than *sru*. Indeed, suppose Σ contains two base types $\mathbf{N}$ and $\mathbf{D}$. $\mathbf{N}$ is the type of natural numbers, while $\mathbf{D}$ contains pairs (x, X), with $x \in \mathbf{N}$ and X a finite set of natural numbers. On these types we have an external function $i : \mathbf{N} \times \mathbf{D} \to \mathbf{D}$ and a constant $\mathbf{e} : \mathbf{D}$, defined by: $i(x, (y, X)) = \text{if } x \in X \text{ then } (y, X) \text{ else } (1 + y, \{x\} \cup X)$, $\mathbf{e} = (0, \{\})$. Note that, from the point of view of $\mathcal{NRC}(\Sigma)$, the values of type $\mathbf{D}$ are *atomic* values as they can only be accessed through i, $\mathbf{e}$, and the equality test. For example, $\pi_1(\mathbf{e})$ is *not* a well-defined expression in $\mathcal{NRC}(\Sigma)$ because it is illegally typed. Consider the query $f : \{\mathbf{N}\} \to \mathbf{D}$ in $\mathcal{NRC}(sri, \Sigma)$, $f \stackrel{\text{def}}{=} sri(i, \mathbf{e})$, with meaning $f(X) = (card(X), X)$, of polynomial (in fact linear) complexity.

Corollary 3. *Any expression in $\mathcal{NRC}(sru, \Sigma)$ equivalent to f has exponential complexity. Specifically, for any equivalent query g in $\mathcal{NRC}(sru, \Sigma)$, there are constants p and c such that the complexity of $g(X)$ is*

$$\text{complex}(g, X) = \Omega(2^{\sqrt[p]{card(X)/c}}) \ .$$

Proof. Define the measure of an object of type $\mathbf{D}$ to be $\#(n, X) = n$. By Theorem 2, we have $card(X) = \#(g(X)) \leq c_g \log^{p_g}(\text{complex}(g, X)) + 0$ (since $\#(X) = 0$). Hence, $\text{complex}(g, X) \geq 2^{\sqrt[p_g]{card(X)/c_g}}$. $\square$

This inefficiency is in contrast to the higher-order translation of Tannen and Subrahmanyam [7], which is both uniform and efficient (that is, preserves complexity classes). A similar situation was described by Colson [10]. He gave examples of functions that can be efficiently computed using primitive recursion when functional input and output are allowed, but cannot be efficiently computed when functional input and output are not allowed. This result, as well as that of Colson, indicates the important effects higher-order functions have on performance.

We should also remark on the *hom* operator of Machiavelli [17], called *dcr* elsewhere [20]. If $sru(u, f, e)$ is well defined, then so is $hom(u, f, e)$ and they compute the same function. The difference is that $hom(u, f, e)$ does not have to obey idempotence axiom. Instead, it is required to satisfy $hom(u, f, e)(O_1 \cup O_2) = u(hom(u, f, e)(O_1), hom(u, f, e)(O_2))$ when O_1 and O_2 are disjoint sets. Consequently, the translation given in Section 3 can also be used to implement sri in terms of hom. More interestingly, the proof of Theorem 2 holds also when hom is used instead of sru. In the view of the result that sri and dcr correspond to the complexity classes PTIME and NC respectively [20], Theorem 2 can be interpreted as saying that there is no uniform translation of a language for PTIME into a language for NC.

Since any uniform translation from sri to sru requires exponential space, it cannot be expressed only over flat relations. Let us denote with $\mathcal{NRC}^1$ the restriction of $\mathcal{NRC}$ to types of set height ≤ 1; it is known [6, 23] that $\mathcal{NRC}^1$ has the same expressive power as the relational algebra. Then, using Theorem 2, we can prove that, over the base type N with constant 0 and external function $succ$, sri is strictly more powerful than sru over flat relations:

Corollary 4. $\mathcal{NRC}^1(sru, \mathsf{N}, 0, succ) < \mathcal{NRC}^1(sri, \mathsf{N}, 0, succ)$.

This result is connected to a result by Immerman [14] stating that $QR[\log^k n] < FO + LFP$, for any $k \geq 1$. That result does not imply our result, since it is not obvious whether $\mathcal{NRC}^1(sru)$ is included in $\bigcup_k QR[\log^k n]$. However, his result is somewhat stronger than ours, because the presence of 0 and $succ$ is not needed.

5 Higher-Order Functions

Consider now an extension of $\mathcal{NRC}(sri, \Sigma)$ and $\mathcal{NRC}(sru, \Sigma)$ to languages with higher-order functions, which we call $\mathcal{HNRC}(sri, \Sigma)$ and $\mathcal{HNRC}(sru, \Sigma)$ respectively. The interesting aspect of these languages is that they are able to use structural recursion in order to compute functions, in the style of Tannen and Subrahmanian's translation of sri into sru with higher-order functions.

Since computing with sets needs an equality predicate on its elements, we do not allow the construction of sets of function in these higher-order languages. Hence we separate the types into two levels: the complex object types s, t and the functional types S, T:

$$s, t ::= b \mid unit \mid s \times t \mid \{s\}$$
$$S, T ::= s \mid t \mid S \times T \mid S \to T$$

The operations at the object level are the same those for $\mathcal{NRC}(sru)$ and $\mathcal{NRC}(sri)$ respectivley, but sru and sri are extended over functions as well:

$$\frac{e : T \quad i : s \times T \to T}{sri(i, e) : \{s\} \to T} \qquad \frac{e : T \quad f : s \to T \quad u : T \times T \to T}{sru(u, f, e) : \{s\} \to T}$$

Also, we have pairing, projections, lambda abstraction, and application at the function level:

$$\frac{e : T}{\lambda x.e : S \to T} \qquad \frac{e_1 : S \to T \quad e_2 : S}{e_1 e_2 : T}$$

$$\frac{e_1 : S \quad e_2 : T}{(e_1, e_2) : S \times T} \qquad \frac{e : S \times T}{\pi_1 e : S} \qquad \frac{e : S \times T}{\pi_2 e : T}$$

In this section we show that every first-order function definable in these higher-order languages is also definable in their first-order fragments. That is, if $f : s \to t$ can be expressed using some expression containing higher-order functions, then we can find another expression having no higher-order function to implement it. The proof requires several technical definitions.

Define the first-order "equivalent" of a type S to be $rel(S)$ as: $rel(unit) \overset{\text{def}}{=} unit$, $rel(\mathbf{B}) \overset{\text{def}}{=} \mathbf{B}$, $rel(b) \overset{\text{def}}{=} b$, $rel(S \times T) \overset{\text{def}}{=} rel(S) \times rel(T)$, $rel(\{s\}) \overset{\text{def}}{=} \{rel(s)\}$, and $rel(S \to T) \overset{\text{def}}{=} \{rel(S) \times rel(T)\}$. Note that if S is a complex object type, then $S = rel(S)$.

Define the "restriction" of the domain of a type S with respect to a finite set b_0 of objects of type b, $restrict_{b_0}(S) \subseteq rel(S)$, by: $restrict_{b_0}(unit) \overset{\text{def}}{=} \{()\}$, $restrict_{b_0}(\mathbf{B}) \overset{\text{def}}{=} \{true, false\}$, $restrict_{b_0}(b) \overset{\text{def}}{=} b_0$, $restrict_{b_0}(S \times T) \overset{\text{def}}{=} \{(x, y) \mid x \in restrict_{b_0}(S), y \in restrict_{b_0}(T)\}$, $restrict_{b_0}(\{s\}) \overset{\text{def}}{=} \{x \mid x \subseteq restrict_{b_0}(s)\}$, and $restrict_{b_0}(S \to T) \overset{\text{def}}{=} \{f \mid f \in \{restrict_{b_0}(S) \times restrict_{b_0}(T)\}$, f is functional$\}$. Note that if b_0 is given, then $restrict_{b_0}(S)$ can be expressed using $\mathcal{NRC}(sri)$, and that $restrict_{b_0}(S) : \{rel(S)\}$.

Define $restrict_{b_0}^{S} : S \to restrict_{b_0}(S)$ to be a partial function "restricting" an object $O : S$ with respect to a finite subset b_0 of objects of type b. Namely: $restrict_{b_0}^{unit}() \overset{\text{def}}{=} ()$; $restrict_{b_0}^{\mathbf{B}}(x) \overset{\text{def}}{=} x$; $restrict_{b_0}^{b}(x) \overset{\text{def}}{=} x$, if $x \in b_0$; $restrict_{b_0}^{S \times T}(x, y) \overset{\text{def}}{=} (restrict_{b_0}^{S}(x), restrict_{b_0}^{T}(y))$, if $restrict_{b_0}^{S}(x)$ and $restrict_{b_0}^{T}(y)$ are defined; $restrict_{b_0}^{\{s\}}(X) \overset{\text{def}}{=} \{restrict_{b_0}^{s}(x) \mid x \in X\}$, if $restrict_{b_0}^{s}(x)$ is defined for each $x \in X$; $restrict_{b_0}^{S \to T}(f) \overset{\text{def}}{=} \{(x, y) \mid x = restrict_{b_0}^{S}(x')$ and $y = restrict_{b_0}^{T}(y')$ where $y' = f(x')\}$, if the latter is functional. In all other cases $restrict_{b_0}^{S}(O)$ is undefined. Note that if $o \in restrict_{b_0}(s)$, then $restrict_{b_0}^{s}(o) = o$. For a first-order function $f : s \to t$, $restrict_{b_0}^{s \to t}(f)$ is precisely the graph of f restricted to b_0.

A function $p : s \to t$ is said to be **internal** in the sense of Hull [13] if $restrict_{b_0}^{t}(p(o)) = p(o)$ for all finite $b_0 \subseteq b$ for which $o = restrict_{b_0}^{s}(o)$. In other words, a function is internal if it does not generate new values.

Proposition 5. *Let all external primitives mentioned in Σ be internal. Let $e : S$ be an expression of $\mathcal{HNRC}(sri, \Sigma)$ with $x_1 : S_1, ..., x_n : S_n$ as free variables. Let b_0 be a finite subset of b that includes all constants $c : b$ occurring in e. Then there is an expression $rel(e) : rel(S)$ of $\mathcal{NRC}(sri, \Sigma)$ with $\bar{x}_1 : rel(S_1), ..., \bar{x}_n : rel(S_n)$ as free variables such that for all $O_1 : S_1, ..., O_n : S_n$, if $restrict_{b_0}^{S_i}(O_i)$ is defined for each i, then $restrict_{b_0}^{S}(e[O_1/x_1, ..., O_n/x_n])$ is defined and equals $rel(e)[restrict_{b_0}^{S_1}(O_1)/\bar{x}_1, ..., restrict_{b_0}^{S_n}(O_n)/\bar{x}_n]$.*

The main idea used in the proof is that hereditarily-finite functions can be represented by hereditarily-finite sets, and hence we can simulate any computation at higher order with some computation over complex objects. So for any signature satisfying the same conditions, we conclude that using higher-order functions at intermediate stages has no influence on the class of first-order functions expressible in our languages.

Theorem 6. *Let all external primitives mentioned in Σ be internal. Suppose $f : s \to t$ is a first-order function in $\mathcal{HNRC}(sri, \Sigma)$, or $\mathcal{HNRC}(sru, \Sigma)$. Then f is also expressible in $\mathcal{NRC}(sri, \Sigma)$, or $\mathcal{NRC}(sru, \Sigma)$ respectively.*

Proof. We prove the case for $\mathcal{HNRC}(sri, \Sigma)$ and $\mathcal{NRC}(sri, \Sigma)$; the other case is similar. Suppose $f : s \to t$ is defined by $\lambda x.e$. Let b_0 be treated as a new constant of type $\{b\}$. Apply the proposition above to e to get $rel(e)$ with $\bar{x}$ as its only free variable and with b_0 appearing as a constant. Let $C : \{b\}$ be the collection of constants $c : b$ appearing in e. Let $D^s : s \to \{b\}$ be the function that extracts objects of type b from its input. This function is readily definable in $\mathcal{NRC}$. Since s and t are complex object types, we know that $s = rel(s)$ and $t = rel(t)$. Then for any $o : s$, we have $f(o) = rel(e)[o/\bar{x}, (C \cup D^s(o))/b_0]$. So $\lambda \bar{x}.rel(e)[(C \cup D^s(\bar{x}))/b_0]$ is an expression in $\mathcal{NRC}(sri, \Sigma)$ implementing f. $\square$

However, in the presence of certain external functions that are not internal, higher-order functions give more expressive power. Indeed, consider the signature Σ containing the base type N and the external functions $+ : \mathsf{N} \times \mathsf{N} \to \mathsf{N}$, $\dot{-} : \mathsf{N} \times \mathsf{N} \to \mathsf{N}$, and $gen : \mathsf{N} \to \{\mathsf{N}\}$. $+$ is the usual addition operation. $\dot{-}$ is the one-sided subtraction operation; that is, $m \dot{-} n = m - n$ if $m > n$ and $m \dot{-} n = 0$ otherwise. gen is the function $gen(n) = \{0, \ldots, n\}$. Then we have

Theorem 7. *1. The class of functions $f : \mathsf{N} \times \ldots \times \mathsf{N} \to \mathsf{N}$ representable in $\mathcal{NRC}(sri, \Sigma)$ coincides with the class of primitive recursive functions [15].*
2. All functions $f : \mathsf{N} \times \ldots \times \mathsf{N} \to \mathsf{N}$ expressible in Godel's system T [12] are also expressible in $\mathcal{HNRC}(sri, \Sigma)$. Hence $\mathcal{HNRC}(sri, \Sigma)$ can express the Ackermann function [12].

Hence, for this particular Σ, $\mathcal{HNRC}(sri, \Sigma)$ is strictly more expressive than $\mathcal{NRC}(sri, \Sigma)$. More, Theorem 1 also implies that $\mathcal{HNRC}(sru, \Sigma)$ is strictly more expressive than $\mathcal{NRC}(sru, \Sigma)$.

6 Conclusion and Future Work

In summary, we presented three results in this paper. First, we exhibited a uniform first-order translation of sri into sru. Second, we proved that any such translation must create very large intermediate data and hence caused a degradation in performance. Third, we proved that every first-order function definable using higher-order structural recursion is also definable using first-order structural recursion. In the course of this work, we have observed several interesting phenomena that we would like to pursue further:

As concluded in Section 4, the ability to define higher-order functions leads to considerably more efficient programs. However, such functions are often excluded from query languages as can be seen from the survey of Abiteboul and Kanellakis [1]. As performance is an important factor in database queries, we should begin to pay serious attention to the use of higher-order functions in query languages.

As remarked in Section 4, sru can be replaced by hom everywhere. Also, there exists a uniform translation from hom to sru, namely going through sri, but which is inefficient. Does a result similar to Theorem 2 hold between sru and hom, stating that *any* uniform translation from hom to sru is inefficient?

In our search for the proof in Section 3, we found that the greatest difficulty was in discovering a u which is both idempotent and associative. For example, let $A \circ B$ be composition of binary relations, and consider the following expression for transitive closure: $tc(R) \stackrel{\text{def}}{=} hom(u, f, e)(R)$, where $e \stackrel{\text{def}}{=} \{\}$, $f(x) \stackrel{\text{def}}{=} R$, and $u(A, B) \stackrel{\text{def}}{=} A \cup B \cup ((A \cup B) \circ (A \cup B))$. Replacing hom with sru will not give us a correct expression, because u is not idempotent. In fact we do not know how to define an efficient transitive closure function using sru. We conjecture that there is no efficient expression for transitive closure in $\mathcal{NRC}(sru)$.

Acknowledgements We thank Peter Buneman and Val Tannen, they provided the inspiration for this paper, as well as some useful simplification. We thank Leonid Libkin for discussions. Suciu is supported by National Science Foundation grants CCR-90-57570 and IRI-90-04137. Wong is supported by Army Reseach Office grant DAALO3-89-C-0031-PRIME. This research was carried out when Wong was at the University of Pennsylvania.

References

1. S. Abiteboul and P. Kanellakis. Database theory column: Query languages for complex object databases. *SIGACT News*, 21(3):9–18, 1990.
2. S. Abiteboul and C. Beeri. On the power of languages for the manipulation of complex objects. In *Proceedings of International Workshop on Theory and Applications of Nested Relations and Complex Objects*, Darmstadt, 1988.
3. S. Abiteboul and V. Vianu. Generic computation and its complexity. In *Proceedings of 23rd ACM Symposium on the Theory of Computing*, 1991.
4. F. Bancilhon, T. Briggs, S. Khoshafian, and P. Valduriez. A powerful and simple database language. In *Proceedings of International Conference on Very Large Data Bases*, pages 97–105, 1988.
5. R. S. Bird and P. Wadler. *Introduction to Functional Programming*. Prentice-Hall International, 1988.
6. V. Breazu-Tannen, P. Buneman, and S. Naqvi. Structural recursion as a query language. In *Proceedings of 3rd International Workshop on Database Programming Languages, Naphlion, Greece*, pages 9–19. Morgan Kaufmann, August 1991.
7. V. Breazu-Tannen and R. Subrahmanyam. Logical and computational aspects of programming with Sets/Bags/Lists. In *LNCS 510: Proceedings of 18th International Colloquium on Automata, Languages, and Programming, Madrid, Spain, July 1991*, pages 60–75.

8. V. Breazu-Tannen, P. Buneman, and L. Wong. Naturally embedded query languages. In *LNCS 646: Proceedings of 4th International Conference on Database Theory, Berlin, Germany, October, 1992*, pages 140–154.

9. L. S. Colby. A recursive algebra for nested relations. *Information Systems*, 15(5):567–582, 1990.

10. L. Colson. About primitive recursive algorithms. *Theoretical Computer Science*, 83:57–69, 1991.

11. P. L. Curien. The $\lambda\rho$-calculus: An abstract framework for environment machines. Technical Report URA 725, Laboratoire d'Informatique, Departement de Mathematiques et d'Informatique, Ecole Normale Superieure, 45 Rue d'Ulm, 75230 Paris Cedex 05, France, 1988.

12. J.-Y. Girard, Y. Lafont, and P. Taylor. *Proofs and Types*, volume 7 of *Combridge Tracts in Theoretical Computer Science*. Cambridge University Press, Cambridge, 1989.

13. R. Hull. Relative information capacity of simple relational database schemata. *SIAM Journal of Computing*, 15(3):865–886, August 1986.

14. N. Immerman. Length of predicate calculus formulas as a new complexity measure. In *Proceedings of 20th Symposium on Foundations of Computer Science, San Juan, Puerto Rico, October 1979*, pages 337–347.

15. L. Libkin and L. Wong. Some properties of query languages for bags. In *Proceedings of 4th International Workshop on Database Programming Languages, New York, August 1993*, pages 97–114.

16. P. Odifreddi. *Classical Recursion Theory*. North Holland, 1989.

17. A. Ohori, P. Buneman, and V. Breazu-Tannen. Database programming in Machiavelli, a polymorphic language with static type inference. In *Proceedings of ACM-SIGMOD International Conference on Management of Data*, pages 46–57, Portland, Oregon, June 1989.

18. H.-J. Schek and M. H. Scholl. The relational model with relation-valued attributes. *Information Systems*, 11(2):137–147, 1986.

19. D. Stemple and T. Sheard. A recursive base for database programming. In *LNCS 504: Next Generation Information System Technology*, pages 311–332, Berlin, 1990.

20. D. Suciu and V. Breazu-Tannen. A query language for NC. In *Proceedings of 13th ACM Symposium on Principles of Database Systems*, pages 167–178, Minneapolis, Minnesota, May 1994.

21. D. Suciu and J. Paredaens. Any algorithm in the complex object algebra needs exponential space to compute transitive closure. In *Proceedings of 13th ACM Symposium on Principles of Database Systems*, pages 201–209, Minneapolis, Minnesota, May 1994.

22. S. J. Thomas and P. C. Fischer. Nested relational structures. In *Advances in Computing Research: The Theory of Databases*, pages 269–307, London, England, 1986. JAI Press.

23. L. Wong. Normal forms and conservative properties for query languages over collection types. In *Proceedings of 12th ACM Symposium on Principles of Database Systems*, pages 26–36, Washington, D. C., May 1993.

Δ-Languages for Sets and Sub-PTIME Graph Transformers*

Vladimir Sazonov and Alexei Lisitsa

Program Systems Institute of Russian Acad. of Sci.,
Pereslavl-Zalessky, 152140, Russia
e-mail: {sazonov,lisitsa}@logic.botik.yaroslavl.su

Abstract. This paper discusses three successively extending versions of a set theoretic Δ-language, as a prototype for "nested" data bases query language. Corresponding finite set operations (data base queries) may be realized in NLOGSPACE under representation of sets by extensional well-founded (acyclic) graphs. (In a previous work for another version of Δ-language an exact correspondence to PTIME-computability was established.) Moreover, each of the mentioned versions of the language is faithfully characterized in terms of corresponding three classes of the graph transformers, the last one being just all transformers definable in the First Order Logic with Transitive Closure operator. For simplicity we are considering here the case of "pure" hereditarily-finite sets, i.e. sets without atoms involved. They are naturally linear ordered, however this order is problematic to formally define in our present case (unlike the case corresponding to PTIME). The related question whether the last class of transformers and corresponding class of queries over HF coincide with all NLOGSPACE-computable ones is left open in this paper.

1 Introduction

Computability over sets (of tuples of sets of tuples of sets, etc.) or over "complex objects" is at present rather popular subject especially in connection with "nested" data bases. There may be distinguished two directions: *typed* (e.g. [1, 10, 15, 18]) and *untyped* (cf. [5, 6, 21, 24, 25, 27, 29]) cases. The first is based on the *direct product* and *powerset* type constructs and presupposes, at least at the beginning, the hyperexponential (i.e. Kalmar elementary) computational complexity. Some additional special efforts are necessary to find restrictions (on the types height, ranges of variables, density/sparsity of data wrt types [10]) to obtain more *tractable* query languages. The second direction is not concerned with exponentiation because it is based on the notion HF of Hereditarily-Finite Sets which may be (of course, non-categorically) axiomatized without any reference (both explicitly and implicitly) to the powerset operation. The tractability of corresponding Δ-languages considered in [24, 25, 27] and below is achieved more straightforward. Also some approach to types within this framework was outlined in [27]. So these two directions seem convergent.

---

* Supported by Russian Foundation of Fundamental Investigations (project 93-011-16016) and partially by INTAS (project 93-972).

Previously considered versions of Δ-language described the class of all PTIME-computable operations over HF-sets wrt to any given (regular) coding of sets. One of these codings is a representation of sets by vertices of *well-founded* graphs[2] with edges corresponding to the membership relation $x \in y$. (It is still unclear which coding and which version of Δ-language are most genuine; cf. Concluding Remarks in [27]).

Note, that analogous representation of sets (of sets of sets ...) by graphs was used also in [5, 6] and [2]. However, in [2] it is considered rather unusual set theory with Antifoundation Axiom which says that arbitrary, even *non-well-founded* graph with a distinguished vertex denotes a uniquely defined set in an *anti*-well-founded universe of sets[3]. We consider corresponding approach in [28].

We confine the discussion on the relation of HF-sets to data bases by the above references and by a general note that nested and HF-like complex data structures seem conceptually more natural to directly represent the states of data bases than e.g. natural numbers or finite strings of symbols or even "flat" relational structures which are more low-level notions (cf. [27] for more details.) This paper is mainly concerned with computational and complexity-theoretic aspect of querying over HF, namely with an attempt to capture the class of (N)LOGSPACE-computable queries.

Remember that the universe HF is defined inductively as a least class of sets such that $\emptyset \in$ HF and if $x_1, \ldots, x_n \in$ HF, $n \geq 0$, then $\{x_1, \ldots, x_n\} \in$ HF.

Of course, for real data base applications we have to consider HF-universe with urelements (or atoms) as in [27]. However, for simplicity we will restrict ourselves here to the "pure" sets.

The key notion for the whole approach is the following definition of (say, PTIME- or LOGSPACE-) *computability* of any operation (query) $Q :$ HF $\rightarrow$ HF where $Q(s) = a$ means for any $s, a \in$ HF that s is a data base *state* and a is an *answer* to the query Q asked about the state s. Given any encoding $\nu :$ Codes $\rightarrow$ HF of states (answers) we say that Q is (PTIME-, etc-) computable wrt ν if the following diagram

$$
\begin{array}{ccc}
\text{HF} & \xrightarrow{Q} & \text{HF} \\
\nu \uparrow & & \uparrow \nu \\
\text{Codes} & \xrightarrow{\tilde{Q}} & \text{Codes}
\end{array}
$$

commutes for some (PTIME-, etc-) computable transformation $\tilde{Q}$ between codes. In other words, for all $c \in$ Codes $Q(\nu(c)) = \nu(\tilde{Q}(c))$ holds.

A general theory of computability over abstract domains with respect to some encoding is developed in [7] as so called numbering theory (with Codes = Natural Numbers)

---

[2] i.e. graphs without infinite chains of edges (vertices) like $\ldots \rightarrow v_{n+1} \rightarrow v_n \rightarrow \ldots \rightarrow v_1 \rightarrow v_0$; for finite graphs, which we actually will consider, this means just *acyclicity* property.

[3] In such an unusual universe there exists a (unique) set Ω satisfying identity $\Omega = \{\Omega\}$ as well as many other more involved analogous examples.

An important example of Codes is the class of all finite acyclic *pointed graphs* (pg), i.e. graphs G with a distinguished point (vertex) p in each. Then let $\nu = C$ be Mostowski's *collapsing* operation which assign to each pg a set $C(G, p) \in HF$ in such a way that

$$C(G, p) = \{C(G, p') : p' \to_G p \text{ for some (predecessor to } p) \text{ point } p' \text{ of } G \} \ .$$

In particular, if p has no predecessors then $C(G, p) = \emptyset$. If, e.g., G consists just of three edges $p_1 \to p_2 \to p_3$ and $p_1 \to p_3$ then $C(G, p_1) = \emptyset, C(G, p_2) = \{\emptyset\}$ and $C(G, p_3) = \{\emptyset, \{\emptyset, \}\}$, etc.

Unfortunately, it is rather tedious and expensive to recognize if any two vertices p_1, p_2 of a well-founded graph G are denoting the same set in the universe HF, i.e. $C(G, p_1) = C(G, p_2)$. (This computational problem proves to be in P-TIME but perhaps not in (N)LOGSPACE $\subseteq$ PTIME due to its P-completeness [6].) Such a procedure was one of the basic tools of PTIME realization of corresponding Δ-language. That is why we are attempting here to find a reasonable graph transformation approach for realizing a version of Δ-language without so numerous identifications of vertices denoting the same set.

In particular, we restrict ourselves to *extensional* [4] acyclic graphs where no such identification is possible, and define some notions of "computable" transformation of such graphs (what may be considered as a kind of *evolving algebra* approach [12]) allowing to effectively (in fact, in (N)LOGSPACE) realize corresponding versions of the Δ-language. Our initial aim to find such a Δ-language and encoding of sets which would correspond *exactly* to (N)LOGSPACE is still unresolved and probably have no good solution. However, it seems important to make more clear the situation and we hope that the results obtained here will be helpful. In fact, it is presented below in Theorems 1–3 an exact correspondence between some three versions of the Δ-language and corresponding three classes of computable transformations of the extensional well-founded graphs. In particular we consider *computability as definability* in FO*, the first order language augmented with the transitive closure construct (cf. [13]). Unfortunately, the third version of the Δ-language corresponding to FO*-transformations is somewhat artificial one. This witnesses that an appropriate defining sub-PTIME-computability over HF is more problematic task than in the case of "flat" data bases [11, 13, 15].

The origins of Δ-language are as follows. A rather weak but natural and elegant class of set theoretic operations, so called *rudimentary* or *basic* operations was considered in [9, ?] with corresponding *Basic Set Theory* [9]. Analogous "predicative" versions of set theory was discussed in [8]. Such a set theory is quite sufficient for many elementary and every-day mathematical considerations. These basic operations constitute a proper subclass of *Primitive Recursive Set Operations* considered in [17]. It was shown in [9] that the basic two valued operations exactly correspond to Δ_0-formulas [19] in the language $\{\in\}$. It was proved in [24, 25] that provably-total Σ-definable operations of KP_0,

---

[4] this is equivalent to saying that any two different points $p_1 \neq p_2$ in G must have different sets of predecessors, i.e. $\{p : p \to_G p_1\} \neq \{p : p \to_G p_2\}$.

Kripke-Platek set theory without foundation axiom, coincide with these basic (rudimentary) operations. Moreover, it was proved in [25] that KP_0, which corresponds to the basic set operations, is nevertheless a conservative extension of the only Extensionality Axiom relative to Δ_0-formulas. It follows that basic operations and Basic Set Theory may be considered as sufficiently reach from one point of view and also as too weak from another.

That is why it was attempted in [24, 25, 27] to extend the class of basic operations and also the Basic Set Theory to more reach versions called there Δ-language and Δ-set theory or Bounded Set Theory (by some analogy with Bounded Arithmetic; e.g. [4, 20, 22]). Bounded Set Theory and its class of Δ-definable or, equivalently, provably computable operations over sets is not reducible to something such weak as Δ_0 and, as was said above, exactly corresponds to PTIME-computability. In this paper we consider more special version of Δ-language under the same name.

2 Δ-Language of Set Theoretic Operations

Define inductively Δ-*formulas* and Δ-*terms* by the clauses

$$\langle \Delta\text{-terms}\rangle ::= \langle\text{variables}\rangle \mid \{a,b\} \mid \cup a \mid \mathrm{TC}(a) \mid \{t(x) : x \in a \& \varphi(x)\}$$

$$\langle \Delta\text{-formulas}\rangle ::= a \in b \mid \varphi\&\psi \mid \varphi \vee \psi \mid \neg\varphi \mid \forall x \in a\varphi(x) \mid \exists x \in a\varphi(x)$$

where φ and ψ are any Δ-formulas, a, b and t are any Δ-terms and $x \notin FV(a)$ is a variable not free in a. Then Δ_0-*formulas* are defined as those Δ-formulas involving only atomic terms (i.e. just variables).

We will use Δ-terms and formulas both as syntactic objects and as denotations of their values in HF. For example, Δ-separation $\{x \in a : \varphi(x)\}$ for $\varphi \in \Delta$ gives the set of all x in the set a for which $\varphi(x)$ holds and is a partial case of the construct $\{t(x) : x \in a\&\varphi(x)\}$ = "the set of all values of $t(x)$ such that ...". Also $x \in \{a,b\}$ iff $x = a$ or $x = b$, $x \in \cup a$ iff $\exists z \in a(x \in z)$ and $x \in \mathrm{TC}(y)$ is equivalent to $x \in^* y$ where $\in^*$ is transitive closure of the membership relation $\in$ on HF, i.e. $x \in^* y$ iff $x \in x_1 \in x_2 \in \ldots \in x_n \in y$ for some $n \geq 0$ and $x_1, \ldots, x_n$ in HF. The meaning of logical symbols & ("and"), $\vee$ ("or"), $\neg$ ("not"), $\forall$ ("for all"), $\exists$ ("exists") is well known. Note, that Δ-formulas involve only *bounded* quantification $\forall x \in a$ and $\exists x \in a$. That is why, according to traditions of mathematical logic, we use the name Δ for our language. These bounded quantifiers have the same meaning as unbounded ones except the variable x ranges only over the set a.

It follows that any Δ-term $t(\bar{x})$ defines a set-theoretic operation $\lambda\bar{x}.t(\bar{x})$: $\mathrm{HF}^n \to \mathrm{HF}$. Let us identify the values **true** and **false** respectively with sets $\emptyset$ and $\{\emptyset\}$. Therefore, $(\Delta\text{-})$formulas may be also considered as a kind of set theoretic terms (operations).

Let us denote by $\lambda\bar{y} \in a.t(\bar{y})$ the graph of a function $t(\bar{y})$ of arguments $\bar{y}$ restricted to the set a. More formally, this is the set in HF of ordered pairs

$\{\langle\langle\bar{y}\rangle, z\rangle : \bar{y} \in a \& z = t(\bar{y})\}$. As usual, ordered singletons, pairs, triples, etc. are defined as $\langle u \rangle \rightleftharpoons u, \langle u, v \rangle \rightleftharpoons \{\{u\}\{u, v\}\}$ and $\langle u, v, w \rangle \rightleftharpoons \langle\langle u, v \rangle, w \rangle$, etc. It follows that $\langle\langle\bar{y}\rangle, z\rangle = \langle\bar{y}, z\rangle$.

For any list of Δ-terms and Δ-formulas $\bar{t}(\bar{y}) = t_0(\bar{y}), t_1(\bar{y}), \ldots, t_n(\bar{y})$ we abbreviate

$$\lambda\bar{y} \in a.[\bar{t}(\bar{y})] \rightleftharpoons \lambda\bar{y} \in a.t_0(\bar{y}), \lambda\bar{y} \in a.t_1(\bar{y}), \ldots, \lambda\bar{y} \in a.t_n(\bar{y}) \ .$$

Note, that by omitting transitive closure operation TC in the definition of Δ-language we obtain a language equivalent to the class of *basic* [9] operations or to *rudimentary* [16] operations. Also, our using the term Δ is not completely fixed in our different papers. In general, it denotes some reasonable, still "bounded" extension of the class of basic (rudimentary) operations. For example, the unrestricted *powerset operation* is considered as intuitively "unbounded".

3 Computability over HF via Graph Transformers

Let us represent any n-tuple of sets $\bar{\tau} \in HF$ by any $(n + 1)$-tuple $\langle T; \bar{\tau}\rangle$ where $\bar{\tau} \in T \in HF$ and T is a *transitive set* (i.e. such that $u \in v \in T$ implies $u \in T$ for all u and v). Moreover, let us consider any such T as a graph with edges to be all the pairs $\langle u, v \rangle$ such that $u \in v \in T$. Then $\langle T; \bar{\tau}\rangle$ is a graph with distinguished vertices $\bar{\tau}$. Evidently, application of collapsing operation from the Introduction to this graph and its distinguished vertices $\bar{\tau}$ will give the same HF-sets $\bar{\tau}$ as the result.

Let we are given also any (general or restricted) notion of *computable* transformation of such tuples (graphs) $\langle T; \bar{\tau}\rangle \mapsto \langle T'; \bar{\tau}'\rangle$. Then we say that $F : HF^n \rightarrow HF$ is called (correspondingly) *computable*, if there exists computable transformation $\tilde{F} : \langle T; \bar{\tau}\rangle \mapsto \langle T'; \tau'\rangle$ such that independently of any transitive $T \ni \bar{\tau}$ we have $\tau' = F(\bar{\tau})$.

This definition of computability over HF is analogous to that based on the commutative diagram in the Introduction with C instead of ν. Note, that they slightly differ because we are considering here only well-founded extensional graphs (i.e. those arising from transitive sets T). This difference is inessential for the case of PTIME-computability, however it is indeed crucial for the case of (N)LOGSPACE. Our aim is to characterize Δ'-definable operations $F : HF^n \rightarrow HF$ for various versions Δ' of Δ-language as those computable in an appropriate sense via corresponding transformations of the above kind. In particular, we are interested just in (N)LOGSPACE-computable transformations. (PTIME-computable case have been considered in [24, 25, 27].)

In the next two sections we consider some class of simple DLOGSPACE-computable transformations which exactly correspond to the Δ-language. Then both the class of transformations and the Δ-language will be extended twice inside NLOGSPACE with preserving this correspondence, the last step giving rise to transformations definable by the First-Order Logic with Transitive Closure operator.

4 Simply Computable Graph Transformers

Given any first-order formula $\varphi(x, \bar{y})$, $\bar{y} = y_0, \ldots, y_s$, possibly with unbounded quantifiers, in the language $\{\in, \in^*\}$ or, shortly, $\in^*$-*formula*, define corresponding *restricted powerset operation* applied to any transitive set T

$$\mathcal{P}_\varphi(T) \rightleftharpoons \{\{x \in T : \varphi^T(x, \bar{y})\} : \bar{y} \in T\}$$

where φ^T is the result of replacing all quantifiers $\forall v$ and $\exists v$, respectively, by $\forall v \in T$ and $\exists v \in T$ with the natural interpretation in T of the language $\{\in, \in^*\}$. The restricted powerset consists of all subsets *definable* by the formula $\varphi(x, \bar{y})$ of x with parameters $\bar{y}$ ranging over T. This formula or, more exactly, the closed *abstract* $\lambda x \bar{y}. \varphi$ defines also an *elementary transformation of the first kind* of arbitrary transitive sets T with any sequence of distinguished elements $\bar{\tau} = \tau_0, \ldots, \tau_k$ of a fixed length $k + 1$ for the input set T and of the length $k + 2$ for the output set $T' = T \cup \mathcal{P}_\varphi(T)$

$$[\![\lambda x \bar{y}. \varphi]\!] : \langle T; \bar{\tau} \rangle \mapsto \langle T \cup \mathcal{P}_\varphi(T); \{x \in T : \varphi^T(x, \bar{\tau})\}, \bar{\tau} \rangle \ .$$

Here $\{x \in T : \varphi^T(x, \bar{\tau})\} \in \mathcal{P}_\varphi(T)$ is an additional distinguished element defined by formula φ, and we agree that τ_i are substituted for y_i and that in the case the length of $\bar{\tau}$ is less than the length of $\bar{y}$ the empty set $\emptyset \in T$ is substituted for the extra y_i's.

Define *elementary transformation of the second kind* as replacing the distinguished values $\bar{\tau} = \tau_0, \tau_1, \ldots, \tau_k$ with a fixed k by any finite sequence $\sigma_{\bar{j}}(\bar{\tau}) = \tau_{j_0}, \tau_{j_1}, \ldots, \tau_{j_m}$ of these values in T defined by a fixed sequence of numbers $\bar{j} = \langle j_0, j_1, \ldots, j_m \rangle$, $j_0, j_1, \ldots, j_m \leq k$:

$$[\![\bar{j}]\!] : \langle T; \bar{\tau} \rangle \mapsto \langle T; \sigma_{\bar{j}}(\bar{\tau}) \rangle \ .$$

Then any finite composition of n elementary transformations is called *simply computable* (in this restricted sense) *transformation* in n steps. For example, the transformation

$$\langle T; \bar{\tau} \rangle \mapsto \langle T \cup \mathcal{P}_\varphi(T); \bar{\tau} \rangle$$

is evidently computable in two steps. Often, by mentioning the transformations of the first kind we, in fact, mean just this slightly more simple one. This transformation is rather natural if we just need to use some values $\{x \in T : \varphi^T(x, \bar{y})\}$, $\bar{y} \in T$, in an extension of T for further computation steps, but *not as the distinguished* ones. The reader himself may easily decide what exactly is meant in each concrete situation. Moreover, it is often unreasonable to mention explicitly (trivial) elementary transformations of the second kind. Our computable transformations will usually begin with a "saturation" of the initial T by suitable sets and then by distinguishing some of them.

Note, that because we interpret any $\in^*$ formula in transitive sets T the *abbreviation* $x = y \rightleftharpoons \forall v(v \in x \leftrightarrow v \in y)$ gives just the ordinary equality relation in T. We shall often use it. For other kinds of formulas with parameters in T

it depends on T whether their truth values in T coincide with the *expected* ones. Therefore, we usually should take care of including in T sufficiently many elements to guarantee this coincidence. For this purpose we will use compositions of (any n copies of) the elementary transformation defined by the abstract $\lambda x u v.(x = u \vee x = v)$. Such a finite composition $[\![\lambda x u v.(x = u \vee x = v)]\!]^n$ is called *a saturation transformations*. Frequently $n = 3$ will suffice.

For example, this transformation will introduce in T all unordered pairs $\{u, v\}$, $u, v \in T$ (because $\{u, v\} = \{x \in T : x = u \vee x = v\}$) as well as ordered pairs $\langle u, v \rangle = \{\{u\}, \{u, v\}\}$, triples $\langle\langle u, v\rangle, w\rangle$ and more long tuples for sufficiently large n.

Evidently, any simply computable transformation $\langle T; \bar\tau \rangle \mapsto \langle T'; \bar\tau' \rangle$ as a finite composition is Δ-definable, $F(\langle T; \bar\tau\rangle) = \langle T'; \bar\tau'\rangle$ (actually without using TC in Δ-operation $F : HF \to HF$ if $\in^*$ is not involved in $\in^*$-formulas defining the above transformation).

Also note, that such simply computable transformations may be considered as transformations over arbitrary *well-founded extensional* graphs with some distinguished vertices. (Remember, that a directed graph is called extensional if different vertices have different sets of predecessors.) The vertices and edges of any such graph correspond to elements of some unique transitive (well-founded) set T and, respectively, to the pairs $\langle u, v \rangle$ s.t. $u \in v \in T$. In fact, this is an *isomorphism*.

Then elementary transformation of the first kind adds a number of new vertices and edges to the given graph G which must (evidently) correspond to the sets $\{x \in G : G \models \varphi(x, \bar y)\}$, $\bar y \in G$, and, respectively, to the membership relation to any such set. Some of these new vertices should be *identified* (literally, or by the corresponding *congruence*[5] relation) one with another and possibly with the old vertices of G, if they correspond to the same set in the universe under consideration. This can be considered as a kind of real computation. Note, that if $\in^*$ is indeed involved in formulas defining transformations then it is reasonable for more *effective* realization to consider graphs G with *two* kinds of edges, corresponding both to $\in$ and $\in^*$ relations[6]. Then $\in^*$ relation in the resulting graph of any elementary transformation could be easily computed from the old version of $\in^*$ by introducing several additional $\in^*$-edges going to new vertices without the tedious direct computing the transitive closure of the resulting version of $\in$; just use the *first-order* formula $y \in^* y' \leftrightarrow y \in y' \vee \exists h.(y \in^* h \& h \in y')$ which allows to compute new version of $\in^*$ by new version of $\in$ and the old version of $\in^*$. Further considerations of this section deal with the computational and descriptional complexity of this procedure and illustrate above sketchy description.

It may be proved that each simply computable transformation of such graphs is DLOGSPACE-computable under a natural coding of graphs by 0-1-matrices. Moreover, these transformations prove to be FO-*computable* (*definable*) because

---

[5] a congruence on a first-order structure is such an equivalence relation which preserves (or commutes with) all predicates and operations of that structure.

[6] what may be considered as a *materialization* of $\in^*$ [3].

they may be simulated by First-Order $\in^*$-formulae defining corresponding graphs over suitable cartesian power $|G|^n$, where $|G|$ is the set of vertices of the graph G with two kinds of edges (isomorphic to initial transitive set $\langle T, \in, \in^* \rangle$) modulo a definable congruence relation on $|G|^n$ (corresponding to the identification of vertices, as mentioned above). More precisely, consider the language $\langle =, \in, \in^*, \emptyset, \{\emptyset\}, \bar{\tau} \rangle$ with $=, \in, \in^*$ interpreted as binary relations with $=$ a congruence relation wrt $\in$ and $\in^*$ and the constants $\emptyset, \{\emptyset\}, \bar{\tau} = \tau_0, \ldots, \tau_k$ interpreted respectively as the "empty-set"-object, the "singleton-set"-object and arbitrary "set"-objects of the intended structure (graph) G. (Without restriction of generality we may consider that transitive sets T considered above always contains elements $\emptyset$ and $\{\emptyset\}$.) Our simply computable transformations may be simulated by FO-formulas in this language denoted as $\bar{x} \approx \bar{y}, E(\bar{x}; \bar{y}), E^*(\bar{x}; \bar{y})$ and a list $\bar{\pi}_0, \ldots, \bar{\pi}_m$ of tuples consisting of the constants $\emptyset, \{\emptyset\}, \tau_0, \ldots, \tau_k$. All these relations $\approx, E$ and E^* are considered as binary relations over tuples $\bar{x}, \bar{y}$ with $\approx$ be a congruence wrt E and E^* be the transitive closure of E. The list of tuples of constants $\bar{\pi}_0, \ldots, \bar{\pi}_m$ corresponds to the distinguished elements of the output structure (graphs).

Let, for example, we have one step transformation $[\![\lambda x \bar{y}. \varphi(x, \bar{y})]\!]$ with $\bar{y} = y_0, \ldots, y_s$. Take $|G|^n$ for $n = s + 2$ and assume that any n-tuple $\langle \bar{y}, z \rangle \in |G|^n$ denotes an "old" element $y_0 \in |G|$ if $z = \emptyset$ and $\langle \bar{y}, z \rangle$ denotes a "new" object $\bar{y}$ if $z \neq \emptyset$. Intuitively, any "new" object $\bar{y}$ represents the set $\{x \in |G| : G \models \varphi(x, \bar{y})\}$. Bearing in mind this interpretation of the tuples $\bar{y}, z$ define formulas E, E^* and $\approx$ as natural analogies and extensions of the relations $\in, \in^*$, and $=$:

$$E(\bar{y}, z; \bar{y}', z') \rightleftharpoons (z = z' = \emptyset \,\&\, y_0 \in y_0') \,\vee$$
$$(z = \emptyset \,\&\, z' \neq \emptyset \,\&\, \varphi(y_0, \bar{y}')) \,\vee$$
$$(z \neq \emptyset \,\&\, z' = \emptyset \,\&\, \exists u (\forall x (x \in u \leftrightarrow \varphi(x, \bar{y})) \,\&\, u \in y_0')) \,\vee$$
$$(z \neq \emptyset \,\&\, z' \neq \emptyset \,\&\, \exists u (\forall x (x \in u \leftrightarrow \varphi(x, \bar{y})) \,\&\, \varphi(u, \bar{y}'))) \ ,$$

$$\bar{y}, z \approx \bar{y}', z' \rightleftharpoons \forall \bar{u} v (E(\bar{u}, v; \bar{y}, z) \leftrightarrow E(\bar{u}, v; \bar{y}', z')) \ ,$$

$$E^*(\bar{y}, z; \bar{y}', z') \rightleftharpoons E(\bar{y}, z; \bar{y}', z') \,\vee$$
$$\exists h \exists u \in^* h(\bar{y}, z \approx u, \ldots, \emptyset) \,\&\, E(h, \ldots, \emptyset; \bar{y}', z'))$$

with $\bar{\pi}_0 \rightleftharpoons \bar{\tau}, \{\emptyset\}$ and $\bar{\pi}_{i+1} \rightleftharpoons \tau_i, \tau_0, \tau_0, \ldots, \tau_0, \emptyset$ for $0 \leq i \leq k$.

5 Δ-Definability and Simple Computability over Graphs

Theorem 1. *For any Δ-term or Δ-formula $t(\bar{y})$ there exists corresponding simply computable transformation*

$$\langle T; \bar{\tau} \rangle \mapsto \langle \tilde{T}; t(\bar{\tau}) \rangle \ .$$

Conversely, any simply computable set theoretic operation $F(\bar{\tau})$ (via some simply computable transformation $\tilde{F} : \langle T; \bar{\tau}\rangle \mapsto \langle T'; F(\bar{\tau})\rangle$ where $F(\bar{\tau})$ depends only on $\bar{\tau}$ and not on $T \ni \bar{\tau}$) is Δ-definable. Moreover, if TC is not allowed in Δ-language and $\in^*$ is not used in the simply computable transformation then only the operation $F'(T; \bar{\tau}) \rightleftharpoons F(\bar{\tau})$ (with the additional argument T) for $\bar{\tau} \in T$ would be guaranteed Δ-definable.

Proof. The converse part of the theorem is evident. Let us only note, that the equality $F(\bar{\tau}) = F'(\mathrm{TC}(\bar{\tau}); \bar{\tau})$ is used in the final step.

Consider the direct part. The induction argument to be successful requires proving more

General statement. *For any list $\bar{t}(\bar{y}) = t_0(\bar{y}), t_1(\bar{y}), \dots, t_n(\bar{y})$ of Δ-terms and Δ-formulas there exists corresponding computable transformation*

$$\langle T\rangle \mapsto \langle \tilde{T}; \lambda\bar{y} \in T.[\bar{t}(\bar{y})]\rangle$$

(with the graphs $\lambda\bar{y} \in T.[\bar{t}(\bar{y})]$ being elements of $\tilde{T}$).

Then the following Lemma will give the required result as formulated in Theorem 1.

Application Lemma. *For any m,n,k there exists computable transformation $\mathrm{App}_{m,n,k}$ such that for any set-theoretic $(m+n+k)$-ary function (considered as a graph) $\lambda\bar{x}\bar{y}\bar{z} \in T.f(\bar{x}, \bar{y}, \bar{z})$, with the tuples $\bar{x}, \bar{y}, \bar{z}$ containing respectively m, n and k variables we have:*

$$\mathrm{App}_{m,n,k} : \langle T; \lambda\bar{x}\bar{y}\bar{z} \in T.f(\bar{x}, \bar{y}, \bar{z}), \bar{\tau}\rangle \mapsto \langle T'; \lambda\bar{x}\bar{z} \in T.f(\bar{x}, \bar{\tau}, \bar{z}), \bar{\tau}\rangle \ .$$

Proof of Application Lemma. We prove the Lemma only for a partial case $m = n = k = 1$. The required transformation $\mathrm{App}_{1,1,1}$ is the composition of elementary transformation of the first kind:

$$[\![\lambda w u \tau \exists x z v(\langle\langle x, \tau, z\rangle, v\rangle \in u \& w = \langle\langle x, z\rangle, v\rangle)]\!]$$

and the elementary transformation of the second kind, omitting the input graph of the function as the distinguished element of the output graph.

$\square$

Proof of General statement. Due to the lack of space we consider only two of many cases of the inductive proof.

If, for example, $t_0(\bar{y})$ is $\mathrm{TC}(a(\bar{y}))$ then, by induction hypothesis, there exists a computable transformation

$$\langle T\rangle \mapsto \langle T'; \lambda\bar{y} \in T.[a(\bar{y}), t_1(\bar{y}), t_2(\bar{y}), \dots]\rangle \ .$$

By composing this transformation with $[\![\lambda x u.(x \in^* u)]\!]$, so that all $\mathrm{TC}(u)$ with $u \in T$ will be available as elements, and then with a saturation transformation which will give all members (tuples) of the set $\lambda\bar{y} \in T.\mathrm{TC}(a(\bar{y}))$ and, finally,

$[\![\lambda z\alpha.\exists\bar{y}uv.[z = \langle\bar{y}, v\rangle \& \langle\bar{y}, u\rangle \in \alpha \& \forall l(l \in v \leftrightarrow l \in^* u)]]\!]$ where $\lambda\bar{y} \in T.a(\bar{y})$ must be substituted for α we obtain the required transformation

$$\langle T\rangle \mapsto \langle\tilde{T}; \lambda\bar{y} \in T.[\text{TC}(a(\bar{y})), t_1(\bar{y}), t_2(\bar{y}), \ldots]\rangle \ .$$

If $t_0(\bar{y})$ is an atomic formula $a(\bar{y}) \in b(\bar{y})$ then, by induction hypothesis, there exists a computable transformation

$$\langle T\rangle \mapsto \langle T', \lambda\bar{y} \in T.[a(\bar{y}), b(\bar{y}), t_1(\bar{y}), t_2(\bar{y}), \ldots]\rangle.$$

By composing this transformation with a saturation transformation and then with the transformation

$$[\![\lambda z\alpha\beta.\exists\bar{y}uv.[(z = \langle\bar{y}, \emptyset\rangle \& \langle\bar{y}, u\rangle \in \alpha \& \langle\bar{y}, v\rangle \in \beta \& u \in v) \vee$$

$$(z = \langle\bar{y}, \{\emptyset\}\rangle \& \langle\bar{y}, u\rangle \in \alpha \& \langle\bar{y}, v\rangle \in \beta \& u \notin v)]]\!]$$

we obtain the required transformation

$$\langle T\rangle \mapsto \langle\tilde{T}, \lambda\bar{y} \in T.[a(\bar{y}) \in b(\bar{y}), t_1(\bar{y}), t_2(\bar{y}), \ldots]\rangle.$$

Other cases are left to the reader.

□
□

6 Δ^*-Definability and $*$-Computability over Graphs

Let us add to Δ-language a new kind of terms r^* to denote the *transitive closure* of any relation (set of pairs) r. The corresponding extended version of Δ-language will be called Δ^*-*language* (with Δ^*-*terms* and Δ^*-*formulas*). This kind of transitive closure also could be called a "horizontal" one unlike the "vertical" $\in^*$ and TC transitive closures considered above.

Simultaneously, let us allow for formulas defining elementary transformations of extensional well-founded graphs to use the following predicate forming construct:

$$[\lambda\bar{x}\bar{y}.\varphi(\bar{x}, \bar{y}, \bar{z})]^*$$

which denotes the *transitive closure* of the relation $\lambda\bar{x}\bar{y}.\varphi(\bar{x}, \bar{y}, \bar{z})$ of two lists variables $\bar{x}$ and $\bar{y}$ of the same length. The free variables $\bar{z}$ serve as parameters. We will use also more short, however ambiguous notation $[\varphi(\bar{u}, \bar{v}, \bar{z})]^*$ for the formula $[\lambda\bar{x}\bar{y}.\varphi(\bar{x}, \bar{y}, \bar{z})]^*(\bar{u}, \bar{v})$ when it is clear from the context which two lists of variables of equal length in φ are considered.

Evidently, $\in^*$ is expressible from $\in$ by this more general $*$-construct. So, instead of so called $\in^*$-formulas we shall consider now so called $*$-*formulas*, i.e. formulas in the language $\in$ only, but with the above $*$-construct. Corresponding transformations of extensional graphs based on these formulae are called $*$-*computable* and immediately generalize simply computable transformations.

As above, it may be proved that each ∗-computable transformation of such graphs is NLOGSPACE-computable (instead of DLOGSPACE for computable transformations of the previous section). Moreover, these transformations may be called FO*-*computable* (*definable*) because they may be simulated by ∗-formulae over suitable cartesian power of the transitive set T (shortly, by FO*-definable[7] transformations in the same way as FO-definable ones). This is also well-known to give rise to NLOGSPACE-computability. (Cf. [13, 14] for the precise correspondence between NLOGSPACE-computability and expressibility by FO*-formulae in finite linear ordered models.)

Then the above Theorem 1 can be reformulated as follows

Theorem 2. *For any list* $\bar{t}(\bar{y}) = t_0(\bar{y}), t_1(\bar{y}), \ldots, t_n(\bar{y})$ *of* Δ^*-*terms and* Δ^*-*formulas there exists corresponding* ∗-*computable transformation*

$$\langle T \rangle \mapsto \langle T'; \lambda \bar{y} \in T.[\bar{t}(\bar{y})] \rangle$$

(with $\lambda \bar{y} \in T.[\bar{t}(\bar{y})]$ elements of T'), *and therefore* (by the same Application Lemma as in Theorem 1) *there exists* ∗-*computable transformation*

$$\langle T; \bar{\tau} \rangle \mapsto \langle \tilde{T}; [\bar{t}(\bar{\tau})] \rangle \ .$$

Conversely, any ∗-*computable set theoretic operation* $F(\bar{\tau})$ *(via some* ∗-*computable transformation* $\bar{F} : \langle T; \bar{\tau} \rangle \mapsto \langle T'; F(\bar{\tau}) \rangle$*) is* Δ^*-*definable. If TC is omitted or replaced by* $\in^*$ *in* Δ^*-*language then only the operation* $F'(T; \bar{\tau}) \rightleftharpoons F(\bar{\tau})$ *(with the additional argument* T*) for* $\bar{\tau} \in T$ *would be guaranteed* Δ^*-*definable.*

Proof. The proof essentially consists in adding to the proof of Theorem 1 the case $t_0(\bar{y})$ is $r^*(\bar{y})$. □

7 Δ^* + C-Definability and FO*-Computability over Graphs

Let us extend Δ^*-language by the following *collapsing* operation $C(\langle g, v \rangle)$ which, given any graph g (i.e. a set of pairs) and a vertex v (just any set in the universe HF), denotes the unique, if any, set x in the universe whose transitive closure $TC(x)$ considered as the graph defined by $\in$-relation is isomorphic to the subgraph of g defined by all finite paths to the vertex v. If the required x does not exist then we set $C(\langle g, v \rangle) \rightleftharpoons \emptyset$. This version of C differs from that one described in the Introduction essentially by restricting the latter to well-founded (finite acyclic) *extensional* graphs.

More exactly, we will consider rather *special* extension Δ^* + *outside* C of Δ^*-language by operation $C(\langle g, v \rangle)$ such that *this operation may occur only in the head of a term*, i.e. C may be applied only to terms with no occurrences of C.

---

[7] i.e. definable in the language FO+TC of [13]; however, the denotation TC have been occupied in our paper (and in axiomatic set theory) for the "vertical" transitive closure in the universe of sets HF. TC in [13] coincides with our "horizontal" ∗-construct.

It is an *open question* whether this restriction is indeed essential for the expressive power of the full $\Delta^* + C$. Unfortunately, only the above restricted version of the language we are able to characterize in the following

Theorem 3. *The class of* FO^**-computable operations* $F : HF^n \to HF$ *(via corresponding* FO^**-definable transformations* $\tilde{F} : \langle T; \bar{\tau} \rangle \mapsto \langle \tilde{T}; F(\bar{\tau}) \rangle$*) coincides with the class of operations definable in the language* $\Delta^* + outside$ *C.*

Proof. For any tuple $\bar{t}$ of terms in Δ^* (which do not involve C) FO^*-computability of the corresponding operations was considered in Theorem 2 and in the note immediately preceding it. The case of operation $C(\tau)$ is treated quite straightforward. It remains to note, that if terms $\bar{t} = t_1, \ldots, t_n$ have a *unique* corresponding FO^*-definable transformation $\langle T; \bar{\tau} \rangle \mapsto \langle \tilde{T}; \bar{t}(\bar{\tau}) \rangle$ and an operation $f(x_1, \ldots, x_n)$ also has corresponding such transformation then $t = f(t_1, \ldots, t_n)$ has too. Finally, take $n = 1$ and $f = C$.

Conversely, let $F(\bar{\tau})$ be n-ary FO^*-computable operation over sets. Then it can be represented as the following $(\Delta^* + outside$ C)-definable operation, in fact a composition:

$$F = C \circ \tilde{F} \circ G$$

where G is an n-ary $\Delta^{(*)}$-definable operation over sets transforming input n-tuple of sets $x_1, \ldots, x_n$ into their well-founded extensional graph representation (with the distinguished n-tuple of its vertices):

$$G(x_1, \ldots, x_n) = \langle \in |_{TC(\{x_1, \ldots, x_n\})}, x_1, \ldots, x_n \rangle \ ,$$

$\tilde{F}$ is evidently also Δ^*-definable and collapsing operation C serves to 'extract' a resulting set from its graph representation. □

8 Concluding Remarks

We left as another *open question* whether some linear order on HF (or on the all transitive sets in HF) may be (uniformly) defined in $\Delta^* + outside$ C or, equivalently, FO^*-computable. In the case of positive answer we would obtain a more strong version of Theorem 3 with 'NLOGSPACE-computable' operations over HF instead of 'FO^*-computable' ones by using the well known representation of NLOGSPACE as FO^*-definability in finite linear ordered structures [13].

In the case of more powerful version of Δ-language from [24, 25, 26] a natural linear order on HF (without urelements, or with *any linear order* on urelements) proves to be definable with the use of some Least Fixed Point Operator, what allowed to characterize exactly corresponding definable set operations as PTIME-computable ones. Unfortunately we are unable to use for this aim *-construct instead LFP. We conclude that the case of HF is not completely similar to the "flat" case because it is problematic also to capture the whole class of (N)LOGSPACE-computable set operations (under some coding) by a Δ-like language. Moreover, even the above capturing FO*-computability by the language $\Delta^* + outside$ C is somewhat disadvantageous because of extremely special using the collapsing operation C in the language.

Nevertheless, some sub-PTIME computable classes of operations over HF was indeed captured by corresponding versions of Δ-language what may be helpful for more effective than PTIME realization of such languages and for the general understanding the whole situation.

Finally note, that many considerations of this paper will succeed also in the case of a more general well-founded universe of sets $\mathcal{V}$ instead of HF which is sufficiently closed under set theoretic operations and may contain also infinite sets (and satisfy, say, all axioms of Zermelo-Frenkel set theory).

9 Acknowledgements

The authors are grateful to anonymous referees for their comments on preliminary version of this paper and useful suggestions.

References

1. Abiteboul, S., Beery, C.: On the power of languages for the manipulation of complex objects. INRIA research report **846** (1988). Abstract in Proc. International Workshop on Theory and Applications of Nested Relations and Complex Objects. Darmstadt (1987)
2. Aczel, P.: Non-Well-Founded Sets. CSLI Lecture Notes. No 14 (1988)
3. Blakely, J.A., Larson, P.A., Tompa, F.W.: Efficiently updating materialized view. Proc. ACM-SIGMOD. 1986. Intern. Conf. on Management of Data. Washington D.C. May 1986. 61–71
4. Buss, S.R.: Bounded Arithmetic. Bibliopolis. Napoli. 1986
5. Dahlhaus, E., Makowsky, J.: The Choice of programming Primitives in SETL-like Languages. ESOP'86. LNCS **213** (1986) 160–172
6. Dahlhaus, E.: Is SETL a suitable language for parallel programming - a theoretical approach. Börger, E., Kleine Buning, H., Richter, M.M. ed. CSL'87. LNCS **329** (1987) 56–63
7. Ershov, Yu.L.: Numberings theory. "Nauka". Glavnaja redakcija phisico-matematicheskoi literatury. Moskva. 1977 (in Russian)
8. Feferman, S.: Predicatively reducible systems of set theory. Proc. Symp. in Pure Math. Vol. **13**, Part II (1974) 11–32
9. Gandy, R.O.: Set theoretic functions for elementary syntax. Proc. Symp. in Pure Math. Vol. **13**, Part II (1974) 103–126
10. Grumbach, S., Vianu, V.: Tractable query languages for complex object databases. Rapports de Recherche N1573. INRIA. 1991
11. Gurevich, Y.: Algebras of feasible functions. FOCS **24** (1983) 210–214
12. Gurevich, Y.: Logic and the challenge of computer science. Trends in Theoretical Computer Science. (E.Borger ed.) Computer Science Press (1988) 1–57
13. Immerman, N.: Languages which captures complexity classes. SIAM J. Comput., **16** 4 (1987) 760–778

14. Immerman, N.: Descriptive and computational complexity. Proc. Symposia in Applied Math. **38** (1989)
15. Immerman, N., Patnik, S., Stemple, D.: The expressiveness of a family of finite set languages. 1991
16. Jensen, R.B.: The fine structure of the constructible hierarchy. Ann. Math. Logic **4** (1972) 229–308
17. Jensen, R.B., Karp, C.: Primitive recursive set functions. Proc. Sympos. Pure Math., vol. **13** part I (1971) 143–176
18. Kuper, G.M., Vardi, M.Y.: A new approach to database logic. Proc. 3rd ACM Symp. on Principles of Database Systems 1984
19. Levy, A.: A hierarchy of formulas in set theory. Mem. Amer. Math. Soc. No. 57 (1965) 76pp. MR 32 N 7399
20. Parikh, R.: Existence and feasibility in arithmetic. JSL, **36** No 3 (1971) 494–508
21. Red'ko, V.N., Basarab, I.A.: Data bases and information systems. News in the life, science and technique; series: "Mathematics, Kybernetics" N6 Moscow. Znanije. (1987) (in Russian)
22. Sazonov, V.Yu.: A logical approach to the problem "P=NP?". Proc., Math. Found. of Comput. Sci. Lect. Not. Comput. Sci. **88** Springer. New York (1980) 562–575 (An important correction to this paper is given in [23], P.490)
23. Sazonov, V.Yu.: On existence of complete predicate calculus in metamathematics without exponentiation. Lect. Not. Comput. Sci. **118** Springer. New York (1981) 483–490
24. Sazonov, V.Yu.: Bounded set theory and polynomial computability. All Union Conf. Appl. Logic., Proc. Novosibirsk (1985) 188–191 (In Russian)
25. Sazonov, V.Yu.: Bounded set theory, polynomial computability and Δ-programming. Application aspects of mathematical logic. Computing systems **122** (1987) 110–132 (In Russian) Cf. also a short English version of this paper in: Lect. Not. Comput. Sci. **278** Springer (1987) 391–397
26. Sazonov, V.Yu.: Bounded set theory and inductive definability. Abstracts of Logic Colloquium'90. JSL **56** Nu.3 (1991) 1141–1142
27. Sazonov, V.Yu.: hereditarily-finite sets, data bases and polynomial-time computability. TCS **119** Elsevier (1993) 187–214
28. Sazonov, V.Yu.: A bounded set theory with anti-foundation axiom and inductive definability. (Presented to the conference CSL'94, Kazimierz, Poland, September 1994) 1994.
29. Sazonov, V.Yu., Leontjev, A.V.: On coding of hereditarily-finite sets, polynomial-time computability and Δ-expressibility. Proc. Conf. Appl. Logic. Novosibirsk , May 1993. Computing systems **146** (1992) 195-198

Partial Strictness in Two-Phase Locking

Eljas Soisalon-Soininen and Tatu Ylönen

Department of Computer Science, Helsinki University of Technology
Otakaari 1, FIN–02150 Espoo, Finland
e-mail: ess@cs.hut.fi, ylo@cs.hut.fi
telefax: +358-0-451 3293, tel: +358-0-4511

Abstract. Two-phase locking is a standard method for managing concurrent transactions in database systems. In order to guarantee good recovery properties, two-phase locking should be strict, meaning that locks can be released only after the transaction's commit or abort. In this paper we show that even exclusive locks can be released immediately after the *commit request* has arrived, without sacrificing any important recovery properties. This optimization is especially useful if the commit operation takes much time compared with the other actions, as for main-memory databases, or if the commits are performed in batches.

1   Introduction

When several transactions operate concurrently on the same database, a mechanism is needed for controlling the concurrency in order to guarantee correctness. That is, we have to ensure that when transactions are run concurrently the consistency of the database is preserved as if the transactions would be run serially. As to concurrency, the formal correctness is based on the notion of serializability, meaning that the interleaved mode of operation has the same result as when the transactions are run one by one.

The most widely used strategy for scheduling concurrent transactions is based on locking. The scheduler locks a data item before a transaction may access it, and no other transaction may access the data item before the lock has been released. Locks are often divided into exclusive and shared locks; several transactions may hold a shared lock on a data item but when one holds an exclusive lock no other transaction may hold any (shared or exclusive) lock on the same data item. In two-phase locking [4], once the scheduler has released the lock for a transaction, it may not subsequently obtain any more locks for that transaction on any data item. It has been shown [13] that two-phase locking is a most general locking strategy that guarantees serializability when the set of transactions may change dynamically.

In addition to guaranteeing serializability the scheduler must reject interleavings that are not recoverable. That is, if a transaction aborts, we must be able to reconstruct the situation we would have arrived at if the aborted transaction had not existed. Moreover, for practical reasons, it is advisable that aborting one transaction does not cause other transactions to abort, i.e., cascading aborts are avoided, and that recovering can be based on so called before images of data items [1]. This leads to the requirement that two-phase locking should be strict [1], meaning that no lock may be released before the transaction's commit or abort has been processed.

There are some obvious cases in which transaction processing according to the rules of strict two-phase locking is too restrictive. In main memory databases [2, 3] no disk accesses are needed for normal reads and writes but, because of possible failures, in commit the changes must be stored into a disk file. Thus performing the commit action is considerably more costly than the other actions, and much more concurrency would be allowed when all locks could be released immediately after the *commit request* has arrived. Another situation in which this early releasing of locks would be very beneficial is when the group commit optimization [6, 8] is applied, i.e., several commits are collected and performed as a batch.

In this paper we shall investigate in detail how good recovery properties can be retained in conjunction with early releasing of locks. In particular, we shall show that for transaction failures, caused for example by deadlocks, strict executions can be guaranteed. For aborts caused by system failures no such guarantee can be obtained, but even then a recoverable execution can be achieved.

The results have been derived in a formal model in which we have added a new action, called the commit request action, into the set of possible transaction steps. We require that the commit request action appears as the second last step in transactions that end with the commit action. Our results say that recoverability is always preserved for early releasing of locks. Moreover, for all aborts that are not preceded by the commit request the strict behaviour can be guaranteed. If an abort occurs after the commit request strictness cannot be guaranteed, and we suggest that in such cases all active transactions are aborted. It should be noted that it is a very rare, though possible, to have an abort after the commit request (e.g., due to a system crash). An abort caused by a deadlock or requested by the application cannot occur after the commit request has been received.

The idea of early releasing of locks is not entirely new. Similar ideas have been used in main-memory databases and some prototypes [3, 5, 8, 9]. Other related work includes [12], where algorithms are given for determining when it is safe to unlock entities while the transaction is still active, and [11], where commit ordering is used in heteregeneous distributed databases. However, no formal presentation of the ideas has previously been available.

This paper is organized as follows. Sections 2 and 3 define the transaction and execution model. Section 4 is the main contribution of this paper; partially strict histories are defined, and it is proven that they maintain recoverability and do not cause cascading aborts except in rare situations that can be handled specially. Section 5 defines partially strict two-phase locking, and proves that it only accepts partially strict histories. Implementation alternatives for commit ordering are analyzed. Section 6 concludes the paper.

2   Transaction Model

A *transaction* T is a finite sequence of actions of the form *Read[x]* (denoted $R[x]$) or *Write[x]* (denoted $W[x]$), where x is an element of a set of *data items*. For a given data item x there is at most one $R[x]$ and at most one $W[x]$ in a transaction. A *committed transaction* is a transaction followed by a special symbol c, and an *aborted transaction* is a transaction followed by a special symbol a. In the sequel, by the term transaction we mean a committed or an aborted transaction. By $R_i[x]$, $W_i[x]$, c_i, and a_i we denote actions of transaction T_i.

Notice that our model slightly differs from that of [1]. For simplicity, we define transactions and histories as total orders of steps, but our results can be derived also in the more general model of [1] where they are partial orders.

Let $\tau = \{T_1, \ldots, T_n\}$ be a set of transactions. A *complete history* of τ is an ordering of the actions of all of the transactions of τ, with the actions within each transaction in the prescribed order. In other words [10], a complete history of τ is an element of the *shuffle* of τ meaning the set of all sequences obtained by interleaving the sequences $T_1, T_2, \ldots, T_n$. A *history* is a prefix of a complete history. A complete history is *serial* if, for every two transactions T_i and T_j appearing in H, all actions of T_i precede all actions of T_j, or vice versa.

Let H be a history of $\tau = \{T_1, \ldots, T_n\}$. We say that transaction T_i is *committed* (resp. *aborted*) in H, if c_i (resp. a_i) appears in H. Transaction T_i is *active* in H if it is neither committed nor aborted. Given a history H, the *committed projection of H*, denoted $C(H)$, is the history obtained from H by deleting all actions that do not belong to transactions committed in H. Two actions of H are said to *conflict* if they both are associated with the same data item x and at least one of them is $W[x]$.

The *serialization graph* for history H of τ, denoted $SG(H)$, is a directed graph whose nodes are the transactions of τ that are committed in H and whose edges are $T_i \to T_j$, $T_i \neq T_j$, where T_i has an action that precedes and conflicts with an action of T_j in H. A history H is called *(conflict-)serializable* if $SG(C(H)) = SG(H_s)$ for some serial history H_s.

3   Recoverable Histories

Let H be a history of a transaction set $\{T_1, T_2, \ldots, T_n\}$. We say that action $R_i[x]$ in T_i *reads from* $W_j[x]$ in T_j in H [1], if H is of the form

$$\ldots W_j[x]\alpha R_i[x] \ldots,$$

where α does not contain a_j or any $W_k[x]$ except possibly when α also contains a_k (the abort action of transaction T_k). We say that transaction T_i *reads from* transaction T_j in H, if for some $R_i[x]$ and $W_j[x]$, $R_i[x]$ reads from $W_j[x]$ in H.

A history H is *not recoverable* [1] if it is of the form

$$\ldots W_j[x] \ldots R_i[x] \ldots c_i \ldots,$$

where $R_i[x]$ reads from $W_j[x]$ and c_j does not occur in H. Otherwise, H is *recoverable*.

In other words, history H is not recoverable if it may be followed by a_j (the abort action of transaction T_j) and the result of transaction T_i is dependent on transaction T_j but T_i has already committed.

Cascading aborts may occur when a transaction reads from another transaction which will be aborted later. We say that a history H *may create cascading aborts* if it is of the form

$$\ldots W_j[x] \ldots R_i[x] \ldots a_j \ldots,$$

where $R_i[x]$ reads from $W_j[x]$, and a_i does not precede a_j in H. Otherwise, H *avoids cascading aborts*.

In other words, history H may create cascading aborts if transaction T_i reads from transaction T_j in H and T_j aborts in H but T_i does not end in H.

A history H is *not strict* if it may create cascading aborts or H is of the form

$$\ldots W_j[x] \ldots W_i[x] \ldots,$$

where transaction T_j has not ended before $W_i[x]$, and some history having H as a prefix contains a_j. That is, it is required that transaction T_i cannot write the same data item as transaction T_j if T_j has not ended yet and may be aborted later. Otherwise, history H is *strict*.

Notice that in practice, of course, an abort may occur for any transaction, and thus the above requirement that transaction T_j may be aborted later seems unnecessary. In the next section, however, we want to distinguish between the case in which an abort is caused by a fairly uncommon system error (such as a system crash) and the case in which the abort is caused by a normal transaction failure. Typical transaction failures come from deadlocks, or when the application wants to abort the transaction.

4 Partially Strict Histories

In this section we want to relax the strictness requirement for histories. The idea is that we want to allow reading and writing from a transaction that has not committed yet but all other actions have been done and, additionally, a request for committing the transaction has arrived. Then, normally, the transaction will commit, and we will prove that the partial strictness obtained in this way will coincide with the true strictness. In practice, in cases of system crash and some unusual errors such as the lack of disk space when writing, we cannot guarantee strict executions. However, these situations are rare, and they can be handled by simply aborting all active transactions. The necessary recoverability will remain in all cases, i.e., even when a commit request is followed by an abort.

In our model, we add a new action c^R to the set of possible actions of transactions. The action c^R meaning the commit request may only occur as the second last action of a transaction. Always when a transaction ends with the action c (commit) it must be preceded by c^R.

We say that a history H is *partially strict* if the following three conditions hold:

(i) whenever H is of the form

$$\ldots W_j[x] \ldots R_i[x] \ldots,$$

where $R_i[x]$ reads from $W_j[x]$, then $c_j{}^R$ precedes $R_i[x]$ in H,

(ii) whenever H is of the form

$$\ldots W_j[x] \ldots W_i[x] \ldots,$$

then a_j or $c_j{}^R$ precedes $W_i[x]$, and

(iii) whenever $c_i{}^R$ precedes $c_j{}^R$ in H, then c_i cannot occur in H without preceding c_j.

Theorem 1. Partially strict histories are recoverable.

Proof. Let H be a partially strict history. For the sake of contradiction assume that H is not recoverable. Then, by definition, H is of the form

$$\ldots W_j[x] \ldots R_i[x] \ldots c_i \ldots,$$

where $R_i[x]$ reads from $W_j[x]$ and c_j does not occur in H. As H is partially strict, we conclude from condition (i) of the definition that $c_j{}^R$ must precede $R_i[x]$. Thus $c_j{}^R$ must precede $c_i{}^R$ implying by condition (iii) that c_j should precede c_i, which is a contradiction. $\square$

Lemma 1. A partially strict history H avoids cascading aborts, provided that a_i cannot follow $c_i{}^R$ in H for any transaction T_i.

Proof. Assume that H may create cascading aborts. Then H is of the form

$$\ldots W_j[x] \ldots R_i[x] \ldots a_j \ldots,$$

where $R_i[x]$ reads from $W_j[x]$, and a_i does not precede a_j in H. Now because $R_i[x]$ reads from $W_j[x]$, we conclude that $c_j{}^R$ must precede $R_i[x]$. Thus, by the assumption of the lemma a_j cannot follow, and we have a contradiction. $\square$

Theorem 2. A partially strict history H is strict, provided that in no continuation of H (which may be H itself) a_i follows $c_i{}^R$ for some transaction T_i.

Proof. Lemma 1 implies that, under the assumption of the theorem, partially strict histories avoid cascading aborts. Then let H be a partially strict history that avoids cascading aborts. If H is not strict, then H is of the form

$$\ldots W_j[x] \ldots W_i[x] \ldots,$$

and there is a history H'

$$\ldots W_j[x] \ldots W_i[x] \ldots a_j$$

that has H as its prefix. Moreover, because H is partially strict, $c_j{}^R$ precedes $W_i[x]$ in H. But by the assumption of the theorem, a_j cannot follow $c_j{}^R$, and we thus conclude that H is strict. $\square$

We have thus shown that partial strictness coincides with strictness if in no execution of transactions the abort action follows the commit request action. This result can be interpreted such that when only transaction failures are present, then the true strictness is obtained through partial strictness. Notice that in the case of a transaction failure such as a deadlock or when the application wants to abort the transaction the commit request action cannot be followed by an abort. This means that under partial strictness property we may well resort to standard recovery strategies when transaction failures occur. For example, they do not cause other transactions to abort, as by Lemma 1 transaction failures do not cascade. System failures must be handled in a different way, and a straightforward solution is to abort all active transactions when a system failure occurs.

5 Partially Strict Two-Phase Locking

In this section we shall show how partial strictness of histories, together with their conflict-serializability [1, 10] can be obtained by two-phase locking.

Let T be a transaction. A *locked transaction* $\bar{T}$ of T is a finite sequence of steps containing all actions of T, and instructions $Rlock[x]$, $Runlock[x]$, $Wlock[x]$, and $Wunlock[x]$ (denoted $Rl[x]$, $Ru[x]$, $Wl[x]$, and $Wu[x]$). Moreover, we assume that $R[x]$ is preceded by $Rl[x]$ or $Wl[x]$ and followed by $Ru[x]$ or $Wu[x]$, respectively, and $W[x]$ is preceded by $Wl[x]$ and followed by $Wu[x]$.

A *locking* of a transaction set $\tau = \{T_1, \ldots, T_n\}$ is a set $\lambda = \{\bar{T}_1, \ldots, \bar{T}_n\}$ of locked transactions, such that the subsequence of $\bar{T}_i$ obtained by deleting all $Rl[x]$, $Ru[x]$, $Wl[x]$, and $Wu[x]$ steps coincides with T_i. If H is a history of τ, then $\bar{H}$ denotes a history of λ that has H as a subsequence. If $\bar{H}$ is a history of λ, the locked version of τ, then H denotes the history of τ obtained from $\bar{H}$ by deleting all lock and unlock instructions.

A history $\bar{H}$ of λ is *legal*, if each $Rl[x]$ is followed by $Ru[x]$ before $Wl[x]$ and each $Wl[x]$ is followed by $Wu[x]$ before another $Wl[x]$ or $Rl[x]$. A history H of τ is *realized* or *accepted* by λ, if there is a legal history $\bar{H}$ of λ that has H as a subsequence. A locking λ of τ is called *(conflict-)safe*, if all histories of τ accepted by λ and projected on committed transactions only are *(conflict-)serializable*.

A locking λ obeys the *two-phase locking* policy [1, 10] if no transaction of λ is of the form where $Rl[x]$ or $Wl[x]$ for some x follows an unlock $Ru[y]$ or $Wu[y]$ for some y. A two-phase locking is *strict* [1] if all unlock instructions follow the abort or commit action in all transactions.

Our claim is that strict two-phase locking is unnecessarily restrictive because locks can be released only after the transaction's commit has been processed. If the group commit [6] optimization is applied, this would mean quite long delays because in group commit several transactions' commits are grouped together in order to save disk writes. We shall show that locks can be released immediately after the commit request operation. This implies that group commits do not cause any extra delays in releasing locks compared with processing the commits one by one.

We say that a two-phase locking is *partially strict* if all unlock instructions follow the abort or commit request action in all transactions. Our goal here is to define such a locking which, in addition to the two-phase property, accepts partially strict histories. An immediate problem is the condition (iii) requiring that whenever $c_i{}^R$ precedes $c_j{}^R$ then also c_i precedes c_j. It is obvious that this requirement, called the *commit ordering*, cannot be achieved by using locks on data items.

Theorem 3. Whenever commit ordering is preserved, a partially strict two-phase locking accept only partially strict histories.

Proof. Let H be a history accepted by a partially strict two-phase locking λ. Then there is a legal history $\bar{H}$ of λ that has H as a subsequence. Assume that H is of the form

$$\dots W_j[x] \dots O_i[x] \dots,$$

where $O_i[x]$ denotes either $R_i[x]$ or $W_i[x]$. Because λ is a two-phase locking and $\bar{H}$ is legal, we conclude that $\bar{H}$ is of the form

$$\dots Wl_j[x] \dots W_j[x] \dots Wu_j[x] \dots O_i[x] \dots.$$

Partial strictness now means that $c_j{}^R$ or a_j precedes $O_i[x]$ implying that the first two conditions of partial strictness are fulfilled. By the assumption that commit ordering is preserved, we conclude that H is partially strict. $\square$

Our next question is how commit ordering can be implemented. We first look at the possibility of using locks. We may introduce into a locking new lock and unlock instructions that are not identified with the data items but with the c^R or c actions or with some specific locking variables (see, e.g., [10]).

Let $\tau = \{T_1, \dots, T_n\}$ be a set of transactions, and let λ be its locking. Here we assume that, in addition to the lock and unlock instructions identified with the data items, a locked transaction may contain steps $Wl[x]$ and $Wu[x]$ where x is not a data item. The requirements for a legal history apply also to these new $Wl[x]$ and $Wu[x]$ steps but the definitions for a two-phase locking and strict and partially strict two-phase locking only apply to lock and unlock steps identified with true data items. We say that λ is *commit locked* if for each transaction T of τ ending with $c^R c$ the transaction $\bar{T}$ is of the form

$$\dots Wl[c^R]\alpha c^R Wl[c] Wu[c^R] c Wu[c],$$

where α does not contain any $R[x]$ or $W[x]$ action.

Theorem 4. A partially strict two-phase locking λ which is commit locked accepts only partially strict histories.

Proof. By Theorem 3 it is enough to show that λ preserves commit ordering. Let H be a history of the transaction set τ obtained from λ by deleting all lock and unlock steps, and assume that H is accepted by λ. For the sake of contradiction, assume that H does not preserve commit ordering, i.e., H is of the form

$$\dots c_i{}^R \dots c_j{}^R \dots c_j \dots c_i \dots$$

for some transactions T_i and T_j of τ. There must be some history $\bar{H}$ of λ that is legal because λ accepts H. But this is clearly impossible because $Wl[c_i{}^R]$ precedes $c_i{}^R$ and $Wl[c_i]$ precedes c_i and $Wu[c_i{}^R]$. Thus we cannot set the lock $Wl[c_j]$ before the action c_i followed by $Wu[c_i]$. This means that no $\bar{H}$ is legal, and thus we conclude that H preserves commit ordering. $\square$

In what extent have we realized commit ordering with commit locks? By Theorem 4 we know that the commit ordering is preserved by commit locks, but are there valid ordering that are forbidden by commit locks? Actually, using commit locks only two commit request operations may be present at a time without processing the next commit. That is, we are able to schedule partially strict histories

$$\ldots c_{i1}{}^R \ldots c_{i2}{}^R \ldots c_{i1} \ldots c_{i3}{}^R \ldots c_{i2} \ldots$$

but not, for example, histories

$$\ldots c_{i1}{}^R \ldots c_{i2}{}^R \ldots c_{i3}{}^R \ldots c_{i1} \ldots c_{i2} \ldots c_{i3} \ldots$$

Given a set $\tau = \{T_1, \ldots, T_n\}$ of n transactions we are able to construct a locking such that all valid orderings of commit request and commit actions will be realized. The question of how such lockings are constructed is discussed in detail in [7]. In our setting, however, the construction of such a locking is not feasible for two reasons. First, the number of locks needed is large ($O(n^2)$). Second, here we consider a dynamic situation in which we do not know in advance how many transactions will arrive.

In practice, however, it is easy to implement the commit ordering by collecting the transactions which have requested to be committed into a queue. The actual commits are then performed in this order. The group commit can be implemented such that always when a certain number of commit requests have arrived the corresponding commits will be done as a batch. Another possibility is to perform the group commit in certain time intervals when all thus far arrived and not yet done commit requests form the batch.

6 Conclusion

We have defined a new variation of the strict two-phase locking policy, called partially strict two-phase locking, that employs early releasing of locks in the sense that all locks of a transaction are released immediately after its commit request has arrived. We have proved formally that all accepted histories are recoverable and, whenever a transaction aborts without a preceding commit request, the recovery properties of strict two-phase locking are preserved. If a transaction must be aborted after its commit request (which can only happen in connection with rare system failures), these properties do not hold and we suggest that then all active transactions are aborted.

The initial motivation for this research was our analysis and implementation of shadow paging (see e.g. [1]) for managing transactions and recovery in database systems [14]. Our shadow paging project was motivated by the need of creating database systems in which recovery would be extremely fast, without sacrificing much or anything of the desirable properties of a complete database management system. For efficiency reasons, in a system based on shadow paging concurrent transactions must be handled such that several transactions commit in a batch. In such an environment, it is important not to hold the transactions' locks until the whole batch has been processed.

References

1. P. A. Bernstein, V. Hadzilacos, and N. Goodman. *Concurrency Control and Recovery in Database Systems*. Addison-Wesley, 1987.
2. D. J. DeWitt, R. H. Katz, F. Olken, L. D. Shapiro, M. R. Stonebraker, and D. Wood. Implementation techniques for main memory database systems. In *ACM SIGMOD*, pages 1–8, 1984.
3. M. H. Eich. A classification and comparison of main memory database recovery techniques. In *Data Engineering*, pages 332–339, 1987.
4. K. P. Eswaran, J. Gray, R. A. Lorie, and I. L. Treiger. The notions of consistency and predicate locks in a database system. *Communications of the ACM*, 19(11):624–633, 1976.
5. D. Gawlick and D. Kinkade. Varieties of concurrency control in IMS/VS Fast Path. *IEEE Database Engineering*, 4:63–70, 1985.
6. J. Gray and A. Reuter. *Transaction Processing: Concepts and Techniques*. Morgan Kaufmann, 1993.
7. G. Lausen, E. Soisalon-Soininen, and P. Widmayer. On the power of safe locking. *Journal of Computer and System Sciences*, 40(2):269–288, 1990.
8. C.-C. Liu and T. Minoura. Effect of update merging on reliable storage performance. In *Data Engineering*, pages 208–213, 1986.
9. C. Mohan, D. Haderle, B. Lindsay, H. Pirahesh, and P. Schwarz. ARIES: A transaction recovery method supporting fine-granularity locking and partial rollbacks using write-ahead logging. *ACM Transactions on Database Systems*, 17(1):94–162, 1992.
10. C. Papadimitriou. *The Theory of Database Concurrency Control*. Computer Science Press, 1986.
11. Y. Raz. The principle of commitment ordering. In *Very Large Data Bases*, pages 292–312, 1992.
12. O. Wolfson. An algorithm for early unlocking of entities in database transactions. *Journal of Algorithms*, 7:146–156, 1986.
13. M. Yannakakis. A theory of safe locking policies in database systems. *Journal of the Association for Computer Machinery*, 29(3):718–740, 1982.
14. T. Ylönen. *Shadow Paging Is Feasible*. Licentiate's thesis, Department of Computer Science, Helsinki University of Technology, 1994.

Unified Transaction Model for Semantically Rich Operations *

Radek Vingralek[1] and Haiyan Ye[1] and Yuri Breitbart[1] and H.-J. Schek[1]

Department of Computer Science, ETH Zurich, CH-8092, Switzerland

Abstract

We present here a unified transaction model for database systems with semantically rich operations. Based on the work in [SWY93], we develop constructive correctness criteria that encompass both serializability and failure atomicity in a uniform manner. As it turns out, an exact characterization of the class of prefix reducible schedules that was introduced for the simple read/write model in [AVA+94] is infeasible. Thus, we propose here two subclasses of prefix reducible schedules and argue that serializability and atomicity can be unified by considering schedules from these classes. We also show that the previously proposed correctness criteria [MGG86a, MGG86b] and [RKS92, RKS93] are subsumed by our model.

1 Introduction

Transaction management in database systems with semantically rich operations [MGG86a, MGG86b, Wei88, HH88, Wei89, HH91, BR92, RKS92, RKS93, LMWF94] is becoming increasingly important. In this paper we develop one such model that is based on commutativity. Such an approach can be captured by a conflict detection method defined on pairs of operation invocations. Importing such a method into a transaction manager allows an extensible approach in providing semantically serializable and semantically atomic transactions. Our main objective is to develop a model that would allow us to reason about transaction atomicity and consistent execution in a uniform manner. Our approach is based on the assumption that with each operation a backward (or undo) operation must be given to undo the observable effects of the operation, if necessary.

Recently, the work by [SWY93, AVA+94] has introduced a unified model of transaction management based on the read/write model. In particular, it introduced the class *PRED* of prefix reducible schedules that captures the correctness criteria of serializability and failure atomicity in a uniform manner. In this paper we generalize the previous work of [SWY93] and [AVA+94]. It turns

* This material is based in part upon work supported by NSF grants IRI-9221947, IRI-9012902 and IRI-9117904 and by grant from Hewlett-Packard Corporation. This work has been performed while Y. Breitbart was on one year sabbatical and R. Vingralek was visiting the database research group at ETH, Zurich.

out that we must distinguish the case where the backward operations have the same conflict behaviour as the forward operations from the case where this does not hold. In the latter case the characterization of prefix reducible schedules given in [AVA+94] for the read/write model is not sufficient to characterize such schedules in a semantically rich model of operations.

To obtain practically feasible protocols, we introduce two incomparable classes of *safe* schedules, each of which is a proper subclass of prefix reducible schedules. We discuss the properties of these schedules and argue that safe schedules are those that practically feasible and allow a uniform treatment of serializability and atomicity in a transaction model with semantically rich operations. Proofs of our results can be found in [VYBS94].

Our definition of commutativity closely relates to the definitions given in [Wei88, Wei89]. However, unlike [Wei88, Wei89], our definition of commutativity considers the effects of the undo related operations in addition to the effects of the forward operations. Moss, Griffith and Graham in [MGG86a, MGG86b] introduced the notion of *revokable* schedules to handle transaction atomicity. We show here that the class of revokable and serializable schedules is a proper subclass of the schedules introduced here. Rastogi, Korth and Silberschatz [RKS92, RKS93] develop a theory of *strict* schedules. It appears that the class of strict schedules from [RKS92, RKS93] is properly contained in the class of schedules introduced here. Thus, our model is more general.

2   Model Description

In this section we define our transaction model. Our model is an extension of a model from [SWY93].

2.1   Operations

A database is a collection of data objects D and a set of operations O (called in the sequel **forward** operations). An operation invocation [Wei88, Wei89] from O is applied to data objects and returns a value to the caller who has invoked the operation. In what follows when we talk about operation, we always mean an operation invocation. We assume that operations from O and only these operations are available to database users and/or transactions to access and manipulate database objects. Consequently, the database states can be inspected only through the return values of operations from O. We assume that in addition to operations from O there are two special termination operations: **abort** (denoted by a) and **commit** (denoted by c).

For each operation o from O we introduce an **undo** or **backward** operation o^{-1} which backs out "recognizable" effects of the corresponding forward operation (i.e., those changes in the database state caused by o that can be detected by other operations through their return values). Let O^{-1} be the set of all undo operations Thus, after executing forward operation o immediately followed by its corresponding backward operation o^{-1}, no "effect" of o is left in the database as far as it can be detected through the return values of any other operation executed after o and o^{-1}. We say that a sequence of operations α is **well-formed** if each undo operation o^{-1} in α is preceded by its corresponding forward operation o.

Definition 1. We call a sequence of operations σ **effect-free** if, for all possible sequences of operations α and β such that $\langle \alpha\ \sigma\ \beta \rangle$ is well-formed, the sequence $\langle \alpha\ \beta \rangle$ is also well-formed and the sequence of the return values of β in the $\langle \alpha\ \sigma\ \beta \rangle$ is the same as in $\langle \alpha\ \beta \rangle$.

We say that o^{-1} is the undo operation for o if and only if sequence $o\ o^{-1}$ is effect-free. In some cases the undo operation does not need to do anything (for example $read^{-1}$ operation in read/write model). Thus, we introduce a **null** operation and denote it by λ. Return value of the null operation is an empty sequence.

We can reasonably assume that whoever designs the forward operation o also provides the undo operation o^{-1}, since it is him/her who knows the semantics of o and thus also knows how to undo it. For example, in the read/write model, for *write* operation of the DBMS, the DBMS maintains a log and uses that information to generate $write^{-1}$ operation. Alternatively, if a high-level interface to a SQL database is provided by using embedded SQL to design an operation o, it is the programmer who designs the undo operation o^{-1}.

2.2 Commutativity

Our notion of conflicting operations is based on the notion of *commutativity* of operations, which we discuss next. Consider sequence $\langle \alpha\ p\ q\ \beta \rangle$. If permuting p and q in the sequence does not change their return values and also return values of β, then we call p and q commutative. There are two possible cases that lead to two alternative definitions of commutativity:

- Permuting p and q in S does not change their return values regardless of which α precedes them in S.
- Permuting p and q in S does not change their return values only for some α.

Thus, we define two notions of commutativity as follows:

Definition 2. We say that two operations p and q from $O \cup O^{-1}$ **state independently commute** if and only if, for all possible operation sequences α and β such that $\langle \alpha\ p\ q\ \beta \rangle$ and $\langle \alpha\ q\ p\ \beta \rangle$ are well-formed, the sequence of the return values of β and the return values of p and of q in $\langle \alpha\ p\ q\ \beta \rangle$ are the same as in $\langle \alpha\ q\ p\ \beta \rangle$.

Definition 3. We say that two operations p and q from $O \cup O^{-1}$ **state dependently commute** with respect to sequence α_0[2] if and only if, for any sequence

---

[2] Note that the sequence α_0 corresponds to existence of some *state* [MGG86a, MGG86b, RKS92, RKS93] in which the two operations commute.

of operations β such that $\langle \alpha_0\ p\ q\ \beta \rangle$ and $\langle \alpha_0\ q\ p\ \beta \rangle$ are well-formed, the sequence of the return values of β and the return values of p and of q in $\langle \alpha_0\ p\ q\ \beta \rangle$ are the same as in $\langle \alpha_0\ q\ p\ \beta \rangle$.

Example 1. Let the database consist of a single set S with the following operations defined on it's elements. S does not contain constants 0 and 1:

SInsert(x)	Inserts element x into S, if it is not already there and returns x. Otherwise it returns constant 0.
SInsert$^{-1}(x)$	If x is a return value of the corresponding forward operation and it is not 0, then it deletes element x from S, otherwise does nothing. It always returns constant 1.
SDelete(x)	Deletes element x from S, if it is there and returns x. Otherwise it returns constant 0.
SDelete$^{-1}(x)$	If x is a return value of the corresponding forward operation and it is not 0, then it inserts element x from S, otherwise does nothing. It always returns constant 1.
Test(x)	Returns YES if element x is in S, otherwise it returns NO.
Test$^{-1}(x)$	Is the λ operation that returns an empty sequence.

The commutativity relation for these operations is shown in Figure 1. As usual, we assume that operations invoked on different elements always commute. Let us illustrate some of the cases:

- $SInsert(x)$ does not commute with itself. Indeed, it is easy to verify that return values in the sequences $\langle\ SDelete(x)\ SInsert_1(x)\ SInsert_2(x)\ \rangle$ and $\langle\ SDelete(x)\ SInsert_2(x)\ SInsert_1(x)\ \rangle$ are not the same. For instance, if the element x exists in S before the execution of the sequences, then $SInsert_1(x)$ returns x in the first sequence and 0 in the second sequence.
- $SInsert^{-1}(x)$ commutes with itself. We know that $SInsert^{-1}(x)$ operations always returns 1. Consequently, it can be only return values of some sequence β that can distinguish $\langle\ \alpha\ SInsert_1^{-1}(x)\ SInsert_2^{-1}(x)\ \beta\ \rangle$ and $\langle\ \alpha\ SInsert_2^{-1}(x)\ SInsert_1^{-1}(x)\ \beta\ \rangle$. Every α must contain both $SInsert_1(x)$ and $SInsert_2(x)$ (to guarantee well-formedness). If any of the two $SInsert$'s returns zero, then one of the two backward operations does not modify the set and thus it is easy to see that no β can distinguish the two sequences. If, on the other hand, both $SInsert$'s return x (this can happen if there is a $SDelete$ in between them), then both undoes delete x and thus no β can recognize the difference between $\langle\ \alpha\ SInsert_1^{-1}(x)\ SInsert_2^{-1}(x)\ \rangle$ and $\langle\ \alpha\ SInsert_2^{-1}(x)\ SInsert_1^{-1}(x)\ \rangle$ since x is removed from the set in both cases.

Any scheduler may execute commutative operations concurrently. In order to design the scheduler, a conflict detection method CON defined on pairs of operation invocations must be provided. CON will return true if the operations conflict and false otherwise. If a concurrency control is based on state-dependent

	SInsert	SDelete	Test	SInsert^{-1}	SDelete^{-1}	Test^{-1}
SInsert	-	-	-	-	-	+
SDelete	-	-	-	-	-	+
Test	-	-	+	-	-	+
SInsert^{-1}	-	-	-	+	-	+
SDelete^{-1}	-	-	-	-	+	+
Test^{-1}	+	+	+	+	+	+

Fig. 1. Commutativity relation

commutativity, it can in general allow more concurrency. However, the mechanism CON to decide whether two operations conflict requires the system to know all prior history.

If the conflict detection method works only on the operation invocations independent of the state, it may still require sophisticated implementation. For example, if applied to SQL operation invocation, we must determine whether two where-predicates are satisfied, i.e., whether the read set and the write set are disjoint. For the rest of the paper we assume that such a conflict detection on operation invocations is provided and this method is *state independent*.

2.3 Perfect Commutativity

The major question we deal with in this paper is a consequence of the following observation. We call a commutativity relation **perfect** if backward operations have the same conflict behaviour as forward operations. Formally, we say that a commutativity relation is **perfect** if for every two operations p and q either p^α commutes with q^β for all possible combinations of $\alpha, \beta \in \{-1, 1\}$ or p^α does not commute with q^β for all possible combinations of $\alpha, \beta \in \{-1, 1\}$ with the exception of λ as a backward operation.

Assume now that a scheduler detected that q commutes with a previous operation p. Then q can be scheduled and executed in parallel with p. However if p^{-1} must be executed afterwards due to an abort and p^{-1} conflicts with q, then it is questionable whether we can compensate effects of p in a correct way. Intuitively, we would like to be "perfect", i.e., if p^{-1} also commutes with q, we can execute p^{-1} without any restriction and without generating an undesirable dependency.

The perfectness is given in the read/write model because the undo of write is another write. However, in the more general model this property is not given a priori. We therefore must deal with non-perfectness and with its consequences.

2.4 Transactions

Database users access the database through **transactions**. A transaction, T_i, is a partial order, $<_i$, of operations (o_i) from O with either *commit* (c_i) or *abort* (a_i)

(but not both) as the maximal element of $<_i$. We say that two operations conflict if and only if they do not commute. A **schedule** S over a set of transactions $\mathcal{T}$ is a partial order $\langle_S$ of all operations of all transactions in $\mathcal{T}$ such that for any transaction T_i in $\mathcal{T}$, $<_i$ is a subset of $<_S$ and any two conflicting operations of different transactions are $<_S$ ordered. If $o_i <_S o_j$ in S, then we say that operation o_i is executed before operation o_j in S. In schedule S we also allow operation $a(T_{i_1}, \cdots, T_{i_k})$ for each transaction $T_{i_1}, \cdots, T_{i_k}$. This operation, called **group abort**, indicates that an abort should be executed for each transaction from $T_{i_1}, \ldots, T_{i_k}$. However, those aborts are executed concurrently.

Transaction T_i is said to be **committed (aborted)** in S if S contains c_i (a_i or $a(\ldots, T_i, \ldots)$) operation(s). Transaction T_i is **active** in S if it is neither committed nor aborted in S.

2.5 Expanded schedules

In order to handle aborted transactions explicitly in a schedule we replace a transaction abort statement with a sequence of transaction undo operations to eliminate the partial effects of an aborted transaction and call the resulting schedule an expanded one. Thus, if a scheduler produces a serializable expanded schedule of transaction operations, where adjacent $o \cdot o^{-1}$ are eliminated from consideration, then issues of serializability and atomicity are treated by such a scheduler in a uniform way. These ideas proposed in [SWY93, AVA⁺94] lead to the introduction of an **expanded schedule**. Following [AVA⁺94], for each schedule $\langle S, <_S \rangle$, we define an expanded schedule $\langle \tilde{S}, <_{\tilde{S}} \rangle$ as follows.

Definition 4 [AVA⁺94]:. Let $S, <_S$) be a schedule, where S is the set of operations and $<_S$ is a partial order over these operations. Its **expansion**, or **expanded schedule**, is a tuple $(\tilde{A}, <_{\tilde{S}})$ where:

1. $\tilde{S}$ is a set of operations which is derived from S in the following way:
   (a) For each transaction $T_i \in S$, if $o_i \in T_i$ and o_i is not an abort operation, then $o_i \in \tilde{S}$.
   (b) Active transactions are treated as aborted transactions, by adding a group abort $a(T_{i_1} \ldots T_{i_k})$ at the end of S, where $T_{i_1} \ldots T_{i_k}$ are all the active transactions in S.
   (c) For each aborted transaction $T_j \in S$ and for every operation $o_j \in T_j$, there exists a backward operation $o_j^{-1} \in \tilde{S}$. An abort operation $a_j \in S$ is changed to $c_j \in \tilde{S}$. Operation $a(T_{i_1} \ldots T_{i_k})$ is replaced with a sequence of $c_{i_1}, \ldots, c_{i_k}$.
2. The partial order, $<_{\tilde{S}}$, is determined as follows:
   (a) For every two operations, o_i and o_j, if $o_i <_S o_j$ then $o_i <_{\tilde{S}} o_j$.
   (b) If transactions T_i and T_j abort in S and their aborts are not $<_S$-ordered, then every two conflicting undo operations of transactions T_i and T_j are in $\tilde{S}$ in the reverse order of the two corresponding forward operations in S. If the forward operations are not $<_S$-ordered, then the two undo operations are in an arbitrary order.

(c) All undo operations of every transaction T_i that does not commit in S follow the transaction's original operations and must precede c_i in $\tilde{S}$.

(d) Whenever $o_n <_S a(T_{i_1}, \ldots, T_{i_k}) <_S o_m$ and some undo operation o_j^{-1} ($j \in \{i_1, \ldots, i_k\}$) conflicts with o_m (o_n), then $o_j^{-1} <_{\tilde{S}} o_m$ ($o_n <_{\tilde{S}} o_j^{-1}$).

(e) Whenever $a(\ldots, T_i, \ldots) <_S a(\ldots, T_j, \ldots)$ for some $i \neq j$, then for all conflicting undo operations of T_i and T_j, o_i^{-1} and o_j^{-1}, $o_i^{-1} <_{\tilde{S}} o_j^{-1}$.

We say that schedule S is **reducible** (RED) [SWY93] if there exists at least one expanded schedule $\tilde{S}$ such that it can be transformed into a serializable schedule by applying the following two rules:

1. **Commutativity rule:** If o_1 and o_2 are two non-conflicting operations in $\tilde{S}$ such that $o_1 <_{\tilde{S}} o_2$ and there is no $p \in \tilde{S}$ such that $o_1 <_{\tilde{S}} p <_{\tilde{S}} o_2$, then the order $o_1 <_{\tilde{S}} o_2$ can be replaced with $o_2 <_{\tilde{S}} o_1$.

2. **Undo rule:** If o and o^{-1} are two operations in $\tilde{S}$ such that there is no $p \in \tilde{S}$ such that $o <_{\tilde{S}} p <_{\tilde{S}} o^{-1}$ then both o and o^{-1} can be removed from $\tilde{S}$.

To illustrate, consider schedule $S_1 : SDelete_1(x) \, SInsert_2(x) \, Test_3(x) \, c_2 \, a_3$. Its expansion is $\tilde{S} : SDelete_1(x) \, SInsert_2(x) \, Test_3(x) \, c_2 \, Test_3^{-1}(x) \, c_3 \, SDelete_1^{-1}(x) \, c_1$ and it is not reducible. On the other hand, schedule $S_2 : SDelete_1(x) \, SInsert_2(x) \, Test_3(x) \, c_2 \, c_1 \, a_3$ with expansion $\tilde{S}_2 : SDelete_1(x) \, SInsert_2(x) \, Test_3(x) \, c_2 \, c_1 \, Test_3^{-1}(x) \, c_3$ is reducible.

Unfortunately, the class of reducible schedules is not prefix-closed and hence cannot be used for online scheduling of transactions [SWY93]. We resolve it by requiring that any reducible schedule be prefix reducible, i.e not only S should be reducible but also any prefix of S must be reducible. For example, schedule S_2 given above is reducible but not prefix reducible, while schedule $S_3 : SDelete_1(x) \, SInsert_2(x) \, Test_3(x) \, c_1 \, c_2 \, a_3$ is prefix-reducible.

3 Unified Transaction Theory

In this section we present our main theoretical results. Our goal is to provide a constructive characterization of prefix reducible schedules in models with semantically rich operations that will easily lead to a construction of schedulers. Such a characterization has been already found for read/write model in [AVA+94]. In the general case, we are still able to provide a constructive graph based characterization of prefix reducible schedules, however its complexity is too high (although polynomial) for design of schedulers. We therefore define subclasses of prefix reducible schedules possessing a simple characterization amenable to a protocol construction.

3.1 Reducible Schedules and Their Characterization

The definition of reducible schedules given in the previous section is not constructive. In this subsection we provide a constructive procedure to decide whether a given schedule is reducible. Consider a pair of operations (o_i, o_i^{-1}) in expanded schedule $\tilde{S}$. If there are no other operations between o_i and o_i^{-1} in $\tilde{S}$, then this pair can be removed using the undo rule. Assume now that there are some operations between o_i and o_i^{-1} in $\tilde{S}$. Let $o_1, \ldots o_n$ be operations between o_i and o_i^{-1} such that each o_l conflicts with o_{l+1}, o_i conflicts with with o_1 and o_n conflicts with o_i^{-1}. Then to eliminate the pair (o_i, o_i^{-1}) we need to break this chain of operations by eliminating at least one operation from the sequence by using undo and commutativity rules. However, if each operation in the sequence belongs to a committed transaction, then none of o_l can be eliminated since no operation of a committed transaction can be eliminated from schedule $\tilde{S}$. In such case, S would not be reducible. Thus in order for S to be reducible, we need to know for each pair (o_i, o_i^{-1}) in $\tilde{S}$ whether it can be removed from the schedule.

Let S be a schedule and $\tilde{S}$ its expansion. To characterize reducibility of schedule S we construct a **reducibility graph** $RG(\tilde{S})$ as follows: The nodes of are *all* operations in $\tilde{S}$. If o_i from T_i $\langle_{\tilde{S}}$-precedes o_j from T_j $(i \neq j)$ and o_i conflicts with o_j, then $RG(\tilde{S})$ contains edge $\langle o_i, o_j \rangle$.

Lemma 5. *Two operations o_i and o_i^{-1} can be moved together by use of the commutativity rule in $\tilde{S}$ if and only if there is no path between o_i and o_i^{-1} in $RG(\tilde{S})$.*

Based on this lemma we can decide whether a given expanded schedule $\tilde{S}$ is reducible using the procedure defined below:

1. For $\tilde{S}$ construct $RG(\tilde{S})$.
2. Find a pair of nodes o_i and o_i^{-1} in $RG(\tilde{S})$ that have no path between them.
3. If such a pair does not exists, exit the loop.
4. If such a pair does exist, remove it from $RG(\tilde{S})$ along with all edges incidental to these nodes and also remove that pair from $\tilde{S}$.
5. Go to step 2.

If, as a result of the procedure, we obtain a serializable schedule of only forward operations, then S is reducible. Otherwise, S is not reducible. To illustrate, consider the following examples:

Example 2. Consider schedule $S_3 : SInsert_1(x)\ SDelete_2(x)\ SInsert_3(x)\ a_1\ a_2$ a_3. Its expansion is $\tilde{S}_3 = SInsert_1(x)\ SDelete_2(x)\ SInsert_3(x)\ SInsert_1^{-1}(x)$ $SDelete_2^{-1}(x)\ SInsert_3^{-1}(x)\ c_1\ c_2\ c_3$. According to the commutativity relation in Example 1, operation $SInsert_1(x)$ conflicts with $SDelete_2(x)$, $SDelete_2(x)$ conflicts with $SInsert_3(x)$, $SInsert_3(x)$ conflicts with $SInsert_1^{-1}(x)$, $SInsert_1^{-1}(x)$ conflicts with $SDelete_2^{-1}(x)$ and $SDelete_2^{-1}(x)$ conflicts with $SInsert_3^{-1}(x)$. There are no other conflicts. The reducibility graph for $\tilde{S}_3$ consists of a single path: $(SInsert_1(x),\ SDelete_2(x),\ SInsert_3(x),\ SInsert_1^{-1}(x),\ SDelete_2^{-1}(x),$ $SInsert_3^{-1}(x))$. Thus, between any two do operation and its corresponding undo operation there is a path. S_3 is not reducible.

Example 3. Consider schedule $S_4 : SDelete_1(x)\ SDelete_2(x)\ SDelete_3(x)\ a_1\ a_2$ a_3. Its expansion is $\tilde{S}_4 = SDelete_1(x)\ SDelete_2(x)\ SDelete_3(x)\ SDelete_1^{-1}(x)$

$SDelete_2^{-1}(x)$ $SDelete_3^{-1}(x)$ c_1 c_2 c_3. Based on the commutativity relation in Example 1, operation $SDelete_1(x)$ conflicts with $SDelete_2(x)$, $SDelete_2(x)$ conflicts with $SDelete_3(x)$, $SDelete_3(x)$ conflicts with $SDelete_1^{-1}(x)$. There are no other conflicts. The reducibility graph for $\tilde{S}_4$ contains path $(SDelete_1(x), SDelete_2(x), SDelete_3(x), SDelete_1^{-1}(x))$ and two isolated nodes $SDelete_2^{-1}(x)$ and $SDelete_3^{-1}(x)$. Consequently, after removing $SDelete_3(x)$ and $SDelete_3^{-1}(x)$ and $SDelete_2(x)$ and $SDelete_2^{-1}(x)$ from the graph, we obtain a graph that does not contain any path between $SDelete_1(x)$ and $SDelete_1^{-1}(x)$. Therefore, also this pair of nodes also can be removed from the graph. Thus, S_4 is reducible.

The above procedure provides a constructive method to decide whether a schedule is reducible. However, the procedure requires $O(n^4)$ operations, where n is the number of operations in S and thus is quite impractical. In Section 3.3 we consider much less complicated procedures that allow us to generate relatively rich subclasses of reducible schedules.

We conclude this subsection by comparing the class of reducible schedules with the class of revokable schedules introduced by Moss, Griffith and Graham [MGG86a, MGG86b]. Their definition in our model can be restated as follows.

Definition 6 [MGG86a, MGG86b]. Schedule S is **revokable** iff for every two transactions T_i, T_j in S and every two operations $o_i \in T_i, o_j \in T_j$ such that $o_i <_S o_j$, a_i does not precede o_j in S and o_i^{-1} is in conflict with o_j then if T_i aborts in S then T_j also aborts in S and either $a_j <_S a_i$ or $a(\ldots, T_i, \ldots, T_j, \ldots) \in S$.

Schedule $SInsert_1(x)$ $SInsert_2(x)$ a_2 a_1 where the commutativity relation is defined as in Fig.1 is both revokable and reducible. Not every reducible schedule is revokable. Schedule $SInsert_1(x)$ $SInsert_2(x)$ a_1 a_2 is not revokable, however, it is reducible. Not every revokable schedule is reducible. Schedule $SInsert_1(x)$ $SInsert_2(x)$ $SInsert_2(y)$ $SInsert_1(y)$ c_1 c_2 is revokable but not reducible, since it is not serializable. It appears that only revokable nonserializable schedules are not reducible.

Theorem 7. *Every revokable and serializable schedule is also reducible.*

3.2 Prefix Reducible Schedules

We restrict now our attention to the class of prefix reducible schedules. In [AVA+94] we characterized the class of prefix reducible schedules in the read/write model. However, straightforward generalization of that result for the transaction model presented here does not work, as we demonstrate below. We first redefine the class of schedules **serializable with ordered termination** (SOT) defined in [AVA+94] for a set of operations O.

Definition 8. A schedule S is **serializable with ordered termination (SOT)** if it is serializable, and for every 2 transactions T_i, T_j in S and every 2 operations $o_i \in T_i, o_j \in T_j$ such that $o_i <_S o_j$, a_i does not precede o_j in S, o_i is in conflict with o_j and o_i^{-1} is in conflict with o_j, the following conditions hold:

1. if T_j commits in S then T_i commits in S and $c_i <_S c_j$.
2. if o_i^{-1} and o_j^{-1} are in conflict, and T_i aborts in S then T_j also aborts in S and either $a_j <_S a_i$ or $a(\ldots, T_i, \ldots, T_j, \ldots) \in S$.

The first condition implies that commit operations of both transactions should be performed in the order of their conflicting operations. Without this condition, the schedule $o_i\ o_j\ c_j\ c_i$ would not be prefix reducible (provided that o_i, o_j and o_i^{-1}, o_j are in conflict). Indeed, consider $o_i\ o_j\ c_j$, which is the prefix of S. Its expansion is $o_i\ o_j\ c_j\ o_i^{-1}\ c_i$. It cannot be reduced since neither operations o_j and o_i^{-1} nor o_i and o_j can be swapped.

The second condition implies that abort operations of conflicting transactions should be performed in the order opposite to the execution of their conflicting operations. Without this condition the schedule $o_i\ o_j\ a_i\ a_j$, where o_i conflicts with o_j, o_j conflicts with o_i^{-1} which, in turn, conflicts with o_j^{-1}, is not reducible, and, thus, is not prefix-reducible.

Theorem 9. *Every prefix reducible schedule is also serializable with ordered termination.*

However, the requirement for a schedule to be SOT is not sufficient to ensure prefix reducibility. In [VYBS94] we give examples of schedules that satisfy SOT, but are not prefix reducible.

The process to decide whether a schedule is prefix-reducible is expensive. To eliminate such complexity, one of the two ways can be followed: either we should restrict the class of prefix reducible schedules or we should impose some restrictions on a commutativity relation. In the next subsection we investigate the first approach and in subsection 3.4 we investigate the second approach.

3.3 Safe Schedules

In order to show that a given schedule is prefix reducible, it is necessary to eliminate all forward-backward operation pairs belonging to aborted transactions by use of commutativity and undo rules. In doing so, it is possible to combine movements of both forward operations towards the backward operations and backward operations towards forward operations. Such a degree of freedom together with the fact that both forward operation and its backward operation can commute with different sets of operations contribute to the difficulties of constructive characterization of $PRED$.

To restrict the $PRED$ class to a class that can be effectively handled by scheduler and/or recovery manager, consider in more details what happens when an undo operation is scheduled. The purpose of the undo operation as we stated earlier is to undo all visible effects of the corresponding forward operation. Consider the situation that after executing $o_1\ o_2 \ldots o_k$ operation o_1^{-1} must be executed. To undo effects of o_1 and also guarantee consistency of the resulting schedule, the scheduler scheduling o_1^{-1} must assure that no operation in the sequence $o_2 \ldots o_k$ would be affected by scheduling o_1^{-1}. This can be achieved in one of the two ways:

- Operations $o_2 \ldots o_k$ do not conflict with o_1 and thus their visible effects are not affected by return value of o_1. Then o_1 can be safely moved to o_1^{-1} and both operations subsequently eliminated by the undo rule.
- Operation o_1^{-1} commutes with every operation in the sequence $o_2 \ldots o_k$. Then o_1^{-1} can be safely moved to o_1 and both operations can be subsequently eliminated by the undo rule.

These two cases can be formalized in the following definition:

Definition 10. Schedule S is **forward safe** (**backward safe**) if and only if for every two transactions T_i, T_j in S and every two operations $o_i \in T_i, o_j \in T_j$ such that $o_i <_S o_j$, T_i does not abort before o_j in S and o_i (o_i^{-1}) is in conflict with o_j the following conditions hold:

1. If T_j commits in S, then T_i commits in S and $c_i <_S c_j$.
2. If T_i aborts in S and $o_j^{-1} \neq \lambda$ then T_j also aborts in S and either $a_j <_S a_i$ or $a(\ldots, T_i, \ldots, T_j, \ldots) \in S$.

There exist forward safe schedules that are not backward safe and vice versa as the example below demonstrates:

Example 4. Consider schedule $S_1 : Test_1(x) \ SInsert_2(x) \ c_2 \ a_1$. Since $SInsert(x)$ is in conflict with $Test(x)$, but $Test^{-1}(x)$ commutes with $SInsert(x)$, the schedule is backward safe, but not forward safe (since the first condition from Definition 10 is not satisfied). Similar ideas can be used to obtain an example of schedule that is forward safe, but not backward safe[VYBS94].

Recall that to guarantee forward safeness we must consider conflicting pairs of forward operations. Alternatively, we must consider conflicting pairs of forward and backward operations to guarantee backward safeness. Consider, for example, a case when transaction T_1 issues several select statements and transaction T_2 subsequently performs some update statements. If transaction T_1 aborts, then T_2 still can commit to guarantee backward safeness, however to guarantee forward safeness T_2 would have to abort. On the other hand, consider, for example, that forward operations of transaction T_1 are followed by forward operations of transaction T_2 which commute with all T_1's forward operations. But some of the backward operations to forward operations of T_1 conflict with some of T_2's forward operations. If transaction T_1 aborts, then transaction T_2 still can commit guaranteeing forward safeness. However, to guarantee backward safeness T_2 would have to abort.

Since the ordering of commit operations reflects conflicts between forward and backward operations rather than between two forward operations, a backward safe schedule is not necessarily serializable. For example, schedule S : $Test_1(x) \ SInsert_2(x) \ Test_2(y) \ SInsert_1(y) \ c_1 \ c_2$ is backward safe, but not serializable. Alternatively, every forward safe schedule is serializable since it is a subclass of **commit ordered** schedules which, in turn, is a subclass of serializable schedules [BGRS91, Raz92]. Every rigorous schedule [BGRS91] is also

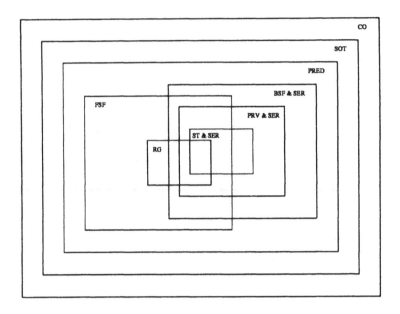

Fig. 2. Relationship between classes

forward safe. On the other hand, schedule $S : SInsert_1(x)\ SDelete_2(x)\ c_1\ c_2$ is forward safe, but not rigorous.

To compare the class of backward and forward safe schedules with **revokable schedules**[MGG86a, MGG86b], we need to make revokable property prefix closed. We therefore introduce the class of **prefix revokable** schedules as follows:

Definition 11. Schedule S is **prefix revokable** iff for every two transactions T_i, T_j in S and every two operations $o_i \in T_i, o_j \in T_j$ such that $o_i <_S o_j$, a_i does not precede o_j in S and o_i^{-1} is in conflict with o_j the following is true:

1. if T_j commits in S then T_i commits in S and $c_i <_S c_j$.
2. if T_i aborts in S then T_j also aborts in S and either $a_j <_S a_i$ or $a(\ldots, T_i, \ldots, T_j, \ldots) \in S$.

It turns out that the class of backward safe schedules is broader than the class of prefix revokable schedules. That is there are schedules that are not prefix revokable and yet are backward safe. For example, consider schedule $S : SInsert_1(x)\ Test_2(x)\ a_1\ a_2$. This schedule is backward safe, but it is not prefix revokable. On the other hand, there are prefix revokable schedules that are not forward safe and forward safe schedules that are not prefix revokable.

The class of *strict* schedules defined in [RKS92, RKS93] as schedules such that if for every two operations in S o_i and o_j such that $o_i <_S o_j$ and o_i^{-1} is in conflict with o_j, then transaction T_i terminates before o_j in S is a subclass of prefix revokable (and consequently also backward safe) schedules. On the other hand, there are prefix revokable schedules that are not strict. Consider for example schedule $S : SInsert_1(x)\ SDelete_2(x)\ c_1\ c_2$. It is easy to see that S is not strict, but it is prefix revokable. Note that S is serial.

As opposed to the read/write model, there is no relationship between strict serializable and rigorous schedules, i.e. there exist strict schedules that are not rigorous and vice versa. Consider schedule $S_1 : Test_1(x)\ SInsert_2(x)\ c_1\ c_2$. The schedule is strict and serializable, but not rigorous. Similarly, a schedule that is rigorous, but not strict can be found in [VYBS94].

Theorem 12. *Every forward safe schedule is prefix reducible. Every backward safe and serializable schedule is prefix reducible.*

The relationship of all the classes introduced in sections 3.1 - 3.3 is shown in Figure 2.

The reader might have observed that in some cases to guarantee safeness (forward or backward) an abort of one transaction might require abort of another transaction. This means that both classes are subject to cascading aborts. We prove, however, the following.

Theorem 13. *The class of rigorous (strict) schedules is the $\subseteq$-maximal subclass of the class of forward (backward) safe schedules that avoids cascading aborts.*

3.4 Perfect Commutativity Relation

The main appeal of models with a perfect commutativity relation lies in their ""isomorphism"" to the read/write model. Namely, serializability with ordered termination becomes an exact characterization of prefix reducible schedules.

Theorem 14. *Let the commutativity relation be perfect. Then the classes of prefix reducible schedules, schedules serializable with ordered termination and backward safe serializable schedules coincide.*

4 Conclusion

In this paper we discussed prefix reducibility within the framework of the general model with semantically rich operations. We have demonstrated that the characterization from [AVA$^+$94], the class schedules serializable with ordered termination, does not suffice to precisely characterize all prefix reducible schedules in this general case. We, however, identified the conditions on the model under which such a characterization is exact.

Acknowledgement

The authors are deeply grateful to Gerhard Weikum, who generously contributed to the ideas described here and whose comments and advise were invaluable. We are also grateful to anonymous referee for his detailed comments and suggestions.

References

[AVA+94] G. Alonso, R. Vingralek, D. Agrawal, Y. Breitbart, A. Abbadi, H. Schek, and G. Weikum. A unified approach to concurrency control and transaction recovery. *Information Systems*, 19(1), 1994.

[BR92] B.R. Badrinath and K. Ramamritham. Semantics-based concurrency control: beyond commutativity. *ACM Transactions on Database Systems*, 17(1), March 1992.

[BGRS91] Y. Breitbart, D. Georgakopoulos, M. Rusinkiewicz and A. Silberschatz. On rigorous transaction scheduling. *IEEE Transactions on Software Engineering*, 17(9), 1991.

[HH88] T. Hadzilacos and V. Hadzilacos. Transaction synchronization in object bases. *Proc. ACM Principles of Database Systems*, 1988.

[HH91] T. Hadzilacos and V. Hadzilacos. Transaction synchronization in object bases. *Journal of computer and system sciences*, 1991.

[LMWF94] N. Lynch, M. Merritt, W. Weihl, and A. Fekete. *Atomic Transactions*. Morgen Kaufmann, San Mateo, CA, 1994.

[MGG86a] J. Moss, N. Griffeth, and M. Graham. Abstraction in concurrency control and recovery management (revised). Tech. rept. coins technical report 86-20., University of Massachusetts at Amherst, March 1986.

[MGG86b] J. Moss, N. Griffeth, and M Graham. Abstraction in recovery management. *ACM SIGMOD Conference*, 15(1), 1986.

[RKS92] R. Rastogi, H. F. Korth, and A. Silberschatz. Strict histories in object-based database systems. Technical report, Matsushita Information Technology Laboratory, 1992.

[RKS93] R. Rastogi, H. F. Korth, and A. Silberschatz. Strict histories in object-based database systems. In *Symposium on Principles of Database Systems*, 1993.

[Raz92] Y. Raz. The principle of commitment ordering, or guaranteeing serializability in a heterogeneous, multiresource manager enviroment using atomic commitment. *Proc. 18th International Conference on Very Large Data Bases*, 1992.

[VYBS94] R. Vingralek, H. Ye, Y. Breitbart, and H.-J. Schek. Unified Transaction Model for Semantically Rich Operations. Technical Report, Department of Computer Science, ETH Zurich, 1994

[SWY93] H.-J. Schek, G. Weikum, and H. Ye. Towards a unified theory of concurrency control and recovery. *Proc. ACM Principles of Database Systems*, 1993.

[Wei88] W.E. Weihl. Commutativity-based concurrency control for abstract data types. *IEEE Transactions on Computers*, 37(12), 1988.

[Wei89] W.E. Weihl. The impact of recovery on concurrency control. *Proc. ACM Principles of Database Systems*, 1989.

[Wei91] G. Weikum. Principles and realization strategies of multilevel transaction management. *ACM Transactions on Database Systems*, 16(1), 1991.

The Dynamic Two Phase Commitment (D2PC) Protocol

Yoav Raz[1]

EMC Corporation, Hopkinton, Massachusetts; raz@emc.com

Since the *Two Phase Commitment* (2PC) protocol is an essential component for *Distributed Transaction Processing*, needed in the commit process of each distributed transaction, a substantial effort has been invested in optimizing its performance. The *Dynamic Two Phase Commitment* (D2PC) protocol is an enhancement of the common (static) *Tree Two Phase Commitment* (T2PC) protocols. Unlike T2PC, with D2PC the commit coordinator is dynamically determined by racing READY (YES vote) messages, on a per transaction basis, rather than being fixed, predetermined. As a result, the protocol commits each transaction participant in minimum possible time, allowing early release of locked resources. This result is true for the various existing variants of T2PC. D2PC subsumes several T2PC optimizations that have been proposed earlier.

1 Introduction

A *transaction* is an execution of a set of programs that access shared *recoverable resources* (e.g., data items). A resource is recoverable if its state, as viewed by the transaction when first accessing this resource, can be restored during the transaction, if has been modified by the transaction. A transaction is characterized by its *atomicity* property: Either it is *committed*, i.e., completes successfully bringing all modified resources to their new, *final state*, or it is *aborted*, returning all modified resources to their *initial state*. A distributed transaction involves several (more than one) *processes*, that may access different recoverable resources. The purpose of *atomic commitment* (AC) protocols (see e.g., [Bern 87]) is achieving consensus among the transaction's processes on whether to commit or abort (on consensus in distributed systems see, for example, [Dwor 84]). Several processes may group to comprise a single *participant* in AC (usually processes that fail together), while the intra participant coordination is done out of the scope of AC (possibly using a separate, internal AC protocol).

AC protocols obey the following general scheme:

- **AC**

  After completing its part in a transaction, each participant votes either YES or NO on the transaction, or votes NO if unable to complete its part successfully (also absence of a vote within a specified time limit may be considered NO). The transaction is committed if all have voted YES. Otherwise it is aborted by all participants.

The *Two Phase Commit* protocol is a special case of AC (2PC; [Gray 78], [Lamp 86], [Moha 83], [Moha 86]; examples of 2PC implementation descriptions and specifications can be found in [DECdtm], [LU6.2], [OSI-CCR], [OSI-DTP], [X/Open-DTP], [Brag 91], [Upto 91]). 2PC has been the most commonly used AC protocol. Since the 2PC protocol is an essential component for *Distributed Transaction Processing*, needed in the commit process of each distributed transaction, a substantial effort has been invested in optimizing its performance. The common variant of 2PC can be described as follows:

---

[1] This work was written while the author was employed by Digital Equipment Corporation. Previous versions appeared as DEC-TR 871.

- **2PC**

  The decision process of whether to commit or abort a transaction is executed in two phases.

  In the *first phase* a preferred participant, the *commit coordinator* (CC) requests the other participants to vote on the transaction. Then votes are logged by each participant and communicated to the CC. The commit coordinator makes the decision whether to commit or abort the transaction (based on the AC scheme above), and logs the decision.

  In the *second phase* the CC communicates the decision to all other participants and the transaction is completed after the CC receives acknowledgment on the decision from all other participants.

In the cases of certain failures occurring with a participant before its voting, the transaction is aborted. A failure occurring after the voting, results in completing the transaction according to the voting, provided that the failure has been recovered. This behavior in cases of failure can be guaranteed by the logged information, which survives certain types of failure. Different variants of 2PC differ in their logging patterns and recovery procedures, and their ability to survive various types of failure.

This work describes a new generic type of 2PC named the *Dynamic Two Phase Commitment (D2PC)* protocol. With D2PC the CC is dynamically determined by racing YES vote messages, on a per transaction basis, rather than being fixed, predetermined. As a result, the protocol commits each participant in minimum possible time, allowing early release of locked resources.

D2PC is the basis for enhancements of the *ISO DTP* and *CCR* standards ([OSI-DTP], [OSI-CCR]; *Amendment 1 on Commit Optimizations* of each standard). D2PC employs the voting strategy of the TREE-COMMIT protocol defined in [Sega 87] and further discussed in [Sega 88] and [Wolf 91]. [Sega 87] shows that TREE-COMMIT commits a transaction on a given communication tree in the minimum elapse time possible for this tree (the time from the first vote of a participant, to the last commitment of a participant). The current work generalizes this result showing that D2PC commits each participant (not just the last to commit) in the minimum possible time for a given tree. Since transactions typically lock resources, and release them upon (local) commitment[1], D2PC guarantees that the total time each resource is locked by a transaction is minimal. Also the correctness of the D2PC protocol (and the correctness of TREE-COMMIT of [Sega 87]) is proven here. This work concentrates on optimizing the case when transactions are successfully committed, which is the common case for current transaction processing technology. The intention of this work is to deal with aspects of D2PC that are unique to this protocol. Thus, procedures for recovery and abort handling are not directly dealt with here. *Any* logging and recovery strategy used for any known T2PC protocol can also be used for D2PC. The description of D2PC and its comparison with T2PC below is general and does not assume any specific variant of T2PC. I.e., for each given variant of T2PC, mainly characterized by its logging and recovery strategy, a respective variant of D2PC that uses the same logging and recovery exists to compare with. Such a respective variant of D2PC exists since also D2PC is a tree protocol with the same message semantics.

The rest of the work is organized as follows: Section 2 describes Tree 2PC protocols. Section 3 describes the D2PC protocol and proves its correctness. Section 4 proves optimality results for D2PC, and section 5 discusses using different communication trees for transaction invocation and termination. Section 6 provides a conclusion.

---

[1] Note that the *read-only* optimization, which allows early release of *read locks* may cause a global serializability violation, if a transaction acquires locks in some participant *after* another participant of the transaction has released read locks following a *read-only* vote.

2 Tree 2PC (T2PC) protocols

2.1 Distributed transactions

A distributed transaction is typically initiated with one participant, the transaction's *root*, and propagated to other participants. The other participants are being invoked recursively, inducing a communication structure that can be modeled as a tree, the *invocation tree*.

The participants and *communication connections* comprise the invocation tree's *nodes* and *edges* respectively. Each invocation either establishes a new communication connection for the transaction's duration, at least, or reuses an existing connection. In any case, at any moment of the transaction's existence, the participants and their connections comprise a tree structure (even two new connections to a same physical participant establish two distinct logical participants, nodes). An invoking node (participant) is the *superior* of the invoked node. The invoked node is the *subordinate* of the invoking node. Two nodes with a common edge are *neighbors* (each one is a neighbor of the other). A node with a single neighbor is a *leaf* in the tree.

A distributed transaction is terminated via an AC protocol. The voting and the decision notification (either commit, or abort) are communicated between participants and a special participant, the CC, also through tree like communication structures, *termination trees*.

Termination trees of a transaction may differ from its invocation tree (e.g., [Sega 88]). However, it is common to use the invocation tree also for termination (e.g., [OSI-DTP]).

2.2 The basic Tree 2PC (T2PC) protocol

The T2PC protocol (also known as *nested* 2PC) is a common type of the 2PC protocol. In T2PC the coordinator does not necessarily directly communicate with the other participants. It may communicate the 2PC information to some participants through other participants, generating any termination tree with the participants as nodes.

A distributed transaction comprises *local subtransactions*, each of them consisting of the portion of the transaction at a single participant. Each local subtransaction has the following states:

- **active** -
  The related local subtransaction's programs are executing. (They are considered executing even if being idle, waiting for input from a neighboring participant or from any other external, interacting source.)

- **prepared** -
  The related local subtransaction's programs have finished executing, and are waiting for no transaction data to arrive from a neighboring participant.

- **ready** -
  The respective participant has voted by sending a message to another participant (a YES vote is carried by a READY message; a NO vote is carried by an ABORT message). When entering this state the participant has already taken all the measures needed to bring modified recoverable resources either to their initial or final states, depending on the voting outcome. This ability remains unharmed by certain types of failure, which depend on implementations' specifics.

- **committed** -
  The respective participant has committed the local subtransaction by bringing all respective recoverable resources to their final state.

- **aborted** -
  The respective participant has aborted the local subtransaction by bringing all respective recoverable resources to their initial state.

- **forgotten** -
  The respective participant has discarded recovery related information of the local subtransaction (including nonvolatile information) .

The possible state transitions are described in Figure 1.

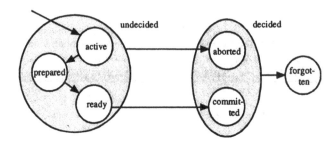

Figure 1: Local subtransaction states and their transitions

A state transition may involve sending/receiving a message(s) to/from a neighbor(s). The following message types are used (following [OSI-CCR]):

- **PREPARE** - A participant is notifying its neighbor that it will not send to it any additional data on behalf of the transaction. In cases when it is a-priori clear that no such data will be sent, the PREPARE message is unnecessary (this is an implicit PREPARE carried by the application's semantics; e.g., when a subordinate "knows" that it is invoked by a single remote procedure call (RPC) with a single returned result).
- **READY** - A participant is notifying (a neighbor) that it has voted YES on the transaction.
- **COMMIT** - A participant is notifying that the transaction has been committed.
- **COMMIT_ACK** (acknowledgment) - A participant is notifying that it has committed the transaction.
- **ABORT** - A participant is notifying that the transaction has been aborted. This message may reflect a NO vote on the transaction by the participant, or a propagation of the decision to abort.
- **ABORT_ACK** (acknowledgment) - A participant is notifying that it has aborted the transaction.

Algorithm 2.1 defines the common T2PC protocol for the case when the transaction is committed.

Algorithm 2.1 - The T2PC Protocol - commitment procedure

Phase One

- A node (participant) sends PREPARE messages when applies (see the semantics of PREPARE above) to every subordinate (when exist). (A nonroot node typically enters the prepared state only after receiving a PREPARE message from its superior. Thus PREPARE messages typically propagate from the root to the leaves.)
- A node in the prepared state, that has received a READY message from all its subordinates (if exist), and has received a PREPARE (typically explicitly) from its superior, sends the superior a READY message and enters the ready state. (This implies that a leaf node sends a READY without receiving READY messages.)

- After receiving a READY message from all its subordinates, when in the prepared state, the root enters the ready state (and is defined to be the CC).

Phase Two

- The root makes the decision to commit (it is the CC), and enters the committed state. Then it sends a COMMIT message to any of its subordinates.
- A nonleaf node that has received a COMMIT message from its superior sends a COMMIT message to any of its subordinates, commits, and enters the committed state.
- A leaf node that receives a COMMIT message commits, enters the committed state and sends a COMMIT_ACK to its superior. Then it enters its forgotten state.
- A node in the committed state that has received a COMMIT_ACK message from all its subordinates, sends a COMMIT_ACK to its superior and enters the forgotten state.
- After receiving COMMIT_ACK from all its subordinates, the root enters the forgotten state.

$$[]$$

Comments:

- The abort case is handled similarly, where ABORT messages are sent to subordinates as soon as possible. READY messages may be replaced with ABORT messages; ABORT messages replace COMMIT messages; ABORT_ACK replace COMMIT_ACK messages.
- Several variants of handling recovery and related logging exist (e.g., *presumed abort, presumed commit*, in [Moha 83], [Moha 84]).

2.3 Variants of T2PC

Several variants of the T2PC protocol (referred to as *commit optimizations*; see for example [LU6.2], [Roth 90], [Sama 93], [Trav 91]) have been implemented to enhance the performance of the basic T2PC protocol. Some variants that relate to D2PC are described below:

- *Implicit PREPARE (unsolicited READY)* and *Multiple Preparing Nodes*.
  A PREPARE message is not sent between neighbors, if by the application's semantics it is clear to both that no more transaction's data will be exchanged between them. In this case a non-root node is allowed to send a PREPARE to another neighbor, even if it has not received one.
- *Transfer of CC*.
  A mechanism exists to transfer the CC role from the root to some other node.
  - Example: *Last subordinate* ("the workstation optimization").
    After sending PREPARE messages to all subordinates but one, the current CC sends a READY message to that last subordinate, and by this transferring to it the CC role.

Comment: The *Read-only* optimization (e.g., [Moha 93]) is not dealt with in this work, bur the results here apply also to that case (e.g., when treating in the analysis READ-ONLY messages that result from a read-only votes as READY messages).

2.4 T2PC instances

For a given transaction, each participant j, in principle, may assume the CC role. We define the T2PC *instance* (T,j) to be the execution of the T2PC protocol for a transaction T on its invocation tree, when the participant j is the CC. n different instances exist for an n participant transaction. It is assumed that for all instances each participant i enters the prepared state at the same time p(i). However, for a given communication tree, with given delays of the connections, each T2PC instance for T may commit the participant i at a different time.

For the rest of the paper, when using T2PC instances, algorithm 2.1 requires some modifications:

1. The CC is considered (substituted for) the *root*, and the relations *superior* and *subordinate* between any two neighbors are redefined as induced by their proximity in the tree to the CC (number of edges on the (single) path between a node and the CC): The closer neighbor is the superior, and the farther is the subordinate.

2. The first bullet in Phase One of algorithm 2.1 is modified to allow multiple preparing nodes. The replacing bullet is the following:

- A node sends an explicit PREPARE message when applies (see the PREPARE semantics in section 2.2 above) to its neighbor, if required (see also implicit PREPARE in section 2.3 above).

3 Dynamic 2PC (D2PC)

D2PC is a modification of T2PC where the CC is dynamically determined by racing READY (YES vote) messages, on a per transaction basis, rather than being fixed, predetermined. For any given transaction D2PC mimics some instance of T2PC. We later see that this instance is optimal (in the set of all instances for a same transaction) in the following sense:

1. It executes the commit decision (i.e., completes phase 1 of 2PC) in minimum time.

2. It commits each participant in minimum time.

Algorithm 3.1 - The D2PC Protocol - commitment procedure[1]

Phase One

- A node sends an explicit PREPARE message when applies (see the PREPARE semantics in section 2.2 above) to its neighbor, if required.

- A node in the prepared state, that has received a READY message from all its neighbors but one, sends to that neighbor a READY message and enters the ready state. (Special case: a prepared leaf node sends a READY without receiving READY messages.)

- A node in the prepared state that has receives a READY message from all its neighbors enters the ready state (and is defined to be a CC).

Phase Two

- A CC makes the decision to commit and enters the committed state. Then it sends a COMMIT message to all its neighbors.

- A nonleaf node that has received a COMMIT message from a neighbor sends a COMMIT message to every other neighbor, commits, and enters the committed state.

- A leaf node that receives a COMMIT message, commits, sends a COMMIT_ACK to its neighbor, and enters the forgotten state.

- A (nonleaf) node (in the committed state) that has received a COMMIT_ACK message from every node to which it has sent a COMMIT, sends a COMMIT_ACK to the node from which it has received the COMMIT message and enters the forgotten state.

- A CC that has received COMMIT_ACK from all its neighbors enters the forgotten state.

[]

---

[1] The enhanced, D2PC based, ISO-DTP protocol provides a detailed specification of commit, abort, and various failure cases. Algorithm 3.1 is a high level abstraction of the commit case, based on the transaction model presented in section 2 above.

Comment: The comments for algorithm 2.1 apply also to algorithm 3.1. The D2PC scheme above can be used with any recovery strategy used for other T2PC variants, and incorporate other optimizations like Read-only (e.g., [Moha 83]).

Theorem 3.1

(i) D2PC determines exactly one CC for each transaction, in the case of half-duplex communication.

(ii) D2PC determines either one CC, or two neighboring CCs, for each transaction, in the case of full-duplex communication (two are determined in the cases where a (single) READY/READY message collision exists).

Proof:

An n node tree has n-1 edges. D2PC implies that in phase 1 READY messages propagate from the tree leafs to the other nodes and every edge in the transaction tree has carried a READY message (at least one), by the end of phase 1.

(i) In the half-duplex case[1] no message collisions are possible, and thus, after one READY message is sent on an edge, no other READY message will be sent in the opposite direction (by the D2PC specification). Every node sees either incoming READY messages only (a CC), or incoming and a single outgoing. In any case no edge of the tree is seen without a READY message. Thus every edge carries exactly one READY message by the end of phase 1, and the total number of READY messages is n-1 (number of edges in an n node tree). Now suppose that K CCs are elected. Examine the READY messages sent by each node. A CC sends no READY. A non CC node sends one READY. Thus the total number of READY messages is n-K. Thus n-K=n-1, implying K=1.

(ii) In the full-duplex case it is possible that two neighboring nodes exchange READY messages, and the edge connecting them carries two READY messages (a double READY edge). Suppose that K double READY edges exist. Thus n-1-K edges carry a single READY. The total number of READY messages sent is n-1-K+2K = n+K-1. Note that by the D2PC rules a node can send one READY at most (possibly none), and thus no more that n READY messages are possible. By the arguments above n+K-1≤ n, implying K≤ 1. Thus, K is 1 at most, and one collision at most of READY messages on an edge is possible, i.e., two neighboring nodes at most can be CCs.

[]

Note that when D2PC has a single CC it exactly executes some instance of T2PC. When two CCs exist, the message exchanges between the two differ from those between two neighbors in T2PC.

Comment: In the case when two CCs exist, it seems that arbitrarily electing one of the two CCs to be the actual CC (e.g., the node that has initiated the connection between the two CCs; each CC are is aware of the other being a CC by noticing a READY messages collision) simplifies failure handling (e.g., ISO-DTP does so).

Theorem 3.2 states the correctness of D2PC (the commit procedure in algorithm 3.1).

Theorem 3.2

D2PC (the commit procedure) terminates on any communication tree, if all nodes have voted YES, and no failure has occurred.

---

[1] Applying D2PC may be impractical for this case, if the overhead of setting the right message direction, as implied by D2PC, is too high.

Proof:

(i) We first show that Phase One terminates correctly on a tree. We use induction on the tree's size n. The claim is true for n=1 and n=2. Suppose that it is true for n≤ k. Examine any tree of size k+1. Let N1 be a leaf in the tree. When N1 enters the prepared state it sends a READY message to its neighbor. After receiving the message the neighbor is not expecting to communicate N1 for the rest of Phase One. Thus N1 can be pruned from the tree temporarily for Phase One. Pruning N1 leaves a size k tree, for which Phase One completes correctly by the induction hypothesis. Thus the claim is true for every k+1 size tree. (Note that the claim (and D2PC) fails for a (nontree) graph with a cycle.)

(ii) By theorem 3.1 either a single or two neighboring CCs exist. By induction on the number of COMMIT message hopes from a CC to a node, we conclude that the COMMIT message is propagated to all nodes. A leaf that has received a COMMIT returns a COMMIT_ACK. A non-leaf node that has received a COMMIT_ACK from each neighbor to which it has sent a COMMIT sends a COMMIT_ACK to the neighbor from which it has received the COMMIT message. Thus the CC eventually receives COMMIT_ACK messages from all the neighbors to whom it has sent a COMMIT.

$$[]$$

4 Comparing D2PC with T2PC instances

We use the following assumptions in modeling the protocols' executions:

- The *Time* of any relevant event in the distributed system is a real number determined by a *global physical clock*[1].

- The duration of a protocol message exchanged between two neighbors (*message delay*) includes all the related time involved with communication, the time for related logging, and related protocol code execution time. Thus, the time interval between a message arriving in a node and triggering a state transition, and a resulting message sent by the node, is considered to be of a size zero in the computations that follow. Since any compared versions of 2PC are assumed to utilize the same logging (and recovery), the compared versions have the same message delays.

- Message delays are assumed to be slowly varying in time relatively to the duration of D2PC for a single transaction. This is typically true in common TP environments, where the transaction nodes reside on autonomous servers with relatively slowly varying communication queue lengths. Also the relatively long logging time supports this assumption.

- The comparison assumes for simplicity that D2PC determines a single CC (this assumption is independent of whether a mechanism to ensure a single CC exists or not; see comment following the proof of theorem 3.1). In the case when two CC exist, an extra READY message, and possibly an extra COMMIT (and COMMIT_ACK) message exist. In this case the last (according to the global clock) CC to enter the committed state is considered the single CC. This assumption implies that when two CCs exist, some nodes involved with D2PC commit even in a shorter time than that calculated below.

4.1 Notation, parameters, and basic formulae

Definition 4.1

A transaction T is modeled as a pair:

---

[1] For mobile nodes the results bellow also apply to a relativistic model of space-time, with physical clocks local to the nodes. This generalization is not analyzed here.

T = (TREE,PREPARED_TIME)

where TREE, the *transaction tree* is the communication tree of T:

TREE = (N,E,d),

N={1,2,...,n} the set of nodes,

E ⊆ NxN is the set of edges, and

d: E → Reals, is the delay function which defines message delays d(i,j) for each edge (i,j) (with possibly d(i,j) ≠ d(j,i)).

Comment: d(i,j) are assumed to be slowly varying functions of time, treated as constants during a transaction.

PREPARED_TIME is the set of times the nodes enter the prepared state. Let p(i) be the time a node i enters the prepared state.

PREPARED_TIME = { p(i) | i is a node in TREE }

[]

A T2PC instance for T where i (a member in N) is the CC is denoted INST(T,i).

In what follows D2PC is compared with T2PC instances of a same transaction. An arbitrary instance I=INST(T,j) is compared with the instance I'=INST(T,k), mimicked by D2PC.

The transaction (communication) tree capabilities are characterized by the message delays d(i,j) on the tree edges. The delay function d(i,j) can be extended to be the total time duration required for a message sent by node i to be received in any node j, when only the tree connections are used, and the intra node delays are negligible. Thus the (extended) delay function d is defined recursively as follows:

(4.1) $d(i,k) = d(i,j) + d(j,k)$ for any nodes i, j, k, where j resides on a path of the tree from i to k, and i and j are neighbors.

Suppose that node i in the transaction tree enters the prepared state at time p(i) (without loss of generality assume that the minimal p(i) is zero). This time depends on both the application and on the way PREPARE messages are sent, as required by the application (implicitly or explicitly). It is assumed that for a given transaction, all the compared T2PC instances, as well as D2PC, have identical sets PREPARED_TIME of p(i) values (i.e., it is up to the application to determine how to bring each node to the prepared state, and this is identical for all T2PC instances and D2PC).

Let r(i) be the time a node enters the ready state (and sends a READY message to its neighbor). Note that the value of r(i) depends on both the time node i enters the prepare state and the latest time a READY is received in node i from a neighbor, i.e.,

(4.2) $r(i) = Max(p(i), Max_{(j \text{ is a neighbor sending READY to } i)}(r(j)+d(j,i)))$
when i is not a CC.

A special case: r(i) = p(i) when i is a non-CC leaf.

Remark: The only reason for a node i to delay entering the ready state and block sending a READY message, violating (4.2), is for the purpose of becoming a CC. This means that for an i that is a CC of a T2PC instance not mimicked by D2PC, the equality in (4.2) is violated, and the left hand side is strictly larger than the right hand side. As a result of this, for different T2PC instances (different CCs) r(i) may take different values for any nonleaf, non-CC i.

Lemma 4.1 is an immediate consequence of (4.2):

Lemma 4.1

If a path of READY messages propagating from node l to node m exists, then

$r(m) \geq r(l) + d(l,m)$

Proof:

Use (4.2) and induction by the order of nodes on the path from l to m.

[]

Let us define the commit decision time for INST(T,j) to be c(j), the time the CC j enters the committed state. At this time the CC sends COMMIT messages to all its neighbors. Any node i that receives a COMMIT message from a neighbor, enters the committed state at time c(i) and sends a COMMIT message to every other neighbor. Thus,

(4.3) $c(j) = r(j)$ for a CC j, and

(4.4) $c(m) = c(l) + d(l,m)$,   if a path of COMMIT messages propagating from nodel to node m exists.

4.2 Directions of READY message flows

We now examine how READY flows of D2PC and instances of T2PC differ. We first make the observation that differences between D2PC and any instance of T2PC only exist for nodes on the (single) path between their respective CCs.

Theorem 4.1

Let I=INST(T,j) and I'=INST(T,k) be two instances of T2PC. Than
(i) Every node in the transaction tree of T, which does not reside on the (single) path between j and k, sends a READY message to the same neighbor for I as for I'.
(ii) Every node on the path between j and k sends a READY to different neighbors for I and I'. Both these neighbors reside on the path between j and k, on opposite sides of the node.

(Note that j does not send a READY for I, and k does not send for I'.)

Proof:

Note first that on any path from a node to a CC, no node receives two READY messages from neighbors on the path (i.e., all the READY messages sent on the path have the same direction on the path). Let i be a node external to the path between j and k. Only the following three cases are possible:

(i) The (single) path from i to k is through j.
Let i' be the neighbor of i on the path from i to j. For both I and I' i sends a READY to i'. The proof is by induction on the number of nodes on the path between i and the CC (j for I and k for I'; the proofs are identical for both cases).

Basis: The number of nodes is 1. If i does not send a READY to i', then i' sends a READY to i. Thus i' has received a READY from the CC. A contradiction to the definition of a CC.

Assume that the claim is true for n nodes on the path. Examine a path with n+1 nodes between i and the CC. The claim is true for i' by the induction hypothesis, since i' has n nodes on its path to the CC. Thus i' sends the READY to its other-than-i neighbor on the path (on the "other side" of the path). This means that i does not receive a READY from i'. Thus it has to send it to i'.

(ii) The (single) path from i to j is through k.
The proof of case (i) above is repeated, when j and k are interchanged.

(iii) The path from i to j does not pass through k, and the path from i to k does pass through j.
In this case the path from i to the CC passes through the path between j and k. Let l be a node on the path from i to the CC, not residing on the path between j and k, but is a neighbor of a node on the path between j and k. Repeat the proof for case (i), when l replaces the CC in the proof.

                                                                                            []

4.3 Time of entering the ready state

Theorem 4.2

Let $I=INST(T,j)$ be any instance, and $I'=INST(T,k)$ the one mimicked by D2PC. Then for every node i in the transaction tree

$r'(i) \leq r(i)$ (times when node i is entering the ready state for I' and I, respectively).

More specifically:

(i) $r'(i) = r(i)$ for i, $i \neq j$, $i \neq k$, that does not reside on the path between j and k.

(ii) $r'(k) = r(k)$

(iii) $r'(i) < r(i)$ for i that resides on the path between j and k.

Proof:

(i) We first show that $r'(i) = r(i)$, for every i that sends the READY message to the same neighbor for both I and I'.

The proof is by induction on the distance m of a node from the farthest leaf (number of edges on the path from the farthest leaf to the node).

For m=0 i is a leaf. If not a CC of I (i=j), this is clearly true, since by (4.2) $r(i)=p(i)$ and $r'(i)=p(i)$.

Now suppose that $r'(i)=r(i)$ for $m \leq l$. Examine a node i where m=l+1. Both $r(i)$ and $r'(i)$ obey the recurrence relation (4.2). The right hand side of the equality includes $p(i')$ which is identical for I and I', and quantities $r(i')$. Since i sends a READY message to the same neighbor for both I and I', i' is a neighbor of i that resides on the longest path from a leaf to i. Thus for i' m=l, and thus $r(i')=r'(i')$ by the induction hypothesis. Thus the right hand side values of (4.2) are equal for I and I', and $r'(i)=r(i)$.

By theorem 4.1 this is true for all nodes that do not reside on the path between j and k.

(ii) By the same arguments given in (i) above we conclude that $r'(k) = r(k)$, where k is the CC of I'.

(iii) Now suppose that i resides on the (single) path from j, the CC of I, to k, the CC for I'. Since k is the CC for I', $r'(j)<r'(i)<r'(k)$ by lemma 4.1. Since j is the CC for I, $r(j)>r(i)>r(k)$ by lemma 4.1. Thus by (ii) we conclude that $r'(i)<r(i)$ and $r'(j)<r(j)$.

(iv) Summarizing (i), (ii) and (iii) we conclude that for every i, $r'(i) \leq r(i)$.

$\square$

4.4 Time of commitment decision

Theorem 4.3

Let $I=INST(T,j)$ be any instance, and $I'=INST(T,k)$ the one mimicked by D2PC. Then

$c'(k) \leq c(j)$

(For any distributed transaction, D2PC completes phase one (i.e., decides the transaction) in a time shorter or equal to the phase one completion time by any instance of T2PC).

Proof:

$c'(k) = r'(k)$	by (4.3).
$r'(k) \leq r(k)$	by theorem 4.2.
$r(k) < r(j)$,	since the CC j of I is the last node to enter the ready state.
$c(j) = r(j)$	by (4.3).
Thus, $c'(k) \leq c(j)$.	

$\square$

4.5 Time of node commitment

A local subtransaction typically locks resources and unlocks them upon (locally) being committed. Thus, it is desired that resources are unlocked as soon as possible, to be utilized by other requesting transactions, which are blocked while waiting for these resources. Theorem 4.4 shows that D2PC commits each node in minimum time.

Theorem 4.4

Let $I=INST(T,j)$ be any instance, and $I'=INST(T,k)$ the one mimicked by D2PC.
Then for every i of T

$c'(i) \leq c(i)$ (commit time of i for I' and I, respectively).

(For any distributed transaction, D2PC delivers the COMMIT message to any node in the transaction tree in a time earlier or equal to the time the COMMIT message is delivered to the node by any instance of T2PC.)

Proof:

(i) Let us first prove the theorem for i=j.

$c(j) = r(j)$	by (4.3); j is the CC of I.
$\geq r(k) + d(k,j)$	by lemma 4.1
$\geq r'(k) + d(k,j)$	by theorem 4.2
$= c'(k) + d(k,j)$	by (4.3); k is the CC of I'.
$= c'(j)$	by (4.4)

(ii) We now generalize the result for any i.

$c(i) = c(j) + d(j,i)$	by (4.4)
$\geq c'(j) + d(j,i)$	by (i) above
$= c'(i)$	by (4.4)

[]

[Sega 87] shows a corollary of theorem 4.4. In our notation it can be phrased as follows:

Corollary 4.1 ([Sega 87])

Let $I=INST(T,j)$ be any instance, and $I'=INST(T,k)$ the one mimicked by D2PC. Also let l be the last committed node for I', and m the last for I. Then $c'(l) \leq c(m)$.

4.6 Number of messages

Theorem 4.5

Let #X be the number of messages of type X sent when executing a protocol over an n node transaction. Then

(i) #READY = #COMMIT = #COMMIT_ACK for both T2PC and D2PC.

(ii) #READY = n-1 for every instance of T2PC, and for D2PC in the half-duplex case.

(iii) n-1 $\leq$ #READY $\leq$ n for D2PC in the full-duplex case.

Proof:

(i) Every node that sends a READY to a neighbor receives a COMMIT from that neighbor. Every node that receives a COMMIT from a neighbor sends a COMMIT_ACK to that neighbor.

(ii) For T2PC and D2PC in the half-duplex case every edge transfers exactly a single READY message. The number of edges is n-1, and the result follows.

(iii) For D2PC in the full-duplex case, one edge, at most, may transfer two READY messages in opposite directions (see proof of theorem 3.1), while every other edge is carrying a single READY message. Thus the result follows, similarly to (ii) above.

[]

Remark: As was noted (see comment following the proof of theorem 3.1), breaking the symmetry between the possible two CCs in the full-duplex case, and electing one to be the CC simplifies the protocol. With some symmetry breaking mechanisms the protocol may result in two CCs exchanging two READY messages, but only one COMMIT, resulting in #READY=#COMMIT+1.

5 On using different trees for invocation and termination

In the analysis above we have assumed that transaction termination with D2PC is carried out using the communication connections of the transaction's invocation tree. However, it is possible that the communication network over the transaction's nodes allows a termination tree with a better (weighted) *average commit time*, when the average is over all the nodes. Furthermore, it is likely that the optimal tree for phase one (voting) is different from the optimal tree for phase two (committing) (e.g., [Sega 88]). In any case, theorems 4.3 and 4.4 ensure that D2PC selects the fastest T2PC instances for any given tree.

The problem of selecting an optimal termination tree for a given transaction T introduces tradeoffs depending on the following factors:

1. The delays in the communication network over the nodes (d(i,j) for neighbors i, j in the network).

2. The time each node is entering the prepared state (in definition 4.1 p(i) for node i).

3. The time required to compute the optimal termination trees (including related communications
   required to propagate the participants' identities and the values p(i)).

4. The time overheads of propagating the solution and establishing the selected communication connections between nodes, when such connections do not already exist.

Since the time values in 2 (when nodes are entering the ready state) are not a-priori known, it is unlikely that they can practically be considered.

Considering only aspect 1 above, [Sega 88] uses a *minimum spanning tree* (minimum total delay, or total cost, for any other cost type considered) to minimize the overall utilization time of the tree connections. However, selecting such a tree does not necessarily reduce the average commit time. The average commit time may be reduced by reducing the *delay diameter*, DD, of the termination tree T, defined by the following expression:

$$DD(T) = \text{Max}_{i,j \text{ nodes of } T}(d(i,j) + d(j,i)).$$

Given the uncertainty involved with the values p(i) (they may vary considerably, depending on instantaneous node conditions), a minimum DD termination tree provides the best worst case scenario for each transaction. The minimum DD tree problem is NP-complete ([Itai 93a]), which means that we do not know any solutions with time complexity better than exponential in the number of participants. However, polynomial time approximations exist ([Itai 93a]; e.g., an O(ne) 2-approximation, when n is the number of participants (nodes), and e is the number of possible direct communication connections between them (edges in the communication network graph)). When all the delays between neighbors in the network are equal, an exact polynomial time solution exists ([Itai 93b]; an $O(n^2 e)$ exact solution, and an O(ne) almost-optimal approximation (with a possible error of a single edge delay)).

6 Conclusion

This work presents and analyzes the Dynamic 2PC (D2PC) protocol. The protocol is shown to commit each transaction participant in the minimum possible time by a Tree 2PC (T2PC) protocol on a given termination tree. The voting strategy of D2PC (TREE-COMMIT in [Sega 87]) is general, and can be utilized also for other tree-based atomic commitment protocols, with the same advantage of optimizing the commit time of each participant. Selecting a termination tree that reduces the average commit time is discussed as well, and selecting a tree with a reduced (minimal, if practical) *delay diameter*, when applicable (e.g., when the selection overhead is amortized over several transactions that use the same termination tree), is proposed.

The D2PC protocol has been generalized to impose constraints preventing nodes from being commit coordinators (e.g., when nodes are not robust enough to guarantee proper recovery from failure). Such constraints may introduce deadlocks in the execution of D2PC. This problem is studied in [Raz 92], where efficient strategies to impose the constraints while guaranteeing deadlock-freedom are presented.

Acknowledgments

A detailed design of D2PC has been developed by the members of the ISO-IEC/JTC1/OSI-DTP&CCR groups. Many thanks are due to all of them for stimulating discussions.

Bruno Traverson provided helpful comments on the protocols' formulations presented here, and Alon Itai and Shlomo Moran contributed algorithms and complexity results for the *minimum-diameter spanning tree* problem. Their contributions are greatly appreciated.

References

[Bern 87]   P. Bernstein, V. Hadzilacos, N. Goodman, *Concurrency Control and Recovery in Database Systems*, Addison-Wesley, 1987.

[Brag 91]   Braginsky, E., "The X/Open Effort", *Proc. 4th Int. Workshop on High Performance Transaction Systems*, Asilomar, CA, September 1991.

[DECdtm]   J. Johnson, W. Laing, R. Landau, "Transaction Management Support in the VMS Operating System Kernel", *Digital Technical Journal*, Vol 3, no. 1, Winter 1991.

Philip A. Bernstein, William T. Emberton, Vijay Trehan, "DECdta - Digital's Distributed Transaction Processing Architecture", *Digital Technical Journal*, Vol 3, no. 1,Winter 1991.

[Dwor 83]   C. Dwork, D. Skeen, "The inherent Cost of Nonblocking Commitment", *Proc. 2nd ACM Symp. on PODC*, pp. 1-11, 1983.

[Dwor 84]   C. Dwork, D. Skeen, "Patterns of Communication in Consensus Protocols", *Proc. 3rd ACM Symp. on PODC*, pp. 143-153, 1984.

[Gray 87]   Gray, J. N., "Notes on Database Operating Systems", *Operating Systems: An Advanced Course*, Lecture Notes in Computer Science 60, pp. 393-481, Springer-Verlag, 1978.

[Itai 93a]   Alon Itai, privat communications.

[Itai 93b]   Alon Itai, Shlomo Moran, privat communications.

[Lamp 76]   Lampson, B., Sturgis, H., "Crash Recovery in a Distributed Data Storage System", Technical Report, Xerox, Palo Alto Research Center, Palo Alto, California, 1976.

[LU6.2]   System Network Architecture - Format and Protocol Reference Manual: Architecture Logic for LU Type 6.2, SC30-3269-3, International Business Machines Corporation,1985.

[Moha 83]   C. Mohan, B. Lindsay, "Efficient Commit Protocols for the Tree of Processes Model of Distributed Transactions", *Proc. 2nd ACM Symp. on PODC*, pp. 76-88, 1983.

[Moha 86]   C. Mohan, B. Lindsay, R. Obermarck, "Transaction Management in the R* Distributed Database Management System", *ACM TODS* 11(4), pp. 378-396, 1986.

[OSI-CCR]   ISO/IEC IS 9804, 9805, JTC1/SC21, *Information Processing Systems - Open Systems Interconnection - Commitment, Concurrency and Recovery service element*, 1989.

[OSI-DTP]   ISO/IEC IS 10026 (1, 2, 3), JTC1/SC21, *Information Processing Systems - Open Systems Interconnection - Distributed Transaction Processing*, 1992.

[Raz 92]   Y. Raz, R. Sijelmassi, B. Traverson, S. Usiskin, "The Constrained Dynamic Two Phase Commit Protocol", Draft, Ottawa, Canada, June 1992. (During the ISO/JTC1/SC21 meeting)

[Roth 90]   Kurt Rothermel, Stefan Pappe, "Open Commit Protocols for the Tree of Processes Model", *Proc 10th IEEE Int. Conf. on Dist. Computing Sys.*, pp. 236-244, 1990.

[Sama 93]   George Samaras, Katheryn Britton, Andrew Citron, C. Mohan, "Two Phase Commit Optimizations and Tradeoffs in the Commercial Environment", *Proc. 9th Int. Conf. on Data Engineering*, pp. 520-529, Viena, Austria, April 1993.

[Sega 87]   Adrian Segall, Ouri Wolfson, "Transaction Commitment at Minimal Communication Cost", *Proc. 6th ACM Symp. on PODS*, pp. 112-118, 1987

[Sega 88]   Adrian Segall, Ouri Wolfson, "Optimal Communication Topologies for Atomic Commitment", *Proc. 6th IEEE Int. Conf. on Data Eng.*, 1988.

[Skee 81]   D. Skeen, "Nonblocking Commit Protocols", *Proc. ACM SIGMOD*, pp. 133-142, 1981.

[Skee 83]   Dale Skeen, Michael Stonebraker, "A Formal Model of Crash Recovery in Distributed Systems", *IEEE Trans. Soft. Eng.* 9(3), pp. 219-227, 1983

.[Trav 91]   Bruno Traverson, Optimization Strategies and Performance Evaluation for the Two Phase Commit Protocol", Doctoral Thesis, University of Paris 6, September 25, 1991.

[Upto 91]   Upton IV, F., "OSI Distributed Transaction Processing - An Overview", *Proc. 4th Int. Workshop on High Performance Transaction Systems*, Asilomar, CA, September 1991.

[Wolf 91]   Ouri Wolfson, "The Communication Complexity of Atomic Commitment and of Gossiping", *SIAM J. Computing*, 20(3), pp. 423-450, June 1991.

[X/Open-DTP]   *X/Open Guide - Distributed Transaction Processing Reference Model*, X/Open Company Ltd., No G120, 1991.

Domain-Independent Queries on Databases with External Functions

Dan Suciu

University of Pennsylvania, Philadelphia, PA 19104
Email: suciu@saul.cis.upenn.edu

Abstract. We investigate queries in the presence of external functions with arbitrary inputs and outputs (atomic values, sets, nested sets etc). We propose a new notion of domain independence for queries with external functions which, in contrast to previous work, can also be applied to query languages with fixpoints or other kinds of iterators. Next, we define two new notions of *computable queries with external functions*, and prove that they are equivalent, under the assumption that the external functions are total. Thus, our definition of computable queries with external functions is robust. Finally, based on the equivalence result, we give examples of complete query languages with external functions. A byproduct of the equivalence result is the fact that Relational Machines are complete for complex objects: it was known that they are not complete over flat relations.

1 Introduction

Database functionalities are important both for practical and for theoretical purposes. E.g. the system O_2 of [9] allows the query language to invoke any method written in the programming language C. The practical integration of external functions in query languages is generally well understood, but the semantics of queries in the presence of external functions has received less attention. [4, 10] offer two distinct definitions for domain independent queries with external functions, but which don't fit languages with fixpoints or other forms of recursions. To the best of our knowledge, no previous attempt has been made to define complete query languages with external functions.

In this paper we propose a new definition of *domain independent queries with external functions* (*ef-domain independence*), in a general setting, namely by allowing the inputs and outputs of the external functions to be scalar values, sets, nested sets, etc. Queries expressed in languages with external functions and fixpoints or other forms of iterations indeed satisfy this definition. We establish the relationship of our notion of domain independence with those in [4, 10]. Next we propose two definitions for *computable queries with external functions* and show that they coincide, when the external functions are total (theorem 16). We take this as evidence for the robustness of the underlying concept. The equivalence is a technically difficult theorem: an interesting byproduct is the corollary that Relational Machines [3] for complex object are complete, while it is known that they are generally not complete for flat relations [5]. Subtle differences separate the two notions of computable queries when the external functions are partial: one definition requires *sequential* computation of the external functions, while the other allows for *parallelism*. The coincidence of the two definitions of computable queries for total external functions enables us to define a robust notion of *complete query languages* with external functions, namely as languages which can express all computable, domain independent queries with total external functions. Finally we give examples of such languages.

Abiteboul, Papadimitrou, and Vianu [2] extend Relational Machines with *reflections*, i.e. the ability to dynamically create queries, and to answer them in constant time; the resulting Reflective Relational Machines are complete. We obtain completeness by a different, orthogonal extension, namely by replacing flat realtions with complex objects. Parallelism arises in Reflective Relational Machines from their ability to compute any first-order query in one parallel step; as a consequence, interesting connections to parallel complexity classes are proven in [2]. The prarallelism implicit in one of our definition of computable queries is of a different nature and consists in the ability of a device to initiate the computation of several external functions in parallel, and to stop when *one* of them terminates.

Chandra and Harel in [7] consider *extended databases* by adding an interpreted domain F to the uninterpreted one D: any given algebraic structure may accompany F. The connection between the two domains is given by functions S going only in one direction, from D to F. Due to their type, these functions can only be applied once, making them strictly less general than external functions considered in [4, 10] and here, which can be repeatedly applied to values in D. The functions on F corresponding to its algebraic structure are also strictly less general than the external functions, because F is already "interpreted".

Abiteboul and Beeri add external functions to their *algebra* and to the *calculus*, and define the notion of *bounded-depth domain independence*. They show that queries expressed both in the *extended algebra* and in the *extended calculus* are bounded-depth domain independent. Similarly, Escobar-Molano, Hull, and Jacobs [10] define *embedded-domain independent queries* with scalar functions (a special case of external functions), and show that any query expressed by an *embedded-allowed* calculus formula are embedded domain independent. But we show here in example 1 that in a language with fixpoints, queries fail to be bounded-depth domain independent or embedded-domain independent.

The first description of a complete query language can be found in [7]: it achieves completeness in a dynamically typed language, by encoding an integer n as a set of tuples of width n. Other complete query languages use different tools to achieve completeness: e.g. object inventions in [1], and untyped sets in [16]. Here we use essentially the same techniques to design complete languages with external functions, w.r.t. our definition of computable queries.

Section 2 reviews some basic database notions and offers an intuition for the constructs to follow. Section 3 defines domain independent queries with external functions (ef-domain independent), shows some of their properties, and establish their relationship with embedded domain independent queries [10]. Section 4 briefly describes the Nested Relational Algebra with external functions, and shows that all queries expressed in this language, possibly extended with iterators, are ef-domain independent. Sections 5 and 6 give the two definitions of computable queries, while section 7 proves their equivalence. Finally we give examples of complete query languages in section 8.

2   Background and Motivation

A database query can be viewed as a (partial) function F mapping any database instance $\mathcal{D} = (D; R_1, \ldots, R_k)$ into some relation $F(\mathcal{D})$ over D. D is the domain of the database instance and $R_1, \ldots, R_k$ are its relations. It is understood that the arities of the relations R_i, as well as the arity of the output relation are fixed. More, it is usually required that the query be be **generic, domain independent** and **computable**. *Generic* means that whenever $\mathcal{D}$ is isomorphic to some structure $\mathcal{D}'$, then the same isomorphism maps $F(\mathcal{D})$ into $F(\mathcal{D}')$; we will assume throughout this paper that all queries are generic in this sense, i.e. map isomorphic database instances to isomorphic outputs. *Domain independence* can be stated as the requirement that, if we replace the domain D with a larger one $D' \supseteq D$, but keep the same relations $R_1, \ldots, R_k$, then the query F returns the same answer on the new database instance $\mathcal{D}' = (D'; R_1, \ldots, R_k)$, i.e. $F(\mathcal{D}) = F(\mathcal{D}')$. Finally, a query is *computable* if there is some Turing Machine which, when started with an encoding of $R_1, \ldots, R_k$ on its tape, halts with an encoding of $F(\mathcal{D})$ on the tape, or diverges, when $F(\mathcal{D})$ is undefined.

Most of the external functions we will consider in this paper, like $+$, *succ*, *make_object*, etc. have infinite domains and codomains. This leads us to consider database instances with an *infinite* domain D (but still with finite relations $R_1, \ldots, R_k$), which is contrary to the traditional view that database instances have *finite* domains.

In the context of complex objects, we consider higher order structures instead of first order ones. Namely we define **complex object types** by the grammar $t ::= d \mid t \times \ldots \times t \mid \{t\}$, and define $dom(t, D)$, for some type t and set D to be: $dom(d, D) \stackrel{\text{def}}{=} D$, $dom(t_1 \times \ldots \times t_n, D) \stackrel{\text{def}}{=} dom(t_1, D) \times \ldots \times dom(t_n, D)$, $dom(\{t\}, D) \stackrel{\text{def}}{=} \mathcal{P}_{fin}(dom(t, D))$. A **database schema** is $\sigma = (t_1, \ldots, t_k)$, while a **database instance** over σ is $\mathcal{D} = (D; R_1, \ldots, R_k)$, with $R_i \subseteq dom(t_i, D)$. The empty product (obtained by taking $n = 0$ in $t_1 \times \ldots \times t_n$) is denoted with *unit*; for any D, $dom(unit, D) = \{()\}$. The notion of a query over flat databases carries over to the complex object databases. The definitions and notations are consistent with those of [11, 16], and all the results in this paper hold also for multisorted databases (with more than one base type: $d, d', \ldots$).

In this paper we consider **databases with external functions**, by augmenting database instances with a number of **external functions** $P_1, \ldots, P_l$. That is a database instance becomes $\mathcal{D} = (D; P_1, \ldots, P_l; R_k, \ldots, R_k)$, where $R_1, \ldots, R_k$ are as before, while $P_1, \ldots, P_l$ are functions "over D". In their simplest form, the external external functions are *scalar*, i.e. of type $D^n \to D$, as in [10], but we allow external functions of any types, i.e. $P_j : dom(d_j, D) \to dom(c_j, D)$, where d_j and c_j are arbitrary types called the **domain** and **codomain** of P_j. A database schema will have then the form $\sigma = (d_1 \to c_1, \ldots, d_l \to c_l; t_1, \ldots, t_k)$. E.g. consider the database schema $\sigma = (\{d\} \to d; d \times d \times d)$. A database instance over σ is $\mathcal{D} = (D; P; R)$, where $P : \mathcal{P}_{fin}(D) \to D$. The relation R can be thought of as containing tuples for persons, with three columns: $SS\#$, $NAME$ and AGE. The function P applied to some set S of social security numbers generates a new $SS\#$ which is not in S, that is $P(S) \notin S$, $\forall S$. Obviously a query over that database may not necessarily be domain independent in the traditional sense, because it has the ability of constructing new social security numbers by calling the function P. The first goal of this paper is to investigate the notion of domain independence of queries with external functions.

Traditionally external functions have been thougth of as *fixed* functions on the universal domain of the database. We give them a broader interpretation here by viewing them as library functions, subject to changes in time. E.g. let $P : D \times D \to D$, be a library function expecting an employee's name and salary, which increases its salary by a quantum. P may incorporate complex knowledge on the company's policy, and may change in time, as the company changes its policy. The following is an example of a query using P: "increase by one quanta the salaries in the *sales* department, by two quanta those in the *business* department, and leave the rest unchanged".

[4], and later [10], present an extension of the notion of domain independence for databases with external functions. Strictly speaking, the *embedded domain independence* of [10] implies the *bounded-depth domain independence* of [4] , but they rely on the same idea. Both notions are used only in conjunction with query languages without recursive queries (or any other kind of iterations), and, as we show in this paper, fail when extended to languages with fixpoints. See example 1 for a fixpoint query which is not embedded domain independent. In this paper we introduce a new notion, called *external-function domain independence* (ef-domain independence), which is more general than the embedded domain independence, and show that all queries expressed in query languages with iterations (fixpoints, loops, structural recursions, etc.) are ef-domain independent.

Our second goal in this paper is to investigate computability of queries in the presence of external functions: we have no knowledge of any previous attempt to define computable queries in the presence of external functions. One way of understanding computable queries is to view external function as oracles: at any point during the computation of a query F, the device computing F may ask the oracle corresponding to some external function P_j for the value of $P_j(x)$, for some x of type d_j: after receiving the answer $y = P_j(x)$, the device may proceed. Note that the active domain, which initially contains all atomic values in $R_1, \ldots, R_k$, is extended dynamically, because the oracles may generate new atomic values. Another way of viewing the external functions, is to restrict them to *computable* functions; then we can encode a computable function as a finite string, e.g. as some program computing that function, or as the Gödel number of the Turing Machine corresponding to that function. The two views give rise to two notions of *computable queries*, and theorem 16 shows that they coincide over databases with *total* external functions.

Previous work [21, 4, 10] has been concerned with identifying recursive sets of first order formulas, which define domain independent queries. We do not address this problem here, but consider only algebraic query languages instead, where all queries are domain independent. We believe that the notion of *embedded allowed formulas* from [10] can be extended to a higher order logic with fixpoints, such that all "embedded allowed" formulas define an ef-domain independent, computable query. We intend to investigate this direction in future work.

3 Domain Independent Queries with External Functions

Before giving the formal definition, we argue for the necessity of considering *partial* external functions, as opposed to *total* ones. The *active domain* of some database instance $\mathcal{D}$ is the set of all atomic values mentioned in its relations. The active domain is always finite, although in this paper the domain may be infinite. Restricting the database domain to the active domain leads naturally to *partial external functions*. Formally, we define:

Definition 1. A **database schema** with external functions is $\sigma = (d_1 \rightarrow c_1, \ldots, d_l \rightarrow c_l; t_1, \ldots, t_k)$; $d_1, c_1, \ldots, d_l, c_l, t_1, \ldots, t_k$ are types. A **database instance** over σ is $\mathcal{D} = (D; P_1, \ldots, P_l; R_1, \ldots, R_k)$, where P_i is a partial function $P_i : dom(d_i, D) \rightarrow dom(c_i, D)$, and R_i is a finite subset of $dom(t_i, D)$. $\mathcal{D}$ is called **total** iff all functions P_i are total, otherwise it is called **partial**.

Next we will define a *morphism* $\psi : \mathcal{D} \rightarrow \mathcal{D}'$ to be a partial, injective function $\psi : D \rightarrow D'$ between the domains of two databases, which "preserves the structure" of theses databases, in a sense to be made precise. For that, we notice that any partial function $\psi : D \rightarrow D'$ can be lifted from the base type to partial functions at any type t, $\psi_t : dom(t, D) \rightarrow dom(t, D')$. Namely $\psi_d \stackrel{\text{def}}{=} \psi$, $\psi_{t_1 \times \ldots \times t_n}(x_1, \ldots, x_n) \stackrel{\text{def}}{=} (\psi_{t_1}(x_1), \ldots, \psi_{t_n}(x_n))$, and $\psi_{\{t\}}(\{x_1, \ldots, x_n\}) \stackrel{\text{def}}{=} \{\psi_t(x_1), \ldots, \psi_t(x_n)\}$. In all cases, $\psi_t(x)$ is undefined whenever one of the subexpressions on the right hand side is undefined. We abbreviate ψ_t with ψ.

Definition 2. Let σ be some database schema, and $\mathcal{D} = (D; \bar{P}; \bar{R})$, $\mathcal{D}' = (D'; \bar{P}'; \bar{R}')$ be two database instances over σ. A **morphism** $\psi : \mathcal{D} \rightarrow \mathcal{D}'$ is a partial injective function $\psi : D \rightarrow D'$, such that (1) for every i, $\psi(R_i)$ is defined and $\psi(R_i) = R_i'$, and (2) for any $x \in dom(d_j, D)$, if $P_j'(\psi(x))$ is defined then so is $\psi(P_j(x))$ and $P_j'(\psi(x)) = \psi(P_j(x))$.

Let us write $e_1 \sqsubseteq e_2$, whenever expression e_1 is undefined, or $e_1 = e_2$. For two functions f_1, f_2, let $f_1 \sqsubseteq f_2$ mean that $\forall x, f_1(x) \sqsubseteq f_2(x)$, or, equivalently, $graph(f_1) \subseteq graph(f_2)$. Then, ψ is a morphism iff $\psi(R_i) = R_i'$ for all i, and $P_j' \circ \psi \sqsubseteq \psi \circ P_j$ for all j (to be precise, $P_j' \circ \psi_{d_j} \sqsubseteq \psi_{c_j} \circ P_j$).

Definition 3. Let σ be a database schema and t some type. A **database query** from σ to t is a partial function F mapping any database instance over σ $\mathcal{D} = (D; \bar{P}; \bar{R})$ to $F(\mathcal{D}) \in dom(\{t\}, D)$. F is **external-function domain independent**, or **ef-domain independent**, iff for every morphism $\psi : \mathcal{D} \to \mathcal{D}'$, $F(\mathcal{D}') \sqsubseteq \psi(F(\mathcal{D}))$.

This notion generalizes those of genericity and domain independence:

Proposition 4. *Suppose that the database schema σ doesn't contain any external functions (i.e. $l = 0$). Then a query is ef-domain independent iff it is generic and domain independent. Also, when σ only contains atomic constants (i.e. functions of type unit $\to d$), then a query is ef-domain independent iff it is C-generic [16] and domain independent.*

Next we look at how an ef-domain independent query behaves on an "approximation" of a database instance. We say that $\mathcal{D}$ **approximates** $\mathcal{D}'$, written $\mathcal{D} \sqsubseteq \mathcal{D}'$, iff $\mathcal{D} = (D; P_1, \ldots, P_l; R_1, \ldots, R_l)$, $\mathcal{D}' = (D'; P_1', \ldots, P_l'; R_1, \ldots, R_l)$ (i.e. they have the same relations), $D \subseteq D'$, and $P_j \sqsubseteq P_j'$, for all $j = 1, l$. Whenever $\mathcal{D} \sqsubseteq \mathcal{D}'$ there is a canonical morphism $\psi : \mathcal{D}' \to \mathcal{D}$ defined by: $\psi(x) = x$ when $x \in D$, and $\psi(x) =$ undefined, otherwise. ψ has the property: $\forall x, \psi(x) \sqsubseteq x$. (Note however that the inclusion function $D \to D'$ is usually not a morphism.) Define a query F to be **monotone** if $\mathcal{D} \sqsubseteq \mathcal{D}'$ implies $F(\mathcal{D}) \sqsubseteq F(\mathcal{D}')$. For any ef-domain independent query F, databases $\mathcal{D} \sqsubseteq \mathcal{D}'$, and canonical $\psi : D' \to D$ we have $F(\mathcal{D}) \sqsubseteq \psi(F(\mathcal{D}')) \sqsubseteq F(\mathcal{D}')$, which proves:

Proposition 5. *Any ef-domain independent query is monotone.*

Next we will connect the notion of ef-domain independent query with that of *embedded domain independent query* defined in [10]. For this, following [10], we define $term^n(\mathcal{D})$, for some database $\mathcal{D}$ and $n \geq 0$, as follows:

$$term^0(\mathcal{D}) \stackrel{\text{def}}{=} atoms(R_1) \cup \ldots \cup atoms(R_k)$$

$$term^{n+1}(\mathcal{D}) \stackrel{\text{def}}{=} term^n(\mathcal{D}) \cup \{atoms(P_j(x)) \mid x \in dom(d_j, term^n(\mathcal{D})), j = 1, l\}$$

where $atoms(R)$ are all values in D mentioned in the relation R. Two databases $\mathcal{D} = (D; \bar{P}; \bar{R})$ and $\mathcal{D}' = (D'; \bar{P}'; \bar{R})$ (note that they have the same relations) are said to *agree to level n* [10] iff (1) $term^{n+1}(\mathcal{D}) = term^{n+1}(\mathcal{D}')$, and (2) for any j, P_j and P_j' agree on any input whose atoms are in $term^n(\mathcal{D})$, i.e. $\forall x \in dom(d_j, term^n(\mathcal{D}))$, $P_j(x) = P_j'(x)$. A query F is called **embedded domain independent at level n**, or **em-domain independent at level n**, if $F(\mathcal{D}) = F(\mathcal{D}')$ whenever $\mathcal{D}$ and $\mathcal{D}'$ agree to level n. Finally we call F **em-domain independent**, if there is some n for which F is em-domain independent at level n (this definition extends the notion of em-domain independence [10] to complex objects and non-scalar external functions).

Intuitively, em-domain independence allows some query to repeatedly apply the external functions at most n times, for some n which is independent on the database instance $\mathcal{D}$. This condition is indeed satisfied by the queries expressed in languages without fixpoints or loops, like those considered in [4, 10], but fails once an iterative construct (like fixpoints) is added to the language (see example 1). For iterative queries, the number n of applications of the external functions is still finite, but may depend on the particular relations $R_1, \ldots, R_k$. To overcome this limitation of em-domain independence, we strengthen it, by switching the quantifiers. We call a query F to be **strongly embedded domain independent (sem-domain independent)**, iff for any database instance $\mathcal{D}$ there is some n such that: for any other database instance $\mathcal{D}'$ which agrees with $\mathcal{D}$ up to level n, it is the case that $F(\mathcal{D}) = F(\mathcal{D}')$. Call n **the level** of F at $\mathcal{D}$. Obviously em-domain independence implies sem-domain independence.

Finally, let us call some query F **continuous** if for any database instance $\mathcal{D}$ for which $F(\mathcal{D})$ is defined, there is some finite approximation $\mathcal{D}_0$ of it ($\mathcal{D}_0$ finite, $\mathcal{D}_0 \sqsubseteq \mathcal{D}$) such that $F(\mathcal{D}_0) = F(\mathcal{D})$. The use of the term "continuous" here is consistent with that of *continuous functions on algebraic cpo's*, see e.g. [17, 12]. All domain independent queries without external functions are continuous.

Proposition 6. *Any sem-domain independent query is continuous. Hence, any em-domain independent query is continuous too.*

Now we can establish the relationship between our notion of ef-domain independence (definition 3) and that of em-domain independence of [10].

Theorem 7. *A query F is ef-domain independent and continuous iff it is sem-domain independent and monotone.*

The proof is given in [18]. On the other hand, ef-domain independence does not imply continuity, as the following example shows. Consider the database schema $\sigma = (d \rightarrow d; d)$, and let F be the query: $F(\mathcal{D}) \overset{\text{def}}{=} R$ if the set $\{P^{(n)}(x) \mid x \in R, n \geq 0\}$ is infinite, and $F(\mathcal{D}) \overset{\text{def}}{=}$ undefined, otherwise, where $\mathcal{D} = (D; P; R)$. F is ef-domain independent, but not continuous.

Certainly, we would expect all queries expressed in a query language with external functions to be continuous: we shall prove indeed in the next section that all *computable* queries are continuous. Hence, we argue that continuity is connected to the property of a query being computable, and should be orthogonal to the notion of domain independence.

The notion of *bounded-depth domain independence* of [4] extends that of em-domain independence by allowing the computation of *inverses* of external functions, that is $P^{-1}(x)$, for P an external function: the two coincide when the set of external functions is closed under inverses.

4 A Language

Let Σ be a **signature**, that is $\Sigma = \{p_1, \ldots, p_l\}$ is a set of l symbols, each symbol p_j having associated two types called *the domain d_j* and *the codomain c_j*, written $p_j : d_j \rightarrow c_j$: we call $p_1, \ldots, p_l$ *external functions*. We defined briefly the Nested Relational Algebra over Σ, $\mathcal{NRA}(\Sigma)$, following the formalism in [6], as an algebra of functions. Namely $\mathcal{NRA}(\Sigma)$ contains: all external functions $p_j : d_j \rightarrow c_j$ in Σ, the identity functions $id_t : t \rightarrow t$, the composition of functions in $\mathcal{NRA}(\Sigma)$, $g \circ f : t_1 \rightarrow t_3$ (for $f : t_1 \rightarrow t_2$ and $g : t_2 \rightarrow t_3$ in $\mathcal{NRA}(\Sigma)$), the projections $\pi_i^n : t_1 \times \ldots \times t_n \rightarrow t_i$, n-tuples of functions $(f_1, \ldots, f_n) : t \rightarrow t_1 \times \ldots \times t_n$ (for $f_i : t \rightarrow t_i$, $i = 1, n$ in $\mathcal{NRA}(\Sigma)$), the empty set $\emptyset : unit \rightarrow \{t\}$, the singleton $\eta : t \rightarrow \{t\}$, the flattening function $\mu : \{\{t\}\} \rightarrow \{t\}$, union $\cup : \{t\} \times \{t\} \rightarrow \{t\}$, map of any function f in $\mathcal{NRA}(\Sigma)$, $map(f) : \{t\} \rightarrow \{t'\}$ (for every $f : t \rightarrow t'$), equality at base type $eq : d \times d \rightarrow \{unit\}$, and negation $not : \{unit\} \rightarrow \{unit\}$. The semantics of map is: $map(f)(\{x_1, \ldots, x_n\}) \stackrel{def}{=} \{f(x_1), \ldots, f(x_n)\}$. We refer the reader to [6] for full details of this language.

Each function $f : \{t_1\} \times \ldots \times \{t_k\} \rightarrow \{t\}$ in $\mathcal{NRA}(\Sigma)$ defines some query F, which on a database instance $\mathcal{D} = (D; P_1, \ldots, P_l; R_1, \ldots, R_k)$ computes the relation $F(\mathcal{D}) \stackrel{def}{=} f(R_1, \ldots, R_k)$. $\mathcal{NRA}(\Sigma)$ is essentially equivalent to Abiteboul and Beeri's *extended algebra without powerset* [4].

Next we add fixpoints to the language, namely $fix(f) : t \rightarrow \{t'\}$ whenever $f : t \times \{t'\} \rightarrow \{t'\}$, with inflationary semantics: $fix(f)(x) = \bigcup_{n \geq 0} y_n$, where $y_0 \stackrel{def}{=} \emptyset$, $y_{n+1} \stackrel{def}{=} y_n \cup f(x, y_n)$ ($fix(f)(x)$ is undefined when $\bigcup y_n$ is infinite). See [11, 13, 19] for fixpoints on complex objects. We denote with $\mathcal{NRA}(\Sigma) + fix$ the extension of $\mathcal{NRA}(\Sigma)$ with the fipxoint construct. While all queries in $\mathcal{NRA}(\Sigma)$ are em-domain independent, the following example proves that the queries in $\mathcal{NRA}(\Sigma) + fix$ are not:

Example 1. Consider $\Sigma = \{p\}$, where $p : d \rightarrow d$ is some unary external function, and let $f : \{d\} \rightarrow \{d\}$ be the query $f(x) = fix(\lambda(x, y).x \cup map(p)(y))(x)$. That is, $f(x)$ applies repeatedly p to all elements of x, until no new element is generated. If the set of all generated elements is finite, then $f(x)$ returns that set; else it is undefined. Then f is sem-domain independent, but not em-domain independent (nor is it bounded-depth domain independent [4]).

Proposition 8. *All queries in $\mathcal{NRA}(\Sigma) + fix$ are ef-domain independent and continuous. Also, queries expressed with other forms of iterations, like loop of [14], the structural recursions sru, sri of [6], and the divide and conquer recursion dcr of [20] are also ef-domain independent and continuous.*

We take the above proposition as evidence that the notion of ef-domain independence is more appropriate for queries with external functions than the notions of em-domain independence or bounded-depth domain independence.

5   Computable Queries

A database query F on databases without external functions is called *decidable* iff there is some Turing Machine T which, whenever presented with an encoding of an input structure $\mathcal{D}$, computes an encoding of $F(\mathcal{D})$ (and diverges when

$F(\mathcal{D})$ is undefined). We will restrict ourselves for the remaining of this paper to database instances with countable domain having some fixed enumeration.

There are two ways of prencenting external functions to T:

1. Require all external functions to be *Turing computable*, i.e. *recursive* [15] (as number theoretic functions), and replace each function P_j by a number e_j which represents the Gödel number of the Turing Machine computing P_j [15]. Thus, T expects as input encodings for $R_1, \ldots, R_k$, as well as l numbers $e_1, \ldots, e_l$, and computes an encoding of $F(\mathcal{D})$.
2. Extend the Turing Machine T with oracles [15], one for each function P_j. Now T will be started only with the encoding of $R_1, \ldots, R_k$ on its tape, but will be allowed to inquire any of its l oracles during the computation.

The second approach is somehow broader, in the sense that it applies to database instances where the external functions are not necessarily computable, a case which is of little interest in practice. But when the external functions are computable and total, then we will prove that the two notions coincide.

$\mathcal{D} = (D; \bar{P}; \bar{R})$ is a *computable database instance* iff all external functions $P_1, \ldots, P_l$ are computable.

Definition 9. A query F is computable iff there is some Turing Machine T such that for any any computable structure $\mathcal{D}$, when T is started with an encoding of $R_1, \ldots, R_k$ and with the Gödel numbers $e_1, \ldots, e_l$ on its tape, halts iff $F(\mathcal{D})$ is defined, and in this case leaves an encoding of $F(\mathcal{D})$ on its tape.

First we prove that any computable, ef-domain independent query is continuous. For this we need the following recursion-theoretic lemma. Let $\varphi_0, \varphi_1, \ldots$ be a standard enumeration of all recursive functions [15].

Lemma 10. *Let* $f : \mathbb{N} \to \mathbb{N}$ *be some recursive function with the property* $\varphi_e \sqsubseteq \varphi_{e'} \Rightarrow \varphi_{f(e)} \sqsubseteq \varphi_{f(e')}$. *Then* $\forall e, \forall x$, *if* $\varphi_{f(e)}(x)$ *is defined, then there is some* e_0 *such that* φ_{e_0} *is a finite function,* $\varphi_{e_0} \sqsubseteq \varphi_e$, *and* $\varphi_{f(e_0)}(x) = \varphi_{f(e)}(x)$.

The lemma essentially says that, whenever f maps encodings of functions to encodings of functions in a monotone way, then $f(e)$ is fully determined by the action of f on the finite approximations of φ_e. The proof is given in [18]. The lemma immediately implies:

Corollary 11. *All computable, ef-domain independent queries are continuous.*

Finally, we can define *complete* query languages, relative to some class $\mathcal{C}$ of database instances.

Definition 12. Let $\mathcal{C}$ be a class of database instances. A query language $\mathcal{L}$ with external functions from a set Σ is **complete** w.r.t. Σ over $\mathcal{C}$ iff it can express all computable, ef-domain independent queries over total databases from $\mathcal{C}$.

The reason for which we require L to be able to express queries over total databases is due to the fact that only in this case do we have a robust notion of computable queries, i.e. the computable queries coincide with the RMC-computable queries, to be defined in the next section.

6   Relational Machines for Complex Objects

The second notion of computable queries is based on a variant of Turing Machines with oracles. In [15], oracles are introduced to compare the relative degrees of computability of number theoretic functions: the interesting cases are when the oracles are non-computable functions. For different purposes, Abiteboul and Vianu in [5] introduce the notion of *loose Generic Machine*, later simplified to *Relational Machines* in [3]. In some sense, these can be also viewed as Turing Machines with oracles, where the oracle performs, on request, first-order transformations on a relational store. The Relational Machines do not gain more computational power than the Turing Machines, but allow a clear separation of the unordered data in the relational store from the ordered data on the tape.

Here we borrow ideas from both extensions of the Turing Machines, and define **Relational Machines for Complex Objects (RMC)** over some signature $\Sigma = \{p_1, \ldots, p_l\}$ of function symbols. A RMC M over Σ is a Turing Machine extended with a fixed number of relational registers, $R_0, R_1, \ldots, R_r$. At each step, M may perform some traditional Turing Machine move, or may affect the relational store in one of the following two ways: (1) it may inspect the content of some register R_i and enter one of two different states, depending on whether R_i is empty or not; we call this a *conditional*, or (2) it may replace the content of some register R_i with $h(R_{i_1}, \ldots, R_{i_k})$, where h is a query in the language $\mathcal{NRA}(\Sigma)$; we call this *an assignment*. In particular h may be one of the external functions in Σ, or may be some expression involving external functions from Σ: we view this assignment as an oracle inquire, asking for the value of h on particular inputs. We keep in mind that h may be partial: if h is not defined for the current values of $R_{i_1}, \ldots, R_{i_k}$, then M gets stuck.

The registers of a RMC are typed, i.e. only values of some type t_i may be stored in R_i, and all RMC's are required to be deterministic.

A RMC computes some database query F as follows: for some database instance $\mathcal{D}$, its k relations are placed in the registers $R_1, \ldots, R_k$ of the RMC, and the machine is started with an empty tape. When (and if) it stops, the result $F(\mathcal{D})$ is in R_0.

Definition 13. Some query F is called **RMC-computable** iff there is some RMC, M, computing F.

Proposition 14. *Any RMC-computable query F is ef-domain independent and continuous.*

As opposed to Relational Machines for flat relations, those for Complex Objects are *complete*, i.e. they can express all computable queries. The difference stems from the ability of a RMC to simulate parallel computations through the use of complex objects. This is a corollary of theorem 16 (see corollary 17), but below we sketch a shorter proof using the following lemma, which is also a key technical tool for theorem 16.

Lemma 15 The Map Lemma. *Let M be some RMC computing the function $F : t \rightarrow t'$. Then there is some RMC M' computing $map(F) : \{t\} \rightarrow \{t'\}$.*

The proof is given in [18]. Now we can prove completeness of RMC's with no external functions. Namely let T be a Turing Machine computing some generic, domain independent query F. We build some RMC M computing F: on some input x, M starts by constructing the active domain of x, say $A = \{o_1, \ldots, o_n\}$, and then generates all $n!$ permutations of A. Each permutation allows M to simulate T [5]. Finally, we use the map lemma to simulate T on all $n!$ orders.

7 Computable Queries Coincide with RMC-Computable Queries on Total Databases

We shall assume in this section that all external functions are computable.

Theorem 16. *Any RMC-computable query is computable. Any ef-domain independent query over total databases is computable iff it is RMC-computable.*

The first implication is easy. For the converse, we have to simulate some Turing Machine T by a Relational Machine for Complex Objects M. The difficulty is that M doesn't have the Gödel numbers $e_1, \ldots, e_l$ for the external functions $R_1, \ldots, R_l$ which T requires: instead, the external functions are hard coded into the Relational Machine M. Thus M has to search for $e_1, \ldots, e_l$, by systematically enumerating the Gödel numbers of all *finite* functions, and by "comparing" their input-output behavior to that of its oracle. The proof is given in [18].

Corollary 17. *Relational Machines are complete for complex objects.*

If we drop the restriction to total databases, then the two notions of computable queries no longer coincide. What distinguish them is the fact that the RMC-computable queries are *sequential*, in a sense related to the notion of *sequential function* in [8], while computable queries need not be.

Definition 18. A query F is **sequential** iff for any database $\mathcal{D} = (D; P_1, \ldots, P_i;$ $R_1, \ldots, R_k)$ for which $F(\mathcal{D})$ is undefined, one of the following holds: (1) For any $\mathcal{D}'$ s.t. $\mathcal{D} \sqsubseteq \mathcal{D}'$, $F(\mathcal{D}')$ is undefined, or (2) $\exists i, \exists x \in dom(d_i, D)$ such that for all $\mathcal{D}' \sqsupseteq \mathcal{D}$, if $F(\mathcal{D}')$ is defined then $P_i(x)$ is defined. We call the pair (i, x) the *sequentiality index* of F at $\mathcal{D}$ [8].

Thus, F is sequential iff it invokes the external functions one at a time: if it gets stuck during the computation on some partial database $\mathcal{D}$ because the external functions are not defined, then there is a certain function P_i and a certain input x to P_i such that F gets stuck while trying to compute $P_i(x)$. One can prove that any function computed by a RMC is sequential, because a RMC applies the external functions one at a time, in a sequential manner:

Proposition 19. *All RMC-computable queries are sequential.*

But the following is an example of a computable, ef-domain independent query which is not sequential:

Example 2. Consider the schema $\sigma = (d \to d; d)$, and the following query F: $F(\mathcal{D}) \stackrel{\text{def}}{=} R$, when $\exists x \in R$ s.t. $P(x) = x$, and $F(\mathcal{D}) \stackrel{\text{def}}{=}$ undefined, otherwise, where $\mathcal{D} = (D; P; R)$. This query is ef-domain independent, and computable. To see that it is computable, suppose $R = \{x_1, \ldots, x_n\}$; a Turing Machine T can perform in parallel the computation steps for $P(x_1), \ldots, P(x_n)$, and stop when one of these computations, say for $P(x_i)$, finishes with $P(x_i) = x_i$. Thus T will not get stuck when some other computation, say for $P(x_j)$, never terminates. However this query is not RMC-computable because it is not sequential. Indeed, consider the partial database in which $R = \{x_1, x_2\}$ and $P(x_1) = P(x_2) =$ undefined. Then $F(\mathcal{D})$ is undefined, but neither $(1, x_1)$ nor $(1, x_2)$ is a sequentiality index for F at $\mathcal{D}$, because we may extend in two different ways the database $\mathcal{D}$ to a database $\mathcal{D}'$, such that F is defined on $\mathcal{D}'$, by either defining $P'(x_1) \stackrel{\text{def}}{=} x_1$ or by defining $P'(x_2) \stackrel{\text{def}}{=} x_2$.

8 Complete Query Languages with External Functions

We give in this section examples of complete query languages with external functions. All use the same technique for gaining completeness: some combination of external functions which allow the representation of natural numbers. Let $\mathcal{L}$ be $\mathcal{NRA}(\Sigma) + fix$, n be some of its types, z a constant of type n, and s a function of type $s : n \to n$. Let $\mathcal{C}$ be a class of databases in which the elements $z, s(z), s^{(2)}(z), \ldots, s^{(k)}(z), \ldots$ are distinct. Then we have:

Proposition 20. *Any such language $\mathcal{L}$ is complete w.r.t. the class $\mathcal{C}$.*

The proof is given in [18]. It follows that the following languages are complete:

Object Inventions Consider some base type ι whose elements are called *object id's*, and some external function $make\_object : \{\iota\} \to \iota$ which "generates" new id's: more precisely, we consider $\mathcal{C}$ to be the class of databases for which $make\_object(x) \notin x$, for all x of type $\{\iota\}$. Intuitively $make\_object(x)$ generates an id which was not present in the set x. It can be thought of as a Skolem function of the following higher order formula, stating that the type ι is infinite: $\forall x : \{\iota\}. \exists y : \iota.y \notin x$. Other base types and/or external functions may be present (recall that we allow for more than one base sort, see section 3). This language satisfies the requirements of proposition 20, by taking $n \stackrel{\text{def}}{=} \{\iota\}$, $z \stackrel{\text{def}}{=} \emptyset$ and $s(x) \stackrel{\text{def}}{=} x \cup \{make\_object(x)\}$. It has been known previously that object inventions in conjunction with fixpoints give rise to complete query languages [1]. Here we use related tools to obtain completeness in the presence of external functions.

Untyped Sets Consider some base type u whose meaning is a restriction of the *untyped sets* in [16]. That is, the class $\mathcal{C}$ of databases we consider interprets u as follows: it contains all finite sets which can be constructed from elements in other base types in $\mathcal{L}$, and from other elements in u. E.g. $x = \{a, \{b, c\}, \{a, \emptyset, \{\{b\}\}\}\}$ is a legal element of u, provided that a, b, c are atomic elements. In particular, all elements of type $\{u\}$ are also of type u, and we consider some external function $include : \{u\} \to u$ to witness that inclusion of types. As any base type, u has an equality operator defined on it. Then $\mathcal{L}$ is complete w.r.t. to $\mathcal{C}$. Indeed, it suffices to take $n \stackrel{\text{def}}{=} u$, $z \stackrel{\text{def}}{=} included(\emptyset)$, and $s(x) \stackrel{\text{def}}{=} include(\{x\})$ in proposition 20. That is, the naturals are represented by the set $\{\emptyset, \{\emptyset\}, \{\{\emptyset\}\}, \{\{\{\emptyset\}\}\}, \ldots\}$.

Natural Numbers Consider N to be one of the base types, and $0, 1, +$ to be among the functions in Σ, and let $\mathcal{C}$ be the class of databases in which $\mathsf{N}, 0, 1, +$ have the standard interpretation. The resulting $\mathcal{L}$ is a complete query language w.r.t. Σ for $\mathcal{C}$: take $z \stackrel{\text{def}}{=} 0$ and $s(x) \stackrel{\text{def}}{=} x+1$ in proposition 20.

9 Conclusions

We have investigated the computability of queries in the presence of external functions. Our techniques do not extend straightforwardly to an investigation of the complexity of queries. E.g. we could define some query F to be in PSPACE either when it is computed by some PSAPCE Turing Machine expecting both an encoding of the relations and the Gödel numbers of the external functions, or when it is computed by some RMC whose tape *and* relational store are polynomially bounded. It is not clear however that these two definitions are equivalent, leaving open the question of what a PSPACE query might be. We intend to address the complexity issues for queries with external functions in the future.

10 Acknowledgments

We thank Victor Vianu, Serge Abiteboul, Catriel Beeri and Rick Hull for commenting on an earlier version of this paper, and the anonymous reviewers for their suggestions. The author was supported by NSF grant CCR-90-57570.

References

1. S. Abiteboul and P. Kanellakis. Object identity as a query language primitive. In *Proceedings of ACM SIGMOD Conference on Management of Data*, pages 159–173, Portland, Oregon, 1989.
2. S. Abiteboul, C.H. Papadimitriou, and V. Vianu. The power of reflective relational machines. In *Proceedings of the 9th IEEE Symposium on Logic in Computer Science*, pages 230–240, Paris, France, July 1994.
3. S. Abiteboul, M. Vardi, and V. Vianu. Fixpoint logics, relational machines, and computational complexity. In *Structure and Complexity*, 1992.
4. Serge Abiteboul and Catriel Beeri. On the power of languages for the manipulation of complex objects. In *Proceedings of International Workshop on Theory and Applications of Nested Relations and Complex Objects*, Darmstadt, 1988. Also available as INRIA Technical Report 846.
5. Serge Abiteboul and Victor Vianu. Generic computation and its complexity. In *Proceedings of 23rd ACM Symposium on the Theory of Computing*, 1991.

6. Val Breazu-Tannen, Peter Buneman, and Limsoon Wong. Naturally embedded query languages. In J. Biskup and R. Hull, editors, *LNCS 646: Proceedings of 4th International Conference on Database Theory, Berlin, Germany, October, 1992*, pages 140–154. Springer-Verlag, October 1992. Available as UPenn Technical Report MS-CIS-92-47.

7. Ashok Chandra and David Harel. Computable queries for relational databases. *Journal of Computer and System Sciences*, 21(2):156–178, 1980.

8. P. L. Curien. *Categorical Combinators, Sequential Algorithms and Functional Programming*. Pitman, 1986.

9. O. Deux. The story of O_2. *IEEE Transactions on Knowledge and Data Engineering*, 2(1):91–108, March 1990.

10. Martha Escobar-Molano, Richard Hull, and Dean Jacobs. Safety and translation of calculus queries with scalar functions. In *Proceedings of 12th ACM Symposium on Principles of Database Systems*, pages 253–264, Washington, D. C., May 1993.

11. Stephane Grumbach and Victor Vianu. Expressiveness and complexity of restricted languages for complex objects. In *Proceedings of 3rd International Workshop on Database Programming Languages, Naphlion, Greece*, pages 191–202. Morgan Kaufmann, August 1991.

12. Carl A. Gunter. *Semantics of Programming Languages: Structures and Techniques*. Foundations of Computing. MIT Press, 1992.

13. Marc Gyssens and Dirk Van Gucht. A comparison between algebraic query languages for flat and nested databases. *Theoretical Computer Science*, 87:263–286, 1991.

14. Marc Gyssens and Dirk Van Gucht. The powerset algebra as a natural tool to handle nested database relations. *Journal of Computer and System Sciences*, 45:76–103, 1992.

15. Jr. Hartley Rogers. *Theory of Recursive Functions and Effective Computability*. MIT Press, 1987.

16. Richard Hull and Jianwen Su. Untyped sets, inventions, and computable queries. In *Proceedings 8th ACM Sumposium on Principles of Database Systems*, pages 347–360, 1989.

17. G. D. Plotkin. Post-graduate lecture notes in advanced domain theory. Department of Computer Science, University of Edinburgh, 1981. Available by email from: kondoh@harl.hitachi.co.jp.

18. Dan Suciu. Domain-independent queries on databases with external functions. Technical Report MS-CIS-94-48/L&C 87, University of Pennsylvania, Philadelphia, PA 19104, October 1994.

19. Dan Suciu. Fixpoints and bounded fixpoints for complex objects. In Catriel Beeri, Atsushi Ohori, and Dennis Shasha, editors, *Proceedings of 4th International Workshop on Database Programming Languages, New York, August 1993*, pages 263–281. Springer-Verlag, January 1994. See also UPenn Technical Report MS-CIS-93-32.

20. Dan Suciu and Val Breazu-Tannen. A query language for NC. In *Proceedings of 13th ACM Symposium on Principles of Database Systems*, pages 167–178, Minneapolis, Minnesota, May 1994. See also UPenn Technical Report MS-CIS-94-05.

21. Rodney W. Topor. Domain-independent formulas and databases. *Theoretical Computer Science*, 52:281–306, 1987.

An Algebra for Pomsets [*]
Extended Abstract

Stéphane Grumbach[1] and Tova Milo[2]

[1] I.N.R.I.A. Rocquencourt, 78153 Le Chesnay, France, Stephane.Grumbach@inria.fr
[2] Dept. Computer Science, Tel-Aviv University, Tel-Aviv, Israel, milo@db.toronto.edu

Abstract. We study languages for manipulating *partially ordered* structures with *duplicates* (e.g. trees, lists). As a general framework, we consider the *pomset* (partially ordered multiset) datatype. We introduce an algebra for *pomsets*, which generalizes traditional algebras for (nested) sets, bags and lists. This paper is motivated by the study of the impact of different language primitives on the expressive power. We show that the use of partially ordered types increases the expressive power significantly. Surprisingly, it turns out that the algebra when restricted to both unordered (bags) and totally ordered (lists) intermediate types, yields the same expressive power as fixpoint logic with counting on relational databases. It therefore constitutes a rather robust class of relational queries. On the other hand, we obtain a characterization of PTIME queries on lists by considering only totally ordered types.

1 Introduction

In the standard approach to database modeling two restrictions are imposed on database relations. (i) The elements are assumed to be un-ordered, and (ii) no duplicates are allowed. The impact of having order on database elements has been studied extensively, and was shown to be significant for the expressive power of query languages. In particular it was shown that fixpoint logic expresses all PTIME functions on ordered inputs [Imm86, Var82]. The impact of allowing duplicates in relations was studied in [GM93, GMK93, LW94]. It was also shown to have a strong effect on the expressive power of query languages, and in particular to result in an increased expressive power. In this paper, we study the interaction between order and duplicates, and the effect that the combined features have on the expressive power of query languages.

Results on the impact of order on the expressive power of languages focus on *ordered domains*. There is another approach to order which was not explored so far, namely the order related to the data types used in the query language, that we call the *internal order*. Observe that many data types allow both multiple occurrences of the same element, and (partial) order on the occurrences (e.g. *lists, trees*). We refer to such data types as *ordered types*. Supporting ordered

---

[*] Work supported in part by the Esprit Project BRA FIDE 2. Work was done while the second author was visiting University of Toronto, and supported by the Institute for Robotics and Intelligent Systems.

types in the data model is essential in databases for advanced applications such as CAD/CAM, Software Engineering, and Text Retrieval [SZL93, ACM93].

Previous research considered *ordered domains* and *internal order* as orthogonal issues. For example, the research on the expressive power of languages focused on languages for manipulating inputs of unordered types like sets and bags, and the intermediate data types used in the computation were also unordered [Var82, Imm86, GM93, GMK93]. This was the case even when the domain of the input was totally ordered. On the other hand, ordered types like lists or trees were mainly used when manipulating inputs of type list or tree [Ric92, GW92, SZL93, CRSV94].

The paper focuses on algebraic languages for manipulating ordered types. We consider the *pomset* (partially ordered multiset) datatype, and present an algebra for *pomsets*. The algebra is an extension of the (nested) relational algebra [AB87]. Our aim is to investigate how the combined use of duplicates and (partial) order affects the expressive power of the languages, and increases the complexity.

Surprisingly, it turns out that the additional expressive power gained by using ordered types with duplicates is similar to that gained by using two well studied primitives — *fixpoint* and *counting*. The use of duplicates introduces counting capabilities, and order enables the simulation of fixpoint. We show that the extension of the relational algebra with un-ordered types with duplicates (like bags) and totally ordered types (like lists) has exactly the same expressive power as FO+FP+C [GO93].

To complete previous works that considered the effect of totally ordered domains on the expressive power of the language, we study here the effect of total internal order. We show that the algebra expresses all PTIME queries on lists. Note that another language for list manipulation, expressing PTIME, was presented in [CRSV94]. This language, however, required the use of nested structures. In contrast, our result shows that all PTIME queries can be expressed even without nesting.

The paper is organized as follows. In the next section, we review some preliminaries and define the type *pomset*. The algebra for pomsets, PALG, is introduced in Section 3. In Section 4, we study properties of the algebra, and in sections 5 and 6, we characterize its complexity and expressive power. Finally, in Section 7, we study the power of the nested algebra.

2 Data Types and Queries

In this section, we introduce formally the various data types, and recall the basic framework of databases and queries over data of complex types. Complexity measures are then defined.

2.1 Partially Ordered Multisets, *pomsets*

We assume the existence of an atomic type U, whose domain is an infinite set of constants. We consider tuples of any arity k, $U^k = [U, ..., U]$. To have a uniform representation for sets, bags, lists, trees, and other ordered types, we use a general data type called *pomset* (partially ordered multiset). Intuitively, a pomset can be viewed as a string with a partial order instead of a total order. The following formal definition (essentially the one of Pratt [Pra84]) is based on labelled partial orders.

Definition 2.1 *A **partial order** is a pair $(V, <)$ where $<$ is an irreflexive transitive binary relation on the vertex set V. A **labelled partial order** (lpo) is a structure $(V, \Sigma, \mu, <)$, where $(V, <)$ is a partial order, and $\mu : V \to \Sigma$ labels the vertices of V with elements of the set Σ.*

*Two lpo's $(V, \Sigma, \mu, <)$ and $(V', \Sigma, \mu', <')$ over the same set of labels Σ are **isomorphic** if there exists a bijection $\tau : V \to V'$ such that for all $u, v \in V$, $\mu(u) = \mu'(\tau(u))$, and $u < v$ iff $\tau(u) <' \tau(v)$.*

*A **pomset** $\langle V, \Sigma, \mu, < \rangle$ is the isomorphism class of an lpo $(V, \Sigma, \mu, <)$. A pomset $\langle V, \Sigma, \mu, < \rangle$ is **finite** if V is finite.*

*Two pomsets $\langle V, \Sigma, \mu, < \rangle$ and $\langle V', \Sigma', \mu', <' \rangle$ are **isomorphic** if there exist bijections $\tau : V \to V'$ and $\nu : \Sigma \to \Sigma'$, such that for all $u, v \in V$ and for all $a \in \Sigma$, $\mu(u) = a$ iff $\mu'(\tau(u)) = \nu(a)$, and $u < v$ iff $\tau(u) <' \tau(v)$.*

Remarks : Pomsets are only defined up to isomorphism to hide the identities of the elements in V, so that only the cardinality of V counts, leaving Σ as the only important set underlying a pomset [Pra84]. This also enables us to assume for the sake of simplicity, that, in any two pomsets, the corresponding sets of vertices are disjoint. This hypothesis is important for algebraic operations. In order to allow algebraic expressions with repeated operands, we assume that a renaming of the vertices is performed on each copy.

Note the difference between lpo's, denoted with "( )", and pomsets, denoted with "⟨ ⟩", and between isomorphisms on lpo's over the same set of labels, and isomorphisms on pomsets. The lpo's are only used to define pomsets, and in the following we shall only consider the latter.

Standard types such as sets, bags, directed acyclic graphs (dags), and lists, are subtypes of the pomset type, and are obtained by restricting the mapping μ and the kind of order in the pomset. For example, sets require μ to be a 1-1 mapping, and no order, bags may have arbitrary μ, but no order, and lists require total order.

If Σ is a collection of objects of **type** T, we denote the type of the pomset $\langle V, \Sigma, \mu, < \rangle$ by $\{T\}$. For a type T, the **domain** of $\{T\}$, is the set of all finite pomsets $\langle V, \Sigma, \mu, < \rangle$ where Σ is a collection of objects of type T. All collection types are defined as usual, assuming *finite* and *homogeneous* collections.

From the implementation view point, a pomset $p = \langle V, \Sigma, \mu, < \rangle$ can be represented by a directed acyclic graph $G = (V, E)$ where each node $v \in V$ has a label in Σ attached to it, (different nodes may have the same label attached to them), and where an edge $(v_1, v_2) \in E$ iff $v_1 < v_2$.[3]

In the graph G, each connected component corresponds to a set of vertices $V' \subseteq V$ that are related to each other by $<$ and not related to other vertices in $V - V'$. We overload the term connected component, and call the (sub)pomset $p' = \langle V', \Sigma, \mu \downarrow_{V'}, <\downarrow_{V' \times V'}\rangle$ corresponding to a connected component V' of the graph G, a *connected component of the pomset p*. A connected component p' of the pomset p may have several isomorphic (with respect to pomset isomorphism) occurrences in p. We say that a connected component **n-belongs** to a pomset if it has exactly n isomorphic occurrences.

We say that a pomset p is *linear* if $<$ defines a total order on V (lists and stacks can be represented by linear pomsets). We say that p is *pseudo-linear* if $<$ defines a total order on each connected component of p.

2.2 Databases and Queries

A **pomset database** is a set of named pomsets. (Following the relational model conventions, we shall sometimes refer to these pomsets as database relations.) A **pomset schema** is an expression $p : T$, where p is a pomset name, and T is a pomset type. An **instance** of p is a pomset of type T. A **database schema** DB is a finite set of pomset schemas with distinct pomset names. An **instance** of DB is a mapping associating a pomset to every pomset schema in DB.

Queries on pomset databases are defined by extending the classical definition of [CH80] for relational queries. A query is a mapping from an input schema **DB** $= \{P_1, ..., P_n\}$ to an output schema **S**$= \{P_0\}$ with a single pomset, mapping instances of the input schema to instances of the output schema. Queries must be computable and generic, i.e. insensitive to isomorphisms on the databases (based on pomset isomorphisms).

Complexity classes of queries are defined straightforwardly by extending the definition for relational queries. We use as complexity measures the time and space used by a Turing machine to produce a standard encoding of the output database, starting from a standard encoding of the input database. The standard encoding of a pomset p is based on some labelled partial order $(V, \Sigma, \mu, <)$, and is similar to that of the binary relations representing μ and $<$. Note that in this encoding, each object in Σ, is repeated as many times as the vertices it labels in V. This encoding may seem inefficient since pomsets can sometimes be encoded more compactly (for example, un-ordered pomsets like bags can be encoded by simply attaching to elements in Σ the number of vertices they label). Nevertheless, this encoding fits with the situation in real database systems, where duplicates are explicitly stored, sometimes precisely to avoid the cost of duplicate elimination.

We consider the **data complexity** of queries, i.e. the complexity of the evaluation of a query in terms of the size of the input databases. For each Turing

---

[3] A compact representation can be obtained by considering a transitively reduced version of the graph [Moh89].

complexity class $\mathcal{C}$ there is a corresponding complexity class of queries, which, for simplicity, we also denote by $\mathcal{C}$.

3 An Algebra for Pomsets

While for un-ordered data types like sets and bags, there is an accepted standard set of algebraic operations, this is not the case for ordered types, and different algebras for manipulating lists and trees exist in the literature [Ric92, GW92, SZL93]. Some of these languages share, however, a common property — to be extensions of the relational algebra, and when restricted to non ordered structures with no duplicates, most of them yield the relational algebra. Following these lines, we present below a uniform algebra for (partially) ordered structures with duplicates, that is a strict extension of the relational algebra. The algebra is designed so that by restricting the order or the number of duplicates, one gets an algebra for manipulating specific kinds of ordered types. For example, when restricted to unordered structures with no duplicates it is the traditional relational algebra. When duplicates are allowed, it is the bag algebra [GM93]. When restricted to total orders, it is an algebra for lists.

To make the results of this paper general and applicable to previously presented languages, we consider a restricted set of operators — the relational algebra operators (adjusted to this context), and a small set of additional operators that are essential for exploiting the order in ordered types.

We first present a simple version of the algebra, that manipulates pomsets of tuples of atomic elements. (Nested pomsets, and the extensions in the algebra needed to enable manipulation of nested structures, are considered in Section 7). We start by presenting the algebraic operators. Next we study their properties, and in particular consider the dependencies of the operations.

The algebra contains a *Tupling* operator $[o_1, \ldots, o_k]$ that builds tuples of type U^k, and *attribute projection* $x.i$ that extracts the ith attribute of a tuple. Singleton pomsets are constructed using the *pomsetting* operator $\{o\}$, that builds a pomset of the form $\langle \{v\}, \{o\}, (v, o), \emptyset \rangle$. (Note that since pomsets are defined up to isomorphism on V, the actual value of v is irrelevant). We shall use below the term *object* to denote a vertex with its associated label.

To construct more complex pomsets we use two classical operations on pomsets which have been considered in the literature [Pra84]. The *additive union* (also called *shuffle* in [Pra84]), and the *concatenation*. Let $p_1 = \langle V_1, \Sigma, \mu_1, <_1 \rangle$, $p_2 = \langle V_2, \Sigma, \mu_2, <_2 \rangle$ be two pomsets of type $\{T\}$. Assume w.o.l.g. that V_1 and V_2 are disjoint.

- *Additive union*, $\uplus$: $p_1 \uplus p_2$ is a pomset containing all the objects in p_1 and p_2, and preserving the order of those objects.
  $p_1 \uplus p_2 = \langle V_1 \cup V_2, \Sigma, \mu_1 \cup \mu_2, <_1 \cup <_2 \rangle$.
- *Concatenation*, $\oplus$: $p_1 \oplus p_2$ is a pomset containing all the objects in p_1 and p_2, preserving the order of the objects, and additionally making all the objects in p_1 smaller than those of p_2. $p_1 \oplus p_2 = \langle V_1 \cup V_2, \Sigma, \mu_1 \cup \mu_2, <_1 \cup <_2 \cup (V_1 \times V_2) \rangle$.

The operations $\uplus$ and $\oplus$ are associative and $\uplus$ is commutative. It turns out that these two operations are not sufficient for building all possible pomsets [Pra84]. This can be done by adding more operations to the language, as further discussed below.

3.1 The Relational and Bag Algebras

The first group of operations that we add to the algebra are the standard union, intersection, and subtraction. These relational operations were extended in [GM93] to handle bags. We now further generalize these operations for pomsets. In bags, all the occurrences of objects with the same label are isomorphic, and thus the operations are defined in terms of the number of occurrences of each label. The generalization to pomsets is based on the observation that in pomsets, objects with the same label may differ due to the relative order of objects. This relative order is captured by the connected components of the pomset. Thus, instead of considering the number of occurrences of individual labels, we define the operators w.r.t. the number of occurrences of the connected components.

Let $p = \langle V, \Sigma, \mu, < \rangle$, $p_1 = \langle V_1, \Sigma, \mu_1, <_1 \rangle$, $p_2 = \langle V_2, \Sigma, \mu_2, <_2 \rangle$ be three pomsets of type $\{T\}$, where $T = [U, ..., U]$. Assume that V_1 and V_2 are disjoint. Let $p' = \langle V', \Sigma, \mu \downarrow_{V'}, < \downarrow_{V' \times V'} \rangle$ be some connected component of p, p_1 or p_2.

- *Union*, $\bigcup$: $p_1 \cup p_2$ is a pomset, s.t. a connected component p' n-belongs to $p_1 \cup p_2$ iff p' r-belongs to p_1 and q-belongs to p_2 and $n = sup(r, q)$.
- *Intersection*, $\bigcap$: $p_1 \cap p_2$ is a pomset, s.t. a connected component p' n-belongs to $p_1 \cap p_2$ iff p' r-belongs to p_1 and q-belongs to p_2 and $n = min(r, q)$.
- *Subtraction*, $-$: $p_1 - p_2$ is a pomset, s.t. a connected component p' n-belongs to $p_1 - p_2$ iff p' r-belongs to p_1 and q-belongs to p_2 and $n = sup(0, r - q)$.

Another group of relational operations that were extended in [GM93] to handle bags are projection (and its more general version MAP), selection, and cartesian product. We now further generalize them for pomsets.

- *Restructuring*, MAP: Assume that φ is an algebra expression[4] mapping objects of type T to pomsets of type $\{T'\}$. $MAP_\varphi(p)$ is a pomset of type $\{T'\}$, obtained by replacing each $v \in V$ in p by the whole pomset $p_v = \varphi(\mu(v))$, preserving order both within and between the p_v's.

This operation is also called in the literature on pomsets the *expansion* operation. (See [Pra84] for a formal definition.) $MAP_{\lambda x \ \{x.1\} \oplus \{x.2\}}$, for instance, denotes the pomset obtained by replacing each tuple by two objects corresponding to the first and second attributes of the tuple, and making the first attribute precede the second in the order.

As another example, $MAP_{\lambda x \ \{[x.1, x.3]\}}$ denotes the projection of each tuple in the pomset on its first and third arguments. For brevity, we shall denote the map

---

[4] φ may contain any algebra operator including MAP and the operators defined below.

operations when applied on pomset of tuples, projecting the attributes $i_1, \ldots, i_n$ by $\Pi_{i_1, \ldots, i_n}$.

- *Selection*, $\sigma_{\varphi = \varphi'}$: Assume that φ, φ' are algebra expressions. $\sigma_{\varphi = \varphi'}(p)$ is the pomset obtained from D by removing all the vertices $v \in V$ not satisfying the equation $\varphi(\mu(v)) = \varphi'(\mu(v))$, and preserving the order of the remaining objects.
- *Cartesian product*, $\times$: Assume $p_1 : \{T_1\}$ and $p_2 : \{T_2\}$. The objects in $p_1 \times p_2$ are obtained from the cartesian product of the objects in p_1 and in p_2. The order on the objects is the lexicographical order.
  $p_1 \times p_2 = \langle V_1 \times V_2, \Sigma^2, \mu_1 \times \mu_2,$
  $\quad \{([x_1, y_1], [x_1, y_2]) \mid (y_1, y_2) \in <_2\} \cup \{([x_1, y_1], [x_2, y_2]) \mid (x_1, x_2) \in <_1\}\rangle :$
  $$\{T_1 \times T_2\}$$

So far we considered only relational algebra operators. An operator important for bags [GM93] is duplicate elimination. This operator can be generalized to pomsets either by (1) considering connected components of the pomsets, and eliminating isomorphic occurrences of the same component, or (2) by considering individual objects and eliminating multiple occurrences of the same label (note that for unordered pomsets, i.e. bags, the two options are identical).

- *Duplicate elimination:*
  Connected components, ϵ : $\epsilon(p)$ is a pomset with exactly one occurrence of each of the non-isomorphic connected components of p.
  Individual objects, ϵ_n : $\epsilon_n(p)$ is a pomset where all the vertices $v \in V$ that are mapped by μ to the same label collapse to one unique vertex with this label, and where the order on the new objects is the maximal order consistent with that of the sources of the objects. More formally:
  $\epsilon_n(p) = \langle V', \Sigma, \mu', <' \rangle$ where $V' \subseteq V$ is such that $\mu' = \mu \downarrow_{V'}$ is 1-1, and for each $v_1, v_2 \in V'$ such that $\mu'(v_1) = a$ and $\mu'(v_2) = b$, $(v_1, v_2) \in <'$ iff there exists $v'_1 \in \mu^{-1}(a)$, $v'_2 \in \mu^{-1}(b)$ such that $(v'_1, v'_2) \in <$, and there is no $v''_1 \in \mu^{-1}(a)$, $v''_2 \in \mu^{-1}(b)$ such that $(v''_2, v''_1) \in <$.

3.2 Special Pomset Operators

To fully exploit the ordered types as a computational device, we need to be able to transform unordered types into partially ordered ones, and vice-versa. The relational and bag operators, do not support this. We introduce two operations which deterministically transform partially ordered pomsets into unordered ones and reciprocally.

- *Order-destroy*, $\oplus^{-1}$: $\oplus^{-1}(p) = \langle V, \Sigma, \mu, \emptyset \rangle$ is an unordered pomset of type $\{T\}$, containing the same objects as p.
- *Listing*, Λ : This operation deterministically maps an **unordered** multiset (i.e. a pomset with an empty order) to a pseudo-linear pomset. More formally, $\Lambda(\langle V, \Sigma, \mu, \emptyset \rangle) = \langle V, \Sigma, \mu, <' \rangle$, where $<'$ is the minimal partial order such that for every label o in Σ with exactly n_o distinct $v_i \in V$

for which $\mu(v_i) = o$, $v_1 <' v_2 <' \ldots <' v_{n_o}$. Otherwise, if $< \neq \emptyset$, then $\Lambda(\langle V, \Sigma, \mu, < \rangle) = (\langle V, \Sigma, \mu, < \rangle)$.

For instance, $\Lambda((\{v_1, v_2, v_3, v_4, v_5\}, \{1, 2\}, \{(v_1, 1), (v_2, 1), (v_3, 1), (v_4, 2), (v_5, 2)\}, \emptyset))$ generates the following partial order[5]: $v_1 < v_2 < v_3$ and $v_4 < v_5$.

To further exploit the internal order in a pomset, we define an operator that enables sequential iteration over components of the pomset, according to their relative order.

Iterator, I: The operator I realizes a structural-recursion [BTBN91] on the pomsets. To simplify the presentation, we first explain how it behaves when applied on totally ordered pomsets (i.e. lists). Let $\emptyset$ denote the empty list of type $\{T\}$. Let $y \neq \emptyset$ be a non empty list of type $\{T\}$, let x be a singleton list of type $\{T\}$ (i.e. a list containing one element), and let $f :\to \{T'\}$, $g : \{T\} \to \{T'\}$, and $h : \{T\}, \{T'\} \to \{T'\}$ be three algebra expressions. The iterator $I_{f,g,h}$ is defined as follows:

- $I_{f,g,h}(\emptyset) = f$,
- $I_{f,g,h}(x) = g(x)$,
- $I_{f,g,h}(x \oplus y) = h(x, I_{f,g,h}(y))$.

Thus, the result of the iterator when applied on the empty list is determined by the algebra expression f. The result when applied on a singleton list is defined by g, and the result when applied on a list of length $n > 1$ is defined recursively by first computing the operator on the last $(n - 1)$ elements, and then using h to take into account the first element.

We next explain how the operator works when applied on partially ordered pomsets. Since lists are totally ordered, the operator can process all the elements of the list sequentially. Partially ordered pomsets do not necessarily have a total order on the individual elements, but the operator can still exploit the relative order of sub-parts of the pomsets. We say that a pomset x is *serial* iff there are two pomsets $x_1, x_2 \neq \emptyset$ such that $x = x_1 \oplus x_2$. A pomset is called *non-serial* otherwise. Every pomset x can be viewed as a concatenation of (one or more) non-serial pomsets $x_1, \ldots, x_n$, such that $x = x_1 \oplus \ldots \oplus x_n$.

Example 3.1 The pomset: $x = \langle \{a, b, c, d, e\}, \{1, 2\},$
$\{(a, 1), (b, 2), (c, 1), (d, 2), (e, 1)\}, \{(a, b), (b, e), (c, d), (d, e), (a, e), (c, e)\} \rangle$
is the concatenation of the non-serial pomsets:
$x_1 = \langle \{a, b, c, d\}, \{1, 2\}, \{(a, 1), (b, 2), (c, 1), (d, 2)\}, \{(a, b), (c, d)\} \rangle$, and
$x_2 = \langle \{e\}, \{1\}, \{(e, 1)\}, \emptyset \rangle$.

It turns out that the non-serial pomsets from which a pomset is composed of can be computed efficiently.

---

[5] Note that since pomsets are defined up to isomorphism on V, the specific order of the v_i's is irrelevant, and thus the operation is deterministic.

Proposition 3.1 Every pomset x has a unique decomposition into non-serial pomsets $x_1, \ldots, x_n$, such that $x = x_1 \oplus \ldots \oplus x_n$. This decomposition can be computed in time polynomial in the size of x.

The algorithm uses the graph representation of a pomset. It is omitted for lack of space. When the iterator is applied to partially ordered pomsets, instead of sequentially processing single elements, it processes sequentially the non-serial pomsets from which the pomset is composed. Thus, for partially ordered pomsets, the iterator is defined by recursion on the serial structure of the pomset. The definition is the same as above, except that now $\emptyset$ denotes the empty pomset, $y \neq \emptyset$ a non empty pomset, and $x \neq \emptyset$ a non-serial pomset.

4 Properties of the Algebra

Let PALG denote the algebra for pomsets containing all the operations as defined above. The algebra PALG is very similar to the relational and bag algebras [GM93]. When restricted to unordered pomsets it is essentially the bag algebra, and if additionally no two vertices are allowed to have the same label (and each operation is followed by duplicate elimination) it yields the relational algebra. We use the notation PALG_θ, to denote the restriction of PALG without the operation θ. We next study the properties and dependencies of the different operations. We first consider the duplicate elimination operator. Note that this operator received much attention in the context of object oriented languages [AK89, BP91]. It was shown in particular that it plays an important role to get complete languages. This operation is also very significant in the context of ordered types. The next propositions shows the limitations of PALG_{ϵ_n}.

Proposition 4.1 PALG_{ϵ_n} can construct only series-parallel pomsets.

Series-parallel pomsets are defined as the smallest class containing singleton pomsets, and closed under parallel ($\uplus$) and series ($\oplus$) composition.

The proof is by induction on the depth of the expressions defining the pomsets. The only delicate operations are $\times$, MAP, σ and the iterator I (omitted).

Note that there are pomsets that are not series-parallel. For example, it was shown in [Moh89] that the N-shaped pomset

$\mathcal{N} = \langle \{a, b, c, d\}, \{1\}, \{(a,1), (b,1), (c,1), (d,1)\}, \{(a,b), (a,d), (c,d)\} \rangle$,

with four objects all labeled with "1", is not series-parallel. It follows that:

Corollary 4.2 Not all pomsets can be constructed in PALG_{ϵ_n}.

It turns out that non series-parallel pomsets can be constructed using the duplicate elimination operator. For example, the N-shaped pomset described above can be constructed in PALG as follows:

$$\mathcal{N} = \Pi_1(\epsilon_n((\{[1,a]\} \oplus \{[1,b]\}) \uplus (\{[1,a]\} \oplus \{[1,d]\}) \uplus (\{[1,c]\} \oplus \{[1,d]\}))).$$

More generally, PALG can construct **all** pomsets.

Proposition 4.3 All pomsets can be constructed using the operators $[]$, $\{\}$, $\uplus$, $\oplus$, ϵ_n, and Π.

The proof is rather straightforward — the construction of arbitrary pomsets is similar to the construction of the N-shaped pomset above (omitted). It follows that:

Corollary 4.4 $\text{PALG}_{\epsilon_n} \subset \text{PALG}$.

Pomsets can be represented in the algebra using the operations $[]$, $\{\}$, $\uplus$, $\oplus$, ϵ_n, and Π, and symbols from $\Sigma \cup V$. We nevertheless often use in the following the semantical notation for pomsets, in terms of a set of vertices V, a labelling function $\mu : V \rightarrow \Sigma$, and a partial order over V.

We next consider the operations that map unordered structures to (partially) ordered structures (listing Λ), and vice-versa (order-destroy $\oplus^{-1}$). We show that these two operators cannot be expressed by other operations.

Proposition 4.5 .

- $\text{PALG}_\Lambda \subset \text{PALG}$
- $\text{PALG}_{\oplus^{-1}} \subset \text{PALG}$

Proof is omitted for lack of space.

5 The Complexity of the Algebra

We next study the complexity of evaluating queries in the pomset algebra. As in the classical relational case, we are aiming for characterizations of PALG in terms of complexity classes of queries. It turns out that some of the operations are rather expensive, but when appropriately restricted, they become tractable.

5.1 Operations on Connected Components

First, consider the four operations $\bigcup, \bigcap, -$, and ϵ, that operate on connected components of pomsets. Note that these operations require a graph isomorphism test. To have a tractable language, these operations must be restricted. Let F be a family of graphs for which graph isomorphism is polynomial, and where the test of membership in F is also polynomial. We restrict the operations so that if the input pomset is not in F, then the result of the operation is the empty pomset. The class of **planar graphs** satisfy these two requirements [HT74, HW74]. We assume in the following that the operations are restricted to pomsets whose (transitively reduced) graph representation is planar. This guarantees tractability of the operations.

5.2 The Iterator

It is important to note that a careless use of the iterator may cause exponential explosion of the size of the result. Consider for example the case where: $f = \emptyset$, $g(x) = a$, and $h(x, y) = y \oplus y$. In this case, if l is a list, then $I_{f,g,h}(l)$ is a list of a's of length $2^{|l|}$.

Consider the algebra containing all the operators described above, including the iterator I. Given an algebra expression e, we call the problem of testing whether there exists an input p for which $e(p)$ is of size $hyper(|\,p\,|)$, the *exponential explosion problem*. It can be shown that that:

Theorem 5.1 The exponential explosion problem is undecidable.

It is easy to verify that every expression in the algebra can be computed in some hyperexponential time in the size of its input. The height of the hyperexponential depends on the number of imbricated iterators. The exponential growth is due to the duplicates generated in the computation. We consider below two restrictions on the language that ensure tractability by restricting the number of duplicates being generated. Both restrictions apply to the use of the iterator I.

Bounded Iterator: The first restriction is similar to the bounded fixpoint operator of [Suc93]. The idea is to restrict the iterator such that the size of the intermediate result in each step of the computation is bounded. The bound is defined using an algebra expression b. The bounded iterator $I_{f,g,h|b}$, when applied on a pomset p, behaves exactly like the unbounded operator, except that it ignores intermediate results whose size is bigger than $b(p)$. More formally:
$$I_{f,g,h|b}(p) = I_{f,g,h'}(p), \text{ where } h'(x, y) = h(x, y) \text{ if } |h(x, y))| < |b(p)|, \text{ and}$$
$$h'(x, y) = y \text{ otherwise.}$$
The key observation is that if only bounded iterators are used in the algebra, then $b(p)$ is guaranteed to be of size polynomial in p, and thus all the intermediate results are of size polynomial in the size of the input.

Let PALG(b) be the algebra containing all the operators of PALG (with the above restrictions on operations on connected components), and where the iterator is bounded. The complexity of PALG(b) is considered in the next theorem.

Theorem 5.2 PALG(b) is in PTIME.

Proof. (Sketch) We prove the result by showing that (i) the maximal number of occurrences of each tuple at any step of the evaluation of the query is bounded by some polynomial in the size of the input, and (ii) all the operations can be computed in polynomial time in the size of their input. The proof is by induction on the number of operations in the expression, and uses Proposition 3.1 to guarantee that the iterator can be computed in polynomial time. □

Duplicate Elimination: Another way to restrict the number of duplicates generated in the computation is to enforce the use of the duplicate elimination operator. We say that an iterator $I_{f,g,h}$ is *duplicate free* if f, g and h have the form $\epsilon_n(f')$, $\epsilon_n(g')$ and $\epsilon_n(h')$ resp., for some algebra expressions f', g', h'. Duplicate free iterators cannot cause exponential explosion of the (intermediate) results[6]. Let PALG(ϵ) be the algebra containing all the operators of PALG, (with the above restrictions on operations on connected components), and where only duplicate free iterator is used. It is easy to see that PALG(ϵ) $\subseteq$ PALG(b), and thus is in PTIME.

We shall see in the following a special case where the two restrictions on the iterator yield equivalent languages. It is open whether in the general case the inclusion is strict.

6 The Expressive Power of the Algebra

We next study the expressive power of the pomset algebra. As in the classical relational case, we are aiming for characterizations of expressiveness of PALG in terms of complexity classes of queries. In particular, we show that even unordered inputs with no duplicates can benefit from the use of ordered data types.

6.1 RALG, BALG, and FO+FP+C

To measure the expressiveness gained by the use of ordered types, we compare the expressive power of the pomset algebra to that of the relational algebra (denoted below as RALG) [Ull88], the bag algebra (denoted as BALG) [GM93], and various extensions of first order logic (FO), such as fixpoint logic (FO+FP), and fixpoint logic with counting (FO+FP+C) [GO93].

The relational and bag algebras can be naturally derived from the pomset algebra by restricting it to respectively unordered structures with no duplicates, and unordered structures. We briefly describe below the language FO+FP+C (for more details see [GO93]).

FO+FP+C is a two-sorted logic, with the sorts *domain* (unordered) and *integer* (with a linear order). The semantics is based on finite structures with a finite segment of the integers. For any finite relational structure $\mathcal{A} = (A, R_1, \ldots, R_n)$, the structure *with a finite segment of the integers* $\mathcal{A}^*$ is defined by: $\mathcal{A}^* = A \cup (\{0, \ldots, n-1\}, \leq)$, where $n = \mid A \mid$. If $\varphi(x)$ is a formula with a free variable x of sort domain, then $\#_x[\varphi(x)]$ is a term of sort integer, interpreted as the cardinality of $\{a \mid \varphi(a)\}$. FO+FP+C allows the manipulation of numbers from 0 to n^k for some k, by using tuples of integers of the form $[i_1, \ldots, i_k]$ where each i_j varies from 0 to $n-1$. In general, we will omit the exact representation of the numbers and consider directly numbers from 0 to some n^k.

---

[6] In fact, a less drastic restriction, where ϵ_n is enforced only after the operations $\times$, MAP, and I, and when h has more than one occurrence of the variable y, is sufficient to prevent exponential explosion. But for the results considered in this paper, the above restrictive definition of the duplicate free iterator is sufficient.

6.2 Expressiveness

When comparing the pomset algebra to RALG, BALG, FO+FP, and FO+FP+C, one consider queries over the same kind of inputs. We thus restrict below our attention to PALG queries mapping set inputs to set outputs. We first show that the pomset algebra is more powerful than the relational and bag algebras.

Theorem 6.1 FO = RALG $\subset$ BALG $\subset$ PALG(ϵ) $\subseteq$ PALG(b).

The strict inclusion of the relational algebra in the bag algebra was proved in [GM93]. Clearly the bag algebra is included in the pomset algebra. The fact that the inclusion is strict follows from the fact that the parity query, $EVEN$ (which is not expressible in BALG [GM93, LW94]), is expressible in PALG.

Proposition 6.2 $EVEN \in$ PALG(ϵ).

Proof: Let R be a relation. The parity of the cardinality of R is expressed by:

$$EVEN(R) \equiv I_{\lambda x; \epsilon_n(\emptyset), \lambda x; \epsilon_n(\{a\}), \lambda x\ y; \epsilon_n(\{a\}-y)}(\Lambda(\mathrm{MAP}_{\{[a]\}}(R))) \neq \{a\}. \square$$

As we show below, the iterator I is very similar to the traditional fixpoint operator. Thus, the fact that FO is strictly included in PALG is not surprising. It turns out however, that PALG is also more expressive than FO+FP.

Theorem 6.3 FO+FP $\subset$ PALG(ϵ) $\subseteq$ PALG(b).

Proof: (Sketch) The inclusion of FO+FP in PALG is proved by induction. (Omitted for lack of space). The strict inclusion follows from the fact that $EVEN$ is not expressible in FO+FP. $\square$

We proved that fixpoint can be simulated in PALG. We next prove that the *counting* construct can also be simulated. In particular, we show that (the tractable portion of) PALG, when restricted to both unordered types (such as sets and bags) and totally ordered types (such as lists) yields exactly the same expressive power as first order logic augmented with fixpoint and counting. Let PALG(b)$|_{u,t}$ (respectively PALG(ϵ)$|_{u,t}$) be the restriction[7] of PALG(b) (respectively PALG(ϵ)) to unordered and totally ordered pomsets.

Theorem 6.4 FO+FP+C = PALG(ϵ)$|_{u,t}$ = PALG(b)$|_{u,t}$.

It is open if the use of general partially ordered types with duplicates further increases the expressiveness of the language. We conjecture that: PALG(b)$|_{u,t}$ $\subset$ PALG(b). More generally, the expressive power resulting from non series-parallel pomsets is badly understood. We conjecture that the query *source*, giving the objects with no predecessor, on N-shaped graphs cannot be expressed in PALG.

---

[7] This restriction is enforced as follows. Whenever, the output of an algebraic operation is neither of the unordered form, $p = \langle V, \Sigma, \mu, \emptyset \rangle$, nor of the totally ordered form, $p = \langle V, \Sigma, \mu, < \rangle$, where $<$ is a linear order over V, then the output is the empty pomset by definition.

6.3 Ordered Input/Output

To complete previous works that considered the impact of totally ordered domains on the expressive power of the language [Imm86, Var82], we study here the effect of having a total internal order. We show that PALG(b) expresses all PTIME queries on ordered types with total internal order and duplicates. It is open if the same result holds for the other tractable version of PALG, PALG(ϵ).

Theorem 6.5 For input/output of type list, PALG(b)=PTIME.

We prove the theorem by showing that the iterator I can be used to simulate the computation of a Turing machine.

Another language for list manipulation, expressing PTIME, was presented in [CRSV94]. To express all PTIME queries, this language required the use of nested structures, i.e. lists of tuples of lists. In contrast, our result shows that all PTIME queries can be expressed even when only flat lists are available.

7 Nesting

We next consider ordered types with nesting. Nesting of structures has been extensively studied in the context of unordered types like sets [HS88, HS89, GV90, GV91] and bags [GM93]. In this section, we study the combined effect of order, nesting, and duplicates. Nested pomsets can be used to represent ordered types with components of some ordered type (e.g. lists of trees). In nested pomsets, every object can be a nested pomset or a tuple with attributes that are nested pomsets. It turns out that nesting increases drastically the expressive power of the language. This is due to the operations linking different levels of nesting.

All the PALG operators presented in Section 3 are extended naturally to handle nested pomsets. The algebra has one additional operator. Let $p = \langle V, \Sigma, \mu, < \rangle$ be a pomset of type $\{T\}$.

- *Powerset, $\mathcal{P}$* : Intuitively, $\mathcal{P}(p)$ computes the set of all sub-pomsets of p. More formally, $\mathcal{P}(p) = \langle V_\mathcal{P}, \Sigma_\mathcal{P}, \mu_\mathcal{P}, \emptyset \rangle$ is an unordered pomset of type $\{\{T\}\}$, where $\mu_\mathcal{P}$ is a 1-1 function, and where for every[8] pomset $p' = \langle V', \Sigma, \mu', <' \rangle$, where $V' \subseteq V$, $\mu' = \mu \downarrow_{V'}$, and $<' \subseteq < \downarrow_{V'}$, there exists $v \in V_\mathcal{P}$ such that $\mu_\mathcal{P}(v) = p'$.

As in the nested relation (bag) algebra, the powerset operator may cause exponential growth of the output, and the resulting language is no longer tractable. We therefore remove the restrictions from the iterator and the other operations and consider the full pomset algebra.

Note that the nested relation (bag) algebra has an additional operator, *set(bag)-destroy*, that is used to destroy one level of set (bag) nesting [AB87, GM93]. This operation can be simulated in PALG using the MAP operator. In

---

[8] Note that since pomsets define isomorphism classes of lpo's, two isomorphic lpo's will have only one occurrence in $\mathcal{P}(p)$.

particular, $\mathrm{MAP}_{\lambda x;x}$ destroys one level of pomset nesting. For every pomset p of type $\{\{T\}\}$, $\mathrm{MAP}_{\lambda x;x}(p)$ is a pomset of type $\{T\}$ obtained by replacing each $v \in V$ in p by a whole pomset $p_v = \mu(v)$, preserving order both within and between the p_v's.

In the rest of this section, we study the effect that different levels of nesting have on the expressive power of PALG. A complex type can be viewed as a tree with nodes representing the tuple and pomset constructors. The **nesting** of a type T is the maximal number of pomset nodes in a path from the root to a leaf. We denote the algebra when restricted to pomsets with nesting of depth k, PALG^k. The simple algebra investigated in previous sections allows only one level of pomsets, thus corresponds to PALG^1. We next consider PALG^2, one stage higher in the nesting hierarchy.

We study the relationship between the nested pomset algebra and the nested relation and nested bag algebras. We denote the nested relation (bag) algebra when restricted to set nesting of depth k, RALG^k (BALG^k) [HS88, GV91, GM93]. We first compare RALG^2, BALG^2 and PALG^2 restricted to queries over (nested) sets.

Theorem 7.1 $\mathrm{RALG}^2 \subset \mathrm{BALG}^2 \subset \mathrm{PALG}^2$.

The strict inclusion of RALG^2 in BALG^2 was proved in [GM93]. It was also shown there that BALG^2 is included in PSPACE. The strict inclusion BALG^2 in PALG^2 follows from the next proposition. Let $\mathcal{E}$ denotes the set of *elementary* queries, i.e. of hyper-exponential complexity.

Theorem 7.2 $\mathrm{PALG}^2 = \mathcal{E}$, for unnested, unordered inputs/outputs.

Proof: (Sketch) We show that every $hyper(i)$-time bounded query over unnested bags can be expressed in PALG^2. The proof is based on an encoding of the configurations of a Turing machine in a set of 4-ary tuples of type $[\{U\}, \{U\}, U, U]$, and using the iterator I to simulate the moves of the machine. $\square$

A similar proof technique leads to the following result.

Theorem 7.3 $\mathrm{PALG}^2 = \mathcal{E}$, for unnested input/output of type list.

The last subject we consider is queries with general partially ordered, nested, input/output.

Theorem 7.4 For every $k \geq 3$, PALG^k expresses exactly all the elementary queries over inputs of nesting $(k-1)$.

The proof is based on an encoding of nested pomsets in nested bags, and using a result from [GM93] (Omitted). Note that a similar result was obtained in [GM93] for BALG^k. It follows that:

Theorem 7.5 $\mathrm{RALG}^k \subset \mathrm{BALG}^k = \mathrm{PALG}^k$, for every $k \geq 3$, and input/output of nesting height $(k-1)$.

8 Conclusion

The pomset datatype generalyzes all the classical collection types manipulated in databases. We proposed an algebra for pomsets which extends classical algebras for sets, bags and lists. When restricted to specific types, we obtain nice equivalences with either logic (FO+FP+C) or complexity classes (PTIME, $\mathcal{E}$). This shows the robustness of the algebra. Nevertheless, the precise expressive power of the full pomset datatype (including non series-parallel) is still an open question.

Acknowledgments: The authors wish to thank Vassos Hadzilacos for technical remarks.

References

[AB87] S. Abiteboul and C. Beeri. On the power of languages for the manipulation of complex objects. In *Proc. Int. Workshop on Theory and Applications of Nested Relations and Complex Objects (extended abstract)*, Darmstadt, 1987. INRIA research report n 846.

[ACM93] S. Abiteboul, S. Cluet, and T. Milo. Querying and updating the file. In *Proc. 19th Int'l Conf. on Very Large Data Bases*, 1993.

[AK89] S. Abiteboul and P. Kanellakis. Object identity as a query language primitive. In *Proc. ACM SIGMOD Int. Conf. on Management of Data*, pages 159–173, 1989.

[AV91] S. Abiteboul and V. Vianu. Generic computation and its complexity. In *Proc. ACM Symp. on Theory of Computing*, New Orleans, May 1991.

[BM92] C. Beeri and T. Milo. Functional and predicative programming in oodb's. In *Proc. 11th Symp. on Principles of Database Systems, San Diego*, 1992.

[BP91] J. Van Den Bussche and J. Paredaens. The expressive power of structured values in pure oodb's. In *Proc. 10th Symp. on Principles of Database Systems*, 1991.

[BTBN91] V. Breazu-Tannen, P. Buneman, and S. Naqvi. Structural recursion as a query language. In *Proc. 3rd Int. Workshop on database programming languages*, pages 9–19, Nafplion, Aug. 1991. Morgan Kaufman.

[CH80] A. Chandra and D. Harel. Computable Queries for Relational Data Bases. *Journal of Computer and System Sciences*, 21(2):156–178, Oct. 1980.

[CRSV94] L.S. Colby, E.L. Robertson, L.V. Saxton and D. Van Gucht. A Query Language for List Based Complex-Objects. In *Proc. 13th ACM Symp. on Principles of Database Systems*, pages 179–189, Minneapolis, May 1993.

[GM93] S. Grumbach and T. Milo. Towards tractable algebras for bags. In *Proc. 12th ACM Symp. on Principles of Database Systems*, pages 49–58, Washington, May 1993.

[GMK93] S. Grumbach, T. Milo, and Y. Kornatzky. Calculi for bags and their complexity. In *4th Int. Workshop on Database Programming Languages*, New-York City, Septembre 1993. Morgan Kaufmann.

[GO93] E. Graedel and M. Otto. Inductive definability with counting on finite structures. In *Proc. of Computer Science Logic 92*, pages 231–247. LNCS, n702, 1993.

[GV90] S. Grumbach and V. Vianu. Playing games with objects. In *Proc. Int. Conf. on Database Theory*, pages 25–38, Paris, dec 1990.

[GV91] S. Grumbach and V. Vianu. Tractable query languages for complex object databases. In *Proc. 10th ACM Symp. on Principles of Database Systems*, pages 315–327, Boulder, May 1991.

[GW92] S. Ginsburg and X. Wang. Towards a unified approach to querying sequenced data. In *Proc. 11th ACM Symp. on Principles of Database Systems*, pages 293–300, San Diego, 1992.

[HS88] R. Hull and J. Su. On the expressive power of database queries with intermediate types. In *Proc. 7th ACM Symp. on Principles of Database Systems*, 1988.

[HS89] R. Hull and J. Su. Untyped Sets, Invention and Computable Queries. In *Proc. 8th ACM Symp. on Principles of Database Systems*, 1989.

[HT74] J.E. Hopcroft and R.E. Tarjan. Efficient planarity testing. *J. of the ACM*, 21:549–568, 1974.

[HW74] J.E. Hopcroft and J.K. Wong. Linear time algorithm for isomorphism of planar graphs. In *Proc 6th ACM Symp. on Theory of Computing*, pages 172–184, 1974.

[Imm86] N. Immerman. Relational queries computable in polynomial time. *Inf. and Control*, 68:86–104, 1986.

[LW94] L. Libkin, L. Wong. New Techniques for Studying Set Languages, Bag Languages, and Aggregate Functions. In *Proc. 13th ACM Symp. on Principles of Database Systems*, pages 155–166, Minneapolis, May 1993.

[Moh89] R. H. Mohring. *Algorithms and Order, I. Rival Ed.*, chapter Computationally Tractable Classes of ordered Sets, pages 105–193. Kluwer Academic Publishers, 1989.

[Pra84] V. Pratt. The pomset model of parallel processes: Unifying the temporal and the spatial. In *Seminar on Concurrency*, pages 180–196, Pittsburgh, 1984. LNCS 197.

[Ric92] J. Richardson. Supporting lists in a data model (a timely approach). In *Proc. 18th Intl. Conf. on Very Large Databases*, Vancouver, 1992.

[Suc93] D. Suciu. Bounded fixpoints for complex objects. In *4th Int. Workshop on Database Programming Languages*, New-York City, Septembre 1993. Morgan Kaufmann.

[SZL93] B. Subramanian, S. B. Zdonik, and T. W. Leung. Ordered types in the aqua data model. In *4th Int. Workshop on Database Programming Languages*, New-York City, Septembre 1993. Morgan Kaufmann.

[Ull88] J.D. Ullman. *Database and Knowledge Base Systems*. Computer Science Press, 1988.

[Var82] M. Vardi. The Complexity of Relational Query Languages. In *Proc. 14th ACM Symp. on Theory of Computing*, pages 137–146, 1982.

On the Power of Stratified Logic Programs with Value Invention for Expressing Database Transformations [*]

Luca Cabibbo

Dipartimento di Informatica e Sistemistica, Università di Roma "La Sapienza"
Via Salaria 113, I-00198 Roma, Italy
cabibbo@infokit.dis.uniroma1.it

Abstract. The expressive power of the family of $\text{ILOG}^{(\neg)}$ languages is investigated. The languages are rule based, with value invention and stratified negation. The chosen semantics for value invention is based on Skolem functor terms. We show that, in presence of value invention, the whole expressive power is achieved using programs made of two strata, and that $\text{ILOG}^{\neq}$ (i.e., the class of programs with non-equality and without negation) express the downward monotone list constructive transformations.

1 Introduction

The study of query languages is a major issue in database theory. Departing from relational calculus and algebra for the relational model of data [8], several extensions to both the languages and model have been investigated, mainly with the goal of gaining in expressive power. The criterion of *genericity* has been widely accepted to limit the class of "interesting" queries to those that *do not* interpret values, i.e., for which the only significant relationships among data are based on (non-)equality of values. Chandra and Harel [7] proposed a completeness criterion for query languages, concerning their ability to express all the Turing computable generic queries.

The addition to relational calculus or algebra of an iterative construct (a fixpoint operator or a *while* iterator) does not lead beyond PSPACE queries, thus a further mechanism is needed to fulfill completeness. On one hand, the language QL of the original proposal in [7] introduces a modification of the data model, allowing unranked relations as well — intuitively, to simulate unbounded space on a Turing machine tape. On the other hand, in [2] the mechanism of *value invention* has been proposed, as a means to introduce new domain elements in temporary relations during computations.

---

[*] This work was partially supported by *MURST*, within the Project "Metodi formali e strumenti per basi di dati evolute", and by *Consiglio Nazionale delle Ricerche*, within "Progetto Finalizzato Sistemi Informatici e Calcolo Parallelo, Obiettivo LOGIDATA+".

Various semantics for value invention within rule-based languages have been investigated. In [1, 2], value invention is embedded in an operational (i.e., fixpoint) semantics. In contrast, according to the so-called *functional approach* (cfr. [5, 13] among others) value invention is related to (a limited use of) Skolem functor terms in the language; in this context, positive programs have a monotonic semantics, which is equivalently characterized in a model-theoretic as well as in a fixpoint fashion.

Another proposal to achieve completeness extends the data model with *complex objects* — built using *set* and *tuple* constructors — allowing for "recursive types" [11]. Unbounded value structures can thus be defined, essentially corresponding to hereditarily finite sets. In [16] the connection between hereditarily finite set construction and value invention is shown, and the two approaches reconciled.

Query languages with value invention may allow for new values in the result of a query; we will call *transformations* this kind of queries, whose semantics is a binary relation rather than a function. For transformation languages, criterions that extend genericity have been proposed (e.g., *determinacy* [1] and *constructivism* [16]).

In this paper we study a family of rule-based transformation languages with value invention, with semantics of invention based on Skolem functors and stratified semantics for negation. The formalism adopted is that of ILOG$^{(\neg)}$ [13], which enjoys all the above characteristics, while keeping away features unneeded for the results shown.

While in a rule-based language *without* invention (i.e., datalog$^{\neg}$) the inflationary semantics for negation is more expressive than the stratified one [14], in languages with invention the two approaches to negation are shown to be equally expressive [12]. Limiting to $i + 1$ the number of strata in allowed stratifications, we consider the family ILOG$^{i,\neg}$, i.e., programs that use i "groups" of negations. In this paper we stress the result of [12], by showing that the whole expressivity is achieved using stratified ILOG$^{\neg}$ programs made of *two* strata, i.e., a positive stratum followed by a semipositive one. The result holds for both *weakly safe* ILOG$^{1,\neg}$ (wILOG$^{1,\neg}$), which expresses queries, and ILOG$^{1,\neg}$, which is shown to express *list constructive transformations*; furthermore, these two languages are proved complete in their respective classes. These results have an analogue in the fact that, in presence of an ordering relation *succ* on the domain elements, stratified datalog$^{\neg}_{succ} \equiv$ datalog$^{1,\neg}_{succ}$, which in turn express the PTIME queries. The analogy is that value invention is expressive enough to build *all* possible orderings on the elements in the active domain of an input instance.

A second group of results concerns the expressive power of the family ILOG$^{\neq}$, i.e., languages without negation that allow just for non-equality comparisons ($\neq$). Because of the chosen semantics for invention, these languages express only monotonic transformations. We extend the notion of monotonicity to general queries (which may be partial functions as well) and transformations, defining *downward monotonicity*. Then, we show that wILOG$^{\neq}$ expresses all the downward monotone queries and ILOG$^{\neq}$ all the downward monotone list constructive transformations. In this case, the analogy with $datalog^\neg_{succ}$ breaks down: it has been shown [3] that $datalog^{\neq}_{succ}$ *fails* to express all the monotone queries in PTIME, even allowing for negation on input relations. This suggests that value invention is more expressive than an ordering relation *succ*, even limiting our attention to polynomial time queries.

This paper is organized as follows. In Section 2 we present the family $ILOG^{(\neg)}$ of languages, with their semantics. Section 3 is devoted to the study of weakly safe languages ($wILOG^{(\neg)}$), which allow for invented values only in temporary relations, so to define queries. In Section 4 we remove the weakly-safety restriction, characterizing $ILOG^{(\neg)}$ languages for transformations.

Because of space limitations, proofs are sketched. Details may be found in [6].

2 Preliminaries

In this section we briefly present the ILOG data model and the family $ILOG^{(\neg)}$ of rule-based languages. For a complete presentation of ILOG we refer the reader to previous works (Hull and Yoshikawa [13]).

2.1 The Data Model

Assume countable sets **Rel** of *relation names* and **Dom** of *domain elements*. Every relation name $R \in$ **Rel** has an associated *arity* $\alpha(R) \geq 0$. A *relational (database) scheme* is a finite set $S = \{R_1, \ldots, R_n\}$ of distinct relation names. A *relational instance* of a relation R is a finite subset of $\mathbf{Dom}^{\alpha(R)}$. A *database instance* over a relational scheme S is a function I that maps every relation $R \in S$ to a relation instance $I(R)$ of R. The *active domain* of an instance I, denoted by $adom(I)$, is the set of all domain elements occurring in I. The set of all instances over a scheme S is denoted by $inst(S)$.

2.2 $ILOG^{(\neg)}$ Syntax

Let a scheme S be fixed. Assume the existence of a countable set of *variables* **Var** disjoint from **Dom**.

A *term* is either a domain element $a \in$ **Dom** or a variable $X \in$ **Var**. An *invention atom* is an expression of the form $R(*, t_1, \ldots, t_m)$, where R is a relation name in S with arity $\alpha(R) = m + 1$, '$*$' is a special symbol called the *invention symbol*, and $t_1, \ldots, t_m$ are terms. A *relation atom* is an expression of the form $P(t_1, \ldots, t_m)$, where P is a relation name in S with arity $\alpha(P) = m$ and $t_1, \ldots, t_m$ are terms. An *equality atom* is an expression of the form $t_1 = t_2$, where t_1, t_2 are terms. A *positive literal* is either a relation atom or an equality atom. A *negative literal* $\neg L$ is the negation of a positive literal L. The negative literal $\neg(t_1 = t_2)$ is called a *non-equality literal* and denoted by $t_1 \neq t_2$; non-equality atoms are (negative) literals as well. In the remainder of the paper we will not consider equality atoms anymore (because we can resort to multiple occurrences of the same term, instead), while non-equality literals will be used.

A *clause* γ is an expression of the form $A \leftarrow L_1, \ldots, L_n$, with $n \geq 0$, where A is either an invention or a relation atom (called the *head of* γ and denoted by *head*(γ)), and $L_1, \ldots, L_n$ is a set of literals (called the *body of* γ and denoted by *body*(γ)). A clause is *range-restricted* if every variable occurring either in its head or in a negative literal or in a (non-)equality literal in its body, occurs in a positive relation literal in its body as well. Hereinafter we will consider only range-restricted clauses. A *rule* is a clause with a non-empty body. A *fact* is a clause with an empty body (that is, an atom A); a fact is *ground* if no variable occurs in it. A clause is an *invention* (*non-invention*, resp.) clause if its head is an invention (relation, resp.) atom.

The relation name appearing in the head of an invention clause is called an *invention relation* name. An ILOG$^{(\neg)}$ *program* is a finite set of clauses, with the condition that no invention relation name appears in the head of a non-invention clause. An ILOG$^{\neg}$ program is *stratified* if it satisfies the *stratification condition* [4]. In the remainder of the paper, unless explicitely stated, we will consider only stratified ILOG$^{\neg}$ programs.

We now consider various sublanguages of ILOG$^{(\neg)}$. An ILOG program is a program in which no negative literal occurs. An ILOG$^{\neq}$ program is a program in which the only negative literals are non-equality literals.

Denote by *sch*(P) the set of relation names occurring in a program P (so that *sch*(P) is a scheme) and by *adom*(P) the finite set of domain elements that explicitly occur in P. An *input-output scheme* (or, simply, *i-o scheme*) for a program P is a pair $(\mathbf{S}, \mathbf{T})$ of schemes, where (i) $\mathbf{S}$ and $\mathbf{T}$ are disjoint subsets of *sch*(P), called the *input* and the *output* scheme, respectively; and (ii) no relation name in $\mathbf{S}$ occurs in the head of a clause in P. For a program P over i-o scheme $(\mathbf{S}, \mathbf{T})$, denoted by $(P, \mathbf{S}, \mathbf{T})$, relations in the input scheme play the role of *extensional* relations, relations in the output scheme that of *target* relations, whereas relations in *sch*(P) but neither in $\mathbf{S}$ nor in $\mathbf{T}$ are viewed as *temporary* relations.

We introduce further sublanguages (that limit the use of "invention" in programs) following analogous definitions in [2].

A program P is *strongly safe* if no invention rule occurs in P; the language of strongly safe ILOG$^{(\neg)}$ programs is denoted by sILOG$^{(\neg)}$. It is apparent that sILOG$^{(\neg)}$ programs *syntactically* correspond to stratified datalog$^{(\neg)}$ programs.

Weak safety is defined relative to an i-o scheme, using the auxiliary notion of "invention-attribute set." An *attribute* is a pair (R, i), where R is a relation name and $1 \leq i \leq \alpha(R)$. Given a program P over i-o scheme $(\mathbf{S}, \mathbf{T})$, the *invention attributes for* $(P, \mathbf{S}, \mathbf{T})$ are the smallest set of attributes such that:

- if R is a relation invention name in *sch*(P), then $(R, 1)$ is an invention attribute for $(P, \mathbf{S}, \mathbf{T})$;
- if (R, i) is an invention attribute for $(P, \mathbf{S}, \mathbf{T})$, $R(\ldots, t_{i-1}, X, t_{i+1}, \ldots)$ is a positive literal in the body of a clause γ in P, and $Q(\ldots, t'_{j-1}, X, t'_{j+1}, \ldots)$ is the head of γ, then (Q, j) is an invention attribute for $(P, \mathbf{S}, \mathbf{T})$.

A program P is *weakly safe wrt* $(\mathbf{S}, \mathbf{T})$ if no invention attribute for $(P, \mathbf{S}, \mathbf{T})$ has the form (R, i), where R is a relation name in $\mathbf{T}$. As it will be clear after discussing the semantics of ILOG$^{(\neg)}$ programs, a program is weakly safe if *invented values* appears only in particular columns of the temporary relations in $sch(P)$, and not in target relations. The language of weakly safe ILOG$^{(\neg)}$ programs is denoted by wILOG$^{(\neg)}$.

2.3 Semantics of ILOG$^{(\neg)}$ Programs

The semantics of an ILOG$^{(\neg)}$ program $(P, \mathbf{S}, \mathbf{T})$ is a binary relation $\varphi_P \subseteq inst(\mathbf{S}) \times inst(\mathbf{T})$, which is defined here in terms of a four-step process, described informally as follows:

1. find the Skolemization $Skol(P)$ of P by introducing Skolem functors;
2. for an instance I, find the set $\phi(I)$ of ground facts that represents I;
3. $Skol(P) \cup \phi(I)$ is essentially a logic program with function symbols; a preferred model $\mathcal{M}_{Skol(P)\cup\phi(I)}$ of $Skol(P) \cup \phi(I)$ (minimal if P is either a positive ILOG or an ILOG$^{\neq}$ program, perfect if it is a stratified ILOG$^{\neg}$ program) can be found via a fixpoint computation; if $\mathcal{M}_{Skol(P)\cup\phi(I)}$ is finite, we call it the *model* of P over I;
4. if the model of P over I is defined, it is something similar to a set of atoms of the language, apart from the presence of Skolem terms. In order to obtain an instance of the output scheme, we must coherently replace functor terms by distinct new values (that is, that do belong neither to $adom(I)$ nor to $adom(P)$) by means of a transformation that is the inverse of ϕ, thus obtaining an instance J over $sch(P)$. Then, the *semantics* $\varphi_P(I)$ of $(P, \mathbf{S}, \mathbf{T})$ over I is the restriction of J to the relation names in $\mathbf{T}$. Otherwise (i.e., if $\mathcal{M}_{Skol(P)\cup\phi(I)}$ is infinite), the *semantics* is *undefined*.

We now formalize some concepts related to "Skolem functors," in order to define the semantics of an ILOG$^{(\neg)}$ program.

Assume a countable set **Fun** of *Skolem functor names*. For each relation name $R \in \mathbf{Rel}$, with arity $n = \alpha(R) \geq 1$, **Fun** contains a $(n-1)$-ary functor f_R, called the *Skolem functor for R*. A *Skolem functor term* is an expression of the form $f_R(t_1, \ldots, t_n)$, where f_R is the n-ary Skolem functor for R and $t_1, \ldots, t_n$ are terms. Then, extend the notion of *term* by considering also Skolem functor terms. The *Skolemization* of a program P, denoted by $Skol(P)$, is obtained by replacing the head of each invention rule in P having the form $R(*, t_1, \ldots, t_n)$ by $R(f_R(t_1, \ldots, t_n), t_1, \ldots, t_n)$.

Then, note that any instance I over a scheme $\mathbf{S}$ is representable by means of a set $\phi(I)$ of ground facts, defined in such a way that, for any relation name $R \in \mathbf{S}$, an atom $R(t_1, \ldots, t_m)$ belongs to $\phi(I)$ if and only if the tuple $(t_1, \ldots, t_m)$ belongs to $I(R)$ (where $t_1, \ldots, t_m$ are domain elements in **Dom**, so they are ground terms).

Now we generalize the notion of instance relative to Skolem functor terms. Given a program P, consider the *Herbrand universe* $\mathcal{U}_P$ *for P* of all the ground terms built using domain elements from **Dom** and Skolem functors for relations in $sch(P)$. The *Herbrand base* $\mathcal{H}_P$ *for P* is the set of all ground facts built using relation names in $sch(P)$ and terms in $\mathcal{U}_P$. A *Herbrand interpretation over P* is a finite subset of $\mathcal{H}_P$. Then, the notions of *Skolemized tuple, Skolemized relational instance*, and *Skolemized database instance over* **S** with respect to a program P are defined in the natural way, referring to the universe $\mathcal{U}_P$ instead of the domain **Dom**. The set of all Skolemized database instances over a scheme **S** wrt a program P is denoted by $S\text{-}inst_P(\mathbf{S})$.

Now, if the model of P over I exists finite, it is a Herbrand interpretation over $sch(P)$, hence it is a Skolemized database instance over $sch(P)$. Thus, limiting our attention to the first three steps of the above algorithm, we introduce the notion of *pre-semantics* of a program P wrt i-o scheme $(\mathbf{S}, \mathbf{T})$ as a partial function $\psi_P : inst(\mathbf{S}) \to S\text{-}inst_P(\mathbf{T})$, that maps I to the Skolemized instance corresponding to $\mathcal{M}_{Skol(P)\cup\phi(I)}$.

Note that the replacement of different Skolem functor terms by different new values (step 4) is defined in a nondeterministic fashion, so that, if Skolem functor terms appear in the model of P over I, then the semantics of P is a binary relation rather than a (partial) function, which considers *all* possible replacements.

2.4 Introductory Examples

The following three examples show the main features of the language; these examples are interesting because they illustrate techniques that are used to prove the results of this paper.

Example 1. Given a unary relation R, assume we want to compute the *enumerations* of the domain elements in R, that is, the listings of the elements in R in any order, without repeats, and enclosed by brackets '[' and ']'. For example, if R contains the elements a and b, then its enumerations are the *lists* [ab] and [ba]; we want to represent these lists.

We use the following program P_{code}, in which values invented in relations $list^{nil}$ and $list^{cons}$ correspond to empty and non-empty lists, respectively; $list^{out}$ is the target relation. Relation *misses* is an auxiliary relation denoting which R's elements are still missing in a list to reach a "total" enumeration.

$$list^{nil}(*) \quad\quad \leftarrow .$$
$$list^{cons}(*, \text{']'}, E) \leftarrow list^{nil}(E).$$
$$misses(RB, X) \quad \leftarrow list^{cons}(RB, \text{']'}, E), list^{nil}(E), R(X).$$
$$list^{cons}(*, X, L) \leftarrow misses(L, X).$$
$$misses(L, Y) \quad \leftarrow list^{cons}(L, X, L'), misses(L', Y), X \neq Y.$$
$$misses^{proj}(L) \quad \leftarrow misses(L, X).$$

$$list^{out}(*, \text{'['}, L) \leftarrow list^{cons}(L, X, L'), \neg misses^{proj}(L).$$

Given an instance I such that $I(R) = \{(a), (b)\}$, the pre-semantics for P_{code} on I contains in $list^{out}$ functor terms $f^{out}(\text{'['}, f^{cons}(a, f^{cons}(b, f^{cons}(\text{']'}, f^{nil}()))))$ and $f^{out}(\text{'['}, f^{cons}(b, f^{cons}(a, f^{cons}(\text{']'}, f^{nil}()))))$, which are the required representations for the enumerations of $I(R)$.

Note that P_{code} is stratified, and made of two strata (the second stratum being composed only of the last clause).

The following example shows that the construction of the "partial" enumerations of a relation can be done without resorting to negation.

Example 2. A *partial enumeration* of a unary relation R is any enumeration of a subset of R (possibly empty).

An ILOG$^{\neq}$ program P_{pcode} that computes the partial enumerations of R can be obtained from P_{code} of Example 1 by replacing its last clause by:

$$list^{out}(*, `[', L) \leftarrow list^{cons}(L, X, L').$$

Finally, we have an example that shows how to perform a transformation that is the inverse of the previous ones.

Example 3. Consider relation $list^{out}$ in which lists of domain elements, enclosed by brackets, are coded using also relations $list^{nil}$ and $list^{cons}$ to keep intermediate lists. Assume we want to compute a relation R containing the domain elements that are components of the input lists.

We use the following program P_{decode}, in which relation *decode* is used to select the lists that have to be decomposed.

$$decode(L') \leftarrow list^{out}(L, `[', L').$$
$$R(X) \leftarrow decode(L), list^{cons}(L, X, L'), X \neq `]'.$$
$$decode(L') \leftarrow decode(L), list^{cons}(L, X, L'), X \neq `]'.$$

Note that P_{decode} is an ILOG$^{\neq}$ program; R will contain the *union* of what can be obtained by decomponing each list in $list^{out}$.

3 Relational Queries

Given relational schemes **S** and **T**, a *database mapping f from* **S** *to* **T**, denoted $f : \mathbf{S} \to \mathbf{T}$, is a partial function from $inst(\mathbf{S})$ to $inst(\mathbf{T})$.

Let C be a finite set of domain elements, out of the domain **Dom**. A database mapping f is C-*generic* if $f \cdot \rho = \rho \cdot f$ for any permutation ρ over **Dom** (extended in the natural way to databases) which leaves C fixed (i.e., for any $x \in C$, $\rho(x) = x$). A database mapping is *generic* if it is C-generic for some finite C. A *query from* **S** *to* **T** is a generic database mapping $f : \mathbf{S} \to \mathbf{T}$.

The class $\mathcal{CQ}$ of *computable queries* [7] is the set of all database mappings f such that f is a query which is Turing computable.

The notion of *genericity* has been introduced to impose that the only significant relationships among data are those based on (non-)equality of values, i.e., values have to be considered as *uninterpreted*, apart from a finite set C of domain elements, which may be fixed by the query. As a consequence of genericity, given a C-generic query q and an input instance I, $adom(q(I)) \subseteq adom(I) \cup C$. This implies that queries are essentially *domain-preserving* database mappings. Proposition 1 shows the connection between C-genericity and the (finite) set of domain elements appearing in a wILOG$^{(\neg)}$ program specifying a query.

A *(database) query language* is a formalism to express queries. Given a query language L, a query q is *expressible in* L if there exists an expression of L whose semantics is the query q. Given two query languages L_1, L_2, we say that L_1 is *weaker than* L_2, denoted $L_1 \sqsubseteq L_2$, if every query in L_1 is expressible in L_2 as well; we say that L_1 and L_2 are *equivalent*, denoted $L_1 \equiv L_2$, if both $L_1 \sqsubseteq L_2$ and $L_2 \sqsubseteq L_1$ hold. We say that L_2 *is more expressive than* L_1, denoted $L_1 \sqsubset L_2$, if $L_1 \sqsubseteq L_2$ but not $L_1 \equiv L_2$.

We may compare query languages to classes of queries as well. Given a query language L and a class C of queries, we say that L *expresses* C, denoted $L \equiv C$, if any query in C is expressible in L. A query language L is *complete* if $L \equiv CQ$, that is, if it expresses the computable queries.

3.1 Languages with Value Invention for Queries

Because of value invention, the semantics of an $ILOG^{(\neg)}$ program is, in general, a binary relation rather than a function, thus not defining a query in the strict sense. In this section we study languages that express only queries.

We have seen that strongly safe $ILOG^{(\neg)}$ programs correspond syntactically to stratified $datalog^{(\neg)}$ programs, which express total queries. Hence, $sILOG^{\neg}$ inherits a lot of well-known results for $datalog^{\neg}$. Among others, we recall that $sILOG^{\neg}$ with inflationary semantics for negation expresses the *fixpoint queries* [2], whereas the stratified semantics is weaker than the inflationary one [14].

We now turn to languages with value invention. It is clear that the semantics of a weakly safe program is always a query.

Proposition 1. *Let P be a $wILOG^{\neg}$ program over i-o scheme $(\mathbf{S}, \mathbf{T})$. Then, the semantics of $(P, \mathbf{S}, \mathbf{T})$ is a C-generic database mapping from $\mathbf{S}$ to $\mathbf{T}$, with $C = adom(P)$.*

In presence of value invention or a similar construct, it has been shown [12] that the expressive power of stratified semantics for negation is the same as inflationary semantics. [1] The following completeness result characterizes the expressive power of weakly safe (stratified) $ILOG^{\neg}$ programs. It is interesting to look at a number of details in its proof to understand further results.

Proposition 2. $wILOG^{\neg}$ *expresses the computable queries.*

Proof (Sketch). Let q be a query. Since q is computable, there is an effective algorithm for its implementation; we refer here to *domain Turing Machines (domTMs)* [11]. We highlight the main differences of domTMs compared with conventional Turing Machines (TMs). Unlike TMs, the alphabet of symbols allowed on a tape is countable (our domain **Dom** plus a finite set W of *working symbols*, corresponding to connectives like parentheses '(' and ')' and brackets '[' and ']'). Moreover, a domTM is equipped with a *register* capable of storing a symbol of the alphabet. In order to keep the control of a domTM finite, moves

---

[1] The proof in [12] refers to COL, a deductive language with untyped sets. There, hereditarely finite set construction is used instead of value invention. Furthermore, COL programs have to be stratified also wrt set construction.

may only refer to a finite subset C of **Dom** (corresponding to a set of interpreted domain elements) and to working symbols in W; in addition, it is possible to specify *generic* moves, based on the (non-) equality between the content of the register and that of the tape cell under the head. The effect of a move is to change the content of the register and/or that of the tape cell under the head, then to possibly move the head.

Given an instance I, an *enumeration* of I is a sequential representation of I on a domTM tape (where domain elements are separated by connectives in W). The difference between instances and enumerations is essentially that instances are *sets* of tuples, whereas enumerations are *sequences* of tuples. The set of all enumerations of an instance I is denoted by $enum(I)$. For example, let I^1 be an instance over $\{R_1, R_2\}$ such that $I^1(R_1) = \{(a)\}$ and $I^1(R_2) = \{(a, b), (b, c)\}$. Then, the enumerations of I^1 (assuming the listing of R_1 preceeds that of R_2) are: $e_1^1 = [(a)][(ab)(bc)]$ and $e_2^1 = [(a)][(bc)(ab)]$.

For any computable query, there exists an *order independent* domTM that computes that query; hence, there exists a domTM M_q which computes q. Thus, given an input instance I, either M_q does not halt on any enumeration of I (i.e., q is undefined on input I), or there exists an instance J such that, for any enumeration e of I, the computation of M_q on e, denoted by $M_q(e)$, halts resulting in an output that is an enumeration of J (i.e., $q(I) = J$). For example, if $M_q(e_1^1) = [(c)(b)]$ and $M_q(e_2^1) = [(b)(c)]$, we assume $q(I^1) = \{(b), (c)\}$.

Our simulation of M_q proceeds as follows:

1. given input instance I, generate the family $enum(I)$ of all enumerations of I, which can be used as input for M_q. Note that, referring to a (substantially) deterministic language like as $ILOG^{(\neg)}$, it is not possible to generate a *single* enumeration of I, so that *all* of them have to be generated;
2. simulate the computation $M_q(e)$ for any enumeration $e \in enum(I)$; the various simulations are performed simultaneously;
3. decode the various output enumerations into instances over the output scheme; denote the result of decoding an output enumeration o by $decode(o)$.

The following can be shown:

1. all the enumerations of an instance can be computed by a stratified $ILOG^{\neg}$ program, where each enumeration is represented by means of a nested Skolem functor term. The technique used is that shown in Example 1, though more complicated because in general we have to deal with n-ary relations, and parentheses to enclose tuples;
2. the simulation of a domTM, starting from an enumeration and producing an output enumeration, can be done by an $ILOG^{\neq}$ program (i.e., without negation). Value invention is used to represent *strings* stored on the tape of the domTM. Termination of a computation happens with a finite number of accrossed global configurations (which are represented by a finite number of strings), whereas a non-termination involves an infinite number of accrossed configurations. Therefore, termination and non-termination correspond to a finite or an infinite number of invented values, resp., and so to a finite or an infinite model for the program performing the simulation;

3. the decoding phase can be done by an ILOG$^{\neq}$ program. The technique used is that of Example 3; intuitively, we perform the *union* of the decoding of the various output enumerations.

Finally, we put together these three subprograms obtaining a single stratified program. To summarize, we have built, starting from q, and so from M_q, a program Q which computes the following query (on input instance I):

$$\varphi_Q(I) = \bigcup_{e \in enum(I)} decode(M_q(e)).$$

The hypothesis of order independence on M_q guarantees that, for any enumeration e of I, $decode(M_q(e)) = q(I)$; hence, $\varphi_Q(I) = q(I)$. □

We now introduce a hierarchy of ILOG$^{\neg}$ sublanguages relative to the number of strata allowed. Let ILOG$^{i,\neg}$ be the class of ILOG$^{\neg}$ stratified programs made of *at most* $i+1$ strata. Thus, ILOG$^{0,\neg}$ (i.e., programs with no negation) syntactically correspond to the language ILOG$^{\neq}$. With respect to the expressive power, we have the following intuitive hierarchy:

$$\text{ILOG}^{\neq} \equiv \text{ILOG}^{0,\neg} \sqsubseteq \text{ILOG}^{1,\neg} \sqsubseteq \ldots \sqsubseteq \text{ILOG}^{\neg}$$

From [14] it descends that the above hierarchy is proper for the family sILOG$^{\neg}$. Surprisingly, for the family wILOG$^{\neg}$ it collapses at the second level:

Theorem 3. wILOG$^{1,\neg}$ *expresses the computable queries.*

Proof (Sketch). The program Q built in the proof of Proposition 2 to implement a query q is made of two strata. In the simulation, the only phase that needs stratified negation is the one that enumerates the input instance. As we have seen, the technique used is that of program P_{code} in Example 1. P_{code} is made of two strata: as output of the first stratum (which contains only ILOG$^{\neq}$ clauses) all the enumerations of R are represented; it is needed only to distinguish the "total" enumerations from those that are just "partial" enumerations of R (i.e., enumerations of subsets of R). To do so, P_{code} resorts once to stratified negation (second stratum), selecting those lists for which *no* R's element is missing.

Intuitively, we can build a two-strata program that computes the enumerations of the various input relations; then, we need to concatenate enumerations of different relations, to obtain enumerations of the global input instance. The claim is that we can do so without resorting to negation anymore, that is, we have a two-strata ILOG$^{\neg}$ program that computes all the enumerations of a relational instances. Hence, the whole computation of the query q can be done by a wILOG$^{1,\neg}$ program. □

We now characterize the expressive power of weakly safe ILOG$^{\neq}$.

For total queries, the notion of monotonicity is defined as follows: a total query $q : \mathbf{S} \rightarrow \mathbf{T}$ is *monotone* if, for any pair of instances I, J over $\mathbf{S}$, $I \subseteq J$ implies $q(I) \subseteq q(J)$. It is well-known [3] that *datalog*$^{\neq}$ expresses only monotone PTIME queries (and thus, total monotone queries). Hence, the same holds for sILOG$^{\neq}$ programs. Unfortunately, this monotonicity result can not be directly generalized to weakly safe ILOG$^{\neq}$ programs, because the latter express partial queries as well.

A (partial) query $q : \mathbf{S} \to \mathbf{T}$ is *downward defined* if, for any pair of instances I, J over $\mathbf{S}$, $I \subseteq J$ and q defined over J implies that q is defined over I as well. A (partial) query $q : \mathbf{S} \to \mathbf{T}$ is *downward monotone* if it is downward defined and, for any pair of instances I, J over $\mathbf{S}$, $I \subseteq J$ and q defined over J implies that $q(I) \subseteq q(J)$.

An example of downward monotone (boolean) query is the one that, given a binary relation representing a directed graph G over a fixed set of nodes, answers the non-empty 0-ary relation $\{()\}$ (meaning *true*) if G is planar and contains a Hamiltonian circuit, answers $\{\}$ (meaning *false*) if G, being planar, does not contain any Hamiltonian circuit, and is undefined if G is not planar. In other words, this query decides, for planar graphs, if they do contain Hamiltonian circuits (this problem being NP-complete [9]), and does not halt on non-planar graphs.

Lemma 4. *Let P be a* wILOG$^{\neq}$ *program. Then, the semantics of P is a downward monotone query.*

The connection with the above class of queries can be strengthened to the following main result of the section.

Theorem 5. wILOG$^{\neq}$ *expresses the downward monotone queries.*

Proof (Sketch). Consider a downward monotone query q and an order independent domTM M_q that implements q. For an instance I, denote by $p\text{-}enum(I)$ the set of all *partial enumerations of I*, that is, the set $p\text{-}enum(I) = \cup_{J \subseteq I} enum(J)$. For example, the set of the partial enumerations for the instance I^1 (proof of Proposition 2) includes, among others, $[][]$, $[(a)][(ab)]$, $[][(bc)]$, and $[(a)][(bc)(ab)]$, the latter being a total enumeration. A program that, starting from I, builds $p\text{-}enum(I)$, is expressible in ILOG$^{\neq}$, where the technique used is that of program P_{pcode} in Example 2 [2]. Hence, we can modify the wILOG$^{1,\neg}$ program Q — which computes q by simulating computations of M_q on all total enumerations of the input instance — into a wILOG$^{\neq}$ program $\tilde{Q}$ which simulates computations of M_q on all partial enumerations of the input instance (recall from the proof of Proposition 2 that the simulation and the decoding phase can be expressed by wILOG$^{\neq}$ programs). The query computed by $\tilde{Q}$ is:

$$\tilde{Q}(I) = \bigcup_{e \in p\text{-}enum(I)} decode(M_q(e)) = \bigcup_{J \subseteq I} \bigcup_{e \in enum(J)} decode(M_q(e)) = \bigcup_{J \subseteq I} q(J).$$

From the downward definition of q, $\tilde{Q}$ is defined on input I if and only if q is; from the (downward) monotonicity, for any $J \subseteq I$, $q(J) \subseteq q(I)$. In turn, $\tilde{Q}(I) = q(I)$. □

---

[2] Note that the construction of $enum(I)$ is non-monotonic, thus it is not expressible in ILOG$^{\neq}$.

4 Database Transformations

In this section we study "queries" for which invented values may appear in the output instance; to distinguish them from the traditional relational queries, we will call them "trasformations." In general, the semantics of a transformation can not be defined as a partial function, because of the nondeterministic choice of the invented values; thus, we have to resort to binary relations.

Given relational schemes S and T, a *database invention mapping f from S to T*, denoted $f : S \rightarrow T$, is a r.e. binary relation $f \subset inst(S) \times inst(T)$. In the following, we denote $(I, J) \in f$ by $J \in f(I)$.

Let C be a finite set of domain elements, out of the domain **Dom**. A database invention mapping f is *C-generic* if, for any permutation ρ over **Dom** which is the identity on C, $I \in f(J)$ implies $\rho(I) \in f(\rho(J))$. A database invention mapping is *generic* if it is C-generic for some finite C.

A *transformation from S to T* is a generic database invention mapping $f : S \rightarrow T$. Given an instance I, we say that a transformation q is defined over I if there exists an instance J such that $J \in q(I)$.

In the literature, to capture the expressive power of languages with value invention, various restrictions to the above class of transformations have been imposed. A first further condition is *determinacy*: a transformation is determinate if it is a generic nondeterministic transformation for which the possible outcomes (wrt a given input instance) are equal *up to renaming* of the invented values. Various transformation languages that have been proposed in the literature (we refer here mainly to IQL [1] and $GOOD$ [10]) lack the ability to express the determinate transformations, because they can not eliminate certain *copies* from result instances. A more precise characterization of these languages is given in [16], where the notion of *(set) constructive transformations* is introduced; in that framework, a strong connection between value invention and *hereditarely finite set construction* is shown.

4.1 Languages with Value Invention for Transformations

Given a ILOG$^{(\neg)}$ program, its semantics turns out to be a transformation. However, neither all the determinate transformations nor all the set constructive ones are expressible in ILOG$^{(\neg)}$. Indeed, it can be shown that certain transformations that are expressible in IQL, are not expressible in ILOG$^{\neg}$: this fact is due to the absence of *sets* in the ILOG data model [13]. A characterization of stratified ILOG$^{\neg}$ programs can be done introducing the notion of *list constructive transformations*, where value invention is connected to *hereditarely finite list construction* [15].

Let D be a subset of **Dom**. The set $HFl(D)$ of *hereditarely finite lists* over D, is the smallest set containing D such that any finite list $(X_1, \ldots, X_n)$ of elements of $HFl(D)$ is an element of $HFl(D)$ as well. Again, we introduce the notion of *HFl-instances* referring to the universe $HFl(\mathbf{Dom})$ instead of **Dom**. Then, the set of HFl-instances over a scheme S is denoted by $HFl\text{-}inst(S)$. A *HFl-transformation from S to T* is a generic partial function $f : inst(S) \rightarrow HFl\text{-}inst(T)$.

Now we show that *HFl*-instances can be represented by Skolemized instances, provided the scheme contains at least a unary and a ternary invention relation. Let R^{nil} and R^{cons} be the unary and ternary required relations, and f^{nil} and f^{cons} the respective Skolem functors; note that f^{nil} is nullary and f^{cons} is binary. Now, $f^{nil}()$ represents the empty list, whereas $f^{cons}(H, T)$ represents a non-empty list with head H and tail T. Hence, any ground term over $\{R^{nil}, R^{cons}\}$ represents a hereditarely finite list, and viceversa. The connection between *HFl*-instances and Skolemized instances is characterized as follows.

Proposition 6. *Let* **S** *be a scheme not containing relations* R^{nil} *and* R^{cons}. *Then:*

- *for any HFl-instance over* **S** *there is an equivalent Skolemized instance over* **S** $\cup \{R^{nil}, R^{cons}\}$; *and*
- *for any Skolemized instance over* **S** $\cup \{R^{nil}, R^{cons}\}$ *there is an equivalent HFl-instance over* **S**.

Theorem 7. ILOG$^\neg$ *expresses the list constructive transformations.*

Proof (Sketch). A list constructive transformations q can always be expressed by an order independent domTM M_q; to build the enumerations of an input instance and to simulate M_q we use the same technique as in the proof of Proposition 2 and Theorem 3. The claim is that the decoding phase can be still correctly expressed by an ILOG$^{\neq}$ program. The crucial point is that, because the semantics of a program is based on its Skolemization, a different value is associated with each different list; more important, the same new value is associated with the same list, even if it is decoded from different declarations, i.e., deriving from computations on different enumerations of the input instance. □

Again, we study the hierarchy induced by the number of strata in programs.

Theorem 8. ILOG$^{1,\neg}$ *expresses the list constructive transformations.*

Proof. In the proof of Theorem 7, negation is used only in the enumerating phase, which can be accomplished in the same way as in the proof of Theorem 3, hence using two strata. □

As a consequence of the above theorem, the hierarchy of stratified programs collapses at the second level, as for weakly safe programs.

For the characterization of ILOG$^{0,\neg}$ = ILOG$^{\neq}$, we need to further extend the notion of downward monotonicity. A transformation $q : \mathbf{S} \to \mathbf{T}$ is *downward monotone* if it is downward defined and, for any pair of instances I, J over $\mathbf{S}$, $I \subseteq J$ and q defined over J implies that there exists a pair of instances K, L such that $K \in q(I)$, $L \in q(J)$ and $K \subseteq L$.

Theorem 9. ILOG$^{\neq}$ *expresses the downward monotone list constructive transformations.*

Proof. Analogue to that of Theorem 5. □

Acknowledgements

The author would like to thank Jan Van den Bussche for the fruitful discussions on the subject of this paper.

References

1. S. Abiteboul and P. Kanellakis. Object identity as a query language primitive. In *ACM SIGMOD International Conf. on Management of Data*, pages 159–173, 1989.
2. S. Abiteboul and V. Vianu. Datalog extensions for database queries and updates. *Journal of Comp. and System Sc.*, 43(1):62–124, August 1991.
3. F. Afrati, S. Cosmadakis, and M. Yannakakis. On Datalog vs. polynomial time. In *Tenth ACM SIGACT SIGMOD SIGART Symp. on Principles of Database Systems*, pages 13–25, 1991.
4. K. Apt. Logic programming. In J. van Leeuwen, editor, *Handbook of Theoretical Computer Science*, pages 493–574. Elsevier Science Publishers (North-Holland), Amsterdam, 1990.
5. P. Atzeni, L. Cabibbo, and G. Mecca. IsaLog: A declarative language for complex objects with hierarchies. In *Ninth IEEE Int. Conf. on Data Engineering*, pages 219–228, 1993.
6. L. Cabibbo. On the power of stratified logic programs with value invention for expressing database transformations. Technical report, Dip. di Informatica e Sistemistica, Università di Roma "La Sapienza", 1994.
7. A.K. Chandra and D. Harel. Computable queries for relational databases. *Journal of Comp. and System Sc.*, 21:333–347, 1980.
8. E.F. Codd. A relational model for large shared data banks. *Communications of the ACM*, 13(6):377–387, 1970.
9. M.R. Garey and D.S. Johnson. *Computers and Intractability*. W.H. Freeman and Company, San Francisco, 1979.
10. M. Gyssens, J. Paredaens, and D. Van Gucht. A graph-oriented object database model. In *Ninth ACM SIGACT SIGMOD SIGART Symp. on Principles of Database Systems*, pages 417–424, 1990.
11. R. Hull and J. Su. Algebraic and calculus query languages for recursively typed complex objects. *Journal of Comp. and System Sc.*, 47(1):121–156, August 1993.
12. R. Hull and J. Su. Deductive query languages for recursively typed complex objects. Technical report, University of Southern California, 1993.
13. R. Hull and M. Yoshikawa. ILOG: Declarative creation and manipulation of object identifiers. In *Sixteenth Int. Conf. on Very Large Data Bases*, pages 455–468, 1990.
14. P.G. Kolaitis. The expressive power of stratified logic programs. *Information and Computation*, 90(1):50–66, January 1991.
15. J. Van den Bussche. *Formal Aspects of Object Identity in Database Manipulation*. PhD thesis, University of Antwerp, 1993.
16. J. Van den Bussche, D. Van Gucht, M. Andries, and M. Gyssens. On the completeness of object-creating query languages. In *33rd Annual Symp. on Foundations of Computer Science*, pages 372–379, 1992.

A Stable Model Semantics for Behavioral Inheritance in Deductive Object Oriented Languages

(Extended Abstract)

Michele Bugliesi[1]

Dip. di Matematica Pura ed Applicata
Università di Padova, Italy
michele@goedel.math.unipd.it

Hasan M. Jamil[2]

Dept. of Computer Science
Concordia University, Canada
jamil@cs.concordia.ca

Abstract. We present a model for deductive object oriented query languages with inheritance and overriding. In this model, we consider a DAG like dynamic *isa* hierarchy and we account for both *value* or *attribute* inheritance and *method* inheritance or *code sharing*. We show that these two types of inheritance can be treated uniformly within an elegant declarative setting. We then propose a novel semantics for the non-monotonic behavior resulting from the combination of overriding, dynamic *self* binding and the dynamic structure of the *isa* hierarchy. This semantics is reminiscent of the stable model semantics of logic programs with negation. We also isolate a syntactic condition that guarantees the existence of a unique stable model for a program. This condition, in its turn, is inspired by the local stratification condition of perfect model semantics for programs with negation. Finally we define a bottom-up procedure that computes the unique stable model of a stratified program.

1 Introduction

There have been several attempts at combining inheritance with deductive programming languages within clean mathematical settings [1, 2, 3, 5, 6, 8, 9, 10, 11, 12, 13, 14]. Inheritance is an essential concept in AI and in object-oriented programming that comprises two main aspects: *structural* and *behavioral* inheritance. Structural inheritance is a mechanism for propagating method declarations and signatures from classes to their subclasses or instances. Behavioral inheritance, on the other hand, propagates method implementations as well as the result of their application.

Logic languages like LOGIN [1] and LIFE [2] incorporate structural inheritance by means of an extended unification algorithm for ψ-terms, complex typed structures that are used for data representation. In [10], Kifer et al. proposed a formalism, called F-Logic, for deductive object oriented database query languages where the semantics of structural inheritance is captured within an elegant model theory and a sound and complete proof theory. F-Logic, together

---

[1] Partially supported by "Progetto Finalizzato Sistemi Informatici e Calcolo Parallelo" of C.N.R. grant n. 93.00898.PF69.

[2] Partially supported by grants from the Canadian Commonwealth Scholarship and Fellowship Plan and the University of Dhaka, Bangladesh.

with other related formalisms, have also addressed the issue of behavioral inheritance. However, there are several aspects of the resulting models that can be objected to in these approaches: we will discuss some of these aspects later on in this paper, but only after having presented our model.

The object oriented language we consider here is loosely related to F-Logic, but the syntax and semantics are quite different. In particular, we consider only behavioral inheritance in our model and, consequently, disregard method signatures and structural inheritance which are peculiar to F-Logic. Similarly to F-Logic, we allow the *isa* hierarchy to be defined dynamically by allowing rules with schema and method components. Within this setting, we consider both value and method inheritance with overriding, multiple inheritance and we focus our attention to only set-valued methods. This choice is motivated by the fact that it allows us to capture the semantics of multiple inheritance in a quite natural and elegant way. Our syntax as well our semantics for set-valued methods is first order in that our variables range over the elements of a set rather than on (the extension of) that set.

We propose the notion of *inheritance by completion* (*i-completion*) of a program and present an abstract semantics that is based on conventional notions of interpretation and satisfaction. This semantics is reminiscent of the stable model semantics of [7]: as in that case, due to the non-monotonic nature of overriding, a program may have more than one stable model, or no stable model at all. However, we isolate a syntactic condition, that we call *i-stratification*, that guarantees the existence of a unique stable model. This condition is reminiscent of the stratification condition of [15] for logic programs with negation, but in our case it constrains the combination of deduction and inheritance with overriding. Reasoning on the i-completion of our programs, we prove that i-stratification is sufficient to guarantee the existence and uniqueness of the stable models. The definition of i-completion provides also the basis for defining a bottom-up computation of the unique stable model of every i-stratified program.

We organize the rest of our paper as follows. In Section 2 we present our model of inheritance and we discuss the informal semantics by means of simple examples. In Section 3 we introduce the notion of i-completion and present the stable model semantics. Then, in Section 4, we introduce the i-stratification condition and we prove the results of existence and uniqueness of stable models. We then address similarities and differences with related work in Section 5, and finally conclude in Section 6 discussing the extensions of the present model that we plan for our future research.

2 The Inheritance Model

In this section we present the salient features of the inheritance model we consider throughout. We do this by introducing a simple deductive object oriented query language with inheritance: the language doesn't account for a number of important object oriented concepts like signatures, structural inheritance, encapsulation, etc. However, it comprises the essential functionalities related to behavioral inheritance: multiple inheritance, overriding, dynamic self binding, set-valued methods, etc.

2.1 Syntax

Every program in this language uses symbols from an alphabet $\langle \mathcal{V}, \mathcal{C}, \mathcal{P} \rangle$ where $\mathcal{V}$ is a denumerable set of variables, $\mathcal{C}$ is a set of data constructors and $\mathcal{P}$ is a set of property (attribute and method) symbols. These components are assumed to be pairwise disjoint. We call *o-terms* the terms built over $\mathcal{C} \cup \mathcal{V}$, and *p-terms* the terms $\mathbf{p} = p_{/a}(args)$ where $p \in \mathcal{P}$ is a property name with arity a, and $args$ is a tuple of o-terms. To ease the notation, we will always denote the property symbols from $\mathcal{P}$ using only their names, with the understanding that every name has an associated unique arity. An o-term is a first order entity in the language and denotes the *object identity* (oid) of a class or instance object. The set of oids is denoted by $\mathcal{O}$.

Atomic and Complex Formulas. *Molecules* and *isa terms* are the atomic formulas of the language. Their structure is defined as follows.
Molecules are statements of the form $o[\mathbf{p}]$, where o is an oid and $\mathbf{p}$ is a p-term (called respectively the molecule's oid and p-term). The intended meaning of a molecule in our language is essentially the same as in F-logic: $o[\mathbf{p}]$ states that property $\mathbf{p}$ holds at object o.
Isa terms are statements of the form $o : c$ or $c :: d$ where o, c and d are o-terms. The intention of an *isa* term is to establish the subclass/membership relation between two objects: $o : c$ states that o is an instance of c, whereas $c :: d$ states that c is a subclass of d. We will often denote with $\sharp$ the type of the *isa* relation between objects: given a class object c, $o\sharp c$ stands for $o : c$ when o is an instance object and for $o :: c$ when o is itself a class object.

Complex formulas are definite clauses of the form $A \leftarrow B_1, \ldots, B_n$ where A and the B_is are molecules and/or *isa* terms. We will call A and the B_is respectively the head and the body literals of the clause and we will assume that all the variables occurring in a clause are universally quantified.

Programs and Queries. As in other object oriented languages, a program in our language specifies which methods/attributes are attached to each object and organizes objects along *isa* hierarchies. Every program can be conceptually viewed as consisting of two parts, each one dedicated to the specification of one of these two components.

Definition 1 (PROGRAMS). A program is a pair $\Gamma : \Pi$ where:

- Γ, the *schema declaration*, is a (possibly empty) set of *isa clauses* whose head is an *isa* term and whose body literals are either *isa* terms or molecules;
- Π, the *property or data definitions*, is a (possibly empty) set of *method clauses* whose head is a molecule and whose body literals are either *isa* terms or molecules.

When the oid in the head molecule of a method clause is a variable, we will assume that there exist an *isa* term $X \sharp o$ in the body to qualify X as an instance or subclass of some object. This assumption does not involve any loss of generality: it serves the only purpose of disallowing clauses like "$X[\mathbf{p}]$." that establish the truth of a property, $\mathbf{p}$ in this case, at *every* object.

The only structural distinction between a method clause and an *isa* clause is that the former has a molecule as its head whereas the latter has an *isa* term. Thus it is possible that the *isa* clauses in the schema and the method clauses in the data definitions of a program depend on each other: the satisfaction of a property at an object may depend on the structure of the *isa* hierarchy (through an *isa* term) and vice versa. Consequently, as in F-Logic, we allow a dynamic structure of the *isa* hierarchy.

2.2 Informal Semantics

The *isa* clauses of the schema organize objects in a DAG-like hierarchy. The interplay between membership and subclassing is subject to the standard condition: every instance of a class is also an instance of all of the super-classes of that class. In other words, where o, c and d are different objects, $o : c$ and $c :: d$ implies that $o : d$. Finally we assume that subclassing and membership are reflexive: an object is always a subclass and an instance of itself.

Each class defines a set of properties (methods and/or attributes) for its instances and subclasses. Every object inherits all the properties that are defined at the objects that are placed higher up in the hierarchy. There are two ways that a property can be inherited, either extensionally or intensionally: we refer to these two types of inheritance respectively as *value inheritance*, and *method inheritance* or *code sharing*.

In the sequel of this section we illustrate the functionalities of inheritance, as well as the interaction of inheritance and overriding by means of a number of simple examples. Later, in section 3, we will formalize these ideas precisely.

Value and Method Inheritance. The difference between value inheritance and method inheritance can be explained as follows. Method inheritance is, in a way, built into our syntax and originates from the interplay between instantiation and the *isa* relations of the schema. Value inheritance, instead, is enforced by our intuitive understanding of the interaction between the *isa* relation and deduction. The following example helps clarify the point.

$$\Gamma_1 ::= \begin{vmatrix} (1) & o : c. \\ (2) & c :: d. \end{vmatrix} \qquad \Pi_1 ::= \begin{vmatrix} (3) & c[q(b)]. \\ (4) & X[p(a)] \leftarrow X : d, def_p \end{vmatrix}$$

The schema states that o is an instance of c and that c is a subclass of d. Given that every object inherits from its class ancestors in the *isa* hierarchy, here we have that o inherits $q(b)$ from its class c. Similarly, o inherits a definition for p from class d: this is because we can substitute o for X in (4) and, since $o : d$ due to the interplay between ":" and "::", clause (4) can be seen as a definition that o inherits from d. If def_p, succeeds, then we will be able to derive $o[p(a)]$.

Note the difference between the two cases. In the former, o is inheriting the extension of a property from its class c: we will say that o value-inherits q from c. In the latter case, it is the intension of the property (the clause defining it) that gets inherited from d to o: accordingly, we will say that o method-inherits p from d.

Overriding. If there were no overriding, we could account for the two types of inheritance in an elegant and easy way. We would simply need to model the relationship between the *isa* relations and substitution/deduction and have our objects be characterized by all the properties they inherit via instantiation and/or deduction in ways similar to those outlined above. With overriding the picture becomes more complex, because there may be conflicts between the types of inheritance and we may want to reject the inheritance of values (or clauses) along the *isa* hierarchies in case properties are redefined at a subclass or instance. Consider for example the following program.

$$\Gamma_2 ::= \begin{vmatrix} (1) & o : c. \\ (2) & c :: d. \end{vmatrix} \qquad \Pi_2 ::= \begin{vmatrix} (3) & c[p(b)]. \\ (4) & X[p(a)] \leftarrow X : d. \end{vmatrix}$$

The point is: how should we answer the query $o[p(X)]$? Both the answers $X = a$ and $X = b$ seem reasonable, because $X = b$ follows from (3) being $o : c$, whereas $X = a$ follows from (4) being $o : d$ implied by the schema. If there were no overriding, then we would certainly accept both the answers as legal and, consequently, say that $\{a, b\}$ is the value of p at o. However, if we assume that inheritance is subject to overriding, then clearly we have a conflict. In this case we claim that the only acceptable answer to the above query is $X = b$, because the inheritance of p from c to o overrides the inheritance of the same property from d to o.

Following the same line of reasoning, if we assume that $w : d$ be part of the schema in the example above, we will interpret the two following clauses:

$$X[t(a)] \leftarrow X : c, def_1.$$
$$X[t(b)] \leftarrow X : d, def_2.$$

as two definitions for t that o and w inherit from their (super)-classes. More precisely, w inherits the second clause from d, whereas o inherits the first clause from c and the second from d. Again, the inheritance of t from c to o overrides the inheritance from d to o. The same arguments apply to the following slightly more complex example.

$$\Gamma_3 ::= \begin{vmatrix} (1) & o : c. \\ (2) & u : c. \\ (3) & c :: d. \end{vmatrix} \qquad \Pi_3 ::= \begin{vmatrix} (4) & c[p(b)]. \\ (5) & u[p(e)]. \\ (6) & X[p(a)] \leftarrow X : d. \end{vmatrix}$$

Here, the expected answer to the query $u[p(X)]$ is $X = e$ rather than $X = b$. This is because the inheritance of p from c to u is overridden owing to the existence of the local definition (5) for p at u.

Multiple Inheritance. The interaction between inheritance and overriding we have outlined above applies to every path in the *isa* hierarchy: each object inherits a property and/or the clauses defining it from the closest ancestors in the hierarchy that define that property. In order to formalize this notion of "closeness", we assume that no pair of immediate ancestors of any given object be connected by an *isa* link. Accordingly, $\Gamma = \{o : c, o : d\}$ is a valid schema whereas $\Gamma' = \{o : c, c :: d, o : d\}$ violates the assumption because o has two immediate ancestors, c and d, that are connected by the link $c :: d$. In our model, Γ' is interpreted as the linear schema $\{o : c, c :: d\}$ where c is closer to o than d. In other words, the model does not distinguish the cases when $o : d$ is asserted or entailed by the schema.

Dynamic Subclassing. In all of the previous programs, we have seen examples of *static* schema definitions, where the *isa* clauses do not depend on the data definitions. Consider now the more complex case of the following program.

$$\Gamma_4 ::= \left|\begin{array}{ll} (1) & o : c \leftarrow o[p(a)]. \\ (2) & o : d. \end{array}\right. \qquad \Pi_4 ::= \left|\begin{array}{ll} (3) & d[p(a)]. \\ (4) & c[p(b)]. \end{array}\right.$$

Note that the *isa* relation between o and c depends now on the satisfaction of $p(a)$ at the object o. Here, inheritance works as before: from $o : d$ and $d[p(a)]$, we can derive $o[p(a)]$ by inheritance from d to o. Then, by standard deduction we derive $o : c$, and hence, $o[p(b)]$ by inheritance from c to o. Therefore, we conclude that the value of p at o is the set $\{a, b\}$.

As a final example, consider adding the *isa* clause $c :: d \leftarrow o[p(a)]$ to the previous program. $\Gamma_4 : \Pi_4$. We obtain the new program (which we adapt from [10]).

$$\Gamma_5 ::= \left|\begin{array}{ll} (1) & o : c \leftarrow o[p(a)]. \\ (2) & c :: d \leftarrow o[p(a)]. \\ (3) & o : d. \end{array}\right. \qquad \Pi_5 ::= \left|\begin{array}{ll} (4) & d[p(a)]. \\ (5) & c[p(b)]. \end{array}\right.$$

As in the previous example, we can derive $o[p(a)]$ from $o : d$ and $d[p(a)]$. Now, however, by standard deduction, we derive not only $o : c$ but also $c :: d$. But this implies that o should inherit p from c, and consequently, that this inheritance should override the inheritance of the same property from d to o. In other words, we shouldn't have used $o : d$ to deduce $o[p(a)]$. However, if we disregard $o : d$, then we are not even allowed to infer $o : c$, and hence we conclude that the value for p at o is the empty set,

Neither one of the two conclusions seems reasonable: indeed this program doesn't seem to have any sensible (determinate) meaning. As we will show in section 4, our semantics *does* classify programs like $\Gamma_5 : \Pi_5$ as *meaningless* programs because they have no stable models.

3 Stable Model Semantics

As in the classical theory of logic programming, an interpretation of a program in our language is a subset of the Herbrand base over the alphabet of the program. The only additional requirement in our theory is that we assume that interpretations be *isa* closed: that means that, whenever $o\sharp c$ and $c :: d$ belong to an interpretation I, we require that $o\sharp d$ be also contained in I. The condition of *isa* closedness provides a formal justification for the equivalence of the two schemas $\{o : c, c :: d, o : d\}$ and $\{o : c, c :: d\}$ we have discussed in the previous section.

Satisfaction in an *isa* closed interpretation is defined exactly as in classical Herbrand interpretations in terms of membership. To account for inheritance in this framework, we introduce the notion of i-completion discussed in the next subsection[1].

3.1 Inheritance by I-completion

We first present the rational behind the idea of i-completion on intuitive grounds. Consider the following program:

$$\Gamma ::= (1) \quad o : c. \qquad \Pi ::= (2) \quad c[p(a)].$$

In every model of this program we would expect to see both $c[p(a)]$ (of course) and $o[p(a)]$ because it can be inferred by value inheritance. However, the fact that $p(a)$ holds at o is not expressed explicitly in the program: it is our idea of the semantics of inheritance that implies it. This is in fact a general issue: value inheritance is not expressed syntactically in our programs; it is a purely semantic mechanism we are attributing to them. In contrast, method inheritance *does* have a syntactic representation owing to substitutions. So the point is: why not model value inheritance in terms of method inheritance so that we can account for value inheritance syntactically the way we do for method inheritance? It is easy to see how this can be accomplished, at least in the previous program: simply, consider the following *completed* program:

$$\Gamma ::= (1) \quad o : c. \qquad \Pi ::= \left| \begin{array}{ll} (2) & c[p(a)]. \\ (3) & o[p(a)] \leftarrow o : c, c[p(a)]. \end{array} \right.$$

Note that clause (3) is inherited by o from c. It states that whenever $p(a)$ holds at c, it also holds at o: exactly as in the original program, with the difference that now the value inheritance from c to o is modeled in terms of the inheritance of clause (3) between the two objects. This simple transformation extends naturally to the general case as suggested in the following definition.

Definition 2 (I-COMPLETION). Let P be a set of clauses and let $[P]$ be the ground closure of P. The *i-completion* of P, denoted by $C(P)$ is the minimal set

---

[1] In [4], we present an alternative semantics based on complex interpretation structures, called β-structures. Using these structures, we are able to capture the functionalities of behavioral inheritance and overriding directly within the definition of satisfaction, without resorting to the notion of i-completion. In [4] we also show the equivalence of the notion of model that results in that framework and the definition of stable model we present in this paper.

of clauses satisfying the following conditions:

1. $[P] \subseteq [C(P)]$
2. $o \updownarrow c \leftarrow B.$ $c :: d \leftarrow B. \in [C(P)]$ $\Longrightarrow$ $o \updownarrow d \leftarrow o \updownarrow c, c :: d. \in [C(P)]$
3. $c[\mathbf{p}] \leftarrow B.$ $o \updownarrow c \leftarrow B. \in [C(P)]$ $\Longrightarrow$ $o[\mathbf{p}] \leftarrow o \updownarrow c, c[\mathbf{p}]. \in [C(P)].$

The effect of i-completing a program is to expose, syntactically, all the inheritance that is implicitly expressed in the original program. As a consequence, the semantics of an i-completed program can be given simply in terms of deduction as it does not need to make reference to inheritance: what in the original program is inferred by value inheritance can be inferred, in the i-completed program, by standard deduction using the clauses added by the i-completion. In both cases, method inheritance is implicitly entailed by substitution.

Clearly, we still need a formal account for overriding, but the use of i-completion allows us to capture the functionalities of inheritance in terms of a standard notion of satisfaction: we can characterize the semantics of an i-completed program simply in terms of its (classical) minimal Herbrand model.

3.2 Overriding

Before we move on to introduce overriding, we put forward the definitions of *local* and *inherited* clauses that, adapted from [8], help formalize this notion.

Definition 3 (LOCAL METHOD CLAUSES). Let cl be a ground (instance of a) method clause. We say that cl is *local* to $o \in \mathcal{O}$ iff $cl = o[\mathbf{p}] \leftarrow B_1, \ldots, B_n$ and there exists no i such that $B_i = o \updownarrow c$ with $c \neq o^2$.

Definition 4 (INHERITED CLAUSES). Let $cl = o[\mathbf{p}] \leftarrow B_1, \ldots, B_n$ be a ground (instance of a) method clause and let I be an interpretation. We say that cl is *inherited by o from c in I* iff there exists i such that $B_i = o \updownarrow c$ and $o \updownarrow c \in I$

Next, we introduce the concepts of *defined* and *inherited* properties. Again, we denote with $\hat{\mathbf{p}}$ the property symbol of the p-term $\mathbf{p}$ and call $\hat{\mathbf{p}}$-clause any clause whose head is $o[\mathbf{p}]$ for some object o. We say that o *defines* a property $p \in \mathcal{P}$ iff there exists a p-clause local to o. Similarly, o *inherits p from d in I* iff o inherits a p-clause from d in I.

Our notion of "overriding" is again inspired by the definition of locality of method clauses proposed in [8]. Overriding comes into play whenever an object o inherits the same property, say p, from different ancestors that are connected by *isa* links in the hierarchy. In every such situation, the conflict is resolved by establishing that o inherits p only from the closest ancestors that define p. This inheritance blocks (overrides) the inheritance of p from all the ancestors of o that are placed higher up in the hierarchy. Note that, since we assume that membership and subclassing are reflexive, it follows that if an object defines

---

[2] Here, and in Definition 5, with "$\dot{=}$" we denote syntactic equality.

a property, then the local definition overrides the inheritance of that property from any of the (proper) ancestors of that object.

The natural consequence of this interpretation is that for every object o, only a subset of the clauses that o inherits from its ancestors are actually "relevant" to the definition of the properties that hold at o itself. The set of relevant clauses corresponding to the overriding rule we have just outlined is defined precisely as follows.

Definition 5 (OVERRIDING-FREE INSTANCES). Let $P = \Gamma : \Pi$ be a program and I be an interpretation. All the ground instances of the *isa* clauses in Γ are *overriding free in* I. Let $cl = o[\mathrm{p}] \leftarrow B_1, \ldots, B_n$ be ground instance of a method clause in Π. cl is *overriding free in* I iff:

- either cl is local to o;
- or there exists a class c such that o inherits cl from c and o does not inherit $\widehat{\mathrm{p}}$ from any $d \neq c$ such that $\{o \natural d, d :: c\} \subseteq I$.

In several respects, this approach results in a model theory that is similar to the model theory of Gulog proposed in [6]: as in that case, it is the syntactic structure of the program that determines the set of "relevant" clauses of a program as well as the ways that overriding affects the inheritance of properties. One important difference is that our notion of overriding in a given interpretation is static, as it is based solely on the existence of an overriding definition (regardless of the satisfaction of the body of the definition in the given interpretation). Furthermore, we generalize the definition of model by allowing the *isa* hierarchy to evolve dynamically during the computation. Let $\mathcal{M}(P)$ denote the minimal model of an (i-completed) program P.

Definition 6 (STABLE MODELS). Let I be an interpretation and let P be an i-completed program. We say that I is a stable model of P iff $I = \mathcal{M}([P]_I)$.

This definition should be contrasted with the corresponding definition of stable models in [7]. As in that case, given an interpretation I, we isolate the subset of the clauses in P that are "relevant" because they are overriding free in I, and then we check whether the remaining clauses are satisfied by I. Note the recursive flavor of the construction: the set of clauses that must be satisfied in order for I to qualify as a model depend on I itself. Also note that, owing to the dynamic nature of the *isa* definitions in the schema, in the construction of a model I, the set $[P]_I$ may be subject to changes as the interpretation I changes. Hence, this construction may or may not be convergent: the following proposition shows that there exist programs that have no stable models.

Proposition 7. Program $\Gamma_5 : \Pi_5$ of section 2 has no stable model.

Proof. We show that that the i-completion of $\Gamma_5 : \Pi_5$, as shown below, has no stable model.

$$\Gamma ::= \left| \begin{array}{ll} (1) & o : c \leftarrow o[p(a)]. \\ (2) & c :: d \leftarrow o[p(a)]. \\ (3) & o : d. \\ (4) & o : d \leftarrow o : c, c :: d. \end{array} \right. \qquad \Pi ::= \left| \begin{array}{ll} (5) & d[p(a)]. \\ (6) & c[p(b)]. \\ (7) & o[p(a)] \leftarrow o : d, d[p(a)]. \\ (8) & o[p(b)] \leftarrow o : c, c[p(b)]. \\ (9) & c[p(a)] \leftarrow c :: d, d[p(a)]. \end{array} \right.$$

Clauses (4), (7), (8) and (9) have been added by i-completion. Let the above i-completed program be called Q: we show that Q has no stable interpretation. First observe that since (4) is subsumed by (3) we can reason independently of clause (4). Similarly, we can disregard clause (9) since it is "written over" in every interpretation (6) being local to c.

Now observe that clauses (1), (2), (3), (5) and (6) are overriding free in every interpretation. Hence, (3), (5) and (6) being unit clauses, if there exists a stable interpretation I, then I must be a superset of $J = \{o : d, d[p(a)], c[p(b)]\}$. Note also that J itself is not stable: in fact, since clause (7) is overriding free in J, $o[p(a)] \in \mathcal{M}([Q]_J)$. Assume now, by contradiction, that there exists a stable interpretation I for Q. We have two possibilities:

1. If $o[p(a)] \in I$, then $o : c, c :: d \in I$ because I is a model for (1) and (2) that are overriding free. But then clause (6) is not overriding free in I and hence $o[p(a)] \notin I$ being I minimal: a contradiction.
2. If $o[p(a)] \notin I$, then neither $o : c$ nor $c :: d$ belong to I being I minimal. But then, clause (7) is overriding free in I. This, in turn, implies that $o[p(a)] \in I$, being I a model. Again, we have a contradiction. □

It is also not difficult to see that there are programs that have more than one stable model. Consider the following new program.

$$\Gamma ::= \left| \begin{array}{ll} (1) & o : c. \\ (2) & o : d. \\ (3) & c :: d \leftarrow o[p(a)]. \\ (4) & d :: c \leftarrow o[p(b)]. \end{array} \right. \qquad \Pi ::= \left| \begin{array}{ll} (5) & d[p(a)]. \\ (6) & c[p(b)]. \\ (7) & o[p(a)] \leftarrow o : d, d[p(a)]. \\ (8) & o[p(b)] \leftarrow o : c, c[p(b)]. \end{array} \right.$$

This program is not i-complete: to complete it we would need to add the following clauses:

(i)	$o : c \leftarrow o : d, d :: c.$	(iii)	$c[p(a)] \leftarrow c :: d, d[p(a)].$
(ii)	$o : d \leftarrow o : c, c :: d.$	(iv)	$d[p(b)] \leftarrow d :: c, c[p(b)].$

However, we can disregard these clauses since (i) and (ii) are subsumed respectively by (1) and (2), whereas (iii) and (iv) are written over in every interpretation owing to the presence of the two local definitions (5) and (6) respectively. Now, call P the above program: every model of P is a superset of $\{o : c, o : d, d[p(a)], c[p(b)]\}$ since (1), (2), (5) and (6) are unit clauses that are always overriding free. Furthermore, owing to the presence of clauses (7) and (8), every model must contain either one of $o[p(a)]$ and $o[p(b)]$, but not both because otherwise we would be led to conclude that the schema of P contains a cycle. Now consider the following two interpretations:

$$I_1 = \{o : c, \; o : d, \; d[p(a)], \; c[p(b)], \; d : c, \; o[p(a)]\}$$
$$I_2 = \{o : c, \; o : d, \; d[p(a)], \; c[p(b)], \; c : d, \; o[p(b)]\}$$

The set of overriding free instances of P in I_1 and I_2 are, respectively, $[P]_{I_1} = [P] \setminus \{(8)\}$ and $[P]_{I_2} = [P] \setminus \{(7)\}$. It is immediate to see that $I_1 = \mathcal{M}([P]_{I_1})$ and $I_2 = \mathcal{M}([P]_{I_2})$ and hence, that I_1 and I_2 are both stable models of P. Furthermore, on the account of the previous observations, we conclude that I_1 and I_2 are actually the only two stable models of this program: yet, neither one is smaller than the other.

4 Existence and Uniqueness of Stable Models

Looking at the previous examples, one notices that the reason why we fail to construct a model is that we have a conflict between the deduction of a property at a given object and the deduction of an *isa* relation for that object. More precisely, the problem is that we use an *isa* relation $o\not\!| c$ to derive a molecule $o[p]$ by value inheritance from c but, having done this, we immediately find out that there exists an intervening object *mid* such that $o\not\!| mid$ and $mid :: c$ and that the existence of *mid* causes $o\not\!| c$ to be overridden for $\hat{p}$. In both the previous examples this is the actual reason why we fail to define a (unique) stable model.

4.1 I-stratification

To obtain a stable model, we will need to constrain the dependency of an *isa* term on a molecule such that if the *isa* term $o\not\!| c$ is used to derive a molecule $o[p]$ by inheritance from c, then we will not, at later stages, derive a new *isa* term $o\not\!| d$ that blocks the inheritance of $\hat{p}$ from c to o. The following definition of stratification ensures this property. Again, let $[P]$ denote the ground extension of P.

Definition 8. Let P be an i-completed program. We say that P is *i-stratified* iff there exists a mapping μ from ground atoms to positive integers such that, for every pair of atoms A and B in $[P]$, the following conditions are satisfied:

1. $\mu(A) \geq \mu(B)$ iff A is the head of a clause of $[P]$ and B is a body literal of that clause;
2. $\mu(A) > \mu(B)$ iff $A = o[p]$ is the head of a clause of $[P]$ and $B = o\not\!| c$ is a body literal of that clause.

The i-stratification mapping μ aims at decomposing a program P in different strata $P^1, \ldots, P^n$ such that $[P]$ can be obtained as the disjoint union of these strata. The intention of condition (2) is to separate clauses defining *isa* relations between objects from clauses defining properties at these objects by placing them at different strata of the program. If there exists an i-stratification $P^1 \cup \cdots \cup P^n$ of P, then it will satisfy the following property. Assume that P^i contains a clause $o[\mathbf{p}] \leftarrow B_1, \ldots, B_n$ and that there exists B_k such that $B_k = o \updownarrow c$: then all the clauses whose head is $o \updownarrow c$ are placed at strata P^j with j strictly lower than i.

The notion of i-stratification, suggests also a way to compute a model of an i-completed program. Let T_P be the following immediate-consequence operator:

$$T_P(I) = \{A \mid A \leftarrow B_1, \ldots, B_n \in P \text{ and } \{B_1, \ldots, B_n\} \subseteq I\} \cup I$$

The intention is to construct a model for a program by repeatedly iterating the T_P operator at each stratum of the program: owing to i-stratification, the set of overriding free instances of each stratum will not be subject to changes as the construction of the model proceeds with iterations at higher strata.

The following theorem shows that the iterated fixed point computation we have just outlined leads indeed to the construction of stable models.

Theorem 9 (EXISTENCE). Let P be an i-complete and i-stratified program and let $P^1 \cup \cdots \cup P^n$ be an i-stratification of P. For every interpretation I, denote with P_I^j the subset of the j-th stratum of $[P]$ consisting of the clauses that are overriding free in I. Finally, let $M_P^\star$ be the interpretation resulting from the following iterated fixed-point computation:

$$M_1 = T_{P^1}^\omega(\emptyset)$$
$$M_i = T_{P^i_{M_{i-1}}}^\omega(M_{i-1}) \quad 1 < i \leq n$$
$$M_P^\star = M_n$$

$M_P^\star$ is a stable model for P.

Proof. We use the following two properties:

1. for every interpretation I, $T_{P^i \cup P^{i+1}}^\omega(I) = T_{P^{i+1}}^\omega(T_{P^i}^\omega(I))$ for every $i = 1, .., n-1$.
2. for every $i = 1, \ldots, n$, $P_{M_{i-1}}^i = P_{M_n}^i$ where we take $M_0 = \emptyset$ by definition.

The first property is a well-known property of stratified programs that carries over directly to i-stratified programs. The proof of the second is omitted for the lack of space and can be found in [4]. To show that $M_P^\star = M_n$ is a stable model, we need to show that $\mathcal{M}([P]_{M_n}) = M_n$. From (1) and (2) above, we can proceed as follows:

$$\mathcal{M}([P]_{M_n}) = T_{P_{M_n}}^\omega(\emptyset) = T_{P^1_{M_n} \cup \cdots \cup P^n_{M_n}}^\omega(\emptyset)$$
$$\text{by (1)} = T_{P^n_{M_n}}^\omega(T_{P^{n-1}_{M_n}}^\omega(\cdots(T_{P^1_{M_n}}^\omega(\emptyset))\cdots))$$
$$\text{by (2)} = T_{P^n_{M_{n-1}}}^\omega(T_{P^{n-1}_{M_{n-2}}}^\omega(\cdots(T_{P^1}^\omega(\emptyset))\cdots)) = M_n$$

We conclude the section with the proof that every i-complete and i-stratified program has exactly one stable model. The proof of this result also shows that the construction of $M_P^\star$ is independent of the choice of the i-stratification of P.

Theorem 10 (UNIQUENESS). Let P be an i-complete and i-stratified program. Let I be a stable model of P. Then $I = M_P^\star$.

Proof. Let I be a stable model and let $P^1 \cup \cdots \cup P^n$ be an i-stratification of P. Then consider the set of overriding free instances $[P]_I = P_I^1 \cup \cdots \cup P_I^n$. Clearly $\mathcal{M}([P]_I) = \mathcal{M}(P_I^1 \cup \cdots \cup P_I^n)$. Let then N_i be the following sequence of sets:

$$N_1 = T_{P_I^1}^\omega(\emptyset)$$
$$N_i = T_{P_I^i}^\omega(N_{i-1}) \quad 1 < i \le n$$
$$N^\star = N_n$$

Since P is i-stratified, clearly $\mathcal{M}([P]_I) = N^\star$. Furthermore, since the minimal model of every i-stratified set of clauses is independent of the i-stratification mapping, the above construction of $\mathcal{M}([P]_I)$ is also independent of the chosen i-stratification of P. Now consider the sequence of sets M_i that result in the construction of $M_P^\star$ using the stratification $P^1 \cup \cdots \cup P^n$. We show, by induction on i, that for every $i = 1, \ldots, n$, $M_i = N_i$.

Base case. First note that for every interpretation I, $P_I^1 \subseteq P^1$. If $P_I^1 \subset P^1$, then P^1 must contain an inherited clause $cl = o[\mathbf{p}] \leftarrow o\natural c, B$ that is overridden in I (for these are the only clauses that can be written over). But then, since P is i-stratified, neither $[P]$ nor P^1 contain any *isa* clause whose head is $o\natural c$. Hence, by iterating T_P on P^1, cl will never produce $o[\mathbf{p}]$ and, consequently, P^1 and $P^1 \setminus \{cl\}$ have the same minimal model. Since this argument applies to all the clauses of P^1 that are not overriding free in I, we have that: $N_1 = \mathcal{M}(P_I^1) = \mathcal{M}(P^1) = M_1$

Inductive step. First notice that, being I stable, $I = \mathcal{M}([P]_I)$ and consequently, $I = N_n$. Then observe that, by construction, $N_i \subseteq I$ for every i: from this we have that $M_{i-1} \subseteq I$ because, by the inductive hypothesis $N_{i-1} = M_{i-1}$. Now we can show that $P_I^i = P_{M_{i-1}}^i$ using the properties of i-completion and i-stratification. Further details can be found in [4]. □

4.2 Remarks

A natural question that arises at this point is how large is the class of programs that have a unique minimal model. A subclass of the programs that enjoy this property is the class of programs that are simple, in the sense of the following definition.

Definition 11 (SIMPLE PROGRAMS). A program $\Gamma : \Pi$ is *simple* if and only if the body of every clause in the schema Γ is constituted solely of *isa* terms.

That these programs have a unique stable model follows as corollary of the results of the previous section. The proof is immediate since the i-completion of every simple program $\Gamma : \Pi$ can be seen as a two-stratum program $P^1 \cup P^2$ where P^1 and P^2 are the i-completions of respectively Γ and Π.

The case of non-simple programs, where the schema and data definitions may depend mutually on each other, is more complex. In this regard, it is interesting to note that the condition of i-stratification is precise enough to distinguish the two programs $\Gamma_4 : \Pi_4$ and $\Gamma_5 : \Pi_5$ of section 2. We already showed that the latter has no stable model: it can now be easily verified that the i-completion of this program, introduced in proposition 7, is not stratified. On the other hand, it is easy to see that the sets of clauses displayed below, define a stratification of (the completion of) $\Gamma_4 : \Pi_4$.

$$P^1 ::= \left| \begin{array}{l} o : d. \\ d[p(a)]. \\ c[p(b)]. \end{array} \right.$$

$$P^2 ::= \left| \begin{array}{l} o : c \leftarrow o[p(a)]. \\ o[p(a)] \leftarrow o : d, d[p(a)]. \end{array} \right.$$

$$P^3 ::= \left| \, o[p(b)] \leftarrow o : c, c[p(b)]. \right.$$

In general, it is hard to give a precise characterization of the class of i-stratified programs. However, our contention is that i-stratification is interesting in itself as a structuring principle: it simply requires that the *isa* relation between two objects be independent of the properties whose satisfaction depends itself on that *isa* relation. As such, i-stratification seems indeed to offer a reasonable principle for writing programs that exploit the power of inheritance in meaningful and practical ways.

5 Discussion on Related Work

In this section we take a very brief look at other proposals that are related to our present work. Readers are referred to [10] for a lucid and comprehensive discussion on the contemporary approaches to inheritance in the literature.

In *L&O* [12], the semantics of inheritance and overriding is given indirectly by translating *L&O* program to logic programs and, hence, it provides little insight into the relationships between inheritance, overriding and deduction.

In F-Logic [10], only structural inheritance is captured semantically within the model theory and the proof theory of the formalism. Counterwise, for behavioral inheritance, the non-monotonic aspects introduced by the combination of overriding and dynamic binding are modeled only indirectly by means of an iterated fixed point construction. Another weakness of F-Logic is that it accommodates only value inheritance: in F-Logic, what gets inherited along the *isa* hierarchy is ground data expressions – values resulting from the application of a method at a superclass – and not method implementations. Method inheritance and overriding, in their turn, are accounted for only indirectly by means of an ad-hoc technique that relies on the higher order features of this formalism. Finally, in F-Logic the problems introduced by the dynamic structure of the schema are solved resorting to a highly non-deterministic semantics: in F-Logic a program might have more than one model and no mechanism is provided so that one can systematically identify an intended or preferred model.

In Gulog [5, 6], Dobbie and Topor develop an elegant semantics for inheritance with overriding that addresses some of the unresolved problems in F-Logic. However, the elegance of their solution is achieved at the expense of a number of restrictions on the inheritance model. In particular, Gulog does not account for value inheritance and, more importantly, it separates the schema declarations from the data definitions thus avoiding the problems introduced by the dynamic subclassing capabilities of F-Logic.

In Orlog [9], Jamil and Lakshmanan developed a model for inheritance based on the notion of inheritance *withdrawal* to capture the idea of *user defined* inheritance and *conflict resolution* in multiple inheritance networks. One of the major shortcomings of this model is that overriding is captured via specification and hence is not deducible. However, by introducing the idea of *locality* of method clauses and the notion of *inheritability* in [8], the above handicap in Orlog is eliminated. However, the proposal in [8] achieved this functionality at the expense of the loss of dynamic subclassing capability.

Behavioral inheritance has been studied also in deductive formalisms like the *Ordered Theories* of [11], in modular languages such as Contextual Logic Programming [13, 14], *SelfLog* [3] and several others. In these proposals, an object is viewed as a set of rules (clauses) that represent the properties that hold at that object. Hence, although the functionalities of inheritance are the same as in object oriented systems, the resulting languages are essentially modular languages that retain the relational flavor of data peculiar to logic programming and, as such, differ from conventional object oriented languages, both syntactically and semantically.

6 Conclusion and Future Research

A desirable extension of the inheritance model we have presented would be to include inheritance with dynamic overriding in ways similar to those proposed for Gulog (and F-Logic, to that matter).

In Gulog, this feature is accounted for by resorting to interpretation structures that carry extra information needed (i) to identify the objects from which a value is inherited and (ii) to resolve the possible conflicts between the inheritance from different ancestors. Our current solution, based on static overriding, simplifies the treatment of overriding for set-valued methods and has also the potential benefit of allowing room for some form of static type checking. However, the extension to dynamic overriding appears to be necessary for several applications, notably for reasoning about inheritance hierarchies in artificial intelligence [16]. Our current work shows that the generalization of the framework we have presented in this paper should be smoothly accomplished by integrating our definition of i-stratification with the i-stratification condition proposed by Dobbie and Topor in [6].

As a further extension, we are currently studying the integration of our model with a corresponding model of structural inheritance. One of the challenges, in this extended framework, is to isolate and define an adequate relation between method inheritance and overriding, as we have defined them here, with the properties of covariance and contravariance for the types of these methods' arguments and results.

References

1. H. Aït-Kaci and R. Nasr. Login: a logic programming language with built-in inheritance. *Journal of Logic Programming*, 3:182–215, 1986.
2. H. Aït-Kaci and A. Podelski. Towards a Meaning of LIFE. Technical Report 11, Digital Paris Research Labs, 1991.
3. M. Bugliesi. A declarative view of inheritance in logic programming. In K. Apt, editor, *Proc. Joint Int. Conference and Symposium on Logic Programming*, pages 113–130. The MIT Press, 1992.
4. M. Bugliesi and M. H. Jamil. A Stable Model Semantics for Behavioral Inheritance in Deductive Object Oriented Languages. Technical Report 6, Dip. di Matematica Pura ed Applicata, Univ. di Padova, 1994.
5. G. Dobbie and R. Topor. A Model for Inheritance and Overriding in Deductive Object-Oriented Systems. In *Sixteen Australian Computer Science Conference*, January 1988.
6. G. Dobbie and R. Topor. A Model for Sets and Multiple Inheritance in Deductive Object-Oriented Systems. Technical report, School of Computing and Information Technology, Griffith University, Nathan Qld 4111, Australia, January 1993.
7. Michael Gelfond and Vladimir Lifschitz. The Stable Model Semantics for Logic Programming. In R. A. Kowalski and K. A. Bowen, editors, *Proc. 5th Int. Conference on Logic Programming*, pages 1081–1086. The MIT Press, 1988.
8. H. M. Jamil. *Semantics of Behavioral Inheritance in Deductive Object-Oriented Databases*. PhD Thesis (in preparation), Department of Computer Science, Concordia University, Canada, 1994.
9. H. M. Jamil and L. V. S. Lakshmanan. Orlog: A Logic for Semantic Object-Oriented Models. In *Proc. of the International Conference on Information and Knowledge Management, Baltimore, Maryland*, pages 584–592, November 1992.
10. M. Kifer, G. Lausen, and J. Wu. Logical Foundations for Object-Oriented and Frame-Based Languages. Technical Report TR-93/06, Department of Computer Science, SUNY at Stony Brook, 1993. (accepted to Journal of ACM).
11. E. Laesen and D. Vermeir. A Fixpoint Semantics for Ordered Logic. *Journal of Logic and Computation*, 1(2):159–185, 1990.
12. F.G. McCabe. *Logic and Objects*. Prentice Hall International, London, 1992.
13. L. Monteiro and A. Porto. A transformational view of inheritance in Logic Programming. In D.H.D. Warren and P. Szeredi, editors, *Proc. 7th Int. Conference on Logic Programming*, pages 481–494. The MIT Press, 1990.
14. L. Monteiro and A. Porto. Syntactic and Semantic Inheritance in Logic Programming. In J. Darlington and R. Dietrich, editors, *Workshop on Declarative Programming*. Workshops in Computing, Springer-Verlag, 1991.
15. Teodor Przymusinski. Perfect Model Semantics. In R. A. Kowalski and K. A. Bowen, editors, *Proc. 5th Int. Conference on Logic Programming*, pages 1081–1096. The MIT Press, 1988.
16. D. S. Touretzky. *The Mathematics of Inheritance Systems*. Morgan Kaufmann, Los Altos, CA, 1986.

A Rewriting Technique for the Analysis and the Optimization of Active Databases

Danilo Montesi[1]* and Riccardo Torlone[2]

[1] Informatics Department, Rutherford Appleton Laboratory,
Chilton, Didcot Oxon, OX11 0QX, UK
[2] IASI–CNR, Viale Manzoni 30, 00185 Roma, Italy

Abstract. We propose a new formal semantics of active databases based on a transaction rewriting technique in the context of the relational model. A user defined transaction, which is viewed here as a sequence of atomic database updates forming a semantic unit, is translated by means of active rules into induced one(s). Those transactions embody active rule semantics which can be either immediate or deferred. Rule semantics, confluence, equivalence and optimization are then formally investigated and characterized in a solid framework that naturally extends a known setting for relational database transactions.

1 Introduction

Active databases are based on rules that allow us to specify actions to be taken by the system automatically, when certain events occur and some conditions are met. It is widely recognized that these *active* rules provide a powerful mechanism for the management of several important database activities (e.g., constraint maintenance and view matherialization [4, 5]), and for this reason, active databases have been extensively investigated and experimented in the last years [2, 3, 6, 9, 11, 14, 15, 16]. However, the various proposals generally suffer from a lack of formal semantics and as a consequence, it turns out that very often active rule processing becomes quickly complex and unpredictable, even for relatively small rule sets [16].

The goal of this paper is to provide a formal approach to active rule processing that relies on a method for rewriting user defined transactions to reflect the behavior of a set of active rules, and to show how known results for transaction equivalence can be used in this framework to pre-analyze properties of transactions and rules.

We start by introducing a simple transaction language, based on a well known model for relational databases [1] in which a transaction is viewed as a collection of basic update operations forming a semantic unit, and a quite general active rule language, whose computational model is set-oriented (like in [16] and differently from other approaches [15]). We consider two different execution models

---

* The work of this author has been partially supported by the ERCIM fellowship *Information and Knowledge Systems*.

for active rules: immediate and deferred [11]. The former has no temporal decoupling between the event, condition and action parts. The latter has a temporal decoupling between the event part on one side and the condition and action parts on the other side. We then define in this context a rewriting process that takes as input a user defined transaction T and a set of active rules and produces a new transaction T' that "embodies" active rule semantics, in the sense that T' explicitly includes the additional updates due to active processing. Under the deferred modality, the new transaction is the original one augmented with some induced actions, whereas, under the immediate modality, the new transaction interleaves original updates and actions defined in active rules. It follows that the execution of the new transaction in a passive environment corresponds to the execution of the original transaction within the active environment defined by the given rules. Other approaches consider rewriting techniques [8, 15], but usually they apply in a restrictive context or are not formal. Conversely, we believe that this formal and simple approach can improve the understanding of several active concepts and make it easier to show results.

As we have said, the execution model of our transactions is based on a relational transaction model [1] which has been extensively investigated. The reason for this choice is twofold. Firstly, we wish to use a well known model within a formal setting and a solid transaction execution model. Secondly, we wish to take full advantage of the results already available on transaction equivalence and optimization [1, 10]. In fact, we are able to formally investigate statically several interesting properties of active rule processing. First, we can check whether two transactions are equivalent in an active database. Then, due to the results on transaction equivalence, we are also able to provide results on confluence. Finally, optimization issues can be addressed. As a final remark, we note that with this approach, run time support of active rule processing turns out to be very close to that of a traditional database system, and so it is simpler to implement than others which are built from scratch [7].

The remainder of this paper is organized as follows. In Section 2, a detailed overview of the approach is presented by using several practical examples. In Sections 3 and 4, we define the basic framework and the rewriting technique respectively. Several results on active rule processing are given in Section 5. Finally, in Section 6, we draw some conclusions and sketch further research issues. Because of space limitation, proofs as well as several technical details are omitted.

2 An overview of the approach

In this section we informally present our approach. The basic idea is to express active rule processing as a four step computation. Let T be a user defined transaction and P be a set of active rules. The first step checks whether P presents some kind of recursion. For the time being, we present a simple characterization and we will not address this issue in detail in the present paper. The second step takes P and T, and transforms the transaction T into an induced one(s) that "embodies" the semantics of the rules in P. In general, during this step several transactions can be generated. These different induced transactions take into account the fact that an update of the original transaction may trigger several rules at the same time, and so the corresponding actions can be executed in different orders yielding different results. In the third step, confluence and optimization issues of active rule processing are investigated by analyzing the transactions computed during the second step. This is done by using (extensions of) techniques for testing equivalence of database transactions [1, 10]. Then, in the last step, according to the results of this analysis, one transaction is finally executed. We point out two important aspects of this approach. Firstly, it relies on a formal basis that allows us to derive solid results. Secondly, the rewriting and confluence/optimization steps can be done statically, without accessing the underlying database, and therefore they can be performed very efficiently at compile time.

As we have said, we will consider the immediate and deferred active rule execution models: the immediate modality reflects the intuition that rules are processed as soon as they are triggered, while deferred modality suggests that a rule is evaluated and executed after the end of the original transaction [11]. Thus, two different rewriting procedures will be given. Specifically, consider a user defined transaction as a sequence of updates: $T = U_1; \ldots; U_k$. This transaction is transformed under the immediate modality into an induced one:

$$T^I = U_1; \bar{U}_1^P; \ldots; U_k; \bar{U}_k^P.$$

where $\bar{U}_i^P$ denotes the sequence of updates computed as *immediate reaction* of the update U_i with respect to a set of active rules P. This reaction can be derived by "unifying" the update U_i with the event part of the active rules. Clearly the obtained updates can themselves trigger other rules, hence this reaction is computed recursively. As noted above, several transactions can be obtained in this way. Note that under the immediate modality the induced transaction is an interleaving of user defined updates with rule actions.

Under the deferred modality, the induced transaction has the form:

$$T^D = U_1; \ldots; U_k; \bar{U}_1^P; \ldots; \bar{U}_k^P.$$

Hence the *reaction is deferred* (or postponed) until the end of the user transaction. Here again the induced updates can themselves trigger other rules, and so the reactions of the original updates are recursively computed, but using the immediate modality.

We now give some examples to clarify the above discussion. Consider the following active rules that react to updates to a personnel database composed by two relations: emp(name,dname,sal) and dep(dname,mgr).

R_1 : WHEN $-\,$dep(X,Y) IF emp(Z,X,W) THEN $-\,$emp(Z,X,W).
R_2 : WHEN $+\,$emp(X,Y,Z) IF emp(X,V,W) AND Y $\neq$ V THEN $-\,$emp(X,V,W).
R_3 : WHEN $+\,$emp(X,Y,Z) IF Z $>$ 50k THEN $+\,$dep(Y,X).

Intuitively, the first rule states that when a department is deleted then all the employees working in such a department must be removed (cascading delete). The second one serves to enforce the constraint that an employee can work in one department only, and states that when an employee tuple (e,d,s) is inserted into the relation emp, then the old tuples where the employee 'e' is associated with a department different from 'd' must be deleted. Finally, the last rule states that if an inserted employee has a salary greater than 50k then he is eligible to be a manager of the department in which he works and so, according to that, a tuple is inserted in the relation dep.

Now, we provide the following simple user defined transaction where first the toy department is removed and then an employee is added to this department with a salary of 60K.

$$T_1 = -\text{dep}(D, M)[D = \text{toy}]; +\text{emp}(\text{bill}, \text{toy}, 60K)^3$$

By inspecting the given active rules, we can easily realize that, at run time, the first update in T_1 will trigger rule R_1, whereas the second update will trigger rules R_2 and R_3. Therefore, under immediate modality, T_1 can be rewritten at compile time into the following transaction by "unfolding" with respect to the active rules (the superscript * denotes an induced update).

$$T_1^I = -\text{dep}(D, M)[D = \text{toy}]; -\text{emp}(Z, X, W)[X = \text{toy}]^*; +\text{emp}(\text{bill}, \text{toy}, 60K);$$
$$-\text{emp}(X', V', W')[X' = \text{bill}, V' \neq \text{toy}]^*; +\text{dep}(\text{toy}, \text{bill})[60K > 50K]^*;$$

The obtained transaction describes the behavior of the transaction T_1 taking into account the active rules under the immediate modality. Note that there is another possible translation in which the last two updates are switched. This is because the second update of the original transaction triggers two rules at the same time (namely R_2 and R_3) and therefore we have two possible execution orders of the effects of these rules. It follows that, in general, a user defined transaction actually induces a *set* of transactions. One of the goals of this paper is to show that in many cases it is possible to statically check whether these transactions are equivalent. If all the induced transactions are equivalent we can state that the active program is "confluent" with respect to the transaction T_1. In this case the execution of one of the obtained transactions implements the expected behavior of the user defined transaction within the active framework.

Let us now turn our attention to the deferred execution model. Assume that we want to move the employee John from the toy to the book department. This can be implemented by means of the following transaction.

$$T_2 = +\text{emp}(\text{john}, \text{book}, 50K); -\text{emp}(\text{john}, \text{toy}, 50K).$$

If we rewrite this transaction taking into account the active rules above under the deferred modality, we have the following possible translation, in which the effect of the rules is postponed to the end of the transaction.

---

[3] The notation $U[C]$ can be read: "perform the update U where the condition C holds".

$$T_2^D = +\text{emp}(\text{john}, \text{book}, 50\text{K}); -\text{emp}(\text{john}, \text{toy}, 50\text{K});$$
$$-\text{emp}(\text{X}, \text{V}, \text{W})[\text{X} = \text{john}, \text{V} \neq \text{book}]^*; +\text{dep}(\text{john}, \text{book})[50\text{K} > 50\text{K}]^*;$$

By inspecting this transaction, we can statically decide that the last update will not be executed (and so it can be discarded) since its condition (namely, 50K > 50K) is independent of the database state and turns out to be false. Moreover, before executing the transaction, we can observe the fact that the second update can be also discarded without altering the overall effect of the transaction, since its effect is included in the effect of the third update. This shows how some optimization can be performed on those induced transactions. The transaction that implements the expected behavior is then as follows.

$$T_2^{D'} = +\text{emp}(\text{john}, \text{book}, 50\text{K}); -\text{emp}(\text{X}, \text{V}, \text{W})[\text{X} = \text{john}, \text{V} \neq \text{book}]^*;$$

In contrast to a user defined transaction, the updates in the derived transactions are not independent, as some updates are indeed "induced" by others. This fact has a consequence on the execution semantics of an induced transaction. Assume for instance that at run-time the execution of an update U in a induced transaction T has a null effect on the database (because, for example, its condition does not hold or its effect is invalidated by a subsequent update). Then, it is reasonable that the updates in T induced (directly or indirectly) by U are not executed as well. Under this interpretation, we need to define a new transaction semantics that takes into account the inducer/induced relationship among updates. Clearly, the techniques to achieve confluence and optimization must take into account this fact.

To clarify the point, consider the transformation of the transaction T_1 under the deferred modality. According to the previous discussion, the rewriting process should generate the following derived transaction.

$$T_1^D = -\text{dep}(\text{D}, \text{M})[\text{D} = \text{toy}]; +\text{emp}(\text{bill}, \text{toy}, 60\text{K}); -\text{emp}(\text{Z}, \text{X}, \text{W})[\text{X} = \text{toy}]^*;$$
$$-\text{emp}(\text{X}', \text{V}', \text{W}')[\text{X}' = \text{bill}, \text{V}' \neq \text{toy}]^*; +\text{dep}(\text{toy}, \text{bill})[60\text{K} > 50\text{K}]^*;$$

However, it is easy to see that the third update invalidates the effect of second one. It follows that the last two updates of the transaction T_1^D, which are induced by such an update, must not be executed at run time. So, the translations of the transaction T_1 under the deferred modality can be simplified as follows:

$$T_1^D = -\text{dep}(\text{D}, \text{M})[\text{D} = \text{toy}]; -\text{emp}(\text{Z}, \text{X}, \text{W})[\text{X} = \text{toy}]^*;$$

So, we need to develop novel techniques to check equivalence and to optimize induced transactions. This will be done by extending the already existing framework for equivalence and optimization in relational databases.

The rest of the paper is devoted to the formalization and characterization of the issues discussed in this section.

3 Active rules and transactions

A *relation scheme* is an object $R(X)$ where R is the name of the relation and $X = \{A_1, \ldots, A_k\}$ is a set of symbols called *attributes*. A *database scheme* is a collection of relation schemes $\mathbf{R} = \{R_1(X_1), \ldots, R_n(X_n)\}$ with distinct relation names. Given a universe D of constant called *domain* and a countable set of variables V, a *relational atom* over a scheme $R(A_1, \ldots, A_k)$ is an object of the form $R(t_1, \ldots, t_k)$ where t_i, for $i = 1, \ldots, k$, is a *term*, that is, a variable or a constant. If every term is a constant then the relational atom is *ground*. A ground relational atom is also called *tuple*.

A *relation r* over a scheme $R(A_1, \ldots, A_k)$ is a set of tuples over R. A *database state s* over a database scheme $\mathbf{R} = \{R_1(X_1), \ldots, R_n(X_n)\}$ is a set of relations $s = \{r_1, \ldots, r_n\}$ over $R_1, \ldots, R_n$ respectively. We will denote by $Inst(\mathbf{R})$ the set of all possible database states over a scheme $\mathbf{R}$.

Together with the relational atoms, we will also use *built-in* atoms based on traditional *comparison predicates* $(=, >, <, \ldots)$. A *literal* is an atom (*positive literal*) or a negated atom (*negative literal*). A *condition* is a set of literals. A *substitution* is a function $\theta : V \to D$, which associates to each variable a constant. Given a relational atom B, a database state s and a substitution θ, we say that θ is a *valuation* of the positive relational literal B (resp., the negative relational literal $\neg B$) on s if there is (there is not) a relation $r_i \in s$ such that $\theta(B) \in r_i$. Similarly, a substitution θ is a valuation of a built-in atom B if $\theta(B)$ is true, according to the usual interpretation of the corresponding comparison predicate. A substitution θ is a valuation of a condition C on a database state s if it is a valuation of each $L_i \in C$ on s. We assume that an empty condition always has at least one valuation on any database state which is the identity. We will consider only *safe* conditions where each variable that occurs in a negative relational literal also occurs in a positive relational literal, and each variable that occurs in a built-in literal also occurs in a relational literal.

Definition 1. An *action* is a relational atom preceded by one of the symbols $\{+, -\}$. A *conditional update U* (or simply an *update*) has the form: $A[C]$, where C is a condition and A is an action such that all the variables occurring in it also occur in C.

A conditional update is executed for those tuples (if any) that verify the specified condition. The *effect* of an update U is a function $\text{EFF}(U) : Inst(\mathbf{R}) \to Inst(\mathbf{R})$ defined as follows:

- $\text{EFF}(+B[C])(s) = s \cup \{\theta(B) : \theta \text{ is a valuation of } C \text{ in } s\}$;
- $\text{EFF}(-B[C])(s) = s - \{\theta(B) : \theta \text{ is a valuation of } C \text{ in } s\}$.

Note that, for sake of simplicity, we do not consider modify operations here.

Update operations are generally executed within *transactions*, that is, collections of data manipulation operations viewed as a semantic atomic unit for recovery and concurrency purposes.

Definition 2. A *user defined transaction* is a sequence of updates of the form: $U_1; \ldots; U_k$ whose effect on a database s is defined as:

$$\text{EFF}(T)(s) = \text{EFF}(U_k) \circ \ldots \circ \text{EFF}(U_1)(s)$$

Definition 3. An *event* is a relational atom preceded by one of the symbols $\{\oplus, \ominus\}$.

An event denotes the fact that a certain update operation has been performed on a database state. We can say that the execution of updates *generate* events which therefore can be viewed as objects tracing update executions.

Definition 4. An *active rule* has the form:

$$E \circ C \rightarrow A$$

where E is an event, C is a condition and A is an action such that: (1) each variable that occurs in a negative literal in the condition also occurs in a positive literal or in the event part, and (2) each variable that occurs in the action also occurs in the condition part. An *active program* P is a set of active rules. An *active database* is a pair (s, P) where s is a database state and P is an active program.

Note that for sake of simplicity, the notation used in Section 2 for active rules is different from the one used here. It is obvious however that one can be reduced to the other in a straightforward way.

The intuitive semantics of an active rule is: "if E succeeds, then evaluate the condition C and if it is true then perform the action A using the bindings of the event and the condition parts". As we have said, one important point here is the temporal relationship between the execution of the various components of a rule. The event part and the condition part have a temporal decoupling under the deferred execution model, whereas, under the immediate execution model there is no temporal decoupling. In our approach, the formal semantics of an active database with respect to a transaction T is given in terms of execution of a transaction T' induced by T and so, it will be defined in the next section along with the definition of the rewriting technique.

4 Transaction transformation

In this section we present the algorithms that transform a user defined transaction into an induced one which embodies the active rules behavior. We consider both the immediate and deferred cases.

4.1 Immediate and deferred transaction transformations

Let us start with some preliminary notion. Let U be an update $A[C]$ and R be an active rule $E \circ C' \to A'$ that does not share any variable with U (this can be easily enforced by means of variable renaming). Then, we say that U *triggers* R if: (1) $A = +B$ and $E = \oplus B'$, or $A = -B$ and $E = \ominus B'$, and (2) there is a substitution θ, called *unifier*, such that $B = \theta(B')$. If an update U triggers a rule $E \circ C' \to A'$ with θ as unifier, then we say that U *induces* the update $\theta(A'[C'])$

As we have said, during translation we need to keep trace of the relationship between inducer and induced update. This is done by subscribing the induced updates in order to encode the inducer, the inducer of the inducer and so on. For instance the update $U_{3;2;1}$ means that it was induced by the update $U_{3;2}$ that in turn was induced by U_3. Thus the original update U_3 induces $U_{3;2}$ that induces $U_{3;2;1}$. The following is a recursive algorithm that computes the reaction of a single update.

Algorithm REACTION
Input: *An active program P and an update U_j.*
Output: *A sequence $\bar{U}_j^P$ of updates induced by U_j.*
begin

$\quad \bar{U}_j^P := <>;$
$\quad i := 1;$
$\quad index := < j >;$
$\quad Triggered(U_j, P) := \{R \in P : R \text{ is triggered by } U_j\};$
$\quad \textbf{while } Triggered(U_j, P) \text{ is not empty do}$
$\quad\quad \text{pick a rule } E \circ C \to A \text{ from } Triggered(U_j, P);$
$\quad\quad \theta := \text{the unifier of } E \text{ and } U_j;$
$\quad\quad index := \text{APPEND}(index, i);$
$\quad\quad U_{index} := \theta(A[C]);$
$\quad\quad \bar{U}_j^P := \text{APPEND}(\bar{U}_j^P, U_{index});$
$\quad\quad \bar{U}_j^P := \text{APPEND}(\bar{U}_j^P, \text{REACTION}(P, U_{index}));$
$\quad\quad i := i + 1;$
$\quad \textbf{endwhile}$
$\quad \textbf{output } \bar{U}_j^P$

end.

Note that, in general, different outputs can be generated by the above algorithm depending on the order in which the available rules are selected in the first step of the loop. Clearly the algorithm can be generalized in such a way that all the possible induced sequences of updates are generated. Moreover, syntactical restriction can be given so that the above algorithm is guaranteed to terminate. The following result is based on the construction of a graph G_P such that the nodes represent the rules in P and there is an edge from a rule $R : E \circ C \to A$ to a rule $R' : E' \circ C' \to A'$ if $A[C]$ triggers R'.

Lemma 5. *If the graph G_P is acyclic then the algorithm* REACTION *is guaranteed to terminate over P and any update U_j.*

Indeed, less restrictive conditions can be given to achieve termination. Also, the algorithm can be modified in order to take into account the presence of some kind of recursion. This is subject of current investigation.

Now let T be a user defined transaction, P be an active program and T_I^P and T_D^P be the transactions obtained by T and P as follows.

- $T_I^P = U_1; \text{REACTION}(P, U_1); \ldots; U_k; \text{REACTION}(P, U_k)$
- $T_D^P = U_1; \ldots; U_k; \text{REACTION}(P, U_1); \ldots; \text{REACTION}(P, U_k)$

We say that T_I^P and T_D^P are *induced* by T and P under the immediate and deferred modality respectively.

We point out that given a user defined transaction and an active program, we may have several different induced transactions (depending on the possible outputs of algorithm REACTION), and even if the number of those induced transactions is always finite, it may be very large. However, this number can be reduced by checking for instance when certain ones are "obviously" equivalent, e.g., when certain rules trivially commute. This is an important problem that will be subject of future investigation.

In the following, we will denote by $\mathbf{T}_I^P$ (respectively $\mathbf{T}_D^P$) the set of all possible transactions induced by a user defined transaction T and an active program P under the immediate (deferred) modality.

4.2   Semantics of induced transaction

As we have said in Section 2, an induced update in an induced transaction is executed only if: (1) the inducing update has been effectively executed or (2) it has not been invalidated afterwards. Then, a new effect semantics EFF' needs to be defined according to that.

Let U be an update, and s be a database state. We denote with $\Delta^+(U, s)$ and $\Delta^-(U, s)$ the *changes* induced by U on s, that is, the tuples that U adds to and deletes from s, respectively. Now, let s' be another database state. We say that the effect of U on s is *visible* on s' if: (1) $\Delta^+(U, s) \cup \Delta^-(U, s) \neq \emptyset$, (2) $\Delta^+(U, s) \subseteq s'$, and (3) $\Delta^-(U, s) \cap s' = \emptyset$.

Now, let $T = U_1, \ldots, U_k$ be an induced transaction and let $T|_j$ denote the transaction $U_1, \ldots, U_j$ composed by the first j components of T ($j \leq k$). Then, the new effect function EFF' is recursively defined as follows, for $1 \leq i \leq k$ and $1 \leq j \leq k$.

$$
\text{EFF}'(T|_j)(s) = \begin{cases} \text{EFF}'(T|_{j-1})(s) & \text{if } U_j \text{ is induced by } U_i \text{ and the} \\ & \text{effect of } U_i \text{ on } \text{EFF}'(T|_{i-1})(s) \\ & \text{is not visible on } \text{EFF}'(T|_{j-1})(s) \\ \text{EFF}(U_j) \circ \text{EFF}'(T|_{j-1})(s) & \text{otherwise} \end{cases}
$$

Note that the above "induced by" relationship between updates can be easily derived on the basis of the indexes associated with the updates. We are now ready to give the semantics of a transaction with respect to an active database.

Definition 6. A *potential effect* of a user defined transaction T on an active database (P, s) under the immediate modality coincides with $\text{EFF}'(T_I^P)(s)$, where T_I^P is a transaction induced by T and P under the immediate modality.

Definition 7. A *potential effect* of a user defined transaction T on an active database (P, s) under the deferred modality coincides with $\text{EFF}'(T_D^P)(s)$, where T_D^P is a transaction induced by T and P under the deferred modality.

5 Analysis of active rule processing

We believe that many interesting problems can be systematically studied in the above formal setting. Among there are: termination, equivalence, optimization and confluence of active databases. Let us go through some of these issues.

5.1 Transaction equivalence

Transaction equivalence has been extensively investigated within the relational model [1, 10]. The major results of this study concern deciding whether two transactions are equivalent and transforming a transaction into an equivalent, but less expensive one. Unfortunately, these results cannot be directly used within our framework because of the different effect semantics defined for transactions. So, we introduce a new notion of transaction equivalence based on the function EFF' as follows.

Definition 8. Two induced transactions T_1 and T_2 are *equivalent* if it is the case that $\text{EFF}'(T_1) = \text{EFF}'(T_2)$.

We now present a method for testing equivalence of induced transaction. The method is based on a set of transformation rules that allows us to transform an induced transaction into a new, equivalent one. We will restrict our attention to the important class of *domain-based* transactions, where the conditions involve only atoms of the form $X = a$ and $X \neq a$. It has been argued in [1] that this is not a strong semantic restriction, but allows us to avoid complex syntactic notation. Moreover, we assume that the transaction is in *first normal form*, that is, every condition in a transaction has a disjoint valuation over any database state. It is possible to show that, similarly to [1], each transaction can be transformed into an equivalent 1NF transaction by "splitting" each update by means of opportune reduction rules.

In the transformation rules we are going to present, we use the notation $S \widehat{\in} T$ to denote that a sequence of updates S occurs in a transaction T. Moreover, $Ind(i)$ denotes the set of updates induced by the update with index i (note that this set can be built by simply inspecting the update indexes). Finally, we make use of the operators RM and SW: the former takes as input a transaction T and a set of indexes I and removes from T the updates with index in I, the latter takes as input a transaction T and a pair of indexes (i, j), and switches the updates in T with those indexes.

Let $\mathcal{R}$ be the following set of transformation rules.

$$(1) \; -A[C_1]_i; -A[C_2]_j \,\widehat{\in}\, T \Rightarrow \text{sw}(T,(i,j)) \qquad \text{if } j \notin Ind(i) \text{ and } C_1 \neq C_2$$
$$(2) \; -A[C_1]_i; -A[C_1]_j \,\widehat{\in}\, T \Rightarrow \text{RM}(T,\{i\} \cup Ind(i))$$
$$(3) \; +A[C_1]_i; +A[C_2]_j \,\widehat{\in}\, T \Rightarrow \text{sw}(T,(i,j)) \qquad \text{if } j \notin Ind(i) \text{ and } C_1 \neq C_2$$
$$(4) \; +A[C_1]_i; +A[C_1]_j \,\widehat{\in}\, T \Rightarrow \text{RM}(T,\{i\} \cup Ind(i))$$
$$(5) \; -A[C_1]_i; +A[C_2]_j \,\widehat{\in}\, T \Rightarrow \text{sw}(T,(i,j)) \qquad \text{if } C_1 \neq C_2 \text{ and } j \notin Ind(i)$$
$$(6) \; -A[C_1]_i; +A[C_1]_j \,\widehat{\in}\, T \Rightarrow \text{RM}(T,\{i,j\} \cup Ind(i) \cup Ind(j))$$
$$(7) \; +A[C_1]_i; -A[C_1]_j \,\widehat{\in}\, T \Rightarrow \text{RM}(T,\{i,j\} \cup Ind(i) \cup Ind(j))$$

Intuitively, rules $(1),(3)$ and (5) state that if the updates are not related, then they can be switched. Rules (2) and (4) state that the execution of two updates with the same effect can be done once only and so we can remove one of them and the corresponding induced updates. Finally, rules (6) and (7) state that the execution of complementary updates can be avoided by removing them and the induced ones. We have the following result.

Theorem 9. *Let T be an induced transaction and T' be a transaction obtained from T by applying rules in $\mathcal{R}$. Then, T is equivalent to T'.*

5.2 Confluence

Confluence is a strong property. Some applications may need a weaker notion. It is sometimes useful to allow an active program P to be non-confluent for certain unimportant relations in the database, but to ensure that P is confluent for other important relations. This was called partial confluence in [2]. We propose another notion of confluence that refers to a given transaction and turns out to be of practical importance.

Definition 10. An active program P is *confluent with respect to a user defined transaction T* under the immediate modality (resp., the deferred modality) if all the induced transaction $T_I^P \in \mathbf{T}_I^P$ ($T_D^P \in \mathbf{T}_D^P$) are equivalent.

Definition 11. An active program P is *strongly confluent* if it is confluent with respect to any user defined transaction T.

The following result is a consequence of Theorem 9 and provides a practical method to test for confluence with respect to a given transaction.

Theorem 12. *Let P be an active program, T be a user defined transaction, $T_I^P \in \mathbf{T}_I^P$ and $T_D^P \in \mathbf{T}_D^P$. Then, P is confluent with respect to T under the immediate modality (resp., deferred modality) if T_I^P (T_D^P) can be transformed into each transaction in $\mathbf{T}_I^P$ ($\mathbf{T}_D^P$) using the rules in $\mathcal{R}$.*

We now introduce another interesting notion of confluence that is independent of a specific transaction. Given an event E, we denote with $\widetilde{E}$ the corresponding update obtained by simply replacing the prefix of E with the corresponding update operation and by considering the variables in E as if they were constants.

Definition 13. An active program P is *locally confluent* if for each rule $E \circ C \to A$ in P, P is confluent with respect to a transaction that involves only $\tilde{E}$.

Note that, by Theorem 12, we can check for local confluence of an active program by using the set of simplification rules $\mathcal{R}$. The following result states that local confluence, although restrictive, is a desirable property for an active program.

Theorem 14. *If an active program is locally confluent then it is strongly confluent.*

This result also gives us an efficient way to check for confluence with respect to a given user defined transaction. Let P be an active program and P_c be the set of rules $E \circ C \to A$ in P such that P is confluent with respect to a transaction that involves only $\tilde{E}$. Actually, the set of rules P_c is the *locally confluent fragment* of P which can be derived one for all, at definition time.

The following result, which directly follows by Theorem 14, provides a characterization of confluence with respect to a user defined transaction T that simply requires one matching of each update in T with the event part of the rules in P.

Corollary 15. *Let P be an active program and T be a user defined transaction. Then, P is confluent with respect to T if the updates in T trigger only rules in P_c.*

5.3 Optimization

One objective of our research is to provide tools for optimizing induced transactions. This is particularly important since, with our approach, an optimization technique for induced transactions yields a method for optimizing the overall activity of active rule processing.

According to [1], two types of optimization criteria for transactions can be considered. The first is related to syntactic aspects (e.g. length and complexity of updates) of a transaction, whereas the second is related to operational criteria such as the number of atomic updates performed by a transaction. The notion of optimality that we use in this section is based on the first criteria but it turns out to be appealing also for the latter. In the following we denote with $|T|$ the length of a transaction, that is the number of insertion/deletion operations involved in the transaction.

Definition 16. Let T and T' be two equivalent induced transactions. Then, T is *simpler* than T' if $|T| < |T'|$

Let us consider the set of transformation rules $\mathcal{R}$ introduced in the previous subsection. It is easy to see that they can be grouped into two classes. The former contains commutativity rules (namely, rules (1), (3) and (5)) whereas the latter consists of simplification rules (namely, rules (2), (4), (6) and (7)). The application of a simplification rule yields a strictly simpler transaction, whereas commutativity rules do not affect the complexity of the translation, but are however useful in order to apply simplification rules. This observation leads to a method for optimizing induced transactions based on the rules $\mathcal{R}$. This method consists of applying a sequence of commutativity rules followed by one simplification rule, until no modification can be performed. We say that a *reduction* of a transaction T based on $\mathcal{R}$ is the transaction obtained from T by applying rules in $\mathcal{R}$ alternating simplification and commutativity rules as long as some simplification rule can be applied. The following theorem, which derives from a result in [10], states that the reduction process always terminates (in polynomial time) and is essentially deterministic regardless of the order of application of the rules.

Theorem 17. *Let T be an induced transaction. Then, (i) a reduction of T based on $\mathcal{R}$ is simpler than T, (ii) each reduction of T based on $\mathcal{R}$ can be generated in polynomial time, and (iii) for each pair of reductions T' and T'' of T based on $\mathcal{R}$, T' can be transformed into T''' by using only commutativity rules in $\mathcal{R}$.*

6 Conclusions and Future Work

We have presented a formal technique that allows us to reduce active rule processing to passive transaction execution. User defined transactions are translated into new transactions that embody the expected rule semantics under the immediate and deferred execution modalities. We have shown that many problems are easier to understand and to investigate from this point of view, as they can be tackled in a formal setting that naturally extends an already established framework for relational transactions. In fact, it turns out that several important results derived for transactions in a passive environment can be taken across to an active one. Firstly, we have been able to formally investigate transaction equivalence in the framework of an active database. Secondly, results on transaction equivalence have been used to check for interesting and practically useful notions of confluence. Finally, optimization issues have also been addressed.

We believe that this approach to active rule processing is very promising for further investigations. From a practical point of view we are studying efficient ways to generate and keep induced transactions, in the context of an implementation of the method on the top of a commercial relational DBMS [13]. From a theoretical point of view we intend to extend the results and to take into account more general frameworks. Finally, the rewriting technique can be applied to other data models such as one based on objects [12].

Acknowledgments

We would like to thank John Robert Kalmus who carefully read an earlier version of this paper and the IDEA group at Politecnico di Milano for fruitful discussions on active database technology.

References

1. S. Abiteboul and V. Vianu. Equivalence and Optimization of Relational Transactions. *Journal of the ACM*, 35(1):70–120, January 1988.
2. A. Aiken, J. Widom, and J. M. Hellerstein. Behavior of Database Production Rules: Termination, Confluence, and Observable Determinism. In *Proc. of the ACM SIGMOD International Conf. on Management of Data*, pages 59–68, 1992.
3. S. Ceri and R. Manthey. Chimera: a model and language for active DOOD Systems. In *Extending Information Systems Technology – Second International East-West Database Workshop, Klagenfurt*, pages 9–21, 1994.
4. S. Ceri and J. Widom. Deriving production rules for constraint maintenance. In *Proc. of the Sixteenth International Conf. on Very Large Data Bases, Brisbane*, pages 566–577, 1990.
5. S. Ceri and J. Widom. Deriving production rules for incremental view maintenance. In *Proc. of the Seventeenth International Conf. on Very Large Data Bases, Barcelona*, pages 577–589, 1991.
6. N. Gehani and H. V. Jagadish. ODE as an active database: constraints and triggers. In *Proc. of the Seventeenth International Conf. on Very Large Data Bases, Barcelona*, pages 327–336, 1991.
7. G. Guerrini, D. Montesi, and G. Rodriguez. Implementing active rules in object-database systems. Technical Report n. 62–94, Politecnico di Milano, 1994.
8. P. W. P. J. Grefen. Combining Theory and Practice in Integrity Control: A Declarative Approach to the Specification of a Transaction Modification Subsystem. In *Proc. of the Nineteenth International Conf. on Very Large Data Bases, Dublin*, pages 581–591, 1993.
9. E. N. Hanson and J. Widom. Rule Processing in Active Database Systems. In *International Journal of Expert Systems*, 6(1):83–119, 1993.
10. D. Karabeg and V. Vianu. Simplification rules and complete axiomatization for relational update transactions. In *Proc. of the ACM Transactions on Database Systems*, 16(3):439–475, September 1991.
11. D.R. McCarthy and U. Dayal. The architecture of an Active Data Base Management System. In *Proc. of the ACM SIGMOD International Conf. on Management of Data*, pages 215–224, 1989.
12. D. Montesi and R. Torlone. A rewriting technique for implementing active object systems. In *Proc. of the International Symposium on Object-Oriented Methodologies and Systems, pag 171–188, Springer-Verlag*, 1994.
13. D. Montesi and R. Torlone. A transaction transformation approach to active rule processing. In *Proc. of the Eleventh International Conference on Data Engineering, Taipei, Taiwan*, 1995. To appear.
14. M. Stonebraker. The integration of rule systems and database systems. *IEEE Trans. on Knowledge and Data Eng.*, 4(5):415–423, October 1992.
15. M. Stonebraker, A. Jhingran, J. Goh, and S. Potamianos. On rules, procedures, caching, and views in data base systems. In *Proc. of the ACM SIGMOD International Conf. on Management of Data*, pages 281–290, 1990.
16. J. Widom and S. J. Finkelstein. Set-Oriented Production Rule in Relational Databases Systems. In *Proc. of the ACM SIGMOD International Conf. on Management of Data*, pages 259–270, 1990.

Sorted HiLog: Sorts in Higher-Order Logic Data Languages

Weidong Chen[*1] and Michael Kifer[**2]

[1] Computer Science and Engineering, Southern Methodist University, Dallas, Texas
75275-0122, U.S.A. Email: wchen@seas.smu.edu

[2] Department of Computer Science, SUNY at Stony Brook, Stony Brook, NY
11794-4400, U.S.A. Email: kifer@cs.sunysb.edu

Abstract. HiLog enhances the modeling capabilities of deductive data
bases and logic programming with higher-order and meta-data constructs,
complex objects, and schema browsing. Its distinctive feature, a higher-
order syntax with a first-order semantics, allows for efficient implementation with speeds comparable to Prolog. In fact, HiLog implementation
in XSB [29, 25] together with tabulated query evaluation offers impressive performance with negligible penalty for higher-order syntax, thereby
bringing the modeling capabilities of HiLog to practical realization.

The lack of sorts in HiLog, however, is somewhat of a problem in database
applications, which led to a number of HiLog dialects such as DataHiLog
[24]. This paper develops a comprehensive theory of sorts for HiLog. It
supports HiLog's flexible higher-order syntax via a *polymorphic* and *recursive* sort structure, and it offers an easy and convenient mechanism
to control the rules of well-formedness. By varying the sort structure
we obtain a full spectrum of languages, ranging from classical predicate
logic to the original (non-sorted) HiLog. In between, there is a number
of interesting higher-order extensions of Datalog with various degrees of
control over the syntax, including second-order predicate calculus with
Henkin-style semantics, as described in [10]. We also discuss the benefits
of using Sorted HiLog for modeling complex objects and for meta programming. Finally, Sorted HiLog can be easily incorporated into XSB,
which makes its practical realization feasible.

---

* Work supported in part by the NSF grant IRI-9212074.
** Work supported in part by the NSF grant CCR-9102159.

1 Introduction

HiLog [6] is a higher-order language for deductive databases and logic programming. It not only expands the limits of first-order logic programming and obviates the need for several non-logical features of Prolog, but also provides important features for databases, including schema browsing and nested and higher-order relations similar to those in COL [1] and LDL [2]. We refer the reader to [6] for the details of these applications. HiLog has been used by many researchers for various ends, such as for specifying types in logic programming [11, 33], for database query languages (e.g., in the Glue-Nail! project [22]), and for object-oriented databases [18]. HiLog has been implemented as part of the XSB system with tabulated query evaluation [29],[3] and it runs at a very impressive speed compared to other deductive databases, such as LDL or Coral [25]. The on-going implementation [26] of C-logic and F-logic [16, 7] in XSB and its integration with HiLog will offer the ability to reason with objects and schema.

The main reason for the popularity of HiLog is its flexible syntax, the simplicity of its semantics, and the fact that its logical entailment is upward-compatible with classical logic. However, at the same time, it was felt that the syntax of HiLog is much too flexible, sometimes making it necessary to impose unwelcome restrictions on the range of logical variables in the program clauses.

Another problem is that HiLog has no higher-order counterparts for various tractable sub-logics of classical logic, such as Datalog, that are all-important in deductive databases. The Herbrand universe (which is the same as the Herbrand base) in HiLog is always infinite due to term application. One unpleasant off-shot of this is that the usual semi-naive bottom-up computation may not terminate, and even proper formulation of complexity results (analogous to those for Datalog) becomes an issue. As a result every query has to be analyzed for "finiteness" before it can be evaluated, even for programs with no applications of function symbols. To overcome this drawback, some researchers attempted to extract useful specialized sub-logics out of HiLog. Examples of this are Relational HiLog [23] and DataHiLog proposed [24]. However, strictly speaking, DataHiLog is not a sublanguage of HiLog in the sense in which Datalog is a sublanguage of classical Horn logic.

The third problem concerns the proof theory. Although HiLog has a sound and complete proof theory, the *direct* resolution-based proof theory of [6] has limitations, which are caused by the fact that Skolemization is not possible in some cases (see [6] for details).

In this paper, we show that all these problems can be rectified with a single mechanism, a *sorted* logic. A superposition of the idea of sorts and HiLog results in what we call *Sorted HiLog*. The idea of using sorts to control syntax is, of course, not new and one may even feel skeptical that applying this idea to HiLog may yield something original. However, as it turns out, a number of problems need to be solved. As they are known in classical logic, sorts are too limited when it comes to supporting the syntax of HiLog. Even the more elaborate theories [9, 14, 28] do not meet the requirements, as they were designed to address different problems. The requisite theory of sorts for HiLog should provide for more control over the syntax and, at the same time, be able to support those features of the syntax that make HiLog an attractive language.

The sort structure proposed in this paper is designed to accommodate both of these (seemingly conflicting) goals. The proposed sort structure is *polymorphic* and *recursive*. The logic itself is independent of the particular choice of a sort structure, and sorts can be viewed as a parameter to the logic. By varying the sort

---

[3] XSB and HiLog can be obtained via the anonymous FTP to *cs.sunysb.edu* in *pub/XSB/*.

structure, we obtain a "continuum" of logic languages, ranging from ordinary HiLog to classical predicate calculus, with various decidable and higher-order extensions of Datalog in between. DataHiLog [24], mentioned earlier, is one of the special cases of Sorted HiLog and so is the second-order predicate calculus with Henkin-style semantics, described in [10, Section 4.4].

Before going into technical details of this paper, it may be useful to give a brief overview of the notions of *sorts* and *types* as they apply to deductive languages.

Historically, *sorts* came from logic, where they were used to separate symbols into (usually disjoint) subdomains. Although sorts do not increase the expressive power of the logic, they may lead to clearer and more concise specifications; they also have been used to speed up automatic proofs [31].

Types, too, originate in logic [8]. However their introduction into logic-based programming languages is primarily due to the influence of functional and object-oriented programming, where it has been shown that sufficiently rich polymorphic type systems would allow the user to write interesting programs and, at the same time, guard against common programming errors.

In principle, logical sorts can be used in a similar way, since an ill-formed term in a program would certainly indicate a programming error. However, sorts lie at the very bottom of any logic — they are part of the very definition of what constitutes syntactically correct formulas in the language of the logic. As such they impose more generic constraints on the well-formedness of terms. For example, an individual term in predicate calculus may not appear as an atomic formula or be applied to other terms.

The work on type systems for logic programs follows two main approaches. One adopts the thesis that the semantics of typed logic programs should be based upon a typed logic [13, 15, 20, 21, 27]. Most of the proposals are designed mainly for predicate calculus like languages and cannot accommodate the flexible syntax of HiLog. The other approach is meta-theoretic in the sense that types are essentially constraints over type-free logic programs [19, 32, 17, 16]. A logic program may have a type-free logical semantics even though it may be ill-typed.

In the meta-logical setting, introducing sorts may be useful for several reasons. First, verifying well-formedness can be a "first cut" at ill-typed programs, since checking for well-formedness with respect to sorts is usually much cheaper than verifying well-typedness with respect to type systems, because the latter are usually much richer. Second, a non-trivial sort structure may significantly improve the efficiency of unification, thereby speeding up query execution. Finally, sorts lead to more natural and concise programs.

In accordance with this philosophy, the sort structure of HiLog does not support such essential elements of a viable type system as parametric and inclusion polymorphism. This is relegated to a richer, meta-level type system [4]. However, our sort system is arity-polymorphic and recursive, and despite its sophistication, well-formedness of HiLog formulas with respect to this sort system can be checked using a linear number of elementary operations such as retrieving the sort declaration of a variable. It should be noted, however, that the framework presented here can be easily extended to include parametric sorts. In contrast, support for inclusion polymorphism (*i.e.*, subsorts) is harder to provide because of complications with unification.[4]

This paper is organized as follows. Section 2 briefly sketches the original HiLog, as described in [6]. Section 3 introduces Sorted HiLog. Section 4 discusses several applications of Sorted HiLog and Section 5 concludes the paper.

Proofs of all theorems and a proof theory for Sorted HiLog can be found in [5].

---

[4] Problems also arise from the interaction of parametric sorts and subsorts. See [12, 4] for some work related to these issues.

2 Overview of HiLog

We assume some familiarity with HiLog, as it has been fairly well-researched in the literature [6, 22, 33, 24, 23, 18]. However, for easier reference, we provide a brief sketch of the syntax and semantics of HiLog.

HiLog is a higher-order logic that allows arbitrary terms to appear in contexts where only predicates and functions may occur in predicate calculus. As a result, higher-order predicates and functions can be defined with ease and, furthermore, higher-order constructs can be parameterized. This, for example, allows the programmer to define generic predicates that accept other predicates as parameters and whose contents depend on these parameters. Despite the fact that HiLog treats predicates and functions as first-class entities, it maintains the semantic simplicity that is characteristic of predicate calculus.

The alphabet of a HiLog language consists of a countably infinite set of variables, $\mathcal{V}$, and a countable set of intensional parameters, $\mathcal{S}$, which is disjoint from $\mathcal{V}$. As usual in logic programming, we adopt the convention by which variables will be denoted via symbols that start with a capital letter. The set of HiLog *terms* is the smallest set that contains variables and intensional parameters, and that is closed under *term application*, i.e., $t(t_1, ..., t_n)$ is a term if $t, t_1, ..., t_n$ ($n \geq 1$) are terms. For instance, $p(X(p), b)(p(p))$ is a term.

Note that the above recursive definition of HiLog terms implies, in particular, that any symbol can be used with different arities (as in most Prologs) and that variables can occur in places that normally are reserved for function symbols.

Atomic formulas in HiLog are just the same as HiLog terms. Therefore, any symbol from $\mathcal{S}$ (and, in fact, any term) may occur in a context where predicates would be expected in classical logic.

Complex formulas are constructed out of the atomic ones using connectives and quantifiers in the standard manner, i.e., $\phi \wedge \psi$, $\neg \eta$, and $(\forall X)(\phi \longleftarrow \psi)$ are formulas, provided that so are ϕ, ψ, and η. (The implication, "$\longleftarrow$", is defined as in classical logic: $\phi \longleftarrow \psi \equiv \phi \vee \neg\psi$.) For instance, the following is legitimate in HiLog:

$$
\begin{aligned}
\text{call}(X) &\longleftarrow X \\
\text{closure}(R)(X, Y) &\longleftarrow R(X, Y) \\
\text{closure}(R)(X, Y) &\longleftarrow R(X, Z) \wedge \text{closure}(R)(Z, Y)
\end{aligned}
\tag{1}
$$

The first clause in (1) defines the familiar Prolog meta-predicate, call, and the other two rules define a parametric predicate, closure(R). Here, the term closure(R) is used in a predicate position, and the symbol closure can be viewed as a higher-order function that applies to binary relations. When it is supplied with an argument, r, it computes the transitive closure of r under the name closure(r).

The semantics of HiLog is designed to capture the different roles an object can play in different contexts. A semantic structure **M** is a quadruple $\langle U, U_{true}, \mathcal{F}, \mathcal{I} \rangle$, where:

- U is a nonempty set, called the domain of **M**;
- $U_{true} \subseteq U$;
- $\mathcal{F}$ associates with each $d \in U$ and each $k > 0$ a k-ary function $U^k \longrightarrow U$, denoted by $d_{\mathcal{F}}^{(k)}$;
- $\mathcal{I}$ associates with each intensional parameter, $a \in \mathcal{S}$, an element in U.

Let ν be a variable assignment that associates to each variable, X, an element $\nu(X) \in U$. This assignment is extended to all terms as follows:

- $\nu(s) = \mathcal{I}(s)$ for every $s \in \mathcal{S}$; and

$$- \nu(t(t_1, ..., t_n)) = \nu(t)_{\mathcal{F}}^{(n)}(\nu(t_1), ..., \nu(t_n)).$$

Let A be an atomic formula. Then $\mathbf{M} \models_\nu A$ holds precisely when $\nu(A) \in U_{true}$. Satisfaction of composite formulas is defined as in predicate calculus. For instance:

- $\mathbf{M} \models_\nu \phi \wedge \psi$ if and only if $\mathbf{M} \models_\nu \phi$ and $\mathbf{M} \models_\nu \psi$;
- $\mathbf{M} \models_\nu \neg\phi$ if and only if it is not true that $\mathbf{M} \models_\nu \phi$;
- $\mathbf{M} \models_\nu (\forall X)\phi$ if and only if for every other variable assignment, μ, that is identical to ν everywhere except on X, $\mathbf{M} \models_\mu \phi$ holds; etc.

One off-shot of the above intensional semantics is that a pair of relations, p and q, are considered equal if and only if the equality $p = q$ can be derived. Thus, it is possible for relations to be unequal ($p \neq q$) even if they consist of the same tuples (*i.e.*, $\forall t(p(t) \longleftrightarrow q(t))$). An extensive discussion of the merits and demerits of intensional vs. extensional semantics appears in [6]. Here we will only mention that equality of relations and sets can be expressed in HiLog via additional axioms [6].

3 Sorted HiLog

In classical logic, it is common to distinguish between different categories of objects via the notion of sorts. In this section we describe Sorted HiLog, an extension of HiLog with a sort structure. Various applications of this enhanced version of HiLog are described in subsequent sections.

Recursive Arity-Polymorphic Sorts. A traditional approach to sorts is to introduce a set of primitive sort names and then define functional sorts using these primitive sorts as building blocks. Each parameter and each variable in the logic language is then assigned a sort. The difficulty in extending this approach to a language like HiLog is two-fold. First, HiLog symbols must be poly-sorted, i.e., they must be acceptable in several different syntactic contexts. For instance, $p(a)$, $q(p(a))$, and $p(p, a)$ should all be considered well-formed, given a suitable sort for p. At the same time, by changing the sort structure we should be able to outlaw some of these contexts, say $q(p(a))$, if desired. Second, HiLog semantics treats every term as a constructor that can be used to build other terms. For instance, $p(a)$ is a term and so are $p(a)(a)$ and $p(a)(a)(a)$. Thus, if $s \to s'$ is the sort for p and s is the sort for a then $p(a)$ is of sort s'. To enable $p(a)$ to act as a constructor in $p(a)(a)$, the sort s' itself has to have internal structure that somehow includes the sort $s \to s'$. This leads us to a realization that a sort-scheme suitable for HiLog must be *recursive*. A formal development follows next.

Let Δ be a set of *sort names*. An *arrow expression* has the form $s_1 \times \cdots \times s_n \to s$, where $s_1, ..., s_n, s$, $n \geq 1$, are sort names. This expression is said to have *arity* $s_1 \times \cdots \times s_n$ (but sometimes we will simply say that the arity is n). The sort names $s_1, ..., s_n$ are *argument* sorts and s is the *target* sort.

A *sort* defined over Δ is any expression of the form $s\sigma$ where $s \in \Delta$ is the *name* of the sort and σ is a (possibly infinite) set of arrow expressions, called the *signature* of that sort. Empty signatures will be omitted, for brevity. A signature, σ, may be infinite, but it is assumed to satisfy the following *uniqueness* and *effectiveness* assumptions:

- *Uniqueness:* For every arity $s_1 \times \cdots \times s_n$, σ has at most one arrow expression of the form $s_1 \times \cdots \times s_n \to s$. (Note, that σ can have several arities, *i.e.*, expressions of the form $s_1 \times \cdots \times s_n$, for any given n.)

- *Effectiveness:* There is an effective "arrow-fetching" procedure that, for every arity, $s_1 \times \cdots \times s_n$, returns the arrow expression $s_1 \times \cdots \times s_n \to s$, if such an expression is in σ (in which case it is unique, by the *uniqueness* property); if σ contains no such expression, the procedure returns some agreed upon symbol, *e.g.*, *nil*.

The idea behind sorts with complex internal structure is that if f is a parameter symbol of sort $s\{a_1, \ldots, a_k, \ldots\}$ then, *as an individual,* it belongs to the domain of s and, *as a term constructor,* it can occur only in the contexts specified by the arrow expressions $a_1, \ldots, a_k, \ldots$.

Note that if $s\sigma$ is a sort and s appears in an arrow expression in σ, then the definition of s acquires recursive flavor. The ability to define recursive sorts is necessary for supporting one important feature of HiLog syntax—terms with several levels of parentheses, such as in (1) above.

For instance, according to the well-formedness rules, below, if the symbols *closure*, X, Y, and P all have the same recursive sort, $s\{s \to s, s \times s \to s\}$, then the terms $closure(P)(X, Y)$ and $closure(P)(X)(Y)(P)$, will be well-formed. Informally, well-formedness holds by the following argument: $closure(P)$ is well-formed and has the sort s because so do *closure* and P separately, and because the signature of s has the arrow expression $s \to s$. Therefore, $closure(P)(X, Y)$ is also well-formed and has the sort s, because the signature of s (which is also the sort of $closure(P)$) has an arrow expression $s \times s \to s$, and because X and Y are variables of the sort s. The well-formedness of $closure(P)(X)(Y)(P)$ is established similarly.

On the other hand, $closure(P)(X, Y)(X, Y, Y)$ is not well-formed because, although the term $closure(P)(X, Y)$ is well-formed and has sort s, this sort does not possess an arrow expression that would allow this term to take three arguments.

Let Σ be a set of sorts over Δ. We say that Σ is *coherent* if different elements of Σ have different names (but elements of Σ having different names may have identical signatures).

We are now ready to define the language of Sorted HiLog. The alphabet of a Sorted HiLog language, $\mathcal{L}$, consists of:

- Δ — a set of sort names.
- Σ — a (possibly infinite) coherent set of sorts defined over Δ.
- For each sort $s \in \Sigma$:
  - $\mathcal{V}_s$ — a set of variables, which must be either empty or countably infinite.
  - $\mathcal{S}_s$ — a countable (empty, finite, or infinite) set of intensional parameters.

Since, according to the coherence requirement, different elements in Σ must have different names, a symbol of any sort, $s\sigma$, can unambiguously be said to have the sort s. Furthermore, without loss of information we can drop the name of any sort (leaving just the signature) if this name does not occur inside σ or in some other signature of Σ. This name can even be dropped from Δ, if we assume that the "anonymous" sorts are unique new symbols, distinct from those mentioned in Δ.

Terms of each sort are defined inductively as follows:

- A variable or an intensional parameter of sort s is a term of sort s.
- If $t_1, \ldots, t_n$, where $n > 0$, are terms of sorts $s_1, \ldots, s_n$, respectively, and t is a term of sort $\bar{s}\{\ldots, s_1 \times \ldots \times s_n \to s, \ldots\}$, then $t(t_1, \ldots, t_n)$ is a term of sort s.

It follows from the above that every term has a unique sort. However, since sorts encode *sets* of arrow expressions, a term can be applicable in many different contexts (even for the same number of arguments there can be several different contexts).

We will also need some control over syntactic formation of atomic formulas. For this purpose we introduce a subset of distinguished sorts, $\Delta_{\text{atomic}} \subseteq \Delta$, that designates certain sorts as being appropriate for atomic formulas. In other words, for a term to be counted as an *atomic formula*, it must have a sort, atm, such that atm $\in \Delta_{\text{atomic}}$. Complex formulas are built out of atomic ones in the standard manner using connectives and quantifiers.

Complexity of Checking Well-Formedness. The following result shows that, despite the polymorphic and recursive nature of sorts in Sorted HiLog, well-formedness of HiLog terms is easy to verify.

Proposition 1 Complexity of Well-Formedness. *Consider a term, T, in ordinary, unsorted HiLog, and let $\mathcal{L}$ be a language of Sorted HiLog. Whether or not T is well-formed as a sorted term in $\mathcal{L}$ can be checked using a sequence of elementary operations that is linear in the size of T, where arrow-fetching and retrieval of the sort declaration of variables and intensional parameters (in Sorted HiLog) are considered to be elementary operations.*[5]

Semantics of Sorted HiLog. The semantics for Sorted HiLog is a refinement of the semantics of ordinary HiLog, which is sketched in Section 2. A semantic structure, **M**, is a quadruple $\langle U, U_{true}, \mathcal{F}, \mathcal{I} \rangle$, where

- U is the domain of **M**; it has the structure of the union $\bigcup_{s \in \Delta} U_s$, where each U_s is *nonempty* and represents the subdomain corresponding to the sort name s;
- U_{true} is a subset of $\cup_{\text{atm} \in \Delta_{\text{atomic}}} U_{\text{atm}}$;[6]
- For each $\bar{s} \in \Delta$, $\mathcal{F}$ associates with each $d \in U_{\bar{s}}$ and each $k \geq 1$ a k-ary function $\mathcal{F}^{(k)}(d) : U^k \longrightarrow U$, denoted by $d_{\mathcal{F}}^{(k)}$. This function is subject to the restriction that if $s_1 \times \cdots \times s_k \to s$ is in the signature of $\bar{s}$ then $d_{\mathcal{F}}^{(k)}$ maps $U_{s_1} \times \ldots \times U_{s_k}$ into U_s;
- $\mathcal{I}$ associates with each intensional parameter, a, of sort $s \in \Delta$ an element $\mathcal{I}(a)$ in U_s.

Intensional equality in Sorted HiLog can be represented by the intensional parameter "=" whose sort may depend on the specific needs. The general theme is, however, that "=" must have signatures composed of the arrow expressions of the form $s \times \cdots \times s \to \text{atm}$, where $s \in \Delta$ and atm $\in \Delta_{\text{atomic}}$. The equality symbol has fixed interpretation under which $(\mathcal{I}(=))_{\mathcal{F}}^{(k)}(u_1, \ldots, u_n) \in U_{true}$ if and only if all $u_1, \ldots, u_n$ coincide in U.

The semantics of terms and formulas is now defined as in HiLog (Section 2) with the only addition that the variable assignments have to respect sorts, i.e., for each $s \in \Sigma$ they must map V_s — the variables of sort s — into U_s, the domain of s. Given a sort-preserving variable assignment, ν, and an atomic formula A, we write $\mathbf{M} \models_\nu A$ precisely when $\nu(A) \in U_{true}$. Satisfaction of complex formulas is defined as in ordinary HiLog.

---

[5] However, it should be noted that, for some sort structures, these may not be constant-time operations. For instance, retrieval of sort declaration may take $log(n)$ time, where n is the size of Σ, and arrow fetching may be arbitrarily complex. This is not the case, however, for the useful logics considered in this paper.

[6] Strictly speaking, it suffices to require only that $U_{true} \subseteq U$, because the elements of $U_{true} - \cup_{\text{atm} \in \Delta_{\text{atomic}}} U_{\text{atm}}$ are intensions of terms that are *not* atomic formulas, and so they have no truth value, anyway.

A model of a formula, ϕ, is any semantic structure, $\mathbf{M}$, such that $\mathbf{M} \models_\nu \phi$, for all ν. If ϕ is closed, then the truth (or falsehood) of $\mathbf{M} \models_\nu \phi$ does not depend on ν, and we can simply write $\mathbf{M} \models \phi$. The logical entailment relation, $\phi \models \psi$, is also defined as is customary in first-order logic: it holds if and only if every model of ϕ is also a model of ψ.

4 Applications

As explained earlier, the main drive behind the introduction of sorts was to provide a way to control the gap between the rigid well-formedness rules of classical predicate calculus and the sometimes-too-flexible syntax of ordinary HiLog, thereby enabling HiLog to better suit practical needs. As we shall see in this section, both predicate calculus and HiLog are special cases of Sorted HiLog—its two extremes, in a sense. We shall also describe several other sort structures with interesting rules of well-formedness, notably, various higher-order extensions of Datalog.

4.1 A Sort Structure for Ordinary HiLog

In ordinary HiLog, any term can be applied to any arbitrary number of terms. To make such expressions into well-formed terms on a Sorted HiLog, let $\Delta = \Delta_{\text{atomic}} = \{\text{atm}\}$ have exactly one symbol and suppose Σ contains exactly one sort:

$$\text{atm}\{\text{atm} \to \text{atm}, \text{atm} \times \text{atm} \to \text{atm}, \text{atm} \times \text{atm} \times \text{atm} \to \text{atm}\dots\} \qquad (2)$$

For instance, if t, a, and b had the sort atm, the term $t(a)(t,b)$ would be well-formed and have the sort atm because:

a	is well-formed and has sort atm;
$t(a)$	is well-formed and has the sort atm, because of the arrow atm $\to$ atm in the signature of t's sort; and
$t(a)(t,b)$	is well-formed because $t(a)$'s sort, atm, has the arrow atm $\times$ atm $\to$ atm in its signature.

The sort structure in (2) defines precisely the well-formedness rules used in ordinary HiLog, as described in Section 2. Notice that even though HiLog allows formation of terms with several levels of parentheses, there is no need for highly nested functional sorts. That is, the components of an arrow expression are all primitive sort names, which is possible because of the recursive structure of atm.

Proposition 2. *The syntax and the semantics of ordinary HiLog of Section 2 and of Sorted HiLog with the sort structure (2) coincide.*

4.2 A Sort Structure for Classical Predicate Calculus

The well-formedness rules of classical logic are fairly rigid: Each intensional parameter is designated to be a predicate or a function symbol and, furthermore, each symbol can be applied only to a fixed number of arguments that corresponds to the arity of the symbol. On top of this, arguments in a term can be constructed only out of function symbols. To capture this notion of well-formedness, let Δ contain the sort names fun_n and pred_n, where $n \geq 0$, for function and predicate symbols, respectively. In addition, Δ has a sort name trm for terms and atm for atomic formulas. The set of sorts for atomic formulas has only one element: $\Delta_{\text{atomic}} = \{\text{atm}\}$. Suppose, further, that signatures in Σ are defined as follows:

$$\begin{array}{ll} \text{fun}_n\{\times^n \text{trm} \to \text{trm}\} & \text{atm}\{\,\} \\ \text{pred}_n\{\times^n \text{trm} \to \text{atm}\} & \text{trm}\{\,\} \end{array} \qquad (3)$$

for each $n \geq 1$, where $\times^n s$ denotes $s \times \cdots \times s$ taken n times. The equality parameter, $=$, is given the sort pred_2. Assuming that only trm has a nonempty set of variables, the language of Sorted HiLog with (3) as a sort system would become isomorphic to the language of first-order predicate calculus.

As shown in [6], in general, logical entailment in ordinary HiLog is *not* identical to the classical logical entailment, even if we restrict our attention to the subset of classical first-order formulas. Consider the following formula:

$$((q(a) \leftarrow r(a)) \land (q(a) \to r(a))) \leftarrow \forall X \forall Y (X = Y)$$

This is a well-formed formula both in predicate calculus and in HiLog. It is a valid HiLog formula, but not in predicate calculus. Therefore, the result, below, cannot be taken for granted (although the proof is routine).

Proposition 3. *The syntax and the semantics of Sorted HiLog with the above sort structure are equivalent to the syntax and the semantics of first-order predicate calculus.*

4.3 Second-Order Calculus with Henkin-style Semantics

If, in the sort structure of the previous subsection, we permit variables of sorts fun_n and pred_n, we obtain a second-order predicate calculus with a semantics equivalent to Henkin's-style semantics described in [10, Section 4.4] (modulo the extensionality and comprehension axioms, which could be added). Due to space limitation, we shall not prove this result here.

The fact that Henkin-style calculus is a special case of Sorted HiLog is somewhat unexpected, since the semantics in [10, Section 4.4] seems radically different from the semantics of HiLog and because ordinary HiLog does not properly extend the aforesaid calculus. It is, therefore, interesting to see how a single semantic framework—HiLog and sorts—can model a wide variety of logics in a uniform way.

4.4 Higher-Order Datalog

Datalog is a sublanguage of pure Horn logic that has been extensively studied in the deductive database community (see, *e.g.*, [30]). The distinctive feature of Datalog is that function symbols with positive arities are not allowed. Due to this restriction, the Herbrand universe of every Datalog program is finite and consists of all the constants in the program.

Ordinary HiLog sketched in Section 2 does not support the notion of constants since any intensional parameter can be used as a function of any arity. However, HiLog with a suitably chosen sort structure is equivalent to Datalog. Moreover, by relaxing the sort structure, we can design various versions of Datalog with higher-order variables and predicates and still maintain finiteness of the Herbrand universe.

Let Δ consist of pred_n, for predicate symbols, where $n \geq 1$; atm, for atoms; and trm, for terms. Suppose $\Delta_{\text{atomic}} = \{\text{atm}\}$, i.e., atm is the only sort for atomic formulas. Let, further, Σ consist of all the sorts in (3), less the sort fun_n, for each $n \geq 1$. Assuming that only the sort trm has a nonempty set of variables, we get ordinary Datalog. Introduction of variables of the sort $pred_n$ ($n \geq 0$) and letting them be used as arguments to other predicate symbols yields a higher-order version of Datalog, which was dubbed DataHiLog in [24].

We can go still further and introduce structural parametric predicate symbols, such as closure(R) in (1). Caution must be taken here to preserve the decidability of Datalog. For instance, suppose that closure has the following sort (where cpred stands for "predicate constructor"):

$$cpred\{pred_2 \rightarrow pred_2\} \tag{4}$$

and let r have the sort $pred_2$. Then, the Herbrand base would no longer be finite, since there would be infinitely many predicates including r, closure(r), closure(closure(r)), ...

However, parametric predicates can still be supported, while maintaining a finite Herbrand universe. To break the recursion in (4), we could introduce a sort, $xpred_n$, for "complex predicates," which is synonymous to $pred_n$ in terms of the signature, but has a different sort name: $xpred_n\{\times^n trm \rightarrow atm\}$, $n \geq 0$.

Then we can modify (4) as follows: $cpred_{n,m}\{\times^n_{i=1} \alpha_i \rightarrow xpred_m\}$, $n, m \geq 0$, where each α_i is either trm or $pred_k$, for some $k \geq 0$. Now, if closure had the sort $cpred_{1,2}$ then closure(r)(X,Y) (where r is of sort $pred_2$) would be a well-formed formula, while closure(closure(r))(X,Y) would be ill-formed, because closure(r) has the sort $xpred_2$, which cannot be input to another application of closure.

4.5 Complex Objects

Complex objects are an extension of relational databases in which arguments of a relation may be relations themselves. In [6], we showed how HiLog can be used to model complex objects by providing "names" for relations. Consider the following example:

person(john, children(john))   children(john)(greg)   children(john)(sarah)

Extensional equality of relations can be approximated by additional axioms [6]. Most languages of complex objects, such as COL [1], use a sorted or typed framework. For instance, person is a binary predicate whose first argument is a term and the second argument is a unary relation, and children is a function, analogous to *data functions* in COL [1], that takes a term as an argument and returns a unary relation. This sort information gets lost when the same program is viewed as a formula in ordinary HiLog.

In contrast, in Sorted HiLog, one can assign sorts so that john, greg, and sarah would have the sort trm; person would have the sort $\{trm \times pred_1 \rightarrow atm\}$; and children would be a data function of the sort $\{trm \rightarrow pred_1\}$, where $pred_1\{trm \rightarrow atm\}$.

4.6 Encapsulation and Modules

A module in logic programming encapsulates a collection of predicate definitions. There are two problems with developing a logical theory of modules. One is to avoid name clashes between predicates used in different modules. The other is to represent a module definition as a logic formula. The latter requires a higher-order framework since predicates can be passed as parameters and returned as results. The development, below, follows the outline of [3].

A program now consists of a finite set of clauses and a finite set of basic module definitions. Each basic module definition consists of a module interface and a body that contains a finite number of clauses. The concrete syntax of a module definition may be the following:

$$\text{closure}(\text{In}, \text{Out}) \{ \begin{array}{l} \text{Out}(X, Y) \longleftarrow \text{In}(X, Y) \\ \text{Out}(X, Y) \longleftarrow \text{In}(X, Z) \wedge \text{Out}(Z, Y) \end{array} \}$$

Here, In is the input predicate variable, and Out is the variable exported by the module; it is instantiated to the transitive closure of In computed by the module. In [3], the above abstract syntax is given meaning using the following formula:

$$\forall \text{In} \exists \text{Out} (\quad \text{closure}(\text{In}, \text{Out}) \\ \wedge \forall X \forall Y (\text{Out}(X, Y) \longleftarrow \text{In}(Y, Y)) \qquad (5) \\ \wedge \forall X \forall Y \forall Z (\text{Out}(X, Y) \longleftarrow \text{In}(X, Z) \wedge \text{Out}(Z, Y)))$$

Notice that encapsulated predicates are represented by existential variables since only variables have local scope in logic and only existentially quantified variables can represent objects inaccessible through other variables. It is precisely this style of quantification that precludes changing the definition of encapsulated predicates from outside the module.

A query or any other clause may use the module closure just as any other predicate, e.g.,

$$? - \text{closure}(\text{parent}, \text{Ancest}) \wedge \text{Ancest}(\text{bill}, X) \wedge \text{closure}(\text{boss}, \text{Mngr}) \wedge \text{Mngr}(X, \text{bob})$$

This query would return all descendants of bill who are managers of bob, provided that parent(a,b) means that a is a parent of b and boss(c,d) stands for "c is a boss of d."

Now, in [3], the expression (5) was understood as a formula in second-order predicate calculus. With the advent of HiLog, it turned out that viewing (5) as a HiLog formula leads to a more tractable semantics of logical modules. If ordinary HiLog gives a satisfactory semantics for modules, then how does Sorted HiLog fit into the picture?

One problem in (5) is that there is an existential quantifier of the kind that cannot be handled directly by most logic programming systems. A natural way to implement modules, then, is to use Skolemization to transform module definitions into ordinary Horn clauses. Since Skolemization preserves unsatisfiability, query answers obtained by refutational proof procedures, such as SLD-resolution, are preserved. Unfortunately, the problem with Skolemization found in ordinary HiLog (see [5]) precludes this natural implementation. In contrast, as is shown in [5], Skolemization in Sorted HiLog can be performed pretty much as in classical logic and, thus, it appears to be a better vehicle for implementing logical modules.

4.7 Sorted Meta Programming

Prolog applications often rely on meta-programming techniques, which require flexibility of the kind HiLog syntax can provide. For instance, consider the following program:

$$\begin{array}{l} \text{call}(A) \longleftarrow A \\ \text{call}(P, X) \longleftarrow \text{ispredicate}(P) \wedge P(X) \\ \text{call}(P, X, Y) \longleftarrow \text{ispredicate}(P) \wedge P(X, Y) \\ \text{call}(P(X), Y) \longleftarrow \text{ispredicate}(P) \wedge P(X, Y) \\ \text{call}(P(X), Y, Z) \longleftarrow \text{ispredicate}(P) \wedge P(X, Y, Z) \\ \text{ispredicate}(\text{ispredicate}) \\ \text{ispredicate}(\text{call}) \\ \text{ispredicate}(p) \qquad \% \text{ for every predicate, p, in the program} \end{array} \qquad (6)$$

Here, call is a meta-predicate[7] that 1) "executes" atomic formulas passed to it as an argument (Clause 1 in (6)); 2) applies predicate symbols to arguments and then executes the resulting atoms (Clauses 2 and 3); and 3) accepts a "partial-load" atoms as a first argument and then applies them to an appropriate number of terms (Clauses 4 and 5).

The problem with the above program is that if call is passed a wrong first argument (that is not an atom, a partial-load atom, or a predicate) the subgoal will simply fail without alerting the user to the problem. Current systems of sorts or types are not expressive enough to handle meta-programs, such as above. However, in Sorted HiLog, ill-formed expressions can be detected at compile time by specifying sorts appropriately. To see this, let Δ contain sort names for:

- function and predicate symbols: fun_n and pred_n, where $n \geq 0$;
- terms: trm;
- ordinary and built-in atomic formulas: atm and sysatm;
- partial-load atomic formulas: partatm;
- meta-predicates call and ispredicate: callsort and ispredsort.

The set of sorts for atomic formulas consists of two elements: $\Delta_{\text{atomic}} = \{\text{atm}, \text{sysatm}\}$. Suppose, further, that signatures in Σ are defined as follows:

$$
\begin{aligned}
&\text{trm} \left\{ \right\} \\
&\text{atm} \left\{ \right\} \\
&\text{sysatm} \left\{ \right\} \\
&\text{fun}_n \left\{ \times^n \text{trm} \to \text{trm} \right\}, \text{ for all } n \geq 0 \\
&\text{ispredsort} \left\{ \begin{array}{l} \text{pred}_n \to \text{sysatm} \\ \text{callsort} \to \text{sysatm} \\ \text{ispredsort} \to \text{sysatm} \end{array} \right\}, \text{ for all } n \geq 0 \\
&\text{pred}_n \left\{ \begin{array}{l} \times^n \text{trm} \to \text{atm} \\ \times^m \text{trm} \to \text{partatm} \end{array} \right\}, \text{ for all } n \geq 0 \text{ and } 1 \leq m < n \\
&\text{callsort} \left\{ \begin{array}{l} \text{atm} \to \text{sysatm} \\ \text{sysatm} \to \text{sysatm} \\ \text{partatm} \times \text{trm} \to \text{sysatm} \\ \text{partatm} \times \text{trm} \times \text{trm} \to \text{sysatm} \end{array} \right\}
\end{aligned}
\tag{7}
$$

Under this sort structure, the above program is well-formed, provided that the variable A in (6) has the sort atm or sysatm; P has sort pred_1, pred_2, or pred_3, as appropriate; and the variables X, Y, and Z are of sort trm. Moreover, passing a non-atom to call in the first clause in (6) will be impossible, since the resulting term will not be well-formed. Similarly, the variables in other clauses in (6) will have to be bound to appropriate entities in order to comply with the above sort structure.

Although sort systems for meta-programming need further investigation, we believe that the polymorphic and recursive sort structure of Sorted HiLog represents a step in the direction towards achieving this goal. One possible extension here is the incorporation of subsorts, as in order-sorted logics [14, 28]. However, a difficulty arises from the interaction between subsorts and recursive poly-sorts. It seems that a "brute-force" approach to such richer sort systems does not lead to an elegant solution.

---

[7] Of course, it is not a meta-predicate in HiLog, but it is in classical logic programming.

5 Conclusion

We presented *Sorted HiLog*, a logic that enhances ordinary HiLog [6] with recursive poly-sorts. The rules of well-formedness for Sorted HiLog enable it to simulate the syntax of a wide range of logic languages, from predicate calculus to the original version of HiLog, as described in [6]. Within this range, we find a pair of decidable, higher-order extensions of Datalog and also the second-order predicate calculus with Henkin-style semantics (see [10, Section 4.4]).

Applications of deductive databases and logic programming demand more flexible syntax than what is offered by languages based on classical predicate calculus (or on the "pure" subset of Prolog). This need is partly filled by the ordinary HiLog, as described in [6]. However, to facilitate understanding and debugging of programs, expressions are often classified into different sorts and restrictions are imposed to guarantee well-formedness. Sorted HiLog is capable of accommodating both of these seemingly conflicting goals. It also appears to capture some important aspects of well-formedness in meta-programs and, we believe, provides a suitable basis for further studies of sort systems for meta programming and schema manipulation. With efficient implementation as part of the XSB system, Sorted HiLog would allow users to choose sort structures for different database applications—all without sacrificing the syntactic flexibility of HiLog.

References

1. S. Abiteboul and S. Grumbach. COL: A logic-based language for complex objects. In *Workshop on Database Programming Languages*, pages 253–276, Roscoff, France, September 1987.
2. C. Beeri, S. Naqvi, O. Shmueli, and S. Tsur. Sets and negation in a logic database language (LDL). Technical report, MCC, 1987.
3. W. Chen. A theory of modules based on second-order logic. In *IEEE Symposium on Logic Programming (SLP)*, pages 24–33, September 1987.
4. W. Chen and M. Kifer. Polymorphic types in higher-order logic programming. Technical Report 93/20, Department of Computer Science, SUNY at Stony Brook, December 1993.
5. W. Chen and M. Kifer. Sorted hilog: Sorts in higher-order logic programming. Technical Report 94/8, SUNY at Stony Brook, 1994. Available via anonymous ftp to *cs.sunysb.edu* in *pub/TechReports/kifer/sorts.ps.Z*.
6. W. Chen, M. Kifer, and D.S. Warren. HiLog: A foundation for higher-order logic programming. *Journal of Logic Programming*, 15(3):187–230, February 1993.
7. W. Chen and D.S. Warren. C-logic for complex objects. In *ACM SIGACT-SIGMOD-SIGART Symposium on Principles of Database Systems (PODS)*, pages 369–378, March 1989.
8. A. Church. A formulation of the simple theory of types. *Journal of Symbolic Logic*, 5:56–68, 1940.
9. A.G. Cohn. A more expressive formulation of many sorted logic. *Journal of Automated Reasoning*, 3:113–200, 1987.
10. H.B. Enderton. *A Mathematical Introduction to Logic*. Academic Press, 1972.
11. T. Fruehwirth. Polymorphic type checking for Prolog in HiLog. In *6th Israel Conference on Artificial Intelligence and Computer Vision*, Tel Aviv, Israel, 1989.
12. J.A. Goguen and J. Meseguer. Eqlog: Equality, types, and generic modules for Logic Programming. In D. DeGroot and G. Lindstrom, editors, *Logic Programming, Functions, Relations, and Equations*. Prentice Hall, 1986.
13. M. Hanus. Polymorphic higher-order programming in prolog. In *Intl. Conference on Logic Programming (ICLP)*, pages 382–397, Lisboa, Portugal, 1989. MIT Press.
14. M. Hanus. Parametric order-sorted types in logic programming. Technical Report 377, Universitaet Dortmund, Fachbereich Informatik, Dortmund, FRG, January 1991.

15. P. Hill and R. Topor. A semantics for typed logic programs. In F. Pfenning, editor, *Types in Logic Programming*, pages 1–62. The MIT Press, 1992.
16. M. Kifer, G. Lausen, and J. Wu. Logical foundations of object-oriented and frame-based languages. Technical Report 93/06 (a revision of 90/14), Department of Computer Science, SUNY at Stony Brook, April 1993. To appear in Journal of ACM. Available in *pub/TechReports/kifer/flogic.ps.Z* by anonymous ftp to *cs.sunysb.edu*.
17. M. Kifer and J. Wu. A first-order theory of types and polymorphism in logic programming. In *Intl. Symposium on Logic in Computer Science (LICS)*, pages 310–321, Amsterdam, The Netherlands, July 1991. Expanded version: TR 90/23 under the same title, Department of Computer Science, University at Stony Brook, July 1990.
18. I.S. Mumick and K.A. Ross. An architecture for declarative object-oriented databases. In *Proceedings of the JICSLP-92 Workshop on Deductive Databases*, pages 21–30, November 1992.
19. A. Mycroft and R.A. O'Keefe. A polymorphic type system for Prolog. *Artificial Intelligence*, 23:295–307, 1984.
20. G. Nadathur and D. Miller. Higher-order horn clauses. *Journal of ACM*, 37(4):777–814, October 1990.
21. G. Nadathur and F. Pfenning. Types in higher-order logic programming. In F. Pfenning, editor, *Types in Logic Programming*, pages 245–283. The MIT Press, 1992.
22. G. Phipps, M.A. Derr, and K.A. Ross. Glue-Nail: A deductive database system. In *ACM SIGMOD Conference on Management of Data*, pages 308–317, 1991.
23. K.A. Ross. Relations with relation names as arguments: Algebra and calculus. In *ACM SIGACT-SIGMOD-SIGART Symposium on Principles of Database Systems (PODS)*, pages 346–353, May 1992.
24. K.A. Ross. On negation in HiLog. *Journal of Logic Programming*, 18(1):27–53, January 1994.
25. K. Sagonas, T. Swift, and D.S. Warren. XSB as an efficient deductive database engine. In *ACM SIGMOD Conference on Management of Data*, pages 442–453, May 1994.
26. Konstantinos F. Sagonas and David S. Warren. A compilation scheme for HiLog. Submitted for publication, 1994.
27. G. Smolka. Logic programming with polymorphically order-sorted types. In J. Grabowski, P. Lescanne, and W. Wechler, editors, *Algebraic and Logic Programming*, volume 343 of *Lecture Notes in Computer Science*, pages 53–70. Springer-Verlag, 1988.
28. G. Smolka, W. Nutt, J.A. Goguen, and J. Meseguer. Order-sorted equational computation. Technical Report SEKI Report SR-87-14, Universität Kaiserslautern, West Germany, December 1987.
29. T. Swift and D.S. Warren. Compiling OLDT evaluation: Background and overview. Technical report, Department of Computer Science, SUNY at Stony Brook, 1992.
30. J.F. Ullman. *Principles of Database and Knowledge-Base Systems, Volume 1*. Computer Science Press, 1988.
31. C. Walther. A mechanical solution of Schubert's Steamroller by many-sorted resolution. *Artificial Intelligence*, 26:217–224, 1985.
32. J. Xu and D.S. Warren. A type inference system for Prolog. In *Joint Intl. Conference and Symposium on Logic Programming (JICSLP)*, pages 604–619, 1988.
33. E. Yardeni, T. Fruehwirth, and E. Shapiro. Polymorphically typed logic programs. In *Intl. Conference on Logic Programming (ICLP)*, Paris, France, June 1991.

The Average Length
of Keys and
Functional Dependencies
in (Random) Databases

J. Demetrovics[1*], G.O.H. Katona[2*], D. Miklos[2*], O. Seleznjev[3**], B. Thalheim[4]

[1] Comp. & Autom. Inst., Hungarian Academy, Kende u. 13-17, H-1111 Budapest
[2] Mathematical Inst., Hungarian Academy, POBox 127, H-1364 Budapest
[3] Moscow State University, Dept. of Mathematics and Mechanics, RU-119 899, Moscow
[4] Cottbus Technical University, Computer Science Inst., POBox 101344, D-03013 Cottbus
h935dem@ella.hu, h1164kat@ella.hu, h1162mik@ella.hu, seleznev@compnet.msu.su,
thalheim@informatik.tu-cottbus.de

Abstract. Practical database applications engender the impression that sets of constraints are rather small and that large sets are unusual and caused by bad design decisions. Theoretical investigations show, however, that minimal constraint sets are potentially very large. Their size can be estimated to be exponential in terms of the number of attributes. The gap between belief and theory causes non-acceptance of theoretical results. However, beliefs are related to average cases.
The theory known so far considered worst case complexity. This paper aims at developing a theory of *average case complexity*. Several statistic models and asymptotics of corresponding probabilities are investigated for random databases. We show that exponential complexity of independent key sets and independent sets of functional dependencies is rather unusual. Depending on the size of relations almost all minimal keys have a length which mainly depends on the size. The number of minimal keys of other length is exponentially small compared with the number of minimal keys of the derived length. Further, if a key is valid in a relation then it is probably the minimal key. The same results hold for functional dependencies.

1 Average Length of Keys

In databases keys play an important role. Records or tuples can be identified, recorded and searched in a unique way. Generally, a key is an attribute (or a combination of several attributes) that uniquely identifies a particular record. Keys are used everywhere in the database to serve as references to tuples identified by values. Keys

---

* Supported by the Hungarian National Foundation of Scientific Research, Grant No. 2575.
** Supported by the German Natural Science Research Council, contract BB-II-B1-3141-211(94).

are generalized to functional dependencies. Those specify the relationship between two attribute sets. In a relation the values of the first set determine the values of the second set. Functional dependencies are used for normalization of database systems. If a database designer knows the complete set of functional dependencies in a given application then unpredictable behavior during updates and update anomalies can be avoided. Therefore, the size of functional dependency and key sets is of great interest. If this size is exponential in the number of attributes then the entire approach becomes unmanageable.

In practical applications it is often the case that sets of keys and sets of functional dependencies are rather small. Based on this observation practioners believe that those sets are small in most applications. If there is an application with a large set of constraints then this application is considered to be poorly designed. This belief of engineers is opposed by theoretical results. It can be proven that key sets and sets of functional dependencies are indeed exponential. Hence the problem which case should be considered the normal one: the observation of practioners or the theory of theoreticians. The solution to this gap between beliefs of practioners and results of theoreticians can be given by developing a theory of average case complexity. There are cases in which worst case complexity really occurs. In most cases, as shown below, worst case complexity is unlikely. Thus, for average case considerations, the observation of practioners is well-founded by the approach to be developed below.

There are several reasons why complexity bounds are of interest. Firstly, most of the known algorithms, e.g. for normalization, depend on the set of all minimal keys or nonredundant sets of dependencies. Therefore, their algorithmic complexity depends on the cardinality of these sets. Secondly, the maintenance complexity of a database depends on the number of integrity constraints are under consideration. Therefore, if the cardinality of constraint sets is large then maintenance becomes infeasible. Furthermore, cardinality gives an indication whether algorithms are of interest for practical purposes since the complexity of most known algorithms is measured by the input length. For instance, algorithms for the construction of a minimal key are bounded by the maximal number of minimal keys. The decision problem whether there is a minimal key with at most k attributes is NP-complete. The decision problem whether two sets of functional dependencies are equivalent is polynomial in the size of the two sets and hence exponential.

Two different approaches can be used for specification of key set behavior:

1. The worst case size is considered.

2. The average case complexity is considered.

Although the second approach is more reliable only very few results are known (Thalheim (1991)). In almost all relations with m tuples on domains with $\mid dom(A_i) \mid = 2$ $(1 \leq i \leq n)$ the average length $av_n(m, 2)$ of minimal keys is bounded by

$$\lfloor \log_2 m \rfloor \ \leq \ av_n(m, 2) \ \leq \ 2 \lfloor \log_2 m \rfloor \ .$$

The worst case complexity has been investigated in a large number of papers (see, for example, Beeri, Dowd, Fagin, Statman (1984), Bekessy, Demetrovics, Hannak, Frankl, Katona (1980), Demetrovics, Katona (1983), Mannila, Raihä (1992),

Thalheim (1992)). The number of keys and minimal keys for Bernoulli databases is investigated in Andreev (1982). Some of his results are close to those presented in sections 3 and 4. However, his techniques use rather complicated graph technique and are not directly generalizable. The number of keys of a relation is determined by the maximal number of elements in a Sperner set. More precisely, given a relational schema $R = (\{B_1, ..., B_n\}, \emptyset)$ and a relation r from $SAT(R)$. Then r has at most

$$\binom{n}{\lfloor \frac{n}{2} \rfloor}$$

different minimal keys. This estimate is sharp, i.e a relation can be constructed with exactly this number of minimal keys.

For the solution, we now use the following approach. We consider random databases of a limited size with a constant number of attributes and restricted domains. Then we derive the likelihood of constraint validity. Next, we show how to estimate probabilities. Based on these results conditions for constraint sets can be derived. The validity of constraints for which the conditions are violated is highly unlikely in the databases under consideration. Finally, the limitations can be omitted and general conditions can be developed.

We can directly apply the results below to the solution of several database problems. Some of them are the following:

· Results of this paper can be directly applied to heuristic support for database design. If the size of relations is restricted by a certain function then the size of minimal keys can be considered in accordance to the expected length. This approach has been used in the design system RAD (Albrecht et al. (1994)).

· Database mining aims at discovering semantics in real existing databases. If any possible constraint or even any possible key is checked database mining is infeasible. However, if we consider the statistic-based approach of this paper we only have to check the validity of a very small portion of constraints provided the size of the database is limited by certain bounds.

· Often stochastic algorithms are applied to solving difficult tasks in databases. Algorithms of the Monte-Carlo or of the Las-Vegas type are more reliable if they can be applied to databases with predictable constraint sets. Thus, our approach can be used to determine in which case such algorithms are useful and in which case they should not be applied.

This short list of application areas for our results is not exhaustive. We feel that the main application of our approach should be database design. The approach restricts the set of constraints to be considered to those which are more likely.

Section 2 discusses the behavior of functional dependencies in random databases after presenting basic notions in Section 2. Sections 4 and 5 are devoted to keys in random databases. Section 6 discusses some extensions of the approach. Proofs of results are given in Seleznjev, Thalheim (1994) and Demetrovics J., Katona G.O.H., and Miklos (1994) and are omitted due to space limitations.

2 Basic notions

We use some definitions of the theory of relational databases. Given sets $D_1, \ldots, D_n$ call *domains*, an n-ary relation R defined over $D_1, \ldots, D_n$ is a subset of the cartesian product $D_1 \times \ldots \times D_n$. An *attribute* is a name assigned to a domain of a relation. Any value associated with an attribute is called attribute value. The attributes names must be distinct. The symbol U will be used to denote the set of all n attribute of R. We assume in sequel that $U = \{1, \ldots, n\}$. A set of attributes $A, A \subseteq U$, is called *key* of R, if for every n-tuple of R the values of attributes in A uniquely determine the values of the attributes in U, i.e. for any $i, j = 1, \ldots, m, i \neq j$ tuples $t_i(A) \neq t_j(A)$, where m denotes the number of tuples in a relation R. Write in sequel $M = m(m-1)/2$. A key A is called a *minimal* key if no any proper subset of A is a key. Consider a relation (or database) R as a matrix with m rows (tuples) and n columns (attributes). Note that this definition of a database implies that some of the tuples can be identical. Let $A \subset U, B \subset U \setminus A$. Following Armstrong (1974), we say that A *determines* B (or B *functionally depends* on A), if there are no tuples in R with the same data in columns A but different in columns B. Denote functional dependency B on A by $A \to B$. We say that R is a random database, if tuples $t_i(U), i = 1, \ldots, m$, are independent and identically distributed random vectors. Assume also that domains $D_i, i = 1, \ldots, m$, be a finite integer sets and distribution of $t(U)$ is defined by probabilities $P\{t(1) = k(1), \ldots, t(n) = k(n)\} = p(k(U))$, $k(U) = (k(1), \ldots, k(n)), k(i) \in D_i, i = 1, \ldots, n$. In further considerations we suppose that distribution $p(k(U))$ are given. We call a random database R *standard Bernoulli database*, if $D_k = \{1, 0\}$ and $t(i), i = 1, \ldots, n$ are standard Bernoulli random variables $P\{t(i) = 0\} = P\{t(i) = 0\} = \frac{1}{2}$, and therefore $p(k(U)) = 2^{-n}$. Say R is a *uniform random database*, if $t(i), i = 1, \ldots, n$ are independent and $P\{t(i) = k(i)\} = |D_i|^{-1}, i = 1, \ldots, n,$, i.e. $p(k(A)) = \prod_{i \in U} |D_i|^{-1}$, where for any finite set $A, |A|$ denotes its cardinality.

Based on information about distribution $p(k(A))$ we study some probability problems of database theory. At first we estimated the probability of existence of functional dependency in a random database. Some more general problems connected with functional dependency and keys are investigated as well. We consider Poisson approximation to the distribution of random number of cases N, when functional dependency fails. Analogously we investigate an asymptotic distribution for a random number of coincidences for a set of attributes X when $a(n) \to \infty$ as $n \to \infty$. Similar results for arbitrary random databases with some uniformity condition for a distribution $p(k(X)) = \prod_{i \in X} |D_i|^{-1}$ are obtained. Asymptotic distribution of a size of a minimal key and mean number of keys in standard Bernoulli database are also investigated. We consider for a set of attributes A in a standard Bernoulli database probability that A is a minimal key. In more general case of arbitrary uniform random database some asymptotic results for this probability can be obtained. Some of the problems in discrete mathematics (i.e. selection of a base for a boolean algebra (Sachkov (1982)), a random strategy of search (Ahlswede, Wegener (1979)) are close to asymptotic results for keys in random databases discussed in Section 4.

3 Functional dependencies in random databases

In some cases a set B functionally depends on a set of attributes A deterministically, e.g. if $t(i) = f_i(t(A)), i \in B$, then clearly $P\{A \to B\} = 1$. But in random databases this property connected also with joint distribution of $t(A)$ and $t(B)$. It is of interest that even for statistically independent random vectors $t(A)$ and $t(B)$ the probability of functional dependency $A \to B$ may be close to 1. We can call this case *artificial dependency*.

The notion of functional dependency can be generalized in the following way. We call that a set of attributes A *almost determines* a set of attributes $B, B \subseteq U \backslash A$, if the number of tuples with *functional independency* condition, i.e. $t(A) = t'(A), t(B) \neq t'(B)$, is a finite number $N = N(n)$, say. Let $m = m(n) \to \infty$ as $n \to \infty, n$ is a number of attributes in R.

Consider at first the case of a uniform random database. Denote by

$$a = a(n) = \sum_{i \in A} \log_2 |D_i|, b = b(n) = |B| \geq 1, \lambda(n) = M \frac{1}{2^a}(1 - \frac{1}{2^b}).$$

For a standard Bernoulli database we have $a(n) = |A|$. The following theorem allows to estimate the distribution function of number of functional independencies N.

Theorem 1 *Let R be a uniform random database, $c_1 \frac{1}{a(n)} \leq \lambda(n) \leq c_0 \frac{a(n)}{\ln a(n)}$, where $0 < c_0 < e^{-2}\frac{1}{2}\ln 2, c_1 > 0$. Then there exists $\gamma > 0$ such that*

$$P\{N = s\} = \frac{\lambda(n)^s}{s!}e^{-\lambda(n)}(1 + O(e^{-\gamma \frac{a(n)}{\ln a(n)}}))$$

as $n \to \infty$, uniformly in $0 \leq s \leq c_0 \frac{a(n)}{\ln a(n)}$.

We can interpret the assertion of Theorem 1 as following. The number of functional independencies has asymptotically Poisson distribution with parameter $\lambda(n)$. Clearly that the case of functional dependency simply follows by Theorem 1 since $P\{A \to B\} = P\{N = 0\}$.

Corollary 1 *Let R be a uniform random database and the conditions of Theorem 1 are valid. Then there exists $\gamma > 0$ such that*

$$P\{A \to B\} = e^{-\lambda(n)}(1 + O(e^{-\gamma \frac{a(n)}{\ln a(n)}})) \text{ as } n \to \infty.$$

To formulate the next corollary we introduce some additional denotations. Write

$$p(\alpha, \beta) = \begin{cases} 0, & \text{if } \alpha = -\infty, \\ \exp\{-2^{-(\alpha+1)}c_\beta\}, & \text{if } |\alpha| < \infty, \\ 1, & \text{if } \alpha = +\infty, \end{cases}$$

where

$$c_\beta = \begin{cases} 1, & \text{if } \beta = +\infty, \\ 1 - 2^{-\beta}, & \text{if } 1 \leq \beta < +\infty. \end{cases}$$

Denote by $\alpha(n) = \sum_{i \in A} \log_2 |D_i| - 2\log_2 m$. And if $\lambda(n) \to \lambda_0, 0 \leq \lambda_0 \leq +\infty$, i.e. $\alpha(n) \to \alpha_0, |\alpha_0| \leq \infty$, as $n \to \infty$, we obtain the following corollary.

Corollary 2 *Let R be a uniform random database. Let $b(n) \to \beta \geq 1$ and $\alpha(n) \to \alpha_0$, as $n \to \infty$, $|\alpha_0| \leq \infty$. Then $P\{A \to B\} \to p(\alpha_0, \beta)$ as $n \to \infty$. Moreover if $|\alpha_0| < \infty$, then for any $s = 0, 1, \ldots$,*

$$P\{N = s\} \to \frac{\lambda_0^s}{s!}e^{-\lambda_0} \text{ as } n \to \infty, \quad \lambda_0 = 2^{-(\alpha_0+1)}c_\beta.$$

Thus the number of functional independencies N converges in distribution to a Poisson random variable with parameter λ_0.

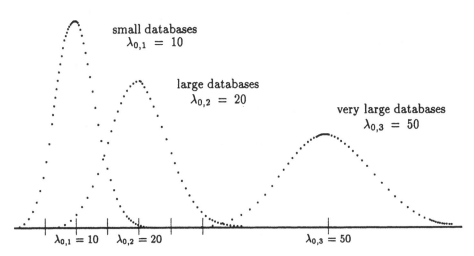

Fig. 1. Poisson distribution of Independencies in Different Databases with Different Parameters

Different distributions are shown in Figure 1. The parameter λ restricts the length of left sides in functional dependencies. Therefore, the size of the database very stongly indicates the length of possible candidates for left sides of functional dependencies. If the database is small then $\lambda_{0,1}$ is small and only sets A with a length in this small interval are likely to be left sides. If the database is large then $\lambda_{0,3}$ is large. The interval is determined by some small portion of possible candidates. Therefore, there exists a subset $\mathcal{F}_0(B)$ of all possible functional dependencies $\mathcal{F}(B)$ with right side B which is likely. This set is much smaller than $\mathcal{F}(B)$ and, for the average case, a functional dependency from $\mathcal{F}(B)$ which is valid in the random database belongs with high probability to $\mathcal{F}_0(B)$. Thus, for example, heuristic algorithms which are used to check validity of functional dependencies from $\mathcal{F}(B)$ should begin with constraints from $\mathcal{F}_0(B)$. In this case, they succeed much faster.

The high in curves depend upon the size of B. If B is smaller then the curves are zoomed up. In this case the intervall with the most probable candidates gets smaller. If B is large then the intervall gets larger. We shall return to these curves during consideration of keys.

In the case of general random database R we introduce some additional denotations. For any tuple $t(U)$ write

$$p(k(A), k(B)) = P\{t(A) = k(A), t(B) = k(B)\},$$
$$p(k(A)/k(B)) = P\{t(B) = k(B)/t(A) = k(A)\},$$

i.e. $p(k(A)/k(B))$ is a conditional probability of the event $t(B) = k(B)$ when $t(A) = k(A)$, $k(A) \in \prod_{i \in A} D_i$, $k(B) \in \prod_{i \in B} D_i$, with cartesian product of domains. Write

$$\lambda(n) = \frac{m(m-1)}{2} \sum_{k(A), k(B)} p(k(A))(1 - p(k(B)/k(A)))p(k(B), k(A)) =$$
$$ME[p(t(A))(1 - p(t(B)/t(A)))].$$

where $M = m(m-1)/2$. Introduce the following uniformity condition. There exist $K_i > 0, i = 1, 2, 3$, such that for any $k(A) \in \prod_{i \in A} D_i$, $k(B) \in \prod_{i \in B} D_i$,

$$\frac{K_1}{2^{a(n)}} \leq p(k(A)) \leq \frac{K_2}{2^{a(n)}}; \qquad p(k(B)/k(A)) \leq K_3 < 1, \qquad (1)$$

where $a(n) = \sum_{i \in A} \log_2 |D_i|$.

Theorem 2 *Let R be a random database with a given distribution $p(k(A), k(B))$. Let the assumptions of Theorem 1 and (1) hold. Then the assertion of Theorem 1 for the number of functional independencies $N = N(n)$ is valid.*

Clearly the analogous corollaries to Corollaries 1 and 2 can be formulated for the case of general random database too.

Corollary 3 *Let R be a random database with given distribution $p(k(A), k(B))$. Let the assumptions of Corollary 1 and (1) hold. Then the assertion of Corollary 1 for $P\{A \to B\}$ is valid.*

Corollary 4 *Let R be a random database with a given distribution $p(k(A), k(B))$ and (1) hold. Let $\lambda(n) \to \lambda_0$ as $n \to \infty, 0 \leq \lambda_0 \leq +\infty$. Then $P\{A \to B\} \to e^{-\lambda_0}$ as $n \to \infty$. Moreover for $|\lambda_0| < \infty$, and for any $s = 0, 1, \ldots,$*

$$P\{N = s\} \to \frac{\lambda_0^s}{s!} e^{-\lambda_0} \quad \text{as } n \to \infty.$$

The results of Theorem 2 explain that the property of functional dependency for a random database with increasing number of tuples m is related to two main factors:

- determination of an attribute set A (probability $p(k(A))$),
- correlation between attribute values in A and B (conditional probability $p(k(B)/k(A))$).

Therefore, in the case that the values in $dom(A_i)$ are not uniformly distributed the results presented in Theorem 1 are valid.

4 Keys in random databases

The asymptotic results and corresponding proofs for probability for a set of attributes A to be a key are very close to the problem of functional dependency when $b(n) = \sum_{i \in B} |D_i| \to \infty$ as $n \to \infty$. But in the case of an uniform random database there is an exact expression for the corresponding probability $P\{R \models A\}$. Write as beforehand $a = a(n) = \sum_{i \in A} \log_2 |D_i|$. For a standard Bernoulli database we have $a(n) = |A|$.

The notion of a key can be generalized in the following way. We call that a set of attributes A a key with a finite number of exceptions, if the number of tuples with $t(A) = t'(A)$ is a finite random variable $N = N(n)$, say. Then $P\{R \models A\} = P\{N = 0\}$. A random number N for a database R means a number of tuples with coincident values for a set of attributes A. Let $m = m(n) \to \infty$ as $n \to \infty$, n is a number of attributes in R.

Consider at first the case of a uniform random database with $\lambda(n) = M2^{-a(n)}$ and $\alpha(n) = a(n) - 2\log_2 m$.

Theorem 3 *Let R be a uniform random database and $m \leq 2^{a(n)}$. Then the following statements are valid:*

(i) $P\{R \models A\} = \prod_{j=1}^{m-1}(1 - j2^{-a(n)})$,

(ii) if $m < 2^{(2-\gamma)a(n)/3}, 0 < \gamma < 2$, then

$$P\{R \models A\} = e^{-\lambda(n)}(1 + O(2^{-\gamma a(n)})) \ as \ n \to \infty,$$

(iii) if $\lambda(n) \to \lambda_0, 0 \leq \lambda_0 \leq \infty$, i.e. $\alpha(n) \to \alpha_0$, as $n \to \infty, |\alpha_0| \leq \infty$, then

$$P\{R \models A\} \to e^{-\lambda_0} = \exp\{-2^{-(\alpha_0+1)}\} \ as \ n \to \infty,$$

(iv) if $\lambda(n) \to \lambda_0$ as $n \to \infty, 0 \leq \lambda_0 < \infty$, then for any $s = 0, 1, \ldots,$

$$P\{N = s\} \to \frac{\lambda_0^s}{s!}e^{-\lambda_0} \ as \ n \to \infty,$$

(v) if $c_1 \frac{1}{a(n)} \leq \lambda(n) \leq c_0 \frac{a(n)}{\ln a(n)}$, where $0 < c_0 < \frac{1}{2}e^{-2}\ln 2, c_1 > 0$. Then there exists $\gamma > 0$ such that

$$P\{N = s\} = \frac{\lambda(n)^s}{s!}e^{-\lambda(n)}(1 + O(e^{-\gamma \frac{a(n)}{\ln a(n)}}))$$

$$as \ n \to \infty \ uniformly \ in \ 0 \leq s \leq c_0 \frac{a(n)}{\ln a(n)}.$$

Therefore, worst case complexity results are highly unlikely. In the remaining cases, if m, n and the size of domains fulfill the conditions *(iv)* or *(v)* then we observe the same behavior as shown in Figure 1.

Consider now a general random database R with a given distribution of a tuple

$$P\{t(A) = k(A)\} = p(k(A)), k(A) \in \prod_{i \in A} D_i.$$

Denote by

$$\lambda(n) = \frac{m(m-1)}{2} \sum_{k(A)} p(k(A))^2 = ME[p(t(A))].$$

and introduce also the following condition (cf. (1)) There exist $K_i > 0, i = 1, 2$, such that for any $k(A) \in \prod_{i \in A} D_i$,

$$\frac{K_1}{2^{a(n)}} \leq p(k(A)) \leq \frac{K_2}{2^{a(n)}}. \tag{2}$$

Theorem 4 *Let R be a random database with a given distribution $p(k(A))$ and for an attribute set A condition (2) hold. Let $\lambda(n) \to \lambda_0$ as $n \to \infty$. Then assertions (iii)-(v) of Theorem 3 are valid.*

The assertion of Theorem 4 can be interpreted in a different way. Denote by ν_n an integer random variable which equals size of a minimal subset B in a set of attributes A, when B is a key, i.e. the size of a minimal key in $A, |A| = c(n)$. Then

$$P\{\nu_n \leq c(n)\} = P\{R \models A, |A| = c(n)\}.$$

Corollary 5 *Let (2) hold and $\lambda(n) \to \lambda_0$ as $n \to \infty, 0 \leq \lambda_0 \leq \infty$. Then*

$$P\{\nu_n \leq c(n)\} \to e^{-\lambda_0} \text{ as } n \to \infty.$$

For a standard Bernoulli database we have $c(n) = a(n) = |A| = \alpha(n) + 2\log_2 m$. Therefore, if $\alpha(n) \to \alpha_0$ as $n \to \infty$ $|\alpha_0| \leq \infty$, then

$$P\{\nu_n \leq a(n)\} = P\{\nu_n - 2\log_2 m \leq \alpha(n)\} \to \exp\{-2^{-(\alpha_0+1)}\} \text{ as } n \to \infty.$$

Thus in the case of a standard Bernoulli database shifted size of a minimal key $\mu_n = \nu_n - 2\log_2 m$ has asymptotically double exponential distribution and values of random variable ν_n concentrates near $2\log_2 m$ as displayed in Figure 1.

We observe that keys are more likely in a very small interval. Therefore, algorithms which search for keys in relations are faster if first this interval is checked.

It means that for large values of $a(n) = |A|$ the random variable $\nu_n - 2\log_2 m$ has an asymptotical double exponential distribution, i.e. $F(x) = \exp(-\exp(-cx))$, $|x| < \infty$ where $c = \ln 2$. The number $\nu_n - 2\log_2 m$ expresses the shifted minimal key length.

Consider now a standard Bernoulli database R and attributes $U, |U| = n$. Assume that we choose a set of attributes A and include an attribute in a set A with probability $p = p(n) = 1 - q(n) \leq 1$, after some random experiment. Denote a random set of attributes by $\mathbf{A}$. Then by Theorem 3(i) $P\{R \models \mathbf{A}/|\mathbf{A}| = k\} = p(n,k) = \prod_{j=1}^{m-1}(1 - j2^{-a(n)})$ and we obtain

$$P\{R \models \mathbf{A}\} = \sum_{k=0}^{n} P\{R \models \mathbf{A}/|\mathbf{A}| = k\}P\{|\mathbf{A}| = k\} = \sum_{k=0}^{n} p(n,k)\binom{n}{k}p^k q^{n-k}.$$

Denote the standard Gaussian distribution function by

$$\Phi(x) = (2\pi)^{-\frac{1}{2}} \int_{-\infty}^{x} e^{-y^2/2}dy.$$

Theorem 5 *Let R be a standard Bernoulli database with a set of attributes $U, n = |U|$.*

(i)Let $n = 2\log_2 m + \alpha(n)$ and $\alpha(n) \to \alpha_0$ as $n \to \infty, |\alpha_0| \leq \infty$. If $nq(n) \to \tau, 0 \leq \tau < \infty$, then $P\{R \models \mathbf{A}\} \to E[\exp^{-2^{-(\alpha_0 - \theta + 1)}}]$ as $n \to \infty$, where θ is a Poisson random variable with parameter τ.

(ii) Let $n = \frac{2}{p}\log_2 m + \beta(n)\left(\frac{nq}{p}\right)^{\frac{1}{2}}$. If $nq(n) \to \infty, q(n) \to q_0 > 0$ as $n \to \infty$, and additionally , $\beta(n) \to \beta_0$ as $n \to \infty, |\beta_0| \leq \infty$, then $P\{R \models \mathbf{A}\} \to \Phi(\beta_0)$ as $n \to \infty$.

We can interpret these results in the following way. Let R be a standard Bernoulli database and K, say, be a number of keys in L selected independently sets $\mathbf{A}_i, i = 1, \ldots, L$. Then every set of attributes $\mathbf{A}_i, i = 1, \ldots, L$, is a key with a probability $P\{R \models \mathbf{A}_i\}$ and we obtain

$$K = \sum_{i=1}^{L} I_i, \qquad E[K] = LP\{R \models \mathbf{A}_1\},$$

where I_i is a indicator function of the event $\{R \models \mathbf{A}_i\}$ and $E[K]$ is a mean number of keys in a sample of L sets.

When $L = 2^n$ and $p = q = \frac{1}{2}$, a random number of keys K can be represented also in the following form. For any set of attribute A_i denote by J_i the indicator function of the event $\{R \models A_i\}, i = 1, \ldots, 2^n$. Then $K = \sum_{i=1}^{2^n} J_i, P\{R \models A_i\} = p(n,k), |A| = k$, and

$$E[K] = \sum_{k=0}^{n}\binom{n}{k}p(n,k) = 2^n \sum_{k=0}^{n}\binom{n}{k}\frac{1}{2^n}p(n,k) = 2^n P\{R \models \mathbf{A}\}.$$

Applying Theorem 5 we have the following asymptotic for a mean number of keys $E[K]$.

Corollary 6 *Let R be a standard Bernoulli database with a set of attributes $U, |U| = n, n = 2\log_2 m + \alpha(n)$ and $p = q = \frac{1}{2}$, $n = 4\log_2 m + \beta(n)n^{\frac{1}{2}}, \beta(n) \to \beta_0$ as $n \to \infty, |\beta_0| \leq \infty$. Then*

$$E[K] \sim 2^n \Phi(\beta_0) \text{ as } n \to \infty.$$

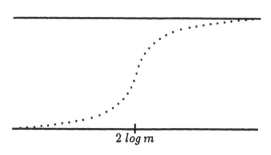

$2 \log m$

Fig. 2. Mean number of Keys Depending on Length

Further, the expectation that K is a key can be displayed as shown in Figure 2. This figure displays the mean number of key depending of the number of attributes and the size m of relations.

Based on this corollary we can show that Monte-Carlo algorithms can be used for checking keys in relations. Randomly attributes are added until the set reaches the size specified by $a(n)$ and m. Then we get keys with a probability $1 - (\frac{1}{2})^k$ for k trials with the Monte-Carlo algorithm.

5 Minimal keys

The methods and results of the previous section can be applied also to the investigation of the probability of the event that a set of attributes $A, |A| = a$, is a minimal key in a random database R. Let R be a standard Bernoulli database with $D_i = \{0, 1\}, i = 1, \ldots, n$, the case when $D_i = \{0, 1, \ldots, d\}, i = 1, \ldots, n$, can be considered in a similar way. Denote by $K(R)$ and $K_{\min}(R)$ the sets of keys and minimal keys in R respectively. Write $A_k = A \setminus \{k\}$, $\mathcal{A}_k = \{A_k \in K(R)\}$, $k = 1, \ldots, a$, and $\mathcal{A} = \{A \in K(R)\} = \{R \models A\}$. Then it follows directly by the definition of a minimal key and Bonferroni inequality (see e.g. Feller (1968), Bender (1974)) for any $r, t = 0, \ldots, M$,

$$|P\{N = r\} - \sum_{j < t} (-1)^j \binom{r+j}{j} S_{r+j}| \leq \binom{r+t}{t} S_{r+t}. \tag{3}$$

that $P\{A \in K_{\min}(R)\}$ can be represented in the following form.

Proposition 1 *Let R be a standard Bernoulli database. Then*

$$P\{A \in K_{\min}(R)\} = P(\mathcal{A}) - \sum_{j=1}^{a(n)} (-1)^{j-1} \binom{a(n)}{j} P(\mathcal{A}_1 \ldots \mathcal{A}_j).$$

Denote by $\lambda = \lambda(n) = M 2^{-a(n)}$.

Theorem 6 *Let R be a standard Bernoulli database and $\lambda(n) \geq \ln \ln a(n) + \lambda_0$. Then there exists $\gamma > 0$ such that for any sufficiently large $\lambda_0 > 0$*

$$P\{A \in K_{\min}(R)\} = e^{-\lambda(n)}(1 - e^{-\lambda(n)})^{a(n)}(1 + O(e^{-\gamma \frac{a(n)}{\ln a(n)}})) \text{ as } n \to \infty.$$

The assumption about lower bound for $\lambda(n)$ in Theorem 6 has a technical character. In the more general case $\lambda(n) \geq \lambda_0 > 0$ we obtain only the following estimate for $P\{A \in K_{\min}(R)\}$.

Proposition 2 *If $\lambda(n) \geq \lambda_0 > 0$ then there exists $\gamma > 0$ such that*

$$P\{A \in K_{\min}(R)\} \leq e^{-\lambda(n)}(1 - e^{-\lambda(n)})^{b(n)}(1 + O(e^{-\gamma \frac{a(n)}{\ln a(n)}})) \text{ as } n \to \infty,$$

where $b(n) = b_0 \frac{a(n)}{\ln a(n)}, b_0 > 0$.

Theorem 6 and Proposition 2 can be used to estimate the asymptotic maximum value of $P\{A \in K_{\min}(R)\}$.

Proposition 3 *If $\lambda(n) \geq \lambda_0 > 0$ then*

$$P\{A \in K_{\min}(R)\} = P(a) \leq P_{\max}(a) = \frac{e^{-1}}{a(n) + 1}(1 + o(1)) \text{ as } n \to \infty,$$

and also $P(a) = P_{\max}(a)$ if and only if $\lambda(n) = \ln(a(n) + 1)(1 + o(1))$ as $n \to \infty$.

The result of Proposition 3 shows that the probability for a set of attributes A to be a minimal key becomes small as $a \to \infty$ and this property does not depend on the relation between number of tuples m and the size of A as in the case of key (cf. Theorem 3). But the following corollary shows that this dependence is important when we consider the conditional probability $P(a/K) = P\{A \in K_{\min}(R)/A \in K(R)\}$.

Corollary 7 *Let $m^2 = 2^{a(n)+1}(\ln a(n) + b(n))$ and $b(n) \to \beta$ as $n \to \infty$, $|\beta| \leq \infty$, and also $b(n) \geq \ln \ln a(n) - \ln a(n) + \lambda_0, \lambda_0 > 0$, then*

$$P(a/K) \to \begin{cases} 0, & \text{if } \beta = -\infty, \\ \exp\{-e^{-\beta}\}, & \text{if } |\beta| < \infty, \\ 1, & \text{if } \beta = +\infty, \end{cases}$$

as $n \to \infty$.

This result can be now compared with worst case complexity of key systems. It means that if m is small or too large then key systems can contain only a very small number of minimal keys. Therefore, worst case complexity results are highly unlikely.

As a straightforward corollary to the previous result we have that if $\lambda(n) = \ln a(n) + b(n)$ and $b(n) \to +\infty$ as $n \to \infty$, then

$$P\{A \in K_{\min}(R)\} \sim P\{A \in K(R)\} \sim e^{-\lambda(n)} \text{ as } n \to \infty. \tag{4}$$

Therefore, if β is unbounded then it is highly unlikely that a set of this size is a key.

This corollary states now the following surprising result:
For any bounded behavior of β , if a set of length $\lambda(n)$ is a key then this set is with high probability also a minimal key.

6   Concluding Remarks

We assumed in previous sections that the initial distribution of tuples in random database R is approximately given. Often a distribution of tuples is unknown. We can generalize the above discussed results to statistical problems for statistical analysis of databases:
  (i) to test of homogeneity of data in R,
  (ii) to test independency of tuples and attributes in a tuple,
  (iii) to fit a distribution of tuples.
  For the first problem we can use for example clustering methods (see e.g. Tou, Gonsales (1974)). Then we can further investigate selected homogeneous clusters. It is possible to use for clusterization some attributes in database or its functionals. For example, a bank database keeps information about residuals in accounts for a long period. Assume that large and active in some sense accounts have different statistical characteristics than small ones. Then we can use as features for clusterization instead of full information the following functionals of attributes:

  − mean residual for accounts for a period,
  − mean residual for accounts with large residuals (greater than a given level),
  − mean absolute values of differences (current and next days).

The independency of different tuples and attributes in R can be verified by some statistical goodness-of-fit tests. To estimate a distribution of a tuple we can use parametric and nonparametric models. The simplest model is a uniform random database. For dependent attributes it is possible to use polynomial or multidimensional Gaussian distribution or histograms, kernel density estimates etc.. For Gaussian distribution we have to modify some previous definitions, e.g., say, $t(A) = t'(A)$ if $|t(k) - t'(k)| < \delta, \delta > 0, k \in A$. To estimate mean characteristics we can use analogous empirical ones, e.g. for $s(n) = E[p(t(A))]$ the statistic

$$\hat{s}(n) = \frac{1}{|S|} \sum_{i,j \in S} I_{\{t_i(A) = t_j(A)\}},$$

where S is a sample of homogeneous tuples and I_C is an indicator function of the event C. The estimate $\hat{s}(n)$ is a standard and optimal in definite sense estimate of $s(n)$. Then we can apply some previous theoretical results with corresponding investigation of statistical errors.

References

1. Ahlswede, R., Wegener, I. (1979).*Suchprobleme*, Teubner B.G., Stuttgart.
2. Albrecht M., Altus M., Buchholz B., Düsterhöft A., Schewe K.-D., Thalheim B. (1994), Die intelligente Tool Box zum Datenbankentwurf RAD. *Datenbank-Rundbrief*, 13, FG 2.5. der GI, Kassel.
3. Andreev, A. (1982), Tests and pattern recognition. PhD thesis, Moscov State University, 1982.
4. Armstrong, W.W.(1974). Depending structures of database relationships. *Information Processing*-74, North Holland, Amsterdam, 580-583.
5. Beeri C., Dowd M., Fagin R., Statman R. (1984), On the structure of Armstrong relations for functional dependencies. *Journal of ACM*, Vol.31, No.1, 30–46.
6. Bekessy A., Demetrovics J., Hannak L., Frankl P., Katona G. (1980), On the number of maximal dependencies in a database relation of fixed order. *Discrete Math.*, 30, 83–88.
7. Bender, E.A. (1974) Asymptotic methods in enumeration. *SIAM Review*, 16, 4, 485-515.
8. Billingsley, P. (1975) *Convergence of Probability Measures*, Wiley, N.Y.
9. Codd E.F. (1970), A relational model for large shared data banks. *Comm. ACM* 13, 6, p. 197–204.
10. Demetrovics J. (1979), On the Equivalence of Candidate Keys with Sperner sets. *Acta Cybernetica*, Vol. 4, No. 3, Szeged, 247 – 252.
11. Demetrovics J. , Katona G.O.H. (1983), Combinatorial problems of database models. Colloquia Mathematica Societatis Janos Bolyai 42, Algebra, Combinatorics and Logic in Computer Science, Gÿor (Hungary), 331–352.
12. Demetrovics J., Katona G.O.H., and Miklos (1994), Functional Dependencies in Random Relational Databases. Manuscript, Budapest.
13. Demetrovics J., Libkin L.O., and Muchnik I.B. (1989), Functional dependencies and the semilattice of closed classes. *Proc. MFDBS-89*, LNCS 364, 136–147.
14. Feller, W. (1968) *An Introduction to Probability Theory and its Applications*, Wiley, N.Y.
15. Gottlob G. (1987), On the size of nonredundant FD-covers. *Information Processing Letters*, 24, 6, 355–360.
16. Mannila H., Räihä K.-J. (1982), On the relationship between minimum and optimum covers for a set of functional dependencies. Res. Rep. C-1982-51, University of Helsinki.
17. Mannila H., Räihä K.-J. (1992), *The design of relational databases*. Addison-Wesley, Amsterdam.
18. Sachkov, V.N. (1982). *An Introduction to Combinatorics Methods of Discrete Mathemathics*, Moscow, Nauka.
19. Seleznjev O., Thalheim B. (1988), On the number of minimal keys in relational databases over nonuniform domains. Acta Cybernetica, Szeged, 8, 3, 267–271.
20. Seleznjev O., Thalheim B. (1994), Probability Problems in Database Theory. Preprint I-3/1994, Cottbus Technical University.
21. Thalheim B. (1987), On the number of keys in relational databases. *Proc. FCT-87-Conf.*, Kazan, LNCS 1987.
22. Thalheim B. (1989), On Semantic Issues Connected with Keys in Relational Databases Permitting Null Values. *Journal Information Processing and Cybernetics, EIK*, 25, 1/2, 11–20.
23. Thalheim B. (1991), *Dependencies in Relational Databases*. Leipzig, Teubner Verlag.
24. Thalheim B. (1992), On the number of keys in relational and nested relational databases. *Discrete Applied Mathematics*, 38.
25. Tou, J., Gonsales, R. (1974). *Pattern Recognition Principles*, Add.-Wesley, London.

Uniformly-Distributed Random Generation of Join Orders

César A. Galindo-Legaria[1,2] *   Arjan Pellenkoft[1]   Martin L. Kersten[1]

[1] CWI
P. O. Box 94079, 1090 GB Amsterdam, The Netherlands

[2] SINTEF DELAB
N-7034 Trondheim, Norway

Abstract. In this paper we study the space of operator trees that can be used to answer a join query, with the goal of generating elements form this space at random. We solve the problem for queries with acyclic query graphs. We first count, in $O(n^3)$ time, the exact number of trees that can be used to evaluate a given query on n relations. The intermediate results of the counting procedure then serve to generate random, uniformly distributed operator trees in $O(n^2)$ time per tree. We also establish a mapping between the N operator trees for a query and the integers 1 through N —i. e. a *ranking*— and describe ranking and unranking procedures with complexity $O(n^2)$ and $O(n^2 \log n)$, respectively.

1 Introduction

1.1 Background

The selection of a join evaluation order is a major task of relational query optimizers [Ull82, CP85, KRB85]. The problem can be stated as that of finding an operator tree to evaluate a given query, so that the estimated evaluation cost is minimum. In practice, the combinatorial nature of the problem prevents finding exact solutions, and both heuristics and randomized algorithms are considered as viable alternatives.

This paper addresses two basic questions related to the space of operator trees of interest: What is the exact size of the space? And, how to generate a random element from the space efficiently? We answer those questions for the class of *acyclic queries* —those whose query graph, defined below, is acyclic. The answer to the second question has a direct application to randomized query optimization, as selection of a random item in the search space is a basic primitive for most randomized algorithms [SG88, Swa89b, Swa89a, IK90, IK91, Kan91, LVZ93, GLPK94].

Acceptable operator trees are subject to restrictions on which relations can be joined together, and counting them does not reduce, in general, to the enumeration of familiar classes of trees —e. g. binary trees, trees representing equivalent

---

* C. Galindo-Legaria was supported by an ERCIM postdoctoral fellowship.

expressions on an associative operator, etc. A variety of techniques are used to enumerate graphs and trees [Knu68, HP73, RH77, GLW82, VF90], but none of them seems to apply directly to our problem.

Previous work has identified restricted classes of queries for which valid operator trees map one-to-one to permutations or to unlabeled binary trees —the first class known as *star* queries, and the second as *chain* queries, see for example [OL90, IK91, LVZ93]— thus solving the counting and random generation problems for those classes. For the general case, since it is easy to generate any valid operator tree non-deterministically, *quasi*-random selection of operator trees has been used in some work on randomized query optimization [SG88, Swa89a]. The term *quasi*-random refers to the fact that every valid tree has a non-zero probability of being selected, but some trees have a higher probability than others and, furthermore, there is no precise characterization of the probability distribution.

Another approach to generate random operator trees is to generate labeled binary trees uniformly at random, until one of them turns out to be a valid operator tree for the query at hand. The validity of an operator tree can be checked efficiently, but the small ratio of valid trees with respect to labeled binary trees renders this method impractical [Swa89a, Swa91].

The paper is organized as follows. The remainder of this introduction defines the space of valid operator trees, and presents some notation and basic properties. Section 2 presents primitives for the construction of operator trees and shows how to efficiently count the number of trees for a given query. Section 3 is devoted to ranking of trees and random generation. Section 4 presents our conclusions.

1.2 Query Graphs and Join Trees

Figure 1 shows the graph representation of a query, called a *query graph*, and two operator trees to answer the query.

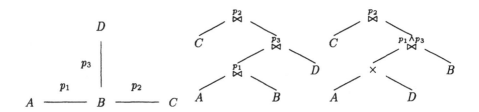

Fig. 1. Query graph and operator trees.

In the query graph, nodes correspond to relations of the database, and undirected edges correspond to join predicates of the query. The graph shown denotes the query $\{(a, b, c, d) \mid a \in A \wedge b \in B \wedge c \in C \wedge d \in D \wedge p_1(a, b) \wedge p_2(b, c) \wedge p_3(b, d)\}$, where A, B, C, D are database relations and p_1, p_2, p_3 are binary predicates. In a database system, such a query is usually evaluated by means of binary operators, and the two operator trees of Fig. 1 can be used to answer this query. The first operator tree requires only relational joins (denoted "⋈"), while the second requires Cartesian products (denoted "×"). For a description of relational operators and query graphs, see, for example, [Ull82, CP85, KRB85]. A Cartesian product is required in the second tree of Figure 1 because we start by combining information from relations A, D, but there is no edge (i. e. predicate) between them in the query graph.

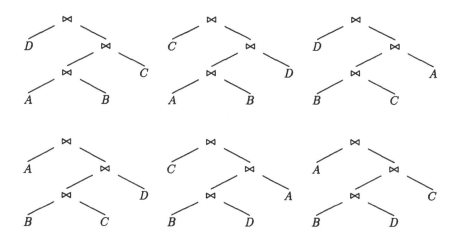

Fig. 2. All join trees of the query graph.

Figure 2 shows all 6 operator trees for the query of Fig. 1 in which only join is required, called *join trees* here. A purely graph-theoretical definition of join trees is given next.

Definition 1. An unordered binary tree T is called a *join tree* of query graph $G = (V, E)$ when it satisfies the following:
- The leaves of T correspond one-to-one with the nodes of G —i. e. leaves$(T) = V$— and
- the leaves of every subtree T' of T induce a connected subgraph of G — i. e. $G|_{\text{leaves}(T')}$ is connected.

Join trees are unordered —i. e. do not distinguish left from right subtree—

because the operator is commutative. There are implementation algorithms that do not distinguish a left and right argument [Gra93], so the selection of left/right argument does not affect the query execution cost. If needed, ordering an operator tree of n leaves requires a binary choice in each of the $n-1$ internal nodes, so there are 2^{n-1} ordered trees for each unordered tree of n relations. This mapping can be easily used to extend our counting and random generation of unordered join trees to the ordered variety.

In the sequel, we omit the operator $\bowtie$ when drawing join trees: A tree of the form $(T_1 \bowtie T_2)$ is written simply as $(T_1.T_2)$. Also, we assume that query graphs are connected and acyclic, i. e. we deal with *acyclic queries*.

1.3 Notation and Basic Properties

We use $\mathcal{T}_G$ to denote the set of join trees of a query graph G, and $\mathcal{T}_G^{v(k)} \subseteq \mathcal{T}_G$ to denote the set of join trees in which a given leaf v is at level k (the level of a leaf v in a tree is the length of the path from the root to v). For example, for the query graph of Fig. 1, Fig. 2 shows that $\mathcal{T}_G$ consists of six trees, $\mathcal{T}_G^{D(1)}$ consists of only two trees, and $\mathcal{T}_G^{B(3)} = \mathcal{T}_G$.

Since our constructions often rely on paths from the root of the join tree to a specific leaf, we introduce an *anchored list* representation of trees. Elements of the anchored list are the subtrees found while traversing the path from the root to some anchor leaf. For list notation, we use square brackets as delimiters and the list construction symbol "|" of Prolog —i. e. $[x|L]$ is the list obtained by inserting a new element x at the front of list L.

Definition 2. Let T be a join tree and v be a leaf of T. The *list anchored on v of T*, call it L, is constructed as follows:
- If T is a single leaf, namely v, then $L = []$.
- Otherwise, let $T = (T_l.T_r)$ and assume, without loss of generality, that v is a leaf ot T_r. Let L_r be the list of T_r anchored on v. Then $L = [T_l|L_r]$.

Then we say that $T = (L, v)$.

Observe that if $T = ([T_1, T_2, \ldots, T_k], v)$ is an element of $\mathcal{T}_G$, then $T \in \mathcal{T}_G^{v(k)}$; that is, the length of anchored list coincides with the level of leaf v in T. In addition, every tree T_i, as well as every suffix-based $T_i' = ([T_i, \ldots, T_k], v)$, for $i = 1, \ldots, k$, is a join tree of some subgraph of G.

The following straightforward observations serve as base cases for our tree counting scheme. Let $G = (V, E)$ be a query graph with n nodes, and let $v \in V$.
- If the graph has only one node, then it has only one join tree T, and v is at level 0 in T; that is, $|\mathcal{T}_G| = \left|\mathcal{T}_G^{v(0)}\right| = 1$, for $n = 1$.
- If the graph has more than one node, then it has no association tree in which v is at level 0; that is, $\left|\mathcal{T}_G^{v(0)}\right| = 0$, for $n > 1$.
- There is no association tree in which v is at level greater than or equal to n; that is, $\left|\mathcal{T}_G^{v(i)}\right| = 0$, for $i \geq n$.

- Since v appears at some unique level in any association tree of G, the total number of association trees is

$$|T_G| = \sum_i \left|T_G^{v(i)}\right| .$$

Our algorithms compute the size of each subset $T_G^{v(0)}, T_G^{v(1)}, \ldots, T_G^{v(n-1)}$ of T_G, for a graph G of n nodes. Therefore, we use a *v-level-partitioned cardinality* $|T_G|_v = \left[\left|T_G^{v(0)}\right|, \left|T_G^{v(1)}\right|, \ldots, \left|T_G^{v(n-1)}\right|\right]$. Clearly, $|T_G|$ can be computed (in linear time) given $|T_G|_v$.

2 Construction and Counting of Join Trees

Our approach to counting join trees is based on two primitive operations that construct join trees of a graph G, given join trees of subgraphs of G. Those operations derive recurrence equations on the number of join trees of a query graph. Together with the base cases presented in Section 1.3, these recurrence equations are used to solve our tree counting problem.

2.1 Graph Extension / Leaf Insertion

Our first operation applies when a query graph G' is extended by adding a new node v and edge (v, w) to yield G. Then any join tree T' of G' can also be extended to a join tree T of G, by inserting a new leaf v somewhere in T'. But by the restrictions on join trees, the new leaf v can be inserted only in certain places.

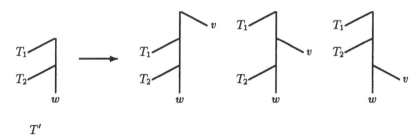

Fig. 3. Construction by leaf-insertion.

Figure 3 illustrates the situation. v has to be inserted somewhere *in the path from the root to w*. Inserting v somewhere else does not produce a valid join tree for G. For example, if in Fig. 3 v is inserted somewhere in T_1 to yield T_1' then $G|_{\text{leaves}(T_1')}$ is not connected, because it excludes node w and therefore edge (v, w), yet it includes v. For this reason, the valid tree T obtained from T' is uniquely determined by the level at which v is inserted. Note, however, that if two edges (v, w_1), (v, w_2) are added instead of just one, then v can be inserted either in the path to w_1 or the path to w_2, and therefore the new tree is not uniquely defined by the insertion level.

Definition 3. Let $G = (V, E)$ be an acyclic query graph. Assume $v \in V$ is such that $G' = G|_{V-\{v\}}$ is connected, and let $(v, w) \in E$. We say G is the *extension by v adjacent to w* of G'.

Definition 4. Let G be the extension by v adjacent to w of G'. Let $T \in T_G$, $T' \in T_{G'}$, with anchored list representations $T = (L, w)$, $T' = (L', w)$. If L is the result of inserting v at position k in L', then T is constructed by leaf insertion from T', and we say T has *insertion pair* (T', k) on v.

The level at which a leaf can be inserted is also clearly restricted. For the same graphs G, G' and join trees T, $T' = (L', w)$ of the above definition, the length of L' is at least $k - 1$ —so that the insertion of a new element v in position k is feasible.

Lemma 5. *Let G be the extension by v adjacent to w of G'. Let $k \geq 1$. There is a bijection between the set $T_G^{v(k)}$ and insertion pairs $\{(T', k) \mid T' \in \bigcup_{i \geq k-1} T_{G'}^{w(i)}\}$.*

Proof. The bijection is given directly by the leaf-insertion operation. $\square$

Lemma 6. *Let G be the extension by v adjacent to w of G'. Let $k \geq 1$. Then,*

$$\left|T_G^{v(k)}\right| = \sum_{i \geq k-1} \left|T_{G'}^{w(i)}\right| .$$

Proof. Follows from Lemma 5, given that $T_{G'}^{w(i)}$, $T_{G'}^{w(j)}$ are disjoint for $i \neq j$. $\square$

Example 1. Let G be a query graph with nodes $\{a, b, c, d, e\}$ and edges $\{(a, b), (b, c), (c, d), (d, e)\}$. From the base cases in Sect. 1.3, $\left|T_{G|_{\{a\}}}\right|_a = [1]$. Then, using Lemma 6 we find $\left|T_{G|_{\{ab\}}}\right|_b = [0, 1]$; $\left|T_{G|_{\{abc\}}}\right|_c = [0, 1, 1]$; $\left|T_{G|_{\{abcd\}}}\right|_d = [0, 2, 2, 1]$; and $|T_G|_e = [0, 5, 5, 3, 1]$.

The computation in the above example is isomorphic to the one used to count unlabeled binary trees in [RH77]. This is the case for *chain queries* —i. e. those with nodes $\{v_1, \ldots, v_n\}$ and edges $\{(v_1, v_2), (v_2, v_3), \ldots, (v_{n-1}, v_n)\}$. Then, as shown in [RH77], the closed form for $|T_G|$ is $1/n \cdot \binom{2n-2}{n-1}$, for a chain query of n nodes. Unfortunately, Lemma 6 is, by itself, insufficient to deal with non-chain queries, as shown in the next example.

Example 2. Take graph G of Example 1, and add a new node f and edge (c, f) to obtain a new graph H. To find $|T_H|_f$ using Lemma 6 we need $|T_G|_c$, but we obtained only $|T_G|_e$ in Example 1. Independently of the order in which we consider the nodes of H, we face the same problem: After a sequence of extensions on a graph in a "chain" fashion, we need to come back to an earlier node to extend from there, but then the necessary counters are not available.

2.2 Graph Union / Tree Merging

A second operation helps to remove the limitation shown in Example 2. The case to consider now is when a query graph G results from the union of two graphs G_1, G_2 that share exactly one common node, say v. Then any two join trees $T_1 \in \mathcal{T}_{G_1}$ and $T_2 \in \mathcal{T}_{G_2}$ can be merged to obtain a join tree $T \in \mathcal{T}_G$. T is obtained by interleaving the subtrees of T_1, T_2 found in the path from the root to the common leaf v.

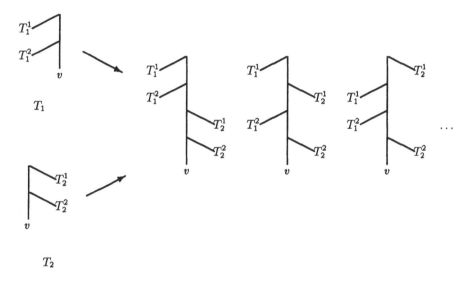

Fig. 4. Construction by tree-merging.

Figure 4 illustrates the situation. We can restrict our attention to the paths from the root to the common node v, in trees T_1, T_2 and the resulting tree T. The path to v in T contains the subtrees found in the paths in T_1, T_2, interleaved in some fashion. In terms of anchored lists, if $T_1 = (L_1, v)$ and $T_2 = (L_2, v)$, then $T = (L, v)$, where list L is a merge of lists L_1, L_2. The merging of two lists L_1, L_2 with respective lengths l_1, l_2 corresponds to the problem of *non-negative integer decomposition* of l_1 in $l_2 + 1$ —that is, a list of $l_2 + 1$ non-negative integers $\alpha = [\alpha_0, \ldots, \alpha_{l_2}]$ such that their sum is equal to l_1. Operationally, the decomposition $[\alpha_0, \ldots, \alpha_{l_2}]$ indicates a merge of L_1, L_2 as follows: Take the first α_0 elements from L_1, then the first element from L_2; now take the next α_1 elements from L_1 and then the second element from L_2, and so on; the last α_{l_2} elements of L_1 follow the last element of L_2. In Fig. 4, for example, the trees shown are obtained by mergings $[2, 0, 0]$, $[1, 1, 0]$, and $[0, 2, 0]$, respectively. Note, however, that if G_1, G_2 share more than one node, then their corresponding trees can be merged in more elaborate ways.

Definition 7. Let $G = (V, E)$ be an acyclic query graph. Assume sets of edges V_1, V_2 are such that $G|_{V_1}, G|_{V_2}$ are connected, $V_1 \cup V_2 = V$, and $V_1 \cap V_2 = \{v\}$. We say G is the *union of* G_1, G_2 *with common node* v.

Definition 8. Let G be the union of G_1, G_2 with common node v. Let $T \in T_G$, $T_1 \in T_{G_1}, T_2 \in T_{G_2}$, with anchored list representations $T = (L, v)$, $T_1 = (L_1, v)$, $T_2 = (L_2, v)$. If L is the result of a merging α of lists L_1, L_2, then T is constructed by tree merging from T_1, T_2, and we say T has *merge triplet* (T_1, T_2, α) *on* V_1, V_2.

Lemma 9. *Let G be the union of G_1, G_2 with common node v. Let $k \geq 1$. There is a bijection between the set $T_G^{v(k)}$ and merge triplets $\{(T_1, T_2, \alpha) \mid T_1 \in T_{G_1}^{v(i)}, T_2 \in T_{G_2}^{v(k-i)}, \alpha$ is an integer decomposition of i in $k - i + 1\}$.*

Proof. The bijection is given by the tree merging operation. □

Lemma 10. *Let G be the union of G_1, G_2 with common node v. Let $k \geq 1$. Then*

$$\left| T_G^{v(k)} \right| = \sum_i \left| T_{G_1}^{v(i)} \right| \cdot \left| T_{G_2}^{v(k-i)} \right| \cdot \binom{k}{i} \ .$$

Proof. Follows from Lemma 9. □

2.3   Counting Join Trees

Our tree-construction operations, and their corresponding count equations, can be applied on query graphs built using graph extension and graph union. We make this construction explicit by means of a *standard decomposition graph*. Algorithms to count and construct trees are implemented by traversals on this decomposition graph.

Definition 11. A *standard decomposition graph* is an operator tree H that builds a query graph G, using the following:
- Constant "v" delivers a graph G with one node v; v is the *distinguished node* of G.
- Unary "$+_v$" takes as input a graph $G' = (V', E')$ with distinguished node w, $v \notin V'$, and delivers a graph G that is the extension on v adjacent to w of G'. The distinguished node of G is v.
- Binary "$\times_v$" takes as input two graphs $G_1 = (V_1, E_1)$, $G_2 = (V_2, E_2)$ both with distinguished node v, $V_1 \cap V_2 = \{v\}$, and delivers a graph G that is the union of G_1, G_2. The distinguished node of G is v.

For example, Fig. 5 shows a query graph G and a standard decomposition graph H for G. It is easy to see that a linear time algorithm obtains standard decomposition graphs for acyclic query graphs. The number of nodes of the standard decomposition is linear in the number of nodes of the query graph it builds. Alternatively, operators in the decomposition graph of G can be interpreted as

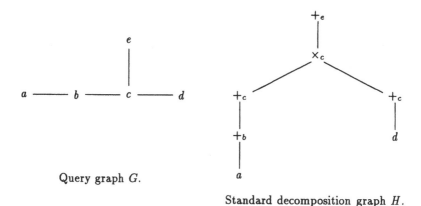

Query graph G.

Standard decomposition graph H.

Fig. 5. Query graph and standard decomposition graph.

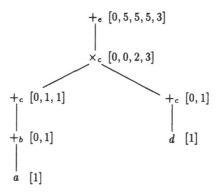

Fig. 6. Counting trees on the standard decomposition graph.

building join trees of G. Adding extra parameters "$+_{v,k}$" and "$\times_{v,\alpha}$" become operators for leaf insertion at k and tree merging on α.

Now, to count the number of join trees of a given acyclic query graph G, we first obtain a standard decomposition H of G, and then apply directly Lemmas 6 and 10 bottom-up on H, to compute a result for each node. In each subexpression H' of H, if H' constructs a graph G' (subgraph of G) with distinguished node v, then at the root of H' we compute $|T_{G'}|_v$. For example, Fig. 6 shows the results of the computation for the query graph of Fig. 5. Note that this query is neither a chain nor a star. The total number of different trees is 18.

Theorem 12. *Let G be a connected, acyclic query graph on n relations. The number of join trees for G can be computed in $O(n^3)$ time.*

Proof. A standard decomposition graph H of G can be constructed in linear time, and the number of nodes of H is linear on n. Then we apply either Lemma 6 or Lemma 10 in each of the $O(n)$ nodes of H. Now, observe that the number of mergings $M(l_1, l_2)$, for lists of size l_1, l_2, satisfies $M(l_1, l_2) = M(l_1, l_2 - 1) + M(l_1 - 1, l_2)$; then a table for $M(l_1, l_2)$, where $l_1, l_2 \leq n$, can be precomputed in $O(n^2)$ time, and evaluating the expression $\binom{k}{i}$ required in Lemma 10 reduces to a simple table lookup. Computing the list of values $|T_{G'}|_{v'}$ at each node of H by either Lemma 6 or 10 does not exceed $O(n^2)$ time. Then, the computation in all the nodes of H requires no more than $O(n^3)$ time. Finally, $|T_G|$ is the result of adding the values in the list $|T_G|_v$ obtained at the root of H. $\qquad\square$

3 Random Generation and Ranking of Join Trees

The bijections given by Lemmas 5 and 9 and the standard decomposition graph can also be used to rank and to generate random join trees. We show how to do this next.

3.1 Generating Random Join Trees

To generate random join trees we can apply the following strategy recursively. Assume a set S is partitioned into sets $S_0, \ldots, S_m$. To generate a random element of S, first select a partition, say S_i, and then generate a random element within S_i. Using a biased probability of selection $|S_i|/|S|$ for each partition, and then generating uniformly from the partition, every element $x \in S_i$ is generated with probability $|S_i|/|S| \cdot 1/|S_i| = 1/|S|$ —i. e. the procedure generates elements from S uniformly at random.

Lemma 13. *Let G be a query graph with n nodes, obtained as the extension by v adjacent to w of G'. Let $1 \leq k_1 \leq k_2 < n$. A random, uniformly distributed T from $\bigcup_{k_1 \leq j \leq k_2} T_G^{v(j)}$ can be obtained as follows:*

1. *Generate a random number r uniformly with $1 \leq r \leq \sum_{k_1 \leq j \leq k_2} \left| T_G^{v(j)} \right|$.*

2. *Find $k = \min_j \left(r \leq \sum_{l=0}^{j} \left| T_G^{v(l)} \right| \right)$.*

3. *Generate a random, uniformly distributed T' from $\bigcup_{i \geq k-1} T_{G'}^{w(i)}$.*

4. *Build T from insertion pair (T', k).*

Proof. A set in the partition $T_G^{v(k_1)}, \ldots, T_G^{v(k_2)}$ is seleted with the appropriate bias in steps 1 and 2, and then an element of the selected partition is generated uniformly in steps 3 and 4 using the bijection of Lemma 5. $\qquad\square$

Lemma 14. *Let G be a query graph with n nodes, obtained as the union of G_1, G_2 with common node v. Let $1 \leq k_1 \leq k_2 < n$. A random, uniformly distributed T from $\bigcup_{k_1 \leq j \leq k_2} T_G^{v(j)}$ can be obtained as follows:*

1. *Generate a random number r uniformly with $1 \leq r \leq \sum_{k_1 \leq j \leq k_2} \left| T_G^{v(j)} \right|$*

2. *Find $k = \min_j \left(r \leq \sum_{l=0}^{j} \left| T_G^{v(l)} \right| \right)$.*

3. *Generate a random number r' uniformly with $1 \leq r' \leq \left| T_G^{v(k)} \right|$.*

4. *Find $i = \min_j \left(r' \leq \sum_{l=0}^{j} \left| T_{G_1}^{v(l)} \right| \cdot \left| T_{G_2}^{v(k-l)} \right| \cdot \binom{k}{l} \right)$.*

5. *Generate random, uniformly distributed T_1 from $T_{G_1}^{v(i)}$, T_2 from $T_{G_2}^{v(k-i)}$, and integer partition of i in $k - i + 1$ α.*

6. *Build T from merge triplet (T_1, T_2, α).*

Proof. A set in the partition $T_G^{v(k_1)}, \ldots, T_G^{v(k_2)}$ is selected with the appropriate bias in steps 1 and 2. The selected set is again partitioned and one of those partitions is in turn selected with the appropriate bias in steps 3 and 4. Finally, an element of the resulting set is selected uniformly in steps 5 and 6. The partition in step 3 and 4, and the uniform selection in steps 5 and 6 use the bijection of Lemma 9. □

Theorem 15. *Let G be a connected, acyclic query graph on n relations. After a preprocessing step of $O(n^3)$ time, uniformly-distributed random join trees for G can be generated in $O(n^2)$ time, given a source of random numbers.*

Proof. By Theorem 12, the standard decomposition graph H of G and the count arrays in the nodes of H can be computed in $O(n^3)$ time. This completes the preprocessing step. To generate a random tree, traverse the decomposition graph recursively from the top, applying the procedure of either Lemma 13 or 14 at each node (except for the "constant" nodes of H, which define a one-node query graph with only one join tree, in which case random selection is trivial). The time taken by either procedure at each node of H is bound by $O(n)$. Therefore, the total time required generate a random tree is $O(n^2)$.

The above scheme generates $O(n)$ random numbers to produce a random join tree. An alternative to obtain a random tree is to generate a single random number, and then unrank such number into a tree, as shown below. The complexity of unranking, however, is higher.

3.2 Ranking and Unranking Join Trees

Mapping the N join trees of a query graph to the integers 1 through N is based on the recursive application of the following idea. Assume we want to rank an element $x \in S$, and S is partitioned into sets $S_0, \ldots, S_m$. If $x \in S_k$, for some $0 \leq k \leq m$, and we can find a *local rank* of x in S_k, then simply set the rank of x in S to be local-rank$(x, S_k) + \sum_{i=0}^{k-1} |S_i|$. Conversely, to unrank the element corresponding to number y under our scheme, first find the set S_k from which the element must be retrieved, where $k = \min_j (y \leq \sum_{i=0}^{j} |S_i|)$. Then find a local number $y' = y - \sum_{i=0}^{k-1} |S_i|$, and finally unrank-local(y', S_k).

Example 3. Applying the idea of ranking based on partitions to the query whose standard decomposition is shown in Fig. 6, the numbers 1 through 5 are assigned to join trees in which leaf e is at level 1; numbers 6 through 10 are assigned to those in which e is at level 2; numbers 11 through 15 are assigned to those in which e is at level 3; and finally 16 through 18 are assigned to those in which e is at level 4.

Lemma 16. *Let G be a query graph with n nodes, obtained as the extension by v adjacent to w of G'. Let $1 \leq k_1 \leq k_2 < n$. The rank r of T in $\bigcup_{k_1 \leq j \leq k_2} T_G^{v(j)}$ can be obtained as follows:*

1. *Find the insertion pair (T', k) of T, where $T' \in T_{G'}$, $k_1 \leq k \leq k_2$.*
2. *Find the rank r' of T' in $\bigcup_{i \geq k-1} T_{G'}^{w(i)}$.*
3. *The rank of T is $r = r' + \sum_{i=0}^{k-1} \left| T_G^{v(i)} \right|$.*

Proof. In step 1, the partition where T belongs is identified by looking at the level of leaf v. In step 2, a local rank of T in its partition is obtained using the bijection of Lemma 5 (assuming some ranking function for the trees in G'). Finally, step 3 adjusts the local rank to the rank in the complete set. □

Lemma 17. *Let G be a query graph with n nodes, obtained as the union of G_1, G_2 with common node v. Let $1 \leq k_1 \leq k_2 < n$. The rank r of T in $\bigcup_{k_1 \leq j \leq k_2} T_G^{v(j)}$ can be obtained as follows:*

1. *Find the merge triplet (T_1, T_2, α) of T, where $T_1 \in T_{G_1}^{v(i)}$, $T_2 \in T_{G_2}^{v(k-i)}$, and α is an integer decomposition of i in $k - i + 1$.*
2. *Find the rank r_1 of T_1 in $T_{G_1}^{v(i)}$, the rank r_2 of T_2 in $T_{G_2}^{v(k-i)}$, and the rank r_3 of α. Set the local rank $r' = (r_3 - 1) \cdot \left| T_{G_2}^{v(k-i)} \right| \cdot \left| T_{G_k}^{v(i)} \right| + (r_2 - 1) \cdot \left| T_{G_k}^{v(i)} \right| + r_1$.*
3. *The rank of T is $r = r' + \sum_{l=0}^{i-1} \left| T_{G_1}^{v(l)} \right| \cdot \left| T_{G_2}^{v(k-l)} \right| \cdot \binom{k}{l} + \sum_{l=0}^{k-1} \left| T_G^{v(l)} \right|$.*

Proof. In step 1, the partition where T belongs is identified from the merge triplet. In step 2, a local rank is obtained, using the bijection of Lemma 9 (assuming some ranking function for trees in G_1 and G_2, and on integer decompositions). Finally, step 3 adjusts the local rank in the complete set. □

Theorem 18. *Let G be a connected, acyclic query graph on n relations. After a preprocessing step of $O(n^3)$ time, join trees of G can be ranked in $O(n^2)$ time and unranked in $O(n^2 \log n)$ time.*

Proof. By Theorem 12, the standard decomposition graph H of G and the count arrays in the nodes of H can be computed in $O(n^3)$ time. This completes the preprocessing step. To rank a tree, at each node of H we have to decompose the tree either into an insertion pair or into a merge triplet, and then use the rules of Lemma 16 or 17 (except for "constant" nodes of H, in which the ranking is trivial). The work per node does not exceed $O(n)$ time, and therefore the work to compute the local ranks for all the nodes takes time $O(n^2)$.

To unrank a tree, we first translate the rank in T_G to a local rank in some $T_G^{v(k)}$. Then, using the rules of Lemmas 16 and 17, we find at each node of H an insertion level k or a merging specification α in a top-down pass of H (except for "constant" nodes of H, in which unranking is trivial). In a bottom-up pass we use the parameters at each node to build the tree. Unranking a merging specification α takes $O(n \log n)$ in the worst case, which bounds all the other computation performed at each node of H. Thus the time required to unrank is $O(n^2 \log n)$. □

4 Discussion

In this paper we described how to efficiently count the number of join trees that can be used to evaluate a given query, and how to generate them uniformly at random. The difficulty of these problems results from the fact that there is no natural one-to-one mapping between join trees and a simple combinatorial structure. Our concept of a standard decomposition graph provides a supporting structure for counting and random generation, because it defines a canonical construction for each tree. The tree constructions are such that they can be counted efficiently by means of a simple traversal of the decomposition graph.

The integers required by our algorithms can become quite large, as is the case with other graph counting/generation problems [vL90]. This eventually limits the applicability of our approach. Nevertheless, our algorithms can be used to a good extent on practical database queries (e. g. certainly for queries of 20 relations, using standard 64-bit integers).

We performed experiments on the selection of join evaluation orders, for query optimization, using the random generation of trees presented here. The results are encouraging. The interested reader is referred to [GLPK94] for more details.

The results we have presented apply only to queries whose graph is *acyclic*. We are currently studying the class of cyclic queries, but the problem is more difficult. Many database problems become significantly more complex when cyclic structures are allowed (see for example [BFMY83]), and the techniques we use for the acyclic case do not seem to extend easily to cyclic queries.

References

[BFMY83] C. Beeri, R. Fagin, D. Maier, and M. Yannakakis. On the desirability of acyclic database schemes. *Journal of the ACM*, 30(3):479–513, July 1983.

[CP85]　 S. Ceri and G. Pelagatti. *Distributed Databases: Principles and Systems*. McGraw-Hill, New York, 1985.

[GLPK94] C. A. Galindo-Legaria, A. Pellenkoft, and M. L. Kersten. Fast, randomized join-order selection —Why use transformations? In *Proceedings of the Twentieth International Conference on Very Large Databases, Santiago*, 1994. Also CWI Technical Report CS-R9416.

[GLW82]   U. Gupta, D. T. Lee, and C. K. Wong. Ranking and unranking of 2-3 trees. *SIAM Journal of Computation*, pages 582–590, August 1982.

[Gra93]   G. Graefe. Query evaluation techniques for large databases. *ACM Computing Surveys*, 25(2):73–170, June 1993.

[HP73]   F. Harary and E. M. Palmer. *Graphical Enumeration*. Academic Press, 1973.

[IK90]   Y. E. Ioannidis and Y. C. Kang. Randomized algorithms for optimizing large join queries. *Proc. of the ACM-SIGMOD Conference on Management of Data*, pages 312–321, 1990.

[IK91]   Y. E. Ioannidis and Y. C. Kang. Left-deep vs. bushy trees: An analysis of strategy spaces and its implications for query optimization. *Proc. of the ACM-SIGMOD Conference on Management of Data*, pages 168–177, 1991.

[Kan91]   Y. C. Kang. *Randomized Algorithms for Query Optimization*. PhD thesis, University of Wisconsin-Madison, 1991. Technical report #1053.

[Knu68]   D. E. Knuth. *The Art of Computer Programming*, volume 1: Fundamental Algorithms. Addison-Wesley, 1968. Second edition, 1973.

[KRB85]   W. Kim, D. S. Reiner, and D. S. Batory, editors. *Query processing in database systems*. Springer, Berlin, 1985.

[LVZ93]   R. S. G. Lanzelotte, P. Valduriez, and M. Zaït. On the effectiveness of optimization search strategies for parallel execution spaces. *Proc. of the 19th VLDB Conference, Dublin, Ireland*, pages 493–504, 1993.

[OL90]   K. Ono and G. M. Lohman. Measuring the complexity of join enumeration in query optimization. *Proc. of the 16th VLDB Conference, Brisbane, Australia*, pages 314–325, 1990.

[RH77]   F. Ruskey and T. C. Hu. Generating binary trees lexicographically. *SIAM journal of Computation*, 6(4):745–758, December 1977.

[SG88]   A. N. Swami and A. Gupta. Optimization of large join queries. *Proc. of the ACM-SIGMOD Conference on Management of Data*, pages 8–17, 1988.

[Swa89a]   A. N. Swami. *Optimization of Large Join Queries*. PhD thesis, Stanford University, 1989. Technical report STAN-CS-89-1262.

[Swa89b]   A. N. Swami. Optimization of large join queries: Combining heuristics and combinatorial techniques. *Proc. of the ACM-SIGMOD Conference on Management of Data*, pages 367–376, 1989.

[Swa91]   A. N. Swami. Distribution of query plan costs for large join queries. Technical Report RJ 7908, IBM Research Division, Almaden, 1991.

[Ull82]   J. D. Ullman. *Principles of Database Systems*. Computer Science Press, Rockville, MD, 2nd edition, 1982.

[VF90]   J. S. Vitter and Ph. Flajolet. Analysis of algorithms and data structures. In J. van Leeuwen, editor, *Handbook of Theoretical Computer Science*, volume A: Algorithms and Complexity, chapter 9, pages 431–524. North Holland, 1990.

[vL90]   J. van Leeuwen. Graph algorithms. In J. van Leeuwen, editor, *Handbook of Theoretical Computer Science*, volume A: Algorithms and Complexity, chapter 10, pages 525–631. North Holland, 1990.

A Probabilistic View of Datalog Parallelization

Sérgio Lifschitz[1]* and Victor Vianu[2]**

[1] PUC-Rio, Depto. Informática, Rua Marquês de São Vicente 225, Rio de Janeiro, RJ 22453-900, Brasil
[2] Univ. of California at San Diego, CSE 0114, La Jolla, CA 92093-0114, USA

Abstract. We explore an approach to developing Datalog parallelization strategies that aims at good *expected* rather than worst-case performance. To illustrate, we consider a very simple parallelization strategy that applies to all Datalog programs. We prove that this has very good expected performance under equal distribution of inputs. This is done using an extension of 0-1 laws adapted to this context. The analysis is confirmed by experimental results on randomly generated data.

1 Introduction

The performance requirements of databases for advanced applications, and the increased availability of cheap parallel processing, have naturally lend great importance to the development of parallel processing techniques for databases. Much of the existing research in this direction has focused on parallelization of Datalog queries. In this paper we investigate parallel processing of Datalog from a probabilistic viewpoint. In contrast to existing work, we propose to guide the design and evaluation of parallelization strategies by *expected* performance. We evaluate the expected performance of parallelization strategies using *0-1 laws*, a powerful tool from logic. We illustrate this approach to design and analysis using a very simple pure parallelization technique, applicable to all Datalog programs. Rather surprisingly, we show that this simple strategy has *provably* very good expected performance. This is backed up with experimental results described in [16] (omitted here).

Most existing approaches to parallel processing of Datalog fall into a few broad categories. In the *pure parallelization* approach, the data (or rule instantiations) are partitioned among a fixed number of sites according to some criteria. Then the Datalog program is run in parallel without communication among the sites. The final result consists of the union of the results at each site. Programs

---

* E-mail: lifschitz@inf.puc-rio.br. This work was done while the author was affiliated with the Ecole Nationale Supérieure des Télécommunications (ENST), Paris, France, and supported in part by CAPES/MEC Brasil under grant #1245/90-13
** E-mail: vianu@cs.ucsd.edu. Work performed in part while visiting ENST Paris, and supported in part by the NSF under grant IRI-9221268.

for which this algorithm is complete (i.e., computes the entire result) are called *sharable* [22] or, in the case of disjoint results at each site, *decomposable*. Sufficient syntactic conditions for decomposability have been provided in [8, 24, 18]. The property of being decomposable was shown undecidable in [23].

The alternative to the pure parallelization approach is to allow *communication* among the sites. Among methods using communication, we can identify two different approaches. One is the so called rule instantiation partitioning strategy [11, 23, 25], which is a pure bottom-up method that parallelizes the evaluation by partitioning the rule instantiations of a program among the sites, such that each site evaluates the same original program but with less data. Since communication ensures completeness, there is no longer a need for restricting programs to ensure decomposability, as in the pure parallelization approach.

Another possibility is the so called rule (or clause) decomposition, where the rules of a program are evaluated in a top-down style, employing *sideways information passing* to focus on relevant facts [21, 13], sometimes considering a pipelined strategy [4]. Such methods are useful primarily when the query goal contains constants. They usually require an initial compilation phase that is expensive. In the presence of constants in the query, optimization techniques like the Magic Sets rewriting method seem to yield better results. A survey of these strategies can be found in [19].

The general paradigm in the approaches described above is to propose heuristics for parallelization, such that the resulting parallel algorithms are always *complete*. Completeness means that the union of the results from each site at the end of the algorithm provides the correct result. Much of the effort and cost in these approaches goes into guaranteeing completeness *in all cases*. As discussed above, this may include inter-site communication during evaluation, pre-processing, or syntactic restrictions on the programs.

Here we explore a somewhat different approach. We argue that the price paid for guaranteeing completeness in all cases is too high and affects adversely the *average* performance. Instead, we propose approaching the issue of completeness from a probabilistic point of view. To illustrate this idea, we examine a parallelization strategy which is extremely straightforward, works on all programs, uses no communication, but which no longer guarantees completeness in all cases. In those cases where incompleteness occurs, a sequential "completion" phase at the end of the parallel processing phase is required. In the worst case, no gain is obtained from the parallelization, since the "completion" portion of the algorithm may be as costly as a purely sequential algorithm. The key to the approach is to show that the cases where incompleteness occurs are rare. Indeed, we prove that for almost all inputs (which is given a precise probabilistic meaning), the result of the parallel phase is complete and the overall performance of the algorithm is much better than the monosite algorithm.

The probabilistic results on the behavior of our parallelization algorithm are obtained using an elegant tool from logic: *0-1 laws* [9]. These establish a connection between logical languages and the probability that properties expressible in these languages are true. Thus, the fact that a property of data is expressible in a language that has a 0-1 law provides information on the probability that the property is true. To use these results, we show that "good" behavior of our parallelization algorithm is a property of data that can be expressed by a sentence that is asymptotically true, in a language having a 0-1 law. This yields the results on the good performance of the algorithm on almost all inputs.

So far, the primary use of 0-1 laws in databases has been as a tool for understanding the expressive power of query languages. For example, this is used to show that the parity of a set is not expressible in languages like FO, *fixpoint*, and *while*. The average complexity of various query languages has been investigated using 0-1 laws in [1]. This also included a probabilistic analysis of certain query optimization algorithms, for which heuristics were then developed in [2]. To our knowledge, the present work is the first to use 0-1 laws in the analysis of concrete parallelization strategies.

The probabilistic results described above should be viewed simply as guiding information towards the design of parallelization algorithms. Indeed, they make the important assumption that no information is available about the database, so all instances are equally likely. For example, this means that if the input is a graph (binary relation), the probability that there is an edge between two nodes is 1/2. This is clearly not true for many applications. Data is often more sparse, or has known structure. The results extend to some of these situations, such as some sparsity assumptions. For example, they remain true for edge probability $1/c$ where c is any constant, and even when the probability is a small function of the number n of nodes, such as $n^{-1/\log\log n}$. However, in applications where more information is available on the structure of data, the pure parallelization algorithm presented here should be considered just as a starting point for the development of algorithms more adapted to that particular application.

Thus, the main contribution of the present paper lies not as much in a specific algorithm, but rather in the idea of guiding the design of parallelization strategies by expected rather than worst-case behavior in the context of known characteristics of data. The algorithm and results presented here illustrate the "limit" situation where all inputs are considered equally likely. The experimental results provided in [16] provide insight into the actual performance of pure parallelization for various types of inputs. Several Datalog queries on graphs are considered. As suggested by the analytical results, in the case of randomly generated graphs the behavior of the algorithm is excellent. Inputs with pre-defined structure, such as acyclic graphs and complete binary trees, are also considered. As expected, the behavior of the algorithm is less impressive for these cases. For acyclic graphs, the pure parallelization algorithm is nonetheless still faster than the sequential algorithm. For complete binary trees however, the pure parallelization algorithm performs worse than the sequential algorithm. This confirms our expectation that the algorithm needs to be adapted to the specific structure of data, in applications where such structure is known.

The paper is organized as follows. We begin with a preliminary section describing some database languages to be used, the notion of asymptotic probability, and 0-1 laws. The following two sections present the pure parallelization algorithm and the analytical results on its performance; this requires developing a variation of 0-1 laws adapted to this context. After providing performance results for all Datalog programs, we identify a large class of programs for which extremely good performance can be shown. The last section contains concluding remarks. The related experimental results can be found in [16].

2 Background

We briefly review in this section several query languages referred to in the development, as well as some basic definitions and results related to 0-1 laws.

2.1 Some query languages

We assume familiarity with the first-order queries, FO, expressed by the relational calculus and algebra.

There are many useful queries that FO cannot express, such as the transitive closure of a graph. Numerous extensions of FO with recursion have been proposed. Most of them converge towards two central classes of queries: *fixpoint* and *while* [5, 6]. These can be defined in various ways: by adding fixpoint operators to FO, looping constructs to relational algebra, or by extensions of Datalog.

In this paper we are interested in the rule-based paradigm, primarily Datalog. A Datalog program is a set of rules of the form

$$A_0(t_0) \leftarrow A_1(t_1), \ldots, A_n(t_n)$$

where each A_i is a relation, t_i are tuples of variables of appropriate arities, and each variable in t_0 occurs in some t_i, $i > 0$. In a Datalog rule as above, $A_0(t_0)$ is called the *head* and $A_1(t_1), \ldots, A_n(t_n)$ the *body* of the rule. The relations occurring in heads of rules are the *intensional* (idb) relations, and the others are *extensional* (edb) relations. For example, the following Datalog program defines a binary relation T containing the transitive closure of a graph G:

$$T(x,y) \leftarrow G(x,y)$$
$$T(x,y) \leftarrow T(x,z), G(z,y).$$

Here, G is extensional and T intensional. Usually, it is assumed that one of the intensional predicates is designated as the *answer*. So, a Datalog program defines a query from instances over its edb relations to instances of the answer idb predicate. For simplicity of exposition, we mostly consider in this paper programs with one binary edb relation G (defining the edges of a graph) and binary answer.

The answer to a Datalog program can be computed by "firing" the rules for as long as new tuples can be inferred. A rule firing consists of finding a substitution of variables by constants such that the body of the rule is satisfied, and adding the head of the rule to the database. A *stage* consists of one firing of all the rules.

Replacing the variables by constants in a rule yields an *instantiation* of the rule. If the body of the instantiation is satisfied then the instantiation is *applicable*. An instantiation whose head has not yet been inferred is *potentially productive*. An instantiation that is both potentially productive and applicable is called *productive*. If P is a Datalog program and $\mathbf{I}$ an input database, $P(\mathbf{I})$ denotes the result of applying P to $\mathbf{I}$.

It is sometimes useful to consider the *expansions* of a Datalog program, obtained by unfolding the program all the way down to edb predicates, starting from the answer predicate, some fixed number of times. (In addition to the edb predicates, expansions may use equalities among the free variables.) Expansions are of the form $\exists \mathbf{u}\gamma$, where γ is a conjunction of atoms of edb predicates or equality. When the program is understood, we denote by Γ_i, $i \geq 0$, the set of expansions obtained by unfolding the program i times, and $\Gamma = \bigcup_{i \geq 0} \Gamma_i$. For the transitive closure program above, $G(x, y) \in \Gamma_0$, $\exists z(G(x, z) \wedge G(z, y)) \in \Gamma_1$, etc. A Datalog program is equivalent to the infinitary disjunction of all formulas in Γ.

While Datalog provides recursion, it defines only monotonic queries. That is, if $\mathbf{I} \subseteq \mathbf{J}$ then $P(\mathbf{I}) \subseteq P(\mathbf{J})$. Thus, FO and Datalog are incomparable. Datalog is subsumed by the *fixpoint* (and therefore *while*) queries.

2.2   0-1 laws

0-1 laws provide an elegant connection between logical languages and the probability that properties expressible in the languages are true. Consider any property σ of inputs. Let $\mu_n(\sigma)$ be the fraction of inputs with n constants which satisfy σ. We say that σ is *almost surely true (or holds almost everywhere)* iff

$$\lim_{n \to \infty} \mu_n(\sigma) = 1.$$

A language L is said to have a 0-1 law if for all properties σ expressible in L, either σ is almost surely true or almost surely false. Surprisingly, it turns out that most of the commonly used query languages have a 0-1 law. This includes FO [9], Datalog, the *fixpoint* and *while* queries [15]. For example, take the property that a graph contains a cycle of length 3. Clearly, this property is expressible in FO. Thus, it is almost surely true or almost surely false. In this case, the property is almost surely true. For several languages, there are algorithms to determine whether a sentence in the language is almost surely true, or if it is almost surely false (e.g., see [12, 14]).

An important class of FO sentences that are almost surely true are the so-called *extension axioms*. For simplicity, we describe extension axioms for directed graphs (a binary relation G). This can be extended to inputs of arbitrary arity. Let k be fixed. The k-ary extension axioms, denoted $\mathcal{A}_k$, are sentences stating that any subgraph of k nodes can be extended by an additional node in all possible ways. More precisely, for each k, $\mathcal{A}_k$ contains all sentences of the form

$$\forall x_1 ... \forall x_k ((\bigwedge_{i \neq j} (x_i \neq x_j)) \Rightarrow \exists y (\bigwedge_i (x_i \neq y) \wedge connections(x_1, ..., x_k; y)))$$

where $connections(x_1, ..., x_k; y)$ is a conjunction of literals containing, for each x_i, one of $G(x_i, y)$ or $\neg G(x_i, y)$, and one of $G(y, x_i)$ or $\neg G(y, x_i)$. For example, for $k = 3$, one of the 4^3 sentences of the form $connections(x_1, x_2, x_3; y)$ is

$$G(x_1, y) \wedge \neg G(y, x_1) \wedge \neg G(x_2, y) \wedge \neg G(y, x_2) \wedge G(x_3, y) \wedge G(y, x_3).$$

There is a close connection between extension axioms and the expansions of Datalog programs. Let $\exists u \gamma$ be one expansion of a Datalog program with binary answer, and let x, y be its free variables. Consider the sentence $\forall x \forall y \exists u \gamma$. If all atoms in γ contain at least one variable in u, then this sentence is implied by a finite set of extension axioms, and is therefore almost surely true. In such case, it follows that the Datalog program produces the complete graph on almost all inputs. This is the case for the transitive closure program above, and for many other programs. However, there are Datalog programs for which this property does not hold, because all its expansions contain some atoms involving just x, y. For example, such is the program

$$T(x, y) \leftarrow G(x, y), G(x, x), G(y, y)$$
$$T(x, y) \leftarrow T(x, z), T(z, y)$$

Indeed, all expansions contain the atoms $G(x, x)$ and $G(y, y)$. This program does not produce the complete graph on almost all inputs.

3 Pure Parallelization

For the sake of simplicity, we describe the algorithm for the case when the input to the query is a graph and the output another graph. For instance, this is the case for the transitive closure and same generation queries. The algorithm and results extend easily to unrestricted arities.

The input to the parallelization algorithm consists of a graph I, a Datalog program P, and a positive integer k. The algorithm uses $C_k^2 = k(k-1)/2$ sites denoted s_{ij} $(0 \leq i < j < k)$ in addition to a central site. It consists of two phases:

– **Parallel phase.** The input database I resides originally in the central site.

1. distribute **I** among the sites as follows: first, construct an arbitrary ordering $\leq$ of the nodes in **I**; then, all arcs of **I** among nodes x such that $x \equiv i \bmod k$ or $x \equiv j \bmod k$ are sent to site s_{ij}. (The *mod* predicate applies to the rank of the node in the ordering $\leq$.)
2. execute P in parallel at all sites s_{ij} (this is done as in the **repeat** loop below, only applied locally).
3. collect all results from the s_{ij} in the central site.
- **Completion phase.** This continues the computation of P in the central site starting from the results collected from the s_{ij}:

repeat until no new facts are inferred
1. Compute all potentially productive instantiations of rules in P (i.e., all instantiations whose heads produce facts not present in the partial result).
2. Add the heads of all applicable instantiations generated in (1) to the partial result.

In the parallel phase, the partitioning of instantiations is based on the *mod* function; this is one way of obtaining a nice, balanced distribution of the data among sites. However, this is not crucial: other functions, and a variety of other partitioning strategies, could be used as well.

In order to evaluate the performance of the above algorithm, we use a common cost model that counts the number of rule instantiations generated by the algorithm (whether applicable/productive or not). The cost of the parallel phase is the maximum of the cost at each site. The cost of the completion phase is the cost of computing the complete answer at the central site starting from the results collected from the sites. The total cost of the parallel algorithm with program P and input **I** is the sum of the costs of the two phases, denoted *parallel-cost*$_{P,k}$(**I**). For comparison purposes, we also consider the purely sequential algorithm which computes the result using just the central site, as in the completion phase above but with no parallel phase. The cost of the sequential algorithm with program P and input **I** is denoted *sequential-cost*$_P$(**I**). The cost measure counting instantiations is a rough abstraction that ignores certain costs, such as:

1. distribution of edges to the sites, and pooling of the partial results to the central site;
2. the cost of computing the potentially productive instantiations in both the sequential and parallel algorithm.

Note that it is consistent to ignore item (2) in both the sequential and parallel algorithms. Item (1) is a communication cost, incomparable to the other costs taken into account, and which can be easily factored in, in the context of a particular machine or architecture. The cost measure we use here is in line with previous investigations related to Datalog, such as [20, 3], where the cost measure is also based on rule instantiations.

4 Expected behavior

We are interested in several aspects of the behavior of the pure parallelization algorithm outlined above. Clearly, its success relies crucially on the assumption that the first, parallel phase, generally produces almost the entire result. Therefore, it is of interest to evaluate the chances that the first phase is complete. In all cases it must be tested whether the parallel phase yielded the complete result, and if not the sequential completion phase must be applied. We are interested in the *total* cost of the pure parallelization algorithm, which includes the test of completeness and the sequential completion phase. We compare this cost to the cost of the purely sequential algorithm.

4.1 An extension of 0-1 laws

To evaluate probabilistically these aspects of our algorithm, we use 0-1 laws. The idea is to describe the behavior of interest as a property of *the input data*, using a language that has a 0-1 law. This guarantees that the behavior almost always or almost never occurs. Finally, it must be determined which of the two holds.

Suppose the pure parallelization algorithm is applied to some query φ. To express the property that the first phase of the algorithm is complete we need to use, besides the relations of the original database, predicates stating that a node belongs to site s_{ij}. This involves the use of the *modulo* predicate. Given a domain ordered by $\leq$ and $k > 1$, we use k predicates $mod_i, 0 \leq i < k$ defined by: $mod_i(x)$ holds iff the rank of x wrt $\leq$ is i modulo k. Stating that x is in s_{ij} is then written, in a language allowing disjunction, as: $mod_i(x) \vee mod_j(x)$.

Let k be fixed and let L be any of the query languages discussed so far. Then $L + mod$ denotes L extended with the predicates mod_i, $0 \leq i < k$. More precisely, let $\mathbf{R}_\leq$ be a database schema including a binary relation $\leq$ (interpreted as an order). A query φ over $\mathbf{R}_\leq$ in the language $L + mod$ is a query in L using relations in $\mathbf{R}_\leq$ *other than* $\leq$, and mod_i, $0 \leq i < k$. Note the following important facts:

(1) All queries in $L + mod$ operate on ordered structures; and,
(2) a query in $L + mod$ over $\mathbf{R}_\leq$ cannot use the ordering $\leq$ directly; however, $\leq$ is used indirectly via the mod predicates.

It is easily seen that, if φ is expressible in L, then the answer to φ at site s_{ij} can be defined by some φ_{ij} in $L + mod$.

Since the statements of interest to us make use of the mod predicates, the 0-1 laws need to be extended to languages using these predicates in addition to database relations. Let σ be a sentence in $L + mod$, over a database schema $\mathbf{R}_\leq$. The asymptotic probability of σ is defined as usual, but counting only *ordered* structures over $\mathbf{R}_\leq$, i.e. finite structures for which $\leq$ provides a total order on the active domain. Extending the 0-1 laws from L to $L + mod$ does not pose any serious problem, although it does require reconstructing the proof of the 0-1 laws for FO and *while* (see [10]) in the presence of *mod*. In particular, the extension axioms now involve the mod_i unary predicates, which act much like a labeling of nodes. Since all languages L discussed here are subsumed by *while*, it is sufficient to show:

Theorem 1. While + mod *has a 0-1 law.*

Note that the restriction that queries in $L + mod$ not use the ordering $\leq$ is essential. Indeed, it is known that the 0-1 law no longer holds for any of the languages considered here if this restriction is removed.

Remark. In the above definition of asymptotic probability we are counting structures over an extended signature containing the order $\leq$ not present in the input. The order is generated nondeterministically by the algorithm. Counting ordered structures over $\mathbf{R}_{\leq}$ is equivalent to counting *runs* of the algorithm on inputs over $\mathbf{R}$. The definition of asymptotic probability of statements describing the behavior of the algorithm could as well have been based explicitly on counting runs of the algorithm. In certain contexts, such as concurrent programs, where counting runs cannot be reduced as easily to counting structures, it may be more appropriate to use a definition based on runs.

4.2 Completeness of the parallelization phase

We now return to Datalog and the pure parallelization algorithm. Consider the property of completeness of the parallelization phase of our algorithm, with C_k^2 sites. For a given Datalog query $\varphi(x, y)$, this can be stated as a property of data by the following sentence, which we denote by $complete_k(\varphi)$:

$$\forall x, y[\varphi(x, y) \leftrightarrow \bigvee_{0 \leq i < j < k} \varphi_{ij}(x, y)].$$

Note that for any language L included in *while*, $complete_k(\varphi)$ is a sentence in the language *while + mod*. Since *while + mod* has a 0-1 law, it follows that $complete_k(\varphi)$ is almost surely true or almost surely false. It turns out that $complete_k(\varphi)$ is in fact almost surely true for all Datalog queries φ, as shown next.

Theorem 2. *For each Datalog query φ,* $complete_k(\varphi)$ *is almost surely true.*

Proof. (Sketch) Let P be a Datalog program expressing the query φ. Again, we assume the only edb predicate is a binary relation G, and the output is also binary. The monotonicity of Datalog implies that, for all instances $\mathbf{I}$ over $\{G, \leq\}$,

$$\forall x, y[\varphi(x, y) \leftarrow \bigvee_{0 \leq i < j < k} \varphi_{ij}(x, y)].$$

Thus, it is sufficient to show that

$$\forall x, y[\varphi(x, y) \rightarrow \bigvee_{0 \leq i < j < k} \varphi_{ij}(x, y)]$$

is almost surely true. Consider the set of expansions Γ of P (see Section 2). Recall that expansions are of the form $\exists \mathbf{u} \gamma$, where γ is a conjunction of atoms of edb predicates (here G) or equalities among free variables. Let α be the conjunction of all atoms in γ whose variables are all free (α is **true** if there are no such atoms), and β the conjunction of the remainder of the atoms in γ. Then $\exists \mathbf{u} \gamma$ is equivalent to $\alpha \wedge \exists \mathbf{u} \beta$. Clearly, there are finitely many nonequivalent α occurring in the expansions in Γ, say $\alpha_1, \ldots, \alpha_m$. For each α_r, pick *one* β_r such that $\alpha_r \wedge \exists \mathbf{u} \beta_r \in \Gamma$. Let

$$\gamma_{ir} = \forall x \forall y \exists \mathbf{u}(mod_i(\mathbf{u}) \wedge \beta_r)$$

where $mod_i(\mathbf{u})$ is the conjunction of atoms $mod_i(z)$ for z occurring in $\mathbf{u}$. Note that each γ_{ir} is almost surely true; indeed, γ_{ir} is implied by a finite set of extension axioms over $\{G, mod_i \mid 0 \leq i < k\}$. So, the conjunction of the γ_{ir} is almost surely true. Let $\mathbf{I}$ be an instance over $\{G, \leq\}$ satisfying this conjunction. Suppose $< a, b > \in \varphi(\mathbf{I})$. There must exist α_r such that $\mathbf{I}$ satisfies $\alpha_r(a, b)$. Also, there exist l, j such that $mod_l(a) \wedge mod_j(b)$, so $\mathbf{I}$ satisfies

$$\alpha_r(a, b) \wedge mod_l(a) \wedge mod_j(b) \wedge \gamma_{lr}.$$

Clearly, this implies that $\mathbf{I}$ satisfies $\varphi_{lj}(a, b)$. $\qquad\qquad \square$

Thus, Theorem 2 shows that for all Datalog programs, it is almost surely true that the parallelization phase of our algorithm provides the complete answer to the query. However, this fact in itself is not sufficient to guarantee the possibility of developing an algorithm which is efficient *overall*, since it must also provide the test of completeness, and carry out the second completion phase if the partial answer is not complete. In the case of Datalog this is facilitated by the monotonicity of Datalog queries, which implies that:

- the parallelization phase always produces a subset of the answer, and
- the answer can be obtained from the output of the first phase by continuing the firing of rules up to a fixpoint.

The above does not generally hold for languages beyond Datalog, including the Datalog¬ languages. Thus, other, possibly less efficient means, must be used in the completion phase for those languages.

4.3 Cost analysis

We next evaluate probabilistically the overall cost of the pure parallelization algorithm compared to the sequential algorithm, for Datalog queries. Recall that the costs of the two algorithms for program P and input $\mathbf{I}$ were defined earlier, and denoted $sequential\text{-}cost_P(\mathbf{I})$ and $parallel\text{-}cost_{P,k}(\mathbf{I})$ for the sequential and parallel algorithms with C_k^2 sites, respectively. For a Datalog program P and input $\mathbf{I}$, let $st_P(\mathbf{I})$ be the number of stages in the sequential evaluation of P on $\mathbf{I}$. We assume the evaluation stops when two consecutive stages yield the same result; so, in all cases $st_P(\mathbf{I}) \geq 2$.

Theorem 3. *Let P be a Datalog program and v the maximum number of variables in a rule in P. Then it is almost surely true that*

$$\text{parallel-cost}_{P,k}(\mathbf{I}) \leq [(2/k)^v + 1/st_P(\mathbf{I})] \times \text{sequential-cost}_P(\mathbf{I}).$$

Proof. (**Sketch**) The core of the proof is to show that the following are almost surely true simultaneously:

(1) the parallel phase produces the complete result (Theorem 2); and,

(2) each fact in the answer is inferred at the same stage in the sequential and parallel evaluations; in particular, the number of stages in the parallel phase equals the number of stages in the sequential evaluation (so, both equal $st_P(\mathbf{I})$).

(1) and (2) are shown along the same lines as the proof of Theorem 2. Now consider an instance $\mathbf{I}$ with n elements for which (1) and (2) hold. The cost ratio is straightforwardly obtained by counting instantiations. Roughly speaking, the $(2/k)^v$ component of the factor is due to the fact that each site holds $2n/k$ elements and there are $(2n/k)^v$ valuations of v variables into these elements; and, the central site holds n elements and there are n^v valuations of v variables into these elements. Finally, the $1/st_P(\mathbf{I})$ component comes from the one iteration at the central site needed to check completeness following the parallel phase. □

Note that the above cost ratio depends critically on the value of $st_P(\mathbf{I})$. For its minimum value (2), the ratio is larger than 0.5, while for high values it approaches the constant $(2/k)^v$. Fortunately, there is a large class of programs, that includes most commonly arising ones, for which the expected ratio is precisely $(2/k)^v$. Recall the notion of *expansion* of a Datalog program, and the notation relating to it (Section 2). We call a Datalog program P *constraint-free* if it has some expansion $\exists \mathbf{u}\gamma$ such that each atom in γ contains at least one variable in $\mathbf{u}$ (recall that such programs were considered at the end of Section 2). All Datalog programs considered in this paper, including the usual transitive closure and same-generation programs, are constraint-free. The program at the end of Section 2 is not (all answers $T(x,y)$ are subject to the "constraints"

$G(x,x), G(y,y)$). It turns out that it can be effectively tested if a given Datalog program P is constraint-free, as outlined next. Let $\mathbf{G}_P$ be the context-free grammar obtained from P as follows. There are no terminals, and its nonterminals are atoms $\nu(R(t))$ where $R(t)$ is an atom occurring in P and ν is a valuation of the variables of t into $\{x, y, @\}$. (Intuitively, @ tracks the existentially quantified variables in the expansions, and x, y track the free variables.) The start symbol is $T(x,y)$ where T is the (binary) answer predicate. For each rule

$$A_0(t_0) \leftarrow A_1(t_1), \ldots, A_n(t_n)$$

in P, $\mathbf{G}_P$ contains all productions

$$\nu[A_0(t_0) \rightarrow A_1(t_1), \ldots, A_n(t_n)]$$

where ν is a valuation of the variables into $\{x, y, @\}$. Finally, $\mathbf{G}_P$ also contains all productions $R(t) \rightarrow \epsilon$ where R is an edb predicate and t a tuple over $\{x, y, @\}$ containing at least one occurrence of @. It can be proven that P is constraint-free iff $\epsilon \in L(\mathbf{G}_P)$. This can be tested in time polynomial in the size of $\mathbf{G}_P$. Note that the size of $\mathbf{G}_P$ is larger than the size of P by a factor of 3^v where v is the maximum number of variables in a rule of P.

One can now show the following:

Theorem 4. *Let P be a constraint-free Datalog program and v the maximum number of variables in a rule of P. Then it is almost surely true that*

$$\text{parallel-cost}_{P,k}(\mathbf{I}) \leq (2/k)^v \times \text{sequential-cost}_P(\mathbf{I}).$$

The expected speedup obtained for constraint-free programs is proportional to some power of the number of sites. Thus, for most programs the expected performance of the parallel algorithm is excellent compared to the sequential one. For example, suppose P is the standard transitive closure program ($v = 3$) and $k = 10$. Then the number of sites is 45 and it can be expected that the parallel cost is $1/125$ of the sequential cost.

Since the above is an *asymptotic* result, the input has to be larger than a certain size before the behavior comes close to that described in the theorem. It is natural to ask whether the behavior actually holds for sizes of practical interest. The answer is positive: the experimental results of [16] show that the behavior actually matches the asymptotic behavior even with relatively few nodes (e.g., 300).

The probabilistic analysis above assumes that all database instances are equally likely. In the example of a single binary relation, this is equivalent to assuming probability $1/2$ for each edge. Consequently, the relation will almost always contain about half of all pairs. Relations are usually more sparse than this. Fortunately, the results hold for probability measures which allow to model at least some sparse graphs. For example, they continue to hold with edge probability $1/c$ where c is any constant, and even $n^{-1/\log\log n}$ where n is the number of nodes in the graph. Experimental results for some sparse graphs are also described in [16].

5 Conclusion

We investigated certain aspects of parallelization strategies for Datalog queries, from a probabilistic viewpoint. The novel ideas of the paper are:

- guiding the design and evaluation of parallelization strategies by *expected* performance; and,
- the use of a powerful tool from logic, 0-1 laws, in the evaluation of the expected behavior of parallelization strategies.

To illustrate the points above, we considered pure parallelization, a particularly simple algorithm that works very well in the limit situation when no information is known *a priori* about the input. The pure parallelization algorithm has the advantage of working for *all* Datalog programs. Using 0-1 laws, we showed that the expected performance of pure parallelization is excellent on arbitrary, random inputs. This is backed up by experimental results on randomly generated data, provided in [16]. In particular, the theoretical expected performance is sometimes reached, even with relatively few nodes. For example, for non-linear transitive closure with 300 nodes and edge probability 1/5, the parallel cost with 10 sites is 0.008 of the sequential one, i.e. exactly the 1/125 ratio given by the theoretical result (Theorem 4).

Experimental results involving "biased" inputs, with various degree of known structure, are also described in [16]. As more assumptions are imposed on input structure, the behavior of pure parallelization degrades. For acyclic graphs it remains nonetheless very good, but far less so than for arbitrary graphs. For highly structured data, like complete binary trees, there is little or no gain from the parallelization. As expected, in such cases pure parallelization needs to be tailored further to the specific situation in order to be practical.

The implementation supporting the above experiments was done using RDL//C [7], a parallel rule-based language on top of a relational DBMS (*SABRINA v7.2*), which supports both declarative production rules and procedural programming based on C code.

References

1. S. Abiteboul, K. Compton and V. Vianu: "Queries are easier than you thought (probably)", *Proc. ACM SIGACT-SIGMOD-SIGART Symp. on Principles of Database Systems*, 1992, pp 23–32.
2. S. Abiteboul and A. Van Gelder: "Optimizing Active Databases using the Split Technique", *Proc. Intl. Conf. on Database Theory*, 1992, pp 171–187.
3. F. Bancilhon and R. Ramakrishnan: "Performance Evaluation of Data Intensive Logic Programs", *Foundations of Deductive Databases and Logic Programming, Ed J. Minker*, 1988, pp 439–517.
4. D.A. Bell, J. Shao and M.E.C. Hull: "A Pipelined Strategy for Processing Recursive Queries in Parallel", *Data and Knowledge Engineering*, 6(5), 1991, pp 367–391.

5. A.K. Chandra: "Programming Primitives for Database Languages", *Proc. ACM Symp on Principles of Programming Languages*, 1981, pp 50–62.

6. A.K. Chandra and D. Harel: "Structure and Complexity of Relational Queries", *J. Computer and System Sciences*, 25(1), 1982, pp 99–128.

7. J.-P. Cheiney, G. Kiernan and C. de Maindreville: "A Database Rule Language Compiler Supporting Parallelism", *Proc. Intl. Symp. on Database Systems for Advanced Applications*, 1993, pp 279–286.

8. S.R. Cohen and O. Wolfson: "Why a Single Parallelization Strategy is not Enough in Knowledge Bases", *Proc. ACM SIGACT-SIGMOD-SIGART Symp. on Principles of Database Systems*, 1989, pp 200–216.

9. R. Fagin: "Monadic Generalized Spectra", *Z. Math. Logik* 21, 1975, pp 89–96.

10. R. Fagin: "Finite-Model Theory: a Personal Perspective", *Proc. Int'l. Conf. on Database Theory*, 1990, pp 3–24.

11. S. Ganguly, A. Silberschatz and S. Tsur: "A Framework for the Parallel Processing of Datalog Queries", *Proc. ACM-SIGMOD Intl. Conf. on Management of Data*, 1990, pp 143–152.

12. E. Grandjean: "Complexity of the First-order Theory of Almost all Structures", *Information and Control*, 52, 1983, pp 180–204.

13. G. Hulin: "Parallel Processing of Recursive Queries in Distributed Archictectures", *Proc. Intl. Conf. on Very Large Data Bases*, 1989, pp 87–96.

14. P.G. Kolaitis and M.Y. Vardi: "The Decision Problem for the Probabilities of Higher-Order Properties", *Proc. IEEE Symp. on Logic in Computer Science*, 1987, pp 425–435.

15. P.G. Kolaitis and M.Y. Vardi: "0-1 Laws for Infinitary Logics", *Proc. IEEE Symp. on Logic in Computer Science*, 1990, pp 156–167.

16. S. Lifschitz: "Stratégies d'évaluation parallèle de requêtes Datalog récursives" (in French), Ph.D. Thesis, Ecole Nationale Supérieure des Télécommunications, Paris, 1994.

17. R. Rado: "Universal Graphs and Universal Functions", *Acta Arith.*, 9, 1964, pp 331–340.

18. J. Seib and G. Lausen: "Parallelizing Datalog Programs by Generalized Pivoting", *Proc. ACM Symp. on Principles of Database Systems*, 1991, pp 78–87.

19. J.D. Ullman: *Principles of Database and Knowledge-Base Systems*, Volumes I and II, Computer Science Press, 1989.

20. J.D. Ullman: "Bottom-up beats Top-down for Datalog", *Proc. ACM Symp. on Principles of Database Systems*, 1989, pp 140–149.

21. A. Van Gelder: "A Message Passing Framework for Logical Query Evaluation", *Proc. ACM-SIGMOD Intl. Conf. on Management of Data*, 1986, pp 155–165.

22. O. Wolfson: "Sharing the Load of Logic-Programming Evaluation", *Proc. Intl. Symp. on Databases in Parallel and Distributed Systems*, 1988, pp 46–55.

23. O. Wolfson and A. Ozeri: "A New Paradigm for Parallel and Distributed Rule-Processing", *Proc. ACM-SIGMOD Intl. Conf. on Management of Data*, 1990, pp 133–142.

24. O. Wolfson and A. Silberschatz: "Distributed Processing of Logic Programming", *Proc. ACM-SIGMOD Intl. Conf. on Management of Data*, 1988, pp 329–336.

25. W. Zhang, K. Wang and S-C. Chau: "Data Partition: a Practical Parallel Evaluation of Datalog Programs", *Proc. Intl. Conf. on Parallel and Distributed Information Systems*, 1991, pp 98–105.

A First Step Towards Implementing Dynamic Algebraic Dependencies

N. Bidoit and S. De Amo*

LIPN – U.R.A. 1507 du CNRS
Université Paris XIII – Institut Galilée
Av. Jean Baptiste Clément, 93430 Villetaneuse, France
bidoit@ura1507.univ-paris13.fr deamo@brufu.bitnet

Abstract. We present a class of dynamic constraints (DADs) which are of pratical interest. The paper investigates in a constructive manner the definition of transaction-based specifications equivalent to DAD-constraint-based specifications. Our study shows the limitation of Abiteboul/Vianu's transaction schemas and proposes a generalization of transaction schemas based on regular expression on transactions.

Key words: Dynamic constraint, Transaction schema, Declarative and Operational specification of database schema.

1 Introduction

In this paper, we investigate the relationship between two paradigms for specifying database histories. The first that forms a crucial component of object-oriented databases, is *operational*: this consists of a predefined set of admissible updates called transactions, and specifies the allowed database histories which are those "generated" by the transactions. The second is *declarative* and consists of temporal logic statements that state dynamic constraints to restrict the database histories to the "good" histories. Both dynamic constraints [10, 11, 14, 15, 19, 9, 13, 1] and operational specifications [3, 4, 6, 8] have been previously investigated, but in isolation. One of the problems raised here is to establish the following connection: given a set of dynamic constraints, is it possible to exhibit a set of transactions such that the set of "good" histories equals the set of "generated" histories. If such a set of transactions exists we say that it has the same effect as the set of constraints.

Why is it important to tackle such a problem ? In the one hand, it is important to have the ability to specify the dynamic behaviour of the database in a declarative manner. For instance at the conceptual level, declarativity allows the designer to concentrate on *what* is to be enforced rather than *how*. On the other hand, at the implementation level, checking constraints is expensive although efficient methods have been proposed for static constraints [18]. Indeed, for static constraints, only few relational database systems provide constraint

---
* This work is partially supported by the French Projects PRC BD3 and PRC IA.

checking mechanisms. Usually database consistency relies on the ability of the programmer to write transactions preserving consistency. In this paper, we enforce dynamic constraints by providing an equivalent operational specification. This approach is history-less. Recall that a transaction is an update program whose input is the database current state. Of course, we need to keep some information about the history of the database in a way similar to [9]. Following this approach, it is obvious that restoring the "previous state" never occurs because a transaction always build a consistent new database.

Recently, transaction schemas [3, 4, 6, 8] have been investigated and their interaction with classical dependencies schemas has been studied [5, 7]. This fundamental pioneer study has been undertaken in the static framework and relationships between transaction schemas and static dependencies have been established with respect to the static database states.

In this paper, we start by investigating the use of Abiteboul/Vianu's transaction schemas as a framework to build operational specifications equivalent to constraint-based specifications, in a dynamic setting. Thus section 2 briefly reviews database terminology and transaction schemas. We study dynamic algebraic dependencies (DADs)in section 3. These dependencies allow one to express that *if some property is true now, then in the past some other property should have hold*. Section 4 investigates the classical notions of correctness and completness of transaction schemas with respect to DAD-schemas. The two first negative results show the limitation of transaction schemas. Roughly speaking, it is not possible to find a transaction schema having the same effect as a set of DADs and moreover it cannot be expected to find a transaction schema having an effect as close as possible to the effect of DADs. Then we restrict our attention to elementary histories that are state sequences where changes from one state to the other is limited to an insertion or deletion of at most one tuple. We show how to build a transaction schema, called elementary, generating exactly the elementary histories satisfying a fixed set of DADs.

The operational specification proposed in Section 5 is a generalization of transaction schema. These generalized transaction schemas have three components: a set of relation schemas, a set of transactions, and a regular expression on transactions. Intuitively, recall that, a state sequence is augmented by a unique transaction call with input the current database state. With the result of section 4, using a unique transaction call allows us to (correctly) update only one tuple at each transition. The idea for recovering (arbitrary) multiple changes is to allow a sequence of elementary transactions to specify a transition. Unfortunately, the fact that an elementary transaction preserves the consistency of the database does not imply that a sequence of elementary transactions does. Regular expression is introduced in the transaction schema in order to restrict the "shape" of the transaction sequences. The main result is a constructive specification of generalized transaction schemas equivalent to sets of DADs. This result is stated for a significant subclass of DADs.

[2] provides proofs and motvating examples which have not been included here because of space limitation. The appendix provides the reader with an example aiming at illustrating the contents of the paper.

2 Preliminaries

We assume that the reader is familiar with basic database concepts [20, 17, 16] and transaction schemas [4, 6]. In order to make the discussion clear, we begin by introducing well-known concepts and notations.

Relational Database and Algebra We assume given a set **Attr** of attributes, a set **Dom** of constants (all attributes have the same domain), a set **Rel** of relation names and a set **Var** of (domain) variables. A relation schema is given by its name R and a set of attributes Attr(R) and is denoted R(Attr(R)). A *free-tuple* is simply a tuple whose values on attributes may be either constants or variables. A *database schema* is a finite set of relation schemas. The set of all possible instances over the relation schema R (resp. over the database schema **R**) is denoted by Inst(R) (resp. by Inst(**R**)).

A relational algebra expression E is defined as in [16] using the following operators: selection ($\sigma_{A=B}$, $\sigma_{A=a}$), projection (Π_X), natural join ($\bowtie$), renaming ($\varrho_{A|B}$), union ($\cup$) and difference ($-$). We use the constant query expression $\{u\}$ whose result on any database instance is $\{u\}$. The set of attributes of the target schema of E is denoted by Tar(E) and the set of relational schemas occuring in E is denoted by sch(E).

Transaction Languages In sections 4 and 5, in order to define transaction schemas we use the language SdetTL (*safe strong deterministic Transaction Language*) defined in [4, 6]. We introduce the constructs of this language in a very informal manner : $\text{ins}_R(u)$ inserts the free tuple u in relation R, $\text{del}_R(u)$ deletes u from R and erase_R erases the contents of relation R. Two constructs are included *composition* (denoted ;) and *iteration* (denoted **while**). To define the syntax of the construct **while** we need to introduce *parameterized relational expressions* and *conditions* : a *parameterized relational expression* on **R** is a relational expression where variables may occur at the place of constants ; an *atomic condition* C over **R** is an expression of the form $E \subseteq F$ where E and F are parameterized relational expressions with Tar(E)=Tar(F) ($u \in E$ (resp. $u \notin E$) denotes $\{u\} \subseteq$ E (resp. $E \subseteq (E - \{u\})$)). and a *condition* C over **R** is a conjunct of atomic conditions. The definition of "C is satisfied by an instance I over **R**" is the usual one.

A *parameterized transaction* (*p-transaction*) over **R** is a basic update $\text{ins}_R(u)$, $\text{del}_R(u)$ or erase_R or more complex updates of the form $t; s$ and **while** C **do** t **done**, where t and s are p-transactions and C is a condition over **R**. The free variables of $\text{ins}_R(u)$ or $\text{del}_R(u)$ are the variables occuring in u. The free variables of $t; s$ are the free variables of t or s. The free variables of **while** C **do** t **done** are the free variables of t which are not variables of C. We explicity identify the parameters $x_1, \ldots, x_n$ in a p-transaction t by writing $t(x_1, \ldots, x_n)$.

A *call* to a p-transaction t is a transaction obtained from t by instantiating its parameters by constants. Call(t) denotes the set of calls to t.

The semantic of SdetTL is very simple to understand. We just discuss the (deterministic) semantics of the **while** construct (see [4, 6] for details). Informally, evaluating a transaction of the form "**while** C **do** t **done**" is done as follows: for each iteration, consider all instantiations of the parameters of the conditions C that makes C true for the current database instance, consider the corresponding set Call of calls to t. Then the result of executing one iteration is the union of the parallel executions of the transactions in Call. The execution of iterations stops when condition C is not satisfied by any instantiation of its parameters.

In what follows, we frequently use the **if** ... **then** ... **else** construct which can obviously be expressed in SdetTL.

3   Dynamic Databases

Intuitively, a dynamic instance of a database keeps the history of the database from its creation to the present time.

Definition 1. Let $\mathbf{R}$ be a database schema. A *dynamic instance* (d-instance) D over $\mathbf{R}$ is a finite sequence of instances over $\mathbf{R}$, $D = (D_0, D_1, \ldots, D_n)$ such that $n \geq 0$ and $D_0 = \phi$. The set of all possible d-instances over $\mathbf{R}$ is denoted by d-Inst($\mathbf{R}$).

The fact that the first state D_0 is empty translates the assumption that the database is empty when created. The last state of a d-instance is the current state of the database. We denote by $|D|$ the size of the sequence D. A d-instance is never a sequence of length 0, it always contains the initial empty state ϕ. We abusively say that a d-instance is *empty* when each states of its sequence is empty. The set of the empty d-instances over $\mathbf{R}$ is denoted $Empty(\mathbf{R})$ or simply $Empty$.

Dynamic Algebraic Dependencies (DADs) Dynamic integrity constraints are introduced in order to restrict the behaviour of the database. Using temporal logic in order to define dynamic properties of databases has been investigated in [9, 13, 10, 11, 15]. Here, we study a class of constraints called *dynamic algebraic dependencies* that are anteriority dependencies and subsume dynamic inclusion dependencies (DIDs) [1]. For the sake of simplicity, we define the syntax of these constraints using database notations.

Definition 2. A *dynamic algebraic dependency* is an expression of the form EF where E and F are relational expressions over the database schema $\mathbf{R}$ such that Tar(E) = Tar(F). E (resp.F) is called the *current property* (resp. the *past property*) of the DAD EF. Let $D = (D_0, D_1, \ldots, D_n)$ be a d-instance over $\mathbf{R}$, the D *satisfies* EF (D $\models$ EF) if $\forall i \in [1 \ldots n]$, $\forall u \in E(D_i)$, $\exists j \in [0 \ldots i-1]$ such that $u \in F(D_j)$.

The constraint given in the *University* Example (2) is a dynamic algebraic dependency. From now on, we will refer to this DAD as UNIV.

A *dynamic inclusion dependency* (DID) is a DAD such that E and F are projections, i.e. $E = \Pi_X [P]$ and $F = \Pi_X [Q]$ for $P,Q \in R$. We note that UNIV is a DID. A DAD *schema* is a pair (R,G), where R is a database schema and G is a finite set of DADs over R. We say that a d-instance D over R *satisfies* G if $D \models g$, for each $g \in G$. The set of d-instances over R satisfying G is denoted by Sat(R,G).

One can easily notice that the set of empty d-instances is always included in Sat(R,G). Thus, we could say that a DAD schema is always consistent. However, when Sat(R,G) is exactly equal to *Empty* this is not appealing because the constraints forbid any information to enter the database. We propose the following notion of consistency :

Definition 3. DAD schema (R,G) is *consistent* when Sat(R,G) $\neq$ *Empty*.

Theorem 4. *Consistency and implication for DADs are undecidable.*

This result is strongly related to the decidability of query containment. These problems are decidable for DIDs for which we provide an axiomatization [1].

4 Transaction Schemas and DADs

A *transaction schema* is a pair (R,T) where R is a database schema and T is a finite set of p-transactions over R [4, 6].

Definition 5. The set of d-instances over R generated by the transaction schema (R,T) is defined by d-gen(R,T) = {D $\in$ d-Inst(R) | $\forall i \in [1..|D|]$, $\exists t \in$ Call(T), $D_i = t(D_{i-1})$} where Call(T) is the set of calls to p-transactions in T. In what follows, "a call to a p-transaction in T" is abbreviated by "a transaction in T".

Our main goal is to investigate the relationship between DADs specifications and transaction schemas. Correctness of the transaction schema (S,T) with respect to the DAD schema (R,G), where $R \subseteq S$, tells us that the d-instances generated by T are satisfying G. Completeness tells us that each d-instance satisfying G can be generated by the transactions in T. Of course a transaction schema (S,T) "has exactly the same effect" as a DAD schema (R,G) when correctness and completeness both hold. The fact that we compare a DAD schema (R,G) with a transaction schema (S,T) where $R \subseteq S$ comes from the need to enrich the database schema R with auxiliary relations in the following. If $\mathcal{D}$ is a set of d-instances over S, we define in the obvious way $\mathcal{D}_R$ the restriction on R of the d-instances in $\mathcal{D}$.

Definition 6. Let (R,G) be a DAD schema and let (S,T) be a transaction schema such that the database schema S contains the database schema R. Then:

- (S,T) is *correct* w.r.t. (R,G) if d-gen(S,T)|$_R$ $\subseteq$ Sat(R,G). A transaction t $\in$ T is correct w.r.t. (R,G) if (S,{t}) is correct w.r.t. (R,G).
- (S,T) is *complete* w.r.t. (R,G) if Sat(R,G) $\subseteq$ d-gen(S,T)|$_R$.

Given a set of DADs G over R, the problem investigated is : does a correct transaction schema (S,T) exist which is complete w.r.t. (R,G) ? Unfortunately, the answer is no.

A DAD EF is *positive* if E does not contain the difference operator.

Theorem 7. *Let (R, G) be a consistent and positive DAD schema. Then for each transaction schema (S, T) correct w.r.t. (R, G), we have d-gen(S, T)|$_R$ $\subset$ Sat(R, G).*

The full paper [2] provides the proof and examples showing that both consistency and positivity are essential to state this result.

Theorem 7 naturally leads to investigate the problem in a more permissive manner: does a correct transaction schema exist which has an effect as close as possible to the effect of G (which generates the biggest subset of Sat(R,G)) ? A natural notion of maximality is defined using inclusion : a transaction schema (S,T) that is correct w.r.t. the DAD schema (R,G) is *maximal* if for each transaction schema (S',T') correct w.r.t. (R,G), we have d-gen(S',T')|$_R$ $\subseteq$ d-gen(S,T)|$_R$. Unfortunately,

Theorem 8. *There exists no transaction schema (S, T) correct w.r.t. the DAD schema (R, G) such that (S, T) is maximal.*

These negative results lead us to generalize the notion of a transaction schema in Section 5. Before, we build specific transaction schemas, called *elementary*. In order to motivate building these elementary transaction schemas, we introduce *elementary* d-instances. A d-instance is *elementary* when changes from one state to the other is limited to an insertion or deletion of at most one tuple. We define Sat$_1$(R,G) as the set of all elementary d-instances over R satisfying G.

Let us look at the *University* Example (see Appendix). In (4), the transaction schema (U,T) is correct w.r.t. (R,G) but is not able to generate the elementary d-instance given in (5). However, the transaction schema (H,T') given in (6) is correct w.r.t. (R,G) and generate exactly Sat$_1$(R,G).

Historical Schemas Without loss of generality, we assume from now on that in the DAD schema (R,G) each relation schema in R has an occurrence in G. The first thing we do when building an elementary transaction schema for a DAD schema (R,G) is to enrich R with additional relation schemas called historical schemas. Historical schemas aim at storing information about the database changes needed in order to "check" the constraints. Thus they are induced by the structure of the DADs in G :

Definition 9. Let (R,G) be a DAD schema such that G = {$E_1F_1,\ldots,E_nF_n$}. For each i, let S_i be a new relation schema and X_i = Tar(F_i). We call $S_i(X_i)$ the *historical relation schema* associated to F_i. H= R $\cup$ {$S_1(X_1),\ldots, S_n(X_n)$} is the *historical schema* associated to (R,G).

These historical schemas are similar to *auxiliary relations* introduced in [9]. However, their semantics are slightly different. The "updates" on relations S_i will be side effects of insertions and deletions on the initial database.

Example 1. Consider $\mathbf{R} = \{P(AB), Q(BC), S(CD), R(AE)\}$ and $G = \{E_1F_1, E_2F_2\}$ where $E_1 = \Pi_{AC}(P \bowtie Q)$, $F_1 = \Pi_{AC}(D_{A=C}(P \bowtie Q) \bowtie S)$, $E_2 = \Pi_{BD}(\Pi_{CD}(P \bowtie S) \bowtie Q)$ and $F_2 = \Pi_{BD}(D_{A=D}(R \bowtie S) \bowtie Q)$. Then the historical schema associated to G is $\mathbf{H} = \mathbf{R} \cup \{S_1(AC), S_2(BD)\}$.

In the *University* Example (2) (see Appendix), the historical schema associated to the DAD schema (U, UNIV) is $\mathbf{H} = \{\text{Prof(Name,Course)}, \text{Stud(Name,Address)}, S(\text{Name})\}$.

Elementary Transaction Schema Given a relational expression E (think of E as being the current property of a DAD EF) and an update μ over a relation Q, we are interested in the relational expression E_μ^+ (resp. E_μ^-) which returns the tuples inserted in (resp. deleted from) the answer to E after performing the update μ. The expressions E_μ^+ and E_μ^- satisfy $E_\mu^+(I) = E(J) - E(I)$ and $E_\mu^-(I) = E(I) - E(J)$ for all $I \in \text{Inst}(\mathbf{R})$ and $J=\mu(I)$. They are defined in such a way that they do not compute E(J). The presentation of E_μ^+ and E_μ^- is skipped because of space limitation (see [2]).

Definition 10. The *elementary* transaction schema associated to the DAD schema $(\mathbf{R}, G)$ is $(\mathbf{H}, T)$ where $\mathbf{H}$ is the historical database schema associated to $(\mathbf{R}, G)$ and T constains for each relation $Q \in \mathbf{R}$ one transaction (i_Q) for inserting a tuple in Q and one transaction (d_Q) for deleting a tuple from Q, given by:
$i_Q(u) = $ **if** $(E_1)_t^+ \subseteq [S_1] \wedge \ldots \wedge (E_n)_t^+ \subseteq [S_n]$ **then** t ; t_{S_1} ; $\ldots$; t_{S_n} **endif**
$d_Q(u) = $ **if** $(E_1)_s^+ \subseteq [S_1] \wedge \ldots \wedge (E_n)_s^+ \subseteq [S_n]$ **then** s ; s_{S_1} ; $\ldots$; s_{S_n} **endif**
with $t = \text{ins}_Q(u)$ and $s = \text{del}_Q(u)$. The transactions t_{S_i} (resp. s_{S_i}) insert in the historical schemas the new tuples that answer the query F_i after the execution of t (resp. s). They are defined by :
$$t_{S_i} = \textbf{while } v \in (F_i)_t^+ \textbf{ do ins}_{S_i}(v) \textbf{ done.}$$
$$s_{S_i} = \textbf{while } v \in (F_i)_s^+ \textbf{ do ins}_{S_i}(v) \textbf{ done.}$$

The transactions hire', register', fire and cancel_registration of *University* Example (6) are the simplified versions of the elementary transactions i_{Prof}, i_{Stud}, d_{Prof} and d_{Stud} respectively.

Theorem 11. *Let $(\mathbf{R}, G)$ be a DAD schema and $(\mathbf{H}, T)$ its associated elementary transaction schema. Then $d\text{-}gen(\mathbf{H}, T)|_{\mathbf{R}} = Sat_1(\mathbf{R}, G)$ and thus $(\mathbf{H}, T)$ is correct w.r.t. $(\mathbf{R}, G)$.*

5 Generalized Transaction Schemas

From the previous section we know that it is impossible to derive an operational specification having the same effect as a set of DADs throught the notion of transaction schemas "à la Abiteboul/Vianu". In this section, we generalize the notion of a transaction schema.

The motivation is the following. A state sequence is augmented by a unique transaction call with input the current database state. Thus the elementary transaction schemas defined in Section 4 allow us to correctly update only one tuple at a time. The idea for recovering multiple changes during one transition is to specify a transation as a sequence of elementary transactions. The non elementary d-instance displayed in (7) of the *University* Example (see Appendix) can be generated using sequences of elementary transactions. Unfortunately, the fact that an elementary transaction preserves the consistency of the database does not imply that a sequence of elementary transactions does. This is illustrated by the d-instance displayed in (8) of the *University* Example (see Appendix) which is generated using sequences of elementary transactions and violates the DAD UNIV. Thus regular expressions on transactions are introduced in order to restrict the "shape" of the transaction sequences.

Definition 12. Let (S,T) be a transaction schema and let e be a regular expression over (the alphabet) T. Then (S,T,e) is a *generalized transaction schema*.

The regular language associated to the regular expression e is denoted by $\mathcal{L}(e)$. If $t \in \mathcal{L}(e)$ and $t = t_1 t_2 \ldots t_n$, a *call* to t is a transaction t', where $t' = t'_1; t'_2; \ldots; t'_n$ and t'_i is a call to t_i, for each $i \in [1 \ldots n]$. The set of calls to transactions in $\mathcal{L}(e)$ is denoted by Call(e). The set of d-instances over S generated by (S,T,e) is defined by d-gen(S,T,e) = { D $\in$ d-Inst(S) | $\forall 0 < i \leq |D|$, $\exists\, t \in$ Call(e), $D_i = t(D_{i-1})$ }.

The notions of correctness and completeness remain the same. At this point of the presentation, we need a notion of preservation of a DAD schema by a generalized transaction schema.

Definition 13. A transaction t over S is said to *preserve* a set of d-instances $\mathcal{D}$ over S iff for each D = $(D_0, \ldots, D_n) \in \mathcal{D}$ we have $(D_0, \ldots, D_n, t(D_n)) \in \mathcal{D}$. We say that (S,T,$e$) *preserves* $\mathcal{D}$ iff each t in $\mathcal{L}(e)$ preserves $\mathcal{D}$.

Let (R,G) be a DAD schema. Let H be the historical schema associated to (R,G). Let D = $(D_0, \ldots, D_n)$ be a d-instance in Sat(R,G). The *historical extension* of D is the d-instance D' over H such that $D'|_R = D$ and for each historical schema S associated to a DAD EF in G, $D'_i(S) = \bigcup_{j=0}^{i} F(D_j)$.

h-ext(R,G) denotes the set of historical extensions of d-instances in Sat(R,G).

Note that (†) if a generalized schema (S,T,e) preserves $\mathcal{D}$ and (ϕ) $\in \mathcal{D}$ then d-gen(S,T,e) $\subseteq \mathcal{D}$ and (††) if d-gen(S,T,e) = $\mathcal{D}$ then (S,T,e) preserves $\mathcal{D}$. Loosely speaking, thinking of S being the historical schema associated to (R,G) and $\mathcal{D}$ being h-ext(R,G), then (†) tells us that preservation implies correctness and (††) tells us that correctness plus completness imply preservation.

The generalized transaction schema (H,T,e) build next will generate exactly h-ext(R,G) and its definition uses the elementary transactions defined in the previous section. As a matter of fact note that :

Lemma 14. *The elementary transactions* i_P, d_P *preserve h-ext(R, G).*

The regular expression For a subclass of DADs, we show how to build a "good" generalized transaction schema from the elementary transaction schema. The step is to exhibit sufficient conditions which ensure that if each transaction of a sequence s preserves h-ext$(\mathbf{R},G)$ then a call to s also preserves h-ext$(\mathbf{R},G)$.

Definition 15. Let $(\mathbf{R},G)$ be a DAD schema, $\mathbf{H}$ its historical schema, let E be a relational expression over $\mathbf{R}$. E is said to be *dynamically decreasing* (d-decreasing) w.r.t. a transaction t over $\mathbf{H}$ if for each d-instance $(D_0,\ldots,D_n)$ in h-ext$(\mathbf{R},G)$ we have
$$E(D_{n+1}) \subseteq \bigcup_{i=0}^{n} E(D_i), \text{ if } D_{n+1} = t(D_n).$$

Note that if E is d-decreasing w.r.t. t and s then it is so w.r.t. $t;s$.

Theorem 16. *Checking dynamic decrease is undecidable.*

Lemma 17. *Let $(\mathbf{R},G)$ be a DAD schema and $\mathbf{H}$ its historical schema. Let t and s be transactions over $\mathbf{H}$ preserving h-ext$(\mathbf{R},G)$. If for each EF in G, F is d-decreasing w.r.t. t or E is d-decreasing w.r.t. s, then $t; s$ preserves h-ext$(\mathbf{R},G)$. It turns out that if E or F are d-decreasing w.r.t. t then t^* preserves h-ext$(\mathbf{R},G)$, where t^* stands for a sequence of calls to t.*

This result can be directly used to show that any call to t in the language of the expression e_m of the *University* Example (9) preserves the DAD schema $(\mathbf{U},\text{UNIV})$.

The problem to deal with general DADs arises when a relational schema P occurs in both the current property (E) and the past property (F). In this case, E and F may not be d-decreasing w.r.t. to the elementary transactions i_P and d_P. For that reason, we will restrict our attention to a subclass of DADs, called *regular*. For a dependency EF in this class, we are able to "separate" transactions which insert into the answers of E from those which insert into the answer of F.

Definition 18. A DAD EF is *regular* when E is a SPJRU query, F is a SPRJ query and the set of relations occuring in F is not included in the set of relations of E (sch(F) $\not\subseteq$ sch(E)). (this class contains consistent DIDs.)

If sch(F)∩sch(E) is empty then there is nothing to do in order to separate transactions inserting on E from those inserting on F. Note that if EF is regular, sch(E)∩sch(F) may not be empty. Thus, we need to introduce some technical modifications on the elementary transactions in order to acomplish the "separation". Let $G = \{E_1F_1,\ldots,E_nF_n\}$:

  arbitrary choose a relation schema $P_i \in \text{sch}(F_i) - \text{sch}(E_i)$.

  for each $R \in \mathbf{R}$ consider the set $\Lambda_R = \{i \mid 0 \leq i \leq n \text{ and } R \in \text{sch}(E_i) \cap \text{sch}(F_i)\}$. Let us assume $\Lambda_R = \{i_1,\ldots,i_k\}$. We define the p-transaction $t_R(\mathbf{x}) = \text{erase}_{P_{i_1}} ; \ldots ; \text{erase}_{P_{i_k}} ; i_R(\mathbf{x})$, where $i_R(\mathbf{x})$ is the elementary transaction inserting on R.

  Now we work with the modified transaction schema $(\mathbf{H},T)$ with $T = \{t_R, d_R \mid R \in \mathbf{R}\}$ (the transactions d_R have not been modified).

Example 2. Consider the DADs of example 1. Let us choose $S \in sch(F_1)-sch(E_1)$ and $R \in sch(F_2)-sch(E_2)$. Then we have:

$\Lambda_P=\{1\}$, $\Lambda_Q=\{1,2\}$, $\Lambda_S = \{2\}$, $\Lambda_R=\phi$.

t_P = erase$_S$;i$_P$, t_Q = erase$_S$; erase$_R$;i$_Q$, t_S = erase$_R$;i$_S$ and t_R = i$_R$.

Lemma 19. For all $R \in \mathbf{R}$ and for all EF in G, t_R preserves G and either E is d-decreasing w.r.t. t_R (when $R \notin sch(E)$) or F is d-decreasing w.r.t. t_R (when $R \in sch(E)$).

In order to exhibit the regular expression e such that the generalized transaction schema $(\mathbf{H},T,e)$ has the same effect as the regular DAD schema $(\mathbf{R},G)$, we use the graph (N,Arc), abusively called G, where $N = \mathbf{R}$ and $(P,Q) \in Arc$ if and only if there exists EF $\in$ G such that $P \in sch(E)$ and $Q \in sch(F)-sch(E)$. Next we only consider the case where the graph G is acyclic (the cyclic case is under study). The partition N_0, ..., N_k of N associated with the topological sorting of G is defined by:

N_0 is the set of nodes in G having no ingoing edges,

N_{i+1} is the set of nodes in the graph obtained by removing the nodes in $\bigcup_{j=0..i}N_j$ from G and having no ingoing edge.

Intuitively, the topological partition of G is the basis of the ordering of the transactions t_Q inserting tuples over the relations schemas Q of $\mathbf{R}$.

Definition 20. Let $(\mathbf{R}, G)$ be an acyclic regular DAD schema and let $(\mathbf{H},T)$ be the slightly modified elementary transaction schema defined above. Let N_0, ..., N_k be the topological partition of G. The *regular expression* associated to $(\mathbf{R}, G)$ is defined by :

$$e = (\sum_{P \in N_1} t_P + \sum_{P \in \mathbf{R}} d_P)^* ... (\sum_{P \in N_k} t_P + \sum_{P \in \mathbf{R}} d_P)^*$$

Example 3. For example 1, we have $N_0 =\{P,Q\}$, $N_1 =\{S\}$ and $N_2=\{R\}$ and the regular expression is:

$$e = (t_P+t_Q+d_P+d_Q+d_S+d_R)^*(t_S+d_P+d_Q+d_S+d_R)^*(t_R+d_P+d_Q+d_S+d_R)^*$$

In the *University* Example (9) (see Appendix), e_m is the regular expression associated to the DAD schema UNIV.

Theorem 21. *Let $(\mathbf{R}, G)$ be an acyclic regular DAD schema. Then, the generalized transaction schema $(\mathbf{H},T,e)$ where $\mathbf{H}$ is the historical schema, T is the modified elementary transaction schema and e is the regular expression associated to $(\mathbf{R}, G)$, is correct and complete w.r.t. the DAD schema $(\mathbf{R}, G)$, that is d-gen$(\mathbf{H},T,e) = h$-ext$(\mathbf{R},G)$.*

6 Conclusions and further work

In this paper we have investigated the relationship between declarative and operational specifications of dynamic databases. We have introduced a class of dynamic constraints, the Dynamic Algebraic Dependencies (DADs) for which the classical problems of consistency and implication are undecidable. We have introduced a generalized notion of transaction schema based on a regular language over an alphabet of transactions. For a signifiant subclass of these constraints, we have given an operational equivalent specification based on generalized transaction schemas. This result is of practical interest because it can be used in order to provide the database application programmer with primitive update programs and programming rules knowing that these primitives and rules are sufficient for writting any (good) update program. One open direction of research is to design the right tools for the programmer.

Clearly, it is important also to investigate other classes of dynamic dependencies. We already have obtained positive results concerning the operational specification of Vianu's Dynamic Functional Dependencies (DFDs) [21] using generalized transaction schemas. For both DADs and DFDs, the regular expressions introduced in transaction schemas are used in a very loose manner and it seems important to carry out a less pragmatic study in order to answer general questions of the kind: what are the temporal-logic-constraint schemas which can be refined to equivalent regular transaction schemas? are there regular transaction schemas not corresponding to any temporal-logic-constraint schemas? These questions are obviously difficult because the parameters which have to be considered are complex. For instance, the choice to use SdetTL could be reconsidered, the limit to put on the use of auxiliary data structures has to be investigated as well as the restriction to regular languages of transactions.

Another interesting direction of future research is given by the tight connection between the general problem presented here and the problem of modelling methods in the framework of object-oriented databases where methods implement object behaviour.

References

1. de Amo, S. , Bidoit N. : Contraintes Dynamiques d'Inclusion et Schémas Transactionnels, Neuviemes Journées Bases de Donnees Avancéees (1993) 401-424
2. de Amo, S., Bidoit N. : Contraintes Dynamiques Algébriques et Schémas Transactionnels. Technical Report, LIPN, Université Paris 13, 1994.
3. Abiteboul, S., Vianu, V. : Transactions and Integrity Constraints, ACM SIGACT/SIGMOD Symp. on Principles of Database Systems (1985) 193-204.
4. Abiteboul, S , Vianu, V. : Transactions Languages for Database update and specification. I.N.R.I.A. Technical Report 715, September 1987.
5. Abiteboul, S , Vianu, V. : A Transaction-based Approach to Relational Database Specification, Journal of the ACM **36** **4** (1989) 758-789.

6. Abiteboul, S , Vianu, V. : Procedural Languages for Database Queries and Updates, Proc. ACM SIGACT-SIGMOD-SIGART Symp. on Principles of Database Systems (1988) 240-250

7. Abiteboul, S , Vianu, V. : The Connection of static constraints vith determinism and boundedness of dynamic specification, Proc. of the Third Int. Conf. on Data and Knowledge Bases (1988) 324-334

8. Brodie, M.L. , Ridjanovic, D. : On the design and specification of database trans-actions, M.L. Brodie, J. Mylopoulos and J.W. Schmidt, editors, On Conceptual Modelling, Springer-Verlag(1984) 277-306

9. Chomicki, J. : History-less Checking of Dynamic Integrity Constraints, Int. Conf. on Data Engineering IEEE (1992) 557-564.

10. Castillo, I.M.V. , Casanova, M.A. , Furtado, A.L. : A Temporal Framework for Database Specifications, Proc. Int. Conf. on Very Large Data Bases(1982) 280-291.

11. Casanova, M.A. , Furtado, A.L. : On the description of database transition con-straints using temporal constraints, H. Gallaire, J. Minker and J.M. Nicolas, editors, Advances in Data Base Theory 2 Plenum Press, New York (1984) 221-236.

12. Casanova, M.A , Fagin, R. , Papadimitriu, C. : Inclusion Dependencies and their Interaction with Functional Dependencies, 1st ACM SIGACT-SIGMOD Conf. on Principles of Database Systems (1982) 171-176.

13. Chomicki, J. , Niwinski, D. : On the Feasibility of Checking Temporal Integrity Constraints, PODS 93.

14. Fiadeiro, J. , Sernadas, A. : Specification and verification of Database Dynamics, Acta Informatica 25 (1988) 625-661

15. Lipeck, U.W. , Saake, G. : Monitoring Dynamic Integrity Constraints Based on Temporal Logic. *Information Systems* 12 (1987), s 255-269.

16. Kanellakis, P.C. : Elements of Relational Database Theory. Handbook of Theoret-ical Computer Science 2 1073-1156.

17. Maier, D.: *The Theory of Relational Databases.* Computer Science Press (1983)

18. Nicolas, J.-M. : Logic for improving integrity checking in relational databases, Acta Informaticae 18 (1982) 227-253

19. Su, J. : Dynamic Constraints and Object Migration, 17th Int. Conf. on Very Large Data Bases (1991) 233-242.

20. Ullman, J.D. : Principles of Database Systems, 2nd Edition, Computer Science Press (1982).

21. Vianu, V. : Dynamic Functional Dependencies and Database Aging., Journal of ACM 34-1 (1987) 28-59

Appendix

Example 4 (University Example).

1. **U** is the *University* database schema including the relation schemas Stud(Name, Address) and Prof(Name,Course).
2. The dynamic constraint saying that *in order to be a professor one should have been a student in the past* is a *dynamic algebraic dependency* over **U** denoted by EF where $E = \Pi_{\text{Name}}[\text{Prof}]$ and $F = \Pi_{\text{Name}}[\text{Stud}]$. The *University* DAD schema is given by (**U**,UNIV) where UNIV denotes the DAD defined above.
3. The d-instance D presented below violates the DAD UNIV :

D_0		D_1		D_2	
Stud	Prof	Stud	Prof	Stud	Prof
ϕ	ϕ	(c,d)	ϕ	(c,d)	(a,b)

4. Consider the transaction schema (**U**,T) where T is the following set of the p-transactions:

$$\text{hire}(x,y) = \textbf{if } (x,z) \in \text{ Stud } \textbf{then } \text{ins}_{\text{Prof}}(x,y)$$
$$\text{register}(x,y) = \text{ins}_{\text{Stud}}(x,y)$$
$$\text{fire}(x,y) = \text{del}_{\text{Prof}}(x,y)$$
$$\text{cancel\_registration}(x,y) = \text{del}_{\text{Stud}}(x,y)$$

It is easy to check that T is correct w.r.t. (**U**,UNIV) that is T generates "good" d-instances.

5. The transaction schema (**U**,T) of item (4) is unable to generate all elementary d-instances satisfying UNIV. The d-instance D described below satisfies UNIV, it is an elementary d-instance, it cannot be generated by (**U**,T) :

D_0		D_1		D_2		D_3	
Stud	Prof	Stud	Prof	Stud	Prof	Stud	Prof
ϕ	ϕ	(a,b)	ϕ	ϕ	ϕ	ϕ	(a,c)

6. Consider the transaction schema (**H**,T') where $\textbf{H} = \{\textbf{U}\} \cup \{S(\text{Name})\}$ is the historical schema associated to (**U**,UNIV) and T' is the set of transactions fire(x,y) and cancel-registration(x,y) together with:

$$\text{hire}'(x,y) = \textbf{if } x \in \text{ S } \textbf{then } \text{ins}_{\text{Prof}}(x,y)$$
$$\text{register}'(x,y) = \text{ins}_{\text{Stud}}(x,y)\text{ins}_S(x)$$

(**H**,T') is correct w.r.t. (**U**,UNIV) and generates all elementary d-instances satisfying UNIV.

7. The elementary transaction schema (**H**,T') of item (6) is unable to generate all d-instances satisfying UNIV. The d-instance D given below (where $c \neq d$) satisfies UNIV and it cannot be generated by (**H**,T') :

D_0		D_1		D_2	
Stud	Prof	Stud	Prof	Stud	Prof
ϕ	ϕ	(a,b)	ϕ	ϕ	(a,c)
					(a,d)

We cannot obtain D_2 from D_1 by executing only one transaction of T'. In order to generate this d-instance, we must execute the *sequence* of transactions hire'(a,c) ; hire'(a,d) in order to perform the transition from D_1 to D_2.

8. If we take arbitrary sequences of transactions in T' in order to update the database **U**, we may obtain a d-instance which violates UNIV. Consider the following d-instance D :

D_0		D_1	
Prof	Stud	Prof	Stud
ϕ	ϕ	(a,b)	(a,c)

The d-instance D violates UNIV. Note that D_1 is obtained from D_0 by the sequence of transactions register'(a,c) ; hire'(a,b).

9. Consider the transaction schema (**H**, T') and the regular expression e_m over T' defined by

$$e_m = (e' + \text{hire'})^* \ (e' + \text{register'})^*$$

where
$$e' = \text{cancel\_registration} + \text{fire}$$

We have that d-gen(**H**,T',e_m)$|_U$ = Sat(**U**,UNIV).

Intuitively, these transactions are correct because a call to hire will effectively hire someone only if the person concerned belongs to the historical relation S of the database i.e. has been a student in the past. It is imporatnt to note that transaction of the regular language defined by e_m does not allow one to hire and register the same person "at the same time" (with the exception of someone who was already registered in the past).

Constraint-Generating Dependencies *

Marianne Baudinet,[1] Jan Chomicki,[2] and Pierre Wolper[3]

[1] Université Libre de Bruxelles, Informatique,
50 Avenue F.D. Roosevelt, C.P. 165, 1050 Brussels, Belgium
Email: mb@cs.ulb.ac.be
[2] Kansas State University, Dept of Computing and Information Sciences,
234 Nichols Hall, Manhattan, KS 66506-2302, U.S.A.
Email: chomicki@cis.ksu.edu
[3] Université de Liège, Institut Montefiore, B28
4000 Liège Sart-Tilman, Belgium
Email: pw@montefiore.ulg.ac.be

Abstract. Traditionally, dependency theory has been developed for un-interpreted data. Specifically, the only assumption that is made about the data domains is that data values can be compared for equality. However, data is often interpreted and there can be advantages in considering it as such, for instance obtaining more compact representations as done in constraint databases. This paper considers dependency theory in the context of interpreted data. Specifically, it studies *constraint-generating dependencies*. These are a generalization of equality-generating dependencies where equality requirements are replaced by constraints on an interpreted domain. The main technical results in the paper are a general decision procedure for the implication and consistency problems for constraint-generating dependencies, and complexity results for specific classes of such dependencies over given domains. The decision procedure proceeds by reducing the dependency problem to a decision problem for the constraint theory of interest, and is applicable as soon as the underlying constraint theory is decidable. The complexity results are, in some cases, directly lifted from the constraint theory; in other cases, optimal complexity bounds are obtained by taking into account the specific form of the constraint decision problem obtained by reducing the dependency implication problem.

1 Introduction

Relational database theory is largely built upon the assumption of uninterpreted data. While this has advantages, mostly generality, it foregoes the possibility of exploiting the structure of specific data domains. The introduction of constraint databases [21] was a break with this uninterpreted-data trend. Rather than defining the extension of relations by an explicit enumeration of tuples, a

---

* This work was supported by NATO Collaborative Research Grant CRG 940110 and by NSF Grant IRI-9110581.

constraint database uses constraint expressions to implicitly specify sets of tuples. Of course, for this to be possible in a meaningful way, one needs to consider interpreted data, that is, data from a specific domain on which a basic set of predicates and functions is defined. A typical example of constraint expressions and domain are linear inequalities interpreted on the reals. The potential gains from this approach are in the compactness of the representation (a single constraint expression can represent many, even an infinite number of, explicit tuples) and in the efficiency of query evaluation (computing with constraint expressions amounts to manipulating many tuples simultaneously).

Related developments have concurrently been taking place in temporal databases. Indeed, time values are intrinsically interpreted and this can be exploited for finitely representing potentially infinite temporal extensions. For instance, in [19] infinite temporal extensions are represented with the help of periodicity and inequality constraints, whereas in [10, 11] and [3] deductive rules over the integers are used for the same purpose. Constraints have also been used recently for representing incomplete temporal information [31, 23].

If one surveys the existing work on databases with interpreted data and implicit representations, one finds contributions on the expressiveness of the various representation formalisms [2, 5, 4], on the complexity of query evaluation [9, 12, 25, 31], and on data structures and algorithms to be used in the representation of constraint expressions and in query evaluation [28, 7, 8, 22]. However, much less has been done on extending other parts of traditional database theory, for instance schema design and dependency theory. It should be clear that dependency theory is of interest in this context. For instance, in [18], one finds a taxonomy of dependencies that are useful for temporal databases. Moreover, many *integrity constraints* over interpreted data can be represented as generalized dependencies. For instance, the integrity constraints over databases with ordered domains studied in [17, 33] can be represented as generalized dependencies. Also, some versions of the constraint checking problem studied in [16] can be viewed as generalized dependency implication problems.

One might think that the study of dependency theory has been close to exhaustive. While this is largely so for dependencies over uninterpreted data (that is, the context in which data values can only be compared for equality) [29], the situation is quite different for dependencies over data domains with a richer structure. The subject of this paper is the theory of these interpreted dependencies.

Specifically, we study the class of *constraint-generating dependencies*. These are the generalization of equality-generating dependencies [6], allowing arbitrary constraints on the data domain to appear wherever the latter only allow equalities. For instance, a constraint-generating dependency over an ordered domain can specify that if the value of an attribute A in a tuple t_1 is less than the value of the same attribute in a tuple t_2, then an identical relation holds for the values of an attribute B. This type of dependency can express a wide variety of constraints on the data. For instance, most of the temporal dependencies appearing in the taxonomy of [18] are constraint-generating dependencies.

Our technical contributions address the implication and the consistency[4] problems for constraint-generating dependencies. The natural approach to these problems is to write the dependencies as logical formulas. Unfortunately, the resulting formulas are not just formulas in the theory of the data domain. Indeed, they also contain uninterpreted predicate symbols representing the relations and thus are not a priori decidable, even if the data domain theory is decidable.

To obtain decision procedures, we show that the predicate symbols can be eliminated. Since the predicate symbols are implicitly universally quantified, this can be viewed as a form of second-order quantifier elimination. It is based on the fact that it is sufficient to consider relations with a small finite number of tuples. This then allows quantifier elimination by explicit representation of the possible tuples. The fact that one only needs to consider a small finite number of tuples is analogous to the fact that the implication problem for functional dependencies can be decided over 2-tuple relations [24]. Furthermore, for pure functional dependencies, our quantifier elimination procedures yields exactly the usual reduction to propositional logic. For more general constraint dependencies, it yields a formula in the theory of the data domain. Thus, if this theory is decidable, the implication and the consistency problems for constraint-dependencies are also decidable. Our approach is based on simple general logical arguments and provides a clear and straightforward justification for the type of procedure based on containment mappings used for instance in [16].

The complexity of the decision procedure depends on the specific data domain being considered and on the exact form of the constraint dependencies. We consider three typical constraint languages: equalities/inequalities, ordering constraints, and linear arithmetic constraints. We give a detailed picture of the complexity of the implication problem for dependencies over these theories and show the impact of the form of the dependencies on tractability.

2 Constraint-Generating Dependencies

Consider a relational database where some attributes take their values in specific domains, such as the integers or the reals, on which a set of predicates and functions are defined. We call such attributes *interpreted*. For the simplicity of the presentation, let us assume that the database only contains one (universal) relation r and let us ignore the noninterpreted attributes. In this context, it is natural to generalize the notion of equality-generating dependency [6]. Rather than specifying the propagation of equality constraints, we write similar statements involving arbitrary constraints (i.e., arbitrary formulas in the theory of the data domain). Specifically, we define *constraint-generating k-dependencies* as follows (the constant k specifies the number of tuples the dependency refers to).

---

[4] Though consistency is always satisfied for equality-generating dependencies, more general constraints turn it into a nontrivial problem.

Definition 1. Given a relation r, a *constraint-generating k-dependency* over r (with $k \geq 1$) is a first-order formula of the form

$$(\forall t_1) \cdots (\forall t_k) \left[[r(t_1) \wedge \cdots \wedge r(t_k) \wedge C[t_1, \ldots, t_k]] \Rightarrow C'[t_1, \ldots, t_k] \right]$$

where $C[t_1, \ldots, t_k]$ and $C'[t_1, \ldots, t_k]$ denote arbitrary constraint formulas relating the values of various attributes in the tuples $t_1, \ldots, t_k$. There are no restrictions on these formulas, they can include all constructs of the constraint theory under consideration, including quantification on the constraint domain. For instance, a constraint $C[t_1, t_2]$ could be $\exists z(t_1[A] < z \wedge z < t_2[A])$.

Note that we have defined constraint-generating dependencies in the context of a single relation, but the generalization to several relations is immediate.

Constraint-generating 1-dependencies as well as constraint-generating 2-dependencies are the most common. Notice that functional dependencies are a special form of constraint-generating 2-dependencies. Constraint-generating dependencies can naturally express a variety of arithmetic integrity constraints. The following examples illustrate their definition and show some of their potential applications.

Example 1. In [18], an exhaustive taxonomy of dependencies that can be imposed on a temporal relation is given. Of the more than 30 types of dependencies that are defined there, all but 4 can be written as constraint-generating dependencies. These last 4 require a generalization of tuple-generating dependencies [6] (see Section 5).

For instance, let us consider a relation $r(tt, vt)$ with two temporal attributes: transaction time (tt) and valid time (vt). The property of r being "strongly retroactively bounded" with bound $c \geq 0$ is expressed as the constraint-generating 1-dependency

$$(\forall t_1) \left[r(t_1) \Rightarrow [(t_1[tt] \leq t_1[vt] + c) \wedge (t_1[vt] \leq t_1[tt])] \right].$$

The property of r being "globally nondecreasing" is expressed as the constraint generating 2-dependency

$$(\forall t_1)(\forall t_2) \left[[r(t_1) \wedge r(t_2) \wedge (t_1[tt] < t_2[tt])] \Rightarrow (t_1[vt] \leq t_2[vt]) \right].$$

Example 2. Let us consider a relation $emp(name, boss, salary)$. Then the fact that an employee cannot make more than her boss is expressed as

$$(\forall t_1)(\forall t_2) \left[[emp(t_1) \wedge emp(t_2) \wedge (t_1[boss] = t_2[name])] \Rightarrow (t_1[salary] \leq t_2[salary]) \right].$$

3 Decision Problems for Constraint-Generating Dependencies

There are two basic decision problems for constraint-generating dependencies.

- *Implication*: Does a finite set of dependencies D imply a dependency d_0?
- *Consistency*: Does a finite set of dependencies D have a non-trivial model, that is, is D true in a nonempty relation?

The implication problem is a classical problem of database theory. Its practical motivation comes from the need to detect redundant dependencies, that is, those that are implied by a given set of dependencies. It is also the basis for proving the equivalence of dependency sets, and consequently for finding covers with desirable properties, such as minimality. The consistency problem has a trivial answer for uninterpreted dependencies: every set of equality- and tuple-generating dependencies has a 1-element model. However, even a single constraint-generating dependency may be inconsistent, as illustrated by $(\forall t)[r(t) \Rightarrow t[1] < t[1]]$. We only study the *implication* problem since the consistency problem is its dual: a set of dependencies D is inconsistent if and only if D implies a dependency of the form $(\forall t)[r(t) \Rightarrow C]$, where C is any unsatisfiable constraint (we assume the existence of at least one such unsatisfiable constraint formula).

The result we prove in this section is that the implication problem for constraint-generating dependencies reduces to the validity problem for a formula in the underlying constraint theory. Specific dependencies and theories will be considered in Section 4, and the corresponding complexity results provided. The reduction proceeds in three steps. First, we prove that the implication problem is equivalent to the implication problem restricted to finite relations of bounded size. Second, we eliminate from the implication to be decided the second-order quantification (over relations). Third, we eliminate the first-order quantification (over tuples) from the dependencies themselves and replace it by quantification over the domain – a process that we call *symmetrization*. This gives us the desired result.

3.1 Statement of the Problem and Notation

Let r denote a relation with n interpreted attributes. Let $d_0, d_1, \ldots, d_m$ denote constraint-generating k-dependencies over the attributes of r. The value of k need not be the same for all d_i's. We denote by k_0 the value of k for d_0.

The *dependency implication problem* consists in deciding whether d_0 is implied by the set of dependencies $D = \{d_1, \ldots, d_m\}$. In other words, it consists in deciding whether d_0 is satisfied by every interpretation that satisfies D, which can be formulated as

$$(\forall r)[r \models D \Rightarrow r \models d_0], \qquad (1)$$

where D stands for $d_1 \wedge \cdots \wedge d_m$. We equivalently write (1) as $(\forall r)[D(r) \Rightarrow d_0(r)]$ when we wish to emphasize the fact that the dependencies apply to the tuples of r.

3.2 Towards a Decision Procedure

Reduction to k-tuple Relations. The following three lemmas establish that when dealing with constraint-generating k-dependencies, it is sufficient to consider relations of size[5] k. Their proofs are straightforward.

Lemma 2. *Let d denote any constraint-generating k-dependency. If a relation r does not satisfy d, then there is a relation r' of size k that does not satisfy d. Furthermore, r' is obtained from r by removing and/or duplicating tuples.*

Lemma 3. *If a relation r satisfies a set of constraint-generating k-dependencies $D = \{d_1, \ldots d_m\}$ and does not satisfy a constraint-generating k_0-dependency d_0, then there is a relation r' of size k_0 that satisfies D but does not satisfy d_0.*

Lemma 4. *Consider an instance (D, d_0) of the dependency implication problem where d_0 is a constraint-generating k_0-dependency. The dependency d_0 is implied by D over all relations if and only if it is implied by D over relations of size k_0; i.e., $(\forall r)[r \models D \Rightarrow r \models d_0]$ iff $(\forall r')[|r'| = k_0 \Rightarrow [r' \models D \Rightarrow r' \models d_0]]$.*

The above lemmas generalize properties of uninterpreted dependencies.

Second-order Quantifier Elimination. By Lemma 4, in order to decide the implication problem, we just need to be able to decide this problem over relations of size k for a given k. Deciding the implication (1) thus reduces to deciding

$$(\forall r')\big[[|r'| = k \wedge D(r')] \Rightarrow d_0(r')\big]. \tag{2}$$

Let $r' = \{t_{x_1}, \ldots, t_{x_k}\}$ denote an arbitrary relation of size k where $t_{x_1}, \ldots, t_{x_k}$ are arbitrary tuples. We can eliminate the (second-order) quantification over relations from the implication (2) and replace it with a quantification over tuples (that is, over vectors of elements of the domain). We get

$$(\forall t_{x_1}) \cdots (\forall t_{x_k})\big[D(\{t_{x_1}, \ldots, t_{x_k}\}) \Rightarrow d_0(\{t_{x_1}, \ldots, t_{x_k}\})\big]. \tag{3}$$

Symmetrization. Next, we simplify the formula (3), whose validity is equivalent to the constraint dependency implication problem, by eliminating the quantification over tuples that appears within the dependencies of $D \cup \{d_0\}$. We refer to this quantifier elimination procedure for dependencies as *symmetrization*. For the sake of clarity, we present the details of the symmetrization process for the case where $k = 2$. The process can be extended directly to the more general case.

For the case where $k = 2$, the formula (3) to be decided is the following.

$$(\forall t_x)(\forall t_y)\big[D(\{t_x, t_y\}) \Rightarrow d_0(\{t_x, t_y\})\big].$$

We can simplify this formula further by eliminating the quantification over tuples that appears in the dependencies $d(\{t_x, t_y\})$ in $D \cup \{d_0\}$. Every such dependency $d(\{t_x, t_y\})$ can indeed be rewritten as a constraint formula $cf(d)$ in the following manner.

---

[5] In what follows, we consider relations as multisets rather than sets. This has no impact on the implication problem, but simplifies our procedure.

1. Let d be a 1-dependency, that is, d is of the form $(\forall t)\big[[r'(t) \wedge C[t]] \Rightarrow C'[t]\big]$. This dependency considered over $r' = \{t_x, t_y\}$ is equivalent to the constraint formula

$$cf(d) : \big[C[t_x] \Rightarrow C'[t_x]\big] \wedge \big[C[t_y] \Rightarrow C'[t_y]\big],$$

which is a conjunction of $k = 2$ constraint implications. Notice that the t_x and t_y appearing in this formula are just tuples of variables ranging over the domain of the constraint theory of interest.

2. Let d be a 2-dependency, that is, d is of the form

$$(\forall t_1)(\forall t_2)\big[[r'(t_1) \wedge r'(t_2) \wedge C[t_1, t_2]] \Rightarrow C'[t_1, t_2]\big].$$

This dependency considered over $r' = \{t_x, t_y\}$ is equivalent to the constraint formula

$$cf(d) : \begin{aligned}&\big[C[t_x, t_y] \Rightarrow C'[t_x, t_y]\big] \wedge \big[C[t_y, t_x] \Rightarrow C'[t_y, t_x]\big] \wedge \\ &\big[C[t_x, t_x] \Rightarrow C'[t_x, t_x]\big] \wedge \big[C[t_y, t_y] \Rightarrow C'[t_y, t_y]\big],\end{aligned}$$

which is a conjunction of $k^k = 4$ constraint implications.

The rewriting of d as $cf(d)$ is what we call the *symmetrization* of d, for rather obvious reasons. It extends directly to any value of k. Notice that for a given k, any j-dependency d is rewritten as a constraint formula $cf(d)$, which is a conjunction of k^j constraint implications. Interestingly, in the case of functional dependencies, symmetrization is not needed. This is due to the fact that the underlying constraints are equalities, which are already symmetric. Hence, in that special case, symmetrization would produce several instances of the same constraint formulas.

Applying the symmetrization process to all the dependencies appearing in the formula (3), we get

$$(\forall t_{x_1}) \cdots (\forall t_{x_k})\big[cf(d_1) \wedge \cdots \wedge cf(d_m) \Rightarrow cf(d_0)\big]. \tag{4}$$

Notice that in formula (4), each tuple variable can be replaced by n domain variables, and thus the quantification over tuples can be replaced by a quantification over elements of the domain. For the sake of clarity, we simply denote by $(\forall *)$ the adequate quantification over elements of the domain (the *universal closure*). Formula (4) thus becomes

$$(\forall *)\big[cf(d_1) \wedge \cdots \wedge cf(d_m) \Rightarrow cf(d_0)\big], \tag{5}$$

where each $cf(d)$ is a conjunction of k^j constraint implications if d is a j-dependency and d_0 is a k-dependency. Thus, we have proved the following theorem.

Theorem 5. *For constraint-generating k-dependencies, with bounded k, the implication problem is linearly reduced to the validity of a universally quantified formula of the constraint theory.*

Example 3. Let us consider the following constraint-generating 2-dependencies over a relation r with a single attribute.

$$d_1 : (\forall x)(\forall y)\big[r(x) \wedge r(y) \Rightarrow x \leq y\big]$$
$$d_2 : (\forall x)(\forall y)\big[r(x) \wedge r(y) \Rightarrow x = y\big]$$

Symmetrizing them produces the following constraint formulas.

$$cf(d_1) : x \leq y \wedge y \leq x \wedge x \leq x \wedge y \leq y$$
$$cf(d_2) : x = y \wedge y = x \wedge x = x \wedge y = y$$

It is clear that these two constraint formulas are equivalent, as they should be.

4 Complexity Results

4.1 Clausal dependencies

In this section, we study the complexity of the implication problem for some classes of constraint-generating dependencies occurring in practice, in particular dependencies with equality, order, and arithmetic constraints. We restrict our attention to atomic constraints and clausal dependencies as defined below.

Definition 6. An *atomic constraint* is a formula consisting of an interpreted predicate symbol applied to terms. A *clausal* constraint-generating dependency is a constraint-generating dependency such that the constraint in the antecedent is a conjunction of atomic constraints and the constraint in the consequent is an atomic constraint.

Notice that a constraint-generating dependency in which the constraint in the antecedent and the constraint in the consequent are both conjunctions of atomic constraints can be rewritten as a set of clausal constraint-generating dependencies (by decomposing the conjunction in the consequent). Essentially all the dependencies mentioned in [18] can be written in clausal form.

Moreover, we assume that the constraint language is *closed under negation.*[6] This is again satisfied by many examples of interest, the most notable exception being the class of functional dependencies. Finally, we study classes of k-dependencies for fixed values of k (mainly $k = 2$). This makes it possible to contrast our results with the results about functional dependencies which are 2-dependencies and for which the implication problem can be solved in $O(n)$.

We proceed by reducing clausal dependency implication to unsatisfiability. More precisely, we negate the result of the symmetrization (formula 5) to obtain

$$(\exists *)\big[cf(d_1) \wedge \cdots \wedge cf(d_m) \wedge \neg cf(d_0)\big], \tag{6}$$

and then move the negation inwards and put the result in conjunctive normal form. Because the constraint language is closed under negation, the implication

---

[6] Note that in this context, the distinction between positive and negative atomic constraints is meaningless.

problem for clausal dependencies can thus be reduced to the unsatisfiability of a formula of the form

$$\Psi = (\exists *) \left[\bigwedge_i \left(\bigvee_j (c_{ij}) \right) \right], \tag{7}$$

where each c_{ij} is an atomic constraint. When $|D| = m$ and d_0 is a k-dependency, the number of clauses in the formula Ψ above is at most equal to $m \cdot k^k$ plus the number of constraints in d_0. The number of literals in each clause is equal to the number of atomic constraints in the dependencies of D, or to 1 for the clauses obtained from the decomposition of d_0. Thus deciding the validity of the implication problem for k-dependencies (k fixed) can be done by checking the unsatisfiability of a conjunction of clauses of length that is linear in the size of $D \cup \{d_0\}$. We can replace the variables in the constraint formulas by the corresponding Skolem constants and view Ψ as a ground formula.

The opposite LOGSPACE reduction, from unsatisfiability to implication, also exists and requires only 1-dependencies.

4.2 Equality and order constraints

We consider here atomic constraints of the form $x\theta y$ where $\theta \in \{=, \neq, <, \leq\}$ over integers, rationals, or reals.[7] This constraint language has two sublanguages closed under negation which we also study: $\{=, \neq\}$-constraints and $\{<, \leq\}$-constraints. We make the additional assumption that *no domain constants appear in the dependencies.* (If this assumption is not satisfied, the complexity usually shifts up. For example, in Theorem 7 the first case becomes co-NP-complete for the integers by the results of [26].)

Theorem 7. *The implication problem for clausal constraint-generating k-dependencies is:*

1. *in PTIME for dependencies with one atomic $\{=, \neq, <, \leq\}$-constraint (no constraints in the antecedent),*
2. *co-NP-complete for dependencies with two or more atomic $\{=, \neq\}$-constraints,*
3. *co-NP-complete for dependencies with two or more atomic $\{<, \leq\}$-constraints.*

Proof Sketch. The first result follows from [30, page 892]. The membership in co-NP for the two remaining cases follows from the fact that checking the satisfiability of a conjunction of equality and order constraints can be done in polynomial time. To prove the lower bounds, we reduce an NP-complete problem to satisfiability of a set of ground clauses with at most two literals corresponding to the formula Ψ above (formula 7). This reduction is then composed with the reduction from unsatisfiability to dependency implication. We use a reduction from GRAPH-3-COLORABILITY for $\{=, \neq\}$-constraints, and from BETWEENNESS [13, page 279] for $\{<, \leq\}$-constraints. Details are omitted due to space limitation.

---

[7] In fact, our lower bounds hold for any infinite linearly-ordered set.

Note that for finite domains of size greater than 2, the implication problem is co-NP-complete even for dependencies with one atomic constraint.

The above results are rather negative. To obtain more tractable classes, we propose to further restrict the syntax of dependencies by typing.

Definition 8. A clausal dependency is *typed* if each atomic constraint involves only the values of one given attribute in different tuples.

The second dependency in Example 1 of Section 2 (i.e., the property of r being "globally nondecreasing") is typed, while the first one (the property of r being "strongly retroactively bounded") and the dependency of Example 2 are not. Functional dependencies are also typed.

Notice that for typed dependencies, the reduction from unsatisfiability to dependency implication given above is not useful for obtaining lower bounds. Indeed, it reduces unsatisfiability to implication of 1-dependencies which are not typed. Furthermore, this reduction cannot in general be adapted to yield typed 2-dependencies. Indeed, because of the symmetrization procedure, the constraint problem obtained from typed 2-dependencies has a particular symmetric structure (for 1-dependencies, there is no symmetrization). The question thus is whether this symmetric structure is sufficient for lowering the complexity of the constraint problem that has to be solved. As shown in the following theorem, the answer is fortunately positive.

Theorem 9. *The implication problem for typed clausal constraint-generating 2-dependencies with at most two atomic $\{=, \neq, <, \leq\}$-constraints is in PTIME $(O(n))$.*

Proof. A typed 2-dependency is of the form

$$(\forall t_x)(\forall t_y)\left[[r(t_x) \wedge r(t_y) \wedge (t_x[i] \; pred_\ell \; t_y[i])] \Rightarrow (t_x[j] \; pred_r \; t_y[j])\right] \qquad (8)$$

where each of $pred_\ell$ and $pred_r$ is one of $\{=, \neq, <, \leq\}$. By Lemma 4, the implication problem for typed 2-dependencies coincides with the implication problem over 2-tuple relations. The remaining steps of the reduction given in Section 3 show how this implication can be reduced to a pure constraint problem. However, since we need to take into account the specific nature of the constraint problem obtained for typed 2-dependencies, our starting point for the proof of this theorem is further upstream. We consider the problem of deciding whether for a typed 2-dependency d_0 and a set D of dependencies of the same kind, $D \models d_0$ over 2-tuple relations, or equivalently whether $D \wedge \neg d_0$ is unsatisfiable over 2-tuple relations. We give a PTIME algorithm for deciding satisfiability (and hence unsatisfiability) over 2-tuple relations of $D \wedge \neg d_0$.

Among the predicates in $\{=, \neq, <, \leq\}$, we distinguish the set *eq-pred* : $\{=, \leq\}$, and the set *diff-pred* : $\{\neq, <\}$. The intuition is that members of *eq-pred* can be satisfied when their arguments are equal, whereas members of *diff-pred* cannot be satisfied in that case. This allows us to define four classes of constraint dependencies:

$$eq\text{-}pred \Rightarrow eq\text{-}pred \quad (9) \qquad\qquad diff\text{-}pred \Rightarrow eq\text{-}pred \quad (11)$$
$$eq\text{-}pred \Rightarrow diff\text{-}pred \quad (10) \qquad\qquad diff\text{-}pred \Rightarrow diff\text{-}pred \quad (12)$$

Notice that (10) and (11) are self-contrapositives, whereas (9) and (12) are each other's contrapositives. We thus only need one of the latter two categories and choose to keep (12). Furthermore, all dependencies of the form (10) are unsatisfiable (over nonempty relations). Indeed, if in (8) one chooses $t_x = t_y$, then $(t_x[i] \; eq\text{-}pred \; t_x[i])$ is true whereas $(t_x[j] \; diff\text{-}pred \; t_y[j])$ has to be false and the implication is false. Thus, if such a dependency occurs in D, this set is trivially unsatisfiable and we can assume without loss of generality that D only contains dependencies of the forms (11) and (12). Similarly, if d_0 is of the form (10), $\neg d_0$ is valid and, since D is always satisfiable by a one tuple relation if it does not contain dependencies of the form (10), $D \wedge \neg d_0$ is satisfiable. We can thus also assume without loss of generality that d_0 is either of the form (11) or of the form (12).

Since the dependencies are typed, each dependency d involves two attributes of the relation r which we refer to as l_d (the one on the left of the implication) and r_d (the one on the right of the implication). We are looking for a 2-tuple model of $D \wedge \neg d_0$. The first step of the procedure is to classify the attributes of the relation r into the set of those that must have a different value in the two tuples of the relation and those that may have the same value. We call the first $diff$-attributes and the second eq-attributes. The set DA of $diff$-attributes is obtained by the following procedure.

The initial extension of DA is obtained from d_0. If d_0 is of the form $diff\text{-}pred \Rightarrow eq\text{-}pred$, then DA initially contains both l_{d_0} and r_{d_0}; whereas if d_0 is of the form $diff\text{-}pred \Rightarrow diff\text{-}pred$, then initially $DA = \{l_{d_0}\}$. One then repeatedly applies the following step until saturation: if there is a dependency d of the form $diff\text{-}pred \Rightarrow diff\text{-}pred$ such that the attribute l_d is in DA, then the attribute r_d is added to DA. This procedure is similar to the one computing the closure of a set of attributes under a set of functional dependencies and hence can be implemented in linear time. From now on, let DA be the set of attributes obtained by this procedure.

A direct consequence of the way in which DA is constructed is that any 2-tuple model in which both tuples give the same value to attributes in DA cannot satisfy $D \wedge \neg d_0$. Furthermore, we claim that if $D \wedge \neg d_0$ has a 2-tuple model, it has a 2-tuple model in which all attributes in DA have different values in the two tuples, and all attributes not in DA have the same value in both tuples. To prove this, assume there is a model and give an arbitrary identical value in both tuples to the attributes not in DA. Since this can only change the truth value of the dependencies in D and of $\neg d_0$ from *false* to *true*, we still have a model.

Thus, in order to find a model for $D \wedge \neg d_0$, it is sufficient to find values for the attributes in DA. We know that these values have to be different and, since we are working in a limited theory, the only relevant property of these values is their order (which one is smaller than the other). Let us call the two possible orders u (up) and d (down). The choice between u and d for each attribute i can be encoded by one boolean proposition $u[i]$ (*true* if the order for i is u, *false* if it is d). The problem thus is to find truth values for the propositions $u[i]$ in such a way that they define a model of $D \wedge \neg d_0$.

To do this, we encode the conditions imposed by the dependencies referring to attributes that are both in DA. Indeed, for dependencies in D (and for $\neg d_0$), if one of the atomic constraints does not refer to an attribute in DA, the dependency ($\neg d_0$) is satisfied whatever the order chosen for the attributes.

We construct the constraints on the propositions u for dependencies in positive form as they appear in D. For $\neg d_0$, one applies the construction to d_0 and negates the result. There are 9 cases of dependencies of the form *diff-pred* $\Rightarrow$ *diff-pred*:

$$\neq \Rightarrow \neq \quad (13) \qquad < \Rightarrow \neq \quad (16) \qquad > \Rightarrow \neq \quad (19)$$
$$\neq \Rightarrow < \quad (14) \qquad < \Rightarrow < \quad (17) \qquad > \Rightarrow < \quad (20)$$
$$\neq \Rightarrow > \quad (15) \qquad < \Rightarrow > \quad (18) \qquad > \Rightarrow > \quad (21)$$

Cases 13, 16, and 19 translate to *true* (we have imposed that attributes in DA have different values in both tuples). Cases 14 and 15 are always unsatisfiable (by symmetry) and thus translate to the constraint *false*. Cases 17 and 21 translate to $(u[l_d] \Rightarrow u[r_d]) \wedge (\neg u[l_d] \Rightarrow \neg u[r_d])$, whereas cases 18 and 20 translate to $(u[l_d] \Rightarrow \neg u[r_d]) \wedge (\neg u[l_d] \Rightarrow u[r_d])$.

There are also 9 cases of dependencies of the form *diff-pred* $\Rightarrow$ *eq-pred*:

$$\neq \Rightarrow = \quad (22) \qquad < \Rightarrow = \quad (25) \qquad > \Rightarrow = \quad (28)$$
$$\neq \Rightarrow \leq \quad (23) \qquad < \Rightarrow \leq \quad (26) \qquad > \Rightarrow \leq \quad (29)$$
$$\neq \Rightarrow \geq \quad (24) \qquad < \Rightarrow \geq \quad (27) \qquad > \Rightarrow \geq \quad (30)$$

Cases 22, 23, 24, 25, and 28 are contradictory and translate to *false*. Cases 26 and 30 translate as 17 and 21 and, similarly, 27 and 29 are translated as 18 and 20.

The result of this encoding is a set of Boolean clauses with at most two literals per clause. Deciding if it is satisfiable can thus be done with the 2-SAT procedure which is in PTIME ($O(n)$) [1].

Theorem 10. *The implication problem for typed clausal constraint-generating 2-dependencies is:*

1. *co-NP-complete for dependencies with three or more atomic $\{=, \neq\}$-constraints,*
2. *co-NP-complete for dependencies with three or more atomic $\{<, \leq\}$-constraints.*

Proof Sketch. Proving the lower bounds in the typed case is more difficult than in Theorem 7 because the reverse reduction, from unsatisfiability of ground clauses to dependency implication that uses 1-dependencies, is not available. We can continue, however, to work with ground clauses as in the proof of Theorem 7 provided the clauses can be mapped back to typed 2-dependencies. The proofs in both cases involve a reduction from SET SPLITTING [13, page 221]. They proceed in two steps. First, we reduce SET SPLITTING to a collection of ground clauses C. Then we show how to construct an instance of the implication problem for typed 2-dependencies whose clausal formulation Ψ (see formula 7) is equisatisfiable with C. Details are omitted due to space limitation.

Theorem 9 yields a new class of dependencies with a tractable implication problem. This class properly contains that of unary functional dependencies and is incomparable with the class of all functional dependencies. Together, Theorems 7, 9 and 10 give a *complete classification* of tractable and intractable classes of untyped and typed 2-dependencies with $\{=, \neq, <, \leq\}$-constraints. The case of typed k-dependencies ($k > 2$) with two $\{=, \neq, <, \leq\}$-constraints is open. (The implication problem for such dependencies with three constraints is clearly co-NP-complete by Theorems 7 and 10.)

4.3 Linear arithmetic constraints

We consider now *linear arithmetic constraints*, i.e., atomic constraints of the form $a_1 x_1 + \cdots + a_k x_k \leq a$ (domain constants are allowed here). We can use directly the results about the complexity of linear programming [27].

Theorem 11. *For linear arithmetic constraints, the implication problem for clausal constraint-generating k-dependencies with one atomic constraint per dependency is in PTIME for the reals, and co-NP-complete for the integers.*

The case of more than one linear arithmetic constraint per dependency remains to be investigated.

5 Conclusions and Related Work

A brief summary of this paper is that constraint-generating dependencies are an interesting concept, and that deciding implication of such dependencies is basically no harder than deciding the underlying constraint theory, which, a priori, was not obvious. The obvious applications of constraint-generating dependencies are constraint database design theory and consistency checking. Apart from the constraint languages considered in this paper, other languages may be relevant as well, for instance the *congruence constraints* that appear in [18]. Also, the impact that the presence of domain constants in equality and order constraints has on the complexity of implication should be fully studied.

Other forms of constraint dependencies can also be of interest. An obvious candidate is the concept of *tuple-generating* constraint dependency. Unfortunately, the implication problem for these dependencies is harder to decide and more closely linked to the underlying theory. Indeed, tuple-generating constraint dependencies can, for example, specify a dense domain.

As far as related work, we should first mention that Jensen and Snodgrass [18] induced us to think about constraint dependencies. We should note that the integrity constraints over temporal databases postulated there involve both typed and untyped constraint-generating dependencies, as well as tuple-generating ones.

Two recent papers on *implication constraints* by Ishakbeyoğlu, Ozsoyoğlu and Zhang [17, 33], as well as a paper on efficient integrity checking by Gupta, Sagiv, Ullman, and Widom [16] contain work fairly close to ours. However, there are several important differences. Foremost, all three papers discuss a fixed language of constraint formulas, namely equality $(=)$, inequality $(\neq)$, and order $(<, \leq)$ constraints, while our results are applicable to any decidable constraint theory thanks to our general reduction strategy. In particular, the papers [33, 16], which were written independently of the first version of this paper, both present results equivalent to our Theorem 5, but formulated in the context of a fixed constraint language. Also, the proof techniques in those papers, based on the theory of conjunctive queries, are quite different from ours. Moreover, the complexity results of [33] are obtained in a slightly different model. Both the number of database literals and the arity of relations in a dependency are considered as parts of the input, while we consider only the latter. We think that our model is more intuitive because it is difficult to come up with a meaningful dependency that references more than a few tuples in a relation. Our intractability results are stronger than those of [33] while our positive characterizations of polynomial-time decidable problems do not necessarily carry over to the framework of [33]. Also, in [17, 33], the tractable classes of dependencies are not defined syntactically but rather by the presence or absence of certain types of refutations.

A clausal constraint-generating dependency (quantifiers omitted)

$$r(t_1) \wedge \cdots \wedge r(t_k) \wedge C_1 \wedge \cdots \wedge C_n \Rightarrow C_0$$

can be viewed as an integrity constraint (in the notation of [16])

$$\textbf{panic} : - r(t_1) \& \cdots \& r(t_k) \& C_1 \& \cdots \& C_n \& \neg C_0.$$

Thus the implication of a dependency by a set of dependencies is equivalent to the subsumption of an integrity constraint by a set of integrity constraints. Therefore the results about the complexity of implication from Section 4 transfer directly to the context of constraint subsumption. The paper [16] applies the results about constraint subsumption to develop techniques for efficient integrity checking. Unfortunately, this application requires introducing constants into constraints, so our complexity results, developed under the assumption that constants do not appear in dependencies, are not applicable here, though our general reduction is.

Order dependencies, proposed by Ginsburg and Hull [14, 15], are typed clausal 2-dependencies over the theory of equality and order (without $\neq$). The order is not required to be total. Ginsburg and Hull provided an axiomatization of such dependencies and proved that the implication problem is co-NP-complete for dependencies with at least three constraints. To prove the lower bound they used, however, dependencies with equality and order constraints, while we proved the lower bounds for both theories separately (Theorem 10). Ginsburg and Hull also supplied a number of tractable dependency classes which are, again, different from ours and involve mainly partial orders.

Acknowledgements. We wish to acknowledge anonymous referees for several helpful comments.

References

1. B. Aspvall, M. Plass, and R. Tarjan. A linear-time algorithm for testing the truth of certain quantified boolean formulas. *Inf. Process. Lett.*, 8(3):121–123, 1979.
2. M. Baudinet. On the expressiveness of temporal logic programming. To appear in *Information and Computation*.
3. M. Baudinet. Temporal logic programming is complete and expressive. In *Sixteenth ACM Symposium on Principles of Programming Languages*, pages 267–280, Austin, Texas, Jan. 1989.
4. M. Baudinet, J. Chomicki, and P. Wolper. Temporal deductive databases. In A. Tansel, et al., editors, *Temporal Databases. Theory, Design, and Implementation*, chapter 13, pages 294–320. Benjamin/Cummings, 1993.
5. M. Baudinet, M. Niézette, and P. Wolper. On the representation of infinite temporal data and queries. In *Tenth ACM Symposium on Principles of Database Systems*, pages 280–290, Denver, Colorado, May 1991.
6. C. Beeri and M. Vardi. A proof procedure for data dependencies. *Journal of the ACM*, 31(4):718–741, Oct. 1984.
7. A. Brodsky, J. Jaffar, and M. J. Maher. Toward practical constraint databases. In *19th International Conference on Very Large Data Bases*, Dublin, Aug. 1993.
8. A. Brodsky, C. Lassez, and J.-L. Lassez. Separability of polyhedra and a new approach to spatial storage. In *Proceedings of the First Workhop on Principles and Practice of Constraint Programming*, Newport, Rhode Island, Apr. 1993.
9. J. Chomicki. Polynomial time query processing in temporal deductive databases. In *Ninth ACM Symposium on Principles of Database Systems*, pages 379–391, Nashville, Tennessee, Apr. 1990.
10. J. Chomicki and T. Imieliński. Temporal deductive databases and infinite objects. In *Seventh ACM Symposium on Principles of Database Systems*, pages 61–73, Austin, Texas, Mar. 1988.
11. J. Chomicki and T. Imieliński. Finite Representation of Infinite Query Answers. *ACM Transactions on Database Systems*, 18(2):181–223, June 1993.
12. J. Cox and K. McAloon. Decision procedures for constraint based extensions of Datalog. In F. Benhamou and A. Colmerauer, editors, *Constraint Logic Programming: Selected Research*. MIT Press, 1993.
13. M. R. Garey and D. S. Johnson. *Computers and Intractability: A Guide to the Theory of NP-Completeness*. W.H. Freeman and Company, New York, 1979.
14. S. Ginsburg and R. Hull. Order dependency in the relational model. *Theoretical Computer Science*, 26:149–195, 1983.
15. S. Ginsburg and R. Hull. Sort sets in the relational model. *Journal of the ACM*, 33(3):465–488, July 1986.
16. A. Gupta, Y. Sagiv, J. D. Ullman, and J. Widom. Constraint checking with partial information. In *Thirteenth ACM Symposium on Principles of Database Systems*, pages 45–55, Minneapolis, MN, May 1994.
17. N. S. Ishakbeyoğlu and Z. M. Ozsoyoğlu. On the maintenance of implication integrity constraints. In *Fourth International Conference on Database and Expert Systems Applications*, pages 221–232, Prague, Sept. 1993. LNCS 720, Springer.

18. C. Jensen and R. Snodgrass. Temporal specialization. In *Eighth International Conference on Data Enfineering*, pages 594–603, Tempe, Arizona, Feb. 1992. IEEE.

19. F. Kabanza, J.-M. Stévenne, and P. Wolper. Handling infinite temporal data. In *Ninth ACM Symposium on Principles of Database Systems*, pages 392–403, Nashville, Tennessee, Apr. 1990.

20. P. Kanellakis. Elements of relational database theory. In J. van Leeuwen, editor, *Handbook of Theoretical Computer Science*, volume B, chapter 17, pages 1073–1158. Elsevier/MIT Press, 1990.

21. P. C. Kanellakis, G. M. Kuper, and P. Revesz. Constraint query languages. In *Ninth ACM Symposium on Principles of Database Systems*, pages 299–313, Nashville, Tennessee, Apr. 1990.

22. P. C. Kanellakis, S. Ramaswamy, D. E. Vengroff, and J. S. Vitter. Indexing for data models with constraints and classes. In *Twelfth ACM Symposium on Principles of Database Systems*, pages 233–243, Washington, DC, May 1993.

23. M. Koubarakis. Representation and querying in temporal databases : the power of temporal constraints. In *Ninth International Conference on Data Engineering*, Vienna, Austria, Apr. 1993.

24. D. Maier. *The Theory of Relational Databases.* Computer Science Press, 1983.

25. P. Revesz. A closed form for Datalog queries with integer order. In S. Abiteboul and P. Kanellakis, editors, *ICDT '90, Proceedings of the Third International Conference on Database Theory*, pages 187–201, Paris, Dec. 1990. LNCS 470, Springer.

26. D. Rosenkrantz and H. B. I. Hunt. Processing conjunctive predicates and queries. In *International Conference on Very Large Data Bases*, pages 64–72, 1980.

27. A. Schrijver. *Theory of Linear and Integer Programming.* John Wiley & Sons, 1986.

28. D. Srivastava. Subsumption in constraint query languages with linear arithmetic constraints. In *Second International Symposium on Artificial Intelligence and Mathematics*, Fort Lauderdale, Florida, Jan. 1992.

29. B. Thalheim. *Dependencies in Relational Databases.* Teubner-Texte zur Mathematik, Band 126. B.G. Teubner Verlagsgesellschaft, Stuttgart, 1991.

30. J. D. Ullman. *Principles of Database and Knowledge-Base Systems – Volume II: The New Technologies.* Computer Science Press, 1989.

31. R. van der Meyden. The complexity of querying indefinite data about linearly ordered domains. In *Eleventh ACM Symposium on Principles of Database Systems*, pages 331–345, San Diego, California, June 1992.

32. M. Vardi. Fundamentals of dependency theory. In E. Börger, editor, *Trends in Theoretical Computer Science*, pages 171–224. Computer Science Press, 1988.

33. X. Zhang and Z. M. Ozsoyoğlu. On efficient reasoning with implication constraints. In *Third International Conference on Deductive and Object-Oriented Databases*, Phoenix, Arizona, Dec. 1993.

Optimization Using Tuple Subsumption

Venky Harinarayan[1] and Ashish Gupta[2]

[1] Department of Computer Science, Stanford University, CA 94305-2140
(venky@cs.stanford.edu)
[2] Department of Computer Science, Stanford. *and* IBM Almaden Research Center

Abstract. A tuple t_1 of relation R *subsumes* tuple t_2 of R, with respect to a query Q if for every database, tuple t_1 derives all, and possibly more, answers to query Q than derived by tuple t_2. Therefore, the subsumed tuple t_2 can be ignored with respect to Q in the presence of tuple t_1 in relation R. This property finds use in a large number of problems. For instance: during query optimization subsumed tuples can be ignored thereby avoiding the computation of redundant answers; the size of cached information in distributed and object oriented systems can be reduced by omitting subsumed tuples; constraints need not be checked and rules need not be recomputed when provably subsumed updates are made. We give algorithms for deciding efficiently when a tuple subsumes another tuple for queries that use arbitrary mathematical functions. We characterize queries for which, whenever a set of tuples $\mathcal{T}$ subsumes a tuple t then one of the tuples in $\mathcal{T}$ also subsumed t, yielding efficiently verifiable cases of subsumption.

1 Introduction

We discuss and formalize the property of *subsumption* in this paper. Subsumption, intuitively, is the identification of the tuples of a database that do not "contribute" to the result of a query. Subsumption is a powerful optimization technique for a variety of problems. In the introduction we give some examples to illustrate and motivate the use of subsumption. The first example illustrates the use of subsumption to optimize integrity constraint checking.

Example 1. This example is from [GW93]. Consider an employee-department relational database with two relations:

$\text{EMP}(E,\ D,\ S)$	*% employee number E in department D has salary S*
$\text{DEPT}(D,\ MS)$	*% some manager in department D has salary MS*

Consider a constraint on the database which asserts that every employee earns less than every manager in the same department. This constraint is expressed as a conjunctive query C [Ull89] such that if C derives **panic** the constraint is violated:

C: **panic** :− $\text{emp}(E, D, S)$ & $\text{dept}(D, MS)$ & $S \geq MS$.

We use upper case letters to refer to the relation corresponding to a particular predicate. For instance, **EMP** refers to the relation corresponding to predicate **emp**.

Suppose tuple **emp**($e1, d1, 50$) is inserted into relation **EMP**. Constraint C will be violated if department $d1$ has a manager whose salary is ≤ 50. However, suppose department $d1$ already has an employee whose salary is 100. Since constraint C is not violated before the insertion, we can infer that no manager in $d1$ earns as little as 100, and therefore **emp**($e1, d1, 50$) does not violate constraint C. We say tuple **emp**($e2, d1, 100$) subsumes tuple **emp**($e1, d1, 50$) with respect to constraint query C.

Consider a scenario where the relation **DEPT** is expensive to access or not accessible at all. Let tuple μ be inserted into **EMP**. If some existing tuple in **EMP** subsumes μ then constraint C can be checked using only relation **EMP** without accessing **DEPT**.

[GW93, GSUW94] build a theory that uses subsumption to verify integrity constraints that are expressable as Select-Project-Join statements that use arithmetic inequalities. The techniques developed there often lead to more efficient constraint checking than naive strategies that do not exploit subsumption. This is especially true in distributed systems and heterogeneous systems where some relations may be very expensive or impossible to access. However, the results in those papers do not extend to queries that use arbitrary mathematical expressions. In addition, in this paper we characterize subsumption in a noncomputational way that yields insight into the problem and opens new avenues for identifying classes of constraints and updates for which subsumption holds. Now we illustrate other applications of subsumption.

Example 2. Consider a distributed database where the relation **EMP** is on site 1 and **DEPT** is on site 2. Let site 2 use view **bad_dept** defined as follows:

$$C: \quad \text{bad\_dept}(D) :- \text{emp}(E, D, S) \ \& \ \text{dept}(D, MS) \ \& \ S \geq MS.$$

Let site 2 cache the relation **EMP** for answering queries on view **bad_dept**. If relation **EMP** has tuples **emp**($e1, d1, 100$) and **emp**($e2, d1, 50$) then both tuples need not be cached in order to answer queries on view **bad_dept**. In particular **emp**($e2, d1, 50$) can be dropped from the cache. In general, all subsumed tuples can be dropped from the cache resulting in a smaller cached relation. The tuples that are not subsumed by any other tuple constitute the *representative* relation. The representative relation for **emp** will be referred to as **emp^r**. Additionally, if relation **EMP** is updated on site 1 and if a subsumed tuple is inserted or deleted, then the cache on site 2 need not be updated!

Example 3. Consider view **bad_dept** defined in Example 2. Note, the view has the same body as the constraint in Example 1 except that the head has arity 1 and not 0. Just as in Example 1, it is straightforward to observe that tuple **emp**($e1, d1, 100$) subsumes tuple **emp**($e2, d1, 50$) with respect to view **bad_dept**. Hence, if tuple **emp**($e2, d1, 50$) is inserted into relation **EMP** and if the relation has a subsuming tuple, then the view update decision can be made without accesing relation **DEPT**.

Finally, tuple subsumption can be used in query optimization. The notion of subsumption can be pushed into a query at optimization time. Hence, each

relation can be reduced to its representative relation before the relation partici-
pates in a join. Techniques currently used, like pushing selections down the query
tree and the use of semi-join algorithms are instances of this general concept of
subsumption. We can do more: in Example 3 the property of subsumption can
be used to replace relation EMP(E, D, S) by

Define emp^r as select $D, \max(S)$ from emp groupby(D) .

and to replace relation DEPT(D, MS) by

Define dept^r as select $D, \min(MS)$ from dept groupby(D) .

The representative relations can be used instead of the original relations to compute bad_dept. Note, the representative relations emp^r and dept^r need not be
explicitly defined or materialized; rather the aggregation can be pushed into the
original query yielding an alternative query plan for the optimizer to choose from.
Thus, subsumption based query rewriting may *introduce* aggregate predicates in
a query that originally did not use aggregation. This rewrite can be done automatically using the theory of subsumption. It has been shown in [CS94] that
pushing aggregate subgoals down a query tree often results in more efficient
plans than the original plan. Thus, we have reason to believe that introducing
aggregate subgoals can result in significant savings; often reducing a $O(n^2)$ time
query to an $O(n)$ query.

We formally define subsumption later in the paper. For now it is sufficient to
define it as follows: consider a query Q on a database consisting of a known set of
tuples $\{t_i\}$ in relation R and some unknown relations $\bar{S}$. Now let us augment the
relation R with a tuple t. If the answer to query Q does not change, independent
of the values of the relations $\bar{S}$, we say that tuple t is subsumed by the set of
tuples $\{t_i\}$ with respect to query Q.

STS Property Consider a query Q and tuple t such that the following property
holds: t is subsumed by a set of tuples $\{t_i, 1 \leq i \leq n\}$ if and only if t is subsumed
by one of the tuples $t_j, 1 \leq j \leq n$ in the set. For such cases we say that single
tuple subsumption is the *strongest* possible check and that the tuple t has the
STS property with respect to query Q. Or in the language of [GSUW94] we say
that single tuple subsumption is the "complete local check"[3]. In the examples
given earlier all the tuples had the STS property with respect to the queries
considered. The following example is an instance where the STS property does
not hold. In such cases we say that multiple tuple subsumption (MTS) holds.

MTS Property Consider a database that stores points (on the number line) in
relation P and line segments in relation L. Let view free_point contain those
points that are not part of any line segment. Let a line segment $l1$ be inserted
into relation L. If $l1$ is a subsegment of some other segment $l2$ that is already in
relation L then we can infer that $l2$ subsumes $l1$ with respect to view free_point
and that the view stays unchanged. We can make the same inference if $l1$ is a
subsegment of (is subsumed by) the union of *two* line segments $l2$ and $l3$. In

---

[3] *Completeness* is formally defined in [GSUW94]

general, $l1$ could be a subsegment of the union of an arbitrary number of existing lines segments without being a subsegment of any one of them. Note, single tuple subsumption is a degenerate case of MTS and is always a *sufficient* check though possibly not the strongest (*complete*) check. The STS property refers to cases where single tuple subsumption *is* the complete check, *i.e.*, the "if and only if" condition stated before holds.

Inferring subsumption by multiple tuples is computationally more expensive than inferring subsumption by a single tuple: checking for MTS may be exponentially more expensive than checking for STS. More importantly, the MTS check may not be expressable in the query language of the database. For instance, for the point-line example above, the general MTS check may use an arbitrary number of tuples and thus checking MTS may involve iterating/recursing over the entire database. Such a check cannot be expressed in a first order language and thus cannot be written as a SQL query (unless some recursive or iterative construct is used). On the other hand, a single tuple check (be it just sufficient or complete) can be written as a single SQL query. We believe STS will lead to efficient optimizations for the applications given earlier.

Thus it is useful to identify classes of queries for which the STS property holds and can be evaluated efficiently.

We consider integrity constraints, 0-ary queries and for these queries we characterize STS in terms of the existence of a "distinguished point". This characterization is a powerful result as it reduces the problem of determining if a k-dimensional unsafe region is contained in a union of m unsafe regions to the problem of determining if a *point* in k-dimensions is contained in one of m k-dimensional regions.

The above characterization enables us to identify classes of queries that use arbitrary mathematical functions as subgoals and for which it is computationally feasible to check STS. The existential characterization holds for a larger class of constraints than those for which we can compute the distinguished point. [GSUW94] considered the problem of checking the STS property for Select-Project-Join statements that use arithmetic comparison operators $<, \leq, >, \geq, =$. The results in [GSUW94] are an example of the more powerful abstraction of the distinguished point, introduced in this paper. Also [GSUW94] considered the restricted case where the STS property holds for a given constraint but does not consider constraints where the STS property may hold for a constraint and a particular tuple but not for the same constraint and some other tuple.

The results of this paper enable subsumption to be checked for queries that use functions like distance, volume, and other more complicated mathematical functions. Such functions appear often in constraint and query specifications [TH93]. Therefore, we need a general theory that deals with subsumption in the presence of arbitrary arithmetic constraints. For instance, consider the following example:

Example 4. Consider a factory floor with a robotic arm that is hinged at one end and rotates in a two dimensional plane. The free end of the arm defines a circular locus. However, the arm does not have 360° rotational freedom. The

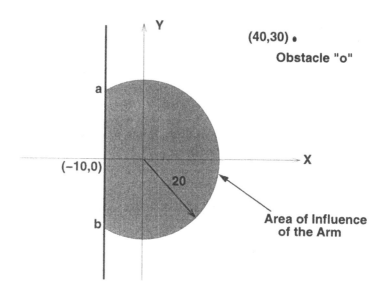

Fig. 1. Figure for Example 4

shaded area in Figure 1 shows the area of influence of the arm.

The factory also has obstacles, like machines, that interfere with the robot's arm if the obstacle is placed close enough to the arm such that some point in the obstacle lies in the shaded area for the arm. We will represent these obstacles as points in the two dimensional plane of motion of the robot arm.

One of the constraints in the above scenario is that an obstacle should not be placed in a position where it can interfere with the arm. This constraint can be represented as the following query that derives the fact **panic** whenever the constraint is violated.

C: **panic** $:-$ $\text{arm}(R, Z)$ & $\text{obstacle}(O, X, Y)$ & $R^2 \geq (X^2 + Y^2)$ & $X \geq Z$.

We assume that the arm is hinged at $[0, 0]$ in the $[X, Y]$ plane. For example, $\text{obstacle}(o, 40, 30)$ says that the point obstacle o is at position $[40, 30]$. $\text{arm}(20, -10)$ says that the arm of robot has radius 20 and that the arm does not go beyond $[-10, Y]$ along the X axis (the line connecting points **a** and **b** in the figure).

In this paper, we consider queries that use arbitrary mathematical functions. We develop theory and algorithms to determine when a tuple subsumes another tuple with respect to a query. We reduce checking for the STS property to a root finding problem and thus show that the STS property depends on the query as well as the subsumed tuple: for a given query only some tuples may satisfy the STS property. We provide a characterization of the STS property for a large class of constraints and also give a sufficient condition for a very general class of constraints.

Paper Outline Section 2 introduces some preliminary notation. Section 3 gives the geometric intuition for single and multiple tuple subsumption. Section 4 describes the class of queries that we will consider. Section 5 has the main results of the paper. We characterize subsumption for the constraint language defined before and give necessary and sufficient conditions for an inserted tuple to satisfy the STS property. We also give sufficient conditions for single tuple subsumption. In the following sections we focus on integrity constraints for simplicity; the results extend to views. We also use the term subsumption henceforth to stand for STS unless otherwise specified.

2 Preliminaries

The integrity constraints of concern in this paper are of the form

$$C: \quad \textbf{panic} :- l(\bar{Y}) \ \& \ r_1(\bar{Z}_1) \ \& \ r_2(\bar{Z}_2) \ \& \ \ldots \ \& \ r_p(\bar{Z}_p) \ \& \ A.$$

where l is the subgoal with a local predicate (relation), the r_is are subgoals with distinct remote predicates (relations) and A is a conjunction of arithmetic subgoals that relate the attributes of l and r_is No r_i is the same as l or any other r_j. Tuples are inserted into relation L and the question of interest is whether some existing tuple(s) in L subsumes the inserted tuples such that the truth value of C remains unchanged. If the answer to the above question is "yes", then the remote relations, that represent inaccessible or expensive information, need not be accessed. The query on the local relation that is used to express the question of subsumption is referred to as the local check.

We denote the set $\bar{Z}_1 \cup \ldots \cup \bar{Z}_p$ by $\bar{Z}$. The variables in $\bar{Y}$ and $\bar{Z}$ are distinct. In order to represent shared attributes between l and r_i the corresponding variables in $\bar{Y}$ and $\bar{Z}_i$ are made equal explicitly in A. Thus for each equijoin there is an equality constraint in A.

It is in A that we are most interested. In this paper we consider A, a conjunction of arithmetic constraints, to be of the following form:

$$f_1(\bar{Z}) \ op_1 \ g_1(\bar{Y}) \ \wedge \ \ldots \ \wedge \ f_k(\bar{Z}) \ op_k \ g_k(\bar{Y}).$$

Here the g_is and f_is are functions that take on all real values and are continuous over their domain. The variables $\bar{Y}$ and $\bar{Z}$ are vectors of reals. Each op_i is either $\geq$ or $=$. This choice of op_i is sufficient to model most operators, since we can change the f_is and g_is. Note however, we cannot model the $\neq$ operator.

For clarity of exposition we will assume that op is $\geq$. The analysis is similar when we allow op to be $=$ (Section 5.3). Thus, the arithmetic subgoals A is:

$$f_1(\bar{Z}) \ \geq \ g_1(\bar{Y}) \ \wedge \ \ldots \ \wedge \ f_k(\bar{Z}) \ \geq \ g_k(\bar{Y}).$$

For a given integrity constraint C, the update we will consider is the insertion of tuple $l(y_1, \ldots, y_n)$ into relation L. The inserted tuple is also denote by $l(\bar{y})$.

3 Geometric Intuition for Subsumption

If tuple $l(y_1, \ldots, y_n)$ is inserted into the local relation integrity constraint C may be violated. Tuple $l(\bar{y})$ may be substituted into C to obtain a partially instantiated constraint violation condition $C(\bar{y})$. Consider an instantiation $\bar{z}$ of the variables $\bar{Z}$ that occur in the remote relations. If the instantiation $\bar{z}$ makes $C(\bar{y})$ true, then $\bar{z}$ violates constraint C with tuple $l(\bar{y})$. The set of all such values of variables $\bar{Z}$ that violate the constraint with $l(\bar{y})$ define the "unsafe" region of the remote database given tuple $l(\bar{y})$. The unsafe region defined by a tuple $l(\bar{y})$ is obtained by computing the $g_i(\bar{y})$ in A, resulting in a set of constraints on $\bar{Z}$. Any $\bar{z}$ which satisfies this set of constraints belongs to the unsafe region of $l(\bar{y})$. For example, for the tuple $\texttt{arm}(20, -10)$ in Example 4, the unsafe region for the remote relation $\texttt{obstacle}$ is given by the shaded area in Figure 1. Geometrically, the unsafe region is defined by the surfaces $f_i(\bar{Z}) \geq g_i(\bar{y})$.

For some tuples $l(y_1, \ldots, y_n)$ the unsafe region is empty, which means that no $r(\bar{z})$ can violate integrity constraint C with tuple $l(y_1, \ldots, y_n)$. Such tuples can be inserted into the local database without any constraint checking and are known as *independent updates* [LS93].

If the tuple to be inserted defines a nonempty unsafe region, we must check that there is no remote tuple $r(\bar{z})$ such that $\bar{z}$ lies in the unsafe region. We can query the remote database and determine if such a tuple $r(\bar{z})$ exists. However, we may be able to avoid this remote access if we use the information available in the local database by using subsumption. In particular, if the unsafe regions of a set of existing tuples contain the unsafe region of the inserted tuple, we can conclude that the inserted tuple does not violate constraint C if the constraint was not violated before. The conclusion can be reached as follows. If a remote tuple violates C with the inserted tuple, *i.e.*, lies in the unsafe region for the inserted tuple then the remote tuple also lies in the unsafe region of some existing tuple. Thus, if we assume that the integrity constraint was not violated before the insertion then we are guaranteed that no such remote tuple exists.

The STS property holds if whenever the unsafe region U of the inserted tuple is contained in the unsafe regions of a set of existing tuples then region U is contained completely in the unsafe region of at least one of the existing tuples. This case is of great practical interest, since the subsumption check looks for only one tuple rather than various subsets of an arbitrarily large set of tuples. The check can therefore be represented using first order language constructs.

In general, subsumption depends on the tuple to be inserted: for a given integrity constraint it may be the case that for only some of the inserted tuples subsumption is the complete local check[4]. Subsumption being the complete local check is equivalent to the existence of what we call a "distinguished" point. We show that when the inequalities in the integrity constraint specification are replaced by equalities, and the resulting equations are solved, the existence of a solution implies that subsumption is the complete local check. The solution is a distinguished point. Some of the constraints obtained by the instantiation of A may be "degenerate," *i.e.*, not contribute to the unsafe region. Such degenerate constraints are eliminated from the set of equations, resulting in a different set of equations to be solved. Then subsumption is characterized by there being a solution to the smaller set of equations. We formalize the idea of degenerate equations later in the paper.

---

[4] Recall that subsumption refers single tuple subsumption

4 Notation

Given integrity constraint C, and inserted tuple $l(y_1, \ldots, y_n)$ the conjunction of arithmetic subgoals A can be instantiated with $l(\bar{y})$ to obtain the following:

$$f_1(\bar{Z}) \geq g_1(\bar{y}) \ \wedge \ \ldots \ \wedge \ f_k(\bar{Z}) \geq g_k(\bar{y}).$$

Let x_i refer to $g_i(\bar{y})$ for $1 \leq i \leq k$. For a given constraint C, we represent the above set of constraints on $\bar{Z}$ by $[x_1, \ldots, x_k]$. If there exists tuples $r_i(\bar{z}_i), 1 \leq i \leq p$ such that $\bar{z}$ satisfies the constraints denoted by $[x_1, \ldots, x_k]$ then inserting tuple $l(\bar{y})$ will violate constraint C.

Definition 1. Region We define $Region(x_1, \ldots, x_k)$ to be the unsafe region associated with $l(\bar{y})$ i.e., the set of all $\bar{z}$ that satisfy the constraints given by $[x_1, \ldots, x_k]$.

$$\bar{z} \in Region(x_1, \ldots, x_k) \Leftrightarrow f_1(\bar{z}) \geq x_1, \ldots, f_k(\bar{z}) \geq x_k.$$

Since we consider only one integrity constraint C, all the unsafe regions in our analysis are obtained by instantiatiating the same A with different values for the variables $\bar{Y}$ i.e., with different tuples of relation L. We use the terms $R, S, \ldots$ to refer to these regions. In other words region R is $Region(v_1, \ldots, v_k)$ for some $[v_1, \ldots, v_k]$.

Definition 2. $\geq$ The relationship $\geq$ between different instantiations of A is defined as:

$$[x_1, \ldots, x_k] \geq [v_1, \ldots, v_k] \Leftrightarrow x_1 \geq v_1, \ldots, x_k \geq v_k.$$

Lemma 3.

$$[x_1, \ldots, x_k] \geq [v_1, \ldots, v_k] \Rightarrow Region(x_1, \ldots, x_k) \subseteq Region(v_1, \ldots, v_k).$$

Definition 4. Distinguished point For a region R, $\bar{z} \in R$ is said to be a distinguished point of R if:

$$\forall S, \bar{z} \in S \Rightarrow R \subseteq S.$$

where R and S are regions obtained from the same constraint C.

In Example 4, **a** and **b** are the distinguished points of the unsafe region (refer Figure 1).

Definition 5. Subsumption as the complete local check Consider the inserted tuple $l(\bar{y})$ and let $R = Region(g_1(\bar{y}), \ldots, g_k(\bar{y}))$. Subsumption is the complete local check for this insertion if the following condition holds:

$$R \subseteq S_1 \cup \cdots \cup S_n \Rightarrow \exists j, 1 \leq j \leq n : R \subseteq S_j.$$

where $R, S_1, \ldots, S_n$ are regions obtained from the same constraint C.

5 Results

5.1 Existentially Characterizing Subsumption

Theorem 6. *Consider constraint C of the form defined in Section 2 and let tuple $l(\bar{y})$ be inserted into relation L. Subsumption is the complete local check for C on inserting $l(\bar{y})$ if and only if for $x_i = g_i(\bar{y}), 1 \leq i \leq k$, $Region(x_1, \ldots, x_k)$ has a distinguished point.*

Theorem 6 is proved in the full version of the paper. It is a very general theorem and does not depend on the expressive power of the constraint language for its validity. The theorem reduces the problem of determining if a k-dimensional unsafe region is contained in a union of m unsafe regions to the problem of determining if a point in k-dimensions is contained in one of m k-dimensional regions. If the problem is indeed reducible, the subsumption (STS) property holds and results in a significant reduction in the complexity of checking subsumption making subsumption an extremely effective optimization in all the applications mentioned in the introduction.

5.2 Computationally Characterizing Subsumption

The following analysis provides a mechanism for identifying the distinguished point for a given class of constraints if such a point exists. In general, the existential characterization of Theorem 6 holds for larger classes of constraints but we may not be able to syntactically identify all these classes. In this section we impose a few restrictions on the constraint language. We require that the g_is be independent of one another. That is, given values for any $g_{i_1}(\bar{Y}), \ldots, g_{i_r}(\bar{Y})$ the possible range of values for $g_i(\bar{Y}), i \notin \{i_1, \ldots, i_r\}$ is unaffected. In other words $g_i(\bar{Y})$ can take on all possible real values, independent of the values of the other g_is. Section 5.3 relaxes the independence assumption.

We now define the Max and Eq functions. Recall that for an inserted tuple $l(\bar{y})$, x_i refers to $g_i(\bar{y}), 1 \leq i \leq k$.

Definition 7. Max We define the Max transform as follows:

$$Max : [x_1, \ldots, x_k] \rightarrow [p_1, \ldots, p_k] .$$

such that

$$Region(p_1, \ldots, p_k) = Region(x_1, \ldots, x_k) \quad \text{and}$$
$$\forall q_1, \ldots, q_k : \{Region(q_1, \ldots, q_k) = Region(x_1, \ldots, x_k) \Rightarrow$$
$$[p_1, \ldots, p_k] \geq [q_1, \ldots, q_k]\}.$$

Geometrically we can think of $Region(x_1, \ldots, x_k)$ as being the "unsafe" region defined by the surfaces $f_i(\bar{Z}) \geq x_i$. Now some of these surfaces (constraints) may be degenerate in that they may not restrict the "unsafe" region at all. The Max transform moves these degenerate surfaces to the maximum extent possible without affecting the original unsafe region $Region(x_1, \ldots, x_k)$. Intuitively, it corresponds to having these surfaces just "touch" (be tangential to) the unsafe region. For instance, consider the robot arm of Example 4. If tuple $\mathbf{arm}(1, -3)$ is inserted then the unsafe region $[1, -3]$ is the shaded circle in Figure 2(A).

However, the line $x = -3$ does not restrict the region. If the Max transform is applied to $[1, -3]$, the line moves to $x = -1$ as shown by the dotted line in Figure 2(B). $Max([1, -3])$ is computed to be $[1, -1]$.

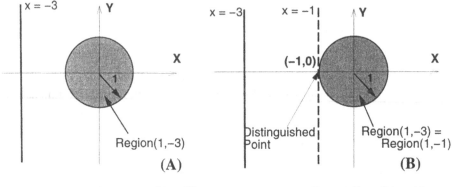

(A)

(B)

Inserting tuple arm(1,-3)

Max([1,-3]) = [1,-1]

Fig. 2.

Definition 8. Eq We define $Eq([x_1, \ldots, x_k])$ to be the set of equations:

$$f_i(\bar{Z}) = x_i.$$

We say that $Eq([x_1, \ldots, x_k])$ has a solution if there is some $\bar{Z} = \bar{z}$ such that $Eq([x_1, \ldots, x_k])$ is true.

Theorem 9. *Consider constraint C of the form defined in Section 2 with the restriction that op is $\geq$ and the g_is are independent. Let tuple $l(\bar{y})$ be inserted into relation L. Subsumption is the complete local check iff $Eq(Max([x_1, \ldots, x_k]))$ has a solution $\bar{z}$, and for $x_i = g_i(\bar{y}), 1 \leq i \leq k$, $\bar{z} \in Region(x_1, \ldots, x_k)$.*

Proof. The intuition for both directions of the proof is based on $\bar{z}$ being a distinguished point of $Region(x_1, \ldots, x_k)$. The details are given in the full version of the paper.

5.3 Extensions

We now relax the restrictions imposed on the set of arithmetic inequalities in constraint C and discuss how Theorem 9 is affected. First we consider the case when the functions g_is in the set of arithmetic inequalities A are not independent. In Section 5.3 we consider the case when the g_is are bounded and may not take all values on the real number line. In Section 5.3 we consider the case when the constraint uses equalities in its set of arithmetic inequalities, *i.e.*, the constraint uses joins. Finally, in Section 5.3 we state a sufficient condition for subsumption. Even though we may not have necessary and sufficient conditions, sufficient conditions are often very useful in using subsumption for constraint checking, view maintenance, or query optimization.

Dependent g_is Theorem 9 is dependent on the constraint language and is contingent on the independence of the g_is, *i.e.*, if the g_is are not independent the theorem does not hold. The existential characterization that ties STS with the existence of a distinguished point still holds. In addition, it is still the case that for inserted tuple $l(\bar{y})$ if $Eq(Max([x_1, \ldots, x_k])$ has a solution $\bar{z} \in Region(x_1, \ldots, x_k)$, subsumption is the complete check. The proof of this statement is identical to that for Theorem 9.

However, the converse, that $Eq(Max([x_1, \ldots, x_k])$ *has to have* a solution if subsumption is the complete check, relies on the independence of the g_is. When the g_is are not independent it can be the case that subsumption is the complete local check and yet there is no solution.

Example 5. An example is the following integrity constraint:

C: **panic** $:- l(X) \,\&\, r(Z) \,\&\, Z \geq -X \,\&\, Z \leq X$.

If we wish to insert the local tuple $l(x)$, the relevant equations are

$$Z = -x \quad \text{and} \quad -Z = -x.$$

These equations have a solution only when $x = 0$ and the solution is $Z = 0$ *in Region$(0, 0)$*. Theorem 9 would indicate that subsumption is the complete local check only when inserting $l(0)$. Actually, subsumption is the complete local check for the insertion of any tuple into the local database.

Bounded g_is In some cases we may want to bound the values of the functions g_is to be in a fixed interval $[a_i, b_i]$ rather than let the values range from $[-\infty, \infty]$. In Example 1 for instance, we may wish to add the constraint that all salaries are positive.

We can augment the original set of arithmetic subgoals A with the subgoals $-a_i \geq -g_i$ and $b_i \geq g_i$ for each g_i, to get a new set of subgoals A'. A' satisfies the format of arithmetic subgoals we have used thus far, since the lower and upper bound subgoals have left hand sides that are merely constant functions of the remote variables $\bar{Z}$. Let us order the subgoals of A' as follows: the first k subgoals are identical to those in A. The $k+1$ and $k+2$ subgoals correspond to the lower and upper bounds of g_1. The $k+3$ and $k+4$ subgoals correspond to the lower and upper bounds of g_2 and so on. In general the lower and upper bound subgoals for g_i are subgoals $k + 2i - 1$ and $k + 2i$ respectively. If A has k subgoals, A' has $3k$ subgoals. When we wish to insert a new tuple $l(\bar{y})$ we instantiate A' with the $g_i(\bar{Y})$ values. Now the set of arithmetic constraints is given by $[x_1, \ldots, x_k, -x_1, x_1, \ldots, -x_k, x_k]$, where $x_i = g_i(\bar{y})$.

From the discussion given above about dependent g_is (which is the case here), if

$$Eq(Max[x_1, \ldots, x_k, -x_1, x_1, \ldots, -x_k, x_k])$$

has a solution in the corresponding region, subsumption holds. It can be shown that

$$Eq(Max[x_1, \ldots, x_k, -x_1, x1, \ldots, -x_k, x_k]) = Eq(Max[x_1, \ldots, x_k])$$

since the last $2k$ subgoals have constants on their right hand sides. Hence it appears that bounded g_is behave the same as unbounded g_is. However, that is not the case.

Example 6. Consider the following query:

C: **panic** $:- l(X, Y)$ & $r(Z)$ & $Z \geq X$ & $-Z \geq -Y$.

If we wish to insert a tuple $l(x, y)$ with $x < y$, we check if $Eq(Max[x, -y])$ has a solution (note, in this case $Max[x, -y] = [x, -y]$, since neither subgoal is degenerate). Clearly there is no solution and hence we conclude subsumption does not hold. This statement is true if X and $-Y$ are unbounded. Consider now X to be restricted to the interval $[a, b]$. If we now wish to insert $l(b, y)$ with $b < y$ we have subsumption, even though $Eq(Max[b, -y])$ has no solution.

Thus when the g_is are bounded, Theorem 9 does not hold as specified. The definitions of Max and Eq need to be modified for the characterization of Theorem 9 to hold.

Let the upper bound for each g_i be b_i (the lower bound does not matter).

$Max : [x_1, \ldots, x_k] \to [p_1, \ldots, p_k]$ is defined as before except if a $p_i \geq b_i$, we replace p_i by the corresponding b_i. This guarantees that $Max([x_1, \ldots, x_k]) \leq [b_1, \ldots, b_k]$ and thus is legal. $Eq([x_1, \ldots, x_k])$ is now defined to be the set of equations:

$f_i(\bar{Z}) = x_i$ *if* $x_i \leq b_i$.
$TRUE$ *if* $x_i = b_i$.

In some sense a subgoal of A does not contribute to the subsumption check if the inserted tuple has the maximum possible value for the corresponding g_i.

With these enhanced definitions of Max and Eq, Theorem 9 holds. The proof is similar and is not stated here.

Joins Until now we considered arithmetic inequalities of the form $f_i(\bar{Z})$ **op** $g_1(\bar{y})$ where **op** was restricted to be $\geq$. Thus joins were not expressible because implicit equalities were not allowed in the constraint specification. In this section we show that the previous restriction was needed only for the sake of simplicity and that the results extend naturally to the case of joins.

In Example 1 we require that an employee's department be the same as that of a manager to compare their salaries. Since we do not allow shared attributes, we rewrite the constraint using an explicit "$=$" to represent the join.

C: **panic** $:-$ **emp**(E, D_E, S) & **dept**(D_M, MS) & $D_E = D_M$ & $S \geq MS$.

When we permit *op* to be either $\geq$ or $=$, without loss of generality we can write the arithmetic subgoals A to be:

$f_1(\bar{Z}) = g_1(\bar{Y}) \wedge \ldots \wedge f_i(\bar{Z}) = g_i(\bar{Y}) \wedge$
$\qquad\qquad f_{i+1}(\bar{Z}) \geq g_{i+1}(\bar{Y}) \wedge \ldots \wedge f_k(\bar{Z}) \geq g_k(\bar{Y})$.

i.e. the first i subgoals are the equality constraints and the remaining subgoals are inequalities. Note, now:

$\bar{z} \in Region(x_1, \ldots, x_k) \Leftrightarrow f_1(\bar{z}) = x_1, \ldots, f_i(\bar{z}) = x_i, f_{i+1}(\bar{z}) \geq x_{i+1}, \ldots, f_k(\bar{z}) \geq x_k$

and

$$[x_1, \ldots, x_k] \geq [v_1, \ldots, v_k] \Leftrightarrow x_1 = v_1, \ldots, x_i = v_i, x_{i+1} \geq v_{i+1}, \ldots, x_k \geq v_k.$$

Theorem 9 holds for the above class of constraints also, and the proof is the same as before (see full version of paper).

A Sufficient Condition For Subsumption We give below a sufficient condition for subsumption to be the complete check. The only requirement for it to hold is that the arithmetic subgoal, A, can be written in the form given in Section 2. There are no restrictions on the g_is for the above lemma to hold.

Lemma 10. *Consider the integrity constraint C:*

C: **panic** :– $l(\bar{Y})$ & $r_1(\bar{Z}_1)$ & $r_2(\bar{Z}_2)$ & $\ldots$ & $r_p(\bar{Z}_p)$ & A.

where A is

$$f_1(\bar{Z} \ op_1 \ g_1(\bar{Y}) \ \wedge \ \ldots \ \wedge \ f_k(\bar{Z}) \ op_k \ g_k(\bar{Y}).$$

Let $l(\bar{y})$ be a tuple inserted into relation L and let $x_i = g_i(\bar{y}), 1 \leq i \leq k$. Subsumption is the complete local check for the inserted tuple if the set of equations:

$$f_1(\bar{Z} = g_1(\bar{Y}) \ \wedge \ \ldots \ \wedge \ f_k(\bar{Z}) = g_k(\bar{Y}).$$

has a solution $\bar{z}$ in $Region(x_1, \ldots, x_k)$,

Proof. Let $Region(x_1, \ldots, x_k) \subseteq Region(v_1^1, \ldots, v_k^1) \cup \ldots \cup Region(v_1^n, \ldots, v_k^n)$ where each $\bar{v}^j$ represents a tuple of relation L. That is, the multiple subsumption property holds for the inserted tuple $l(\bar{y})$. Now consider a particular point $\bar{z}$ in the unsafe region for $l(\bar{y})$.

$\bar{z} \in Region(x_1, \ldots, x_k) \Rightarrow \exists j : \bar{z} \in Region(v_1^j, \ldots, v_k^j)$.
　　　　　　% *i.e., $\bar{z}$ must be in the unsafe region for some tuple $\bar{v}^j$.*
a:　$\Rightarrow \forall i, f_i(\bar{z}) \geq v_i^j$　% *that is, the arithmetic subgoals A must be satisfiable* given $\bar{z}$ and $\bar{v}^j$.

If the conditions of the lemma hold, then $f_i(\bar{z}) = x_i$. Therefore, substituting x_i for $f_i(\bar{z})$ in (a) we obtain:

$\forall i, x_i \geq v_i^j$
$\Rightarrow [x_1, \ldots, x_k] \geq [v_1^j, \ldots, v_k^j]$
$\Rightarrow Region(x_1, \ldots, x_k) \subseteq Region(v_1^j, \ldots, v_k^j)$.

Thus subsumption is the complete local check.

6 An Example

Consider the integrity constraint $C1$:

$C1$: **panic** :– $\text{emp}(D, S_E, OT, Rate)$ & $\text{manager}(D, S_M, Bonus)$ &
　　　　$S_M \geq S_E$ & $Bonus \leq OT * Rate$.

We can rewrite $C1$ this in the our constraint language as follows:

$C1$: **panic** :– $\text{emp}(D_E, S_E, OT, Rate)$ & $\text{manager}(D_M, S_M, Bonus)$ &
　　　　$D_M = D_E$ & $S_M \geq S_E$ & $- Bonus \geq -OT * Rate$.

Now let's say we want to insert emp("*sales*", 30000, 400, 30) into the local emp database. We first compute the g_is (the functions that appear on the right-hand-side of the arithmetic subgoals above):

$g_1(\text{emp}("sales", 30000, 400, 30)) = "sales".$

$g_2(\text{emp}("sales", 30000, 400, 30)) = 30000.$

$g_3(\text{emp}("sales", 30000, 400, 30)) = -12000.$

Now we check if there can be a **manager** tuple that can cause a constraint violation; we check to see if the unsafe region $Region("sales", 30000, -12000)$ is empty. In this case we find it is not empty: A sales manager who earns more than 30000 but who has a bonus less than 12000 would cause a violation. If the unsafe region was empty we could have gone ahead and inserted the tuple without any further checks. Thus, we proceed by checking if subsumption is the complete local check. We find it is, since the solution $D_M = "sales", S_M = 30000$ and $Bonus = 12000$ satisfies Lemma 10. We now query the emp database to find if there is any $\text{emp}(D_E, S_E, OT, Rate)$, such that $[D_E, S_E, -OT * Rate] \leq ["sales", 30000, -12000]$. If there is one such tuple (a sales employee who earned less than 30000 but made more than 12000 in overtime wages) already in the database, then inserting the new tuple will not violate constraint $C1$. If no such tuple exists in the DB, then we require a conventional constraint check that queries the **manager** relation.

For this constraint $C1$, we can determine that subsumption is the complete check for all tuples to be inserted. So we can parameterize the inserted tuple and derive an SQL query at compile time such that this query is the complete local check for subsumption.

7 Conclusions

We considered the property of subsumption, *i.e.*, when can a tuple be ignored with respect to a query given some other tuples in the same relation. Subsumption finds many uses: in intelligent caching, in query optimization, in optimizing integrity constraint checking, and in efficient incremental view maintenance. We illustrate these uses and then give the intuition behind subsumption. We consider multiple tuple subsumption (when many tuples together subsume one tuple) and single tuple subsumption (when just one tuple is sufficient to subsume another tuple). We are especially interested in the latter case because it is the more practical case and can be implemented using first order languages like SQL without recursion.

We consider integrity constraints, 0-ary queries, in this paper in order to simplify our analysis. For a large class of such queries we characterize subsumption in terms of the existence of a "distinguished point". This characterization is a powerful result as it reduces the problem of determining if a k-dimensional unsafe region is contained in a union of m unsafe regions to the problem of determining if a *point* in k-dimensions is contained in one of m k-dimensional regions.

The above characterization enables us to identify classes of queries that use arbitrary mathematical functions as subgoals and for which subsumption is computationally feasible. That is, the existential characterization holds for a larger class of constraints than those for which we can compute the distinguished point. This result enables us to generate automatic query rewrite and view maintenance algorithms for such queries.

By providing a formal basis for subsumption we hope to identify, apply and possibly unify optimization techniques in the many areas mentioned in the introduction. In particular, query optimization is a promising application for subsumption, since we can now automatically generate aggregate subgoals during query rewriting. We are also currently exploring how results from computational geometry can yield efficient subsumption checking algorithms. The intuition in Section 3 gives an idea of how geometry results tie into subsumption. We are looking at other ways of correlating subsumption with properties of mathematical functions. For instance, the linearity of functions, number of variables, independence of the variables, etc.

Acknowledgements

We would like to thank Anand Rajaraman, Jeff Ullman, and Jennifer Widom for valuable comments and feedback on the ideas presented in this paper. The authors' research was supported by NSF grants IRI–91–16646 and IRI–92–23405, by ARO grant DAAL03–91–G–0177, and by Air Force Grant F33615–93–1–1339.

References

[CS94] Surajit Chaudhuri and Kyuseok Shim. Including Group-By in Query Optimization. To appear in *Proceedings of the Twentieth International Conference on Very Large Databases (VLDB)*, 1994.

[GSUW94] Ashish Gupta, Shuky Sagiv, Jeffrey D. Ullman, and Jennifer Widom. Constraint Checking with Partial Information. In *Proceedings of the Thirteenth Symposium on Principles of Database Systems (PODS)*, 1994.

[GW93] Ashish Gupta and Jennifer Widom. Local Checking of Global Integrity Constraints . In *Proceedings of ACM SIGMOD 1993 International Conference on Management of Data*, pages 49–59.

[LS93] A.Y. Levy and Y. Sagiv. Queries independent of updates. In *Proceedings of the Nineteenth International Conference on Very Large Data Bases*, pages 171–181, Dublin, Ireland, August 1993.

[TH93] Sanjai Tiwari and H. C. Howard. Constraint Management on Distributed AEC Databases. In *Fifth International Conference on Computing in Civil and Building Engineering*, pages 1147–1154. ASCE, 1993.

[Ull89] J. D. Ullman. *Principles of Database and Knowledge-Base Systems*, volume 2. Computer Science Press, New York, 1989.

Deterministic and Non-Deterministic Stable Model Semantics for Unbound DATALOG Queries*

Domenico Saccà

DEIS Dept., Università della Calabria, 87030 Rende, Italy

sacca@ccusc1.unical.it

Abstract. There are presently many proposals to extend the notion of stable model to the domain of partial interpretations. This paper is concerned with the analysis of the expressive powers of such types of stable model under various versions of deterministic semantics for unbound (i.e., without ground terms) queries on DATALOG programs with negation. Various versions of non-deterministic semantics are also proposed and their expressive powers are fully characterized as well.

1 Introduction

The notion of *stable model* [8] and its various refinements [2, 6, 19, 21, 22, 27, 29] represent an interesting solution to the problem of providing a formal semantics to logic programs where rules contain negative literals in their bodies [3]. In this paper we shall consider four types of stable models: the *partial stable* models of [22] (corresponding to the three-valued stable models of [19] and the strongly-founded models of [21]), the *total stable* models of [8], the *maximal stable* models of [22] (corresponding to the partial stable models of [21], the preferred extensions of [6], the regular models of [29] and the maximal stable classes of [2]) and the *least undefined stable* models of [22].

Although multiple stable models exist for the same program, it is possible to enforce a deterministic semantics so that the intrinsic non-determinism is only used to increase the expressive power. We shall consider three versions of deterministic semantics [1, 24]: (i) the *possibility* semantics, which takes the union of all stable models of the given type, (ii) the *definite* semantics, which takes their intersection if at least one stable model exists or the empty set otherwise, and (ii) *certainty* semantics which differs from definite semantics only when there exists no stable model for it infers the whole Herbrand base. (Thus, certainty semantics, despite its name, may be more credulous than possibility semantics!)

A DATALOG⁻ query is of the form $< \mathcal{LP}, G >$ where $\mathcal{LP}$ is a DATALOG⁻ program (i.e., function-free logic program with negation in the rule bodies) and G is the query goal. In [20] we have studied the expressive power of deterministic

---

* Work partially supported by the CNR project "Sistemi Informatici e Calcolo Parallelo" and by a MURST grant (40% share) under the project "Sistemi formali e strumenti per basi di dati evolute".

semantics for *bound queries*, i.e., DATALOG⁻ queries for which the query goal is ground. In this paper we analyze the expressive power of deterministic semantics for *unbound queries* where G is not ground. A nice result is that the expressive power of unbound queries under a given deterministic semantics, measured in terms of the complexity of recognizing whether a tuple belongs to the answer of a query, is strongly related to the expressive power of bound queries under the same semantics. We shall also give a characterization in terms of the complexity of recognizing whether a relation consists of exactly all the answer tuples.

Finally, we shall conjecture that deterministic semantics for unbound queries is not much effective since it requires to specify which solution is to be selected for any problem admitting multiple solutions. This requires introducing low-level details to single out a unique solution so that a finding problem is eventually transformed into an optimization problem thus increasing the complexity. We shall then propose to integrate deterministic and non-deterministic semantics using queries with two goals: a ground goal selects the stable models which have certain properties and a non-ground one non-deterministically returns the solution computed by any of the selected models. The expressive power of various combinations of semantics for such queries will be fully characterized as well.

2 Preliminary Definitions and Results

2.1 Logic Programs

We assume that the reader is familiar with the basic terminology and notation of logic programming [16]. Only non-standard or specific terminology and notation are presented next.

A *logic program* (or, simply, a *program*) $\mathcal{LP}$ is a finite set of rules. Each *rule* of $\mathcal{LP}$ has the form $Q \leftarrow Q_1, ..., Q_m$. where Q is a atom (*head* of the rule) and $Q_1, ..., Q_m$ are literals (*goals* of the rule). Let $H(r)$ and $G(r)$ represent, respectively, the head of r and the set of all goals of r. A rule with no goals is called a *fact*.

The *ground instantiation* of $\mathcal{LP}$ is denoted by $ground(\mathcal{LP})$; the *Herbrand universe* and the *Herbrand base* of $\mathcal{LP}$ are denoted by $U_{\mathcal{LP}}$ and $B_{\mathcal{LP}}$, respectively.

A ground atom $A \in B_{\mathcal{LP}}$ and its negation, i.e., the literal $\neg A$, are said to be the *complement* of each other. Moreover, if B is a ground literal, then $\neg B$ denotes the complement of B.

Let X be a set of ground literals A such that either A or $\neg A$ is in $B_{\mathcal{LP}}$. Then $\neg X$ denotes the set $\{\neg A | A \in X\}$, X^+ (resp., X^-) denotes the set of all positive (resp., negative) literals in X; moreover, $\overline{X}$ denotes all elements of $B_{\mathcal{LP}}$ which do not occur in X, i.e., $\overline{X} = \{A | A \in B_{\mathcal{LP}}$ and neither A nor $\neg A$ is in $X\}$.

Given $X \subseteq (B_{\mathcal{LP}} \cup \neg B_{\mathcal{LP}})$, X is a *(partial) interpretation* of $\mathcal{LP}$ if it is *consistent*, i.e., $X^+ \cap \neg X^- = \emptyset$. Moreover, if $X^+ \cup \neg X^- = B_{\mathcal{LP}}$, the interpretation X is called *total*.

Given an interpretation I and a ground literal A, A is *true* if $A \in I$, *false* if $\neg A \in I$ or *undefined* otherwise. Obviously A is true if and only if $\neg A$ is false and conversely.

Given an interpretation I and $X \subseteq B_{\mathcal{LP}}$, X is an *unfounded set w.r.t. I* if for each rule $r \in ground(\mathcal{LP})$ with $H(r) \in X$, $G(r) \subseteq I$ or $G(r) \cap X \neq \emptyset$. The union of all unfounded sets w.r.t. I is also an unfounded set w.r.t. I and is called the *greatest unfounded set.*

Given an interpretation I, I is *founded* (or *justified* [29]) if $I^+ = T^\infty_{\mathcal{LP}(I)}(\emptyset)$, where T is the classical *immediate consequence transformation* and $\mathcal{LP}(I)$ denotes the logic program that is obtained from $ground(\mathcal{LP})$ by (i) removing all rules r such that there exists a negative literal $\neg A \in G(r)$ and $\neg A \notin I^-$, and (ii) by removing all negative literals from the remaining rules.

2.2 Stable Models

An interpretation M is a *P-stable (partial stable)* model of $\mathcal{LP}$ if (a) it is founded, and (b) $\neg M^-$ is the greatest unfounded set w.r.t. M. Thus an interpretation M is a P-stable model iff both M^+ consists of all derivable ground literals (see condition a) and any ground literal that is granted not to be derivable (i.e., it is in some unfounded set), is declared false (see condition b).

The set of P-stable models of $\mathcal{LP}$ is a non-empty lower semilattice w.r.t. the subset operator [22]. The bottom element is called the *well-founded* model [27] which is then contained in any P-stable model of $\mathcal{LP}$. The top elements of the semilattice are called *M-stable (maximal stable)* model for they are not contained in any other P-stable model. *L-stable (least undefined stable)* models are those M-stable models that verify the following minimal undefinedness requirement: a P-stable model M is L-stable if there exists no P-stable model N such that $\overline{N}$ is a proper subset of $\overline{M}$. The definition of *T-stable (total stable)* models is the final step toward a criterium of minimum undefinedness as it requires that $\overline{M} = \emptyset$; unfortunately, existence is not any-more guaranteed. In fact, every program has at least one P-stable, M-stable and L-stable model but not necessarily a T-stable model. Obviously, if a T-stable model exists then the notions of T-stability and L-stability coincide [22].

Example 1. Consider the following program:

$$b \leftarrow a(1), \neg c.$$
$$c \leftarrow a(1), \neg b.$$
$$p \leftarrow b, \neg p.$$
$$d \leftarrow a(2), \neg p, \neg e.$$
$$e \leftarrow a(2), \neg p, \neg d.$$
$$q \leftarrow \neg d, \neg q.$$

where the predicate symbol a is defined by the following facts: $a(1)$. and $a(2)$.

The P-stable models are: $M_1 = \{a(1), a(2)\}$, $M_2 = \{a(1), a(2), b, \neg c\}$, $M_3 = \{a(1), a(2), \neg b, c, \neg p\}$, $M_4 = \{a(1), a(2), \neg b, c, \neg p, \neg d, e\}$, $M_5 = \{a(1), a(2), \neg b, c, \neg p, d, \neg e, \neg q\}$. M_1 is the well-founded model; M_2, M_4 and M_5 are the M-stable models; M_5 is also both L-stable and T-stable.

Suppose now that the predicate symbol a is defined only by the fact $a(1)$. Then the P-stable models are: $M_1 = \{a(1), \neg a(2), \neg d, \neg e\}$, $M_2 = \{a(1), \neg a(2),$

$\neg d$, $\neg e$, b, $\neg c\}$, $M_3 = \{a(1)$, $\neg a(2)$, $\neg d$, $\neg e$, $\neg b$, c, $\neg p\}$. M_1 is the well-founded model; M_2 and M_3 are the M-stable models; M_3 is also L-stable but not T-stable. □

Let PS, WS, MS, LS and TS be the sets of models of a logic program LP that are P-stable, well-founded, M-stable, L-stable and T-stable, respectively. Each of such sets can be considered as the *intended models* of LP. ¿From now on, XS will denote any of the sets of intended models, i.e., XS will stand for PS, WS, MS, LS or TS.

We consider three versions of semantics for each type of stable model: the *possibility* (or *credulous*) semantics, the *certainty* (or *skeptical*) semantics [1, 24] and a variation of certainty semantics, called the *definite* semantics. The difference between the two latter semantics arises only when the set of stable models is empty; in this case, any atom A is inferred from certainty semantics whereas it is not from definite semantics. It turns out that the two definitions differ only for total stable models as the sets of all other stable models are never empty for any program. The three versions of semantics are formally definite next.

Let XS be the set of stable model for the program LP and A be a ground literal. Then

1. A is a $\exists_{XS}$ (*possible*) inference of LP if A is in any model in XS;
2. A is a $\forall_{XS}$ (*certain*) inference of LP if A is in every model in XS;
3. A is a $\overline{\forall}_{XS}$ (*definite*) inference of LP if XS is not empty and A is in every model in XS.

2.3 Bound DATALOG Queries

A DATALOG⁻ program LP is a logic program with negation in the rule bodies but without functions symbols [4, 13, 25]. Some of the predicate symbols (*EDB predicates*) correspond to database relations and do not occur in the head rules. The other predicate symbols are called *IDB predicates*. EDB predicate symbols are also seen as relation schemes on a countable domain domain U and, therefore, they represent a relational database scheme, say DB_{LP}. A database D on DB_{LP} is a set of finite relations $D(q)$, one for each q in DB_{LP}. The family of all databases on DB_{LP} is denoted by $\mathbf{D}_{LP}$. Given $D \in \mathbf{D}_{LP}$, LP_D will denote the following logic program:

$$LP_D = LP \cup \{q(t).|q \in DB_{LP} \wedge t \in D(q)\}.$$

A (*bound* DATALOG⁻) *query* Q is a pair $< LP, G >$, where LP is a DATALOG⁻ program and G is a ground literal (the *query goal*). The set of all queries is denoted by $\mathbf{Q}$.

The *database collection* of $Q =< LP, G >$ w.r.t. the set of stable models XS under the *possibility* (resp., *certainty*, and *definite*) version of semantics is the family of all databases D in $\mathbf{D}_{LP}$ for which G is a $\exists_{XS}$ (resp., $\forall_{XS}$, and $\overline{\forall}_{XS}$) inference of LP_D —- denoted by $DB^{\exists}_{XS}(Q)$ (resp., $DB^{\forall}_{XS}(Q)$, and $DB^{\overline{\forall}}_{XS}(Q)$).

The *expressive power* of a type of semantics is given by the class of the database collections of all possible queries, i.e., $DB^{\exists}_{\chi S}[\mathbf{Q}] = \{DB^{\exists}_{\chi S}(Q)|Q \in \mathbf{Q}\}$, $DB^{\lor}_{\chi S}[\mathbf{Q}] = \{DB^{\lor}_{\chi S}(Q)|Q \in \mathbf{Q}\}$ and $DB^{\bar{\lor}}_{\chi S}[\mathbf{Q}] = \{DB^{\bar{\lor}}_{\chi S}(Q)|Q \in \mathbf{Q}\}$.

Note that we follow the *data complexity* approach of [28] for which the size of the query is assumed to be a constant whereas the database is the input variable; therefore, the expressive power coincides with the complexity class of the problems of recognizing each query database collection and it will be compared with database complexity classes, defined as follows. Given a Turing machine complexity class C (for instance $\mathcal{P}$ or $\mathcal{NP}$), a relational database scheme $\mathbf{R}$, and a set $\mathbf{D}$ of databases on $\mathbf{R}$, $\mathbf{D}$ is C-*recognizable* if the problem of deciding whether D is in $\mathbf{D}$ is in C. The *database complexity class DB-C* is the family of all C-recognizable database sets (for instance, DB-$\mathcal{P}$ is the family of all database sets that are recognizable in polynomial time).

2.4 Expressive Powers for Bound Queries

The following results about the complexity of stable models and their expressive power for bound queries under the various types of deterministic semantics are known in the literature.

Fact 1 *Given a* DATALOG¬ *program* $\mathcal{LP}$, *a database* D *in* $\mathbf{D}_{\mathcal{LP}}$, *and an interpretation* M *for* $\mathcal{LP}_D$,

1. *deciding whether* M *is a P-stable or T-stable model for* $\mathcal{LP}_D$ *is in* $\mathcal{P}$;
2. *deciding whether* M *is a M-stable or L-stable model for* $\mathcal{LP}_D$ *is co$\mathcal{NP}$-complete;*
3. *deciding whether a T-stable model for* $\mathcal{LP}_D$ *exists is* $\mathcal{NP}$-*complete.*

Proof. The proof of (1) is simple. The proof of (2) can be found in [20] and the part (3) was first proven in [17]. $\qquad\square$

Under the possibility semantics, P-stable models capture the whole class DB-$\mathcal{NP}$ while they express only a subset of polynomial queries under the definite semantics. In the latter case, their expressive power coincides with the one of well-founded models.

Fact 2
   (1) $DB^{\exists}_{\mathcal{PS}}[\mathbf{Q}] = DB$-$\mathcal{NP}$ *and* (2) $DB^{\bar{\lor}}_{\mathcal{PS}}[\mathbf{Q}] = DB^{\bar{\lor}}_{\mathcal{WS}}[\mathbf{Q}] = DB^{\exists}_{\mathcal{WS}}[\mathbf{Q}] \subset DB$-$\mathcal{P}$.

Proof. The proof of (1) can be found in [20]; the expressive power of well-founded model has been studied in [27]. $\qquad\square$

Under the possibility semantics T-stability keeps the same expressive power of P-stability but, under definite semantics, it captures the whole class DB-$\mathcal{D}^p$. Observe that the expressive power of T-stable models only gets to DB-$co\mathcal{NP}$ under the certainty semantics; as this is the expressive power of all queries admitting a stable model for any database, we can say that the extra-power of definite semantics comes from the fact that existence of a T-stable model is not guaranteed.

Fact 3

(1) $DB^{\exists}_{TS}[\mathbf{Q}] = DB\text{-}\mathcal{NP}$ and (2) $DB^{\vee}_{TS}[\mathbf{Q}] = DB\text{-}\mathcal{D}^p$;

(3) $DB^{\bar{\vee}}_{TS}[\mathbf{Q}] = DB\text{-}co\mathcal{NP}$ and (4) $DB^{\bar{\vee}}_{TS}[\mathbf{Q}^T] = DB^{\vee}_{TS}[\mathbf{Q}^T] = DB\text{-}co\mathcal{NP}$, where $\mathbf{Q}^T$ is the set of all queries for which a T-stable models exists for every possible database.

Proof. The proof of (3) is given in [23]; the other proofs can be found in [20]. □

Under the possibility semantics M-stable models have the same expressive power as P-stable and T-stable models but, under definite semantics, their expressive power tremendously increases and gets to the second level of the polynomial hierarchy. The expressive power of L-stable models gets to this level also under the possibility semantics, i.e., definite and possibility semantics have complementary expressive power in this case.

Fact 4

(1) $DB^{\exists}_{MS}[\mathbf{Q}] = DB\text{-}\mathcal{NP}$ and (2) $DB^{\bar{\vee}}_{MS}[\mathbf{Q}] = DB\text{-}\Pi^p_2$.

(3) $DB^{\exists}_{LS}[\mathbf{Q}] = DB\text{-}\Sigma^p_2$ and (4) $DB^{\bar{\vee}}_{LS}[\mathbf{Q}] = DB\text{-}\Pi^p_2$.

Proof. See [20]. □

Note that, in order to let total stable models achieve the same expressive power as L-stable models, it is necessary to switch to disjunctive DATALOG¬ as shown in[7].

In the next section we shall evaluate the expressive power of P-stable, T-stable, M-stable and L-stable models for unbound queries. We shall assume that the reader is familiar with the basic notions of complexity classes [12, 18] and of query language complexity evaluation (see, for instance, [1, 5, 7, 11, 13, 14, 15, 24, 28]).

3 Expressive Powers for Unbound Queries

3.1 Deterministic Semantics

In this section we shall study the expressive power of stable models for non-bound DATALOG¬ queries, i.e., the query goals are not ground. For simplicity but without substantial loss of generality, we shall assume that the query goal is a literal and that no term in it is ground.

Definition 1. An *unbound* (DATALOG¬) *query* is a pair $\mathcal{UQ} = <\mathcal{LP}, r(\mathbf{X})>$ where $\mathcal{LP}$ is a DATALOG¬ program, r is an IDB predicate symbol and $\mathbf{X}$ is a list of variables. Given a database D on $\mathcal{DB}_{\mathcal{LP}}$, the *answer* of $\mathcal{UQ}$ on D under the $\exists_{\mathcal{XS}}$ (resp., $\bar{\forall}_{\mathcal{XS}}$ or $\forall_{\mathcal{XS}}$) semantics is the (possibly empty) relation $\mathbf{r} = \{\mathbf{t} \mid r(\mathbf{t})$ is a $\exists_{\mathcal{XS}}$ (resp., $\bar{\forall}_{\mathcal{XS}}$ and $\forall_{\mathcal{XS}}$) inference of $\mathcal{LP}_{\mathbf{D}}\}$ and is denoted by $\mathcal{UQ}^{\exists}_{\mathcal{XS}}(D)$ (resp., $\mathcal{UQ}^{\bar{\forall}}_{\mathcal{XS}}(D)$ and $\mathcal{UQ}^{\forall}_{\mathcal{XS}}(D)$). □

Definition 2. Given a database scheme $\mathcal{DB}$ and a relation symbol $r \notin \mathcal{DB}$, both on a countable domain U, a *database mapping* from $\mathcal{DB}$ to r is a recursive function which maps every database D on $\mathcal{DB}$ to a finite (possibly empty) relation on r and which is invariant under an isomorphism on $U - W$, where W is any finite subset of U. □

Thus, for every stable model semantics, an unbound query $\mathcal{UQ}$ defines a mapping from $\mathcal{DB}_{\mathcal{LP}}$ to the query predicate symbol r that is invariant under an isomorphism on $U - W$, where W is the finite set of constants occurring in $\mathcal{LP}$. Therefore, the expressive power of stable model semantics can be measured by the class of database mappings that can be defined by all possible unbound queries.

A typical measure of complexity for a database mapping is [10, 7, 1]: given a database mapping $DM : \mathcal{DB} \to r$ and a Turing machine complexity class C, DM is *C-recognizable* if for each D on $\mathcal{DB}$, deciding whether a tuple $\mathbf{t}$ is in $DM(D)$ can be done in C time. Note that $DM(D)$ is polynomially bound on the size of D.

To characterize the expressive power of unbound queries we shall some time need the following notation: a database mapping $DM : \mathcal{DB} \to r$ is C_1/C_2-recognizable if both deciding whether $DM(D) \neq \emptyset$ for any D on DB is in C_1 and the restriction of DM to the family of all D on DB for which $DM(D) \neq \emptyset$ is C_2-recognizable.

We shall also use another complexity measure, that is borrowed from the analysis of finding problems: given a database mapping $DM : \mathcal{DB} \to r$ and a Turing machine complexity class C, DM is *C-rel(ation)-recognizable* if for each D on $\mathcal{DB}$ and $\mathbf{r}$ on r, deciding whether $\mathbf{r} = DM(D)$ can be done in C time. Moreover DM is C_1/C_2-recognizable if both deciding whether $DM(D) \neq \emptyset$ for any D on DB is in C_1 and the restriction of DM to the family of all D on DB for which $DM(D) \neq \emptyset$ is C_2-rel-recognizable.

The following interesting relationships between the two measures hold.

Lemma 3. *Let DM be a database mapping. Then*

1. *if DM is $\mathcal{P}$-recognizable then it is $\mathcal{P}$-rel-recognizable;*
2. *if DM is $\mathcal{NP}$ or $co\mathcal{NP}$-recognizable then it is $\mathcal{D}^p$-rel-recognizable;*
3. *if DM is $\mathcal{D}^p$-recognizable then it is $\mathcal{D}^p$-rel-recognizable;*
4. *if DM is Σ_2^p or Π_2^p-recognizable then it is $\mathcal{D}_2^p$-rel-recognizable, where $\mathcal{D}_2^p$ is the class of all problems that can be defined as the conjunction of a problem in Σ_2^p and a problem in Π_2^p;*
5. *if DM is $\mathcal{NP}$-rel-recognizable then it is $\mathcal{NP}$-recognizable;*
6. *if DM is Σ_2^p-rel-recognizable then it is Σ_2^p-recognizable.* □

The reverse implications do not in general hold. For instance, deciding whether a relation consisting of a set of nodes represents a kernel for the directed graph (corresponding to the input database) is in $\mathcal{P}$, whereas deciding whether a node (i.e., a tuple) is in the kernel is $\mathcal{NP}$-complete. Also deciding whether a set of nodes represents a maximum clique for a graph is $co\mathcal{NP}$-complete, whereas deciding whether a node is in a maximum clique is $\mathcal{D}^p$-complete [12, 18].

The next results show that the expressive powers of unbound queries under possibility semantics is strongly related to the expressive powers of bound queries.

Theorem 4. *Let DM be a database mapping. Then*

1. *DM is expressible by an unbound query under the $\exists_{\mathcal{XS}}$ semantics, where $\mathcal{XS} = \mathcal{PS}, \mathcal{TS}$ or $\mathcal{MS}$, if and only if DM is $\mathcal{NP}$-recognizable;*
2. *DM is expressible by an unbound query under the $\exists_{\mathcal{LS}}$ semantics if and only if DM is Σ_2^p-recognizable.*

Proof. Let DM be a database mapping from a database scheme $\mathcal{DB}$ to a relation symbol r. In the proof we refer to a generic type $\mathcal{XS}$ of stable models. Let $DB_{\mathcal{XS}}^\exists[Q] = DB\text{-}C$ be the expressive power of all bound queries under $\exists_{\mathcal{XS}}$ semantics. Observe that $C = \mathcal{NP}$ for $\mathcal{XS} = \mathcal{PS}, \mathcal{TS}$ and $\mathcal{MS}$ because of the parts (1) of Facts 2, 3 and 4, respectively; furthermore, by the part (3) of Fact 4, $C = \Sigma_2^p$ for $\mathcal{XS} = \mathcal{LS}$. The proof of the only-if part is simple and is omitted. As for the if-part, suppose now that DM is C-recognizable. Consider the database scheme $\mathcal{DB}' = \mathcal{DB} \cup \{r\}$ and the database collection $\mathbf{D}'$ on $\mathcal{DB}'$ defined as: $\{D \cup \{\mathbf{r}\} | D$ is any database on $\mathcal{DB}$ and $\mathbf{r} \subseteq DM(D)\}$. It is easy to see that $\mathbf{D}'$ is a C-recognizable database collection. So there exists a bound query $Q' =< \mathcal{LP}', G >$ such that $\mathcal{DB}_{\mathcal{LP}'} = \mathcal{DB}'$ and $DB_{\mathcal{XS}}^\exists(Q') = \mathbf{D}'$. Let $\mathcal{LP} = \mathcal{LP}' \cup \{r_1, r_2, r_3, r_4\}$ where:

$$
\begin{aligned}
r_1 &: \quad r(X) \leftarrow \neg \mathbf{f}(X). \\
r_2 &: \quad \mathbf{f}(X) \leftarrow \neg r(X). \\
r_3 &: \quad r(X) \leftarrow \neg G, \mathbf{f}(X). \\
r_4 &: \quad \mathbf{f}(X) \leftarrow \neg G, r(X).
\end{aligned}
$$

We have that $\mathcal{DB}_{\mathcal{LP}} = \mathcal{DB}$, r is now an IDB predicate symbol and $\hat{r}$ is a new IDB predicate symbol. Given a database D on $\mathcal{DB}$, the rules r_1 and r_2 allow to select a set of ground atoms with r as predicate symbol, thus they enable the selection of any relation on r. But any selection which will not eventually make G true will be invalidate by the rules r_3 and r_4; so all and only all subsets of $DM(D)$ will be eventually selected. Hence, because the union of all subsets of $DM(D)$ yields $DM(D)$, we have that, given the unbound query $UQ =< \mathcal{LP}, r(X) >$, $UQ_{\mathcal{XS}}^\exists(D) = DM(D)$. $\qquad\square$

The next result shows that the characterization in terms of relation recognizability is less precise.

Corollary 5. *Let DM be a database mapping. Then*

1. *sufficient and necessary conditions for DM to be expressible by an unbound query under the $\exists_{\mathcal{PS}}, \exists_{\mathcal{TS}}$ or $\exists_{\mathcal{MS}}$ semantics are, respectively: DM is $\mathcal{NP}$-rel-recognizable and DM is $\mathcal{D}^p$-rel-recognizable;*

2. *sufficient and necessary conditions for DM to be expressible by an unbound query under the $\exists_{\mathcal{CS}}$ semantics are, respectively: DM is Σ_2^p-rel-recognizable and DM is $\mathcal{D}_2^p$-rel-recognizable.* □

Thus, under relation recognizability and possibility semantics, we have singled out a lower bound and an upper bound for the class of database mappings that are expressed by unbound queries for each type of stable model. Observe that each class contains database mappings that are complete for its upper bound but does not coincide with it; thus inclusions are proper (obviously, provided that the polynomial hierarchy does not collapse).

Next we analyze the expressive powers of unbound queries under definite semantics.

Theorem 6. *Let DM be a database mapping. Then*

1. *DM is expressible by an unbound query under the $\overline{\forall}_{\mathcal{PS}}$ semantics (i.e., the well-founded semantics) if and only if DM is $\mathcal{P}'$-recognizable, where $\mathcal{P}' = DB_{\mathcal{PS}}^{\overline{\forall}}(\mathbf{Q}) \subset \mathcal{P}$;*
2. *DM is expressible by an unbound query under the $\overline{\forall}_{\mathcal{MS}}$ or $\overline{\forall}_{\mathcal{CS}}$ semantics if and only if it is Π_2^p-recognizable.*

Proof. Let DM be a database mapping from a database scheme $\mathcal{DB}$ to a relation symbol r. In the sequel we refer to a generic type $\mathcal{XS}$ of stable models, where $\mathcal{XS} = \mathcal{PS}$, $\mathcal{MS}$ or $\mathcal{CS}$. Let $DB_{\mathcal{XS}}^{\overline{\forall}}[\mathbf{Q}] = DB\text{-}C$ be the expressive power of all bound queries under $\overline{\forall}_{\mathcal{XS}}$ semantics. Recall that $C = \mathcal{P}'$ for $\mathcal{XS} = \mathcal{PS}$ by the part (2) of Fact 2, and $C = \Sigma_2^p$ for $\mathcal{XS} = \mathcal{MS}$ and $\mathcal{CS}$ by the parts (2) and (4) of Fact 4, respectively. Again the proof of the only-if part is omitted. As for the if-part suppose that DM is C-recognizable. Consider the database scheme $\mathcal{DB}' = \mathcal{DB} \cup \{r\}$ and the database collection $\mathbf{D}'$ on $\mathcal{DB}'$ defined as: $\{D \cup \{r\}|D$ is any database on $\mathcal{DB}$ and $\mathbf{r} \subseteq DM(D)\}$. As $\mathbf{D}'$ is a C-recognizable database collection, there exists a bound query $Q' = < \mathcal{LP}', G >$ such that $\mathcal{DB}_{\mathcal{LP}'} = \mathcal{DB}'$ and $DB_{\mathcal{XS}}^{\overline{\forall}}(Q') = \mathbf{D}'$. Without loss of generality, we assume that G is equal to an IDB predicate symbol with arity 0, say g. Let K be the set of predicate symbols consisting of r and of all IDB predicate symbols of $\mathcal{LP}'$. We construct a program $\mathcal{LP}$ as follows:

- we modify the arity of every predicate symbol in K by adding k new arguments, where k is the arity of r,
- we modify every rule in $\mathcal{LP}'$, say

$$\mathbf{p(X) \leftarrow c, q_1(X_1), ..., q_n(X_n).}$$

where C is a (possibly empty) conjunction of literals with predicates symbols in $\mathcal{DB}$ and q_i $(1 \leq i \leq n$ and $n \geq 0)$ is a predicate symbol in K, with the rule

$$\mathbf{p(X, Y) \leftarrow r(Y, Y), c, q_1(X_1, Y), ..., q_n(X_n, Y).}$$

where $\mathbf{Y}$ is a list of distinct variables non occurring in the rule, and

– we add the fact $r(\mathbf{X}, \mathbf{X})$ so that for each possible k-tuple $\mathbf{t}$, $r(\mathbf{t}, \mathbf{t})$ is true.

Note that $\mathcal{DB}_{\mathcal{CP}} = \mathcal{DB}$ and r is now an IDB predicate symbol with arity $2 \times k$. The ground instantiation of $\mathcal{CP}$ consists of a ground occurrence of the program $\mathcal{CP}'$ for each possible tuple $\mathbf{t}$ on r; so $g(\mathbf{t})$ will be in a $\mathcal{XS}$ stable model of the corresponding occurrence iff $\mathbf{t}$ is in $DM(D)$. As the various occurrences are independent from each other, an $\mathcal{XS}$ stable model for the overall program $\mathcal{CP}$ is equal to the union of a $\mathcal{XS}$ stable model of each replicated program. As an $\mathcal{XS}$ (for $\mathcal{XS} = \mathcal{PS}$, $\mathcal{MS}$ or $\mathcal{LS}$) stable model exists for any program, we have that, given the unbound query $\mathcal{UQ} = < \mathcal{CP}, g(X) >$, $\mathcal{UQ}^{\forall}_{\mathcal{XS}}(D) = DM(D)$. (Note that for $\mathcal{XS} = \mathcal{TS}$, it may happen that for some $\mathbf{t} \notin DM(D)$ there exists no T-stable model for the corresponding occurrence of $\mathcal{CP}'$; then $\mathcal{CP}$ would have no T-stable model even though $DM(D)$ is not empty — thus the proof is not applicable to T-stable models.) □

Also for unbound queries, certainty semantics is less expressive than definite semantics for T-stable models.

Proposition 7. *Let DM be a database mapping. Then*

1. *DM is expressible by an unbound query under the $\forall_{TS}$ semantics if and only if DM is coNP-recognizable;*
2. *DM is expressible by an unbound query under the $\overline{\forall}_{TS}$ semantics if and only if DM is $\mathcal{D}^P$/coNP-recognizable.* □

For the sake of presentation we omit to include the proof of the above proposition. We just point out that the proof is based on the part (4) of Fact 3 stating that every coNP-recognizable database collection can be defined by a query for which a T-stable model exists for every database.

Corollary 8. *Let DM be a database mapping. Then*

1. *necessary condition for DM to be expressible by an unbound query under the $\overline{\forall}_{PS}$ semantics is that DM is P-rel-recognizable;*
2. *necessary condition for DM to be expressible by an unbound query under the $\overline{\forall}_{TS}$ or $\forall_{TS}$ semantics is that is $\mathcal{D}^P$-rel-recognizable.*
3. *necessary and sufficient conditions for DM to be expressible by an unbound query under the $\overline{\forall}_{MS}$ or $\overline{\forall}_{LS}$ semantics are, respectively: DM is $\mathcal{D}^P_2$-rel-recognizable and DM is NP-rel-recognizable.* □

Having characterized the expressive power of unbound queries under possibility and definite semantics of various types of stable models is not satisfactory as, in our belief, such semantics on unbound queries does not have practical validity. In fact, collecting the tuples of a query answer from a number of distinct models requires a rather awkward and obscure style of writing DATALOG¬ programs; moreover, it often happens that a program solving a decision problem cannot be used to solve the associated finding problem, particularly in the case it admits multiple solutions.

Example 2. Take the bound query $Q =< \mathcal{LP}, \neg no\_kernel >$ where $\mathcal{LP}$ is:

```
s(W) ←              v(W), ¬connected_to_S(W), ¬ŝ(W).
ŝ(W) ←              v(W), ¬s(W).
connected_to_S(X) ← s(Y), e(Y, X).
no_kernel ←         ŝ(Y), ¬connected_to_S(Y), ¬no_kernel.
```

and the EDB predicate symbols v and e define the vertices and the edges of a directed graph. It is easy to see that $\neg no\_kernel$ is in a P-stable model M iff the sets s and $\hat{s}$ selected by M cover v, no two nodes in s are adjacent and there exists no node in $\hat{s}$ that is not adjacent to some node in S, i.e., iff S is a kernel. This query, under the possibility and definite semantics of T-stable models, defines the graph kernel problem. In order to actually get a kernel, we can just fire the unbound query $\mathcal{UQ} =< \mathcal{LP}, s(X) >$ only when the kernel is not unique, otherwise the query would return the union of all kernels under the possibility semantics and the intersection of all kernels under the definite semantics!   □

To get the wanted result of the finding problem we have to rewrite the program in such a way that the union or intersection of tuples will work correctly — and this is not practical in many situations. But our criticism to deterministic semantics for unbound queries is motivated not only by the intrinsically-obscure programming style but also by the fact that, in our belief, any determinism (or even a restricted type of non-determinism such as the semideterminism [26]) is not appropriate for unbound queries. In fact, as an unbound query often corresponds to a problem with multiple solutions, determinism requires introducing into the query some properties which single out exactly one of the possible solutions; such properties typically involve some low-level details (e.g., fixing some order) which are difficult to encode, data dependent and, besides, they could even increase the complexity of the query. For instance, for the graph kernel problem, we have to specify which kernel is to be returned when the kernel is not unique, e.g., by enforcing the selection of the kernel whose list of vertices is first in some lexicographic order — this corresponds to transforming a finding problem into an optimization problem. In particular, the graph kernel query is not any-more $\mathcal{NP}$-recognizable but it becomes $\mathcal{DP}$-recognizable.

In the next subsection we resume the potential non-determinism of stable models to provide a simple and efficient formulation of unbound queries as well as the precise characterization of their expressive power.

3.2 Non-Deterministic Semantics

To deal with unbound queries we here propose to combine the expressive strength of possibility or definite semantics in defining decision problems with the "cut" capability of the intrinsic non-determinism of stable models [9, 21, 22]. Thus we define an unbound query as composed by two goals; the first one is ground and allows to select the stable models in which it is true and the second one is unbound and is to be unified with any of the selected stable models.

Definition 9. An *non-deterministic unbound query* $\mathcal{NQ}$ is a triple $< \mathcal{LP}, G,$ $r(\mathbf{X}) >$, where $\mathcal{LP}$ is a DATALOG⌐ program, G is a ground literal, r is an IDB predicate symbol and $\mathbf{X}$ is a list of variables. The *answer set* of $\mathcal{NQ}$ for a database D on $\mathcal{DB}_{\mathcal{LP}}$ under the $\exists_{\mathcal{XS}}$ (resp., $\overline{\forall}_{\mathcal{XS}}$ or $\forall_{\mathcal{XS}}$) semantics, denoted by $\mathcal{NQ}^{\exists}_{\mathcal{XS}}(D)$ (resp., $\mathcal{NQ}^{\overline{\forall}}_{\mathcal{XS}}(D)$ and $\mathcal{NQ}^{\forall}_{\mathcal{XS}}(D)$), is the empty set if G is not a $\exists_{\mathcal{XS}}$ (resp., $\overline{\forall}_{\mathcal{XS}}$ and $\forall_{\mathcal{XS}}$) inference of $\mathcal{LP}_D$ or otherwise the set of (possibly empty) relations $r_i = \{t | r(t) \in M_i\}$ on r such that for each $M_i \in \mathcal{XS}$ for which both G is true in M_i and no ground atom with r as predicate symbol is undefined. □

In practice it is sufficient to non-deterministically return any relation in the answer set. Observe that the restriction that a relation in the answer set be fully defined does not reduce the expressive power (possibly except for M-stable models under the possibility semantics as it will discussed later); moreover, the restriction corresponds to a natural writing of unbound queries.

Example 3. The mixed query $< \mathcal{LP}, \neg no\_kernel, s(\mathbf{X}) >$ on the program of Example 2 with $\exists_{\mathcal{TS}}$ or $\overline{\forall}_{\mathcal{TS}}$ semantics filters the T-stable models corresponding to the selection of a kernel and returns the kernel recognized by any of these models. □

Definition 10. Given a database scheme $\mathcal{DB}$ and a relation symbol r, both with a countable domain U, a *database relation mapping DRM* : $\mathcal{DB} \xrightarrow{\#} r$ is a (possibly partial) recursive function which maps every database on $\mathcal{DB}$ to a finite (possibly empty) set of finite (possibly empty) relations on r and is invariant under an isomorphism on $U - W$, where U is the domain of $\mathcal{DB}$ and W is any finite subset of U. □

Thus, a non-deterministic unbound query $\mathcal{NQ}$ expresses a database relation mapping $\mathcal{DB}_{\mathcal{LP}} \xrightarrow{\#} r$.

To characterize the expressive power of non-deterministic unbound query, the notion of C-recognizability is not appropriate as two tuples may belong to different relations in the answer set. So we shall use C-rel-recognizability, thus our measure is based on the complexity of recognizing whether a relation is in the answer set. As shown next, also in this case the expressive powers of non-deterministic unbound queries are characterized by means of the expressive powers of bound queries.

Theorem 11. *Let DRM be a database relation mapping. Then*

1. *DRM is expressible by a non-deterministic unbound query under the $\exists_{\mathcal{XS}}$ semantics, where $\mathcal{XS} = \mathcal{PS}, \mathcal{TS}$ or $\mathcal{MS}$, if and only if it is $\mathcal{NP}$-rel-recognizable;*
2. *DRM is expressible by a a non-deterministic unbound query under the $\exists_{\mathcal{LS}}$ semantics if and only if it is Σ^p_2-rel-recognizable.*

Proof. Let *DRM* be a database relation mapping from a database scheme $\mathcal{DB}$ to a relation symbol r. Suppose that there exists a non-deterministic unbound query $\mathcal{NQ} =< \mathcal{LP}, G, r(\mathbf{X}) >$ such that $\mathcal{DB}_{\mathcal{LP}} = \mathcal{DB}$, r is an IDB predicate symbol of $\mathcal{LP}$, and for each D on $\mathcal{DB}$, $DRM(D) = \mathcal{NQ}^{\exists}_{\mathcal{XS}}(D)$. Let $\mathbf{r}$ be a relation on r; we want to verify whether $\mathbf{r}$ is in $DRM(D)$. We guess an interpretation M of $\mathcal{LP}_D$ and we check in polynomial time whether G is M and for each tuple $\mathbf{t}$ on r, $r(\mathbf{t})$ is in M if $\mathbf{t} \in \mathbf{r}$ and $\neg r(\mathbf{t})$ is in M otherwise. Moreover, depending on $\mathcal{XS}$ we perform the following additional test:

- if $\mathcal{XS} = \mathcal{PS}$ or $\mathcal{MS}$, we verify whether M is a P-stable model — this test is in $\mathcal{P}$ by the part (1) of Fact 1;
- if $\mathcal{XS} = \mathcal{TS}$, we verify whether M is a T-stable model — this test is in $\mathcal{P}$ by the part (1) of Fact 1;
- if $\mathcal{XS} = \mathcal{LS}$, we verify whether M is an L-stable model — this test is in $co\mathcal{NP}$ by the part (2) of Fact 1.

It is easy to see that $\mathbf{r}$ is in $DRM(D)$ iff all the above tests succeed. Observe that for $\mathcal{XS} = \mathcal{MS}$ we can just check whether M is P-stable and not M-stable (that is instead $co\mathcal{NP}$-complete by the part (2) of Fact 1) because of the condition that no ground atom with r as predicate symbol is undefined in M; in fact, if such a P-stable model M exists, no $r(\mathbf{t})$ is undefined in the $\mathcal{MS}$ stable model containing M as well. It turns out that $\mathbf{r}$ is in $DRM(D)$ iff DRM is $\mathcal{NP}$-rel-recognizable for $\mathcal{XS} = \mathcal{PS}, \mathcal{MS}$ or $\mathcal{TS}$ and Σ^p_2-rel-recognizable for $\mathcal{XS} = \mathcal{LS}$. For the sake of presentation, we omit to include the proof of if-part. $\square$

Note that the restriction on the full definiteness of the relation is necessary only for the proof of the only-if part for M-stable models. The problem of whether the expressive power increases in this case is open, but our conjecture is that it does not.

For the characterization of the expressive powers for definite and certainty semantics, we use the notation of C_1/C_2-rel-recognizability, i.e., a database relation mapping $DRM : \mathcal{DB} \xrightarrow{\#} r$ is C_1/C_2-rel-recognizable if both DRM is C_1-decidable (i.e., deciding whether $DRM(D) \neq \emptyset$ for any D on DB is in C_1) and for each D on DB for which $DRM(D) \neq \emptyset$, deciding whether a relation $\mathbf{r}$ belongs to $DRM(D)$ is in C_2.

Theorem 12. *Let DRM be a database relation mapping. Then*

1. *DRM is expressible by a non-deterministic unbound query under the $\overline{\forall}_{TS}$ semantics if and only if it is $\mathcal{D}^p/\mathcal{NP}$-rel-recognizable;*
2. *DRM is expressible by a non-deterministic unbound query under the $\forall_{TS}$ semantics if and only if it is $co\mathcal{NP}/\mathcal{NP}$-rel-recognizable;*
3. *DM is expressible by a non-deterministic unbound query under the $\overline{\forall}_{MS}$ semantics if and only if it is $\Pi^p_2/\mathcal{NP}$-rel-recognizable;*
4. *DM is expressible by a non-deterministic unbound query under the $\overline{\forall}_{LS}$ semantics if and only if it is Π^p_2/Σ^p_2-rel-recognizable.* $\square$

The proof can be found in the full paper. Observe that, as the definite semantics of P-stable model is deterministic, it does not make sense to consider non-determinism in this case.

We conclude by summarizing in the table of Figure 1 the results about the expressive power of stable models for unbound queries under deterministic and non-deterministic semantics.

	P-Stable	T-Stable	M-Stable	L-stable
	(a) Deterministic Semantics			
Possibility	= $\mathcal{NP}$-rec. $\subseteq \mathcal{D}^P$-rel-rec. $\supseteq \mathcal{NP}$-rel-rec.	= $\mathcal{NP}$-rec. $\subseteq \mathcal{D}^P$-rel-rec. $\supseteq \mathcal{NP}$-rel-rec.	= $\mathcal{NP}$-rec. $\subseteq \mathcal{D}^P$-rel-rec. $\supseteq \mathcal{NP}$-rel-rec.	= Σ_2^p-rec. $\subseteq \mathcal{D}_2^p$-rel-rec. $\supseteq \Sigma_2^p$-rel-rec.
Definite	= $\mathcal{P}'$-rec. $\subseteq \mathcal{P}$-rel-rec.	= $\mathcal{D}^P/co\mathcal{NP}$-rec. $\subseteq \mathcal{D}^P$-rel-rec.	= Π_2^p-rec. $\subseteq \mathcal{D}_2^p$-rel-rec. $\supseteq \mathcal{NP}$-rel-rec.	= Π_2^p-rec. $\subseteq \mathcal{D}_2^p$-rel-rec. $\supseteq \mathcal{NP}$-rel-rec.
Certainty	see definite	= $co\mathcal{NP}$-rec. $\subseteq \mathcal{D}^P$-rel-rec.	see definite	see definite
	(b) Non-Deterministic Semantics			
Possibility	$\mathcal{NP}$-rel-rec.	$\mathcal{NP}$-rel-rec.	$\mathcal{NP}$-rel-rec.	Σ_2^p-rel-rec.
Definite	N/A	$\mathcal{D}^P/\mathcal{NP}$-rel-rec.	$\Pi_2^p/\mathcal{NP}$-rel-rec.	Π_2^p/Σ_2^p-rel.-rec.
Certainty	N/A	$co\mathcal{NP}/\mathcal{NP}$-rel-rec.	see definite	see definite

Fig. 1. *Expressive Powers of Stable Models for Unbound Queries*

References

1. Abiteboul S., Simon E., and V. Vianu, "Non-deterministic languages to express deterministic transformations", *Proc. ACM PODS Symp.*, 1990, pp. 218-229.
2. Baral V. and V. Subrahmanian, "Stable and extension class theory for logic programs and default logic", *Journal of Automated Reasoning*, 1992, pp. 345-366.
3. Bidoit N., "Negation in Rule-based Database Languages: a Survey", *Theoretical Computer Science 78*, 3, 1991, pp. 3-83.
4. Ceri S., Gottlob G. and L. Tanca, *Logic Programming and Databases*, Springer-Verlag, Berlin, Germany, 1990.
5. Chandra A., and D. Harel, "Structure and Complexity of Relational Queries", *Journal of Computer and System Sciences 25*, 1, 1982, pp. 99-128.
6. Dung P., "Negation as Hypotheses: an abductive foundation for logic programming", *Proc. 8th Conf. on Logic Programming*, 1991, pp. 3-17.
7. Eiter T., Gottlob G. and H. Manila, "Expressive Power and Complexity of Disjunctive DATALOG", *Proc. ACM PODS Symp.*, Minneapolis, USA, May 1994, pp. 267-278.
8. Gelfond M., and V. Lifschitz, "The Stable Model Semantics for Logic Programming", *Proc. 5th Int. Conf. and Symp. on Logic Programming*, MIT Press, Cambridge, 1988, pp. 1070-1080.
9. Giannotti F., Pedreschi D., Saccà D. and C. Zaniolo, "Non-Determinism in Deductive Databases", *Proc. 2nd Conference on Deductive and Object-Oriented Databases, Proc. of DOOD 91, LNCS 566*, Springer-Verlag, 1991, pp. 129-146.

10. Gurovich Y., "Logic and the Challenge of Computer Science", in E. Borger (ed.), *Trends in Theoretical Computer Science*, Computer Science Press, 1988.
11. Immerman N., "Languages which Capture Complexity Classes", *SIAM Journal on Computing 16*, 4, 1987, pp. 760-778.
12. Johnson D.S., "A Catalog of Complexity Classes", in J. van Leewen (ed.), *Handbook of Theoretical Computer Science*, Vol. 1, North-Holland, 1990.
13. Kanellakis P.C., "Elements of Relational Database Theory", in J. van Leewen (ed.), *Handbook of Theoretical Computer Science*, Vol. 2, North-Holland, 1991.
14. Kolaitis P.G., "The Expressive Power of Stratified Logics Programs", *Information and Computation 90*, 1991, pp. 50-66.
15. Kolaitis P.G. and C.H. Papadimitriou, " Why not Negation by Fixpoint?", *Journal of Computer and System Sciences 43*, 1991, pp. 125-144.
16. Lloyd J.W., *Foundations of Logic Programming*, Springer-Verlag, Berlin, Germany, 1987.
17. Marek W. and M. Truszcynski, "Autoepistemic Logic", *Journal of the ACM 38*, 3, 1991, pp. 588-619.
18. Papadimitriou C., *Computational Complexity*, Addison-Wesley, Reading, MA, USA, 1994.
19. Przymusinski T.C., "Well-founded Semantics Coincides with Three-valued Stable Semantics", *Fundamenta Informaticae 13*, 1990, pp. 445-463.
20. Saccà D., "The Expressive Power of Stable Models for DATALOG Queries with Negation", in *Informal Proceedings of 2nd Work. on Structural Complexity and Recursion-theoretic methods in Logic Programming*, Vancouver, Canada, 1993, pp. 150-162.
21. Saccà D. and C. Zaniolo, "Stable Models and Non-Determinism in Logic Programs with Negation", *Proc. ACM PODS Symp.*, 1990, pp. 205-218.
22. Saccà D. and C. Zaniolo, "Determinism and Non-Determinism of Stable Models", unpublished manuscript, 1992.
23. Schlipf J.S., "The Expressive Powers of the Logic Programming Semantics", *Proc. ACM PODS Symp.*, 1990, pp. 196-204.
24. Schlipf J.S., "A Survey of Complexity and Undecidability Results in Logic Programming", *Proc. Workshop on "Structural Complexity and Recursion-Theoretic Methods in Logic Programming*, Washington D.C., USA, Nov. 1993, pp. 143-164.
25. Ullman J.D., *Principles of Database and Knowledge Base Systems*, Vol 1-2, Computer Science Press, 1989.
26. Van de Bussche J. and D. Van Gucht, "Semi-determinism", *Proc. of ACM PODS Symp.*, 1992, pp. 191-201.
27. Van Gelder A., Ross K. and J.S. Schlipf, "The Well-Founded Semantics for General Logic Programs", *Journal of the ACM 38*, 3, 1991, pp. 620-650.
28. Vardi M.Y., "The Complexity of Relational Query Languages", *Proc. ACM Symp. on Theory of Computing*, 1982, pp. 137-146.
29. You J. and L.Y. Yuan, "Three-valued Formalization of Logic Programming: is it needed? *Proc. of ACM PODS Symp.*, 1990, pp. 172-182.

Revision programming, database updates and integrity constraints

V. Wiktor Marek and Mirosław Truszczyński

Department of Computer Science
University of Kentucky
Lexington, KY 40506-0027
{marek,mirek}@cs.uky.edu

Abstract. We investigate revision programming, a logic-based mechanism for describing changes in databases and enforcing certain type of integrity constraints. We show that revisions justified by an initial database and a revision program can be computed by a sequential execution of the rules of the program (with subsequent check of the applicability of the rules). In general, a program may determine none, exactly one or many justified revisions of a given initial database. We exhibit two classes of programs, *safe* and *stratified*, with the property that for every initial database a **unique** justified revision exists. We study the complexity of basic problems associated with justified revisions. Although the existence problems are NP-complete, for safe and stratified programs justified revisions can be computed in polynomial time.

1 Introduction

We study a formalism for stating and enforcing integrity constraints in databases. Integrity constraints can be described in the language of first-order logic, which is quite expressive and allows us to formulate a wide range of constraints. However, there is a problem: if no restrictions on the syntax of integrity constraints are imposed, the classical semantics of the language of first-order logic does not entail a mechanism for *enforcing* them. In this paper, we describe a version of the first-order logic language consisting of rules rather than formulas. In that we follow the approach of logic programming [vEK76, Apt90] but our class of rules is much more general. Our system allows us to specify integrity constraints in a declarative fashion similarly as in the case of the standard first-order language (or logic programming). What is more important, it provides an imperative interpretation to these integrity constraints and, consequently, a mechanism to enforce them, given the initial state of a database. In this paper we will study basic properties of our formalism and we will argue that it is a convenient tool for describing updates on databases and integrity constraints which databases must satisfy.

There are fragments of first-order logic that can be given an imperative interpretation. For example, as first pointed by Van Emden and Kowalski [vEK76], definite Horn programs have least Herbrand models and these models can be described in a procedural fashion. This match between declarative first-order logic semantics and procedural treatment of rules in logic programming disappears for wider classes of theories. Logic programming writes clauses in such a way as to underline their imperative, computational, character. Namely, a logic program clause is any expression of the form

$$\gamma \leftarrow \alpha_1, \ldots, \alpha_k, \neg\beta_1, \ldots, \neg\beta_m,$$

where α_i, β_i and γ are propositional atoms (the restriction to the propositional case is not needed; we adopt it for the sake of simplicity of discussion). It is interpreted as a mechanism for computing γ after α_i, $1 \le i \le k$, have been computed and after it has been established that β_i, $1 \le i \le m$, cannot be computed. This last part is somewhat controversial. Several proposals were made to formalize the requirement "β_i cannot be computed". They led to different semantics for logic programs [Cla78, Fit85, VRS91]. One of the most successful is the semantics of stable models [GL88]. The key idea behind the stable model semantics is to select a tentative model M, regard atoms not in M as those that cannot be computed, and use this information in the van Emden-Kowalski computation process. If M is what is produced as the result, M is a *stable* model. Hence, $\neg\beta$ is interpreted as **absence from a tentative model**, while positive literals have to be computed.

We will consider updates (insertions and **deletions**), and integrity constraints which, in the case of some data being present in a database and some data being absent from the database, require that some other data be present in (absent from) the database. The formalism of logic programs with stable semantics is not expressive enough to be directly employed as a specification language for database updates and integrity constraints. Logic program clauses can only compute new atoms and, thus, can only model rules which require items be inserted into databases. But they cannot model deletions. No logic program clause can express an imperative rule *"(under some conditions) delete a record"*, since negative literals are not allowed in the head. Second, less troublesome limitation, of logic programming is that logic programs compute from the empty set of atoms while updates and integrity constraints must be enforced on arbitrary databases. DATALOG [Ull88] overcomes this difficulty.

In this paper, we present a system which allows us to form rules with negative literals in the head. We call it *revision programming*. For revision programs, we describe a semantics of justified revisions. This semantics describes, for a given set of atoms, all "justified" ways in which to modify it in order to satisfy the constraints specified by a revision program. Consequently, our formalism can be used to formulate and process integrity constraints and updates.

Revision programming extends logic programming and the notion of a justified revision generalizes that of a stable model. It is different, though, from logic programming with classical negation [GL90].

We have introduced revision programs and justified revisions in [MT94]. We have studied there basic properties of revision programming, mentioned a simple application to belief revision and considered analogies with logic programming. In this paper, we discuss applications of revision programming to study updates and integrity constraints in databases and investigate results on algorithmic aspects of revision programming. We introduce two classes of programs, *safe* and *stratified*, for which justified revisions are unique and can be computed efficiently.

Techniques developed here are based on the work of Reiter [Rei80] and Gelfond and Lifschitz [GL88]. However, motivations as well as some key ideas come from database theory. First, we treat programs as input-output devices, as it is the case in DATALOG [Ull88]. Second, our language is similar to that used by Abiteboul and Vianu [AV90, AV91] in their work on extensions of DATALOG admitting deletions. Stratified programs were studied (in a different setting) by Manchanda and Warren [MW88], who assigned to them a Kripke-style semantics.

2 Preliminaries

In this section we present basic concepts of revision programming introduced in [MT94]. We will encode a database D as a theory consisting of ground atomic formulas of a certain first-order language. Namely, for each k-ary relation R in the database schema we have a predicate symbol p_R whose intended meaning is: $p_R(x_1, \ldots, x_k)$ if and only if $(x_1, \ldots, x_k) \in R$. Then, each tuple $(a_1, \ldots, a_k)$ of R is represented by the ground atom $p_R(a_1, \ldots, a_k)$.

Definition 1. Let U be a denumerable set. We call its elements *atoms*. A *revision in-rule* or, simply, an *in-rule*, is any expression of the form

$$\mathbf{in}(p) \leftarrow \mathbf{in}(q_1), \ldots, \mathbf{in}(q_m), \mathbf{out}(s_1), \ldots, \mathbf{out}(s_n), \tag{1}$$

where p, q_i, $1 \leq i \leq m$, and s_j, $1 \leq j \leq n$, are all in U. A *revision out-rule* or, simply, an *out-rule*, is any expression of the form

$$\mathbf{out}(p) \leftarrow \mathbf{in}(q_1), \ldots, \mathbf{in}(q_m), \mathbf{out}(s_1), \ldots, \mathbf{out}(s_n), \tag{2}$$

where p, q_i, $1 \leq i \leq m$, and s_j, $1 \leq j \leq n$, are all in U. All in- and out-rules are called *rules*. Expressions $\mathbf{in}(a)$ and $\mathbf{out}(a)$ are called *literals*. Literals $\mathbf{in}(p)$ and $\mathbf{out}(p)$ are called the heads of the rules (1) and (2). The head of a rule r is denoted by *head*(r). A collection of rules is called a *revision program* or, simply, a *program*. The set of all literals appearing in a program (as the heads of the rules in a program) is denoted by *var*(P) (*head*(P), respectively). A database D *satisfies* a rule (1) (rule (2), respectively) if $p \in D$ ($p \notin D$, respectively), or if there is i, $1 \leq i \leq m$, such that $q_i \notin D$, or if there is i, $1 \leq i \leq n$, such that $s_i \in D$. A database D satisfies a revision program P if D satisfies each rule in P. The notion of a *model* corresponds in a natural way to the notion of satisfaction.

In order to apply revision programming to a database D, we need to take for U the set of all ground atomic formulas $p_R(a_1, \ldots, a_k)$. Here $a_1, \ldots, a_k$ are descriptors of appropriate attributes. Notice that we need an atom $p_R(a_1, \ldots, a_k)$ for each tuple $(a_1, \ldots, a_k)$ which *potentially* appears in D, not only those which *actually* appear there. To specify the insertion of $(a_1, \ldots, a_k)$ into a relation R of D we can use an in-rule: $\mathbf{in}(p_R(a_1, \ldots, a_k)) \leftarrow$. Similarly, the deletion can be specified as an out-rule $\mathbf{out}(p_R(a_1, \ldots, a_k)) \leftarrow$. More generally, rules of type (1) describe integrity constraints of the form: if tuples $q_1, \ldots, q_m$ are in a database and tuples $s_1, \ldots, s_n$ are not in the database, then tuple p is in the database. Rules of type (2) have a similar interpretation, except that they stipulate that tuple p be **not in** the database.

We use revision programs as means to specify integrity constraints. We assume some initial state D_I of a database. If D_I satisfies all constraints in a revision program P, no change in D_I is necessary. If, however, D_I does not satisfy P, we use P as an input-output device to **enforce** on D_I the constraints it represents. That is, we produce several (possibly none) databases D_R each of which satisfies the constraints of P. Moreover, we do so in such a way that each change (insertion, deletion) necessary to transform D_I into D_R is **justified**.

Example 1. Consider a database $D_I = \{a, b, d, f\}$. Let P be the program:

(1) $\mathbf{in}(c) \leftarrow$ (2) $\mathbf{out}(a) \leftarrow \mathbf{in}(c)$ (3) $\mathbf{in}(d) \leftarrow \mathbf{in}(c)$
(4) $\mathbf{out}(b) \leftarrow \mathbf{in}(d)$ (5) $\mathbf{out}(a) \leftarrow \mathbf{out}(b)$ (6) $\mathbf{in}(e) \leftarrow \mathbf{in}(b)$

Rule (1) tells us that c must be inserted into the resulting database. Hence, a must be deleted and d must be inserted (rules (2) and (3)). Note that d is in the database so, actually, no action is needed. Then, by rule (4) we must eliminate b. Next, since b is deleted, we must eliminate a (it has already been deleted so no additional action is needed). Finally, since we do not have b, there is no need to insert e. Hence, the resulting database D_R will consist of $\{c, d, f\}$.

Despite the fact that revision rules have an imperative flavor and sometimes, as in Example 1, there is no problem with computing the transformed database, in general it is by no means obvious how revision programs should operate.

Example 2. Let D_I consist of b and c. Let the program P consist of clauses:

(1) $\mathbf{out}(c) \leftarrow \mathbf{in}(b)$ (2) $\mathbf{out}(b) \leftarrow \mathbf{in}(c)$

A straightforward approach is to observe that premises of both rules are satisfied in D_I. Hence, both rules should "fire" and both b and c should be eliminated. The resulting database is empty and it indeed satisfies (1) and (2). However, there are problems with this approach. First, it is enough to eliminate only **one** of these elements to satisfy **both** constraints expressed by the program P. Second, with respect to the resulting database, no deletion has a justification any more (premises of rules (1) and (2) are no longer satisfied). Third, there is no way to sequentially execute the rules (as in Example 1) and obtain the empty database as the result. The other possibility is not to take D_I into account at all. But then, there is no reason to "fire" any rule. Hence, the same database D_I results from the process and it does not even satisfy the constraints! Clearly, the intended meaning of rules (1) and (2) is to enforce that at most one of b and c is in the database. Since both elements are in D_I to start with, the "parsimonious" way to enforce both constraints is to select for D_R either $\{b\}$ or $\{c\}$.

We will now present a construction introduced in [MT94], which describes a mechanism for enforcing rules in revision programs. It is based on the notion of *necessary change* — the change that is entailed by a program alone, that is, without references to any databases.

Definition 2. Let P be a revision program. Let Q be the Horn program obtained from P by treating each literal in P as a separate propositional variable. Let M be the least model of Q. We call M *necessary change basis* for P and denote it by $NCB(P)$. The *necessary change* for P (or, *determined by P*) is defined as the pair (I, O), where $I = \{a : a$ is an atom and $\mathbf{in}(a) \in M\}$ and $O = \{a : a$ is an atom and $\mathbf{out}(a) \in M\}$. If $NCB(P)$ does not contain any pair $\mathbf{in}(a)$, $\mathbf{out}(a)$, that is, if $I \cap O = \emptyset$, then P is called *coherent*.

In general, necessary change is not sufficient to compute a revised database. The initial database as well as a tentative final one (used in a way reminiscent of the construction of stable models [GL88]) must be taken into account.

Definition 3. [MT94] Let P be a revision program and let D_I and D_R be two databases.

1. The reduct of P with respect to (D_I, D_R) is defined in two stages:
   Stage 1: Eliminate from P every rule of type (1) or (2) such that $q_i \notin D_R$, for some i, $1 \le i \le m$, or $s_j \in D_R$, for some j, $1 \le j \le n$. The resulting program is denoted by P_{D_R}.
   Stage 2: From the body of each rule that remains after Stage 1 eliminate each $\mathbf{in}(a)$ such that $a \in D_I$ and each $\mathbf{out}(a)$ such that $a \notin D_I$.
2. The program resulting from P after both stages are executed is called the *reduct of P with respect to* (D_I, D_R) and is denoted by $P_{D_R}|D_I$.
3. Let (I, O) be the necessary change determined by $P_{D_R}|D_I$. If $I \cap O = \emptyset$ (that is, if $P_{D_R}|D_I$ is coherent) and $D_R = (D_I \cup I) \setminus O$, then D_R is called a *P-justified revision of* D_I and the pair $\langle D_I, D_R \rangle$ is called a *P-justified transition*.

Informally, in order to treat D_R as a P-justified revision of D_I, we need to have justifications for every deletion and insertion that are needed to transform D_I into D_R. The justification must be valid **after** the revision. Hence, only rules of $P|D_R$ can be used as justifications. In addition, the initial status D_I of the database must be taken into account (Stage 2). If the necessary change entailed by the resulting program $P_{D_R}|D_I$ converts D_I into D_R, D_R is a P-justified revision of D_I.

Example 3. We will illustrate now the concepts of reduct and justified revision. Let P be a revision program consisting of the following revision rules:

(1) $\mathbf{out}(b) \leftarrow \mathbf{in}(c)$ (2) $\mathbf{out}(c) \leftarrow \mathbf{in}(b), \mathbf{in}(d)$
(3) $\mathbf{in}(a) \leftarrow \mathbf{out}(b), \mathbf{in}(c)$ (4) $\mathbf{out}(d) \leftarrow \mathbf{in}(a), \mathbf{in}(b)$

Suppose that $D_I = \{b, c, d\}$. There are two P-justified revisions of D_I: $\{b, d\}$ and $\{a, c, d\}$. Let us consider the second possibility, leaving the first one for the reader as an exercise. We have

$$P_{\{a,c,d\}} = \{\mathbf{out}(b) \leftarrow \mathbf{in}(c);\ \mathbf{in}(a) \leftarrow \mathbf{out}(b), \mathbf{in}(c)\}$$

and

$$P_{\{a,c,d\}}|D_I = \{\mathbf{out}(b) \leftarrow;\ \mathbf{in}(a) \leftarrow \mathbf{out}(b)\}.$$

Consequently, $NCB(P_{\{a,c,d\}}|D_I) = \{\mathbf{in}(a), \mathbf{out}(b)\}$. Thus $I = \{a\}$, $O = \{b\}$. Since $(D_I \cup \{a\}) \setminus \{b\} = \{a, c, d\}$, $\{a, c, d\}$ is indeed a P-justified revision.

Now we show an example of a database which is not a P-justified revision of D_I. Consider $D = \{a, b, c\}$. Then,

$$P_{\{a,b,c\}}|D_I = \{\mathbf{out}(b) \leftarrow;\ \mathbf{out}(d) \leftarrow \mathbf{in}(a)\}.$$

In this case, $NCB(P_{\{a,b,c\}}|D_I) = \{\mathbf{out}(b)\}$. Since $D \neq D_I \setminus \{b\}$, D is not a P-justified revision of D_I.

The following result describes the most fundamental properties of satisfaction and necessary change.

Theorem 4 [MT94]. *1. Let P be a revision program and let (I, O) be the necessary change determined by P. Then, for every model M of P, $I \subseteq M$ and $O \cap M = \emptyset$.*

2. If a database D satisfies a revision program P then D is a unique P-justified revision of D.

3. Let P be a revision program and let D_I be a database. If a database D_R is a P-justified revision of D_I, then D_R is a model of P.

Revision programming can be viewed as a generalization of logic programming. Given a logic program clause $C = p \leftarrow q_1, \ldots, q_m, \mathbf{not}(s_1), \ldots, \mathbf{not}(s_n)$ we define the revision rule $r(C)$ as

$$\mathbf{in}(p) \leftarrow \mathbf{in}(q_1), \ldots, \mathbf{in}(q_m), \mathbf{out}(s_1), \ldots, \mathbf{out}(s_n). \tag{3}$$

In addition, for a logic program P, we define the corresponding revision program $r(P)$ by

$$r(P) = \{r(C): C \in P\}. \tag{4}$$

Theorem 5 (Stability theorem, [MT94])). *Let P be a logic program. A set of atoms M is a model of P if and only if M is a model of $r(P)$. A set of atoms M is a stable model of P if and only of M is an $r(P)$-justified revision of $\emptyset$.*

Two other properties of revision programming are listed below.

Theorem 6 (Minimality theorem, [MT94]). *Let P be a revision program and let D_I be a database. If D_R is a P-justified revision of D_I, then $D_R \div D_I$ ($\div$ stands for the symmetric difference) is minimal in the family $\{D \div D_I : D$ is a model of $P\}$.*

By $\overline{D}$ the complement of D i.e. $At \setminus D$. The program P^D called *dual* of P arises from P by simultaneous substitution of **in** for **out** and conversely.

Theorem 7 (Duality theorem, [MT94]). *Let P be a revision program and let D_I be a database. Then, D_R is a P-justified revision of D_I if and only if $\overline{D_R}$ is a P^D-justified revision of $\overline{D_I}$.*

3 Sequential revision process

Our definition of P-justified revisions has a certain "global" character. It is based on two operators that are applied to programs rather than to individual rules. First of these operators assigns the reduct to a revision program, the other one assigns to the reduct the necessary change it implies. Hence, P-justified revisions of D_I can be viewed as the results of applying all rules of P to D_I "in parallel". In this section, we will present a different description of P-justified revisions. We will show that P-justified revisions of D_I are exactly those databases D_R which can be obtained from D_I by executing all rules of P **one by one** according to some enumeration of the rules in P. This property of the semantics of P-justified revisions is similar to the notion of *serializability* in transaction management.

Let C be a revision rule and let D be a database. If D satisfies the body of the rule C, then C is *applicable* with respect to D (D-*applicable*, for short). Let P be a revision program. We define

$$AR_P(D) = \{C \in P : C \text{ is } D\text{-applicable}\}.$$

For example, the rule $\textbf{in}(c) \leftarrow \textbf{in}(a), \textbf{out}(b)$ is not D-applicable for $D = \{a, b\}$ and it is D-applicable for $D = \{a, d\}$.

If a rule C is D-applicable then its conclusion can be executed on the database D and, according to the type of the head of C, an atom will be inserted to or deleted from D. Assume that a certain well-ordering $\prec$ of the rules of P is given. Then, the following *sequential revision process* can be considered: in each step select the first rule according to $\prec$ which has not been selected before and which is applicable with respect to the **current** state of the database. Modify the database according to the head of the selected rule. Stop when a selection of a rule is no longer possible. The question that we deal with in this section is: how the results of such revision process relate to P-justified revisions?

Example 4. Let $D = \emptyset$ and let P consist of the following two rules:

(1) $\textbf{in}(c) \leftarrow \textbf{out}(b)$ (2) $\textbf{in}(b) \leftarrow \textbf{in}(c)$.

Let us process the rules in the order they are listed. Rule (1) is applicable with respect to $D = \emptyset$. Hence, the update $\textbf{in}(c)$ is executed and we get a new database $D_1 = \{c\}$. The second rule is the first D_1-applicable rule not applied yet. Hence, the update $\textbf{in}(b)$ is executed. Consequently, the next database $D_2 = \{b, c\}$ is obtained. Since there are no other rules left, the process stops. Notice, however, that rule (1) is not D_2-applicable. Hence, the justification for inserting c is lost and D_2 should not be regarded as a revision of D. Observe that D_2 is not a P-justified revision of D.

Example 4 shows that there are cases when processing rules sequentially does not lead to a P-justified revision. The problem is that some of the rules applied at the beginning of the process may be rendered inapplicable by subsequent updates. But there is yet another source of problems.

Example 5. Let $D = \{a\}$ and let P consist of the following three rules:

(1) **in**$(c) \leftarrow$ **out**(b) (2) **in**$(d) \leftarrow$ **in**(a) (3) **out**$(c) \leftarrow$ **in**(d).

Let us process the rules in the order they are listed. After using rule (1) we get a new database: $D_1 = \{a, c\}$. Then, rule (2) is D_1-applicable and after the update we obtain the database $D_2 = \{a, c, d\}$. Finally, we apply rule (3) and produce the database $D_3 = \{a, d\}$. Notice that all the rules applied in the process are D_3-applicable. But D_3 is not a model of the program P and sets of inserted and deleted atoms are not disjoint. Hence, it cannot be regarded as a possible revised version of D. Observe also that, since D_3 is not a model of P it is not a P-justified revision of D.

Example 5 shows another case when processing rules of the program according to some ordering does not yield a P-justified revision. It turns out that Examples 4 and 5 capture all such cases.

We will now formally define the *sequential revision process* and provide a precise formulation of the statement above. The approach we take is similar to our earlier result in which default extensions (and, hence, also stable models of logic programs) are characterized as results of some sequential computation by means of default rules (program clauses) [MT93].

Let D_I be a set of atoms (a database) and let P be a revision program. Both D_I and P may be infinite. Let $\{r_\xi\}_{\xi < \eta}$ be the enumeration of rules in P (here and below, we will use Greek letters to denote ordinals) corresponding to some well-ordering $\prec$ of P. We define an ordinal η^*, a sequence of ordinals $\{\xi_\gamma\}_{1 \leq \gamma < \eta^*}$ and two sequences of sets $\{I_\gamma\}_{\gamma < \eta^*}$ and $\{O_\gamma\}_{\gamma < \eta^*}$ as follows. First, we define

$$I_0 = \emptyset, \quad O_0 = \emptyset.$$

Let $\alpha \geq 1$ be on ordinal number. Assume that we have already defined I_γ and O_γ, for $\gamma < \alpha$ and ξ_γ for $1 \leq \gamma < \alpha$. Set

$$I = \bigcup_{\gamma < \alpha} I_\gamma, \quad O = \bigcup_{\gamma < \alpha} O_\gamma, \quad D = (D_I \cup I) \setminus O$$

and

$$A = AR_P(D) \setminus \{r_{\xi_\gamma} : 1 \leq \gamma < \alpha\}.$$

(The set D describes the database prior to step α in the construction, the set A consists of all rules that are applicable with respect to the database D and have not been applied in the construction until now.) If $A = \emptyset$ then we stop the construction and set $\eta^* = \alpha$. Otherwise, we define

$$\xi_\alpha = \min\{\xi : r_\xi \in A\}.$$

Next, if $head(r_{\xi_\alpha}) = \mathbf{in}(a)$, define

$$I_\alpha = I \cup \{a\}, \quad O_\alpha = O.$$

Otherwise, if $head(r_{\xi_\alpha}) = \mathbf{out}(a)$, define

$$I_\alpha = I, \quad O_\alpha = O \cup \{a\}.$$

If $I_\alpha \cap O_\alpha \neq \emptyset$, define $\eta^* = \alpha + 1$ and stop.

After the construction terminates, define $I_R = \bigcup_{\gamma < \eta^*} I_\gamma$, $O_R = \bigcup_{\gamma < \eta^*} O_\gamma$ and $D_R = (D_I \cup I_R) \setminus O_R$. Note that η^* and the sequences $\{I_\gamma\}_{\gamma < \eta^*}$, $\{O_\gamma\}_{\gamma < \eta^*}$, and $\{\xi_\gamma\}_{1 \leq \gamma < \eta^*}$ depend on the well-ordering $\prec$ of P. We suppressed $\prec$ in the notation in order to simplify it. Let us also observe that if P is finite, all ordinal numbers appearing in the construction are also finite.

The process described above is called the *sequential revision process* for the ordering $\prec$ and a database D_I. Its *result* is a database D_R. In Examples 4 and 5 we saw that the result of a sequential revision process is not necessarily a P-justified revision of D_I. We will now investigate conditions under which it is so.

A well-ordering of a revision program P is called *a posteriori consistent* for D_I if all the rules of P that were applied in the corresponding sequential revision process are applicable with respect to the resulting database D_R. It is called *sound for a database* D_I if $I_R \cap O_R = \emptyset$. The ordering considered in Example 4 is not *a posteriori* consistent for $D_I = \emptyset$, The ordering given in Example 5 is not sound for $D_I = \{a\}$.

Theorem 8. *Let P be a revision program and let D_I be a database. A database D_R is a P-justified revision of D_I if and only if there exists a well-ordering of P which is a posteriori consistent and sound for D_I and such that D_R is the result of the corresponding sequential revision process.*

Theorem 8 states that P-justified revisions correspond to a well-motivated class of orderings of the revision program P. It allows us to construct a P-justified revision of D_I by means of a process in which rules are applied sequentially one by one, assuming an a posteriori consistent and sound ordering of P can be found.

4 Complexity and algorithms

We will now study the complexity of problems involving justified revisions. For related results see [EG92]. We will also present algorithms for computing justified revisions given a finite revision program and a finite initial database. We use a certain "localization" result.

Theorem 9 (Localization Theorem). *Let P be a revision program. A database D_R is a P-justified revision of a database D_I if and only if*

1. $D_R \cap var(P)$ *is a P-justified revision of $D_I \cap var(P)$, and*
2. $D_R = (D_R \cap var(P)) \cup (D_I \setminus var(P))$.

Problems concerned with justified revisions can be grouped into into three broad categories:

Existence: Does a justified revision exist?
Membership_in_some: Does an atom a belong to some justified revision?
Membership_in_all: Does an atom a belong to all justified revisions?

These questions can be further specialized. Let us start with the existence problem. It has three versions:

E1 Given a finite revision program P, decide whether there is a P-justified transition.
E2 Given a finite revision program P and a finite database D_I, decide whether there is a database D_R such that D_R is a P-justified revision of D_I.
E3 Given a finite revision program P and a finite database D_R, decide whether there is a database D_I such that D_R is a P-justified revision of D_I.

Given a finite program P and two finite sets D_I and D_R one can check in linear time whether D_R is a P-justified revision of D_I.

Check_Justified_Revision(P, D_I, D_R)
(1)   Compute the program P_{D_R} (as in Stage 1 of Definition 3)
(2)   Compute the reduct $P_{D_R}|D_I$ (as in Stage 2 of Definition 3)
(3)   Encode $P_{D_R}|D_I$ as a Horn program Q (as in Definition 2)
(4)   Compute the least model M of Q
(5)   Decode from M the necessary change (I, O) for $P_{D_R}|D_I$
(6)   **if** $I \cap O \neq \emptyset$ **then return**$\{$false$\}$
(7)   **else if** $D_R \neq (D_I \cup I) \setminus O$ **then return**$\{$false$\}$
(8)   **else return**$\{$true$\}$

Steps (1), (2), and (6) - (8) correspond to Definition 3. Steps (3) - (5) correspond to Definition 2. Hence, it is easy to see that **Check_Justified_Revision** correctly checks whether D_R is a P-justified revision of D_I. Notice also that step (4) can be accomplished in time proportional to the size of Q [DG84]. Hence, the whole algorithm can be implemented to run in time linear in the size of P, D_I and D_R.

By Theorem 9 it follows that each of problems E1 - E3 is in NP. Problem E2 is, in fact, NP-complete. It follows from the observation that under the restriction to programs consisting of in-rules only and to the case $D_I = \emptyset$, problem E2 becomes equivalent to the question whether a logic program has a stable model (Theorem 5), which is known to be NP-complete [MT91]. Since the satisfiability problem is polynomically reducible to E1, E1 is NP-complete. Problem E3 is simpler. If D_R

is not a model for P the answer is NO. Otherwise, D_R is a P-justified revision of itself. Since checking whether D_R is a model of P can be accomplished in time linear in the size of P and D_R, problem E3 can be solved in linear time, too. These observations are summarized in the following theorem.

Theorem 10. *Problems* E1 *and* E2 *are NP-complete. Problem* E3 *can be decided in time linear in the size of* P *and* D_R.

Next, we will consider versions of the Membership_in_some problem.

MS1 Given a finite revision program P and an element a, decide whether there exists a P-justified transition $\langle D_I, D_R \rangle$ such that $a \in D_I$ if and only if $a \in D_R$ (informally, decide whether there is a P-justified transition which does not change the status of a).

MS2 Given a finite revision program P and an element a, decide whether there is a P-justified transition $\langle D_I, D_R \rangle$ such that $a \in D_I$ if and only if $a \notin D_R$ (informally, decide whether there is a P-justified transition which changes the status of a).

MS3 Given a finite revision program P, an element a and a database D_I, decide whether there is a database D_R such that D_R is a P-justified revision of D_I and $a \in D_R$.

MS4 Given a finite revision program P, an element a and a database D_R, decide whether there is a database D_I such that D_R is a P-justified revision of D_I and $a \in D_I$.

MS5 Given a finite revision program P, an element a and a database D_I, decide whether there is a database D_R such that D_R is a P-justified revision of D_I and $a \notin D_R$.

MS6 Given a finite revision program P, an element a and a database D_R, decide whether there is a database D_I such that D_R is a P-justified revision of D_I and $a \notin D_I$.

For these problems, we have the following result.

Theorem 11. *Problems* MS1 - MS3 *and* MS5 *are NP-complete. Problems* MS4 *and* MS6 *are in the class* P.

Membership_in_All problems can be defined as the complements of Membership_in_Some problems. One can use Theorem 11 to establish their complexity.

We will now present two algorithms for computing all P-justified revisions for a given database D_I. The first of these algorithms, **Guess_and_Check**, is based directly on the definition of justified revisions and on Theorem 9. The idea is to try every possibility for a P-justified revision for D_I. Theorem 9 allows us to restrict the search space to subsets of the universe $var(P)$.

Guess_and_Check(P, D_I)
(1)   Compute $U = var(P)$
(2)   Compute $D_I' = D_I \cap var(P)$

(3)   for all subsets D_R' of U repeat:

(4)   if **Check_Justified_Revision**(P, D_I', D_R')

(5)   **then** output $D_R' \cup (D_I \setminus U)$ as a P-justified revision of D_I.

Steps (1) and (2) can be implemented to run in time linear in the size of P and D_I. The loop (3) is executed 2^n times, where n is the size of the universe $var(P)$. Each execution of the loop takes time linear in the size of P and D_I, Hence, the algorithm runs in time $O((m + n)2^n)$, where $n = |var(P)|$ and $m = |D_I|$.

The next algorithm is based on the sequential revision process idea. Namely, it is based on Theorem 8 which states that all P-justified revisions of D_I can be found if all possible orderings of rules in P are considered. In the description given below, I stands for all elements inserted until now, O stands for all elements removed until now and D stands for the current database, R consists of all the rules that were already applied and A stands for the rules that can be applied in a current stage. If the algorithm does not generate any output, D_I has no P-justified revisions.

Sequential_Revision_Process(P, D_I)

(1)   for all total orderings $\prec$ of P repeat:

(2) $I := \emptyset$

(3) $O := \emptyset$

(4) $D := D_I$

(5) $R := \emptyset$

(6) $A := AR_P(D) \setminus R$

(7)   **while** $I \cap O = \emptyset$ **and** $A \neq \emptyset$ **do**

(8) $r := \prec$-first rule in A

(9)   **if** $head(r) = \mathbf{in}(a)$ **then** $I := I \cup \{a\}$ **else if** $head(r) = \mathbf{out}(a)$ **then** $O := O \cup \{a\}$

(10) $R := R \cup \{r\}$

(11) $A := AR_P(D) \setminus R$

(12)   **if** $I \cap O = \emptyset$ **and** $AR_P(D) = R$ **then** report "D is a P-justified revision of D_I"

Both algorithms are exponential. High complexity of computing justified revisions is a serious problem. Fortunately, there are wide classes of programs whose computational properties are much better. We discuss them in the next section.

5 Safe programs

We will now discuss two types of revision programs, *safe* and *stratified*, for which the task of finding a P-justified revision can be solved in polynomial time.

Definition 12. A revision program P is *safe* if

1. there is no a such that $\mathbf{in}(a) \in var(P)$ and $\mathbf{out}(a) \in head(P)$

2. there is no a such that $\mathbf{out}(a) \in var(P)$ and $\mathbf{in}(a) \in head(P)$

For example, program $P_1 = \{\mathbf{in}(a) \leftarrow \mathbf{out}(b)\}$ is safe. Similarly, $P_2 = \{\mathbf{in}(a) \leftarrow \mathbf{out}(b), \mathbf{out}(c) \leftarrow, \mathbf{out}(d) \leftarrow \mathbf{in}(a), \mathbf{out}(b) \leftarrow\}$ is also safe. Program $P_3 = \{\mathbf{in}(a) \leftarrow \mathbf{out}(b), \mathbf{in}(b) \leftarrow \mathbf{out}(a)\}$ is not safe.

Safeness is a syntactic condition and it can be checked in linear time. Safe revision programs have several other nice properties similar to the properties of Horn logic programs.

Theorem 13. *Let P be a safe revision program. Then, for every database D_I:*

1. *There is a unique D_R such that $\langle D_I, D_R \rangle$ is a P-justified transition.*
2. *The family of sets $\{D \div D_I : D$ is a model of $P \}$ has a least element. It is the set $D_R \div D_I$, where D_R is a unique P-justified revision of D_I.*
3. *For every well-ordering $\prec$ of P, the result of the sequential revision process for $\prec$ and D_I is the unique P-justified revision for D_I.*
4. *The unique P-justified revision for D_I can be computed in time proportional to the total size of D_I and P.*

The proof of Theorem 13 is based on the following useful lemma.

Lemma 14. *Let P be a safe program and let D be any database. Then the necessary change (I, O) determined by $P|D$ has the property that $(D \cup I) \setminus O$ is a P-justified revision of D.*

Lemma 14 implies a deterministic, polynomial-time algorithm for computing justified revisions for **safe** programs.

Lemma 14 together with Duality Theorem 7 allows for an estimate of arithmetic complexity of revisions by means of safe programs. The subsequent result is the analogue of the fundamental result on the complexity of the least model of the Horn logic program [Smu68, AN78].

We first need some definitions.

Definition 15. [EHK81]

1. A subset $A \subseteq \omega$ is called a *d.r.e. set* (difference of r.e. sets) if there are r.e. sets B, C such that $A = B \setminus C$.
2. A subset $A \subseteq \omega$ is *weakly d.r.e.* if both A and $\omega \setminus A$ are d.r.e. sets.

The class of d.r.e. sets is not closed under complements in the very same way as r.e. sets are not closed under the complements. The weakly d.r.e sets play the role of "recursive" sets with respect to d.r.e. sets. More on d.r.e. sets can be found in [EHK81].

Theorem 16. *Let D be a recursive database and P be a recursive safe program. Then the result of P-justified revision of D is a weakly d.r.e. set.*

A converse result holds for a slightly modified class of revision programs.

As in logic programming, some of useful properties of safe programs can be extended to a wider class of programs.

Definition 17. Let P be a revision program and let $\langle P_\xi \rangle_{\xi < \eta}$ be a partition of P. We say that $\langle P_\xi \rangle_{\xi < \eta}$ is a *stratification* of P if for every $\xi < \eta$:

1. P_ξ is safe, and
2. $\{a : \mathbf{in}(a) \in head(P_\xi) \text{ or } \mathbf{out}(a) \in head(P_\xi)\} \cap$
$$\bigcup_{\alpha < \xi} \{a : \mathbf{in}(a) \in var(P_\alpha) \text{ or } \mathbf{out}(a) \in var(P_\alpha)\} = \emptyset.$$

Safe programs are stratified. Notice also that revision programs obtained from locally stratified logic programs under the interpretation described in Section 2 are stratified according to Definition 17.

To test if a finite revision program P is stratified, one can use a modified version of the algorithm of Apt, Blair and Walker [ABW88]. It takes linear time in the size of P. Moreover, also in linear time, one can establish a partition of P into strata $\langle P_m \rangle_{m < n}$.

Theorem 18. *Let P be a stratified revision program. Then for every database D_I there exists a unique database D_R such that $\langle D_I, D_R \rangle$ is a P-justified transition.*

As in the case of safe programs, one can show that given a finite stratified revision program P and an initial database D, the unique P-justified revision of D can be computed in linear time (in the total size of P and D).

Consider a stratification $\langle P_\xi \rangle_{\xi < \eta}$ of a stratified program P. A well-ordering $\prec$ of P *agrees* with the the stratification $\langle P_\xi \rangle_{\xi < \eta}$ if whenever $\xi_1 < \xi_2 < \eta$ then every rule in P_{ξ_1} $\prec$-precedes every rule in P_{ξ_2}. It is easy to see that such orderings exist. Now, we can generalize Theorem 13(3) and (4).

Theorem 19. *Let P be a stratified revision program and let D_I be a database. Then:*

1. *For every stratification $\langle P_\xi \rangle_{\xi < \eta}$ of P and for every well-ordering $\prec$ of P which agrees with the stratification $\langle P_\xi \rangle_{\xi < \eta}$, the result of the sequential revision process for $\prec$ and D_I is the unique P-justified revision of D_I.*
2. *If, in addition, P and D_I are finite, then the unique P-justified revision of D_I can be computed in time proportional to the total size of P and D_I.*

Acknowledgements

This work was partially supported by National Science Foundation under grants IRI-9012902 and IRI-9400568.

References

[ABW88] K. Apt, H.A. Blair, and A. Walker. Towards a theory of declarative knowledge. In J. Minker, editor, *Foundations of deductive databases and logic programming*, pages 89–142, Los Altos, CA, 1988. Morgan Kaufmann.

[AN78] H. Andreka and I. Nemeti. The generalized completeness of Horn predicate logic as a programming language. *Acta Cybernetica*, 4:3–10, 1978.

[Apt90] K. Apt. Logic programming. In J. van Leeuven, editor, *Handbook of theoretical computer science*, pages 493–574. MIT Press, Cambridge, MA, 1990.

[AV90] S. Abiteboul and V. Vianu. Procedural languages for database queries and updates. *Journal of Computer and System Sciences*, 41:181–229, 1990.

[AV91] S. Abiteboul and V. Vianu. DATALOG extensions for database queries and updates. *Journal of Computer and System Sciences*, 43:62–124, 1991.

[Cla78] K.L. Clark. Negation as failure. In H. Gallaire and J. Minker, editors, *Logic and data bases*, pages 293–322. Plenum Press, 1978.

[DG84] W.F. Dowling and J.H. Gallier. Linear-time algorithms for testing the satisfiability of propositional horn formulae. *Journal of Logic Programming*, 3:267–284, 1984.

[EG92] T. Eiter and G. Gottlob. On the complexity of propositional knowledge base revision, updates and counterfactuals. In *ACM Symposium on Principles of Database Systems*, pages 261–273, 1992.

[EHK81] R.L. Epstein, R. Haas, and R.L. Kramer. Hierarchies of sets and degrees below $0'$. In M. Lerman, J.H. Schmerl, and R.I. Soare, editors, *Logic Year 1979-80*, pages 32–48. Springer Verlag, 1981. S.L.N. in Mathematics 859.

[Fit85] M. C. Fitting. Kripke-Kleene semantics for logic programs. *Journal of Logic Programming*, 2:295–312, 1985.

[GL88] M. Gelfond and V. Lifschitz. The stable semantics for logic programs. In R. Kowalski and K. Bowen, editors, *Proceedings of the 5th international symposium on logic programming*, pages 1070–1080, Cambridge, MA., 1988. MIT Press.

[GL90] M. Gelfond and V. Lifschitz. Logic programs with classical negation. In D. Warren and P. Szeredi, editors, *Proceedings of the 7th international conference on logic programming*, pages 579–597, Cambridge, MA., 1990. MIT Press.

[MT91] W. Marek and M. Truszczyński. Autoepistemic logic. *Journal of the ACM*, 38:588–619, 1991.

[MT93] W. Marek and M. Truszczyński. *Nonmonotonic logics; context-dependent reasoning*. Berlin: Springer-Verlag, 1993.

[MT94] W. Marek and M. Truszczyński. Revision specifications by means of revision programs. In *Logics in AI. Proceedings of JELIA '94*. Lecture Notes in Artificial Intelligence. Springer-Verlag, 1994.

[MW88] S. Manchanda and D.S. Warren. A logic-based language for database updates. In J. Minker, editor, *Foundations of Deductive Databases and Logic Programming*, pages 363–394, Los Altos, CA, 1988. Morgan Kaufmann.

[Rei80] R. Reiter. A logic for default reasoning. *Artificial Intelligence*, 13:81–132, 1980.

[Smu68] R.M. Smullyan. *First-order logic*. Berlin: Springer-Verlag, 1968.

[Ull88] J.D. Ullman. *Principles of Database and Knowledge-Base Systems*. Computer Science Press, Rockville, MD, 1988.

[vEK76] M.H. van Emden and R.A. Kowalski. The semantics of predicate logic as a programming language. *Journal of the ACM*, 23(4):733–742, 1976.

[VRS91] A. Van Gelder, K.A. Ross, and J.S. Schlipf. Unfounded sets and well-founded semantics for general logic programs. *Journal of the ACM*, 38:620 – 650, 1991.

Some Positive Results for Boundedness of Multiple Recursive Rules

Ke Wang

Department of Information Systems and Computer Sciences
National University of Singapore
Lower Kent Ridge Road, Singapore 0511

Abstract. Following results are sketched in this extended abstract: (1) Datalog recursive programs where each rule has at most one subgoal called *unit recursions* are shown to be bounded, with an effective construction of equivalent non-recursive programs. (2) A *generalized chain program*, which allow IDB predicates of arbitrary arity and remove the uniqueness condition of chain variables, is bounded if and only if it is a unit recursion. (3) The characterization of uniform unboundedness for linear sirups in [NS] is extended to a substantial superclass called class C^+. (4) Boundedness for class C^+ with multiple exit rules is decidable in polynomial space. (5) Predicate boundedness is decidable in doubly exponential time for a large class of Datalog programs that properly contains all connected monadic programs. (6) For binary linear programs, program boundedness is decidable if each recursive predicate is defined by at most one recursive rule; predicate boundedness is also decidable if each recursive predicate is mutually recursive with one another.

1 Introduction

This abstract presents some positive results of the boundedness problem for logic programs with multiple rules and multiple recursive predicates. The boundedness problem is to answer whether a given recursive program is equivalent to a non-recursive program, i.e., whether the program is *bounded*. Detecting bounded programs is a powerful optimization technique as a bounded program needs only a fixed number of iterations in evaluation or can simply be replaced by a non-recursive program. Unfortunately, this problem is undecidable in many cases, which include, among others, programs with a single recursive rule [Ab], linear programs with one binary IDB predicate [Va], and programs with two linear recursive rules and one initialization rule [Va]. Because of the inherent difficulty of boundedness problem, the positive results in earlier work [HKMV, Io, Na, NS, Va] have been obtained mainly for programs of a single recursive rule except for monadic programs [CGKV], some strongly restricted chain rules [AP, BKBR, Gu] that correspond naturally to productions of a context-free grammar, as well as typed rules with a single predicate (not only a single IDB predicate) [S]. There is a lack of positive results for more general rules.

The following are the contributions in this paper.

- (Section 3) Datalog programs in which each recursive rule has at most one subgoal are bounded. Such programs are called *unit recursions* in this paper. The result is also extended to a more general case, called *pseudo-unit recursions*, where each recursive rule has at most one recursive subgoal and the variables in all non-recursive subgoals occur in the recursive subgoal. A construction of a non-recursive program that is equivalent to a unit recursion (resp., pseudo-unit recursion) is presented. The constructed non-recursive program may have many rules, but each rule is very simple and the depth of the program is very small, a feature desirable for parallel evaluation.

- (Section 4) Reduction of boundedness to finiteness of CFL for "chain rules" [AP, BKBR, Gu] is extended to more general programs, called *generalized chain programs*. It is shown that a generalized chain program is bounded if and only if it is a unit recursion. In all "chain rules" studied previously in the literature, uniqueness of chain variables has been a crucial requirement for mapping rules to productions of a CFG. Our generalization is substantial in that IDB predicates of arbitrary arity are allowed and uniqueness of chain variables is no longer required.

- (Section 5) We extend the characterization of uniform unboundedness for linear sirups in [NS] to a superclass of the class C defined there, which we call class C^+. For a linear sirup in C^+, the restriction that no linking variables are mapped to persistent variables, which is a crucial requirement in [NS], is removed. All linear sirups efficiently identified as in C by methods in [NS] as well as more linear sirups can be efficiently identified as in C^+ by a method given in this paper.

We also extend the language (or automata) theoretic approach in [CGKV] for monadic programs to arbitrary Datalog programs. In particular,

- (Section 6) We show that boundedness (not just uniform boundedness) for linear sirups with a recursive rule in class C^+ and with multiple exit rules is decidable in polynomial space. Positive results of boundedness were obtained in [NS] only for a refinement of class C with one strongly restricted exit rule.

- (Section 7) We show that predicate boundedness is decidable in doubly exponential time for a large class of arbitrary Datalog programs that properly contains all connected monadic programs [CGKV].

- (Section 8) We show that program boundedness is decidable for binary linear programs in which each recursive predicate is defined by at most one recursive rule and that predicate boundedness is also decidable if each recursive predicate is mutually recursive with one another. These results generalize the decidability of boundedness for linear binary sirups in [Va].

- In the spirit of [CGKV], it follows immediately from our results that containment problem is decidable for programs considered in Sections 6,7 and 8.

Due to compactness of the presented materials, certain knowledge of work in [CGKV, Gu, Na, NS, Va] is helpful in reading the paper.

2   Preliminary

A program has an *IDB graph* in which nodes are IDB predicates of the program and there is a directed edge $< q, p >$ if q occurs in the body of a rule whose head predicate is p; we say that this rule *contributes* to this edge. An IDB predicate q is *useful* to an IDB predicate p if there is a (directed) path from q to p in the IDB graph; otherwise, q is *useless* to p. A *sirup* consists of one recursive rule and some number of exit rules. A *monadic* program is a program in which all IDB predicates have arity one.

A DB of a program P is a set of ground predicate instances, called *tuples*, for the predicates in P. An EDB is a DB in which the set of tuples for the IDB predicates in P is empty. For each DB or EDB I, $q_P^i(I)$ denotes the set of tuples for an IDB predicate q that can be derived by at most i applications of rules in P, and let $q_P^\infty(I) = \cup_{i \geq 0} q_P^i(I)$. A program P_1 is *contained* (resp., *uniformly contained*) in a program P_2 wrt q if $q_{P_1}^\infty(I) \subseteq q_{P_2}^\infty(I)$ for every EDB (resp., DB) I. P_1 is *equivalent* (resp., *uniformly equivalent*) to P_2 wrt q if P_1 is contained (resp., uniformly contained) in P_2 wrt q and vice versa. q is *bounded* (resp., *uniformly bounded*) in P if there exists some k, depending only on P, such that for every EDB (resp., DB) I, $q_P^\infty(I) = \cup_{i=0}^k q_P^i(I)$. This testing is called *predicate boundedness* problem. P is *bounded* (resp., *uniformly bounded*) if q is bounded (resp., uniformly bounded) in P for every IDB predicate q in P. This testing is called *program boundedness* problem. It is known that q is bounded (resp., uniformly bounded) in P if and only if P is equivalent (resp., uniformly equivalent) to a non-recursive program wrt q. Note that: (1) decidability of program boundedness does not necessarily imply decidability of predicate boundedness and (2) uniform boundedness implies boundedness.

Let q be an IDB predicate in a program P. A *partial q-expansion* is a conjunction of predicate instances that can be generated by some sequence of backward applications of rules in P beginning with an instance of q containing distinct distinguished variables (dv's). See [NS] for a detailed definition of backward applications of rules. A *q-expansion* is a partial q-expansion that contains only EDB predicates. The relation specified by a q-expansion $A_1, \ldots, A_n$ is

$$\{(v_1, \ldots, v_i) \mid (\exists w_1) \ldots (\exists w_j)(A_1 \wedge \ldots \wedge A_n)\},$$

where v's are dv's and w's are non-distinguished variables (ndv's, i.e., existential variables) introduced by backward applications. Given an EDB I, $q_P^\infty(I)$ is equivalent to the infinite union of the relations specified by all q-expansions. It was shown in [Na] that q is bounded in P if and only if for q-expansions $C_0, C_1, \ldots$ there is some $N \geq 1$ such that for every $n > N$, the relation specified by C_n is contained in C_m for some $m \leq N$. Note that C_n is contained in C_m if and only if there is a *containment mapping* from C_m to C_n [CM].

3   Boundedness of Unit and Pseudo-Unit Recursions

We first consider programs in which each recursive rule has only one subgoal. We show that such programs are always bounded by constructing a non-recursive equivalent program.

3.1 Unit Recursions

Definition 1. *A recursive rule in a program is a* unit rule *if it has exactly one subgoal; otherwise, it is a* non-unit rule. *A program is a* unit recursion *if every recursive rule in it is a unit rule.*

Clearly, a program P is not a unit recursion if and only if the IDB graph of P has a cycle on which at least one edge is contributed by a non-unit rule in P. We will call such cycles *non-unit cycles*.

Example 1. *Consider a program consisting of the following rules:*

$$
\begin{aligned}
r_1 &: \quad p(x,y,z) : -q(x,y,z,z) \\
r_2 &: \quad r(z,x,y) : -p(x,y,z) \\
r_3 &: \quad q(x,x,y,z) : -r(x,y,z) \\
r_4 &: \quad q(w,x,y,z) : -e(w,x,y,z) \\
r_5 &: \quad v(x,y,z) : -r(x,y,w), e'(w,y,z) \\
r_6 &: \quad p(x,y,y) : -v(x,y,z), q(z,w,x,y) \\
r_7 &: \quad r(x,z,y) : -p(x,y,z), u(x,y)
\end{aligned}
$$

This program is not a unit recursion because non-unit rules r_5, r_6, r_7 contribute to edges of a cycle in the IDB graph. However, a program consisting only of the first five rules is a unit recursion, since in this case r_5 is not a recursive rule and all recursive rules r_1, r_2, r_3 are unit rules.

The next example illustrates some basic idea of constructing an equivalent non-recursive program for a unit recursion.

Example 2. *Consider the unit recursion given by the first five rules $r_1, \ldots, r_5$ in Example 1. We want to find a non-recursive program equivalent to this program wrt $Q = \{q, v\}$. Suppose that the relation for q receives a "canonical" tuple t, i.e., a tuple consisting of distinct variables, through initialization rule r_4. Other tuples can be derived from t by applying recursive rules r_1, r_2, r_3. In applying rules, we treat variables in t as unknown values so that they can be equated or replaced with constants if necessary for applying a rule. For instance, to apply r_1 to t the last two variables in tuple t must be equated. Assume we have derived all tuples from t by applying rules r_1, r_2, r_3 in this manner. Let t' be any derived tuple for q (or r). The variables in t' must appear in the original tuple t because all rules are safe. Let t'' be obtained from t by equating or replacing (with constants) whatever variables that were equated or replaced in the derivation of t'. Then the derivation of t' (from the corresponding tuple in e) can be represented by a rule $q(t') : -e(t'')$ (or $r(t') : -e(t'')$). If we so construct a rule for each derived t', the recursive rules r_1, r_2, r_3 can be removed because each derivation has been represented by one of these new rules. As a result, the program becomes non-recursive and equivalent to the original program wrt $\{q, v\}$.*

In the above example, the canonical tuple for q is transformed by a block of mutually recursive rules into tuples for predicates, q and r, that are useful for answering the query, q and v. In each transformation, we are interested in the mapping from the initial tuple (possibly with some variables equated or replaced by constants) to the final derived tuple, not the intermediate steps in the transformation. If each recursive rule is a unit rule, there are only a bound number of such mappings and each mapping can be represented by a non-recursive rule. In fact, we can effectively construct all non-recursive rules representing mappings.

Theorem 2. *Let P be a unit recursion and let Q be a set of query predicates. a non-recursive program equivalent to P wrt Q can be constructed effectively.*

Due to space limitation, the construction is omitted here.

3.2 Pseudo-Unit Recursions

Now we extend the algorithm in subsection 3.1 to more general programs.

Definition 3. *A recursive rule in a program is a pseudo-unit rule if it has the form*

$$p : -q, e_1, \ldots, e_k, \quad k \geq 0$$

where (a) q is mutually recursive with p and none of $e_1, \ldots, e_k$ is mutually recursive with p, (b) every variable that appears in some of $e_1, \ldots, e_k$ also appears in q. A program is a pseudo-unit recursion if every recursive rule is a pseudo-unit rule.

The attachment $e_1, \ldots, e_k$ in the above pseudo-unit rule can be considered as "conditions" on tuples for the subgoal q. By modifying the concept of mappings defined for unit recursions to account for such "conditions", we can effectively construct all non-recursive rules that represent mappings as in subsection 3.1. So we have

Theorem 4. Let P be a pseudo-unit recursion. For any non-empty set Q of query predicates, a non-recursive program equivalent to P wrt Q can be constructed effectively.

4 Generalized Chain Programs

In this section, we consider several classes of programs for which the condition of unit recursion is both necessary and sufficient for boundedness.

Definition 5. *A program P is a generalized chain program if for every predicate p there are two distinct positions h_p and t_p, called the head position and the tail position of p, such that every rule in P has the form (up to reordering of subgoals):*

$$q(\mathbf{x}) : -q_1(\mathbf{y}_1), \ldots, q_k(\mathbf{y}_k), \quad k \geq 1,$$

where (a) $\mathbf{x}[h_q] = \mathbf{y}_1[h_{q_1}]$, $\mathbf{x}[t_q] = \mathbf{y}_k[t_{q_k}]$, and (b) for $1 \leq i < k$, $\mathbf{y}_i[t_{q_i}] = \mathbf{y}_{i+1}[h_{q_{i+1}}]$ and are (not necessarily distinct) ndv's. (We use $\mathbf{u}[i]$ to denote the ith argument of $\mathbf{u}$) A generalized chain program is simple if in each rule a ndv appears in at most one head position (or tail position). A program is stationary if every rule in the program has the form $q(\mathbf{x}) : -q_1(\mathbf{x}), \ldots, q_k(\mathbf{x})$, where $\mathbf{x}$ is a vector of distinct dv's.

A stationary program is obviously bounded. Unlike all previously studied "chain rules" [AP, BKBR, Gu], we do not require that ndv's as chain variables be distinct. Even the most restricted class of simple generalized chain programs contains properly all chain programs in [AP, BKBR, Gu].

Theorem 6. (1) Every uniformly connected program in [Gu] that is not stationary is a simple generalized chain program. (2) Every general chained program in [Gu] is a simple generalized chain program. The converse is not true for each of (1) and (2).

Example 3. Consider the following simple generalized chain program:

$$q(x_1, x_2, x_3) : -q(u, x_2, u), q(x_1, u, x_3),$$

where $h_q = 2$ and $t_q = 3$. This rule is uniformly connected but not general chained [Gu]. The following simple generalized chain program:

$$q(x_1, x_2, x_3) : -q(x_1, u, z), q(z, x_2, x_3),$$

where $h_q = 1$ and $t_q = 3$, is general chained but not uniformly connected [Gu].

Rule bodies in a generalized chain program are considered naturally as strings of predicate instances in the order they are written, so are partial expansions generated by such programs. In the following, we reduce boundedness of some generalized chain programs to finiteness of CFL. We associate with each Datalog program P and each IDB predicate q a CFL $L(P, q)$ generated by a grammar CFG $\Gamma(P, q)$ given below: With each EDB predicate b we associate a terminal symbol t_b, and with each IDB predicate p we associate a non-terminal symbol v_p. The productions of $\Gamma(P, q)$ are obtained by replacing in each rule of P all occurrences of predicates by the corresponding grammar symbols, deleting all the variables in the rules, and turning $:-$ into $\rightarrow$. The starting symbol of $\Gamma(P, q)$ is v_q, the symbol associated with q. The *graph* of a CFG is a directed graph that contains all non-terminal symbols as nodes, and contains a directed edge $< A, B >$ whenever there is a production $A \rightarrow \alpha$ such that B is in α.

Theorem 7. Let P be a simple generalized chain program and q be an IDB predicate. q is bounded in P if and only if $L(P, q)$ is finite.

The proof is essentially the same as in [Gu], that is, the uniqueness of variables in head (resp., tails) positions implies that the mapping from a q-expansion C_l to a q-expansion C_m always maps the ith predicate instance in C_l to the ith predicate instance in C_m. In the following, we consider reduction of some non-simple subclasses. The first such subclass is based on the observation that the above uniqueness is only required for head (resp., tail) positions of instances of the *same* predicate, since containment mappings preserve predicates.

Let P be a generalized chain program. Given two predicates p and q, we say that p is *directly left* (resp., *directly right) dependent* on q if either $p = q$ or there is a rule in P such that p is the head predicate and q is the predicate of the first (resp., last) subgoal in the body. The *left* (resp., *right) dependency* is defined to be the transitive closure of the direct left (resp., right) dependency.

Definition 8. *Let P be a generalized chain program and r be a rule in P. r is type 1 wrt P if the following conditions hold: if a ndv u occurs in two tail positions t_p and t_q in the body of r, then p and q are not right dependent on a common predicate, and if a ndv u occurs in two head positions h_p and h_q in the body of r, then p and q are not left dependent on a common predicate. P is type 1 if every rule in P is type 1 wrt P.*

For a generalized chain program of type 1, it can be shown that in any expansion variables at the head position in two instances of the same predicate are pairwise distinct. So we have

Theorem 9. Let P be a type 1 generalized chain program and q be an IDB predicate. q is bounded if and only if $L(P, q)$ is finite.

Reduction to finiteness of a CFL also holds as long as in any expansion all predicate instances sharing variables at head (or tail) positions are no more than a fixed number of predicate instances apart. In the following, an IDB predicate is called *recursion-related* in a program if either it is recursive or it can be reached from a recursive predicate in the IDB graph of the program.

Definition 10. *Let P be a generalized chain program and r be a rule in P. r is type 2 wrt P if for every recursion-related predicate instance p in the body of r, subgoals on the left of p and subgoals on the right of p have disjoint variables at all head (or tail) positions. P is type 2 if every rule in P is type 2 wrt P.*

However, disjointness of variables is not required for non-head (or non-tail) positions on the two sides.

Theorem 11. Let P be a type 2 generalized chain program and q be an IDB predicate. q is bounded if and only if $L(P, q)$ is finite.

Since for each q-expansion there is a word in $L(P, q)$ of the same length, as a corollary of proofs of the above reduction, boundedness of the above programs in fact implies boundedness of length of expansions, as stated in the following corollary.

Corollary 12. Let P be a generalized chain program that is either simple, or type 1, or type 2. An IDB predicate q is bounded in P if and only if q-expansions in P have a bounded length.

But q-expansions have a bounded length if and only if all recursive rules defining predicates useful to q are unit rules (as defined in Section 3). So we have an efficient characterization of boundedness for the above programs.

Theorem 13. Let P be a generalized chain program that is either simple, or type 1, or type 2. Let q be an IDB predicate. If P has no useless predicates to q, then the following are equivalent. (1) $L(P, q)$ is finite. (2) q is bounded in P. (3) The IDB graph of P has no non-unit cycle. (4) P is a unit recursion.

Based on Theorem 13, we can show that boundedness and uniform boundedness coincide for each of the above three subclasses of generalized chain programs.

Theorem 14. Let P be a generalized chain program that is either simple, or type 1, or type 2. Let q be an IDB predicate. Assume that P contains no useless predicates to q. Then q is bounded in P if and only if q is uniformly bounded in P.

5   Extending the A/V Graph Approach

In [NS], uniform boundedness for a linear sirup in a class called C is characterized by absence of chain generating paths in the A/V graph of the linear sirup. Unfortunately, membership in C is difficult to test and only some sufficient conditions are given there. We now extend that characterization to a superclass of C, called C^+, so that more programs can be efficiently identified to suit the characterization. See [NS] for definitions of *A/V graphs, persistent variables, linking variables, chain generating paths*. Non-persistent variables are variables (dv's or ndv's) that are not persistent.

Definition 15. *Let r be the recursive rule of a linear sirup defining an IDB predicate q. A non-persistent variable V in r is called a* target link *if for any pair C_i and C_j of q-expansions with $i \neq j$, whenever C_i maps to C_j, no instance of V is mapped to a persistent variable. r is in class C^+ if either it has no chain generating paths or has a chain generating path on which all linking variables (i.e., ndv's on this path) are target links.*

Note that a linear sirup is in class C if and only if all linking variables are target links. But for class C^+, being target links is required only for the linking variables on a single chain generating path. The following generalizes results in [NS].

Theorem 16. (1) $C \subset C^+$. (2) For every $r \in C^+$, r is uniformly unbounded if and only if r has a chain generating path.

Finding all target links is not an easy task. The following theorem finds enough target links so that all programs identified as in class C by all lemmas in [NS] (i.e., Lemmas 4.5, 4.6, 4.7, and 4.8) as well as some other programs can be efficiently identified as in class C^+. We first define a relationship between two predicate instances.

Definition 17. *Let r be the recursive rule of a linear sirup. Let e and e' be two (not necessarily distinct) predicate instances in the body of r. $e \leq e'$ if all following conditions hold: (a) they are instances of the same predicate, (b) if position t in e has a persistent variable X, then position t in e' has X, (c) if position t in e has a target link, then position t in e' has a non-persistent variable, and (d) if positions t and s in e share a variable, then positions t and s in e' share a variable.*

Intuitively, $e \leq e'$ is a necessary (but not necessarily sufficient) condition for an instance produced by e to be mapped to an instance produced by e' in any containment mapping between expansions generated by the linear sirup.

Theorem 18. Let r be the recursive rule in a linear sirup and V be a variable in r. Then V is a target link if one of the following holds. (1) (Basis) V is a ndv appearing in a non-repeating EDB predicate in r. (2) V is a ndv appearing in an EDB predicate e in r such that, for every other EDB predicate e' in r with $e \leq e'$, if V appears in a position t in e then a non-persistent variable appears in position t in e'. (3) V is a non-persistent dv that can be reached from a target link in the A/V graph of r. (4) V is a ndv such that, for two identical copies B and B' of the set of EDB predicate instances in the body of r, V is always mapped to some non-persistent variable in every containment mapping from B to B'.

Observe that these rules identify as target links only variables in r whose instances are never mapped to persistent variables in all potential containment mappings.

Example 4. Consider the rule r

$$t(X, Y, Z) : -t(X, U, V), a(X, X), a(V, Z), e(U, Y)$$

There is a chain generating path that contains U as the only ndv. By Theorem 18(1), U is a target link, so r is in C^+ and is not uniformly bounded by Theorem 16. Observe that X is a persistent variable that occurs in some linking position of a, since V is a linking variable (on a different chain generating path). Thus [NS] can not identify r as a member in class C and therefore can not tell if r is uniformly bounded, even though r may be indeed in C.

For the rest of the paper, we extend the language-theoretic approach in [CGKV] for monadic programs to programs of arbitrary arity.

6 Decidable Boundedness of C^+ Class

Testing boundedness is harder than testing uniform boundedness. Decidability of boundedness was given in [NS] only for a refinement of class C with one strongly restricted exit rule. By extending the language-theoretic technique [CGKV] we can show that boundedness for the whole class C^+ with arbitrary exit rules is decidable, as stated in the following theorem.

Theorem 19. Boundedness for linear sirups with a recursive rule in C^+ and multiple exit rules is decidable in polynomial space.

Proof idea: We extend the language-theoretic characterization of unboundedness for monadic programs to programs in C^+. Assume P is a linear sirup with a recursive rule r in class C^+. If r has no chain generating path then P is bounded [NS]; otherwise, r has a chain generating path on which all linking variables are target links. By unfolding r a certain number of times, boundedness of P can be reduced to boundedness of a linear sirup in which the recursive rule has the form (Theorem 4.1, [HKMV])

$$r' : \quad p(X_1, \ldots, X_k, Y_1, \ldots, Y_l) : -p(X_1, \ldots, X_k, Z_1, \ldots, Z_l), A$$

where X's, Y's, and Z's are vectors of distinct variables and they share no variables, A is a conjunction of EDB predicates. Moreover, $r \in C^+$ implies that $r' \in C^+$, and there must be some integer $1 \le m \le l$ such that position $k + m$ of p is on a chain generating path (in the A/V graph of r') on which all linking variables are target variables. Clearly, Y_m is connected to Z_m in G_A and Z_m is a target link, where $G_A = (V, E)$ is the *variable graph* of F [CGKV], such that V is the set of variables occurring in A and $< X, Y > \in E$ if X and Y occur in the same predicate instance in A. Without loss of generality, assume the exit rules have the same head as r' and have the bodies $B_1, \ldots, B_n$. By a reduction in [CGKV] (i.e., Proposition 5.4), no generality is lost by assuming that each graph G_{B_j} is connected. $B_1, \ldots, B_n$ are called *initialization bodies* and A is called a *recursive body*.

The following extends the language treatment in [CGKV] to the above linear sirup. Let A^i (resp., B_j^i) be a variant of A (resp., B_j), where all variables carry a superscript i and if $i > 1$ Y_j^i are replaced by variables Z_j^{i-1}, $1 \le j \le l$. Initially, view A^1 (resp., $B_{i_1}^1$) as a conjunctive query where all variables except for dv's are existentially quantified and this one body is the *leaf*. Inductively, suppose that C is a conjunctive query, A^k is a recursive body that is the leaf of C, and $B_{i_{k+1}}$ is an initialization body. Note that A^k contains variables $Z_1^k, \ldots, Z_l^k$, which are also in A^{k+1} (resp., $B_{i_{k+1}}^{k+1}$). Then C, A^{k+1} (resp., $C, B_{i_{k+1}}^{k+1}$) can be viewed as a conjunctive query C', where all variables except for dv's are existentially quantified and where A^{k+1} (resp., $B_{i_{k+1}}^{k+1}$) is the leaf of C'. Let $\Sigma_r = \{a\}$ be the *recursive alphabet* and $\Sigma_i = \{b_1, \ldots, b_n\}$ be the *initialization alphabet*. It is important to see that each conjunctive query is uniquely determined by a word in $(\Sigma_r \cup \Sigma_i)^*$. We can show that the language-theoretic characterization of unboundedness for connected monadic programs, i.e., Proposition 3.2 in [CGKV], is still valid for the above linear sirup. The key argument is that if there is a containment mapping from a p-expansion C_i to a p-expansion C_j, then there is a containment mapping from C_i to the prefix of C_j that contains no more than c bodies, for some fixed integer c. In particular, the position $k + m$ of p plays the role of the position of an unary recursive predicate in a monadic program, in that all variables Z_m^i are connected by EDB predicates and none of them is mapped to a persistent variable (because Z_m is a target link). The presence of variables in other positions of p does not affect the above argument. The rest of treatment is then a copy of [CGKV], because it depends only on language features that make no difference in our case.

7 Persistence-free and Connected Datalog Programs

We show that boundedness is decidable for a large class of Datalog programs that are not necessarily sirups. The general idea is to prevent "linking variables" from being mapped to "persistent variables". First we need these terms for general rules.

Definition 20. *Let P be a Datalog program, q an IDB predicate, and t a position of q. The position q^t is persistent wrt an IDB predicate p in P if for every $k > 0$ there is a partial p-expansion in which an instance of q contains a variable V at position t and the instance is at least k predicate instances away from the very first predicate containing V; otherwise, q^t is persistence-free wrt p in P. An IDB predicate p is persistence-free in P if q^t is persistence-free wrt p for every IDB predicate q and every position t of q.*

We create a directed graph for testing existence of persistence: G_{per} has a node p^t for each recursive predicate p and each position t of p; G_{per} has an (directed) edge from p^t to q^s if and only if there is a recursive rule with a p instance in the head and a q instance in the body such that the variable in position t in the head appears in position s in that q instance in the body.

Proposition 21. *q^t is persistence-free wrt p if and only if no node of form p^s reaches a cycle containing node q^t in G_{per}.*

The following definition generalizes the connectivity defined for monadic programs [CGKV] to Datalog programs.

Definition 22. *An IDB predicate p is connected in P if there is a choice of a position for each IDB predicate useful to p such that for each rule $q(X)$: $-A, q_1(Y_1), \ldots, q_n(Y_n)$ $(n \geq 0)$, G_A is connected and $X, Y_1, \ldots, Y_n$ are in G_A, where q is useful to p, A is the conjunction of the EDB predicates in the rule, and $X, Y_1, \ldots, Y_n$ are variables in the chosen positions of predicates $q, q_1, \ldots, q_n$, respectively. (The rule is an exit rule when $n = 0$) The chosen positions, if they exist, are called linking positions.*

It is easy to see that every IDB predicate of a connected monadic program [CGKV] is persistence-free and connected (We need only consider monadic programs where the variable in the head does not appear in any IDB predicate in the body, as the general case can be reduced to this case [CGKV]). An efficient algorithm for testing connectivity and finding linking positions will be given in the full paper.

Theorem 23. Predicate boundedness for predicates that are both persistence-free and connected is decidable in doubly exponential time.

Proof idea: The idea is the same as Theorem 19, i.e., simulating a monadic program. Linking positions plays essentially the role of the single position of unary IDB predicates in a monadic program. Unlike Theorem 19, we have to use the general argument based on the tree language and tree automata [CGKV]. The time is doubly exponential because predicate boundedness for monadic programs is doubly exponential [CGKV].

However, the reduction of boundedness of unconnected programs to boundedness of connected ones for monadic programs in [CGKV] does not apply here, because the connectivity used in that reduction is weaker than the connectivity used here, although the two notions coincide for monadic programs.

8   1-branching Binary Linear Programs

It was previously known that boundedness is decidable for linear binary sirups but is undecidable for multiple recursive rules even with a single IDB predicate [Va]. We now show some positive results for linear binary programs, not necessarily sirups, where each predicate is defined by at most one recursive rule. First, we extend the decidability for binary linear sirups in [Va] to a slightly general version. In a sirup in [Va], all non-recursive predicates in the body of the recursive rule must be EDB predicates. A *generalized linear sirup* has a recursive rule of the form $p : -A, p$ (arguments are omitted here) and one or more non-recursive rules, where A is a conjunction of non-recursive predicates. In other words, non-recursive IDB predicates are allowed in the body of a generalized sirup. This generalization appears to be nontrivial because removing such non-recursive IDB predicates simply by unfolding them using non-recursive rules may result in more than one recursive rule, therefore, no longer a sirup. However, no generality is lost by assuming that each non-recursive rule has only EDB predicates in the body. We assume a generalized binary linear sirup has a recursive rule of the form $p(X, Y) : -A, p(U, V)$, for variables X, Y, U, V. Consider the following cases.

Case 1: X, Y, U, V are all distinct, and each of X and Y is connected to some of U and V in graph G_A and vice versa. By unfolding the recursive rule at most once, we can assume that X is always connected to U in G_A. We may also assume that for each exit rule with a body B, G_B is connected, since the general case can be reduced to this case by a reduction in [CGKV]. (Note that this is so only for exit rules) Now we remove all non-recursive IDB subgoals in

A by unfolding them using non-recursive rules. In each resulting recursive rule with the set A_i of EDB predicates, X is still connected to U in G_{A_i}. Therefore the first position of p can be chosen as the linking position. Now the predicate p is persistence-free and connected in the program under consideration. Then from Theorem 23, the boundedness is decidable.

Other cases: As in [Va], all other cases can be proved to be either bounded or reducible to monadic programs with a single recursive rule. It is important to see that those reductions do not depend on the absence of non-recursive rules. So we have

Theorem 24. Boundedness for generalized binary linear sirups is decidable.

Now we consider more general rules defined below.

Definition 25. *A program P is 1-branching if every recursive predicate is defined by at most one recursive rule.*

A 1-branching program may have more than one recursive predicate. In the following, we show that program boundedness is decidable for binary linear 1-branching programs. We first show that program boundedness is reduced to programs with at most one mutual recursion.

Let P be an arbitrary Datalog program. Let $I_1, \ldots, I_k$ be a partial ordering of the scc's of IDB graph of P such that no predicates in I_i depend on predicates in I_j for $j > i$. Let R_i be the set of rules in P that define predicates in I_i. $\{R_1, \ldots, R_k\}$ is a partition of rules in P.

Theorem 26. (1) P is bounded if and only if for $i = 1, \ldots, k$ in order, $R_{i-1}^n \cup R_i$ is bounded, where R_{i-1}^n is a non-recursive program equivalent to $R_1 \cup \ldots \cup R_{i-1}$, and $R_0^n = \emptyset$. (2) P is uniformly bounded if and only if for every R_i, the set of recursive rules in R_i is uniformly bounded.

Corollary 27. (1) Program boundedness for 1-branching linear programs is reducible to boundedness for generalized linear sirups of the same arity. (2) Uniform program boundedness for 1-branching linear programs is reducible to uniform boundedness for linear sirups of the same arity. (3) Predicate boundedness and program boundedness coincide for 1-branching linear programs in which each recursive predicate is mutually recursive with one another.

Proof idea: Consider a 1-branching linear program consisting of three recursive rules $p : -A, q, \quad q : -B, r$, and $r : -C, p$, where A, B, C are conjunctions of non-recursive predicates. By unfolding these recursive rules, p can be defined by a linear recursive rule of form $p : -A, B, C, p$ and some number of non-recursive rules. Once p is so defined, q and r can be defined by p and other predicates non-recursively. As a result, we need only deal with a generalized linear sirup. This reduction also holds in general in light of Theorem 26.

From Corollary 27 and Theorem 24, we have

Theorem 28. (1) Program boundedness is decidable for 1-branching binary linear programs. (2) Predicate boundedness is decidable for 1-branching binary linear programs in which each recursive predicate is mutually recursive with one another.

Using the reduction of Corollary 27 and some known decidability for linear sirups in [Na, NS, HKMV], boundedness and uniform boundedness of many 1-branching linear programs of arbitrary arity can be shown to be decidable. Finally, in the spirit of [CGKV] (i.e., Proposition 7.1), we can show

Theorem 29. (1) Predicate containment is decidable in polynomial space for linear sirups in C^+ (with multiple exit rules). (2) Predicate containment is decidable in doubly exponential time for persistence-free and connected predicates. (3) Predicate containment is decidable for 1-branching binary linear programs in which each recursive predicate is mutually recursive with one another.

References

[Ab]   Abiteboul, S.: Boundedness is undecidable for Datalog programs with a single recursive rules. IPL 32 (1989), pp. 281-287

[AP]   Afrati, F., Papadimitriou, C.H.: The parallel complexity of simple chain queries. ACM PODS, 1987, pp. 210-213

[BKBR]   Beeri, C., Kanellakis, P.C., Bancilhon, F., Ramakrishnan, R.: Bounds on the propagation of selection into logic programs. ACM PODS, 1987, pp. 214-226

[CGKV]   Cosmadakis, S., Gaifman, H., Kanellakis, P.C., Vardi, M.Y.: Decidable optimizations for datalog logic programs. ACM Symp. on Theory of Computing, 1988, pp. 477-490

[CM]   Chandra, A.K., Merlin, P.M.: Optimal implementation of conjunctive queries in relational databases. ACM Symp. on Theory of Computing, 1977, pp. 77-90

[GMSV]   Gaifman, H., Mairson, H., Sagiv, Y., Vardi, M.Y.: Undecidable optimization problems for database logic programs. Proc. of 2nd IEEE Symposium on Logic in Computer Science, 1987, pp. 106-115

[Gu]   Guessarian, I.: Deciding boundedness for uniformly connected Datalog programs. Lecture Notes in Computer Science 470, ICDT 1990, pp. 395-405

[HKMV]   Hillebrand, G.G., Kanellakis, P.C., Mairson, H.G., Vardi, M.Y.: Tools for datalog boundedness. ACM PODS, 1991, pp. 1-12

[Io]   Ioanidis, Y.E.: A time bound on the materialization of some recursively defined views. VLDB, 1985, pp. 219-226

[NS]   Naughton, J., Sagiv, Y.: A decidable class of bounded recursions. ACM PODS, 1986, pp. 227-236

[Na]   Naughton, J.: Data independent recursion in deductive databases. JCSS 38 (1989), pp. 259-289

[S]   Sagiv, Y.: On computing restricted projections of representative instances. ACM PODS, 1985, pp. 171-180

[Va]   Vardi, M.Y.: Decidability and undecidability results for boundedness of linear recursive queries. ACM PODS, 1988, pp. 341-351

Increment Boundedness and Nonrecursive Incremental Evaluation of Datalog Queries
(Extended Abstract)

Guozhu Dong[1] *   and   Jianwen Su[2] **

[1] Department of Computer Science
University of Melbourne
Parkville, Vic. 3052, Australia
dong@cs.mu.oz.au

[2] Department of Computer Science
University of California
Santa Barbara, CA 93106, U.S.A.
su@cs.ucsb.edu

Abstract. Given a recursive (datalog) query, the nonrecursive incremental evaluation approach uses nonrecursive (datalog) programs to compute the difference of the answers to the query against successive databases between updates. The mechanism used in this approach is called a "First-Order Incremental Evaluation System" (FOIES). We show that for two large classes of datalog queries, called "generalized (weakly) regular queries", FOIES always exist. We also define "increment boundedness" and its variations, which generalize boundedness. Increment bounded queries are shown to have FOIES of certain forms. We also relate increment boundedness to structural recursion, which was proposed for bulk data types. We characterize increment boundedness using the "insertion idempotency", "insertion commutativity", and "determinism" properties of structural recursion. Finally, we show that the increment boundedness notions are undecidable and a decidable sufficient condition is given.

1 Introduction

Recursive query optimization has been a focus of the study on the datalog language over the last several years (see [17] and recent PODS, SIGMOD, VLDB, DOOD proceedings). Most recently, query evaluation against databases that are frequently updated is studied in [8, 6, 5, 7, 10]. Specifically, to repeatedly evaluate the same (computationally expensive) recursive query on a database that is being updated between successive query requests, it should be possible to use the difference between successive database states and the answer to the query in one state to reduce the cost of evaluating the entire query in the next state. It is considered as "desirable" if one can use nonrecursive queries to

---

* This author gratefully acknowledges support of Australian Research Council (ARC) through research grants and the Centre for Intelligent Decision Systems.
** Work supported in part by NSF grants IRI-9109520 and IRI-9117094. Part of work was done while visiting the University of Melbourne with partial support from an ARC grant to G. Dong.

compute the differences. In [8, 6, 5, 7], these ideas were abstracted in the so-called "first-order incremental query evaluation system" (or FOIES), and some interesting results were given; and in [15] a similar class called Dyn-FO was investigated as a complexity class. In this paper we continue our investigation in this direction by studying further on FOIES and by exploring some related query optimization issues.

Boundedness of datalog programs is one of the most-studied issues in the deductive database community [13, 14, 19, 18, 1, 12, 4]. In this paper we introduce and examine a related property, "increment boundedness", of datalog programs. Intuitively, a datalog program P is increment bounded if, to derive a new model after inserting one edb fact, one only needs to apply T_P^k for some fixed k (instead of T_P^ω).

On the other hand, the notion of "structural recursion" by insertion was proposed in [3] as a paradigm to specify database queries. Briefly speaking, a query defined by structural recursion consists of a base clause on the empty set, and a recursive clause on "inserting an element to a set".

In this paper, we establish close relationships between the three notions: FOIES, increment boundedness, and structural recursion. This paper has the following contributions: First, we extend our earlier results [7] on the existence of FOIES for (weakly) regular queries to wider classes of queries, "generalized (weakly) regular queries". These queries allow predicates of arbitrary arities, unlike in the (weakly) regular case where only binary chain rules are permitted in the recursive part. Second, increment boundedness and its variations are defined and shown to be equivalent to some subclasses of FOIES. Third, we characterize increment boundedness by the "insertion idempotency", "insertion commutativity", and "determinism" properties of structural recursion and show that commutativity is equivalent to increment boundedness for a syntactic class of programs. Fourth, undecidability results for increment boundedness and its variations are presented and a decidable sufficient condition is given. Increment boundedness turns out to be remarkably different from boundedness.

This abstract is organized as follows. Section 2 reviews some basic terminologies. Section 3 discusses generalized (weakly) regular queries. Section 4 presents the notion of increment boundedness and some results on them. Section 5 provides the characterizations of increment boundedness through structural recursion; and Section 6 focuses on the decision issues. Proofs are sketched or omitted in this extended abstract; full proofs will be included in the full version.

2 Preliminaries

We briefly review datalog and some necessary notions, and then present the definition of a FOIES.

We assume the existence of three pairwise disjoint infinite sets of *constants, variables*, and *predicates*. Built-in predicates such as equality are disallowed. Each predicate has a positive *arity*. An *atom* is a formula of the form $q(t_1, ..., t_k)$, where q is a predicate and $t_1, ..., t_k$ are variables or constants. A *fact* is an atom without variables. A *(datalog) program* is a finite set of rules of the form $A \leftarrow A_1, ..., A_n$, where $n \geq 1$, A and $A_1, ..., A_n$ are atoms and each variable in A occurs in some A_i. Let P be a program. We call a predicate occurring in P *intensional* (*idb*) if it occurs in the head of some rule in

P, and *extensional* (*edb*) otherwise. We use $idb(P)$ to denote the set of all idb predicates in P. For each set D of facts and each nonnegative integer i, let $T_P^i(D)$ denote the set of facts having derivation trees of depth at most i; each fact in D is considered to have a derivation tree of depth zero; and let $T_P^\omega(D) = \bigcup_{i=0}^{\infty} T_P^i(D)$. A *(datalog) query* is a pair (P, p), where P is a program, and p an (answer) idb predicate; for each set D of edb facts, the *answer* to the query is the set of facts over p in $T_P^\omega(D)$.

We now turn to FOIES, which use nonrecursive programs to maintain models of programs after insertion of facts. The nonrecursive programs need to differentiate facts in the old state (before an insertion) and facts in the new state (after the insertion). We adopt the following notation: for each predicate q, we shall use (i) q^o (*o* for old) as a predicate to represent facts over q computed or stored in the old database state, and (ii) q to represent facts over q that are asserted (either through insertion or through derivation) in the new state. For each set I of facts, let I^o be the set of facts obtained from I by replacing each predicate q with q^o. If S is a set of predicates, the restriction of I to those with predicate in S is denoted $I|_S$. We write $I|_p$ for $I|_{\{p\}}$.

Definition. A *FOIES* for a query (P, p) is a triple $\langle P_p, S, P_\delta \rangle$, where:

- S is a set of idb predicates containing p;
- P_p is a (possibly recursive) program, called the *initial program*, such that P_p and P are equivalent regarding their common idb predicates, i.e., $T_{P_p}^\omega(D)|_{idb(P) \cap S} = T_P^\omega(D)|_{idb(P) \cap S}$ for each set D of edb facts; and
- P_δ is a nonrecursive program, called the *incremental program*, such that, for each set D and each singleton set Δ of edb facts, P_δ derives the new least model of P_p containing $D \cup \Delta$ from Δ and the old least model of P_p containing D, i.e., $T_{P_p}^\omega(D \cup \Delta)|_S = T_{P_\delta}^\omega([T_{P_p}^\omega(D)|_S]^o \cup \Delta)|_S \cup T_{P_p}^\omega(D)|_S$.

A FOIES $\langle P_p, S, P_\delta \rangle$ for (P, p) is *space-free* if $S \subseteq idb(P)$.

Intuitively, a FOIES of a query always stores the answer on the current database. It may also store some auxiliary relations (predicates in S other than p). When the database changes, the FOIES uses the stored answer (and possibly auxiliary relations) to nonrecursively compute the new answer (and the new auxiliary relations). Space-free FOIES do not use any auxiliary relations. The following example illustrates the notion of FOIES.

Example 2.1. Consider the program P_1 computing the transitive closure of an edb predicate q: $\{p(x, z) \leftarrow q(x, z);\ p(x, z) \leftarrow q(x, y), p(y, z)\}$. Let $P_p = P_1$, $S = \{p\}$, and P_δ be the program

$$
\begin{array}{ll}
p(x, z) \leftarrow q(x, z) & p(x, z) \leftarrow q(x, y), p^o(y, z) \\
p(x, z) \leftarrow p^o(x, y), q(y, z) & p(x, z) \leftarrow p^o(x, y_1), q(y_1, y_2), p^o(y_2, z)
\end{array}
$$

Then $\langle P_p, S, P_\delta \rangle$ is a FOIES for (P_1, p). To illustrate how the FOIES works, suppose $D = \{q(1, 2), q(2, 3),\ q(4, 5), q(5, 6)\}$ and $\Delta = \{q(3, 4)\}$. Then $T_{P_p}^\omega(D) = D \cup \{p(i, j) \mid 1 \le i < j \le 3, 4 \le i < j \le 6\}$. To compute $T_{P_p}^\omega(D \cup \Delta)$ from $T_{P_p}^\omega(D)$ using P_δ, the facts in $T_{P_p}^\omega(D)$ are marked with the superscript o to indicate that they were facts before inserting the fact $q(3, 4)$; the predicate q (resp. p) in P_δ denotes the additional set of facts that are added (resp. derived) for q (resp. p). Thus, the additional fact for q is $q(3,4)$, and the additional facts for p are $\{p(i,j) \mid i \in [1..3] \text{ and } j \in [4..6]\}$.

Note that, to get the new paths after a q edge is added using this FOIES, only four (one if the new edge is treated as a pair of constants) joins are needed. Thus we have transformed the computation of a recursive program into the computation of a nonrecursive one (with the help of stored results). □

3 Generalized Regular Queries

In this section, we define "generalized (weakly) regular queries", which are subclasses of generalized chain queries, and extend the results on FOIES for subclasses of chain queries reported in [7] to generalized (weakly) regular queries. The results are new and the proofs require nontrivial new techniques.

The main results are Theorems 3.3, 3.5 and 3.6. Theorem 3.3 says that generalized regular queries (defined syntactically) have FOIES, Theorem 3.5 that generalized regular queries augmented by adding non recursive initializations having a property called "cci" have FOIES, and Theorem 3.6 that the cci property is decidable for non recursive programs which implies that the extended class, generalized weakly regular queries, is decidable. (This is because the class is defined syntactically except the cci property.)

A datalog rule r is a *generalized chain rule* if it has the following form:

$$r : p_0(\bar{x}_0, \bar{x}_n) \leftarrow p_1(\bar{x}_0, \bar{z}_0, \bar{x}_1), ..., p_i(\bar{x}_{i-1}, \bar{z}_{i-1}, \bar{x}_i), ..., p_n(\bar{x}_{n-1}, \bar{z}_{n-1}, \bar{x}_n) \quad (1)$$

where $\bar{x}_0, ..., \bar{x}_n, \bar{z}_0, ..., \bar{z}_{n-1}$ are disjoint (possibly empty) sequences of variables. Note that *chain rules* are special generalized chain rules, where $\bar{x}_0, ..., \bar{x}_n$ are distinct single variables and $\bar{z}_0, ..., \bar{z}_{n-1}$ are all empty sequences of variables. A *generalized chain program* is a finite set of generalized chain rules; and a *generalized chain query* is a query (P, p), where P is a generalized chain program. Similar to chain queries, each generalized chain query $Q = (P, p)$ can be associated with a context-free grammar G_Q constructed as follows. The terminals (nonterminals) are the edb (idb) predicates; the start nonterminal is p; and for each rule in P of the form (1) there is a production of the form $p_0 \rightarrow p_1 p_2 \cdots p_n$.

A query Q is *generalized regular (g.r.)* if G_Q is right-linear, i.e., the only nonterminal in the right hand side of each production is the rightmost symbol.

Obviously, each chain query (program) is also generalized chain; each regular (chain) query [7] is also generalized regular. In particular, transitive closure can be expressed by a g.r. query. For nonrecursive generalized chain queries, the next proposition follows from a result in [7].

Proposition 3.1. Each nonrecursive generalized chain query is a conjunctive query, but not vice versa. □

We now give an example of a g.r. chain query which is not a chain query, together with a FOIES for it.

Example 3.2. Let $Q = (P_2, p)$ be a query, where $P_2 = \{p(x) \leftarrow s(x,y), p(y); \ p(x) \leftarrow q(x)\}$. Q represents the propagation of signals q through a network s of logical "or" gates ($s(x, y)$ means the gate x has y as an input wire). Q is g.r. but not a (regular) chain query. Q also has a FOIES. Indeed, let $S = \{p, t\}$, where $t(x, y)$ denotes x is "on" whenever y is "on" and

$$P_p = \left\{ \begin{array}{l} t(x, y) \leftarrow s(x, y) \\ t(x, z) \leftarrow t(x, y), t(y, z) \\ p(x) \leftarrow q(x) \\ p(x) \leftarrow t(x, y), q(y) \end{array} \right\},$$

$$P_\delta = \left\{ \begin{array}{ll} t(x, y) \leftarrow s(x, y) & p(x) \leftarrow q(x) \\ t(x, z) \leftarrow t^o(x, y), s(y, z) & p(x) \leftarrow t^o(x, y), q(y) \\ t(x, z) \leftarrow s(x, y), t^o(y, z) & p(x) \leftarrow t(x, y), q^o(y) \\ t(x, z) \leftarrow t^o(x, y_1), s(y_1, y_2), t^o(y_2, z) \end{array} \right\}$$

It can be verified that $\langle P_p, S, P_\delta \rangle$ is a FOIES for Q but Q has no space-free FOIES. Observe that P_p computes the entire transitive closure of s, whereas P_2 only computes the part reachable from constants in q.

Theorem 3.3. Each g.r. (generalized regular) query has a FOIES.

The proof idea is similar to the one used in [7] for regular (chain) queries. To construct a FOIES for a g.r. query, we first find a regular expression E corresponding to the grammar, and E uses only symbols from the set of idb predicates, "(", ")", "$\cup$", and "+". This can be done by standard procedures [2]. For example, for P_2, the regular expression is $(s^+ q) \cup q$. We then use an auxiliary relation for each subexpression of E and the incremental program is obtained inductively according to (roughly) the syntax tree of E. The basis for both [7] and here is that all new derived facts after inserting a fact A can be obtained by using the old derived facts and A a bounded number of times. The proof and construction for the g.r. case, however, require some new techniques. The modification to this proof, as well as to the proofs of other results, is needed due to the following difference between chain and generalized chain programs:

Note that chain programs consist of rules of the form (1) where all $\bar{z}_i$'s are empty and each $\bar{x}_i$ is a single variable. Consequently, chain queries operate on graphs where each edge has two constants as nodes. On the other hand, generalized chain queries operate on hypergraphs where each hyperedge may have three nodes, each being a sequence of constants. Specifically, a fact $q(a_1, ..., a_k)$ corresponds to many hyperedges, e.g., for each $j \in [1..(k-1)]$, it can be used as a hyperedge from $a_1, ..., a_j$ to $a_{j+1}, ..., a_k$ (there are many other ways where the middle constants do not connect other constants in the edges before and after this edge).

We now consider "generalized weakly regular queries".

We say $p[j_1, j_2, j_3]$ is a *partition* of a predicate p if j_1, j_2, j_3 are nonnegative integers such that $j_1 + j_2 + j_3 = $ arity of p. Each rule r of form (1) above is said to *use* the partition $p_i[|\bar{x}_{i-1}|, |\bar{z}_{i-1}|, |\bar{x}_i|]$ for each $i \in [1..n]$ ($|\bar{x}|$ denotes the length of $\bar{x}$). Intuitively, r uses $p_i[j_1, j_2, j_3]$ if facts over p_i may be unified with an atom $p_i(\bar{x}_{i-1}, \bar{z}_{i-1}, \bar{x}_i)$ such that the first j_1 constants are identical to the last j_1 constants of the preceding fact, the last j_3 constants are identical to the first j_3 constants of the following fact, and the middle j_2 constants are not restricted.

A set D of facts over a predicate q is called $q[j_1, j_2, j_3]$-*cartesian closed* if, $q[j_1, j_2, j_3]$ is a partition of q and, whenever $q(\bar{a}_1, \bar{c}_1, \bar{b}_1)$ and $q(\bar{a}_2, \bar{c}_2, \bar{b}_2)$ are in D where $|\bar{a}_1| = |\bar{a}_2| = j_1$ and $|\bar{b}_1| = |\bar{b}_2| = j_3$, there is some $\bar{c}$ so that $q(\bar{a}_1, \bar{c}, \bar{b}_2)$ belongs to D.

This notion is a special case of embedded multivalued dependency (with an empty left-hand-side [16]). Note that D is always $q[j_1, j_2, j_3]$-cartesian closed if either D is a singleton set, or $j_1 = 0$ or $j_3 = 0$.

The notion of cartesian-closed sets is important for incremental evaluation since it allows us to extend results on single fact to sets: the insertion of a cartesian-closed set will behave like the insertion of a single fact in incremental evaluation, which can be dealt with by FOIES for generalized regular queries.

Definition. A program P has k-*cartesian-closed increment* (k-*cci*) w.r.t. a partition $p[j_1, j_2, j_3]$ if $k \geq 0$ and for each set D and singleton set Δ of edb facts, there are k $p[j_1, j_2, j_3]$-cartesian-closed sets $C_1, ..., C_k$ satisfying

$$T_P^\omega(D \cup \Delta)|_p - T_P^\omega(D)|_p \subseteq \cup_{i=1}^k C_i \subseteq T_P^\omega(D \cup \Delta)|_p.$$

P has *cci* w.r.t. $p[j_1, j_2, j_3]$ if it has k-cci w.r.t. $p[j_1, j_2, j_3]$ for some k.

Example 3.4. Program $P_3 = \{p_1(x, y) \leftarrow q_1(x, u, v), q_5(v, w, z), q_3(z, y)\}$ has 1-cci w.r.t. $p_1[1, 0, 1]$. Intuitively, for each database D and each set Δ of one edb fact, let

$$C = \begin{cases} \{p_1(a, d_2) \mid q_5(c, d, d_1) \text{ and } q_3(d_1, d_2) \text{ in } D \text{ for some } d \text{ and } d_1\}, \\ \qquad \text{if } \Delta \text{ has the form } \{q_1(a, b, c)\} \\ \{p_1(a_2, b_1) \mid q_1(a_2, a_1, a) \text{ and } q_3(b, b_1) \text{ in } D \text{ for some } a_1\}, \\ \qquad \text{if } \Delta \text{ has the form } \{q_5(a, c, b)\} \\ \{p_1(c, b) \mid q_1(c, d_1, d_2) \text{ and } q_5(d_2, d, a) \text{ in } D \text{ for some } d, d_1 \text{ and } d_2\}, \\ \qquad \text{if } \Delta \text{ has the form } \{q_3(a, b)\} \end{cases}$$

Then C is cartesian closed, and $P_3(D \cup \Delta) - P_3(D) \subseteq C \subseteq P_3(D \cup \Delta)$ hold.

An empty (binary) program has 1-cci w.r.t. $p_1[1, 0, 1]$, since the empty set is cartesian closed. Program $P_4 = \{p_1(x, y) \leftarrow q_1(x, u, v), q_5(v, u, z), q_6(z, u, y)\}$ also has 1-cci w.r.t. $p_1[1, 0, 1]$.

Program $P_5 = \{p_1(x, y) \leftarrow q_4(x, y), q_2(u, v)\}$ does not have cci w.r.t. $p_1[1, 0, 1]$. Indeed, for each $k \geq 0$, suppose D is a set of q_4 facts such that D is not the union of any k cartesian-closed sets. Then $P_5(D \cup \{q_2(a, b)\}) - P_5(D)$ is not bounded by any k cartesian-closed sets in $P_5(D \cup \{q_2(a, b)\})$, violating the two containments in the above definition.

We next define "generalized weakly regular" queries which may allow nonrecursive initialization.

Definition. A query (P, p) is *generalized weakly regular* (*g.w.r.*) if $P = P_c \cup P_r$ satisfies the following:

1. P_c is non recursive;
2. Each predicate in the heads of rules in P_r does not occur in P_c;

3. For each $q \in idb(P_c)$, let P_c^q be the set of rules defining q. The program Q_q with only one idb-predicate (i.e., q), modified from P_c^q by eliminating all other idb predicates through expansion, has cci for each partition $q[j_1, j_2, j_3]$ of q used by P_r.
4. (P_r, p) is a g.r. query (viewing idb predicates in P_c as edb predicates).

Since the nonrecursive initialization part of a g.w.r. query has cci, Theorem 3.3 can be generalized:

Theorem 3.5. Each g.w.r. (generalized weakly regular) chain query has a FOIES. $\square$

Finally, we consider the decision problem for cci. It turns out that the decidability and undecidability results in [7] can also be extended (nontrivially) to the case with partitions. In the following, we state the results and two key lemmas used in proving the decidability result.

Theorem 3.6. It is decidable if a nonrecursive program has cci w.r.t. a partition $p[i, j, k]$; undecidable if a recursive program has cci w.r.t. $p[i, j, k]$. $\square$

A program P is nonredundant if P cannot be syntactically simplied by removing "elements" from it, i.e., (i) P is not equivalent to any of its proper subsets and (ii) P is not equivalent to any P' obtained by removing atoms from its rule bodies.

Lemma 3.7. A nonredundant, nonrecursive program P with a single idb-predicate has cci w.r.t. $p[i, j, k]$ iff $\{r\}$ has cci w.r.t. $p[i, j, k]$ for each $r \in P$. $\square$

For each set S of atoms and each atom A, we say two variables x and y are (S, A)-connected if there is a sequence $A_1, ..., A_\ell$ ($\ell \geq 1$) of atoms from S such that, x occurs in A_1, y occurs in A_ℓ, and A_i and A_{i+1} share a variable x_i not occurring in A for each $1 \leq i < \ell$. For examples, for $S = \{q_1(x, u, v), q_2(z, u, y)\}$ and $A = q(v, v, z)$, x and y are (S, A)-connected; however, for $A' = q(v, u, z)$, x and y are not (S, A')-connected. If two variables occur in a common atom in S, then they are (S, A)-connected for every A. Note that (S, A)-connectivity reduces to the usual connectivity when A contains no variable.

For each sequence of variables $\bar{x}$, we define $V(\bar{x})$ to be the set of variables occurring in $\bar{x}$. We also extend V to atoms naturally.

Lemma 3.8. A rule $r : p(\bar{x}, \bar{y}, \bar{z}) \leftarrow A_1, ..., A_m$ has cci w.r.t. $p[|\bar{x}|, |\bar{y}|, |\bar{z}|]$ iff for each $i \in [1..m]$,

1. $V(\bar{x}) \cap V(\bar{z}) \subseteq V(A_i)$; and
2. either $V(\bar{x}) \subseteq V(A_i)$, or $V(\bar{z}) \subseteq V(A_i)$, or for each $x \in V(\bar{x}) - V(\bar{z})$ and each $z \in V(\bar{z}) - V(\bar{x})$, x, z are not (S, A_i)-connected (where $S = \{A_j | 1 \leq j \leq m\}$).
$\square$

For example, P_3 in Example 3.4 has 1-cci w.r.t. $p[1, 0, 1]$ according to this lemma. Indeed, let $A_1 = q_1(x, u, v)$, $A_2 = q_5(v, w, z)$ and $A_3 = q_3(z, y)$. Then $V(\bar{x}) \cap V(\bar{z}) = \emptyset \subseteq V(A_i)$ for each $i \in [1..3]$. For each $i \in \{1, 3\}$, we have either $V(\bar{x}) \subseteq V(A_i)$, or $V(\bar{z}) \subseteq V(A_i)$. Furthermore, x, y are not (S, A_2)-connected where $S = \{A_1, A_2, A_3\}$.

4 Increment Boundedness and FOIES

We define a new property, called "increment boundedness", for datalog programs and establish two equivalence relationships with space-free FOIES and FOIES that are syntactically constructible from the programs. A characterization of increment boundedness using "structural recursion" is given in the next section and decision problems are discussed in Section 6.

Intuitively, a program P is ℓ-increment bounded ($\ell \geq 1$) if, upon an insertion of one edb fact A into a database D, the new minimal model $T_P^\omega(D \cup \{A\})$ can be obtained by apply T_P^ℓ (instead of the usual T_P^ω) to the previous minimal model $T_P^\omega(D)$ and the new fact A. Hence, an ℓ-increment bounded program needs no recursion to update its minimal model upon insertion. This concept is closely related to the popular bounded class [9] but with some interesting distinct behavior. Formally, we have:

Definition. Suppose P is a datalog program.

- For each $\ell \geq 1$ [and each edb predicate q], P is ℓ-increment bounded (ℓ-IB) [w.r.t. q] if
$$T_P^\omega(D \cup \{A\}) = T_P^\ell(T_P^\omega(D) \cup \{A\})$$
for each set D of edb facts and for each edb fact A [over q].
- P is increment bounded (IB) if it is ℓ-IB for some fixed ℓ.
- P is generalized increment bounded (GIB) if there is some nonrecursive program Q such that
$$T_P^\omega(D \cup \{A\}) = T_Q(T_P^\omega(D) \cup \{A\})$$
for each set D of edb facts and for each edb fact A.

We also denote by ℓ-IB (resp., IB, GIB) the set of programs which are ℓ-IB (resp., IB, GIB).

Example 4.1. Let P_6 be P_6 in Example 2.1 except the o superscript is removed. Note that the predicate p holds the transitive closure of q. P_6 is increment bounded (by Theorem 4.2). In fact, P_6 is 1-IB: Suppose p contained the transitive closure of q before the insertion. Then after inserting a q fact, the new closure is obtained by applying $T_{P_6}^1$ once. However, the equivalent program P_1 in Example 2.1 is not even increment bounded. Indeed, for each $\ell \geq 1$, $T_{P_1}^\omega(D \cup \{A\}) \neq T_{P_1}^\ell(T_{P_1}^\omega(D) \cup \{A\})$, where $D = \{q(i, i+1) \mid 0 \leq i \leq 2\ell, i \neq \ell\}$ and $A = q(\ell, \ell+1)$. □

Example 4.1 indicates that IB is not semantic. (A property is semantic if it is closed under substitution by equivalent programs [9].) Recall that a program P is *bounded* if there is an integer ℓ such that $T_P^\omega(D) = T_P^\ell(D)$ for each set D of edb facts. It follows that each bounded program is also increment bounded but not vice versa.

Theorem 4.2. Let (P, p) be a query. If P is ℓ-IB, then (P, p) has a FOIES (and the FOIES can be constructed from P by syntactic changes). Furthermore, P is GIB iff (P, p) has a space-free FOIES. Consequently, each IB query has a space-free FOIES; but the converse is not true.

For proving the first statement, for each ℓ-IB query (P, p), we construct a FOIES $(P, idb(P), Q_\ell)$, where, roughly, Q_ℓ is obtained by "expanding" P up to ℓ times (all derivation trees of height $\leq \ell$) and marking appropriate predicates with superscript o. To be more precise, consider an arbitrary rule in the expansion:

$$A \leftarrow B_1, \ldots, B_m, C_1, \ldots, C_n$$

where each B_i is an idb atom and C_j is an edb atom. Then, for each proper subset M of $[1..n]$, Q_ℓ includes the following rule:

$$A \leftarrow B_1^o, \ldots, B_m^o, C_1', \ldots, C_n'$$

where C_j' is C_j if $j \notin M$ and C_j' is C_j^o otherwise. (If $C = p(t_1, \ldots, t_k)$, then by C^o we mean $p^o(t_1, \ldots, t_k)$.)

The second statement is easily verified from the definitions. For the last statement, the standard TC program P_1 (Example 2.1) has a space-free FOIES, but is not IB.

Example 4.3. Let P_1 be as in Example 2.1. Then, for (P_1, p), there is a space-free FOIES. Let P_6 be P_6 in Example 2.1 except the o superscript is removed, as considered in Example 4.1. Then there is a space-free FOIES $\langle P_6, \{p\}, P_6' \rangle$ for (P_6, p), where P_6' is constructed as above, and it happens that $P_6' = P_6$ (in Example 2.1).

It can be verified that the original transitive closure query (P_1, p) and the or-gate propagation query Q in Example 3.2 do not have FOIES constructed in this way. □

The following result shows that there is a strict hierarchy among the classes.

Theorem 4.4. $\forall \ell \geq 1$, ℓ-IB $\subseteq\neq$ $(\ell + 1)$-IB. Also, $\cup_{\ell \geq 0} \ell$-IB = IB $\subseteq\neq$ GIB.

Proof. Obviously the containments hold. The first containment is proper because we can write inefficient datalog programs that delays output; for example, for $\ell = 1$, the two-rule program $\{p_1(x) \leftarrow q(x); \ p_2(x) \leftarrow q(x), p_1(y)\}$ is 2-IB, but not 1-IB. The second containment is proper since the standard TC program P_1 (Example 2.1) belongs to GIB but not to IB. □

In terms of the number of iterations needed for evaluating IB queries, we have:

Theorem 4.5. If (P, p) is an IB query, then the number of iterations needed to derive $T_P^\omega(D)|_p$ using semi-naive evaluation method is at most linear in the number of facts in D.

Finally, similar to the boundedness problem of whether a given program is equivalent to some nonrecursive program, it is also interesting to know when a given program is equivalent to some IB program.

5 FOIES and Structural Recursion

Structural recursion [3] was proposed as a database programming paradigm on "bulk" types such as sets or relations. Structural recursion can be performed based either on insertion or on union. Under the insertion approach, the computation (query) on an input set S is divided into the computation on a subset which contains all but one element of S, followed by the computation for inserting the remaining element. The computation on the subsets of S is done recursively in that manner.

Since both FOIES and structural recursion accomplish computation in a similar way, it is interesting to know how FOIES relates to structural recursion.

We consider Datalog programs having the special forms of space-free FOIES corresponding to the IB property as discussed Theorem 4.2. We give two characterizations of such IB programs using structural recursion. The first shows the equivalence of four properties: (i) IB, (ii) determinism, (iii) idempotency, and (iv) the combination of weak idempotency and commutativity. The second refines the first by establishing the equivalence of IB and commutativity for connected datalog programs. The restrictions on programs are shown necessary to guarantee this equivalence.

Roughly, structural recursion by insertion allows inductive definition of mappings on sets by inserting one element at a time, where each element may be inserted more than once. Formally, given a constant e and a function ϕ, we define a mapping g as follows[3]:

$$\begin{array}{ll} fun & g(\emptyset) = e \\ | & g(Insert(A, S)) = \phi(A, g(S)) \end{array}$$

Following [3], we will write in combinator style $\Psi(e, \phi)$ for g. The typing is $\Psi(e, \phi) : \{\alpha\} \to \beta$, provided that $e : \beta$ and $\phi : \alpha \times \beta \to \beta$.

The mapping g is called *deterministic* if, for all appropriate S, $g(S)$ has exactly one value, that is, $\phi(A_1, \phi(A_2, ..., \phi(A_m, e))) = \phi(B_1, \phi(B_2, ..., \phi(B_n, e)))$ whenever $A_1, ..., A_m$ and $B_1, ..., B_n$ are sequences satisfying $\{A_1, ..., A_m\} = S = \{B_1, ..., B_n\}$. The following two properties imply determinism [3]: If ϕ is a function whose typing is $\alpha \times \beta \to \beta$, then (i) ϕ is called *(insertion) idempotent* if

$$\phi(A, \phi(A, \phi(A_1, \phi(A_2, ..., \phi(A_m, e)...)))) = \phi(A, \phi(A_1, \phi(A_2, ..., \phi(A_m, e)...)))$$

for all $A, A_1, ..., A_m$ ($m \geq 0$) of type α, and (ii) ϕ is called *(insertion) commutative* if

$$\phi(A, \phi(B, \phi(A_1, \phi(A_2, ..., \phi(A_m, e)...)))) = \phi(B, \phi(A, \phi(A_1, \phi(A_2, ..., \phi(A_m, e)...))))$$

for all $A, B, A_1, ..., A_m$ ($m \geq 0$) of type α. We further define ϕ to be *weakly idempotent* w.r.t. e if $\phi(A, \phi(A, e)) = \phi(A, e)$ for all A.

The proposition below shows the relationship among determinism, idempotency, and commutativity for general functions. As it will be seen later, (b) shows an interesting difference between structural recursion using general function and using datalog mappings.

Proposition 5.1. (a) Determinism $\equiv$ idempotency + commutativity. (b) Idempotency and commutativity are incomparable. (c) Commutativity + weakly idempotency imply idempotency. $\Box$

---

[3] *Insert* is a set constructor so that *Insert*(A, S) returns the set obtained by inserting A (an element) into a set S.

For each program P and each positive integer ℓ, define I_P^ℓ by $I_P^\ell(A, S) = T_P^\ell(S \cup \{A\})$. We will write I_P^1 as I_P. From here on we assume that e is the empty set $\emptyset$.
The next theorem presents the first characterization for IB.

Theorem 5.2. If ℓ is a positive integer, then (a) P is ℓ-IB *iff* (b) I_P^ℓ is idempotent *iff* (c) $\Psi(\emptyset, I_P^\ell)$ is deterministic *iff* (d) I_P^ℓ is commutative and weakly idempotent.

Proof. By Proposition 5.1, we have (d) implies (b), and so (c) and (d) are equivalent; and we have (c) implies (b). It is easy to prove that (a) and (b) are equivalent and that (b) implies (c). □

As an aside, from the equivalence of (b) and (c) it is easily seen that the expressive power of structural recursion using datalog is confined to datalog. That is, all deterministic mappings defined by using datalog mappings in structural recursion by insertion are themselves datalog mappings.

Corollary 5.3. A query (P, p) has a space-free FOIES if for some ℓ, one of the following conditions holds: (1) I_P^ℓ is idempotent, (2) $\Psi(\emptyset, I_P^\ell)$ is deterministic, or (3) I_P^ℓ is commutative and weakly idempotent. □

We now give results on the relationships between commutativity and IB for datalog programs.

Proposition 5.4. Commutativity does not imply IB in general: There are constant-free (nonrecursive or recursive) programs P such that I_P is commutative but not idempotent. Consequently, commutativity for datalog mappings does not imply IB and determinism.

Proof. Let P_7 be the nonrecursive program consisting of the following two rules:

$$
\begin{aligned}
r_1: \quad & p_1(x) \leftarrow q(x) \\
r_2: \quad & p_2(x) \leftarrow q(x), p_1(y)
\end{aligned}
$$

Then I_{P_7} is not idempotent:

$$I_{P_7}(q(1), \emptyset) = \{q(1), p_1(1)\} \neq I_{P_7}(q(1), I_{P_7}(q(1), \emptyset)) = \{q(1), p_1(1), p_2(1)\}.$$

To see that I_{P_7} is commutative, let $A_0, \ldots, A_m$ $(m \geq 1)$ be a sequence of facts. Let c be a constant occurring in some A_i. From r_1 we see that the following two statements hold:

$$
\begin{aligned}
p_1(c) &\in I_{P_7}(A_0, I_{P_7}(A_1, I_{P_7}(A_2, \ldots, I_{P_7}(A_m, \emptyset) \ldots))), \\
p_1(c) &\in I_{P_7}(A_1, I_{P_7}(A_0, I_{P_7}(A_2, \ldots, I_{P_7}(A_m, \emptyset) \ldots))).
\end{aligned}
$$

Since $m \geq 1$, there are p_1 facts in each of the following two sets:

$$
\begin{aligned}
& I_{P_7}(A_1, I_{P_7}(A_2, \ldots, I_{P_7}(A_m, \emptyset) \ldots)), \\
& I_{P_7}(A_0, I_{P_7}(A_2, \ldots, I_{P_7}(A_m, \emptyset) \ldots)).
\end{aligned}
$$

Hence, from r_2 we see that the following two statements hold:

$$
\begin{aligned}
p_2(c) &\in I_{P_7}(A_0, I_{P_7}(A_1, I_{P_7}(A_2, \ldots, I_{P_7}(A_m, \emptyset) \ldots))), \\
p_2(c) &\in I_{P_7}(A_1, I_{P_7}(A_0, I_{P_7}(A_2, \ldots, I_{P_7}(A_m, \emptyset) \ldots))).
\end{aligned}
$$

So commutativity follows. □

Theorem 5.5. If P is a connected[4] and constant-free datalog program, then P is ℓ-IB iff I_P^ℓ is idempotent *iff* I_P^ℓ is commutative.

Proof. Suppose P is a connected and constant-free datalog program. By Theorem 5.2, it suffices to show that I_P^ℓ is weakly idempotent.

We call two sets of facts S_1 and S_2 disconnected if there are no facts $A_1 \in S_1$ and $A_2 \in S_2$ such that A_1 is connected to A_2 in $S_1 \cup S_2$. Clearly T_P^ℓ maps disconnected sets to disconnected sets, and $T_P^\ell(D_1 \cup D_2) = T_P^\ell(D_1) \cup T_P^\ell(D_2)$ for all disjoint sets D_1 and D_2 of facts.

Let A be an arbitrary fact, and B a fact not[5] using any constants in A. Then

$$I_P^\ell(A, I_P^\ell(B, \emptyset)) = T_P^\ell(T_P^\ell(\{B\}) \cup \{A\}), \quad \text{by definition of } I_P^\ell$$
$$= T_P^\ell(T_P^\ell(\{B\})) \cup T_P^\ell(\{A\}), \quad \text{since } \{A\} \text{ and } \{B\} \text{ are disconnected.}$$

Similarly, $I_P^\ell(B, I_P^\ell(A, \emptyset)) = T_P^\ell(\{B\}) \cup T_P^\ell(T_P^\ell(\{A\}))$. Suppose I_P^ℓ is commutative. Then

$$I_P^\ell(A, I_P^\ell(B, \emptyset)) = I_P^\ell(B, I_P^\ell(A, \emptyset)).$$

Since P is connected and A and B are disconnected, we get $T_P^\ell(\{A\}) = T_P^\ell(T_P^\ell(\{A\}))$, that is, $I_P^\ell(A, \emptyset) = I_P^\ell(A, I_P^\ell(A, \emptyset))$. □

Corollary 5.6. A query (P, p) has a space-free FOIES if P is connected and constant-free and I_P^ℓ is commutative for some ℓ. □

6 Decision Problems for Increment Boundedness

We consider here the decision issues for the increment bounded properties. The main results of the section show that they are all undecidable. The results also raise an interesting contrast between boundedness and increment boundedness: While they are both undecidable for the general case, for a fixed ℓ, ℓ-boundedness is decidable [4] but ℓ-IB is still undecidable.

In [9], it was shown that undecidability of boundedness can be translated into undecidability for many other properties. The translation, however, is not applicable to our context because none of the IB notions is semantic.

Theorem 6.1. It is undecidable for an arbitrary datalog query Q if Q is GIB; if Q is IB.

Proof. In [7], it was shown that it is undecidable if a query has a space-free FOIES. By Theorem 4.2, it follows easily that GIB is also undecidable. By using a direct reduction from the halting problem, IB can also be shown undecidable. □

---

[4] Two atoms are *directly connected* if they share a variable or constant. Given a set S of atoms, two atoms in S are *connected in S* if either they are directly connected, or there is an atom C in S which is connected to both of them in S. A rule $A \leftarrow A_1, ..., A_m$ is *connected* if for each $i, j \in [1..m]$, A_i, A_j are connected in $\{A_1, ..., A_m\}$. A program is *connected* if each rule is connected.

[5] Here we assume that there are unbounded number of constants.

We next consider ℓ-IB for a fixed ℓ. It turns out to be again undecidable which is interesting compared to the decidability of ℓ-boundedness.

Theorem 6.2. It is undecidable whether P is ℓ-IB w.r.t. q for arbitrary datalog programs P and arbitrary edb predicate q.

The proof is based on the following lemma, which shows that ℓ-boundedness for databases that are least models of some datalog program is undecidable.

Definition. For datalog programs P_α, P_β, P_α is ℓ-*bounded* ($\ell \geq 1$) w.r.t. P_β if for each set D of edb facts $T_{P_\alpha}^{\ell+1}(T_{P_\beta}^\omega(D)) \subseteq T_{P_\alpha}^\ell(T_{P_\beta}^\omega(D))$.

Lemma 6.3. Let $\ell \geq 1$ be fixed. It is undecidable if a program is ℓ-bounded w.r.t. another.

Proof. The proof is based on a reduction using a similar technique as in [11]. (The reduction simulates the checking of whether the input database describes a halting configuration of a Turing machine starting from an empty tape.) □

In view of the undecidability results, it is interesting to give some sufficient yet decidable conditions for ℓ-IB. In the following we provide a sufficient condition (in Proposition 6.5) which is based on "uniform query containment relative to a program P" ($\subseteq_P^u$).

Definition. Let P be a datalog program and Q_1, Q_2 two queries. Q_1 is *uniformly contained in Q_2 relative to P*, denoted $Q_1 \subseteq_P^u Q_2$, if for each model D of P, $Q_1(D) \subseteq Q_2(D)$.

Intuitively, the problem of uniform relative query containment is to consider containment under certain "integrity" constraints specified by some datalog program.

Lemma 6.4. For an arbitrary program P and two conjunctive queries Q_1, Q_2, it is decidable if $Q_1 \subseteq_P^u Q_2$. □

Thus the following provides a decidable sufficient condition for ℓ-IB:

Proposition 6.5. Suppose P is an arbitrary datalog program. Then P is ℓ-IB if, for each edb fact $A = q(\bar{a})$ where q occurs in P, $T_{P_A}^{\ell+1} \subseteq_P^u T_{P_A}^\ell$, where P_A is obtained as follows: For each rule r containing q in the rule body, add each rule r' to P_A, where r' is obtained by unifying one or more q atoms in the body of r with A. □

Acknowledgments

The authors are grateful to the anonymous referees for their helpful comments on an earlier version of the paper.

References

1. S. Abiteboul. Boundness is undecidable for datalog programs with a single recursive rule. *Inf. Process. Lett.*, 32(6), October 1989.

2. A. V. Aho, J. E. Hopcroft, and J. D. Ullman. *The Design and Analysis of Computer Algorithms*. Addison-Wesley Publishing Company, 1974.

3. V. Breazu-Tannen, P. Buneman, and S. Naqvi. Structural recursion as a query language. In *Proceedings of the Third International Workshop on Database Programming Languages: Bulk Types and Persistent Data*, pages 9–19, 1991.

4. S. Chaudhuri and M. Vardi. On the equivalence of recursive and nonrecursive datalog programs. In *Proc. ACM Symp. on Principles of Database Systems*, 1992.

5. G. Dong and J. Su. First-order incremental evaluation of datalog queries (extended abstract). In *Proc. 4th Int. Workshop on Database Programming Languages*, 1993.

6. G. Dong and J. Su. First-order on-line computation of transitive closure queries. In *Proc. of 16th Australian Computer Science Conference*, pages 721–729, 1993.

7. G. Dong, J. Su, and R. Topor. First-order incremental evaluation of datalog queries. Technical report, Dept. of Comp. Sci., Univ. of Melbourne, 1993. (Submitted to AMAI).

8. G. Dong and R. Topor. Incremental evaluation of datalog queries. In *Proc. Int'l Conference on Database Theory*, pages 282–296, Berlin, Germany, Oct. 1992.

9. H. Gaifman, H. Mairson, Y. Sagiv, and M. Y. Vardi. Undecidable optimization problems for database logic programs. *Journal of the Association for Computing Machinery*, 40(3):683–713, 1993.

10. A. Gupta, I. S. Mumick, and V. S. Subrahmanian. Maintaining views incrementally. In *Proc. ACM SIGMOD Int. Conf. on Management of Data*, pages 157–166, 1993.

11. G. Hillebrand, P. Kanellakis, H. Mairson, and M. Vardi. Undecidable boundedness problems for datalog programs. Technical Report RJ 8739, IBM Almaden Research Center, San Jose, CA, Apr. 1992.

12. G. Hillerbrand, P. Kanellakis, H. Mairson, and M. Vardi. Tools for Datalog boundedness. In *Proc. ACM Symp. on Principles of Database Systems*, 1991.

13. Y. Ioannidis. A time bound on the materialization of some recursively defined views. In *Proc. of Int. Conf. on Very Large Data Bases*, 1985.

14. J. Naughton and Y. Sagiv. A decidable class of bounded recursion. In *Proc. ACM Symp. on Principles of Database Systems*, pages 227–236, 1987.

15. S. Patnaik and N. Immerman. Dyn-FO: A parallel dynamic complexity class. In *Proc. ACM Symp. on Principles of Database Systems*, pages 210–221, 1994.

16. J. D. Ullman. *Database and Knowledge-Base Systems*, volume 1. Computer Science Press, 1988.

17. J. D. Ullman. *Database and Knowledge-Base Systems*, volume 2. Computer Science Press, 1989.

18. R. van der Meyden. Predicate boundedness of linear monadic datalog is in PSPACE. Technical Report SCS&E Report 9205, Univ. of New South Wales, 1992.

19. M. Vardi. Decidability and undecidability results for boundedness of linear recursive programs. In *Proc. ACM Symp. on Principles of Database Systems*, pages 341–351, 1988.

Approximation in Databases

Leonid Libkin

AT&T Bell Laboratories
600 Mountain Avenue, Murray Hill NJ 07974, USA
email: libkin@research.att.com

Abstract. One source of partial information in databases is the need to combine information from several databases. Even if each database is complete for some "world", the combined databases will not be, and answers to queries against such combined databases can only be approximated. In this paper we describe various situations in which a precise answer cannot be obtained for a query asked against multiple databases. Based on an analysis of these situations, we propose a classification of constructs that can be used to model approximations.

A major goal is to obtain universality properties for these models of approximations. Universality properties suggest syntax for languages with approximations based on the operations which are *naturally* associated with them. We prove universality properties for most of the approximation constructs. Then we use them to design languages built around datatypes given by the approximation constructs. A straightforward approach results in langauges that have a number of limitations. In an attempt to overcome those limitations, we explain how all the languages can be embedded into a language for conjunctive and disjunctive sets from [17], and demonstrate its usefulness in querying independent databases.

1 Introduction

The idea of using approximate answers to queries against databases with partial information has been known in the database literature for more than ten years. In his classical papers, Lipski [18, 19] suggested to use two approximations to answer queries for which a precise answer can not be found. The *lower approximation* consists of those objects for which one can conclude with certainty that they belong to the answer to the query. The *upper approximation* consists of those objects for which one can conclude that they may belong to the answer.

However, it was not until ten years later that it was observed by Buneman, Davidson and Watters [3] that those pairs of approximations may not only be regarded as results of query evaluation, but may also be used as a representation mechanism for certain kinds partial data. Moreover, this kind of partiality is different from traditional models such as null values and disjunctive information. If a query is asked against several databases, the combined database may not be complete even if each database is complete for some "world". Hence, incompleteness shows up in the form of an *answer to query*, rather than (or in addition to) incompleteness of the stored data as in the classical models.

Example: Querying independent databases

Simple approximations. Consider the following problem. Assume that we have access to two relations in a university database. These relations, Employees and CS1 (for teaching the course CS1), are shown below.

Assume that our query asks to compute the set TA of teaching assistants. Suppose that only TAs can teach CS1 and that every TA is a university employee. To make the example easier to understand, we make an assumption that the Name field is a key. We use nulls $\perp$ to make both relations have the same set of attributes. Let us outline how the TA query can be answered. Since every person in CS1 is a TA, CS1 gives us the certain part of the answer. Moreover, every TA is an employee, hence finding people in Employees who are not represented in CS1 gives us the possible part of the answer to the TA query.

Employees:

Name	Salary	Room
John	15K	$\perp$
Ann	17K	$\perp$
Mary	12K	$\perp$
Michael	14K	$\perp$

CS1:

Name	Salary	Room
John	$\perp$	076
Michael	$\perp$	320

A pair of relations CS1 and Employees is called a *sandwich* (for TA), cf. [3]. The Employees relation is *an upper bound:* every TA is an employee. The CS1 relation is *a lower bound:* every entry in CS1 represents a TA. We are looking for the set of TA – something that's in between; hence the name. Notice that the records in CS1 and Employees are *consistent:* for every record in CS1, there is a record in Employees consistent with it. That is, they are joinable (in the sense of [4, 24]) and their join can be defined. For example,

$$\boxed{\text{John}|15\text{K}|\perp} \vee \boxed{\text{John}|\perp|076} = \boxed{\text{John}|15\text{K}|076}$$

(Note that taking this join makes sense only if Name is a key.)

Hence, a sandwich (for a query Q) is a pair of relations U and L such that U is an upper bound or an upper approximation to Q, L is a lower bound or a lower approximation to Q, and U and L are consistent.

Let U and L be a pair of consistent relations. What is the semantics of the sandwich (U, L)? That is, the family of possible answers to Q that U and L approximate. To answer this question – at this stage, only informally – we appeal to the idea of representing partial objects as elements of ordered sets. In a graphical representation, ordered sets will be shown as triangles standing on one of their vertices that represents the minimal, or bottom element. The side opposite to it represents maximal elements. In our interpretation the order means "being more informative", and maximal elements correspond to complete descriptions, i.e. those that do not have any partial information at all.

The graphical representation of a sandwich (U, L) is shown in the first picture in figure 1. Trapezoids standing on U and L represent graphically elements of the whole space which are bigger than an element of U or L respectively. The semantics of a sandwich is a family of sets such as the one denoted by three bullets in the picture. Such sets X satisfy two properties. First, each element of the lower approximation contributes to at least one element of X, i.e. $\forall l \in L \exists x \in X : l \leq x$. Second, each element of X is approximated by an element of the upper approximation, i.e. $\forall x \in X \exists u \in U : u \leq x$.

In the example in figure 1, L is assumed to have two elements, each of them being under an element shown as a bullet, and those are in turn above some elements of U. Therefore, (U, L) satisfies the consistency condition.

Under the assumption that the Name field is a key, one can replace certain nulls in relations CS1 and Employees by corresponding values taken from the other relation. The reason is that certain tuples are joinable, and corresponding joins can be taken to infer missing values. One such join was shown above. Since Name is a key, we know that there is only one John and we assume that the

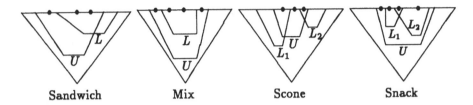

Figure 1. Models of approximations and their semantics

same John is represented by both databases. Hence we infer that he is in the office 076 and his salary is 15K. Similarly for Michael we infer that he is in the office 320 and his salary is 14K.

We can regard the newly constructed relations as another approximation for TA. But this one satisfies a much stronger consistency condition than sandwiches: every record in the lower approximation is at least as informative as some record in the upper approximation. Such pairs, called *mixes*, were introduced in [10]. Semantics of mixes is defined in·exactly the same way as semantics of sandwiches: we look at sets that represent all elements of the lower approximation and whose elements are representable by the upper approximation. In Figure 1, a set shown by four bullets is such.

Approximating by many relations. Let us consider a more complicated situation. Assume that CS1 has two sections: $CS1_1$ and $CS1_2$, and each section requires a teaching assistant. Assume that we have a pool of prospective TAs for each section that includes those graduate students who volunteered to TA for that section. Suppose that the selection of TAs has been made, and those selected have been entered in the database of employees, while the database of prospective TAs remained unchanged. This is represented by an example below:

Employees

Name	Salary	Room
John	15K	$\perp$
Ann	17K	$\perp$
Mary	12K	$\perp$
Michael	14K	$\perp$

$CS1_1$

Name	Salary	Room
John	$\perp$	076
Jim	$\perp$	$\perp$

$CS1_2$

Name	Salary	Room
Michael	$\perp$	320
Helen	$\perp$	451

Since all the selections have been made, at least one of prospective TAs for each section is now a TA, and therefore is represented in Employees. Thus, both $CS1_1$ and $CS1_2$ contain at least one entry consistent with the Employees relation. Hence, this new approximation differs from sandwiches and mixes in two ways.

1. The lower approximation is not a single relation but a *family of relations*.
2. The consistency condition does not postulate that all elements in the lower approximation are consistent with the upper approximation, but rather that there *exists* an element in each of the subrelations of the lower approximation that is consistent with the upper.

Such approximations are called *scones*, cf. [21]. We shall denote the lower approximation by $\mathcal{L}$ and its components by L_1, L_2 etc. The graphical representation of a scone with two-element $\mathcal{L}$ is shown in Figure 1.

The semantics of a scone is a family of sets X that satisfy two properties. First, each set in the lower approximation contributes at least one element to X. That is, $\forall L \in \mathcal{L} \exists l \in L \exists x \in X : l \leq x$. Second, each element of X is approximated by some element of U. This is the same condition as for mixes and sandwiches.

Now assume that the Name field is a key. Since there is no entry for Jim in Employees, then Jim could not have been chosen as a possible TA for a section of CS1. Similarly, Helen can be removed from $CS1_2$. Hence, one can remove Jim and Helen from $CS1_1$ and $CS1_2$ and infer some of the null fields as we did before in order to obtain mixes from sandwiches. In the new approximation that we obtain, the condition expressing consistency is much stronger: now every element of every set in the lower approximation is at least as informative as some element of the upper approximation. Such constructions are called *snacks*, see [20, 21]. (The reason for this name is that they were initially thought of as – not quite correctly, as we shall show – as "many sandwiches", hence snacks.)

The graphical representation of a snack with a two-element $\mathcal{L}$ is given in Figure 1. The semantics of snacks is defined precisely as the semantics of scones. For example, in Figure 1 the four-bullet set is in the semantics of $(U, \{L_1, L_2\})$. Thus, it is only the consistency condition that makes scones different from snacks.

Finally, what if we have arbitrary data coming from two independent databases that may not be consistent? For instance, there may be anomalies in the data that ruin various consistency conditions. Then we need a model that would not require any consistency condition at all. Such a model was introduced in [16]. Since it is in essence "all others put together", it is called *salad*.

Goals of the paper and organization. The main problem that we address in this paper is *building the general theory of approximate answers to queries against independent databases*. In particular, we address the following questions.

- What are the formal models of approximations? Is it possible to classify those models according to some general principle?
- Do approximations corresponds to (a combination of) known datatypes?
- How do we program with approximations?

Note that the problems of approximation have been studied by the datalog community; see, for example, [6, 7]. There are, however, major differences between the problems that are addressed. In papers like [6, 7] information is complete, and using approximations reduces the complexity of query evaluation. For example, upper and lower envelopes are defined as datalog programs whose result would always be superset (subset) of a given program P. If P is a recursive program, envelopes are usually sought in the class of conjunctive queries. Secondly, approximating relations are usually defined as subset or superset.

In contrast, in our approach the reason for approximating is incompleteness of information. Approximations arise as best possible answers to queries that one can get, and not as best answers that can be computed within a given complexity class. Moreover, the notions of approximations that arise are much more sophisticated than simple subsets and supersets.

The paper is organized in follows. In section 2 we explain the approach of [4, 15] to databases with partial information that treats database objects as subsets of some partially ordered space of descriptions. The meaning of the ordering is "being more informative". Then we explain a "data-oriented" paradigm for the query language design [5]. It is based on incorporating operations *naturally* associated with datatypes into a query language [2]. To find such operations, one describes the semantic domains of those datatype via *universality properties*.

In section 3 we use the ordered semantics to give formal models of approximations and classify them. The main part of the paper is section 4 in which we show that most of the constructs possess universality properties. This tells us what the important operations on approximations are. We also obtain results of a new kind, saying that some constructs do not possess universality properties.

In section 5 we discuss programming with approximation. We explain problems with using the data-oriented approach together with operations arising from the universality properties. Then we we suggest an encoding of approximation constructs with *or-sets* [14, 17] and explain how the language for or-sets from [17] is suitable for programming with approximations.

2 Preliminaries

Partial objects and ordered sets. Most models of partiality of data can be represented via orderings on values, e.g. [1, 13, 9]. In [4, 15, 17] a general approach to the treatment of partial information in the context of ordered sets has been developed. Here we present the basics of that approach.

First, elements of base types are ordered. For example, if there are three kinds of nulls – no information **ni**, existing unknown **un** and nonexisting **ne** – then the ordering is given by $\mathbf{ni} < \mathbf{un} < v$ and $\mathbf{ni} < \mathbf{ne}$, where v is any nonpartial value. For more examples, see [1, 4, 16].

Complex objects are constructed from the base objects by using the record and the set type constructors. Hence, one has to lift an order to records and sets. Lifting to records is done componentwise: [Name: Joe, Age:$\perp$] $\leq$ [Name: Joe, Age: 28]. Lifting an order to sets is harder. This problem also arises in the semantics of concurrency, where a number of solutions have been proposed, see [11]. Here we consider two, which turn out to be suitable for our problems. Given an ordered set $\langle A, \leq \rangle$, its subsets can be ordered by the *Hoare ordering* $\sqsubseteq^\flat$ (generalized subset) or the *Smyth ordering* $\sqsubseteq^\sharp$ (generalized superset):

$$X \sqsubseteq^\flat Y \Leftrightarrow \forall x \in X. \exists y \in Y. x \leq y \qquad X \sqsubseteq^\sharp Y \Leftrightarrow \forall y \in Y. \exists x \in X. x \leq y$$

In early work on representing partiality via orders, the problem of choosing the right ordering was not considered. Recently, in [17, 16] a theory for deciding which order is suitable for which collection was developed. It turns out that $\sqsubseteq^\flat$ is suitable for sets and $\sqsubseteq^\sharp$ is suitable for or-sets [14, 17]. Or-sets, denoted by the angle brackets, are sets of exclusive possibilities, i.e. [Name: Joe, Age:$\langle 25, 27 \rangle$] says that Joe is 25 or 27 years old.

Orderings suggest a natural approach to the *semantics of partiality*: an object may denote any other object that is above it. For example, [Name: Joe, Age:$\perp$] denotes the set $\{$[Name: Joe, Age:n] $\mid n \in \mathbb{N}\}$. Hence, we define the semantic function for the database objects of the same domain D as $\llbracket o \rrbracket = \{o' \in D \mid o' \geq o\}$. This semantics leads us to an important observation. Since sets are ordered by $\sqsubseteq^\flat$, then for any set X we have $\llbracket X \rrbracket = \llbracket \max X \rrbracket$, where $\max X$ is the set of maximal elements of X. For any or-set X we have $[X] = [\min X]$, where $\min X$ is the set of minimal elements of X. Elements of $\max X$ and $\min X$ are not comparable; such subsets of ordered sets are called *antichains*. Therefore, the ordered semantics suggests that the database objects are represented as antichains in certain posets, cf. [4, 15].

The idea of using orderings to represent partiality has been quite fruitful. A general theory of partial information based on orderings was developed in [16]. The reader is referred to [4, 16] for further examples.

Data-oriented programming. In this subsection we give an overview of the *data-orientation* as a programming language paradigm (cf. [5]) and demonstrate one instance of this approach: a language for sets.

Databases are designed using some data models, e.g. relational, complex object, etc. To program with data, it is necessary to represent the concept of a data model in a programming language. The best way to do it is to use *type systems*. This often allows *static type-checking* of programs which is particularly important in handling large data as run-time errors are very costly. To ensure that the type system is not too restrictive and does not limit the programmer's freedom, we allow all type constructors to be polymorphic, *e.g.* the set type constructor can be applied to any type, the product type constructor can be applied to any pair of types etc. For example, types of complex objects are given by the grammar $t ::= b \mid [l_1 : t, \ldots, l_n : t] \mid \{t\}$, where b ranges over base types.

It was suggested in [5] that one use *introduction* and *elimination* operations associated with a type constructor as primitives of a programming language. The introduction operations are needed to construct objects of a given type whereas the elimination operations are used for doing computations over them. For example, record formation is the introduction operation for records, and projections are the elimination operations.

Databases work with various kinds of collections. To find the introduction and elimination operations, it was suggested in [2] to look for operations *naturally* associated with collections. To do so, one often characterizes the semantic domains of collection types via *universality properties*, which tell us what the introduction and the elimination operations are.

Assume that we have a collection type constructor (like sets, bags etc.) that we denote by $C(\cdot)$ and a type t. By *universality property* we mean that the following is true about $[C(t)]$, the semantic domain of type $C(t)$ of collections of elements of type t. It is possible to find a set Ω of operations on $[C(t)]$ and a map $\eta : [t] \to [C(t)]$ such that for any other Ω-algebra $\langle X, \Omega \rangle$ and a map $f : [t] \to X$ there exists a unique Ω-homomorphism f^+ that makes the first diagram in figure 2 commute.

If we are successful in identifying η and Ω, then we can make them the *introduction* operations. The reason is that now any object of type $C(t)$ can be constructed from objects of type t by first embedding them into type $C(t)$ by means of η, and then constructing more complex objects using the operations from Ω. The *elimination* operation is a higher-order operation that takes f as an input and returns f^+.

Now let us see what these operations are for sets. The semantic domain of $\{t\}$ is $\mathbb{P}_{\text{fin}}([t])$, the finite powerset of elements of t. For any set X, $\mathbb{P}_{\text{fin}}(X)$ is the free semilattice generated by X. Thus, Ω consists of $\emptyset$ and $\cup$ and η is the singleton formation: $\eta(x) = \{x\}$ of type $t \to \{t\}$. Then f^+ is given by

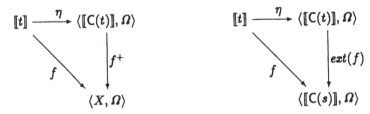

Figure 2. Structural recursion and *ext*

$$
\begin{aligned}
\textbf{fun } f^+[e,u](\emptyset) &= e \\
|\quad f^+[e,u](\{x\}) &= f(x) \\
|\quad f^+[e,u](A\cup B) &= u(f^+[e,u](A), f^+[e,u](B))
\end{aligned}
$$

This operation f^+, often called **structural recursion** [2], depends on e and u which are interpretations of the operations of Ω on its range. Notice that if e and u do not supply the range of f^+ with the structure of a semilattice, then f^+ may not be well-defined (see what happens if e is 0, f is $\lambda x.1$, and u is $+$.) To overcome this, one can require that e be interpreted as $\emptyset$ and u as $\cup$. Generally, the simplest way to ensure well-definedness is to require that $\langle X,\Omega\rangle$ be $\langle [\![C(s)]\!],\Omega\rangle$ for some type s. Thus, we obtain the second diagram in figure 2.

The unique completing homomorphism is called $ext(f)$, the extension of f. Its semantics in the case of sets is $ext(f)\{x_1,\ldots,x_n\} = f(x_1)\cup\ldots\cup f(x_n)$ (that is, it "extends" f to sets.) This function is well-defined. Using ext together with η, $\emptyset$, $\cup$, projections and record formation, conditional and the equality test gives us precisely the nested relational algebra [2] but the presentation is nicer than the standard ones, such as in [8]. This approach to the language design has proved extremely fruitful and allowed to solve some open problems and develop languages for other collections. The reader who is interested in other applications of this approach and in mathematical constructions behind it is referred to [23].

In order to apply the data-oriented paradigm to the approximation constructs, we first need formal models of those, and then the universality properties for those models.

3 Formal models of approximations

In this section we reexamine the approximation constructs by applying the idea of representing objects with partial information as elements of ordered sets. We need the notion of *consistency* in posets: $x,y\in A$ are consistent (written $x\updownarrow y$) if $x,y\le z$ for some $z\in A$. For records consistency means joinable, as in [24].

Recall that a *sandwich* is given by an upper approximation U and a lower approximation L that satisfy the following consistency condition: for every $l\in L$, there is $u\in U$ such that u and l are consistent. Representing objects in approximating sets as elements of some posets, we can formally define *sandwiches* over a poset $\langle A,\le\rangle$ as pairs (U,L) of finite antichains that satisfy the consistency condition: $\forall l\in L\,\exists u\in U: u\updownarrow l$ [3].

The consistency condition for mixes says that every element in the lower approximation is at least as informative as some element of the upper. Thus, a *mix* [10] over a poset $\langle A, \leq \rangle$ is a pair of finite antichains (U, L) satisfying the following consistency condition: $\forall l \in L \; \exists u \in U : u \leq l$ (*i.e.* $U \sqsubseteq^{\natural} L$.)

In a scone, the lower approximation is a family of sets. The consistency condition says that for each set in the lower approximation, at least one element is consistent with an element of the upper. Hence a *scone* [21] over $\langle A, \leq \rangle$ is a pair $(U, \mathcal{L})$ where U is a finite antichain, and $\mathcal{L} = \{L_1, \ldots, L_k\}$ is a family of finite nonempty antichains which is itself an antichain with respect to $\sqsubseteq^{\natural}$. That is, $L_i \not\sqsubseteq^{\natural} L_j$ if $i \neq j$. The consistency condition is $\forall L \in \mathcal{L} \; \exists l \in L \; \exists u \in u : u \Uparrow l$.

Snacks are obtained from scones exactly as mixes are obtained from sandwiches: by using the assumption about keys, additional information is inferred. Thus, the consistency condition is similar to that of mixes, and *snacks* [20, 21] can be defined as pairs $(U, \mathcal{L})$ where U is a finite antichain, and $\mathcal{L} = \{L_1, \ldots, L_k\}$ is a family of finite nonempty antichains which is itself an antichain with respect to $\sqsubseteq^{\natural}$. The consistency condition for snacks is $\forall L \in \mathcal{L} \; \forall l \in L \; \exists u \in u : u \leq l$.

One can see that there are three main parameters that may vary and give rise to new constructs. First, the lower approximation is either a set or a set of sets. Second, the consistency condition is of form

$$\mathbf{Q} l \in L \; \exists u \in U \; C(u, l) \quad \text{for simple lower approximations and}$$
$$\forall L \in \mathcal{L} \; \mathbf{Q} l \in L \; \exists u \in U \; C(u, l) \quad \text{for multi-set lower approximations,}$$

where $\mathbf{Q}$ is either $\forall$ or $\exists$ and $C(u, l)$ is a condition that relates u and l. Third, the condition $C(u, l)$ is either $u \leq l$ or $u \Uparrow l$.

Thus, we have eight constructions since each of the parameters – the structure of the lower approximation, the quantifier $\mathbf{Q}$ and the condition $C(u, l)$ – has two possible values. For constructs with a simple lower approximation we use notation $\mathcal{P}$, for constructs with multi-set lower approximation we use $\boldsymbol{\mathcal{P}}$. The superscript consists of the quantifier $\mathbf{Q}$, followed by $\wedge$ if $C(u, l)$ is $u \Uparrow l$. For constructs with no consistency condition we use the superscript $\emptyset$.

Ten possible constructs that arise are shown below. We denote the family of sandwiches over A by $\mathcal{P}^{\forall \wedge}(A)$, mixes by $\mathcal{P}^{\forall}(A)$, snacks by $\boldsymbol{\mathcal{P}}^{\forall}(A)$ etc.

L-part	type of consistency condition (quantifier–condition)				
	$\forall \quad u \leq l$	$\forall \quad u \Uparrow l$	$\exists \quad u \leq l$	$\exists \quad u \Uparrow l$	no condition
one set	$\mathcal{P}^{\forall}$ (mix)	$\mathcal{P}^{\forall \wedge}$ (sandwich)	$\mathcal{P}^{\exists}$	$\mathcal{P}^{\exists \wedge}$	$\mathcal{P}^{\emptyset}$
family of sets	$\boldsymbol{\mathcal{P}}^{\forall}$ (snack)	$\boldsymbol{\mathcal{P}}^{\forall \wedge}$	$\boldsymbol{\mathcal{P}}^{\exists}$	$\boldsymbol{\mathcal{P}}^{\exists \wedge}$ (scone)	$\boldsymbol{\mathcal{P}}^{\emptyset}$

Order and semantics. The approximation constructs being representations of partial data, they can be ordered themselves in terms of being more informative. We define $\sqsubseteq^{\mathbb{B}}$ and $\sqsubseteq^{\mathbb{B}}_f$, called *the Buneman orderings* [3, 10], as follows. ($\sqsubseteq^{\mathbb{B}}_f$ is used for *families* of sets in the lower approximations.)

$$(U, L) \sqsubseteq^{\mathbb{B}} (U', L') \text{ iff } U \sqsubseteq^{\natural} U' \text{ and } L \sqsubseteq^{\natural} L'$$
$$(U, \mathcal{L}) \sqsubseteq^{\mathbb{B}}_f (U', \mathcal{L}') \text{ iff } U \sqsubseteq^{\natural} U' \text{ and } \forall L \in \mathcal{L} \; \exists L' \in \mathcal{L}' : L \sqsubseteq^{\natural} L'$$

Claim. *The approximations must be ordered by the Buneman orderings.* $\quad\square$

The reader is referred to [16] for the rationale behind this claim. It is justified by proving the results similar to those proved in [17, 16] for sets, or-sets and bags. Thus, when we consider approximation constructs $\mathcal{P}^i(A)$ and $\boldsymbol{P}^i(A)$, where $i \in \{\forall, \exists, \forall\wedge, \exists\wedge, \emptyset\}$, we assume that they are ordered by $\sqsubseteq^{\boldsymbol{B}}$ and $\sqsubseteq^{\boldsymbol{B}}_{\boldsymbol{f}}$ respectively.

Because of the space limitation, we only offer the definition of the semantic functions. The reader is invited to apply them to the examples in section 1 and obtain sets of TAs that can be approximated by Employees and CS1. For simple approximations, $[\![(U, L)]\!]$ is defined as $\{X \in \mathbb{P}_{fin}(A) \mid U \sqsubseteq^{\flat} X$ and $L \sqsubseteq^{\flat} X\}$. For constructions with multi-element lower approximations $[\![(U, \mathcal{L})]\!]$ is defined as $\{X \in \mathbb{P}_{fin}(A) \mid U \sqsubseteq^{\flat} X$ and $\forall i : {\uparrow}L_i \cap X \neq \emptyset\}$.

4 Universality properties of approximations

The flavor of the results. Before we give the results about universality of $\mathcal{P}^i(A)$ and $\boldsymbol{P}^i(A)$, let us give a quick overview. The desired result would be to obtain the first diagram in figure 3, where $\eta(x) = (\{x\}, \{x\})$ for $\mathcal{P}^i(A)$ and $\eta(x) = (\{x\}, \{\{x\}\})$ for $\boldsymbol{P}^i(A)$. That is, every *monotone* map f can be extended to a *monotone homomorphism* f^+. Unfortunately, this is not always possible and here is the reason. Let $x{\uparrow}y$ in A. If $\mathcal{P}^{\forall\wedge}(A)$ or $\boldsymbol{P}^{\exists\wedge}(A)$ were free algebras generated by A, then there would be a way to construct the sandwich $(\{x\}, \{y\})$ and the scone $(\{x\}, \{\{y\}\})$ from the singletons $\eta(\cdot)$. But this way must use the information about consistency in A and therefore can not be "universal"!

Therefore, we shall settle for less by making the generating poset convey the information about consistency in A. We define the *consistent closure* of A as

$$A{\uparrow}A = \{(a, b) \mid a \in A, b \in A, a{\uparrow}b\}$$

The consistent closure of A can be embedded into $\mathcal{P}^i(A)$ and $\boldsymbol{P}^i(A)$ (where $i \in \{\exists\wedge, \forall\wedge\}$) by means of the functions $\eta^{\dagger}(x, y) = (\{x\}, \{y\})$ and $\eta^{\dagger}(x) = (\{x\}, \{\{y\}\})$. Since $A{\uparrow}A$ interacts in a certain way with the structure of approximations, we shall seek the result like the one in the second diagram in figure 3. In this case we say that $\mathcal{P}^i(A)$ or $\boldsymbol{P}^i(A)$ is freely generated by $A{\uparrow}A$ *with respect to the class C of monotone maps*.

We need two kinds of algebras defined in [22]. A *bisemilattice* $\langle B, +, \cdot \rangle$ is an algebra with two semilattice (idempotent, commutative, associative) operations. It is called *distributive* if both distributive laws hold. A *left normal band* $\langle B, * \rangle$ is an algebra with an idempotent associative operation $*$ such that $x*y*z = x*z*y$.

In what follows, we describe the algebras, admissibility conditions on functions that determine the class C (when needed), then give the interpretation of the algebraic operations, and then present the results.

Universality of $\mathcal{P}^{\vee}(A)$ (mixes)

Algebra. A *mix* algebra $\langle M, +, \square, e \rangle$ has partially ordered carrier M, one monotone binary operation $+$ and one monotone unary operation $\square$. $\langle M, +, e \rangle$ is a semilattice with identity e, and in addition the following equations must hold: 1) $\square(x + y) = \square x + \square y$. 2) $\square\square x = \square x$. 3) $\square x \leq x$. 4) $x + \square x = x$. 5) $x + \square y \leq x$.

Interpretation of operations. The ordering is interpreted as $\sqsubseteq^{\boldsymbol{B}}$. For the operations, $(U, L) + (V, M) = (\min(U \cup V), \max(L \cup M))$, $\square(U, L) = (U, \emptyset)$ and $e = (\emptyset, \emptyset)$.

Theorem 1 [10]. $\mathcal{P}^{\vee}(A)$ *is the free mix algebra generated by A.* $\qquad\square$

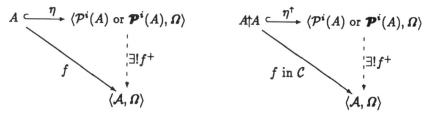

Figure 3. Universality results

Universality of $\mathcal{P}^{\vee\wedge}(A)$ (sandwiches)

Theorem 2. *For no Ω is $\mathcal{P}^{\vee\wedge}(A)$ the free ordered Ω-algebra generated by A.* $\square$

However, we can overcome this by using the consistent closure and mix algebras with the same interpretation of operations. Let M be a mix algebra. A monotone map $f : A{\uparrow}A \to M$ is called *admissible* (or sandwich-admissible) if $f(x,y) + f(z,y) \le f(x,y)$ and $\Box f(x,y) = \Box f(x,z)$.

Theorem 3. $\mathcal{P}^{\vee\wedge}(A)$ *is the free mix algebra generated by $A{\uparrow}A$ with respect to the admissible maps.* $\square$

Universality of $\mathcal{P}^{\exists}(A)$

Algebra. $\langle B, \oplus, * \rangle$ is called a *distributive bi-LNB algebra* if: 1) $\oplus$ and $*$ are left normal band operations. 2) All distributive laws between $*$ and $\oplus$ hold. 3) $a \oplus (b * c) = a \oplus b$. 4) $(a * b) \oplus b = (b * a) \oplus a$. Order: $a \le b := b \oplus a = a * b$.
Interpretation. $(U, L) \oplus (V, M) = (\min(U \cup V), L)$ and $(U, L) * (V, M) = (U, \max(L \cup M))$.

Theorem 4. $\mathcal{P}^{\exists}(A)$ *is the free distributive bi-LNB algebra generated by A.* $\square$

Universality of $\mathcal{P}^{\theta}(A)$

Algebra. In a *bi-mix* algebra $\langle B, +, \Box, \Diamond \rangle$, $\langle B, +, \Box \rangle$ is a mix algebra, $x = \Box x + \Diamond x$ and $\langle B, +, \Diamond \rangle$ is a dual mix algebra, i.e. $\Diamond$ is a closure ($\Diamond$ is monotone, $\Diamond x \ge x$, $\Diamond\Diamond x = \Diamond x$ and $\Diamond(x + y) = \Diamond x + \Diamond y$), and $x + \Diamond x = x$ and $x + \Diamond y \ge x$.
Interpretation. $+, \Box$ and e are interpreted as for mixes, and $\Diamond(U, L) = (\emptyset, L)$.

Theorem 5. $\mathcal{P}^{\theta}(A)$ *is the free bi-mix algebra generated by A.* $\square$

Universality of $\boldsymbol{P}^{\vee}(A)$ (snacks)

Algebra. A *snack* algebra is a bisemilattice $\langle B, +, \cdot \rangle$ in which $+$ has the identity e (i.e. $x + e = e + x = x$.) Order: $x \le y$ iff $x \cdot y = x$.
Interpretation. $(U, \mathcal{L}) + (V, \mathcal{M}) = (\min(U \cup V), \max^{!}(\mathcal{L} \cup \mathcal{M}))$ and $(U, \mathcal{L}) \cdot (V, \mathcal{M}) = (\min(U \cup V), \max^{!}\{\min(L \cup M) \mid L \in \mathcal{L}, M \in \mathcal{M}\})$ where $\max^{!}$ means family of maximal elements w.r.t. $\sqsubseteq^{!}$. e is interpreted as $(\emptyset, \{\emptyset\})$.

Theorem 6. (see also [22, 21]) $\boldsymbol{P}^{\vee}(A)$ *is the free snack algebra generated by A.*

Universality of $\boldsymbol{P}^{\vee\wedge}(A)$

Theorem 7. Let Ω_+ be a set of operations on $\boldsymbol{P}^{\vee\wedge}(A)$ such that $+$ is a derived operation. Then $\boldsymbol{P}^{\vee\wedge}(A)$ is not the free ordered Ω_+-algebra generated by A. $\quad\square$

Universality of $\boldsymbol{P}^{\exists}(A)$

Theorem 8. Let Ω_+ be a set of operations on $\boldsymbol{P}^{\exists}(A)$ such that $+$ is a derived operation. Then $\boldsymbol{P}^{\exists}(A)$ is not the free ordered Ω_+-algebra generated by A. $\quad\square$

Universality of $\boldsymbol{P}^{\exists\wedge}(A)$ (scones)

Algebra. A *scone* algebra is an algebra $\langle Sc, +, *, e\rangle$ where $+$ is a semilattice operation with identity e, $*$ is a left normal band operation, $+$ and $*$ distribute over each other, the absorption laws hold and $e * x = e$. In other words, a scone algebra is an "almost distributive lattice" – commutativity of one of the operations is replaced by the law of the left normal bands.

Order. $x \cdot y = x * y + y * x$ is a semilattice operation. Then $x \le y$ iff $x \cdot y = x$.

Interpretation. Operations $+$ and e are interpreted as for snacks and $(U, \mathcal{L}) * (V, \mathcal{M}) = (U, \max^\sharp\{\min(L \cup M) \mid L \in \mathcal{L}, M \in \mathcal{M}\})$.

Admissibility. A monotone function $f : A \to Sc$ from a poset A to a scone algebra Sc is called *scone-admissible* if, for any two consistent pairs $x\mathord{\uparrow}y_1$ and $x\mathord{\uparrow}y_2$ such that $x, y_i \le z_i, i = 1, 2$, the following holds:

$$(f(x) * e + f(z_1)) * f(y_1) * f(y_2) = (f(x) * e + f(z_2)) * f(y_1) * f(y_2)$$

A monotone map $f : A\mathord{\uparrow}A \to Sc$ is called *admissible* if $f(u, l) * f(v, m) = f(u, m) * f(w, l)$ and $f(u, l) * e = f(u, m) * e$.

Theorem 9. *1)* $\boldsymbol{P}^{\exists\wedge}(A)$ is the free scone algebra generated by $A\mathord{\uparrow}A$ with respect to the admissible maps.
2) $\boldsymbol{P}^{\exists\wedge}(A)$ is the free scone algebra generated by A with respect to the scone-admissible maps.
3) Let Ω_{Sc} be a set of operations on scones such that $+, *$ and e are derived operations. Then $\boldsymbol{P}^{\exists\wedge}(A)$ is not the free ordered Ω_{Sc}-algebra generated by A. $\quad\square$

Universality of $\boldsymbol{P}^{\emptyset}(A)$

Algebra. A *salad algebra* $\langle Sd, +, \cdot, \square, \Diamond\rangle$ has two semilattice operations $+$ and $\cdot$ and two unary operation $\square$ and $\Diamond$, and the following equations hold: 1) $x \cdot (y + z) = x \cdot y + x \cdot z$. 2) $x = \square x + \Diamond x$. 3) $\square(x + y) = \square x + \square y = \square x \cdot \square y = \square(x \cdot y)$. 4) $\Diamond(x + y) = \Diamond x + \Diamond y$. 5) $\Diamond(x \cdot y) = \Diamond x \cdot \Diamond y$. 6) $\square x \cdot \Diamond y = \square x$. 7) $\Diamond x \cdot \Diamond y + \Diamond x = \Diamond x$. 8) $\Diamond\Diamond x = \Diamond x$. 9) $\square\square x = \square x$.

Interpretation. $+$ and $\cdot$ are interpreted as for snacks, and $\square$ and $\Diamond$ as for $\mathcal{P}^{\emptyset}(A)$.

Theorem 10. $\boldsymbol{P}^{\emptyset}(A)$ is the free salad algebra generated by A. $\quad\square$

Summing up, there are four kinds of operations naturally associated with the approximations: union operations (like $+$), pairwise union operations (like $\cdot$), skewed versions of the above (like $\oplus$ and $*$) and modal operations ($\square$ and $\Diamond$.)

5 Programming with approximations

In this section we consider programming with approximations. First, we turn the universality properties of approximation constructs into programming syntax. The languages thus obtained have a number of drawbacks. To overcome their problems, we look at the semantic connection between approximations and sets and or-sets, that suggests an encoding of the approximation constructions.

Using universality properties. Because of the space limitations, we consider only mixes and sandwiches. We consider them as *type constructors*. That is, for any type t we now have new types t *mix* and t *sand* such that $[\![t\ mix]\!] = \mathcal{P}^\triangledown([\![t]\!])$ and $[\![t\ sand]\!] = \mathcal{P}^{\triangledown\wedge}([\![t]\!])$. Since mixes possess universality property, we can define structural recursion on them. Similarly, structural recursion can be defined on sandwiches, but the second clause must be different since sandwiches are generated by $A\!\uparrow\!A$ rather than A. See figure 4.

$$
\begin{array}{llll}
fun\ f^+(\emptyset,\emptyset) & = e & fun\ f^+(\emptyset,\emptyset) & = e \\
|\quad f^+(\eta(x)) & = f(x) & |\quad f^+(\eta^\uparrow(x,y)) & = f(x,y) \\
|\quad f^+(M_1 + M_2) & = u(f^+(M_1), f^+(M_2)) & |\quad f^+(S_1 + S_2) & = u(f^+(S_1), f^+(S_2)) \\
|\quad f^+(\square M) & = h(f^+(M)) & |\quad f^+(\square S) & = h(f^+(S))
\end{array}
$$

Figure 4. Structural recursion on mixes (left) and sandwiches (right)

Structural recursion has a number of parameters: in addition to f, they include e, u and h prescribing its action in all possible cases of constructing a new mix/sandwich. Similarly to the case of sets, one might ask if, by setting these parameters in such a way that they do not obey the laws of the equational theory, one may write ill-defined programs. This is indeed the case. In fact,

Theorem 11. *It is undecidable whether the structural recursion on mixes or sandwiches is well-defined for a given choice of e, u and h.* □

The solution that worked for sets was to impose syntactic restrictions on the general form of structural recursion. In the case of mixes a similar restriction yields $mix\_ext(f) = f^+[(\emptyset, \emptyset), f, +, \square]$ of type t *mix* $\to s$ *mix*, provided f sends elements of type t to s *mix*. But this alone does not eliminate the need to verify preconditions when we use the ordered semantics. Functions agree with the ordered semantics iff they are monotone [16]. Thus, monotonicity of f is needed for well-definedness of mix_ext. Now if we disregard the second components in mixes, then we obtain the structural recursion on sets. Hence, its restriction to the ext operator gives us the nested relational algebra. However,

Theorem 12. *If sets are ordered by $\sqsubseteq^\flat$, then it is undecidable whether the semantics of an expression in the nested relational algebra is a monotone function.*

We can observe the same phenomenon for other approximations. Thus, turning universality properties into syntax, we encounter a number of problems. Most operations used in the universality properties for approximations are not as intuitive as union or intersection. All approximations have different equational characterizations, and there are several forms of structural recursion and the *ext* primitives. A language that contains all of them is going to be too complicated to comprehend even for a theoretician, let alone a programmer. Verification of preconditions can not be taken care of by the compiler as the preconditions are undecidable – even for the *ext* operations when the ordered model is used. Therefore, we need a unifying framework for programming with approximations.

Using or-sets. Recall that or-sets are sets of disjunctive possibilities: an or-set $\langle 1, 2, 3 \rangle$ denotes an integer which is 1, or 2 or 3. A language or-$\mathcal{NRL}$ was proposed in [17]. Its type system includes, in addition to sets and records, the or-set type constructor $\langle t \rangle$. Its expressions include those in the nested relational algebra and an or-set analog for each set operation. In addition, there is an operation of type $\{\langle t \rangle\} \to \langle \{t\} \rangle$ which essentially converts a conjunctive normal form into disjunctive normal form by picking one element from each or-set in the input.

If we look at how approximations are ordered, and recall that $\sqsubseteq^\flat$ is used for sets and $\sqsubseteq^\natural$ is used for or-sets, then this suggests the following encoding of the approximation constructs. In fact, there is a very close semantic connection between or-sets and approximations that further justifies this connection [16].

Approximations	Encoding
t *mix*, t *sand* and similar	$\langle t \rangle \times \{t\}$
t *snack*, t *scone* and similar	$\langle t \rangle \times \{\langle t \rangle\}$

To show that this encoding can be used to program with approximations, let $\mathcal{L}_\star$ be the language obtained from the restricted form of structural recursion (*ext*) for each approximation $\star$ that admits a universality property. Then

Theorem 13. *Using the encoding of approximation constructs with sets and or-sets, the following can be expressed in or-$\mathcal{NRL}$.*
1. All operations on approximations arising from the universality properties.
2. Orderings on approximations and tests for the consistency conditions.
3. All languages $\mathcal{L}_\star$. □

This encoding has been used in practice. In [12] it was shown how OR-SML, an SML based DBPL whose core language is essentially or-$\mathcal{NRL}$ can be used to define the promotion operation of [3], which forces a sandwich into a mix using assumptions about keys. It was also shown that a simple change in the program allows to drop the key assumption, getting an or-set of possible solutions.

6 Conclusion

All existing papers on approximate answers to queries against independent databases ([3, 10, 20, 21]) did not address two important problems, which we have to look at in order to build a general theory. First, we need a classification of models. In each of those papers, only one or two models are considered. The second problem is programming with the approximation constructs. In its rudimentary form it was considered in [3], but no general principles were known.

Our goal was to address these two problems. Using the approach to partial information based on representing partiality via orders on objects, we have given formal models of approximate answers to queries. We have characterized most of the approximation constructs via their universality properties. Finally, we have used the operations given by the universality properties as primitives of a language, and shown that the language arising this way can be embedded into the language for conjunctive and disjunctive sets from [17].

A number of open problems remain. For two constructs no universality results are known, and we strongly suspect that negative results can be proved. Standard procedures for querying independent databases, implemented in the language of [17], admit some interesting optimizations that must be further studied. It may be interesting to explore the connection between our approach and more traditional work on approximations [6, 7] that was mentioned earlier.

Acknowledgements. I would like to thank Peter Buneman, Tim Griffin, Carl Gunter, Elsa Gunter, Paris Kanellakis, Hermann Puhlmann, Anna Romanowska and especially Achim Jung for their help.

References

1. J. Biskup. A formal approach to null values in database relations. In: *"Advances in Data Base Theory"*, Volume 1, Prenum Press, New York, 1981.
2. V. Breazu-Tannen, P. Buneman, and L. Wong. Naturally embedded query languages. In *LNCS 646: Proc. ICDT-92*, pages 140–154, Springer-Verlag.
3. P. Buneman, S. Davidson, A. Watters. A semantics for complex objects and approximate answers. *JCSS* 43(1991), 170–218.
4. P. Buneman, A. Jung, A. Ohori. Using powerdomains to generalize relational databases. *Theoretical Computer Science* 91(1991), 23–55.
5. L. Cardelli. Types for data-oriented languages. In *LNCS 303: Proc. EDBT-88*.
6. S. Chaudhuri. Finding nonrecursive envelopes for database predicates. In *PODS-93*, pages 135–146.
7. S. Chaudhuri, Ph. Kolaitis. Can Datalog be approximated? In *PODS-94*, pages 86–96.
8. L. Colby. A recursive algebra for nested relations. *Inf. Syst.* 15 (1990), 567–582.
9. G. Grahne. *"The Problem of Incomplete Information in Relational Databases"*. Springer, Berlin, 1991.
10. C. Gunter. The mixed powerdomain. *Theoretical Computer Science* 103 (1992), 311–334.
11. C. Gunter. *"Semantics of Programming Languages"*. The MIT Press, 1992.
12. E. Gunter and L. Libkin. OR-SML: A functional database programming language for disjunctive information and its applications. *LNCS 856: Proc. DEXA-94*, pages 641–650.
13. T. Imielinski and W. Lipski. Incomplete information in relational databases. *J. ACM* 31(1984), 761–791.
14. T. Imielinski, S. Naqvi, and K. Vadaparty. Incomplete objects — a data model for design and planning applications. In *Proc. SIGMOD-91*, pages 288–297.
15. L. Libkin. A relational algebra for complex objects based on partial information. In *LNCS 495: Proc. MFDBS-91*, pages 36–41, Springer-Verlag.
16. L. Libkin. *"Aspects of Partial Information in Databases"*. PhD Thesis, University of Pennsylvania, 1994.
17. L. Libkin and L. Wong. Semantic representations and query languages for or-sets. In *PODS-93*, pages 37–48.
18. W. Lipski. On semantic issues connected with incomplete information in databases. *ACM Trans. Database Systems* 4 (1979), 262–296.
19. W. Lipski. On databases with incomplete information. *J. ACM* 28 (1981), 41–70.
20. T.-H. Ngair. *"Convex Spaces as an Order-theoretic Basis for Problem Solving"*. Technical Report MS-CIS-92-60, University of Pennsylvania, 1992.
21. H. Puhlmann. The snack powerdomain for database semantics. In *LNCS 711: Proc. MFCS-93*, Springer Verlag, 1993, pages 650–659.
22. A. Romanowska and J.D.H. Smith. *"Modal Theory: An Algebraic Approach to Order, Geometry and Convexity"*. Heldermann Verlag, Berlin, 1985.
23. V. Tannen. Tutorial: Languages for collection types. In *PODS-94*, pages 150–154.
24. C. Zaniolo. Database relations with null values. *JCSS* 28 (1984), 142–166.

Datalog Queries of Set Constraint Databases

Peter Z. Revesz

Department of Computer Science and Engineering
University of Nebraska–Lincoln, Lincoln, NE 68588, USA

Abstract. Extension of the relational database model to represent complex data has been a focus of much research in recent years. At the same time, an alternative extension of the relational database model has proposed using constraint databases that finitely describe infinite relations. This paper attempts to combine these two divergent approaches. In particular a query language called Datalog with set order constraints, or $Datalog^C\mathbf{P(Z)}$, is proposed. This language can express many natural problems with sets, including reasoning about inheritance hierarchies. $Datalog^C\mathbf{P(Z)}$ queries over set constraint databases are shown to be evaluable bottom-up in closed form and to have DEXPTIME-complete data complexity.

1 Introduction

Many non-traditional applications, such as computer-aided design and scientific databases, require storing and reasoning with complex-objects. The same applications also tend to require efficient constraint-solving over various numerical domains. There are several new data model and query language proposals that address either of the two requirements separately. For example, object-oriented query languages and extensions of rule-based languages with sets address the former and constraint logic programming and constraint query languages address the latter requirement.

The present paper addresses both requirements. It combines CLP\CQL style constraint solving with non-finite, non-atomic data types, namely sets over the finite and infinite subsets of the integers. A different approach that goes beyond the CLP\CQL style and addresses both requirements is considered within the "constraint objects" model of [27]. Also, [1, 12] survey the use of set constraints in different aspects of program analysis.

There are several logic programming languages that allow the use of set type data, for example, LDL [29], CORAL [24], and ELPS [22]. These languages however do not allow the use of set constraints within the input (or output) database. The purpose of this paper is to consider the generalization of Datalog with set order constraints permitted within both the database and the program. The resultant language, $Datalog^C\mathbf{P(Z)}$, fits well within both the constraint logic programming [14] and the constraint query languages [18] frameworks that allow the use of finitely representable infinite relations.

The latter framework advocates set-at-a-time bottom-up evaluation of queries in closed-form. A closed-form means that all possible tuple answers to a query are represented finitely by an output constraint database that has the same type of constraints as the input constraint database. The advantage of this is that set-at-a-time processing is faster, requires less access to secondary storage [19] and closed-form evaluation allows the addition of aggregate operators as is done recently in [8]. However, even without the addition of aggregate operators constraint query languages can be quite expressive.

Many types of non-ground databases were used before in both constraint logic programming and constraint query languages in general (e.g. [2, 4, 9, 10, 11, 13, 15, 17, 23, 25, 26, 28, 30]) and with particular view to temporal database applications (e.g. [3, 6, 7, 16, 20, 21]). However, constraint databases with set order constraints were not considered before. As the following example shows many interesting problems can be solved using set order constraints.

Example 1.1 Consider the inheritance hierarchy in Figure 1. This inheritance hierarchy is more complicated than traditional ones, because it contains *indefinite information*. Each class in the hierarchy has some lower and upper bounds on its set of elements. The lower bound tells only which persons are in the class, while the upper bound tells which persons may be in the class. Any set in between the two is a possible solution. For example, the given constraint for the Employee class allows two possible solutions, one is $\{Al, Bob, Carl\}$ the other is $\{Al, Bob, Carl, Dave\}$. (We use character strings instead of ID numbers to make the example clearer.)

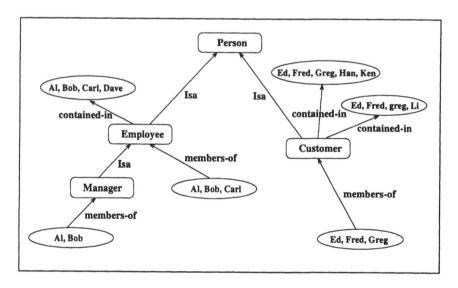

Figure 1: The inheritance hierachy

Suppose we also know that *Joe* is not a customer, which is an information that is not represented in the inheritance hierarchy. Then all the informations can be represented in a constraint database as shown below.

$root(Person)$
$subclass(1, Person, Employee)$
$subclass(2, Person, Customer)$
$subclass(1, Employee, Manager)$

$no\_subclasses(Person, 2)$
$no\_subclasses(Employee, 1)$
$no\_subclasses(Manager, 0)$
$no\_subclasses(Customer, 0)$

$inbounds(Person, \hat{p})$
$inbounds(Employee, \hat{e}) := \{Al, Bob, Carl\} \subseteq \hat{e}, \hat{e} \subseteq \{Al, Bob, Carl, Dave\}$
$inbounds(Manager, \hat{m}) := \{Al, Bob\} \subseteq \hat{m}$
$inbounds(Customer, \hat{c}) := \{Ed, Fred, Greg\} \subseteq \hat{c}, \hat{c} \subseteq \{Ed, Fred, Greg, Li\},$
$\qquad\qquad\qquad\qquad\quad \hat{c} \subseteq \{Ed, Fred, Greg, Han, Ken\}, Joe \notin \hat{c}$

$next(0, 1)$
$next(1, 2)$

A natural question is to find the tightest lower and upper bounds for each class implied by the entire inheritance hierarchy. This can be done by:

$upper\_bound(c_2, \hat{s_2}) := subclass(n, c_1, c_2), upper\_bound(c_1, \hat{s_1}), \hat{s_2} \subseteq \hat{s_1},$
$\qquad\qquad\qquad\qquad inbounds(c_2, \hat{s_2})$
$upper\_bound(c, \hat{s}) \quad := root(c), inbounds(c, \hat{s})$

$lower\_bound(c, \hat{s}) := inbounds(c, \hat{s}) lower\_bound2(n, c, \hat{s}), no\_subclasses(c, n).$
$lower\_bound2(n, c, \hat{s}) := lower\_bound2(m, c, \hat{s}), lower\_bound(c_2, \hat{s_2}), \hat{s_2} \subseteq \hat{s}$
$\qquad\qquad\qquad\qquad next(m, n), subclass(n, c, c_2)$
$lower\_bound2(0, c, \hat{s})$

The intuitive idea is that the upper bound of a superclass is also an upper bound of its subclasses. Similarly, the lower bound of a subclass is a lower bound of its superclass. For example, the program will find the upper bound for the class Manager to be $\hat{m} \subseteq \{Al, Bob, Carl, Dave\}$, and the lower bound for the class Person to be $\{Al, Bob, Carl, Ed, Fred, Greg\} \subseteq \hat{p}$. $\square$

A generally accepted measure of performance of a query evaluation is *data complexity*, which was introduced by Chandra and Harel [5], and by Vardi [31]. Data complexity measures the complexity of answering a fixed query in terms of the size of the database. The rationale behind data complexity is that the size of the database dominates the query size by several orders of magnitude for most applications. For example, the program above can remain fixed and the size of the inheritance network may still grow to include hundreds of classes.

This paper shows that for $Datalog^C P(Z)$ queries the least model and the fixpoint semantics coincide (Theorem 4.1). Moreover, a finite representation of the fixpoint can be computed bottom-up in closed form in an algebraic manner (Theorem 4.2).

This paper also shows that $Datalog^C P(Z)$ queries have DEXPTIME-complete data complexity (Theorem 4.5). In addition, the tuple recognition problem for $Datalog^{C}\mathbf{P}(\mathbf{Z})$ queries can be done in DEXPTIME in general (Theorem 4.3) and in linear NSPACE for piecewise linear queries (Theorem 4.4).

Section 2 describes some basic definitions. Section 3 describes an algebra for set order constraint databases. Section 4 presents the closed form query evaluation algorithm, the fixpoint theorem, the tuple and the data complexity results. Section 5 compares $Datalog^{C}\mathbf{P}(\mathbf{Z})$ with related languages. Finally Section 6 lists some open problems.

2 Basic Concepts

Let $\mathbf{N}$ denote the set of natural numbers and $\mathbf{Z}$ the set of integers. For any $D \subseteq \mathbf{Z}$, we denote by $P(D)$ the set $\{B : B \subseteq D\}$, by $\overline{P(D)}$ the set $\{\mathbf{Z} \setminus B : B \subseteq D\}$, and by $P(D)^{+}$ the set $P(D) \cup \overline{P(D)}$.

Let $\hat{v}, \hat{u}$ be set variables. Set variables range over the *intensional domain* $P(\mathbf{Z})$. A *set-order constraint* is of the form $\hat{u} = \hat{v}, \hat{u} \subseteq \hat{v}, \hat{c} \not\subseteq \hat{v}$ where $\hat{c} \in \mathbf{P}(\mathbf{Z})$, $c \in \hat{v}$ or $c \notin \hat{v}$ where $c \in \mathbf{Z}$. The relations $=, \subseteq, \not\subseteq$ are interpreted as the usual ordering on sets of integers. We interpret $c \in \hat{v}$ as equivalent to $\{c\} \subseteq \hat{v}$, and $c \notin \hat{v}$ as equivalent to $\hat{v} \subseteq \{\mathbf{Z} \setminus c\}$.

Our database framework is set up as follows. Let $\phi(\hat{x_1}, \ldots, \hat{x_k})$ be a conjunction of set order constraints over distinct variables $\hat{x_1}, \ldots, \hat{x_k}$. We call ϕ a *constraint tuple*. We call an expression of the form $A(\hat{x_1}, \ldots, \hat{x_k}) :\!- \phi(\hat{x_1}, \ldots, \hat{x_k})$ a *generalized relational tuple*, where $\hat{x_1}, \ldots, \hat{x_k}$ are distinct variables, and A is a relation symbol with arity k. We consider each generalized relation to be a finite set of generalized relational tuples.

We view each generalized relational tuple $A(\hat{x_1}, \ldots, \hat{x_k}) :\!- \phi(\hat{x_1}, \ldots, \hat{x_k})$ as a finite decription for a possibly infinite number of ground relational tuples $A(t_1), \ldots, A(t_n)$, where each $t_i \in P(\mathbf{Z})^k$ and t_i satisfies ϕ, i.e. $t_i \models \phi$ in the standard sense. Therefore, we are dealing with special types of unrestricted (finite or infinite) relational databases with basic data type of sets of integers instead of integers.

Note 1. As the inheritance hierarchy example shows, we may use both integer and set of integers data types in a query. This could be easily done by fixing each argument of a relation to be either of type $\mathbf{Z}$ or of type $\mathbf{P}(\mathbf{Z})$. For simplicity in the rest of this abstract we assume that the data type of each argument in each relation is $\mathbf{P}(\mathbf{Z})$.

The syntax of $Datalog^{C}\mathbf{P}(\mathbf{Z})$ programs we consider is that of traditional Datalog where the bodies of the rules can also contain a conjunction of set order constraints. More precisely, a $Datalog^{C}\mathbf{P}(\mathbf{Z})$ program P is a finite set of rules of the form:

$$A_0 :\!- A_1, A_2, \ldots, A_l.$$

where the expression A_0 (the rule *head*) must be an atomic formula of the form $R(\hat{x_1}, \ldots, \hat{x_n})$, and the expressions $A_1, \ldots, A_l$ (the rule *body*) must be atomic formulas of the form $R(\hat{x}_1, \ldots, \hat{x}_n)$ where R is some predicate symbol, or a set order constraint described above.

2.1 Set-Graphs

For this section let D be any fixed finite set of integers. We start with the basic definitions of *set-orders* and *set-graphs*.

Definition 2.1 Let $\hat{x}$ and $\hat{y}$ be any two integer set variables. Given some assignment to the variables, a *set-order* constraint $\hat{x} \subseteq \hat{y}$ holds if and only if $\hat{x}$ is contained in $\hat{y}$. A *set-order* constraint $\hat{x} = \hat{y}$ holds if and only if $\hat{x}$ and $\hat{y}$ are equal in the given assignment. □

Definition 2.2 Let $\hat{x}_1, \ldots, \hat{x}_n$ be a set of integer set variables. Then a *set-graph* is any graph that has n vertices labeled $\hat{x}_1, \ldots, \hat{x}_n$ and at most 2^D other vertices with distinct labels that are elements of $P(D)^+$ and has between any pair of distinct vertices at most one undirected edge labeled by $=$ or one directed edge labeled by a set-order $\subseteq$. □

In the following we will always assume when talking about edges that an edge labeled by $=$ is undirected and an edge labeled by $\subseteq_g$ is directed. The direction in the latter case is necessary only to make it clear which vertex is contained in the other. We will assume that if a directed edge from vertex $\hat{v}$ to another vertex $\hat{u}$ has label $\subseteq$ on it, then $\hat{v} \subseteq \hat{u}$ is the set-order constraint that is represented within the set-graph. Two examples of set-graphs are shown in Figure 2.

Definition 2.3 A set-graph G is *consistent* if and only if there is a sets of integers assignment $\mathcal{A}$ to the variables in the vertices that satisfies all the set-order labels on the edges. We denote this as $\mathcal{A} \models G$. □

Set-Graphs provide an alternative representation of generalized tuples which are conjunctions of integer set-order constraints. That is spelled out in Lemma 2.1. which helps to simplify the problem of evaluating $Datalog^C \mathbf{P}(\mathbf{Z})$ queries. We can assume later that the generalized input database has only set-graphs as generalized tuples.

Lemma 2.1 Let C be any conjunction of set-order constraints over variables $\hat{x}_1, \ldots, \hat{x}_k$, integer set constants and constraints $=, \subseteq$. Let D be the union of all integer constants in C. Then
(a) C can be represented as a finite disjunction of set-graphs over vertices labeled by $\hat{x}_1, \ldots, \hat{x}_k$ and elements of $P(D)^+$. Moreover, any assignment $\mathcal{A}$ satisfies C if and only if $\mathcal{A}$ is a consistent assignment to at least one of the set-graphs in the representation.
(b) In each set-graph, each variable is equal to exactly one set constant or has at most one set constant lower bound and at most one set constant upper bound. □

3 An Algebra for Relations in Set-Graph Form

In this section we describe the three basic operations on set-graphs. These operations are called *shortcut* (Definition 3.1), *merge* (Definition 3.2), and *subsume* (Definition 3.3).

Based on the shortcut and the merge operators, we define later the *generalized project* and the *generalized natural join* operators that work on generalized relations composed of a finite number of set-graphs. These replace the corresponding operators of relational algebra, while the subsume operator replaces duplicate elimination.

Definition 3.1 Let G be a set-graph with vertices $\hat{y}, \hat{v}_1, \ldots, \hat{v}_n, \hat{L}_y, \hat{U}_y, \hat{L}_1,$ $\hat{U}_1, \ldots, \hat{L}_n, \hat{U}_n$, where each $\hat{L}_i, \hat{U}_i \in P(D)^+$. Then a *shortcut* operation over vertex $\hat{y}$ transforms G into an output set-graph over vertices $\hat{v}_1, \ldots, \hat{v}_n$ and $\hat{L}'_1, \hat{U}'_1, \ldots, \hat{L}'_n, \hat{U}'_n$ as follows.

First, for each $0 < i, j, \leq n$ do the following.

If $\hat{v}_i = \hat{y}$ and $\hat{y} = \hat{v}_j$ are edges in G, then add $\hat{v}_i = \hat{v}_j$ as undirected edge to G.
If $\hat{v}_i = \hat{y}$ and $\hat{y} \subseteq \hat{v}_j$ are edges in G, then add $\hat{v}_i \subseteq \hat{v}_j$ as a directed edge to G.
If $\hat{v}_i \subseteq \hat{y}$ and $\hat{y} = \hat{v}_j$ are edges in G, then add $\hat{v}_i \subseteq \hat{v}_j$ as a directed edge to G.
If $\hat{v}_i \subseteq \hat{y}$ and $\hat{y} \subseteq \hat{v}_j$ are edges in G, then add $\hat{v}_i \subseteq \hat{v}_j$ as a directed edge to G.

For each vertex combine all lower bounds into one. Do the same for the upper bounds. Check that the constraint between $\hat{L}_y$ and $\hat{U}_y$ holds. If it does not hold, then do not return a set-graph. Otherwise delete $\hat{L}_y$ and $\hat{U}_y$ if they become isolate vertices.

Second, if $\hat{v}_i \subseteq \hat{v}_j$ and $\hat{v}_j \subseteq \hat{v}_i$, then delete these directed edges and replace them with $\hat{v}_j = \hat{v}_i$. Also delete $\hat{y}$ and all edges incident on $\hat{y}$. □

The intuition behind the shortcut operation is that just erasing $\hat{y}$ and the edges incident on $\hat{y}$ is not enough, because they imply set-order constraints about other vertices and that information would be lost. We need to explicitly preserve that information. The first part of the operation does exactly that. It is easy to see that it tests all possible cases in which two edges incident on $\hat{y}$ can imply a new set-order constraint.

The first part only adds (undirected or directed) edges to the graph. As a result of the first part, it could happen that the graph will have multiple edges between some pair of vertices $\hat{v}$ and $\hat{w}$. The second part cleans up these multiple edges. It deletes all directed edges from $\hat{v}$ to $\hat{w}$ except the one with the largest set-order constraint. By symmetry, it does the same for all directed edges from $\hat{w}$ to $\hat{v}$. Note that the set-graph returned by the shortcut operation may be inconsistent by Definition 2.3. Consistency is not checked by the shortcut operation.

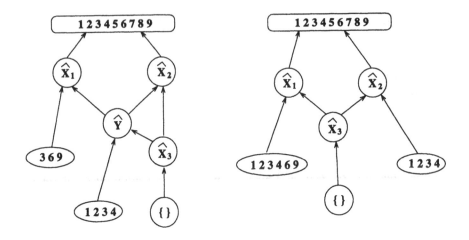

Figure 2: Example of a shortcut

An example of the shortcut operation is shown in Figures 2. The input set-graph is on the left, and the set-graph obtained by shortcutting over vertex $\hat{y}$ is on the right. Besides deleting $\hat{y}$ the shortcut creates two new edges from $\{1, 2, 3, 4\}$ to $\hat{x}_1$ and from $\{1, 2, 3, 4\}$ to $\hat{x}_3$. However, the first edge will be combined with the already existing lower bound for $\hat{x}_1$.

Definition 3.2 Let G_1 and G_2 be two set-graphs over some (maybe different) subsets of the variables $\hat{v}_1, \ldots, \hat{v}_n$ and the set constants $c_1, \ldots, c_{4n}$, where each $c_i \in P(D)^+$. Then a *merge* operation on G_1 and G_2 creates a set-graph G with vertices $\hat{v}_1, \ldots, \hat{v}_n, \hat{L}_1, \hat{U}_1, \ldots, \hat{L}_n, \hat{U}_n$ as follows. First, for each vertex $\hat{v}_i$ that occurs in both G_1 and G_2 combine the lower bounds. Do the same for the upper bounds. Second, for each $0 < i, j \le n$ do the following.

If there is no edge between $\hat{v}_i$ and $\hat{v}_j$ in G_1 and G_2, then do nothing.
If there is an edge between $\hat{v}_i$ and $\hat{v}_j$ in only one of G_1 or G_2, then add that edge to G.
If $\hat{v}_i = \hat{v}_j$ is an edge in both G_1 and G_2, then add $\hat{v}_i = \hat{v}_j$ as an edge to G.
If $\hat{v}_i \subseteq \hat{v}_j$ in G_1 and $\hat{v}_i = \hat{v}_j$ in G_2 are edges, then add $\hat{v}_i = \hat{v}_j$ as an edge to G.
If $\hat{v}_i \subseteq \hat{v}_j$ in G_1 and $\hat{v}_i \subseteq \hat{v}_j$ in G_2 are edges, then add $\hat{v}_i \subseteq \hat{v}_j$ as an edge to G.
If $\hat{v}_i \subseteq \hat{v}_j$ in G_1 and $\hat{v}_j \subseteq \hat{v}_i$ in G_2 are edges, then add $\hat{v}_i = \hat{v}_j$ as an edge to G.
□

For the merge operation any assignment that satisfies the output set-graph should satisfy both of the input set-graphs. This is ensured by checking that the corresponding edges in the two input set-graphs are compatible and by adding always the edge which has the stricter set-order constraint to the output.

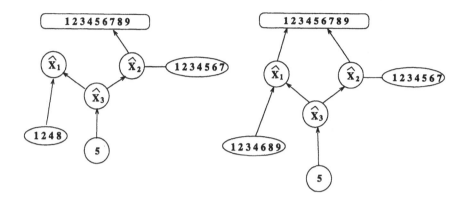

Figure 3: Example of a merge

An example of the merge operation is shown in Figure 3. The input set-graphs are the one on the right of Figure 2 and the one on the left of Figure 3. The result of the merge is shown on the right of Figure 3.

Definition 3.3 Let G_1 and G_2 be two set-graphs over the same set of variables $\hat{v}_1, \ldots, \hat{v}_n$ and set constants $\hat{L}_1, \hat{U}_1, \ldots, \hat{L}_n, \hat{U}_n$, where each $\hat{L}_i, \hat{U}_i \in P(D)^+$.

We say that G_1 *subsumes* G_2 when either (1) $\hat{v}_i \subseteq \hat{v}_j$ or $\hat{v}_i = \hat{v}_j$ is an edge in G_2 exactly when $\hat{v}_i \subseteq \hat{v}_j$ is an edge in G_1 or (2) $\hat{v}_i \subseteq \hat{v}_j$ is an edge in both G_1 and G_2. $\square$

For set-graph A to subsume another set-graph B, for each corresponding directed edge A must have a larger set-order constraint than B has. We now show the semantic correctness of the operations defined, that is, we show that the operations are consistency preserving.

Lemma 3.1 Let G be a set-graph over variables $\hat{y}, \hat{v}_1, \ldots, \hat{v}_n$ and constants $\hat{L}_y, \hat{U}_y, \hat{L}_1, \hat{U}_1, \ldots, \hat{L}_n, \hat{U}_n$, where each $\hat{L}_i, \hat{U}_i \in P(D)^+$. Let G' be the set-graph obtained by shortcutting over $\hat{y}$ in G (if exists). Let $\hat{a}_0, \hat{a}_1, \ldots, \hat{a}_n$ be any sequence of integer sets. Then $\hat{a}_0, \hat{a}_1, \ldots, \hat{a}_n \models G$ if and only if G' exists and $\hat{a}_1, \ldots, \hat{a}_n \models G'$. $\square$

For the merge operation we want to show that the *and* of the input set-graphs is consistent if and only if the output set-graph is consistent.

Lemma 3.2 Let G_1 and G_2 be two set-graphs over some (maybe different) subsets of the variables $\hat{v}_1, \ldots, \hat{v}_n$ and over constants $\hat{L}_1, \hat{U}_1, \ldots, \hat{L}_{2n}, \hat{U}_{2n}$, where each $\hat{L}_i, \hat{U}_i \in P(D)^+$. Let G be the set-graph obtained by merging G_1 and G_2 (if exists). Then for any assignment $\mathcal{A} = \{\hat{a}_1, \ldots, \hat{a}_n\}$, $\mathcal{A} \models G_1$ and $\mathcal{A} \models G_2$ if and only if G exists and $\mathcal{A} \models G$. $\square$

For the subsume operation we want to show that if $\mathcal{A}$ is a consistent assignment to a set-graph G, then $\mathcal{A}$ is also a consistent assignment to any set-graph that G subsumes. Note that the reverse may not be true. Our evaluation method uses only the first direction.

Lemma 3.3 Let G_1 and G_2 be two set-graphs over variables $\hat{v}_1, \ldots, \hat{v}_n$ and set constants $\hat{L}_1, \hat{U}_1, \ldots, \hat{L}_n, \hat{U}_n$, where each $\hat{L}_i, \hat{U}_i \in P(D)^+$. If G_1 subsumes G_2, then for any assignment $\mathcal{A} = \{\hat{a}_1, \ldots, \hat{a}_n\}$ if $\mathcal{A} \models G_1$, then $\mathcal{A} \models G_2$. $\square$

We say that a relation is in set-graph form if it consists of a set of set-graphs. We also say that a program is in set-graph form if the conjunction of set order constraints in each rule forms a set-graph. Similarly to Lemma 2.1, it is possible to transform each program to set-graph form. Let R be a relation in set-graph form with arity k. Then we define the generalized project operation $\hat{\pi}_{\hat{x}_i} R$ as returning the set of consistent set-graphs in R with all but the ith variable shortcut over. This then can be generalized to projecting out several variables at a time.

Similarly, let R_1 and R_2 be two relations in set-graph form. Then we define the generalized join operation on the two relations, denoted $R_1 \bowtie R_2$, as the set of consistent set-graphs that results from pairwise merging set-graphs in R_1 with set-graphs in R_2.

4 A Query Evaluation Algorithm for $Datalog^C\mathbf{P}(\mathbf{Z})$

Next we describe the query evaluation algorithm. The input of the query evaluation algorithm is a $Datalog^C\mathbf{P}(\mathbf{Z})$ program over a generalized database in set-graph form. The output of the query evaluation algorithm is another generalized database in set-graph form.

Each set-graph with k variables is a finite representation of a possibly infinite set of set constant tuples, i.e., G represents $\{(\hat{c}_1, \ldots, \hat{c}_k) : (\hat{c}_1, \ldots, \hat{c}_k) \models G\}$. Clearly, a set of set constant tuples can be represented by many different disjunctions of set-graphs. However, we define the model of programs independent of any particular representation.

Definition 4.1 Let $\mathcal{M}$ be the set of all possible set constant tuples over the integers. Let P be a $Datalog^C\mathbf{P}(\mathbf{Z})$ program and d be a database in set-graph form. Let $\mathcal{D}$ be the set of set constant tuples implied by d. The function T_P from and into $\mathcal{M}$ is defined as follows.
$T_P(\mathcal{D}) = \{t \in \mathcal{M} :$ there is a rule $R_0 :- R_1, \ldots, R_k, C$ in P and an instantiation θ
such that $R_0\theta = t$, $R_i\theta \in \mathcal{D}$ for each $1 \leq i \leq k$, and $C\theta$ holds.$\}$
Now we prove that for $Datalog^C\mathbf{P}(\mathbf{Z})$ programs the least model and the least fixpoint coincide.

Theorem 4.1 For any $Datalog^C\mathbf{P}(\mathbf{Z})$ program P, Least Model of P = Least Fixpoint of T_P. $\square$
Next we show that the least fixpoint can be computed in finite time, in an algebraic manner by the following algorithm.

Query Evaluation Algorithm
INPUT: $Datalog^C\mathbf{P}(\mathbf{Z})$ program P and a set of set-graphs G_i for each database

relation R_i. For the defined relations $G_i = \emptyset$.
OUTPUT: The least fixpoint model of P in set-graph form.
REPEAT

For each i let $H_i = G_i$.
For each rule r_j of the form $R_0(\hat{x}_1, \ldots, \hat{x}_m) :\!- R_1(\ldots), \ldots, R_k(\ldots), C$
in P, where $R_0, R_1, \ldots, R_k$ are relation symbols, C is a set-graph, and
the set of variables in the rule is $S = \{\hat{x}_1, \ldots, \hat{x}_m, \hat{y}_1, \ldots, \hat{y}_n\}$ do the
following:
(1) $F_j = \rho_{j,1}(G_1) \bowtie \ldots \bowtie \rho_{j,k}(G_k) \bowtie C$.
(2) $F'_j = \hat{\pi}_{\hat{x}_1, \ldots, \hat{x}_m} F_j$.
(3) Delete all inconsistent set-graphs from F'_j
(4) Add to G_0 each set-graph in F'_j that does not subsume another in
G_0.

UNTIL $H_i = G_i$ for each i
In the algorithm each ρ is a renaming operator fitting to a fixed subgoal of a
rule.

Theorem 4.2 Let Q be any $Datalog^C P(Z)$ program and let d be any database
in set-graph form. Let $\mathcal{D}$ be the set of set constant tuples implied by d. The
query evaluation algorithm will find a closed form for $Q(d)$ which is a finite
representation of the fixpoint of T_P on $\mathcal{D}$. $\square$
Next we consider the upper bound of the problem of tuple recognition.

Theorem 4.3 For any fixed $Datalog^C P(Z)$ program Q with output relation A,
variable database d, and set constant tuple $(\hat{c}_1, \ldots, \hat{c}_k)$, we can test whether
$A(\hat{c}_1, \ldots, \hat{c}_k) \in \mathcal{M}_Q$ in DEXPTIME in the size of d. $\square$
A tighter bound can be shown for *piecewise linear* programs.

Theorem 4.4 For any fixed piecewise linear $Datalog^C P(Z)$ program Q with out-
put relation A and variable database d, we can test whether $A(\hat{c}_1, \ldots, \hat{c}_k) \in \mathcal{M}_Q$
in NSPACE(n) where n is the size of d. $\square$
Let's consider now the data complexity of query evaluation.

Theorem 4.5 There is a fixed yes/no program Q in $Datalog^C P(Z)$ such that
deciding whether $Q(d)$ is yes for variable database d is DEXPTIME-complete.

Proof. The upper bound follows by Theorem 4.3. The lower bound is by simulation of deterministic exponential time bounded Turing machines. At first we
show that we can express the successor function for values between 1 and 2^s
using only $O(s)$ space. The idea is to encode the binary notation of each number as some subset of $\{s1, s0, \ldots, 21, 20, 11, 10\}$, where $i1$ or $i0$ will be present
according to whether in the binary encoding the ith digit from the right is 1 or
0, respectively. For example, let $s = 4$. Then the number 9 can be represented
as $\{41, 30, 20, 11\}$.

We first create a relation $digit(\hat{n}, \hat{i}, \hat{x})$ which is true if and only if in the binary notation of n the ith digit from the right is x.

$digit(\hat{n}, \{1\}, \{0\}) :— 10 \in \hat{n}, 11 \notin \hat{n}.$
$digit(\hat{n}, \{1\}, \{1\}) :— 11 \in \hat{n}, 10 \notin \hat{n}.$

$\ldots$

$digit(\hat{n}, \{s\}, \{0\}) :— s0 \in \hat{n}, s1 \notin \hat{n}.$
$digit(\hat{n}, \{s\}, \{1\}) :— s1 \in \hat{n}, s0 \notin \hat{n}.$

We also add to the input database the facts $next(\{0\}, \{1\}), \ldots, next(\{s - 1\}, \hat{s})$ and the fact $no\_digits(\{s\})$ and $time\_bound(\{s1, \ldots, 11\})$ that describe that we have s binary digits in each number and the largest number is 2^s. Note that the size of the database is $O(s)$. Now we express the successor relation $succ(\hat{n}, \hat{m})$ which is true if and only if $m = n + 1$ for any $n, m \leq 2^s$.

$succ(\hat{n}, \hat{m}) \qquad :— succ2(\hat{n}, \hat{m}, \hat{s}), no\_digits(\hat{s}).$

$succ2(\hat{n}, \hat{m}, \hat{i}) \qquad :— succ2(\hat{n}, \hat{m}, \hat{j}), next(\hat{j}, \hat{i}), digit(\hat{n}, \hat{i}, \hat{x}), digit(\hat{m}, \hat{i}, \hat{x}).$
$succ2(\hat{n}, \hat{m}, \{1\}) :— digit(\hat{n}, \{1\}, \{0\}), digit(\hat{m}, \{1\}, \{1\}).$
$succ2(\hat{n}, \hat{m}, \hat{i}) \qquad :— succ3(\hat{n}, \hat{m}, \hat{j}), next(\hat{j}, \hat{i}), digit(\hat{n}, \hat{i}, \{0\}), digit(\hat{m}, \hat{i}, \{1\}).$

$succ3(\hat{n}, \hat{m}, \hat{i}) \qquad :— succ3(\hat{n}, \hat{m}, \hat{j}), next(\hat{j}, \hat{i}), digit(\hat{n}, \hat{i}, \{1\}), digit(\hat{m}, \hat{i}, \{0\}).$
$succ3(\hat{n}, \hat{m}, \{1\}) :— digit(\hat{n}, \{1\}, \{1\}), digit(\hat{m}, \{1\}, \{0\}).$

During the simulation the successor relation will be used for counting the current position on the tape and the running time. □

5 Comparison with Other Languages

It is worthwhile to compare $Datalog^{C}P(Z)$ with the Datalog with integer order query language $Datalog^{<}Z$. In [25] the data complexity of $Datalog^{<}Z$ queries is shown to be in PTIME if the size of each constant in the database is logarithmic in the size of the entire database and to be in DEXPTIME in general. In [10] the expression complexity in general is shown to be DEXPTIME-complete. We show that the data complexity in general is also DEXPTIME-complete.

Theorem 5.1 There is a fixed yes/no program Q in $Datalog^{<}Z$ such that deciding whether $Q(d)$ is yes for variable database d is DEXPTIME-complete.

Proof. The upper bound is from [25]. The proof of the lower bound is similar to Theorem 4.5. Hence we only show that the digit relation can be expressed. The idea is to represent each number i by a pair of constraints: $-1 <_i x$ and $x <_{2^s - (i+1)} 2^s$.

We start by representing the value of each digit using a constraint interval, where the gap-value is one less than the actual value. For example, the value of the fifth digit from the right we represent as: $weight(5, s_1, s_2) :— s_1 <_{15} s_2$

We also add to the input database the facts $next(0, 1), \ldots, next(n-1, n)$ and $no\_digits(s)$. Note that each number can be expressed as the sum of a subset of the values of the n digits. Hence the digit relation can be expressed as follows.

$$single\_integer(n) :- no\_digits(s), digit(n, n, s, d)$$
$$digit(x_3, x_2, j, 1) :- next(i, j), digit(x_1, x_2, j, d), weight(j, x_1, x_3)$$
$$digit(x_1, x_3, j, 0) :- next(i, j), digit(x_1, x_2, j, d), weight(j, x_3, x_2)$$
$$digit(x_1, x_2, 0, 0) :- -1 < x_1, x_2 < 2^s$$

□

An interesting difference between $Datalog^C P_{(Z)}$ and $Datalog^< Z$ is that the former is DEXPTIME-hard even if the size of each constant in the database is logarithmic in the size of the entire database.

It is also interesting to see what happens when we retrict $Datalog^C P_{(Z)}$ programs to be *safe* and apply them only to ground non-first-normal form databases. Here safety means the restriction that in each rule each argument variable in the head relation must occur as an argument variable of one of the relations in the rule body. This restriction prevents creation of new sets not in the input database. Hence, for any fixed query, the number of tuples we can have in the output relation is only a polynomial in the size of the input database. Therefore:

Theorem 5.2 Safe $Datalog^C P_{(Z)}$ programs over databases in which each relation is a set of set constant tuples have PTIME data complexity. □

6 Open Problems

We presented $Datalog^C P_{(Z)}$ queries as a first step towards incorporating complex objects into constraint logic programming. There are many open questions regarding nesting within sets. How could that be incorporated? Also, it is possible to have set operators like *union* allowed in the queries if they are restricted to certain binding patterns or "adorments". Can suitable "capture rules" be developped for such programs? Toman et al. [28] combine periodicity constraints with integer gap-order constraints. Is it possible to have the three types of constraints in the same language? What would be the data complexity of the resulting language?

References

1. A. Aiken. Set Constraints: Results, Applications and Future Directions. *Proc. 2nd Workshop on Principles and Practice of Constraint Programming*, 171–179, 1994.
2. F. Afrati, S.S. Cosmadakis, S. Grumbach, G.M. Kuper. Linear vs. Polynomial Constraints in Database Query Languages. *Proc. 2nd Workshop on Principles and Practice of Constraint Programming*, 152–160, 1994.
3. M. Baudinet, M. Niette, P. Wolper. On the Representation of Infinite Temporal Data and Queries. *Proc. 10th ACM PODS*, 280–290, 1991.
4. A. Brodsky, J. Jaffar, M. J. Maher. Toward Practical Constraint Databases, *Proc. VLDB*, 1993.

5. A.K. Chandra, D. Harel. Computable Queries for Relational Data Bases. *Journal of Computer and System Sciences*, 21:156–178, 1980.
6. J. Chomicki. Polynomial Time Query Processing in Temporal Deductive Databases. *Proc. 9th ACM PODS*, 379–391, 1990.
7. J. Chomicki, T. Imielinski. Finite Representation of Infinite Query Answers. *ACM Transactions of Database Systems*, 181–223, vol. 18, no. 2, 1993.
8. J. Chomicki, G. Kuper. Measuring Infinite Relations, *Proc. Workshop on Constraints and Databases*, 1994.
9. A. Colmerauer. *An Introduction to Prolog III. CACM*, 28(4):412–418, 1990.
10. J. Cox, K. McAloon. Decision Procedures for Constraint Based Extensions of Datalog. In: *Constraint Logic Programming*, MIT Press, 1993.
11. M. Dincbas, P. Van Hentenryck, H. Simonis, A. Aggoun, T. Graf, and F. Berthier. The Constraint Logic Programming Language CHIP. *Proc. Fifth Generation Computer Systems*, 1988.
12. N. Heintze, J. Jaffar. Set Constraints and Set-Based Analysis. *Proc. 2nd Workshop on Principles and Practice of Constraint Programming*, 1-17, 1994.
13. S. Grumbach, J Su. Finitely Representable Databases. *Proc. 13th ACM PODS*, 289–300, 1994.
14. J. Jaffar, J.L. Lassez. Constraint Logic Programming. *Proc. 14th ACM POPL*, 111–119, 1987.
15. J. Jaffar, S. Michaylov, P.J. Stuckey, R.H. Yap. The CLP(R) Language and System. *ACM Transactions on Programming Languages and Systems*, 14:3, 339-395, 1992.
16. F. Kabanza, J-M. Stevenne, P. Wolper. Handling Infinite Temporal Data. *Proc. 9th ACM PODS*, 392–403, 1990.
17. P.C. Kanellakis, D.Q. Goldin. Constraint Programming and Database Query Languages. *Proc. 2nd TACS*, 1994.
18. P. C. Kanellakis, G. M. Kuper, P. Z. Revesz. Constraint Query Languages. *Proc. 9th ACM PODS*, 299–313, 1990. Final version to appear in *Journal of Computer and System Sciences*.
19. P.C. Kanellakis, S. Ramaswamy, D.E. Vengroff, J.S. Vitter. Indexing for Data Models with Constraints and Classes *Proc. 12th ACM PODS*, 1993.
20. M. Koubarakis. Representing and Querying in Temporal Databases: the Power of Temporal Constraints. *Proc. Ninth International Conference on Data Engineering*, 1993.
21. M. Koubarakis. Complexity Results for First-Order Theories of Temporal Constraints. *Int. Conf. on Knowledge Representation and Reasoning*, 1994.
22. G. M. Kuper. Logic Programming with Sets. *Journal of Computer and System Sciences*, 41, 44-64, 1990.
23. J. Paradeans, J. Van den Bussche, D. Van Gucht. Towards a Theory of Spatial Database Queries. *Proc. 13th ACM PODS*, 279–288, 1994.
24. R. Ramakrishnan, D. Srivastava, S. Sudarshan. CORAL: Control, Relations and Logic. *Proc. VLDB*, 1992.
25. P. Z. Revesz. A Closed Form Evaluation for Datalog Queries with Integer (Gap)-Order Constraints, *Theoretical Computer Science*, vol. 116, no. 1, 117-149, 1993. (Preliminary version in *3rd ICDT*, 185–201, 1990.)
26. D. Srivastava. Subsumption and Indexing in Constraint Query Languages with Linear Arithmetic Constraints. *Proc. 2nd International Symposium on Artificial Intelligence and Mathematics*, 1992.

27. D. Srivastava, R. Ramakrishnan, P.Z. Revesz. Constraint Objects. *Proc. 2nd Workshop on Principles and Practice of Constraint Programming*, 274–284, 1994.
28. D. Toman, J. Chomicki, D.S. Rogers. Datalog with Integer Periodicity Constraints. *Proc. ILPS*, 1994.
29. S. Tsur and C. Zaniolo. LDL: A Logic-Based Data-Language. *Proc. VLDB*, pp 33-41, 1986.
30. P. Van Hentenryck. *Constraint Satisfaction in Logic Programming*. MIT Press, 1989.
31. M. Vardi. The Complexity of Relational Query Languages. *Proc. 14th ACM Symposium on the Theory of Computing*, 137–145, 1982.

Space Usage in Functional Query Languages

Serge Abiteboul and Gerd Hillebrand

INRIA Rocquencourt, BP 105, F-78153 Le Chesnay cedex, France

Abstract. We consider evaluation strategies for database queries expressed in three functional query languages: the complex value algebra, the simply typed lambda calculus, and method schemas. Each of these query languages derives its expressive power from a different primitive: the complex value algebra from the *powerset* operator, the simply typed lambda calculus from *list iteration*, and method schemas from *recursion*. We show that "natural" evaluation strategies for these primitives may lead to very inefficient space usage, but that with some simple optimizations many queries can be evaluated with little or no space overhead. In particular, we show: (1) In the complex value algebra, all expressions with set nesting depth at most 2 can be evaluated in PSPACE, and this set of expressions is sufficient to express all queries in the polynomial hierarchy; (2) In the simply typed lambda calculus with equality and constants, all query terms of order at most 5 (where "query term" is a syntactic condition on types) can be evaluated in PSPACE, and this set of terms expresses exactly the PSPACE queries; (3) There exists a set of second-order method schemas (with no simple syntactic characterization) that can be evaluated in PSPACE, and this set of schemas is sufficient to express all PSPACE queries.

1 Introduction

A number of database languages with a functional flavor have been proposed, including, for instance, relational algebra [9] and FQL [6]. The algebra for complex values [1], which generalizes Codd's Algebra, is of the style [4] based on a small set of operations that can be composed. An alternative approach based on variables and λ-abstractions is used in [15]. Yet a third one with an object-oriented flavor is considered in the method schema model of [2]. These approaches seem to lead to a very inefficient use of space. In this paper, we present techniques for avoiding (or at least limiting) waste of space in the complex value algebra, λ-calculus, and method schema frameworks.

In the complex value algebra, we reconsider a nice result of [24] that states that any algebraic query expressing transitive closure essentially requires exponential space if evaluated naturally. We exhibit an evaluation technique that allows to compute a large class of queries (including TC) using only polynomial space. For such queries, we avoid computing powersets but instead produce a stream of elements that are treated by subsequent operators. More precisely, the tree of the algebraic expression can be viewed as a tree-network of processors with one processor for each vertex in the expression. Data flows through the edges of the tree towards the root. Each processor has a polynomial space local memory and produces the result of evaluating the corresponding subexpression as a stream that goes to its parent in the tree.

The algebra wastes space for two reasons: (1) the functional framework (and that is somewhat corrected by our technique), (2) the lack of explicit recursion/iteration, which has to be simulated using *powerset*. The other two languages that are considered provide iteration and recursion, respectively. In both cases, we can show that within PSPACE, we can avoid unnecessary waste of space. The techniques in both cases come down to representing functions extensionally as tables. These tables can be viewed in some sense as the relations used in a fixpoint evaluation.

We study the evaluation of database queries expressed in Church's *simply typed λ-calculus* [8] with equality and constants, TLC$^=$ for short. The computation of PTIME queries was considered in [14]. It was shown that the order 4 fragment of TLC$^=$ expresses exactly the PTIME queries. The proofs are based on an order-efficient representation of relational algebra and fixpoint queries as λ-terms and a space- and time-efficient evaluation strategy for such terms. We generalize here these techniques to define a space-efficient evaluation strategy for the order 5 fragment of TLC$^=$. Indeed, we provide a characterization of PSPACE in terms of the order 5 fragment of TLC$^=$. As a consequence, all PSPACE problems can be computed in this functional language using polynomial space and not more.

Finally, we extend the method schemas of [2] to allow higher-order methods, which can receive other methods as arguments and which may return methods. We show that second-order method schemas can simulate *while* queries (and thus express all PSPACE queries) and that with a space-efficient evaluation strategy, the simulation can be carried out in PSPACE. However, our evaluator cannot evaluate *all* second-order method schemas in PSPACE, so at this point we do not know whether second-order method schemas express exactly the PSPACE queries.

The paper is organized as follows. Each of the next three sections addresses one particular paradigm. Section 2 deals with the algebra for complex values, Section 3 with the simply typed λ-calculus, and Section 4 with method schemas. Since the techniques used for method schemas are similar to those introduced in Section 3, our presentation in Section 4 will be mostly informal and sketchy. We conclude in Section 5 with a summary of the paper and with some directions for further research.

2 The Complex Value Algebra

In this section, we first recall the algebra and calculus for complex values [1]. We then discuss how some simple queries are evaluated in this algebra "naturally" with a poor usage of space. We finally present techniques to improve space usage. In particular, we present a general evaluator that computes all queries with "set-nesting 2" in polynomial space.

Let us briefly review the relevant definitions. We assume the existence of the following countably infinite and pairwise disjoint sets of atomic elements: relation names $\{R_1, R_2, \ldots\}$, attributes $\{A_1, A_2, \ldots\}$, constants $D = \{d_1, d_2, \ldots\}$. The abstract syntax and the interpretations of *sorts* are given by:

1. $\sigma = D \mid \langle B_1 : \sigma, \ldots, B_k : \sigma \rangle \mid \{\sigma\}$, where $k \geq 0$ and $B_1, \ldots, B_k$ are distinct attributes,
2. $[\![D]\!] = D$
3. $[\![\{\sigma\}]\!] = \{\{v_1, \ldots, v_j\} \mid v_i \in [\![\sigma]\!], i = 1, \ldots, j\}$,
4. $[\![\langle B_1 : \sigma_1, \ldots, B_k : \sigma_k \rangle]\!] = \{\langle B_1 : v_1, \ldots, B_k : v_k \rangle \mid v_j \in [\![\sigma_j]\!], j = 1, \ldots, k\}$,

where σ denotes a sort and $[\![\sigma]\!]$ its interpretation. An element of a sort is called a *complex object*. A complex object of the form $\langle \ldots \rangle$ (resp., $\{\ldots\}$) is said to be a *tuple* (resp., a *set*). The tuple fields are viewed as unordered. We therefore do not distinguish, for instance, between sorts $\langle A : D, B : D \rangle$ and $\langle B : D, A : D \rangle$, or between objects $\langle A : 2, B : 2 \rangle$ and $\langle B : 2, A : 2 \rangle$. Note also that (because of the empty set) a complex object may belong to more than one sort.

A *(database) schema* is a pair $(\mathcal{R}, \mathcal{S})$ where $\mathcal{R}$ is a set of relation names and $\mathcal{S}$ is a function from $\mathcal{R}$ to sorts. A *(database) instance* $\mathcal{I}$ of a schema $(\mathcal{R}, \mathcal{S})$ is a function from $\mathcal{R}$ such that:

$$\text{for each } R \text{ in } \mathcal{R}, \mathcal{I}(R) \in [\![\{\mathcal{S}(R)\}]\!].$$

The *complex value algebra*, denoted by ALG^{cv}, is a (many-sorted) algebra extending relational algebra to complex values. It contains set operations (e.g., intersection, union, difference, setting, set flattening) that include a powerset operation, tuple operations (e.g., selection, projection, tupling, tuple flattening), and cross product. For a definition of these operations and others, see [1].

The *complex value calculus*, denoted by CALC^{cv}, is a (many sorted) calculus based on higher-order logic over finite domains. For each sort, we assume the existence of a countably infinite set of variables of that sort. Let $(\mathcal{R}, \mathcal{S})$ be a schema. A constant or a variable is a *term*. If $t_1, \ldots, t_k$ are terms and $B_1, \ldots, B_k$ distinct attributes, then $\langle B_1 : t_1, \ldots, B_k : t_k \rangle$ is a term; furthermore, if the t_i are of the same sort, $\{t_1, \ldots, t_k\}$ is a term. The sorts of terms are defined in the obvious way. (Note again that a term may have several sorts because of the empty set.) A *positive literal* is an expression of the form: (1) $R(t)$, where $R \in \mathcal{R}$ and t is of sort $\mathcal{S}(R)$, (2) $t = t'$, or (3) $t \in t'$ (with the appropriate sort restrictions[1]). *Formulas* are defined from atomic formulas using the standard connectors and quantifiers: $\wedge, \vee, \neg, \forall, \exists$. A *query* is an expression of the form $\{x \mid \psi\}$ where x is the only free variable in ψ. The *answer* to a query q on an instance $\mathcal{I}$, denoted $q(\mathcal{I})$, is defined analogously to the relational model. We assume that the domain consists of only those constants occurring in $\mathcal{I}$, so the answer to a query is always finite.

The equivalence of the algebra and the calculus has been shown in [1]. A similar result for the (in some sense more general) logical data model was shown earlier [22]. It is also known [19, 21] that ALG^{cv} (respectively, CALC^{cv}) expresses the *elementary queries*, i.e., the queries that are computable [7] in hyperexponential time (space) with respect to the database size.

---

[1] Strictly speaking, the symbols $=$ and $\in$ are also many sorted.

An essential difference between relational calculus and complex value calculus is that the latter can express transitive closure [1] whereas the former cannot [3]. Indeed, this is done very simply with the following CALC^{cv} query:

$$\{y \mid \forall x(closed(x) \wedge contains\_R(x) \rightarrow y \in x)\}$$

where

- $closed(x) \equiv \forall u, v, w (\langle A\colon u, A'\colon v\rangle \in x \wedge \langle A\colon v, A'\colon w\rangle \in x \rightarrow \langle A\colon u, A'\colon w\rangle \in x)$,
- $contains\_R(x) \equiv \forall z(R(z) \rightarrow z \in x)$,
- $sort(x) = \{sort(R)\}$, $sort(y) = sort(z) = sort(R)$, $sort(u) = sort(v) = sort(w) = \mathbf{dom}$.

Intuitively, the formula specifies the set of pairs y such that y belongs to each binary relation x containing R and transitively closed. It is interesting to consider the algebraic expression for transitive closure proposed in [1]. In a schematic form, it looks like:

$$\bigcap \sigma(powerset(D \times D)),$$

where D is a query computing the set of domain elements and σ a query expression filtering the relations that contain R and are closed transitively. The operator $\bigcap$ takes the intersection of the relations that passed the test. Observe that this construction requires by essence exponential space in the database size because of powerset. Indeed, in a recent paper [24], it is shown that "any expression in ALG^{cv} needs exponential space to compute transitive closure." Now, let us examine this statement more closely. There is a basic assumption underlying it: expressions are evaluated in the "natural" manner; and for this particular style of evaluation, TC requires exponential space. We are concerned here with more sophisticate evaluation techniques that allow for a better management of space.

We consider three such evaluation strategies. The first two are of little interest and are here only to highlight the limits of what we may expect to prove:

The cheater evaluator. By [26], we know that PSPACE corresponds to partial fixpoint logic (or the language *while*). There is a simple way of coding partial fixpoint queries into complex value expressions. The evaluator, called *cheater*, works as follows. Before starting the computation, *cheater* tests whether this is (syntactically) a translation of a partial fixpoint. If yes, the query is evaluated using PSPACE. Otherwise, the standard (perhaps exponential space) computation is performed. Therefore,

For each query q in PSPACE, there is an expression in ALG^{cv} that computes q and is evaluated by *cheater* in PSPACE.

From this, it is clear that evaluators have to be ranked also by the esthetics of the optimization.

The second-order logic evaluator. Given an expression in the powerset algebra like the one for transitive closure above, we can translate it into a calculus expression. Then, one can check whether this calculus expression is in second-order logic, i.e., whether quantifications are over domain elements or sets of domain elements (not sets of sets). If yes, one can evaluate the expression in

PSPACE. Otherwise, we go with the standard evaluation. Using this technique, we have a slightly weaker "result" since some PSPACE queries (e.g., quantified formula) would require exponential space unless the polynomial hierarchy (PH) and PSPACE coincide.

We next consider a last evaluator called the *space-careful evaluator*. This evaluator provides a generic optimization technique that (sometimes) allows to avoid going to exponential space. To simplify, we first assume that an ordering of the domain elements is provided. We will remove this assumption at the end of the section.

The only operation that introduces exponential space is *powerset*. The space-careful evaluator avoids when possible to compute a powerset—when this cannot be avoided, the standard potentially EXPSPACE computation is used. Our evaluator only works for expressions of set nesting 2. (We consider "deeper" expressions at the end of the section.) The *set nesting* of an algebraic expression is n if the type-tree of each intermediary result has at most n set-constructions on any path from the root to a leaf. For instance, $\{\langle\{D\}, D\rangle\}$ is of set nesting 2, and $\{\{\{D\}\}\}$ is of set nesting 3.

The *space-careful* evaluator works as follows. Let E be an algebraic expression. This expression can be viewed as a tree. With each vertex of the tree we associate a processor. Each vertex can produce for its parent a stream of relations or tuples. The parent may at any time require the first relation/tuple in the output stream of a child and the next one in the stream. We will see that each of these processors require only a polynomial local space, so the evaluator is PSPACE.

For the example above, the powerset vertex produces a stream of sets and this stream is filtered by the next processors. A last processor receives a stream of relations and computes the intersection keeping the intermediate results in its local store. Observe that we do not require that a stream be duplicate-free. So a stream can be viewed as a representation of a list (and not a set). We deal with duplicate elimination later.

More precisely, the leaves of the tree are base relations, and since we are assuming a total ordering of the database, there is clearly a processor that produces the tuples of the relation one at a time. Each internal vertex implements the corresponding operation of the algebra. We illustrate this with some examples:

1. The projection of a relation is implemented as follows. To produce its output stream, the projection processor resets its child and then asks for the elements of its input stream, one at a time, and produces the projection (possibly with duplicates).

2. For powerset, since set nesting is limited to 2, the input stream is of set nesting 1. Thus it is of polynomial size and can be loaded into the local store. The elements of the powerset are then produced one at a time in lexicographical order on the output stream.

3. An intersection of two sets of sets is implemented as follows: iterate over the first stream, and for each X in this stream, iterate over the second stream;

if X is found in that second stream, X is delivered on the output stream.

Before stating the main result of the section, we make two observations, the first is on duplicate elimination and the second on the absence of order:

1. If a result is of set nesting 1, we can store it in some local store and eliminate duplicates. If the set nesting is 2, consider a tree that computes the solution possibly with duplicates. Say its root is processor *sol_with_dup*. We add a processor *dup_elim* that receives the stream produced by *sol_with_dup* and receives also a duplicate-free enumeration of the candidate solutions. For each candidate solution X, *dup_elim* examines the entire stream produced by *sol_with_dup* to see whether X is in there.

2. The absence of order is not a problem since we are presenting an implementation. At the implementation level, we have a representation of data elements that provides an ordering that we can use in the computation. Observe that since algebra expressions are order-independent, the result will not depend on the ordering.

In the following, we assume that our devices write the result (without duplicates) on a write-only/write-once output tape and that the size of this output tape is not counted. One can show:

Theorem 1. *Each algebraic expression in ALG^{cv} of set nesting at most 2 can be evaluated with the space-careful evaluator in* PSPACE.

A straightforward consequence is that for each query q in second-order logic (i.e., the polynomial hierarchy), there is an expression in ALG^{cv} (indeed, the "natural translation" of the $CALC^{cv}$ expression q) that computes q and is answered by the *space-careful* evaluator in PSPACE. In particular, queries such as TC, which requires EXPSPACE with the natural evaluation, or *even* (is the cardinality of an input set even?), which is not even expressible in *while* (the natural order-free counterpart of PSPACE), are both computed using polynomial space resources.

On the other hand, there is still a big gap between the actual space complexity of TC and the space required by its evaluation with the *space-careful* evaluator. Furthermore, we would like to be able to compute *all* PSPACE queries using polynomial space. But, the iteration required by a partial fixpoint requires an extra level of set nesting (unless PSPACE = PH.) This suggests the following open problems:

Open Problem 2 *(a) Find a "nice" evaluator such that for each query q in* PSPACE, *there is an expression in ALG^{cv} that computes q and is evaluated in* PSPACE. *(b) Similarly, for* PTIME.

In the statement of the problems, we use the word "nice". Indeed, observe that *cheater* satisfies (a) if we remove this word. The difference between *cheater* and *space-careful* is that the optimization used in the former is based on detecting some particular syntactic patterns, whereas the latter does not attempt to modify the query but tries to save space when performing the evaluation. Clearly, we need formal criteria for nicety.

3   The Simply Typed Lambda Calculus

As our next topic, we study database queries expressed in Church's *simply typed λ-calculus* (with equality and constants). We briefly review the way databases and queries can be represented as typed λ-terms and mention previous results obtained for these representations. Then, we generalize the techniques of [14] to define a space-efficient evaluation strategy for order 5 λ-terms, which leads to a characterization of PSPACE in terms of the order 5 fragment of TLC$^=$.

The simply typed λ-calculus [8] (TLC for short) is a very basic functional framework built around the concepts of *abstraction* and *function application*, and it forms the backbone of most modern functional programming languages (e.g., ML [11, 23], Miranda [25], and Haskell [18]). Let us briefly review its definition (cf. [5, 17]).

The syntax of TLC *types* is given by the grammar $T \equiv t \mid (T \rightarrow T)$, where t ranges over a set of *type variables*. Thus, α is a type, as are $(\alpha \rightarrow \beta)$ and $(\alpha \rightarrow (\alpha \rightarrow \alpha))$. As usual, the type $\alpha \rightarrow \beta \rightarrow \gamma$ stands for $\alpha \rightarrow (\beta \rightarrow \gamma)$. The *order* of a type is defined as $\operatorname{order}(t) = 0$ for a type variable t, and $\operatorname{order}(\sigma' \rightarrow \sigma'') = \max(1 + \operatorname{order}(\sigma'), \operatorname{order}(\sigma''))$. TLC *terms* are given by the grammar $\mathcal{E} \equiv x \mid (\mathcal{E}\mathcal{E}) \mid \lambda x.\mathcal{E}$, where x ranges over a set of *expression variables*, and the condition of *well-typedness*. As usual, the term $P Q R$ stands for $(P Q) R$. For lack of space, we have to assume that the reader is familiar with the notion of *well-typedness* in TLC and with α- and β-reduction. We denote by $\rhd$ the transitive closure of α- and β-reduction. A term is in *normal form* if it does not $\rhd$-reduce to another term.

We obtain the simply typed λ-calculus *with equality and constants* (TLC$^=$ for short) by enriching the simply-typed λ-calculus syntax with: (1) a countably infinite set $\{o_1, o_2, \ldots\}$ of atomic constants of type o (some fixed type variable), and (2) a function constant Eq of type $o \rightarrow o \rightarrow \tau \rightarrow \tau \rightarrow \tau$ (for some fixed type variable τ different from o). For every pair of constants o_i, o_j, we add to $\rhd$ the reduction rule

$$Eq\, o_i\, o_j \;\rhd\; \begin{cases} \lambda x\, \lambda y.\, x & \text{if } i = j, \\ \lambda x\, \lambda y.\, y & \text{if } i \neq j. \end{cases}$$

Note that $\lambda x\, \lambda y.\, x$ and $\lambda x\, \lambda y.\, y$ are the usual λ-calculus encodings of the Boolean values *True* and *False*. For every pair of terms P, Q of type τ, $(Eq\, o_i\, o_j\, P\, Q)$ reduces to P if $i = j$ and to Q if $i \neq j$. Thus, the term $(Eq\, o_i\, o_j\, P\, Q)$ is the equivalent of "if $o_i = o_j$ then P else Q".

Just as TLC, TLC$^=$ is Church-Rosser and strongly normalizing, and principal types can be inferred from unadorned terms. (See [5, 17, 20] for a discussion of these concepts.)

Relations are represented in TLC$^=$ as follows. Let $O = \{o_1, o_2, \ldots\}$ be the set of constants of the TLC$^=$ calculus. For convenience, we assume that this set of constants also serves as the universe over which relations are defined.

Definition 3. Let $r = \{(o_{1,1}, o_{1,2}, \ldots, o_{1,k}), \ldots, (o_{m,1}, o_{m,2}, \ldots, o_{m,k})\} \subseteq O^k$ be a k-ary relation over O. An *encoding* of r, denoted by $\bar{r}$, is a TLC$^=$ term

$$\lambda c.\, \lambda n.$$

$$(c\, o_{1,1}\, o_{1,2} \ldots o_{1,k}$$
$$\quad (c\, o_{2,1}\, o_{2,2} \ldots o_{2,k}$$
$$\quad \ldots$$
$$\quad (c\, o_{m,1}\, o_{m,2} \ldots o_{m,k}\, n) \ldots)),$$

in which every tuple of r appears exactly once. If r contains exactly one tuple $(o_{1,1}, o_{1,2}, \ldots, o_{1,k})$, we also allow $\lambda c.\, c\, o_{1,1}\, o_{1,2} \ldots o_{1,k}$ as an encoding of r.[2]

The encoding $\bar{r}$ can be thought of as a generalized Church numeral that not only iterates a given function a certain number of times, but also provides different data at each iteration. Note that there can be many encodings of a relation, depending on how the input is ordered.

If r contains at least two tuples, the principal type of $\bar{r}$ is $(o \rightarrow \cdots \rightarrow o \rightarrow \sigma \rightarrow \sigma) \rightarrow \sigma \rightarrow \sigma$, where σ is a free type variable.[3] The order of this type is 2, independent of the arity of r. We abbreviate this type as o_k^σ. Instances of this type, obtained by substituting some type expression θ for σ, are abbreviated as o_k^θ. It is fairly easy to see that any closed normal-form term of type o_k^σ is an encoding of a relation.

In [14], a hierarchy of functional query languages based on fixed-order fragments of TLC$^=$ is defined:

Definition 4. The language of *typed list iteration* of order i with equality, denoted as TLI$_i^=$, is the set of all closed (i.e., not containing any free variables) TLC$^=$ terms Q that can be typed as $Q : o_{k_1}^{\theta_1} \rightarrow o_{k_2}^{\theta_2} \rightarrow \cdots \rightarrow o_{k_l}^{\theta_l} \rightarrow o_k^\sigma$, where $l, k_1, \ldots, k_l$ and k are non-negative integers, $\theta_1, \ldots, \theta_l$ are types of order $\leq i$, and σ is a type variable different from o.

Note that a TLC$^=$ term Q of type $o_{k_1}^{\theta_1} \rightarrow o_{k_2}^{\theta_2} \rightarrow \cdots \rightarrow o_{k_l}^{\theta_l} \rightarrow o_k^\sigma$ has the property that whenever $\bar{r}_1, \ldots, \bar{r}_l$ are encodings of relations of arities $k_1, \ldots, k_l$, the expression $(Q\, \bar{r}_1, \ldots, \bar{r}_l)$ is closed, well typed, and of type o_k^σ. Hence its normal form must be an encoding of a relation, i.e., Q defines a mapping from encodings of relations to encodings of relations. Thus, the somewhat obscure typing constraint in the definition of TLI$_i^=$ is merely a syntactic condition to guarantee the proper semantic behavior of query terms.

It was shown in [15] how to express relational algebra, Datalog$^\neg$, and complex object algebra queries as typed λ-terms acting on λ-calculus representations of relations or complex values. In [14], it is proved that TLI$_0^=$ expresses at least the first-order queries[4] and that TLI$_1^=$ expresses exactly the PTIME queries. The proofs are based on an order-efficient representation of relational algebra and fixpoint queries as λ-terms and a space- and time-efficient evaluation strategy for such terms.

---

[2] This is because $\lambda c.\, c\, o_{1,1}\, o_{1,2} \ldots o_{1,k}$ is an η-reduct (see [5] for a definition of η-reduction) of $\lambda c.\, \lambda n.\, c\, o_{1,1}\, o_{1,2} \ldots o_{1,k}\, n$.

[3] If r is empty or contains only one tuple, this type is only an instance of the principal type of $\bar{r}$.

[4] Under certain assumptions about the ordering of the input, it can be shown that TLI$_0^=$ expresses *exactly* the first-order queries, cf. [13].

In the following, we extend the results of [14] to obtain a characterization of PSPACE. This provides a sublanguage of TLC$^=$ which expresses PSPACE and such that each query in this language can be evaluated in PSPACE. We highlight the main arguments of the proof. A detailed presentation of the technique can be found in [13].

Theorem 5. *The database queries definable by TLI$_2^=$ query terms are exactly the* PSPACE *queries.*

The proof involves two parts: An encoding of generic PSPACE computations as TLI$_2^=$ queries and an evaluation algorithm that evaluates arbitrary TLI$_2^=$ queries in PSPACE. For lack of space, we only consider the latter part here.

The main idea of the evaluation algorithm is to represent λ-terms not as syntactic objects, but as *tables* describing their functional behavior. For example, a term $f: o \rightarrow o$ is represented as the binary relation $\{(o_i, o_j) \mid (f\, o_i) \rhd o_j\}$, which describes how f acts on constants. When evaluating a particular query, it suffices to record the behavior of f on the constants appearing in the input database, so f can be represented by a table of size quadratic in the size of the active domain. Thus, the evaluator is essentially a *semantic* evaluator— it manipulates *values* of terms (in a certain simple model) rather than terms themselves. (Observe that a purely syntactical evaluator might require up to doubly exponential space to evaluate a TLI$_2^=$ expression of the form *Crank Q Nil*: If Q does not eliminate duplicate tuples, the size of the result can increase by a polynomial factor at each step of the iteration.)

To make the discussion more precise, consider a fixed TLI$_2^=$ term Q applied to inputs $\overline{r_1}, \ldots, \overline{r_l}$. Without loss of generality, we may assume that Q is of the form $\lambda R_1 \ldots \lambda R_l. \lambda c. \lambda n. Q'$, where the variables $R_1, \ldots, R_l$ receive the input relations and the $\lambda c. \lambda n.$ part is the beginning of the output of the query (which is again an encoding of a relation). The evaluation of the query consists of determining the relation encoded by the normal form of $\lambda c. \lambda n. Q'[R_1 := \overline{r_l}, \ldots, R_l := \overline{r_l}]$. When evaluating the body of this term, we can treat the variables c and n as *constants* associated with the fixed types $o \rightarrow \cdots \rightarrow o \rightarrow \tau \rightarrow \tau$ and τ, respectively, where the number of o's is given by the arity of the output of Q, and τ is some type variable different from o. (For convenience, we pick the same variable that is used in the typing $Eq: o \rightarrow o \rightarrow \tau \rightarrow \tau \rightarrow \tau$ and we assume that no variables other than o and τ appear in the type of Q.)

The evaluation of $Q'[R_1 := \overline{r_1}, \ldots, R_l := \overline{r_l}]$ involves the manipulation of terms whose types are built from the type variables τ and o and whose symbols are either variables or constants drawn from the set $\{o_1, \ldots, o_N, Eq, c, n\}$ (where $\{o_1, \ldots, o_N\}$ is the active domain of the input). Let T be the set of simple types containing only the type variables τ and o and for each type $\gamma \in T$, let $\mathcal{E}_\gamma$ be the set of TLC$^=$ terms of type γ built from $o_1, \ldots, o_N, Eq, c, n$ and variables with types in T. Let $\overline{\mathcal{E}}_\gamma$ be the set of terms in $\mathcal{E}_\gamma$ which are closed (i.e., built from $o_1, \ldots, o_N, Eq, c, n$ and bound variables) and in normal form. It is easy to see that $\overline{\mathcal{E}}_o$ contains just the constants $\{o_1, \ldots, o_N\}$ and that $\overline{\mathcal{E}}_\tau$ consists of all lists of the form

$$(c\, o_{1,1}\, o_{1,2} \ldots o_{1,k}\, (c\, o_{2,1}\, o_{2,2} \ldots o_{2,k} \ldots (c\, o_{m,1}\, o_{m,2} \ldots o_{m,k}\, n) \ldots)),$$

where $m \geq 0$ and the $o_{i,j}$ are drawn from the set $\{o_1, \ldots, o_N\}$. Thus, each term in $\overline{\mathcal{E}}_\tau$ represents a relation $\{\langle o_{i,1}, \ldots, o_{i,k}\rangle \mid 1 \leq i \leq m\} \subseteq D^k$.

For the output of a query, the exact normal form of $Q'[R_1 := \overline{r_1}, \ldots, R_l := \overline{r_l}]$ does not matter—the evaluation algorithm merely has to determine the relation that it represents. Thus, it can identify terms in $\overline{\mathcal{E}}_\tau$ that represent the same relation, or, more generally, terms in $\overline{\mathcal{E}}_\gamma$ that represent the same mapping from relations to relations, the same operator on mappings, etc. More formally, we introduce an equivalence relation $\sim_\gamma$ on every set $\overline{\mathcal{E}}_\gamma, \gamma \in T$, by defining

$$t \sim_0 t' \iff t \equiv t'$$
$$t \sim_\tau t' \iff t \text{ and } t' \text{ represent the same relation}$$
$$t \sim_{\alpha \to \beta} t' \iff \forall s \in \overline{\mathcal{E}}_\alpha : \mathrm{nf}\,(ts) \sim_\beta \mathrm{nf}\,(t's),$$

where nf (ts) denotes the normal form of ts.

We can view equivalence classes in $\overline{\mathcal{E}}_0$ as constants from D and equivalence classes in $\overline{\mathcal{E}}_\tau$ as k-ary relations over D. More interestingly, we can view equivalence classes in $\overline{\mathcal{E}}_{\alpha \to \beta}$ as mappings from equivalence classes in $\overline{\mathcal{E}}_\alpha$ to $\overline{\mathcal{E}}_\beta$:

Lemma 6. *Let* $t \sim_{\alpha \to \beta} t'$ *and* $s \sim_\alpha s'$. *Then* nf $(ts) \sim_\beta$ nf $(t's')$.

Since we are only interested in the equivalence class of the normal form of $Q'[R_1 := \overline{r_1}, \ldots, R_l := \overline{r_l}]$, it suffices to manipulate equivalence classes of terms during the evaluation of the query, rather than actual λ-terms. Thus, an intermediate result t of type $\alpha_1 \to \cdots \to \alpha_m \to \beta$, where β is o or τ, can be stored as a table describing the action of t on each vector of equivalence classes from $\overline{\mathcal{E}}_{\alpha_1} \times \cdots \times \overline{\mathcal{E}}_{\alpha_m}$, rather than the term t itself. This "extensional" representation of intermediate results has the advantage that there is a fixed bound on the size of the representation that depends only on the size of the input and the type of the term. Unfortunately, the bound is quite large. For example, there are exponentially many equivalence classes in $\overline{\mathcal{E}}_\tau$ (one for each k-ary relation over D), and thus a table describing an order 1 term, such as the "accumulator value" passed between stages of an iteration, would have to be of exponential size.

However, there is an important optimization that can be made. On closer inspection of the structure of terms in $\overline{\mathcal{E}}_\alpha$, where α is an order 1 type in T, one finds that such terms cannot define arbitrary functions of their inputs. For example, if α is of the form $\tau \to \cdots \to \tau \to$ o, it is easy to see that the only terms in $\overline{\mathcal{E}}_\alpha$ are constant functions of the form $\lambda x_1 : \tau \ldots \lambda x_i : \tau . o_j$. If α is of the form $\tau \to \cdots \to \tau \to \tau$, the only terms in $\overline{\mathcal{E}}_\alpha$ are functions of the form

$$\lambda x_1 \ldots x_i : \tau . (c\, o_{1,1}\, o_{1,2} \ldots o_{1,k}\, (c\, o_{2,1}\, o_{2,2} \ldots o_{2,k} \ldots (c\, o_{m,1}\, o_{m,2} \ldots o_{m,k}\, y) \ldots)),$$

where $m \geq 0$ and $y \in \{x_1, \ldots, x_i, n\}$. In both cases, the equivalence class of a term in $\overline{\mathcal{E}}_\alpha$ can clearly be represented in polynomial space. More generally, if $\alpha \in T$ is an arbitrary order 1 type and t is a term in $\overline{\mathcal{E}}_\alpha$ that takes p inputs of type τ and q inputs of type o, then once the inputs of t of type o have been instantiated with constants, the resulting term is of type $\tau \to \cdots \to \tau \to \tau$ or $\tau \to \cdots \to \tau \to$ o and its normal form must therefore take one of the forms listed above. If this normal form is computed for each of the (polynomially many) possible assignments of constants to the inputs of t of type o and the results are arranged in a table, we obtain a description of the equivalence class of t of polynomial size.

Using this polynomial-size representation of the equivalence classes of order 1 terms, the evaluation of a query $\lambda R_1 \ldots \lambda R_l. \lambda c. \lambda n. Q'$ on input $\overline{r_1}, \ldots, \overline{r_l}$ now proceeds as a recursive descent into Q'. Subexpressions of order 1 are fully evaluated and turned into a table as soon as they are encountered. Subexpressions of order 2 or more are evaluated only when applied to enough arguments to bring the overall type down to 1, in which case the result fits into polynomial space. Thus, redexes $(\lambda x. M) N$ are evaluated according to the rule: If the order of N is 1 or 0, evaluate N to obtain its equivalence class and evaluate M in an environment where x is bound to the equivalence class of N. If the order of N is 2 or more, evaluate M in an environment where x is bound to N itself. In other words, redexes up to order 2 are evaluated in applicative order and redexes of higher order are evaluated in normal order. One can show that (with certain technical modifications, see [13]), this evaluation procedure can be implemented using a polynomial-size stack and a polynomial-size heap. Thus, the other direction of the theorem follows.

The proof of the theorem implies in particular:

Corollary 7. *For each query q in* PSPACE, *there is a query in* $TLI_2^=$ *that computes q and that can be evaluated in* PSPACE.

To conclude this section, we note that similar techniques can be used to show that EXPTIME and $TLI_3^=$ coincide [13].

4 Method Schemas

We show now that the evaluation techniques developed for the simply typed λ-calculus above can also be applied to *method schemas*, which may be viewed as an object-oriented extension of the simply typed λ-calculus. The main new language features that we consider here are *recursion* (which replaces list iteration as the main control structure) and *name overloading* resolved by *late binding*. Originally, method schemas were defined in a strictly first-order setting: methods could not operate on other methods. We loosen this restriction here by introducing second-order method schemas and we show that all PSPACE queries can be expressed by second-order method schemas that are evaluable in polynomial space using the "extensional representation" technique of the previous section. Due to space limitations, our presentation will be sketchy and in particular, we refer to [2] for a formal presentation of the original model.

Method schemas are a simple programming formalism for OODBs, based on applicative program schemas with additional features such as *classes*, *methods*, *inheritance*, *name overloading*, and *late binding*. They are intended to model the object/class/method paradigm of object-oriented programming in the same way that applicative program schemas [10, 12] model traditional programming languages. Method names in a method schema fall into two categories: *base methods*, whose interpretation is part of the input, and *coded methods*, which are defined in a *method schema* in terms of base methods and possibly other coded methods. One may view base methods, coded methods, and method schemas as functional analogs of EDB predicates, IDB predicates, and Datalog programs. For example, the following method schema declares a base method *Price* of type *Basepart* → *Int* and defines a coded method *Cost*, whose expansion depends on whether its argument is of class *Part* or *Basepart*:

$$Price @ Basepart : Int$$

$$Cost @ Part = \lambda x. Sum(Assemblingcost(x), Cost(Subparts(x)))$$

$$Cost @ Basepart = \lambda x. Price(x)$$

Informally, the input to a method schema is a finite set of objects, each one belonging to a unique class, and a set of interpretations for the base methods as functions over the set of objects. Given an input, the evaluation of a method invocation $m(e_1, \ldots, e_k)$, where $e_1, \ldots, e_k$ are variable-free expressions, proceeds recursively as follows. First, $e_1, \ldots, e_k$ are evaluated to produce objects $o_1, \ldots, o_k$. Then, if m is a base method, the return value is obtained from the interpretation of m. If m is a coded method, the term is rewritten according to the definition of m that applies for the classes of the o_i's. (The result is undefined if there is no applicable definition.) Thus, the evaluation of a coded method proceeds essentially by applicative-order β-reduction, augmented by a late binding process to do name resolution.

It is known that over ordered databases (encoded in a functional way), method schemas express exactly the PTIME queries [16]. We briefly sketch how this is obtained. We consider queries over finite ordered relational databases. The input of a query consists of a finite ordered universe O (w.l.o.g an initial segment of the positive integers) and some relations $R_1, R_2, \ldots, R_l$ over O, and the output is another relation R over O.

We encode the input in the method schema framework as follows. The elements of the universe are represented by objects $\{o_0, \ldots, o_{n-1}\}$. Of these, objects $\{o_1, \ldots, o_{n-1}\}$ are assigned class *Number* and object o_0 is assigned class *Zero*, which is a subclass of *Number*. We use a separate class for o_0 to facilitate Boolean tests: a conditional of the form "if $x = 0$ then P else Q" can be expressed as $Test_{P,Q}(x)$, where $Test_{P,Q}$ is defined as $Test_{P,Q} @ Zero = P$, $Test_{P,Q} @ Number = Q$. The ordering of the universe is represented by a unary base method *Pred* of type *Number* → *Number*, which computes the predecessor function, and a zero-ary base method *Max: Number*, which returns the largest element in the universe, i.e., o_{n-1}. Finally, for each k-ary database relation R, there is a k-ary base method r of type $(Number, \ldots, Number) \to Number$ coding the *characteristic function* of R, i.e., such that $r(x_1, \ldots, x_k)$ returns o_0 if the tuple represented by $(x_1, \ldots, x_k)$ does not belong to R and some other object if it does. (Thus, the test "if $(x_1, \ldots, x_k) \in R$ then P else Q" can be expressed as $Test_{Q,P}(r(x_1, \ldots, x_k))$.)

We represent a query by a coded method q of type $(Number, \ldots, Number) \to Number$ that codes the characteristic function of the result. That is, if $q(\mathbf{x})$ reduces to an object of class *Number*, then the tuple represented by $\mathbf{x}$ is considered part of the output; if $q(\mathbf{x})$ reduces to an object of class *Zero*, then the tuple represented by **x** is not considered part of the output. For example, the query computing the union of two relations r, s is represented by the coded method $q = \lambda\mathbf{x}.\, r(\mathbf{x}) \vee s(\mathbf{x})$ (where the disjunction is not actually part of the language, but can be simulated similarly to the "if-then-else" statement above).

As defined above, method schemas are strictly first-order: methods cannot operate on other methods. We study here an extension of this framework where methods are first-class citizens that can be passed to and returned by other methods. For instance, we allow definitions such as

$$Compose = \lambda f.\, \lambda g.\, \lambda x.\, f(g(x)),$$

which defines an operator that composes two methods.

This extension raises the question of how to handle name resolution in the presence of functional arguments. For our purposes, a very simple solution suffices, where method overloading is not allowed to discriminate on the signature of functional arguments. That is, name resolution simply ignores all functional arguments of a method and picks the applicable definition based on the classes of the remaining arguments. Furthermore, a method returned as a result of a method invocation cannot be overloaded at all because it does not have a name. This is certainly not the best possible approach, but since our main concern here are evaluation techniques, we will not dwell on the issue.

Recall that over ordered databases, (first-order) method schemas express exactly the PTIME queries. We next show that second-order method schemas (where "order" is defined as in the λ-calculus section) can simulate *while* queries and thus express all PSPACE queries.

The essential ingredient for a simulation of *while* queries is the ability to iterate a first-order query an exponential number of times. The iteration can be easily implemented using recursion; what is more difficult is to terminate the recursion. For this, we need to maintain a counter whose value is decremented for each level of recursion and which terminates the recursion once its value reaches zero. In the simulation of PTIME queries by first-order method schemas in [16], tuples of objects are used for this purpose, since they allow counting up to some polynomial value. To implement an exponential counter, we use second-order methods. More precisely, we encode a counter as a first-order method with domain O^k and range $\{o_0, o_{n-1}\}$, with the convention that o_0 means *False* and o_{n-1} means *True*. Such a method may be viewed as a bit string of length n^k, where each bit contains the value of the method for one k-tuple of arguments. Observe that there are 2^{n^k} such methods and that they can easily be ordered. For instance, one can choose the method

$$Bigmax = \lambda x_1 \ldots x_k.\, True$$

as the maximal element and it is a rather tedious but straightforward exercise to code second-order methods *Decr* and *IsZero* to do decrement and test for zero.

Finally, let us describe how to perform an exponential iteration of a relational query using the counter technique we have just developed. Suppose we are given a relational algebra expression $\varphi(R, R_1, R_2, \ldots, R_l)$ and we want to iterate the mapping $R \mapsto \varphi(R, R_1, R_2, \ldots, R_l)$, starting from the empty relation. We first obtain, using the techniques of [16], a second-order method M_φ computing $R \mapsto \varphi(R, R_1, R_2, \ldots, R_l)$. Observe that M_φ takes a relation, i.e., a first-order method, as argument and returns a new first-order method. Now we use the following code:

$$Fix_\varphi \ = Crank_\varphi(\emptyset, Bigmax)$$
$$Crank_\varphi = \lambda R. \lambda C. \text{if } IsZero(C) \text{ then } R \text{ else } Crank_\varphi(M_\varphi(R), Decr(C))$$

where $\emptyset$ is a first-order method representing the empty relation of the same arity as R and the "if-then-else" statement is coded as shown earlier.

This completes the simulation of *while* queries, so we have:

Theorem 8. *Under the representation conventions listed above, second-order method schemas over ordered databases can express every* PSPACE *query.*

Let us now discuss how to evaluate second-order method schemas. As in the λ-calculus, it is easy to construct examples where an "intensional representation" of functional arguments and results as λ-terms may lead to doubly exponential space usage. The remedy is again to represent first-order methods *extensionally*, i.e., as tables describing their action on constants, very much like base methods. Thus, whenever the interpreter encounters a first-order method expression $\lambda x_1 \ldots \lambda x_k. e$, it evaluates $e[\mathbf{x}: = \mathbf{o}]$ for each k-vector of constants $\mathbf{o}$ and stores the result in a table indexed by $\mathbf{o}$. With this evaluation strategy, the code of Fix_φ above can be executed in PSPACEas follows. We start with the term $Crank(\emptyset, Bigmax)$. The extensions of $\emptyset$ and $Bigmax$ are computed and substituted for the formal parameters R, C in the definition of $Crank$. We now have subterms $IsZero(C)$, $M_\varphi(R)$ and $Decr(C)$. Since the extensions of R and C are known, each one of these can be fully evaluated to produce another extension (or an object in the case of $IsZero(C)$). Depending on the value returned by $IsZero(C)$, the computation either terminates and returns the current value of R, or proceeds with another invocation of $Crank$, using the previously computed extensions as arguments. Note that this is a tail-recursive call, so there is no need to maintain a stack to unwind the recursion. Thus, the only storage used during the computation is a polynomial-size workspace holding the current values of the formal parameters R and C in extension format (plus some additional polynomial workspace required by the $IsZero$, M_φ, and $Decr$ methods). Therefore, we have:

Theorem 9. *For each query q in* PSPACE, *under the representation conventions listed above, there exists a second-order method schema over ordered databases that computes q and can be evaluated in* PSPACE.

Observe that we do not guarantee here that every query expressed using second-order method schemas can be evaluated in PSPACE. Indeed, it is easy to find examples of second-order method schemas that cannot be evaluated in PSPACE by the evaluator described above. However, we conjecture that all second-order method schemas can be evaluated in EXPTIME by translating them into an inflationary fixpoint query over an exponential domain, similar to the translation of first-order method schemas to an inflationary fixpoint query over a polynomial domain in [16].

To conclude this section, let us briefly compare the evaluation of second-order method schemas and of $TLI_2^=$ query terms. In both cases, the main optimization is a polynomial-size representation format for functions of order 1, based on computing the extension of the function. However, the evaluation of $TLI_2^=$ terms is complicated by the fact that such terms may contain redexes $(\lambda x. M)N$ where the order of N is greater than 1. Thus, the evaluation algorithm has to alternate judiciously between applicative and normal order reduction and the proof of the PSPACE resource bound becomes more difficult. In the second-order method schema case, the order of N is always at most 1 and thus the reduction can always be carried out in applicative order. On the other hand, due to the presence of recursion, it is impossible to obtain any bound on the number of method invocations originating from a particular call, so the evaluation algorithm cannot evaluate all second-order method schemas in PSPACE, but only those which are either of polynomially bounded recursion depth or tail-recursive with exponentially bounded recursion depth.

5 Conclusions

We have studied space-efficient evaluation strategies for three functional query languages: the complex value algebra with set nesting 2, typed list iteration of order 2, and method schemas of order 2. For the complex value algebra, a stream-based implementation of *powerset* led to a PSPACE evaluator for all queries in the polynomial hierarchy, and for $TLI_2^=$ and second-order method schemas, an extensional representation of order 1 terms led to a PSPACE evaluator for all queries in PSPACE. Furthermore, we showed that $TLI_2^=$ expresses exactly the PSPACE queries.

The following problems are still open: (1) Find a "nice" evaluator such that for each query q in PSPACE, there is an expression in ALG^{cv} that computes q and is evaluated in PSPACE. Similarly, for PTIME. (2) Characterize the expressive power of $TLI_k^=$ for $k > 3$. (3) Characterize the expressive power of second-order and higher-order method schemas.

References

1. S. Abiteboul and C. Beeri. *On the Power of Languages for the Manipulation of Complex Objects.* INRIA Research Report 846, 1988.

2. S. Abiteboul, P. Kanellakis, S. Ramaswamy, and E. Waller. *Method Schemas.* Technical Report CS-92-33, Brown University, 1992. (An earlier version appeared in *Proc. 9th ACM PODS,* 1990).

3. A. V. Aho and J. D. Ullman. Universality of Data Retrieval Languages. In *Proc. 6th ACM POPL,* pp. 110–117, 1979.

4. J. Backus. Can Programming be Liberated from the von Neumann Style? A Functional Style of Programming and its Algebra of Programs. *CACM* 21(8):613–641, 1978.

5. H. Barendregt. *The Lambda Calculus: Its Syntax and Semantics.* North Holland, 1984.

6. P. Buneman, R. Frankel, and R. Nikhil. An Implementation Technique for Database Query Languages. *ACM Trans. Database Syst.* 7(2):164–186, 1982.

7. A. K. Chandra and D. Harel. Computable Queries for Relational Data Bases. *JCSS*, 21(2):156–178, 1980.

8. A. Church. *The Calculi of Lambda-Conversion.* Princeton University Press, 1941.

9. E. F. Codd. A Relational Model of Data for Large Shared Data Banks. *CACM*, 13(6):377–387, 1970.

10. B. Courcelle. Recursive Applicative Program Schemes. In J. van Leeuwen, editor, *Handbook of Theoretical Computer Science*, Vol. B, pp. 459–492. Elsevier, 1990.

11. M. J. Gordon, R. Milner, L. Morris, M. Newey and C. P. Wadsworth. A Metalanguage for Interactive Proof in LCF. In *Proc. 5th ACM POPL*, pp. 119–130, 1978.

12. S. Greibach. *Theory of Program Structures: Schemes, Semantics, Verification.* Springer LNCS 36, 1975.

13. G. Hillebrand. *Finite Model Theory in the Simply Typed Lambda Calculus.* Ph.D. thesis, Brown University, 1994. Available by anonymous ftp from ftp.cs.brown.edu:/pub/techreports/94/cs94-24.ps.Z.

14. G. Hillebrand and P. Kanellakis. Functional Database Query Languages as Typed Lambda Calculi of Fixed Order. In *Proc. 13th ACM PODS*, pp. 222–231, 1994.

15. G. Hillebrand, P. Kanellakis, and H. Mairson. Database Query Languages Embedded in the Typed Lambda Calculus. In *Proc. 8th IEEE LICS*, pp. 332–343, 1993.

16. G. Hillebrand, P. Kanellakis, and S. Ramaswamy. Functional Programming Formalisms for OODB Methods. In *Proc. of the NATO ASI Summer School on OODEs*, Turkey 1993. To appear in Springer LNCS.

17. J. R. Hindley and J. P. Seldin. *Introduction to Combinators and λ-Calculus.* Cambridge University Press, 1986.

18. P. Hudak and P. Wadler, editors. *Report on the Functional Programming Language Haskell.* Technical Report YALEU/DCS/RR656, Dept. of Computer Science, Yale University, 1988.

19. R. Hull and J. Su. On the Expressive Power of Database Queries with Intermediate Types. *JCSS* 43(1):219–267, 1991.

20. P. Kanellakis, J. Mitchell, and H. Mairson. Unification and ML Type Reconstruction. In J.-L. Lassez and G. Plotkin, editors, *Computational Logic: Essays in Honor of Alan Robinson*, pp. 444–479. MIT Press, 1991.

21. G. Kuper and M. Y. Vardi. On the Complexity of Queries in the Logical Data Model. *TCS* 116:33–58, 1993.

22. G. M. Kuper and M. Y. Vardi. The Logical Data Model. *ACM Trans. Database Syst.* 18(3):379–413, 1993.

23. R. Milner. The Standard ML Core Language. *Polymorphism*, 2(2), 1985. (An earlier version appeared in *Proc. of the 1984 ACM Symposium on Lisp and Functional Programming*.)

24. D. Suciu and J. Paredaens. Any Algorithm in the Complex Object Algebra with Powerset Needs Exponential Space to Compute Transitive Closure. In *Proc. 13th ACM PODS*, pp. 201–209, 1994.

25. D. A. Turner. Miranda: A Non-Strict Functional Language with Polymorphic Types. In J.-P. Jouannaud, editor, *Functional Programming Languages and Computer Architecture*, pp. 1–16. Springer LNCS 201, 1985.

26. M. Y. Vardi. The Complexity of Relational Query Languages. In *Proc. 14th STOC*, pp. 137–146, 1982.

Lecture Notes in Computer Science

For information about Vols. 1–814
please contact your bookseller or Springer-Verlag

Vol. 851: H.-J. Kugler, A. Mullery, N. Niebert (Eds.), Towards a Pan-European Telecommunication Service Infrastructure. Proceedings, 1994. XIII, 582 pages. 1994.

Vol. 852: K. Echtle, D. Hammer, D. Powell (Eds.), Dependable Computing – EDCC-1. Proceedings, 1994. XVII, 618 pages. 1994.

Vol. 853: K. Bolding, L. Snyder (Eds.), Parallel Computer Routing and Communication. Proceedings, 1994. IX, 317 pages. 1994.

Vol. 854: B. Buchberger, J. Volkert (Eds.), Parallel Processing: CONPAR 94 – VAPP VI. Proceedings, 1994. XVI, 893 pages. 1994.

Vol. 855: J. van Leeuwen (Ed.), Algorithms – ESA '94. Proceedings, 1994. X, 510 pages.1994.

Vol. 856: D. Karagiannis (Ed.), Database and Expert Systems Applications. Proceedings, 1994. XVII, 807 pages. 1994.

Vol. 857: G. Tel, P. Vitányi (Eds.), Distributed Algorithms. Proceedings, 1994. X, 370 pages. 1994.

Vol. 858: E. Bertino, S. Urban (Eds.), Object-Oriented Methodologies and Systems. Proceedings, 1994. X, 386 pages. 1994.

Vol. 859: T. F. Melham, J. Camilleri (Eds.), Higher Order Logic Theorem Proving and Its Applications. Proceedings, 1994. IX, 470 pages. 1994.

Vol. 860: W. L. Zagler, G. Busby, R. R. Wagner (Eds.), Computers for Handicapped Persons. Proceedings, 1994. XX, 625 pages. 1994.

Vol: 861: B. Nebel, L. Dreschler-Fischer (Eds.), KI-94: Advances in Artificial Intelligence. Proceedings, 1994. IX, 401 pages. 1994. (Subseries LNAI).

Vol. 862: R. C. Carrasco, J. Oncina (Eds.), Grammatical Inference and Applications. Proceedings, 1994. VIII, 290 pages. 1994. (Subseries LNAI).

Vol. 863: H. Langmaack, W.-P. de Roever, J. Vytopil (Eds.), Formal Techniques in Real-Time and Fault-Tolerant Systems. Proceedings, 1994. XIV, 787 pages. 1994.

Vol. 864: B. Le Charlier (Ed.), Static Analysis. Proceedings, 1994. XII, 465 pages. 1994.

Vol. 865: T. C. Fogarty (Ed.), Evolutionary Computing. Proceedings, 1994. XII, 332 pages. 1994.

Vol. 866: Y. Davidor, H.-P. Schwefel, R. Männer (Eds.), Parallel Problem Solving from Nature - PPSN III. Proceedings, 1994. XV, 642 pages. 1994.

Vol 867: L. Steels, G. Schreiber, W. Van de Velde (Eds.), A Future for Knowledge Acquisition. Proceedings, 1994. XII, 414 pages. 1994. (Subseries LNAI).

Vol. 868: R. Steinmetz (Ed.), Multimedia: Advanced Teleservices and High-Speed Communication Architectures. Proceedings, 1994. IX, 451 pages. 1994.

Vol. 869: Z. W. Raś, Zemankova (Eds.), Methodologies for Intelligent Systems. Proceedings, 1994. X, 613 pages. 1994. (Subseries LNAI).

Vol. 870: J. S. Greenfield, Distributed Programming Paradigms with Cryptography Applications. XI, 182 pages. 1994.

Vol. 871: J. P. Lee, G. G. Grinstein (Eds.), Database Issues for Data Visualization. Proceedings, 1993. XIV, 229 pages. 1994.

Vol. 872: S Arikawa, K. P. Jantke (Eds.), Algorithmic Learning Theory. Proceedings, 1994. XIV, 575 pages. 1994.

Vol. 873: M. Naftalin, T. Denvir, M. Bertran (Eds.), FME '94: Industrial Benefit of Formal Methods. Proceedings, 1994. XI, 723 pages. 1994.

Vol. 874: A. Borning (Ed.), Principles and Practice of Constraint Programming. Proceedings, 1994. IX, 361 pages. 1994.

Vol. 875: D. Gollmann (Ed.), Computer Security – ESORICS 94. Proceedings, 1994. XI, 469 pages. 1994.

Vol. 876: B. Blumenthal, J. Gornostaev, C. Unger (Eds.), Human-Computer Interaction. Proceedings, 1994. IX, 239 pages. 1994.

Vol. 877: L. M. Adleman, M.-D. Huang (Eds.), Algorithmic Number Theory. Proceedings, 1994. IX, 323 pages. 1994.

Vol. 878: T. Ishida; Parallel, Distributed and Multiagent Production Systems. XVII, 166 pages. 1994. (Subseries LNAI).

Vol. 879: J. Dongarra, J. Waśniewski (Eds.), Parallel Scientific Computing. Proceedings, 1994. XI, 566 pages. 1994.

Vol. 880: P. S. Thiagarajan (Ed.), Foundations of Software Technology and Theoretical Computer Science. Proceedings, 1994. XI, 451 pages. 1994.

Vol. 881: P. Loucopoulos (Ed.), Entity-Relationship Approach – ER'94. Proceedings, 1994. XIII, 579 pages. 1994.

Vol. 882: D. Hutchison, A. Danthine, H. Leopold, G. Coulson (Eds.), Multimedia Transport and Teleservices. Proceedings, 1994. XI, 380 pages. 1994.

Vol. 883: L. Fribourg, F. Turini (Eds.), Logic Program Synthesis and Transformation – Meta-Programming in Logic. Proceedings, 1994. IX, 451 pages. 1994.

Vol. 884: J. Nievergelt, T. Roos, H.-J. Schek, P. Widmayer (Eds.), IGIS '94: Geographic Information Systems. Proceedings, 1994. VIII, 292 pages. 19944.

Vol. 885: R. C. Veltkamp, Closed Objects Boundaries from Scattered Points. VIII, 144 pages. 1994.

Vol. 886: M. M. Veloso, Planning and Learning by Analogical Reasoning. XIII, 181 pages. 1994. (Subseries LNAI).

Vol. 887: M. Toussaint (Ed.), Ada in Europe. Proceedings, 1994. XII, 521 pages. 1994.

Vol. 888: S. A. Andersson (Ed.), Analysis of Dynamical and Cognitive Systems. Proceedings, 1993. VII, 260 pages. 1995.

Vol. 889: H. P. Lubich, Towards a CSCW Framework for Scientific Cooperation in Europe. X, 268 pages. 1995.

Vol. 890: M. J. Wooldridge, N. R. Jennings (Eds.), Intelligent Agents. Proceedings, 1994. VIII, 407 pages. 1995. (Subseries LNAI).

Vol. 891: C. Lewerentz, T. Lindner (Eds.), Formal Development of Reactive Systems. XI, 394 pages. 1995.

Vol. 892: K. Pingali, U. Banerjee, D. Gelernter, A. Nicolau, D. Padua (Eds.), Languages and Compilers for Parallel Computing. Proceedings, 1994. XI, 496 pages. 1995.

Vol. 893: G. Gottlob, M. Y. Vardi (Eds.), Database Theory – ICDT '95. Proceedings, 1995. XI, 454 pages. 1995.